1395

RIEL

MAGGIE SIGGINS

RIEL

A LIFE
OF
REVOLUTION

HarperCollins*PublishersLtd*

The publisher acknowledges permission to reprint the following: portions of *Selected Poetry of Louis Riel*, translated by Paul Savoie and edited by Glen Campbell, Exile Editions Ltd, 1993; portions of *Gabriel Dumont Speaks*, translation copyright © 1993, Michael Barnholden, Talon Books Ltd., Vancouver, B.C.; portions of *The Diaries of Louis Riel*, edited by Thomas Flanagan, Hurtig Publishers, 1993; and translations of Louis Riel's poems by Wilfrid Dubé.

Many quotations from letters and poems written by Louis Riel appearing in this volume have been translated from the French originals published in *The Collected Writings of Louis Riel/Les ecrits complets de Louis Riel*, ed. F.G. Stanley et al., University of Alberta Press, 1985.

First Edition

Canadian Cataloguing in Publication Data

Siggins, Maggie, 1942-
Riel : a life of revolution

Includes index and bibliographical references.
ISBN 0-00-215792-6 (bound)   ISBN 0-00-638052-2 (pbk.)

1. Riel, Louis, 1844-1885.   2. Metis — Prairie Provinces — Biography.
3. Red River Rebellion, 1869-1870.   4. Riel Rebellion, 1885.   I. Title.

FC3217.1.R53S54 1994   971.05'1   C94-931576-1
F1060.9.R53S54 1994

94 95 96 97 98 99 ❖ EB 10 9 8 7 6 5 4 3 2 1

Printed and bound in the United States

For Mike, Bill, Fangfang and Yaya,
each one an inspiration

CONTENTS

Acknowledgements / ix
Prologue / xv

Part I: Emergence / 1
Part II: Triumph / 67
Part III: Exile / 189
Part IV: Tragedy / 325

Epilogue / 446
Addendum One / 449
Addendum Two / 452
Addendum Three / 453
Notes / 460
Bibliography / 486
Index / 498

ACKNOWLEDGEMENTS

I would like to thank my researcher, Tracy Stevens, for her dedication, insight and great skill in digging up the vast amount of material relating to Louis Riel. That she is Métis herself added a special dimension to this project.

I would like to express gratitude to Wilf Dubé, who translated many of the difficult Riel poems with such verve and insight. Thanks also to Exile Editions for allowing the use of translations by Paul Savoie from the book *Selected Poetry of Louis Riel*. While much of the mundane translation of the writings and documents of Riel and others was done by myself, I greatly appreciate the help I received from Joanne Bonneville, Julienne Morissette, Karina Fleury and Lorraine Chelle McConwell, who tackled the more difficult materials.

I would like to acknowledge the enormous value of the five-volume *Collected Writings of Louis Riel* in the writing of this manuscript. Published in 1985 by the University of Alberta Press, with general editor George F.G. Stanley, the *Collected Writings* seems to me to represent the best in academic scholarship.

Also essential to my research were the Saskatchewan Archives Board, the Provincial Archives of Manitoba, the Hudson's Bay Company Archives, the Provincial Archives of Alberta and the Glenbow-Alberta Institute Archives.

Finally I would like to thank two people who were inspirations throughout the writing of this book: my husband, Gerald B. Sperling, who is always my first reader and best editor, and Iris Skeoch, publisher of HarperCollins, who remained wonderfully helpful and enthusiastic.

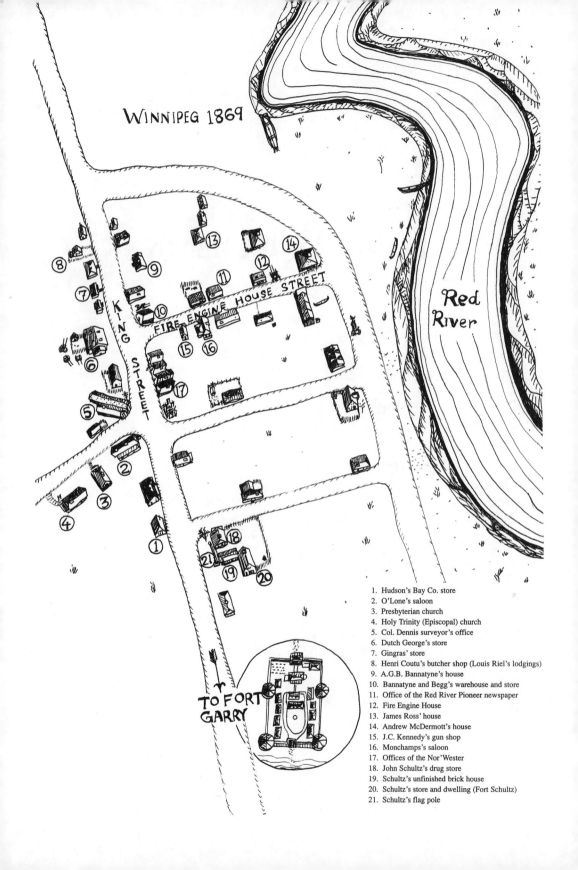

WINNIPEG 1869

Red River

KING STREET

FIRE ENGINE HOUSE STREET

TO FORT GARRY

1. Hudson's Bay Co. store
2. O'Lone's saloon
3. Presbyterian church
4. Holy Trinity (Episcopal) church
5. Col. Dennis surveyor's office
6. Dutch George's store
7. Gingras' store
8. Henri Coutu's butcher shop (Louis Riel's lodgings)
9. A.G.B. Bannatyne's house
10. Bannatyne and Begg's warehouse and store
11. Office of the Red River Pioneer newspaper
12. Fire Engine House
13. James Ross' house
14. Andrew McDermott's house
15. J.C. Kennedy's gun shop
16. Monchamps's saloon
17. Offices of the Nor'Wester
18. John Schultz's drug store
19. Schultz's unfinished brick house
20. Schultz's store and dwelling (Fort Schultz)
21. Schultz's flag pole

THE RED RIVER SETTLEMENT
1869

STONE FORT
(LOWER)

ST. ANDREW'S

ST. PAUL'S
MISSION

KILDONAN
& Town

WINNIPEG

ST. JOHN'S

HOUSE WHERE
LOUIS RIEL
WAS BORN

HEADINGLY

ASSINIBOINE RIVER

(UPPER) FORT GARRY

ST. CHARLES   ST. VITAL

ST. BONIFACE

STE. ANNE
des CHENES
(OAK POINT)

ST. NORBERT

RIVIERE SALE

STE. AGATHE

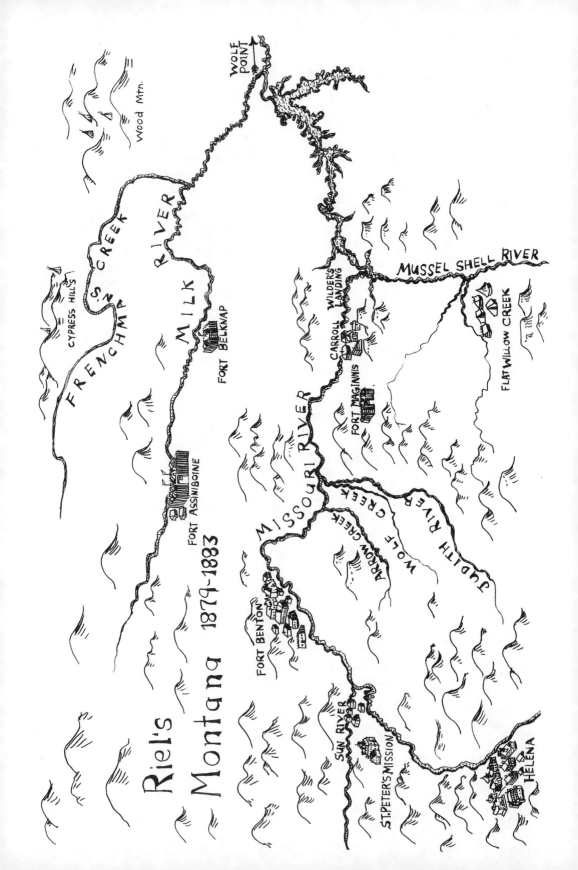

Riel's
Montana 1879-1883

WOLF POINT

Wood Mtn.

CYPRESS HILLS

FRENCHMAN CREEK

MILK RIVER

FORT BELKNAP

MUSSEL SHELL RIVER

FLATWILLOW CREEK

CARROLL

WILDER'S LANDING

FORT MAGINNIS

FORT ASSINIBOINE

MISSOURI RIVER

JUDITH RIVER

WOLF CREEK

ARROW CREEK

FORT BENTON

SUN RIVER

ST. PETER'S MISSION

HELENA

VILLAGE of BATOCHE

CARLTON TRAIL

TRAIL TO ST. LAURENT

SOUTH SASKATCHEWAN RIVER

HUMBOLT TRAIL

NORTH SASKATCHEWAN RIVER

SOUTH SASKATCHEWAN RIVER

Prince Albert

Fort Carlton

St. Laurent

St. Louis de Langeuin

Duck Lake

Beardy's Reserve

Batoche

One Arrow's Reserve

Gabriel's Crossing

Fish Creek

Clarke's Crossing

Humbolt

Saskatoon

PROLOGUE

Oh my God! How has Death become my fiancée, with all the horror I feel towards her?

And how can it be that the more she repels me, the more she seeks me out? *

AUGUST 2, 1885

It was a perfect prairie day. The drought had mysteriously broken; orange lilies, white primrose and rich pink prickly roses had come alive and were running amuck in the luxuriant grasses. The sky was a stunning azure, without a speck of cloud. A breeze played about.

As W.W. Harkins, Willy to his friends, bumped along in the little buggy, he thought to himself, this is exactly what the prairies are supposed to look like, which didn't give him much comfort. He was very nervous. He had convinced his paper, the *Weekly Star* of Montreal, to cough up the money to send him here, and he wasn't at all sure of success. He'd pulled as many strings as he could, with his cronies in the Conservative Party, the few officers he knew in the North-West Mounted Police, the lawyers he drank with, but he wasn't sure anything had come of it. Since he wasn't exactly a favourite with the publisher anyway, failure would likely mean his job.

Three miles west of the shack town of Regina, he spotted the Mountie

---

* The original punctuation, spelling and grammar found in Riel's poetry and journals have not been changed, unless the meaning was hopelessly unclear.

headquarters. Driving up to the main building, he braced himself, then asked for the man in charge, Inspector R. Burton Deane. Much to his amazement he was told that everything had been arranged. He would be the first person to interview the notorious Louis Riel since the Métis leader had given himself up two and a half months before.

The prison that held the condemned man had formerly been the guard house, a wooden structure, single storey, with a long slanting roof overhanging little windows, all heavily barred. Six Mounties in brilliant scarlet uniforms paced up and down outside, two more guarded the entrance and inside yet another stood at attention before the cell. Harkins thought the security around Jesse James would not have been any heavier.

The reporter was led not to Riel's cell, but to another airy room set up as a makeshift office. He sat tense, waiting, until he heard a banging down the corridor.

Two guards accompanied a burly, handsome man into the rather cramped quarters. In his right hand he carried an iron ball that was attached by a coarse chain to a shackle around his ankle. Harkins was taken aback by this, but his embarrassment was soon relieved, for the prisoner, bowing low, clasped his hand warmly and exclaimed, "Ah, my young friend, I am happy to meet you. I have seen you at work in the courtroom last week."

"I'm pleased to meet you, Mr. Riel. My request now is to interview you for my paper."

"The *Montreal Star*, oh, yes, I recollect it is a well-known newspaper. I am surely glad to meet its representative."

Harkins then suggested they sit down. Riel did so, depositing the iron weight on the floor beside him.

A few days before, in the crowded Regina courtroom, the reporter had watched as the curious had scrambled around Riel, much to the annoyance of the Mounties on guard, asking him for his autograph. Harkins hesitated at first, but then did exactly the same thing—"if your patience is not exhausted by previous experience."

Riel took up a sheet of NWMP supply paper and penned the following:

> To the Readers of *The Star*:
> I have devoted my life to my country. If it is necessary for the happiness of my country that I should now cease to live, I leave it to the Providence of God.
> Louis Riel

Any sharp journalist would have asked the essential question, and W.W. Harkins was no slouch. "Have you any hopes of escaping the scaffold?"

Riel paused, forming his reply carefully. Then his eyes burrowed into the reporter: "Yes, yes, that is a subject I like to converse about. Humanly speaking nothing can save me. Do I look excited?" he continued with a flash of a smile. "No—I do not, for I will be preserved from death at this critical hour through the divine and saving influence of our Lord Jesus Christ."

> *Death lies beside me in my bed. When sleep begins to close my eyes, she whispers. Her voice touches the bottom of my heart; it says that sleep is a rehearsal for death. "Notice," she says, "how sleep comes to you. That is almost how I will greet you on the day you will have to meet me."*

Relaxing a little, Harkins noted how impressively handsome this man was at forty years of age. Somewhat tall, and broad-shouldered without an ounce of fat, he had thick, curly hair, auburn-brown, worn long but nicely kept, a prominent, straight nose, a heavy brown beard, rather thin lips and those eyes—dark, glistening, expressive, as mesmerizing as they had often been described.

The reporter asked him why he sometimes called himself Louis "David" Riel. At that the Métis leader rifled through his pockets and eventually pulled out a well-worn piece of paper. "This is my marriage certificate," he explained. "As you will observe, I was married in Montana to a Cree woman. Well, listen and I will read." He turned the document over and read the reverse side. "I, Louis Riel, on this the occasion of my marriage, and in conformity with a custom prevailing in Catholic countries, hereby have taken in addition to my name the title of 'David'.

"When I was being hunted in the woods of St. Norbert like a wild beast, my friend Dubuc—he's a judge now—named me David after the great prophet who also spent years in the wilderness. I love and admire David so why shouldn't I take his name?"

> *Death reveals how much she is attached to me. She speaks tenderly, saying: "I am your wife. I don't want to turn my back on you. You'll never hear me say I'm leaving you. I follow faithfully wherever you go. I am always trying to embrace you for I love you. My only desire is to have and possess you."*

Harkins realized at that point that Riel had grabbed hold of the conversation and that it would be no small matter to get a word in edgewise. But then, why would he want to? This was front-page stuff. He did manage one question: "For how many years have you been aware that you possessed the gift of prophecy?" Since 1874, Riel responded matter-of-factly. The reporter began madly scribbling down his words.

"On the eighteenth of December 1874, while [I was] standing alone on a mountaintop near Washington, D.C., the same spirit that appeared to Moses in the midst of clouds of flame appeared to me in the same manner. I was astonished. I was dumbfounded. It was said to me: 'Rise, Louis David Riel, you have a mission to accomplish for the benefit of humanity.' The words, spoken in Latin, were addressed to me: I received my divine notification with uplifted arms and bowed head." Since then, said Riel, he had dedicated himself to humankind. And always with practical results. "And the province of Manitoba? Without our provisional government it would still be nothing more than a colony tied to the apron strings of Canada. I deserve to be called the Father of Manitoba."

> *When everyone, even your relatives and friends, has fled from you, deserted the place where you have been put, I, Death, whom you don't love and whom you fear so much, I will be your constant companion. Who can separate me from you? Who will come to take you from my arms? Who will disturb our union when I press you to my breast in the grave?*

The journalist noticed that Riel's manner of speaking had changed. At first, he had spoken tremulously in a low undertone, but slowly his passion was aroused until finally he stood upright, his huge head with its curly hair dancing from side to side in time with his gesticulations. He spoke with terrible earnestness. His eyes burned as if they contained some secret fire. His shirt was pulled open revealing his sun-browned rugged chest. From his throat hung a scapular which was flung to and fro by the breeze from the open window and his excited movements.

"My future will be a glorious one," he cried, "but what it will be, I cannot reveal to you. That would be a breach of the divine confidence."

The reporter was trying desperately to put to the Métis leader the question he had been itching to ask from the beginning. "Why did you murder Thomas Scott?" Riel looked as though he had swallowed a rotten plum, but he squared his shoulders, ready to reply. Then the door burst open and a police officer announced that time was up.

Harkins shook Riel's hand, as the Métis leader bowed low. The door clanged shut and prisoner and guards alike were gone. The reporter thought he could hear the prisoner mumbling to himself as he walked along the corridor.

> *Death is playing with me. My fear is her amusement.*

PART I
EMERGENCE

· 1 ·

Indian Blood throbs in me:
And I praise my ancestors
Who have in the sweetest tone
Taught me the Huron Carol.

The Red River is a sash of muddy brown water which loops with grandeur and daring through the Red River Valley. Jig-jagging alongside it is the little Seine, more creek than river. At the point of land where these two waterways meet, now an industrial area of Winnipeg, in a thatched-roofed house made of logs and mud plaster, Louis Riel was born. His mother always remembered that October 22, 1844, was a particularly beautiful sunny morning.

It's not outlandish to view these rivers, the Red and the Seine, as representing the double edge of Riel's persona, two forces, often antithetical, that etched deeply his short but incredibly eventful life.

The very essence of Louis Riel is contradiction. He was a handsome, smartly dressed, highly educated prude who enthralled his adoring constituency, the illiterate, risk-taking, pleasure-loving Métis buffalo hunters. His was a conservative political philosophy and yet he led a desperate, violent rebellion against the very political establishment he had once supported. He was a devout Catholic, yet his heart-felt religion was laced with Indian spiritualism, and he didn't hesitate to thumb his nose at meddling clergy, who promptly labelled him a heretic. Most important: only one branch of the Riel family shows Indian heritage—his paternal grandmother was a mixed-blood, all his other ancestors were French Canadian—and yet he symbolizes to this day the courage, pride and accomplishments of what is now seen as the Métis golden age.

Family tradition has it that Louis Riel was born in a house owned by his maternal grandfather, Jean-Baptiste Lagimodière. By the year of Riel's birth, Lagimodière was a prosperous farmer, a land owner of consequence and a prominent member of the Red River Settlement's bourgeoisie. His name is not found among the ranks of the Métis and French-Canadian dissidents who were rattling the cages of the governing establishment during those years. Although his was a most adventuresome past, Lagimodière was deeply conservative, a man who believed in the predestined hierarchy of his society, who respected authority for authority's sake. He was to have a profound influence on his grandson.

The first Lagimodière ancestor to immigrate to Quebec, Samuel Lecompte, sieur de la Vimaudière, arrived from France in 1693. He described himself as a "surgeon". His offspring thrived and multiplied over the years, with the family name somehow metamorphosing from Vimaudière into Lagimodière.

Louis Riel's grandfather Jean-Baptiste was born in December 1778 on the family farm near St. Antoine-sur-Richelieu on the east bank of the St. Lawrence River, 135 miles north of Montreal. His mother, Josephte Beauregard, died at age thirty-three shortly after giving birth to her third child, and Jean-Baptiste, eight years old at the time, and his two siblings were taken under the wing of an aunt. She lived near Maskinongé, in the diocese of Trois-Rivières, the main commercial centre and the seat of regional government. At the heart of this busy town was the governor's mansion, the Ursuline monastery and the Récollets' cathedral. Not surprisingly, the set pieces of Jean-Baptiste's character were deference to authority and devotion to church.

From the town's inception the fur trade had been Trois-Rivières's *raison d'être*. The precious cargo was shipped from the northern forests down the St. Maurice and warehoused in the town, which in turn distributed supplies to the traders heading north again. As the fur business spread farther west, the Trois-Rivières region became one of the incubators hatching young men—from noblemen's illicit offspring to farmers' sons—who were determined to escape the narrow confines of their church-dominated parishes and turn a quick profit from that plushest of gold—the beaver pelt.

By the second half of the eighteenth century, the *coureurs de bois*, middlemen between Indian trappers north of Lake Superior and Montreal merchants, had established themselves as romantic, adventurous role models for young men stuck in the deep poverty that was New France at the time. As the European developed his passion for stylish top hats made of felt from beaver pelts, the fur trade boomed, and the mechanism required to carry on this prosperous business grew more complex. The hired hands, the voyageurs, became lowly paid cogs in a complicated commercial machine. Most of the young adventurers of Trois-Rivières and other towns were hired on as contract servants, toiling eighteen hours a day in the harshest conditions to transport supplies over the Canadian Shield into the heart of the North American continent and carry the precious furs back to Montreal. The voyageur remains a precious Canadian legend. Tough, exuberant, lascivious, full of chip-on-the-shoulder pride and bravado, he was the muscle-power that drove the Montreal-based fur trade.

When Jean-Baptiste Lagimodière first headed west in 1799 at age twenty-one, he probably started out as a voyageur for the North West Company. If his was a standard contract, he would have signed on for three years.

Lagimodière began his career at a time when the St. Lawrence–based fur trade was in the grip of violence and chaos. The merchant aristocracy of Montreal were engaged in cut-throat competition that featured theft, murder and a free flow of liquor to Indian trappers. There was, however, one advantage that resulted from this brawl—more workers were needed and higher wages paid. Jean-Baptiste Lagimodière was one of those who benefited.

By 1804, however, a truce had finally been called and the fur barons amalgamated into one big enterprise, the mighty North West Company. Immediately all the extra voyageurs and others who had been hired at the height of the rivalry were considered superfluous. At this point Lagimodière probably lost his job and began a new career, as a hunter of bison and trapper of beaver attached only loosely to the fur companies, thereby joining the ranks of the freemen, *les gens libres*—a wild, dangerous, sometimes enchanting existence.

Freemen often spent the cold winters in log huts or Indian lodges in the shelter of the wooded Red River Valley, trapping beaver and otter and surviving on the abundance of white fish, water-birds and their eggs, and small game. But the fur-bearing animals in the area were becoming scarcer and trappers began ranging west and north, as far as the Peace River, spending months far removed from any human contact, to seek out the beaver with the thickest, glossiest, blackest pelts. These would be transported to the forts of the North West or Hudson's Bay companies, depending on where the best deal could be negotiated. These rugged men also hunted bison, both for their own consumption and to supply others—the fur company outposts quickly came to rely on them for their very existence.

As well as being hunters and trappers, some freemen developed into inventive entrepreneurs. They set up shop along the brigade routes, trading buffalo robes for the winterers' leather garments, operating primitive taverns and restaurants—one such outfit specialized in freshly baked bread—preparing slabs of bark and resin with which the voyageurs could repair their canoes, even at times acting as pimps, procuring the services of an Indian woman for some raunchy bourgeois. There is no record of Jean-Baptiste Lagimodière engaging as a petty trader. He was, however, a skilful hunter and trapper, and when he returned home to Trois-Rivières in 1805, he cut a dashing figure.

Certainly Marie-Anne Gaboury must have thought so, for she was smitten at once.

By all accounts, Marie-Anne was gorgeous. With lovely golden hair, bright blue eyes and pale complexion, a gift of her Normandy ancestors, she was often described as "petite", "dainty", "dignified". The fifth child of Charles Gaboury, a farmer, and his wife, Marie-Anne Tessier, she was born on August 2, 1780, near Maskinongé. By the time Jean-Baptiste arrived home, Marie-Anne had worked eleven years as an assistant housekeeper to the parish priest at Saint Joseph Church in Maskinongé. She was already twenty-five years old and everybody, her family and friends, wondered what she was waiting for. Why wasn't she married? The family's account has it that she was so lively and quick-witted that the thought of life with a dull farmer didn't appeal to her. But Jean-Baptiste Lagimodière was something quite different.

He made quite an impression that winter he spent in Lower Canada. He must have seemed wildly romantic, dark and good-looking, with the muscular build of a woodsman, and dressed in his fur trader's costume—typically a jacket of buckskin fringed with wild horse hair, moccasins beautifully beaded, a *capote* (over-cape) of caribou skin, all set off by an impressive otter-skin cap. One cold winter night, the parish organized a soirée featuring Lagimodière as guest speaker. Apparently he was superb at spinning tales of adventure, and not unreasonably Marie-Anne fell madly in love with him. The Lagimodière family were considered respectable, hard-working people and so the Gabourys, per-haps worried that their daughter might otherwise be doomed to spinsterhood, quickly gave their blessing. The couple were married on April 21, 1806, at the Saint Joseph Church.

In later years Marie-Anne claimed that, before their marriage, Jean-Baptiste had given every indication that his life as reckless woodsman was over, that he was prepared to settle down and work the family's farm. But as the warm spring breezes arrived that May and the ice on the river began breaking up, Jean-Baptiste twitched with impatience as he watched the voyageurs assembled at Lachine to prepare for their journey west. He finally admitted that he could not give up the thrill of life in the Northwest.

There had been similar situations in the past—the well-brought-up, reli-giously devout young woman marrying a man of the woods. He would go off to do his hunting and trapping and she would remain at home, bearing the children that resulted from his infrequent visits, and above all preserving his link with church and "civilization". Headstrong and spirited, and encouraged by the advice of the village priest (who may have heard Jean-Baptiste's confessions of promiscuity and concluded that his wife had better not leave his side), Marie-Anne astonished everyone by brushing aside this tradition. She would become the first white woman from the Canadas to take on the incredibly harsh, arduous existence that was a fur-trapper's life. Although she would live to the ripe old age of ninety-five, she would never return to Lower Canada, or see her family again.

Marie-Anne probably wasn't aware of it, but there was a most compelling reason for her to accompany her husband. She was in competition for Jean-Baptiste's affection—he already had a wife and three children who were anxiously awaiting his return.

The fur traders who ventured early into the wilderness of the Canadian Northwest could never have survived without the help of Indian women. These marriages, *à la façon du pays* ("according to the custom of the country"), were encouraged by Natives and Europeans alike for they established an economic symbiosis which fuelled the St. Lawrence–based fur trade. The Indian woman ground corn to make sagamité, chopped firewood, collected berries, snared hares and partridges and caught fish, which frequently saved the white traders from starvation and scurvy. She also provided her man with a never-ending supply of moccasins from deer or moose skins, and she netted the intricate webbing which gave the essential snowshoe its support. She collected wattappe (roots from the spruce tree) and with the resulting twine repaired his canoe, she dressed the beaver and otter furs and prepared the staple food of the Northwest—the famous pemmican, a mixture of buffalo meat, fat and berries. She also acted as a guide, a language teacher, and perhaps most important, an adviser on the traditions and customs of various Indian tribes with which her husband must deal. Some of these marriages were long and happy, even after the husband had left the fur trade. More typically, the Native woman was unceremoniously dumped as soon as the white had no further use for her; she and her children would simply melt back into her family's clan—at an emotional and physical sacrifice that can only be imagined.

Not long after he arrived in the West, Jean-Baptiste Lagimodière had begun living with a Chipewyan woman, and the union had produced three daughters. That after his marriage to a white woman he should abandon his country wife was not unusual, but that he should come back, with a new bride in tow, to the very place where his first family awaited his return seems unnecessarily insensitive and cruel. And Marie-Anne Gaboury too must have found it most unpleasant.

The journey from Lachine to the Red River had been as gruelling as every-one had warned her that it would be, lodged in the bottom of the huge canoe. Packed around with a mountain of supplies, she could hardly shift position without precipitating a tip-over. The hundreds of portages covered such rough ground, through mud, woods, bog, over rocky outcrops, that Jean-Baptiste had to carry his wife. Two storms which struck while the brigade crossed Lake Superior were so ferocious even the hardened voyageurs were unnerved; one canoe actually tipped over and several men drowned. Marie-Anne would later recite the details of that voyage again and again to her grandchildren, including Louis Riel, telling them how terrified she had been and how she had so fervently prayed to the Blessed Virgin Mary.

When the flotilla arrived at Fort William just in time for the boisterous, drunken celebration that was the great annual rendezvous of all Nor'Westers, Marie-Anne, having lived in the sedate respectability of the parish church for so many years, must have been just as shocked as she was at the terrible weather. She imparted to her grandchildren a lesson that Louis Riel for one never for-got—drunkenness is the font of all evil.

In July the brigade finally arrived at the North West Company trading post located at the point where the Red and Assiniboine rivers meet (now downtown Winnipeg). This had been a favourite gathering spot for trappers and traders since the famous French explorer Pierre de La Vérendrye had built an advance depot in 1738 called Fort Rouge. But Jean-Baptiste and Marie-Anne stayed only a short time before they began another five-day journey southward down the Red River heading for the little community of Pembina (presently situated at the Canada–U.S. border).

This was a favourite place for the buffalo; they gathered in the rolling, heavily wooded hills just where the Red meets the Pembina River. By 1801, free traders, their Indian wives and Métis children had built the first crude log shacks not far from a North West Company trading post called Fort Daer. When Jean-Baptiste and Anne-Marie arrived, about a half-dozen families were encamped there; Anne-Marie's lasting impression was that of the wives and their dress—"Canadian style" in brightly coloured shirts, short gowns, petticoats and leggings made of deer skin.

Their dress was a kind of metaphor for the diverse and colourful people that populated Canada's Northwest at the time. Since the very first French explorers and fur traders had made their way to the Great Lakes and beyond, they had mated with Indian women, and their offspring had come to be called Métis. By the late 1690s, the traders had set down permanent roots in the vast Canadian West, and over the next century their children would form a distinct cultural group, connected with the St. Lawrence–based fur trade. When the

French fur trade was reorganized under Anglo management, British traders formed liaisons with Métis, so that names like Grant, Bruce and McGillis popped up. But these people were quickly absorbed into the French culture. Not only were the Métis hunters of buffalo and trappers of furs, but they were natural entrepreneurs, serving as guides, interpreters, ferrymen, mail carriers.

As well as the Métis, there was another distinct group of mixed-bloods. These were the offspring of Scots and Brits who worked for the Hudson's Bay Company. Referred to often as Half-breeds or Country-born, they were English-speaking and Protestant. The sons were sometimes sent back to Great Britain to be educated, and they often served as the clerks, and occasionally even factors, for the Hudson's Bay Company.

Of course, the largest and most powerful group on the prairie at the time was the Indians—the Ojibwa, Cree, Assiniboine, Sarcee, Blackfoot, Blood Stoney, Peigan, Chipewyan, Beaver and Sekani. With the exception of the Sioux, who resided primarily in the United States, the relations between the mixed-bloods and Indians were most often peaceful and accommodating. The Métis in particular acted as a buffer, a link between Natives and whites.

This was the interesting world that greeted Marie-Anne on her arrival in the West. The Lagimodières set up housekeeping in a large tent near the Pembina fur-trading post—not far from where Jean-Baptiste's country wife and children lived.

How Lagimodière thought he could avoid disaster is hard to imagine, but naturally his Cree wife was horribly upset when she discovered Marie-Anne at his side. The Lagimodière family history, which totally ignores the feelings or rights of the original wife, claims that at first the Cree was very friendly towards Marie-Anne, doing her many favours to help ease the burden of camp life. But according to this legend, she was only waiting for the right moment to poison the young French Canadian. Some accounts say Lagimodière's dogs were exposed first and died slow painful deaths, thus saving Marie-Anne's life.

Whether the legend is true or not, Jean-Baptiste quickly packed up camp and moved his bride some forty miles away to a spot called Grand Camp at the head of the Pembina River where buffalo hunters traditionally gathered in summer and autumn. By the beginning of January 1807, however, the couple had moved backed to Fort Daer.* Marie-Anne was expecting her first child, and her husband realized she would need the help of other women during the birth.

---

* At this point Lagimodière's Indian family disappears from written history, never to be heard of again. Some have suggested that the wife's family insisted she join a clan in another location to keep the peace.

She delivered the baby in a squatting position, her moccasinned feet digging into a mat of moss, her upper body tied to a spruce pole for support. The baby was a girl with bright blue eyes and flaxen yellow hair which the Indian and Métis women loved to fondle, born on January 6, the birthday of the ruling king, George III. Given that the infant's birthplace was a teepee, the Lagimodières bestowed on her a rather unlikely name—Reine, honouring his most gracious majesty. Marie-Anne was said to have cried as she baptized the infant herself, lamenting that there was no priest within thousands of miles to do a proper job.

At the end of May, Lagimodière announced to Marie-Anne that they were moving. The Red River Valley was beginning to be over-trapped and he knew the beaver pelts found deep in the wilderness of the Rocky Mountains foothills were much more abundant and more valuable. He had formed a partnership with three other French-Canadian trappers, known to history only as Chalifoux, Bellegarde and Paquin, all married to Cree women, to better exploit this opportunity.

Up to that point, Lagimodière, like most of the French freemen, had dealt exclusively with the North West Company, primarily because the Montreal traders offered a better deal than their rival, the Hudson's Bay Company. While the Nor'Westers were offering freemen like Lagimodière hard cash for their beaver pelts, the Company would still only deal in goods.

James Bird, the HBC factor at Fort Edmonton on the North Saskatchewan River, realized what a mistake this was; in 1807 he wrote his superiors in London that more furs were received from freemen than from all the Native tribes, with the exception of the Iroquois, combined. The year before he had met Jean-Baptiste Lagimodière and had been impressed with his integrity and his trapping skill. Without waiting for permission from London, Bird offered cash, £12 Canadian per standard weight, a pound more than the Nor'Westers' price, and Lagimodière snapped up the deal. He became a staunch loyalist of the Hudson's Bay Company and remained so ever after.

At the end of May 1807, with Marie-Anne's baby safely stored in a papoose filled with moss, the group of four French-Canadian freemen and their wives took off in two canoes for a 1,200-mile trip. In the first portion, they travelled down the Red River to Lake Winnipeg and then up the Saskatchewan River until they reached Cumberland House, a Hudson's Bay Company post. There, a huge crowd was eagerly waiting to catch their first glimpse of a white woman. They must have regarded Marie-Anne with some awe since one of the partners, arriving before the main party, had announced that she was a kind of witch who could kill them by merely looking at them. This story was apparently concocted to protect her against the "savages".*

After a week's rest, the party set out along the Saskatchewan for Fort Edmonton. While they were preparing camp one night, their canoes tied to willows along the riverbanks, there occurred the incident that provided the most terrifying tale in Marie-Anne's bedtime story repertoire.

Lagimodière and his partners were sitting around the fire, chatting and enjoying a pipe, a fifth man named Bouvier who had joined them en route was gathering kindling nearby, and the women were preparing the tents for the night. Suddenly Bouvier let out a terrifying shriek. The other men grabbed their guns and, running into the woods, were horrified to find their companion being mauled by a huge black bear, her two cubs at her side. Lagimodière managed to shoot the bear and save Bouvier's life, but the man's face had been so badly clawed that his eyes and nose had all but disappeared. Marie-Anne nursed Bouvier for the rest of the journey, but he remained blind and crippled for the rest of his life.

The Lagimodières spent almost three years, from the summer of 1808 to the spring of 1811, in the Edmonton area. It was an important fur-trading area, attracting Blackfoot, Assiniboine, Sarcees, Blood and Cree. Marie-Anne never entirely got over her fear of people she considered "savage warriors", even though they performed many kindnesses for her.

During most of the winter Jean-Baptiste was away tending his snares and his wife was left alone under the protection of the factor of Fort Edmonton. In the spring and summer, however, Marie-Anne, who had quickly become a superb horsewoman, would follow Jean-Baptiste on long forays across the prairies hunting buffalo.

In August of 1808, Marie-Anne was riding a new horse, a bag of provisions hanging on one side, counterweighted by her child in a papoose on the other. The horse had often been used in buffalo hunts and as soon as the animal spotted a herd in the distance, it took off in wild flight. Marie-Anne clung desperately to the horse's mane until at last Jean-Baptiste cut across the runaway's

---

Marie-Anne seems to have had an ambivalent attitude towards Native peoples. While she didn't hesitate to adopt their way of life when her family's comfort was at stake— the baby's papoose, for example—and she made friends of the Métis and Indian wives of other freemen, she told her family that, no matter what the circumstances, she always dressed as "a proper French woman". A flatiron for pressing clothes, which weighed two and a half pounds, was carried by Marie-Anne from Quebec—the first flatiron in Canada's wilderness. It remained a precious family treasure.

path and halted it. Hours later, the young woman gave birth to her second baby. It was a boy whom they named Jean-Baptiste Elzéar but whose nickname Laprairie stuck with him all his life.

In the spring of 1809 the Lagimodières were involved in an experience so frightening that it soured Marie-Anne forever on life in the north.

The previous winter, news had reached Fort Edmonton that the wives of Jean-Baptiste's partners, all living with their Cree families at the time, had been killed in a horrible massacre perpetrated by their enemies, the Sarcee. These women had become close friends of Marie-Anne's and she wept for them.

When spring arrived the Lagimodières, as usual, went out onto the prairies to hunt buffalo. On one of their first nights camping, Jean-Baptiste woke to find their horses had either been stolen or wandered away. He took after them on foot and his wife was left alone. That evening a group of Sarcee surrounded her lodge. Although Marie-Anne was scared out of her wits, she had enough sense to remain hospitable towards them. When Jean-Baptiste arrived back in camp, the chief informed him that the couple would be held hostage until the safe return of members of his tribe who were trading at Fort Edmonton. The Lagimodières somehow escaped during the night but they knew the Indians would follow them. After five days at full gallop, their two babies strapped to the horses, they reached the banks of the Saskatchewan and Fort Edmonton, just as the Sarcee came in sight.

The experience so unnerved Marie-Anne that she remained at the fort that summer while Jean-Baptiste hunted buffalo. The following spring, 1810, however, she regained her courage and set out once again. Her third baby, a girl they named Josephte after Jean-Baptiste's mother, was born that summer somewhere in the Cypress Hills and she was thereafter called La Cyprès.

With three small children to look after, Marie-Anne was growing tired of the uncertain life of a fur trader's wife. As well, the profits from the business were not nearly as large as Jean-Baptiste had anticipated, and he began thinking of other ways of earning his living. When news reached the Lagimodières in 1811 that a colony of Europeans was to be established at the Red River Valley, Lagimodière decided to establish his base there. The family left Fort Edmonton for good that summer.

They must have been surprised when they arrived back at Red River. For the year before, on the high ground just at the elbow formed by the junction of the Red and Assiniboine rivers, the North West Company had built a huge trading post called Fort Gibraltar. Eighteen-foot palisades enclosed a beehive of buildings—two residences for forty-odd workers, stables, carpentry and blacksmith shops, a meat-house and kitchens, stores and an icehouse, atop of which sat a wooden watchtower. The grandest structure of all was a large and comfortable house occupied by the bourgeois (bosses).

Fort Gibraltar had become the nerve centre for the Nor'Westers' trade. Here was the warehouse where pemmican was collected and distributed to the canoe brigades scattered throughout the fur company's far-flung empire. In the region of the fort resided several hundred families, mostly Métis but some Indians, and a handful of English-speaking Half-breeds. The people lived in lodges or clusters of log cabins. Gardens full of potatoes and other vegetables and some wheat were planted, but this was only a sideline, for they were engaged in a much more profitable business. They were among the most successful fur-trappers and hunters of buffalo in the West. Most of them still dealt primarily with the North West Company, and their loyalty was to the trader-bourgeoisie, the "winterers" who ran the enterprise.

The Lagimodières spent the winter of 1811–12 in Pembina, Jean-Baptiste once again hunting bison and trapping furs, Marie-Anne giving birth to her fourth child, Benjamin. In the spring of 1812 the family moved back to Red River and Jean-Baptiste built a rough board hut, without windows or a wooden floor, twelve miles south of Fort Gibraltar, in an area now known as St. Charles. This was supposed to be a temporary home, but Marie-Anne and the children would end up living there, in isolation, for six years. Meanwhile, the family waited in anticipation until at last that August a hundred exhausted and hungry settlers, the first guinea-pigs of Lord Selkirk's infamous experiment, arrived at Red River.

Thomas Douglas, fifth Earl of Selkirk, was the scion of a dynasty that had played an influential role in the affairs of Scotland for centuries. Strikingly good-looking in a blond, effete way, he had been educated in arts at the University of Edinburgh, where the philosophy that young men of his social stature, wealth and influence should spend their lives promoting the common good was drummed into him. After graduation he toured France, meeting many of the intellectuals connected with the French Revolution. He absorbed a fundamental lesson from this experience: that highly placed gentlemen with humanitarian instincts must act to relieve the suffering of the downtrodden, for if they didn't the oppressed might resort to rebellion and violence. Heads might even roll.

On his return to Scotland, Thomas Douglas amazed his parents by deciding to work on the family farm. He toiled from dawn to dusk like a common labourer, in the process developing an appreciation for the land and a romantic ideal of the peasant. While touring northern Scotland, he also saw first-hand the incredible damage done by the Highland clearances—it had been discovered that raising sheep was more profitable than renting land to dirt farmers.

Thomas Douglas was overwhelmed by the plight of the poor crofter evicted from his land, and vowed to do something to help. After 1799, when he became earl, he set in motion the schemes that had boiled forth from his by now highly developed sense of *noblesse oblige*.

In 1802, after reading *Voyages* by the explorer Alexander Mackenzie, he proposed to the British Home Secretary that a settlement of Scottish immigrants be established along the Red River. His scheme was turned down as totally unfeasible. Undaunted, the following year he organized his first colonization scheme, settling eight hundred people on Prince Edward Island. This proved successful and he followed with another group of crofters at Lake St. Clair in Upper Canada. But the land there was low and marshy and would require costly drainage before it could be farmed. Most of the settlers fled as soon as they could.

Selkirk's reputation as an idealist and humanitarian began to tarnish. He dreamed up his colonization schemes in the comfort of his Scottish castle; he never accompanied his guinea-pigs, never personally supervised their shelter, food or distribution of land. Foolish, irresponsible, impulsive, fanatical were epithets soon heard whenever Selkirk's name was raised, as it often would be in Britain and Canada during the first decades of the nineteenth century.

In 1807 Selkirk married beautiful Jean Wedderburn, heiress to a considerable fortune in Hudson's Bay Company stock. Armed with his and his wife's interests, Selkirk persuaded the HBC stockholders to permit him to establish a colony of Scottish settlers at Red River. He would shoulder the expense of this scheme in return for a sizeable grant of land from the Company in what was known as Rupert's Land. And what a grant it was: 116,000 square miles, almost as large as the British Isles including Ireland, it extended south from Lake Winnipeg deep into what are now Minnesota and North Dakota,* and on the west far into Saskatchewan almost to the source of the Assiniboine River. Included in this magnificent gift were North West Company fur-trading posts which had been in operation for years, ignoring the Hudson's Bay Company's claim that the land had been granted to them by the British crown and providing the livelihood of Métis and Indians who certainly did not relish suddenly becoming subjects of an unknown Scottish lord. Indeed, the central contradiction of the Selkirk story is that although he was acting from a heart-felt concern for the Scottish Highland squatters, he didn't give two figs for the Indians, the Métis, the French Canadians, who had lived and thrived in the vast region which he now claimed as his own.

---

* *These areas did not become American territory until 1815, when the Treaty of Ghent concluded the War of 1812.*

On August 29, 1812, about a hundred ragtag, exhausted men—a mixture of Irish, Orkneymen, Glaswegians and Highlanders—arrived at Red River. They were the advance party, mostly labourers, for Lord Selkirk's settlers, and they had just suffered a year-long nightmare of a journey. During a horrendous winter at York Factory, many of Selkirk's first pioneers had died of exposure, starvation and scurvy. After an exhausting six-hundred-mile journey inland, they finally stumbled ashore at Red River, where they found almost nothing had been done in preparation for their arrival—there was no shelter, no warehouse to store seed, no stocks of food supplies. Many would have liked to see Lord Selkirk strung up right there.

Two months later the second contingent of seventy settlers arrived, and this time women and children were included.

Selkirk's settlers were supposed to begin growing their own food the moment they arrived at Red River, never mind that it was already fall and that their farm implements consisted solely of hoes pathetically inadequate for breaking the virgin prairie soil. They had never used snowshoes; they had never hunted large game; they had no idea how to make pemmican. It finally occurred to the man Selkirk had placed in charge and given absolute power, Miles Macdonell, that if the settlers were to have any hope of surviving the winter, they must travel the seventy miles to Pembina, where the buffalo traditionally gathered and where some two hundred Canadian freemen (including Louis Riel's grandfather) and Métis had already established the Fort Daer colony. The Indians who for centuries had resided in the neighbourhood, the Saulteaux, led by Chief Peguis, guided the settlers on the long journey; the children were given ponies to ride but most of the women had to walk the seventy miles. And the Saulteaux didn't hesitate to demand payment for their services. One settler had to hand over an antique gun once carried by his father at the Battle of Culloden; a woman had to give up her wedding ring. Settled in at Pembina in tents or huts, the Selkirk contingent spent the winter trying to track down scarce buffalo. Had it not been for the kindness and hunting skill of the Métis and freemen, the colony would have been devastated.

Actually, the settlers' predicament turned into something of a windfall for Jean-Baptiste Lagimodière. He was hired by Governor Macdonell for the goodly sum of £30 a year to organize hunting expeditions. With fifteen Métis and French-Canadian freemen under his supervision, he brought in as many as seven bison at a time. If that winter had not been so unusually mild, Lagimodière and the others could have provided for the settlers, but the buffalo remained far in the north. The shortage became obvious by December, and by April people were living on fish supplied by Métis, roots they dug up for themselves and the odd big game that Lagimodière and his cohorts managed to bag.

In the spring of 1813, the colonists returned to Red River, and began to till the soil in earnest. There were many disasters, among them flocks of ravenous blackbirds and pigeons so thick they were thought to be black clouds. A very small crop was harvested, so that settlers were forced to return to Pembina that winter. It was a cycle that would repeat itself for many years; Canada's history has seldom seen such suffering and deprivation as the Selkirk settlers endured, all the result of a Scottish lord's pipe dream. Still, there were enough people, the Lagimodières included, determined to see the colony prevail that it might naturally have evolved into a thriving community without bloody confrontations—if it had not been for the shortsightedness and stupidity of Macdonell, a rash, stubborn tyrant of a man, a Canadian Scot who had never been out West before but thought he knew everything.

There was no question that Miles Macdonell was faced with a terrible problem. In autumn 1813, Selkirk sent out another contingent of forty-odd settlers; mass starvation was a real threat. But the governor's solution to the crisis seemed designed to court disaster. He issued an order limiting the amount of pemmican that could be transported and he followed the proclamation by confiscating four hundred bags of North West Company foodstuffs. The following year he forbade the exporting of the vital commodity altogether. This embargo effectively cut the lifeline to hundreds of Nor'Wester employees scattered across the continent.

When the proclamation was tacked to the gate of Fort Gibraltar, it was received first with incredulous laughter and then with deep resentment. It marked the start of a fierce war between Nor'Westers and their allies and the supporters of the Hudson's Bay Company and the Selkirk settlement. Kidnapping, theft and murder quickly became acts of this unfortunate drama.

The North West Company had been bitterly opposed to the formation of a permanent agricultural settlement from the beginning. The partners realized that if political control in the Red River Valley devolved to the rival Hudson's Bay Company, the days of their mighty fur company would be numbered. As though to lay truth to their fears, almost as soon as Governor Macdonell arrived, he began buying furs from the Saulteaux, never mind that he had been promoted as the administrator of the Red River Settlement, not a trader. He was doing it only to maintain the friendship of the Indians, he claimed, but the Nor'westers naturally concluded that he was very much in bed with the HBC. Then Macdonell committed the final faux pas; he ordered the bourgeois of all North West depots on Selkirk land to vacate their posts. The Nor'Westers believed that even though they didn't have a land grant from the British crown, they certainly had squatters' rights, rights of first possession; in fact they felt they had as much authority to governor the Red River area as Selkirk's representative. They resolved to destroy the Red River colony and the audacious Governor Macdonell with it.

The method of attack was often ingenious. Duncan Cameron, one of the North West Company's experienced wintering partners and a man with a finely tuned Machiavellian mind, arrived in Red River in June of 1814. He immediately set out to woo Lord Selkirk's settlers, welcoming them to the well-stocked Fort Gibraltar, presenting gifts of scarce tea, sugar and liquor, and charming them by reminiscing, in their native Gaelic, about the beauty of their homeland. The North West Company, he promised, would transport them in company canoes to Upper Canada and guarantee free, tillable farm land in "civilized surroundings". By June of 1815, more than half of the original families had taken up his offer—they considered it their "blessed salvation"—and quit the colony for good.

The Nor'Westers' main defence against the threat of a permanent settlement, however, was the Métis, not only those located near Red River, but those throughout the entire Northwest. Lord Selkirk's vision had the mixed-bloods taking up land and becoming stable farmers in his colony. But Selkirk was a deeply ingrained racist, a typical imperialist of his age, who believed whites and Métis were "unequally evolved races"; in his land distribution scheme, the Europeans were to settle around the Assiniboine and Red rivers and the Métis were to be kept on the periphery. Governor Macdonell was even more intolerant; he openly condemned unions between whites and Indians and he announced that he would discourage the mingling of the two races. Certain that the Métis were purposely driving the bison away from the colony, he issued a decree forbidding them to hunt the buffalo on horseback, although this might have resulted in starvation for everybody. Naturally this attitude did not endear Macdonell to a people who were experiencing the first stirrings of nationalism, a sense that as far as surviving on the prairies and northern woodlands were concerned, they were far more masterly than any Scottish settler. Most would ally themselves with the North West Company; many would resort to bloody violence.

The third force in the Red River Valley consisted of the hundred or so freemen, mostly French Canadian but some Scottish immigrants as well, who were far more ambivalent in their feelings towards the conflict. Many simply wandered off into the prairies to hunt buffalo, thereby escaping the growing tension at Red River. Jean-Baptiste Lagimodière did nothing of the sort; he remained totally devoted to Lord Selkirk, his colony, and the Hudson's Bay

Company. He helped the Selkirk settlers harvest their grain crop, hauled their timber and other goods with his Red River carts, continued to hunt large game to feed them. His devotion remained firm long after other freemen had become alienated by Macdonell and his tyrannical manner. Lagimodière had been brought up to respect authority even in the guise of the British Hudson's Bay Company.

During the winter of 1815 the violence intensified, until finally Governor Macdonell, realizing that he had few supporters even among the English-speaking Half-breeds, resigned his post and went into hiding. The Métis continued to torment the settlement, stealing horses, killing cattle, digging up fences, ruining crops by encouraging horses to gallop through the fields, dragging off ploughs. Defections among the settlers increased so that by the second week in June 1815 only eighteen loyalists were left. Macdonell finally gave himself up to the Nor'Westers—to avoid blood-shed, he claimed. He was promptly detained and sent back to Montreal to be dealt with. These victories only added to the Métis sense of power, and on June 27 they issued a proclamation ordering that the colony be vacated. As the settlers boarded the six boats, along with their possessions and their small flock of sheep, they saw smoke billowing up from the Hudson's Bay Company's Fort Douglas. The Métis had set fire to the heart of their colony.

The Lagimodières must have watched all this with great fear, for they were now branded as Selkirk sympathizers; indeed their cabin had become a kind of outlet where buffalo meat was bought and sold. Fortunately, most of the Métis left Red River for the west and south to hunt buffalo. Still, the Lagimodières must have breathed a deep sigh of relief when, on August 19, Colin Robertson, a seasoned North West winterer who had switched allegiance and joined the Hudson's Bay Company, showed up in the colony with the set-tlers in tow—he had come across them huddled on the banks of Lake Winnipeg and persuaded them to return. Robertson quickly understood that a most precarious situation existed in the colony and asked Jean-Baptiste to per-form the most difficult feat of his life. He was to travel to Montreal, on foot in dead of winter, to warn Lord Selkirk, newly arrived from Scotland, of the grave peril his colony faced.

On October 17, 1815, Lagimodière tied on his snowshoes, shouldered his long rifle, and hugged his wife and children goodbye.

Meanwhile, Colin Robertson, as interim governor of the colony, had set out to appease the Métis, paying large sums for pemmican and furs, and distributing quantities of rum and tobacco. As well, as a show of force, he captured Fort

Gibraltar and arrested the Nor'Wester Duncan Cameron. His carrot-and-stick tactics seemed to be working; a brief period of peace ensued—until newly appointed "Governor-in-chief of all of Rupert's Land" Robert Semple blundered into the colony. A man of great self-importance, with a full-blown superiority complex, Semple immediately upset Robertson's fragile truce. He demolished Fort Gibraltar, rafting the stockades downstream to the HBC's Fort Douglas and burning what was left. Nothing could have infuriated the Métis more; the North West fort had come to symbolize their long success as hunters and trappers of the plains. The news of the destruction spread like wildfire across the prairies. Acts of revenge followed immediately.

The leader of the Métis was actually an English-speaking Half-breed. Cuthbert Grant was the twenty-three-year-old son of a Scottish North West wintering partner and a Cree mother, who had been educated in Scotland and Montreal and who had returned to the West as a bourgeois for the North West Company. In May 1816 his "cavalry" of Métis sharpshooters overtook a Hudson's Bay brigade, seizing the pemmican and furs. When word of the destruction of Fort Gibraltar reached them, Grant's little army attacked the Hudson's Bay Company's Brandon House in retaliation. The supplies found there were included with the other cargo, some 1,150 pounds of pemmican, to be transported to Lake Winnipeg, where a party of bourgeois and voyageurs were waiting to carry supplies to North West Company posts. This was in contravention of the embargo on pemmican imposed by Selkirk authorities, but it didn't deter Grant. The Métis battalion, travelling on the traditional route to the west, was only three miles from Fort Douglas when Governor Robert Semple spotted them.

Brushing aside warnings from the older settlers, Semple and a party of two dozen volunteers rode out to intercept Grant and his men. The two sides met in a shady grove of trees known as Seven Oaks on the afternoon of June 19. The Métis and Indians, some wearing war paint, immediately fanned out on either side of Grant. Semple, arrogant as ever, approached the Métis envoy, François Firmin Boucher, who had been designated by Grant to negotiate with the settlers. Boucher apparently asked Semple why Fort Gibraltar had been destroyed and called him a "damn rascal"; Semple, stunned by what he considered the Métis's insolence, made a grab for Boucher's gun while seizing the reins of his horse. Boucher slid from his mount and ran for the Métis line. Shots rang out. Twenty minutes later, twenty-one settlers, including Governor Semple, were dead. Only one Métis was killed. The Battle of Seven Oaks was considered by the Métis as a great victory, the birth of their ethnic pride and the idea that they were a separate people, a separate nation.

Marie-Anne Lagimodière was one of those who watched the massacre from the HBC's Fort Douglas. After Jean-Baptiste had set out on his journey, she had moved there with her brood—the fifth child, Pauline, had been born in 1813. In the Lagimodière tradition, she had helped the Selkirk colonists, working during harvest, cutting hay. Now she and her children were branded as Hudson's Bay Company loyalists and she feared for their lives. Realizing that the victorious Métis would soon occupy the fort, the weary Selkirk settlers once again packed up for a quick escape. Marie-Anne was determined not to leave Red River without her husband. Fortunately, the evening after the Seven Oaks battle, Peguis, the chief of the Saulteaux, who considered himself a "blood brother" of Jean-Baptiste's, came to the fort and offered shelter to Madame Lagimodière and her family. While she was embarking for the short trip across the Red River, Marie-Anne was so frightened she fainted, upsetting the canoe, dumping herself and the children into the water. Three or four Saulteaux warriors were on hand to rescue them.

Marie-Anne and her family spent the summer as guests of Chief Peguis and his wife in their lodge. When the cool fall arrived they moved into a wooden hut on the east side of the Red River, opposite Fort Gibraltar, built by an old friend of the Lagimodières', the freeman Bellehumeur. The subsequent months were extremely difficult for Marie-Anne; it had been such a long time since Jean-Baptiste had set out on his journey, she was sure something terrible had happened to him. How was she, a woman alone in the wilderness, supposed to provide for and protect her five children?

While all the commotion was going on at Red River, Jean-Baptiste had been making his way eastward battling a winter that was truly ferocious. By the time he reached Kingston his food supplies had disappeared and he had been forced to eat boiled moss and even the carcass of a small dog to survive. Finally on March 10, 1816, he arrived in Montreal and went directly to the residence of Lord Selkirk. There is a marvellous painting by Adam Sherriff Scott, shown often in Canadian rotogravures of the 1920s, which captures the excitement of this event. There is a grand ball going on at Selkirk's elegant home. The women are decked out in lovely pastel, low-cut gowns; their bosoms all seem to be heaving in unison. The gentlemen are attired in formal evening wear or elegant military dress. Lagimodière has just burst in. Obviously servants have tried to prevent the woodsman from entering the ballroom, for one has been harshly brushed aside and has fallen on his behind, the other is trying to restrain the intruder without success. Lagimodière is dressed pure woods—antelope-skin leggings and coat, *ceinture fléchée*, (the famous L'Assomption sash), a red cap. He sports a heavy black beard. He is seeking Lord Selkirk, who stands in the centre of the room looking alarmed and very effete, his beautiful wife at his side. In Lagimodière's hand is the leather sack containing the precious dispatches he has carried 1,800 miles. Although the scene is probably apocryphal, Lagimodière's feat was truly courageous. Over the next century he would evolve into a mythic folk hero, a wonderfully romantic symbol—if one that remains today somewhat primitive and simple-minded—of the Canadian wilderness.

After indulging in a couple of weeks' rest and a shopping spree buying fancy clothes for himself* and his family, Lagimodière set out to retrace his route. This time he was armed with letters from Selkirk giving instructions to his men at Red River. The North West Company bosses, however, had learned of his mission—their network of spies in Montreal was amazing—and were determined not to let Jean-Baptiste through. On June 16, he and three companions were nabbed by ten Indians loyal to the North West Company near Fond du Lac (Superior, Wisconsin). They were then escorted to the North West wilderness headquarters at Fort William. They were eventually released, but they were stripped of everything—food, knives, guns and powder, tents, even personal things that Lagimodière held dear, including his *ceinture fléchée*, his rum and all the expensive gifts he had bought in Montreal. The group might have starved to death if a Métis, Pierre-Paul Lacroix, hadn't found them at Rainy River near present-day Fort Frances, Ontario.

It was almost Christmas 1816 when Jean-Baptiste finally reached Red River and appeared at Bellehumeur's little house. The family was joyfully reconciled. And he brought good news—Lord Selkirk was on his way to personally re-establish his colony.

After Lagimodière had arrived to warn him of the danger at Red River, Selkirk had sprung into action. Unable to persuade the government to provide him with a military escort—Lower Canadian politicians thought him a meddler who was seriously undermining the fur trade—he had hired four officers and seventy soldiers. These were chiefly foreigners—Germans, French, Italians and Swiss—who had fought for Britain during the Napoleonic battles and who had been brought to Canada during the War of 1812. On arrival at Red River, they were to be granted parcels of land for their service. (They were, however, old soldiers, not farmers, and few evolved into the model settlers which Lord Selkirk had anticipated.) Selkirk, by this time, was in a dither, exultant one moment, depressed the next—all the time coughing blood into his handkerchief.

---

* *He likely was spending the fee he had received—£50—for his services; Marie-Anne was to receive an annual indemnity of £7 for ten years if Jean-Baptiste perished while performing his duties.*

The tuberculosis which would eventually kill him was advancing at an alarming rate. When the news of the Seven Oaks tragedy reached him, his determination turned into frenzy.

On August 13, 1816, Selkirk and his bodyguards occupied Fort William and arrested (illegally, as it turned out) several senior Nor'Westers. In January 1817, an advance party of thirty-five mercenaries under the command of the infamous Miles Macdonell set out to recapture Fort Douglas at Red River. Since by now many Métis, including Grant, were away buffalo hunting, Lord Selkirk's little army, arriving under cover of night, captured the fort without firing a shot.

In July 1817, to the salute of cannon and loud cheers, Selkirk finally arrived at the Red River Settlement. He remained for three months, once again attempting to forge his utopian dream in the wilderness. The Saulteaux, who had remained friendly to the Hudson's Bay Company—they took to calling Selkirk "Father"—sold him their land along the Red River, an act they would ultimately deeply regret. A surveyor set to work imposing order on the colony's physical contours and about 150 of the original settlers who had fled after Seven Oaks returned.

Naturally there were rewards to be handed out to the faithful. For generations a sword presented in gratitude by Lord Selkirk to Jean-Baptiste was displayed prominently in the Lagimodière household; ironically this symbol of deference to authority was hung near the casket of Louis Riel as he lay in state in the family home after he had been hanged for treason.

Of more immediate material advantage was the grant of land bestowed on Lagimodière. It was triangular in shape, wedged between the Red and Seine rivers. In 1882, one of Lagimodière's sons would sell this land, along with other parcels he had acquired in the area, for $100,000—a fortune in those days.

The year 1818 was wonderful for Marie-Anne. Her husband spent the winter cutting logs to build a comfortable house with large windows, a real door and a roof of thatch, their first permanent home since their marriage twelve years before (the very place their grandson, Louis Riel, would be born twenty-six years later). During that summer, the Lagimodières finally moved in, and Marie-Anne marked the occasion by planting a field of corn.

On July 16, she experienced the most memorable event of all. The first Catholic missionaries destined for permanent residence finally reached Red River. Marie-Anne would later tell her grandchildren that she cried for joy when Father Joseph Provencher, a tall, handsome man, and Father Sévère Dumoulin stepped from their canoe. Only days later, over a hundred Métis and Indian children were baptized; Marie-Anne was called upon to be godmother of them all. She was the only Catholic white woman, and the clergy considered aboriginal adults unsuitable. Only three of the five Lagimodière children could be baptized immediately; the older two, at nine and eleven years, had to be trained in Catholic catechism first.

The missionaries made no plans to immediately set up schools; saving the souls of "savages" was their first priority. One of the great sacrifices Marie-Anne made when she came west was the education of her children. None of them learned more than the rudiments of reading and writing; most were totally illiterate, including Louis Riel's mother, Julie.

During 1817–18, the Red River colony began to take shape. Lord Selkirk made plans for bridges, roads and churches, and promised a well-stocked store would soon open. His mercenaries, allocated land near the Lagimodières, chose to build their houses, all thirty-one of them, close together, European style, creating the settlement's first artery, called German Street. And the colonists planted a giant crop—peas, potatoes, pumpkins, Indian corn, barley and, most important, wheat, which seemed to spring from the ground that early summer. It was the first indication that the valley might indeed be as fertile as the dreamers had predicted. Then, just as the corn was on the ear and the barley ripe, the grasshoppers arrived, clouds so thick they blackened the sky. Crops, gardens, every piece of greenery in the colony was destroyed by the ravenous insects within hours.

The grasshoppers reappeared for four consecutive, miserable years, destroying the wheat crop each time. Bread came to be considered the greatest of luxuries. The entire colony again moved to Pembina for the winter; again only the buffalo hunts organized by Jean-Baptiste Lagimodière and the Métis kept the settlement from starvation.

After another disastrous crop in 1821, the next three years produced fairly good harvests. For the first time there was real hope in the air. The stable population now stood at four hundred, and forty-two new houses were built in one year. But as if to make amends for any small progress the settlers might enjoy, calamity struck once again.

The winter of 1824–25 was cold and severe; in December an incredible blizzard descended which lasted for days, killing most of the horses out grazing. Then the buffalo mysteriously and suddenly evaporated.

Thirty-three people lost their lives that winter. One family, a husband, wife and three children, were buried inside their shelter in the snow for five days and nights, without food or fire, before they were finally dug out. The woman and two of the children survived, but the others perished.

Out on the prairie, Jean-Baptiste Lagimodière was desperately trying to find food when he came across several families huddled together for warmth; two children had already frozen to death. As he approached he realized that they were raving mad, out of their minds with hunger. They had already eaten their dogs and horses and even their leather shoes. Lagimodière had just bagged a couple of rabbits and he was able to cook them with some kindling he carried. He then helped the settlers back to the main camp at Pembina.

But that was only the beginning of the tragic year of 1825. On May 2, when the ice on the Red River finally broke up, the water seemed to be running far more swiftly than normal. Even the Indians were startled. Then the rivers began to swell, the water rising nine feet in twenty-four hours. By May 5, fifty houses along the riverbanks were first battered by huge ice blocks and then swallowed by the surge; trees were torn up by their roots and cattle swept away. The settlers fled to the higher ground of Bird's Hill and Silver Heights, and from there watched the demolition with dread. The water continued to rise until May 21, turning the prairie for miles around into a huge, turbulent sea.

The Lagimodières lost everything and Marie-Anne had finally had enough. Already a mass exodus from Red River was taking shape—most of the ex-mercenaries would leave—and she pleaded with her husband to return to Lower Canada. His only reply was that if the priests were brave enough to remain, then so were they. He set to work building yet another house.

In fact, that disastrous year was the nadir of the colony's misery. The summer of 1828 produced a bumper harvest, and after that, although hardships continued to plague the settlement, the threat of starvation eased. During the 1830s, prosperity was in the air and the Lagimodière family became one of the most successful in the colony.

Jean-Baptiste continued to hunt bison and, to a lesser degree, trade furs, but slowly these means of livelihood were replaced by agriculture. By 1832 he had established himself as a farmer with some 27.5 acres planted; by 1849 he was seeding 75 acres, the largest farm in St. Boniface, the town named after the newly established Catholic church, and he kept nearly a hundred head of cattle. He was involved in the transportation business and by 1843 owned fourteen Red River carts and oxen.

Marie-Anne had given birth to three more children—Romain in 1819, Julie in 1822 and Joseph in 1825. At a time of high child mortality, and despite the incredible hardships the family had endured over the years, not one of the Lagimodière offspring died before adulthood. All four sons, Laprairie, Benjamin, Romain and Joseph, joined their father's thriving farm and transport operations. The girls married well and had many children. Marie-Anne's one sadness involved her eldest daughter, the one they called Reine after King George. In 1822, at age fifteen, she married a French-Canadian settler, Joseph Lamer. After the disastrous flood of 1826, the Lamers and their two children fled to the United States. Marie-Anne wouldn't see her eldest daughter again for forty-two years.

Jean-Baptiste's favourite child seems to have been the dark-haired, dreamy little girl with high cheekbones and saucer eyes named Julie. In 1843, at age twenty-one, she would marry a handsome, flamboyant young Métis, five years her senior, who had bought some land near her family's. A year later she would give birth to her beloved first child, a boy they called Louis after his father, Jean-Louis Riel.

The first Riel to immigrate to Lower Canada arrived at the turn of the eighteenth century; a document dated August 3, 1700, notarizes a concession of land from Dame Louise Bissot, seigneuresse of Lavaltrie (located directly across the St. Lawrence from where Jean-Baptiste Lagimodière was born) to Jean Riel (or Riol as it was then spelled). Riel had not emigrated from France as one might have supposed, but from the parish of Saint Peter, County Limerick, Ireland. During the sixteenth and seventeenth centuries Ireland and France, both Catholic countries, were sometime allies in their struggle with Protestant England, and many Irish soldiers fought in French campaigns, particularly those of Louis XIV. Fishermen of the ocean ports also travelled freely between the two nations and populations inevitably intermixed. This apparently was the case with Jean Riel's family, who may originally have been fishermen from Brittany.

After Jean settled in Lower Canada in 1700, the next three generations of Riels continued to reside in the Lavaltrie area. By the 1780s, however, the family had moved to Berthierville, just south of Maskinongé; in all likelihood the Riels knew the Lagimodières.

Louis Riel's grandfather Jean-Baptiste Riel was born at Berthierville in April 1785. Like Jean-Baptiste Lagimodière, he dreamed of travelling west, and at age fifteen years and eight months, he signed up as a voyageur with the North West Company. He likely started out as a *mangeur de lard* ("pork eater", so called because of the bits of pork they mixed into their gruel), a member of a twelve-man crew who transported supplies as far as the head of Lake Superior (Rainy Lake) and then carried furs back to Montreal. He probably then graduated into the ranks of *les hommes du nord*, the Northmen, the elite of the fur trade, who delivered their precious cargo to depots deep in the Northwest where they would spend the winters. By about 1809, Jean-Baptiste Riel was wintering permanently at the North West Company's fort at Île-à-la-Crosse.

Situated on the lake of the same name (so called because the Indians played lacrosse on its frozen surface during winters), on the Upper Churchill River, this Indian meeting-place was a strategic pemmican depot during the expansion of the fur trade into the Athabasca region. Jean-Baptiste Riel probably met Jean-Baptiste Lagimodière during the years the Lagimodière family trapped near Fort Edmonton.

Riel spent the long winter nights in the company of an old friend, another North West Company *engagé* named Louis Boucher. Boucher also hailed from Berthierville, Quebec; his family and Riel's had known each other for generations. Boucher had come west much earlier than Riel and had married a Chipewyan, Marie-Joseph LeBlanc. In 1811, Boucher decided to move his family back east, but by that time Jean-Baptiste Riel had fallen in love with their daughter. The following year, Riel and Marguerite Boucher began living together (there were no priests in the area to consecrate a marriage). The only Indian blood, therefore, that the Riel family could boast of and which could legitimize them as Métis came from Marguerite's mother.

The Chipewyans traditionally lived along the Churchill River system* and their life was harsh. In the sparse northern forest, resources were scarce and starvation, especially in the frigid winters, was always a threat. In small bands they ranged over thousands of miles searching for caribou, although moose, bear, beaver and fish were also part of their diet. Their talent in using every scrap of any animal they killed, fashioning clothing, moccasins and even tents from caribou skin, for example, was considered astonishing. They quickly understood the financial advantages offered by the fur business and were drawn into the trading orbit of the Hudson's Bay Company in the early eighteenth century.

The Inuit to the north and Cree to the south were their traditional enemies, but before Europeans brought guns, warfare was not an all-consuming passion; daily life was too precarious to allow for frequent outbreaks of war. The fur traders pushing into the Athabasca brought the Chipewyans the weapons they needed to ward off their enemies, but they also brought smallpox. Samuel Hearne, who traded in the area in the 1780s, estimated that ninety percent of the Chipewyans had been wiped out by the disease. Hearne probably exaggerated, but by 1800 the epidemic had left the Chipewyan nation a shadow of its former self. The fur trade changed the Indian in other ways too; the profit motive infused competition and individualism into a society that had been primarily communal in character. This was to have a devastating effect on the Chipewyan and other Indian nations.

Chipewyan women had always been considered near perfect mates for the European fur traders. They were used to a hard life; their endless round of domestic chores was made even more onerous because they were constantly on the move. It was their job to pack up and transport their families' goods—they would even harness themselves to their sleighs to haul their heavy cargo through

---

* *With the Beaver and Slaves, the Chipewyans are part of what is often called the Dene Nation. They speak Athapaskan, quite different from the Algonkian language of their southern neighbours.*

water or wet snow. They were, needless to say, incredibly strong. They were also known for their high spirits, unfailing honesty and devotion to their families.

The Chipewyans were most often Hudson's Bay Company loyalists; indeed, their relationship with the North West Company was often very sour. In the 1790s the Nor'Westers, desperate to keep their monopoly in the Athabasca area, took to strong-arming the Indians into trading exclusively with them. They even began seizing their women in payment of debt. Whether Marie-Joseph LeBlanc had been coerced into marrying Louis Boucher is not recorded. Whatever the case, the relationship must have been a loving one, for Boucher took his Chipewyan wife with him when he returned to the East, and they legitimized their marriage in the Berthierville parish church.

Jean-Louis Riel, the first of Jean-Baptiste Riel's and Marguerite Boucher's seven children, was born on June 7, 1817, at Île-à-la-Crosse. He lived there until he was five, when his father decided to move the family to Lower Canada. Jean-Baptiste Riel had suddenly lost his job and there was no hope of finding another in the fur country.

In 1821, after a ferocious struggle with its rival the mighty North West Company was absorbed by the Hudson's Bay Company; its world-famous name disappeared, and its trading posts and knowledgeable employees would now be controlled by a rich and powerful monopoly based in London.

As usual, those who suffered the most from these high-finance manipulations were the lowest on the totem pole—the Métis and French-Canadian voyageurs and labourers. George Simpson, the anointed governor of the new HBC, was the ultimate penny-pincher; he carried out a consolidation of services so extreme that by the end of 1824 only about a third of those who had previously been employed by the two fur companies still held their jobs. At Île-à-la-Crosse, the North West Company's fort was closed and most of its employees fired, Jean-Baptiste Riel among them.

The Riels had always been a deeply religious family, and the fact that their marriage had been legitimized by one of the newly arrived priests at Red River in 1818 meant a great deal to them. When the family returned to Berthierville in 1822, Jean-Louis, aged five years, was immediately baptized at the parish church, his grandfather Louis Boucher standing by his side.

The Riel family remained in Berthierville for about five years, until they moved to Mont-Saint-Hilaire, a forestry town twenty miles east of Montreal on the Upper Richelieu River. There's no record of how Jean-Baptiste provided for his family, although he was probably in some trade, but his first-born, Jean-Louis, received a fairly good education. As an adolescent he learned the craft of carding wool, and worked in a wool factory for a few years. This experience would eventually help him earn his living in the Red River settlement.

There is some indication that Jean-Louis Riel was involved in the Lower Canadian Rebellion of 1837. For one thing, Louis-Joseph Papineau, the leader of the insurrection, remained his idol throughout his life. Although only twenty, Riel already had a highly developed sense of justice and a flamboyant personality to go with it. Possibly he joined in the rabble-rousing meetings where fiery orators advocated the violent overthrow of the colonial government. However, by the time open revolt broke out, Jean-Louis Riel had left for the Northwest.*

Following in the steps of his father, he signed on with the Hudson's Bay Company as a voyageur, a middleman (meaning his spot was in the middle of the canoe). But unlike his father he did not ply the great water highway between Lachine, Quebec, and fur-trading posts of the far Northwest. Times had changed and so had the voyageur's job.

Rainy River flows into the lake of the same name, which straddles the Ontario and Minnesota borders. It had long been a crucial depot for the voyageurs travelling north; in fact, for some years their *canots du nord* were built there. When the two fur companies amalgamated in 1821, Lac la Pluie remained an important trading post for Indian fur-trappers. This cargo was shipped, not to eastern Canada, but to York Factory on Hudson Bay, and from there to Europe. Voyageurs, including Riel, were stationed permanently at Rainy Lake.

HBC records first mention Jean-Louis Riel on October 30, 1837. On that date, he bought two moose skins, likely to make moccasins and other apparel, fifteen litres of maple sugar and six yards of plain jerkin from the company stores. He was one of twenty-seven HBC servants assigned to Rainy Lake, including the chief factor and apprentices. Riel's job paid him the rather lowly sum of seventeen pounds a year, about average. Interestingly, his ethnicity was listed as "native" rather than "Canada"; although he had spent most of his adult life in Quebec, his grandmother's origins still labelled him, at least in the West.

Over the next couple of years his work description changed to labourer, one of nine such employees at Rainy Lake. He worked at odd jobs; one company journal reveals how he spent several days digging up rich black earth around the portage, dumping it in the kitchen garden, then adding large quantities of dung, in preparation for next year's vegetable crop. This was menial work which must have seemed a little demeaning to a man of his education but, since he spoke no English, the language of the HBC, there was little opportunity to advance. His contract stipulated a three-year term of service and he

---

* It may have been that his family was eager to have the hot-headed young man clear of trouble, and that his father used his connections to get him a job with the Hudson's Bay Company.

may have planned to return east when his time was up in the fall of 1840. If so he would have been accompanied by a family, for he was already living with a young Métis woman. Nothing much is known about her except that she was connected, in some way, with the Catholic mission. That the two set up a household can be deduced from Riel's credit account with the Hudson's Bay Company: his debt tripled to seven and a half pounds, and items he bought now included fine cotton and sewing needles.

In 1839, there is a brief notation beside Riel's name in the company accounts—"goes to Canada, left at Norway House". According to the Riel family account, Jean-Louis's young wife died during childbirth and he was so distraught that the Hudson's Bay Company released him from his contract early, so that he could return to Mont-Saint-Hilaire. The baby, raised by her Métis grandmother, was named Marguerite after Riel's mother. Riel did not abandon this daughter; over the years he apparently kept in touch with her and may have sent money for her education. In 1859 she married Jean-Baptiste Zastre, and the couple eventually settled in Manitoba.

On June 3, 1842, Jean-Louis Riel entered the novitiate of the Oblates of Mary Immaculate at Mont-Saint-Hilaire. Why he decided to become a missionary is not known, although it may have had something to do with his wife's premature death and his deep religious commitment. But he never took his vows, and probably remained in the seminary for only a few months. Since he passionately kept his Catholic faith until his death, his disappointment probably had more to do with his temperament. He was a man of firm conviction, headstrong and fiery in expressing his beliefs—hardly someone who could easily knuckle under to the discipline imposed by a religious order.

By the spring of 1843, Jean-Louis was anxious to return to the West. He had heard that Father Provencher was about to set up mission classes at St. Boniface and he wanted the job as schoolmaster. Through Oblate connections, Riel approached Bishop Ignace Bourget of Montreal, who not only wrote him a letter of recommendation but also lent him enough cash for the trip and to set him up at Red River (the money was quickly paid back). The bishop had supported the *patriotes* during the Rebellion of 1837–39 and may have met Jean-Louis at the time. Unfortunately, when Riel arrived at Red River, he found that a group of the Sisters of Charity, better known as the Grey Nuns, had just completed their gruelling two-month voyage from Montreal and were in the process of setting up a school. Since there was no teaching job available, he decided he would eventually go into business for himself as a miller, and bought a river lot next to the Lagimodière family. It wasn't long before he became enchanted with their youngest daughter, Julie, and asked for her hand in marriage.

· 2 ·

In my rapture my eyes can hold
Onto my mother's warm stare.
My brothers and sisters are there.
I am at my father's knees.
Crouched and in tears I hear him pray.

The Lagimodières were delighted when Jean-Louis Riel asked for their daughter's hand in marriage. In the Red River Settlement, thoroughbred French-Canadian women were highly sought after and had no need to "marry down" to half-bloods. Nevertheless, Riel, although he was a Métis, was well educated, articulate, devout and charming. There was only one catch: Julie flatly refused. She was not interested in marrying anybody.

Even as a child she had been utterly devoted to her Roman Catholic faith. Bishop Provencher had high hopes that she might be tempted by the religious life and she too could see herself forever "in the arms of Jesus". Only after inner struggle and after experiencing a terrifying vision of God did she finally consent. She married Jean-Louis Riel on January 21, 1844, in the chapel of St. Boniface Cathedral.

As wife and mother, Julie took her responsibility as nurturer of the Catholic faith most seriously. Daily attendance at mass, continuous prayers, obedience to priestly edicts and a fatalistic acceptance of life's sorrows were central to her daily life. Her son Louis would later paint this portrait of his early childhood: "Family prayers, the rosary were always in my eyes and ears. And they are as much a part of my nature as the air I breathe. The calm reflective features of my mother, her eyes constantly turned towards heaven, her respect, her attentions, her devotion to her religious obligations left upon me the deepest impression of her good example." But there was more to Julie Riel than that. Behind that serene, compliant countenance there was a woman of great strength who would be brave enough to castigate a bishop when her son's reputation was being maligned. Nor was she merely a passive, unquestioning follower of Catholic canon; she possessed a rich, imaginative spirituality.

She had spent her formative years with Métis and Indian children and she must have been touched by Native myth and belief. Divine revelation, the direct intervention of the spirits, the realization that unpredictable, mystical forces are continuously at play and must be appeased, was very much part of her inner world. This was dramatically illustrated by the vision she experienced just before her marriage, recorded some years later by her daughter Henriette. Julie was just leaving church after confiding in "Jesus, the prisoner of love." Henriette's account continues, "She [Julie] was suddenly enveloped in flames. Dazzled, frightened, she raised her eyes and there in the clouds, she saw an old man, flashing with light and encircled with fire, who in a powerful voice boomed out, Disobedient child ... when you return to your home you will tell your parents that you will obey them." Echoes of similar vivid encounters with the Almighty would resound, an oratorio of passion, throughout Louis Riel's life.

Louis's early childhood was a particularly happy one. For one thing, he was adored by his parents. In the three years after Louis's birth, Julie had two more babies, Élie and Philomène, but both died in infancy, which may have been one reason she so cherished her eldest. His closest sibling was Sara, born in 1848. The two children developed a passionately affectionate relationship which lasted their entire lives. In a letter to her brother in 1883, she would say of their early years together, "Little Sara enjoyed good times; you and I were so happy."

Some of their more pleasurable moments were spent with their Lagimodière grandparents, who lived nearby. Grandpère Baptiste, as he was called, then operated a grist mill by the Seine River, and the Riel children loved exploring the dense woods of maple, poplar and willow surrounding it. While the Lagimodières and Riels were distinctly not a part of the buffalo-hunting population of Red River, Louis and Sara must have played with Indian and Métis children, because both were fluent in Cree by the time they went to school.

Colouring all of Riel's early years was the intense religious instruction he received. He would later write, "My earliest years were scented with the sweet perfume of faith, for my beloved father permitted no person to speak evil in my presence." His first confession at age seven, his confirmation and his first communion at St. Boniface Cathedral on March 25, 1857, were not merely ceremonies which an active young boy was forced to endure. For Riel they were intense emotional experiences.

Riel's piety—the very first words he supposedly spoke as an infant were Jesus, Mary and Joseph—turned him into something of a prig and a momma's boy. His sister Henriette described one telling incident when a young school-mate snatched Louis's cap and then taunted him. Riel lost his temper but rather than give the boy a good punch, he yelled out, "I shall ask my mother if it's all right to fight you; if she says yes then we'll meet again."

But there was another sharp contour of Riel's religious upbringing that was to become a fundamental part of his adult character; he was imbued with a sense of justice and charity towards others. These sensibilities were spawned at a time when his community was seething with discontent and transgression. And they were very much shaped by his beloved father, who happened to be the leader of the revolutionary forces.

There was much to rebel against, for the government of the Red River Settlement was totally undemocratic, and often tyrannical. Lord Selkirk had died in 1820, but his estate continued to control the settlement, designating the gover-nor, who had near absolute powers, and a three-man council. Other important officials such as magistrates and sheriffs were also appointed. After 1825 the Hudson's Bay Company took over this job from Selkirk's heirs. When, in 1836, the Company finally bought the colony, the London board of directors continued to appoint the Red River administration, although the council was expanded to between eight and twelve members, sometimes including a Métis representative; Cuthbert Grant was a member for some years. Still, it was an autocratic govern-ment which seldom listened to the population, especially if their grievances were contrary to the Hudson's Bay Company's interests—which they often were. The councillors were considered by many as mere "toadies" of the HBC.

By the 1840s the shape of the Red River Settlement had evolved loosely into a cross, with the Red River forming the stem and the Assiniboine and little Seine the arms. Scattered along its length were small villages, clusters of distinct reli-gious and ethnic groupings; in fact the population, which in 1849 stood at 5,391, was as segregated as Lord Selkirk had originally planned.

The commercial heart of the colony was the Hudson's Bay Company's Upper Fort Garry, which stood on a steep bank facing the Assiniboine River near the junc-tion of the Red, on the same spot as the North West Company's old Fort Gibraltar.

The huge quadrangle enclosed about four acres. Its thick walls, made of wood and stone and standing fifteen feet high, were punctuated by ten stone bastions. Inside sat a fine stone house which was the residence of the settle-ment's governor, accommodation for company clerks and officers, a well-used public store, granaries, blacksmith and carpentry shops, a courthouse and, of course, a jail.

Close to Fort Garry was the Anglican St. John's Cathedral, rather dilapidated in 1849, and around it was starting to sprout the hub of the Settlement's wheeling and dealing which would soon become the village of Winnipeg. Here the retired Hudson's Bay Company employees, the "commissioned gentlemen", almost all prosperous free traders, set up their businesses. These people, many originally from the Orkney Islands, would quickly congeal into a wealthy, powerful Anglo elite.

Running along either side of the Red for four miles north to Frog Plain was the community of Kildonan. Here the Selkirk settlers had at last established themselves on orderly, prosperous farms, each with a neat barn and hard-working windmill. Adapted from the river-lot system of French Canada, each farm fronted on the Red and many stretched westward to the prairie meadows where hay was communally grown.

Farther north, near the Stone Fort, was situated the community of St. Andrew consisting of English Half-breeds. And directly north was located the St. Paul mission where the Saulteaux Indians had settled.

If the commercial heart of settlement sat on the Red River's west bank, its spiritual core, its soul, loomed large on the east side. Like a cardinal among a flock of blackbirds, the elegant St. Boniface Cathedral dominated its rustic surroundings.

Father Provencher's first church had been a chapel in his log house. By 1825, a church of oak with a bell tower *cum* steeple was completed, but it was soon deemed not grand enough—especially since, by this time, Provencher had been named a bishop. In 1833, St. Boniface Cathedral began taking shape, and it would have been just as much at home in the Quebec town of Maskinongé, so similar was it to contemporary French-Canadian churches. Built of stone, it was an enormous and expensive undertaking, boasting two soaring twin towers from which three bells, weighing together 1,600 pounds, clanged throughout the day. The cathedral was also distinguished by a huge central window designed "*à la gothique*", an intricate frescoed ceiling painted by Grey Nuns, and religious artifacts gaudy and colourful enough to appeal to the Métis passion for the dramatic. It was to dominate the Red River Settlement, a symbol of Catholic proselytism in the Canadian West,* the victory of civilization over "barbarity", until a fire destroyed it in 1860. For Louis Riel, growing up in its long shadow, it would come to symbolize the power and splendour of his native religion.

Around and south of St. Boniface evolved the small French-speaking Catholic communities, St. Vital, St. Norbert, St. Charles, Ste. Agathe. Living here

---

* *There is irony here, as Provencher spent so much time and energy building his huge monument that he had little left over to administer to the "heathens" ... i.e., the Native peoples living in the Northwest.*

were the half-dozen pioneering families from Quebec, the remnants of Selkirk's mercenaries, a few Swiss settlers, the last of the Quebec freemen—Lagimodière among them—and Métis who tended to be part of the bourgeoisie, those with small businesses and farmers such as the Riels (although hunters and trappers also inhabited these villages). The largest grouping in Red River's population in 1849 were the buffalo-hunting Métis, who had settled far west along the Assiniboine River at a spot on the wide open prairie called White Horse Plains.

As early as 1814, a nucleus of French-Canadian and Half-breed free traders had chosen the spot as their home base. After the amalgamation of the two fur giants, many of those who lost their jobs joined them and began careers as independent pemmican suppliers. When the Hudson's Bay Company shut down Fort Daer at Pembina in 1822, the large Métis community there began looking for somewhere to relocate. Their exodus was not just a result of the fort closing; prairie fires had devastated the area around Pembina and, as well, the Sioux were a continuous and terrifying threat. That year news reached them that Cuthbert Grant had taken up Governor Simpson's offer of free land at White Horse Plains. The leader of the Seven Oaks confrontation was still considered a great hero and many Métis were willing to follow his lead. By 1849 Grant had become the patriarch of a river-front village boasting a population of 169 families, appropriately called Grantown but better known as White Horse Plains.

Bishop Provencher and Governor Simpson had both hoped that the colony would serve as an enticement to transform the nomad Métis into model farmers, but their expectations were certainly not realized. White Horse Plains became home base for the Red River buffalo hunters.

For years, the Métis were chastised for their dedication to the buffalo hunt*; farming, with its nose-to-the-grindstone work ethic and supposedly "civilizing" influence, was judged to be a more worthy occupation than chasing bison around the plain. The missionaries waged unrelenting war against the Half-breeds' nomadic life. For one thing, it was hardly possible to exert moral influence on a

---

* *The buffalo-hunting industry and the way of life it spawned have given many white historians the ammunition they needed to expound their racist view of the Métis. For example, George F. Stanley wrote in 1960, "... the French half-breed were indolent, thoughtless and improvident, unrestrained in their desires, restless, clannish and vain. Life held no thought of the morrow. To become the envied possessor of a new suit, rifle or horse, they would readily deprive themselves and their families of the necessities of life." A close look at the dynamics of the pemmican trade reveals that a successful buffalo hunter would have been anything but "indolent" or "improvident". During the hunt, he worked harder than any farmer, and he certainly faced much greater danger.*

people who were never around. Yet there's no doubt that without the Métis's remarkable skill in hunting the bison, the population at Red River would have starved to death during the many years of crop failure. When bread wasn't available, fresh and frozen buffalo steaks, tongues, jerky and fat were. As well, the fur trade would not have developed into a vast, transcontinental industry without the systematic production of pemmican—by 1840 the HBC was purchasing 100,000 pounds a year for its workers, and this had doubled by 1870. For almost half a century, pemmican production was the only business that produced real currency in the Red River community—a worker's wages, payment for land, children's school fees were all paid for in packets of dried buffalo meat mixed with fat. (British pound sterling was also used on occasion, but seldom in day-to-day transactions.)

Since the beginning of the Red River Settlement, independent buffalo hunters such as Lagimodière had found it advantageous to congregate in larger groups, primarily for protection against Sioux attack. By 1826, the pattern of the famous mass hunting expeditions had been set. Twice a year, in June and September, as many as 2,700 Métis men, women and children, and their Indian confrères, would converge on the flat prairies near Pembina. This massive camp was set up in a huge circle encompassed by hundreds of carts and a triple layer of tents. Bedlam always ensued: old friends exchanged gossip, men gambled passionately, fiddlers sang out dance after dance, children squealed in play, priests hastily heard confessions and married young couples, dogs barked, expensive, fast, highly trained horses, decked out in bridles entwined with brightly coloured beads, twitched impatiently. It was left to the women, of course, to undertake the serious task of actually making the preparations for the great trek.

Elections were held for ten guides and ten captains, including a supreme leader called the war chief, or "*le président*". As well, twelve councillors or elders were chosen who with the chief and captains formed a "provisional government" which would formulate the laws of the chase—no hunting on the Sabbath, no running the buffalo before the order was given, etc.—and arbitrate disputes. (On vitally important issues, the entire hunting population was consulted and a decision made only if the majority agreed.) Each of the captains selected ten "soldiers". Their job was to see that the regulations were adhered to, to protect their group against Indian attack, and to ensure that no theft of personal property occurred. There were few infractions and when there was a problem, disciplinary action, usually some form of public ridicule such as name-calling and taunting, was severe and immediate. The hunt became a precise, highly disciplined but also fundamentally democratic organization, a modus operandi which would be part of Louis Riel's insurrections against the establishment in years to come.

After the priest said a final, good-luck mass, the expedition got under way. Hundreds of Red River carts pulled by either horses or cattle, piled high with blankets, tents, ammunition, axes and butchering knives, groaned loudly as if in agony. The caravan stretched for as long as six miles, in staggered formation to cut the dust. It was orderly—if that most dangerous of enemies, the Sioux, were sighted, it could, in a quick moment, halt and wheel into corral formation.

When a herd was finally spotted, the caravan would position itself downwind so as not to catch the attention of the huge animals. The hunters, disciplined and in concert, would advance cautiously. As soon as the public crier yelled "*Allez,*" they took after the maddened, panic-stricken beasts, dust flying like a thick cloud. The free-for-all that resulted was as wild and deadly as a battle of gladiators.

As soon as the bulls became aware of danger they surrounded the females, stamping the ground, bellowing in terror, and it was not easy to penetrate their line of defence; many hunters lost their lives trying to do so. But tender cow and calf meat was the most valuable so it was the cows and calves the Métis went after. Usually one hunter would kill about a half-dozen of the unfortunate creatures at each run, but sometimes more fell; the renowned hunter Baptiste Parenteau once slaughtered sixteen cows with as many shots in a single chase. Indeed, the bloodbath was unrelenting. In 1845, the year after Louis Riel was born, the September hunt yielded 1,776 bison.

Camp was established near the hunting ground and there the women set to work butchering the catch. If it was the spring hunt, they made pemmican. Cut into fine strips, the meat was spread out on grids where it dried in the sun. It was then pounded until almost powder. To this was added melted buffalo fat and sometimes berries. The concoction was laboriously kneaded and then stuffed into buffalo-hide sacks.

As the years passed, an even more lucrative money-maker came into fashion—buffalo robes. Such was the cash paid for the robes that Métis, Indians and white men alike began an unrelenting, foolish slaughter that would lead to the near extinction of the buffalo and a life of destitution for the hunters.

Only a portion of the plains hunters' livelihood was provided by the buffalo hunt. The Métis continued to trap for furs, and they farmed—potatoes, corn, wheat and other vegetables—and fished in lakes Winnipeg and Manitoba for sturgeon, white fish and golden eye. As years went by, their freighting business became more complex; some Métis had dozens of the amazing lightweight wooden carts, with their huge wheels, which in spring and summer swarmed like ants throughout the Red River basin. Of course, the Métis continued to work for the Hudson's Bay Company as labourers, boatmen, packmen and trip-men. Despite these jobs and their reliance on HBC manufactured goods, they lived fiercely independent lives, influenced only slightly by the "civilizing" priests and even less so by the governing power.

The Métis of Red River would have been even more prosperous and inde-pendent if they had been allowed to follow their instincts for competition and free enterprise. But they were tied tightly to the Hudson's Bay Company. Prices were arbitrarily fixed. Any hunter, Métis or Indian, caught doing business in furs or buffalo with an independent trader, especially an aggressive Yankee, was punished. The early Red River historian, Alexander Ross, wrote the following account of the hardship imposed by these HBC rules:

> A half-breed, in his rambles through the wilderness, stumbles on an Indian in great distress, either for want of food or the inclemency of the weather; he applies to the half-breed for relief, offers him some furs, the only thing he possesses. The half-breed cannot afford to give for nothing what he has got; and if he accepts of what the Indian offers him, he breaks the law, although by the act he saves the Indian's life!

No wonder that, despite HBC threats, smuggling flourished. The dusty Red River trails that ran south to Pembina and beyond to the bustling frontier town of St. Paul, Minnesota, were busy with a traffic of buffalo robes, tongues and pemmican, while such items as blankets, tea kettles, butchering knives and pipe tobacco travelled north. In 1843 the first regular cart service between Pembina and St. Paul was inaugurated and in 1845 the famous American trader Norman Kittson established a trading post at Pembina itself. (He offered such good prices for fur, partly paid in real gold, that Métis dedication to smuggling grew by leaps and bounds and was eventually labelled "Kittson's fever".)

At first the HBC officials turned a blind eye to the illicit trade; the Métis, after all, were a well-armed, powerful group. In 1835 the Council of Assiniboia imposed a duty of seven and a half percent on all exports and imports, but the reaction to this was so severe that it was cut back to four and a half percent. Even so, by the mid-1840s the situation was becoming desperate; the HBC was being outsmarted by the wily Yankees and the draining off of trade was serious. The Company grew determined to enforce its monopoly. HBC agents, so-called "police", took to breaking into Métis homes and ransacking them in a search for illicit furs which were seized without payment and never returned. Personal mail was opened, Métis carts arbitrarily searched. Public flogging was even introduced for "theft", defined as removal of goods from Company jurisdiction without paying the export fee. Yet the amounts paid for furs and buffalo robes in Pembina and St. Paul were so much higher, the prices charged for manufactured goods so much lower, that the smugglers merely took a wider berth on the prairie, and under cover of night continued their southward journeys.

The imperial government finally realized that the Métis were in open revolt. In 1846, four hundred British soldiers arrived at Fort Garry, supposedly to protect the colony against American annexationists. But since they left as soon as Métis rumblings of discontent quieted down, the real reason for their presence was obvious. The people of Red River grew even angrier.

All along, they had tried hard to have their grievances redressed through peaceful channels. In 1835 they had petitioned the HBC for a definition of their rights, particularly those pertaining to their farmland, and had been told in effect that they didn't have any. In 1845, with the help of famous Métis lawyer Alexander Kennedy Isbister, the British Colonial Office had been sent a petition with a thousand signatures—including Jean-Louis Riel's—asking for, among other things, a say in how the colony was governed. Despite Isbister's best efforts, nothing had come of it. Finally, in 1849, the Métis and the mighty Hudson's Bay Company confronted each other in a showdown. The mixed-bloods won hands down.

Jean-Louis Riel was their most articulate and flamboyant leader, even though he himself was not directly involved in the smuggling business. His in-laws, the Lagimodières, did own eighteen Red River carts at the time and likely dabbled in free trade, but they were not interested in messy protest—only the second son, Benjamin, would become involved in the political turmoil. They may, however, have encouraged their eloquent son-in-law to act as their front man, a strong, persistent voice for their complaints.

After his marriage Riel himself had begun farming his land, and by 1849 he owned a house—a neat, white-washed log cabin—a stable, seventeen head of livestock, an assortment of farm implements, two Red River carts and a canoe. Ten acres of farmland were under cultivation. But Jean-Louis's ambition did not stop at the plough; he saw himself as a businessman, part of the merchant elite that was then evolving in Red River. Given his experience carding wool in Quebec—water power had been an integral part of the operation—he decided to become a miller. He convinced the Council of Assiniboia—through the intervention of Bishop Provencher, who was a council member—to purchase a simple carding machine and ship it from Quebec. The deal was a complicated one: the mill would be set up on his land near the Seine River, he would operate it and take the proceeds, but the ownership of the machinery would remain with the Hudson's Bay Company. Riel quickly became disillusioned with the terms of his agreement with the HBC, and dismantled the operation that same year. His dispute with the company may have stiffened his political backbone, made him eager to thumb his nose at the establishment.

Probably, though, it was simply his nature to jump into the thick of the fray. He likely saw in the HBC and its toady, the Assiniboia Council, the same black cloud of inequity and oppression that had led to the Papineau rebellion of 1837 in Lower Canada. Since his arrival in the Red River Settlement, he had met many allies, in particular the extraordinary priest Georges-Antoine Belcourt.

Belcourt had passed the winter of 1846–47 at St. Boniface working as a carpenter and teacher, and Riel had spent many evenings talking with him. The two became fast friends. It was a phenomenon that would surface again in the Riel family history; the alliance with strong-minded, free-thinking clerics whose activism would lead to battles with the establishment church.

Belcourt, a thin-faced, ascetic-looking man, was fourteen years older than Jean-Louis Riel, having been born in Quebec in 1803. He was ordained a priest in 1827 and came to the Northwest as a missionary in 1830. In 1833 he established the mission of Baie-St-Paul, thirty miles west of the Red River Settlement on the Assiniboine, which he periodically administered to for the next ten years. He was one of the few clergy of any religious denomination who truly appreciated Native culture and who had the genuine interests of the Indians and Métis at heart. He learned the language of every Indian nation he spent time with, which made him unique among the missionaries of the time. Not surprisingly, he quickly engendered envy among his colleagues. As early as 1839, Bishop Provencher was criticizing him for not sharing the Saulteaux dictionary he was preparing. Belcourt merely replied that he wasn't finished; in fact it would take another eight years.

Early on, Belcourt had developed a deep antipathy to the Hudson's Bay Company; he couldn't abide what he considered the company's wicked treatment of the Indian and Métis population. Fluent in English, he formed a liaison with free trader Norman Kittson to encourage the Métis to look beyond the HBC influence. (Bishop Provencher charged that all Belcourt wanted to do was engage in the lucrative fur trade himself.) Belcourt was also a major instigator of the anti–Hudson's Bay Company petition presented by the Métis to the British government in 1846. Predictably, the priest came to be despised by the establishment as a dangerous troublemaker. HBC governor George Simpson put pressure on the Archbishop of Quebec to recall Belcourt and breathed a sigh of relief when, in 1847, the priest left the West. Bishop Provencher was Simpson's accomplice in this recall, and, because of this, became discredited in the eyes of the Native population. But neither he nor Simpson had reckoned on the wrath of the Métis of White Horse Plains—233 families signed a petition demanding Belcourt's return, pointing out that he was the only person interested in protecting their rights and the only one who could prevent bloodshed. Simpson finally agreed, but only if the priest promised not "to interfere in the politics of the country." Belcourt flatly refused the condition, and then did an impressive end-run around the Red River establishment. He took over the Catholic mission at Pembina, in American territory, and from that base carried on guerrilla tactics against Simpson and the HBC.

One of the first things Belcourt did was to convince three hundred Métis to move to Pembina; those who remained in Red River visited the rebel priest often, paying no attention to Bishop Provencher's admonishments. Jean-Louis Riel was among them.

In 1846, a year before Belcourt moved to Pembina, Red River carts which he had hired to transport supplies from Pembina had been stopped and searched by HBC "police". There was no sign of the illegal trafficking in furs which the HBC had expected, but the missionary was arrested anyway. Riel led a mob of furious, armed Métis in a march on Fort Garry. HBC chief factor Alexander Christie could do nothing but release Belcourt, and it was Jean-Louis Riel who carried the priest in triumph on his shoulders to the steps of St. Boniface Cathedral.

The following year, on a tip from the priest, Riel led another angry delegation of armed men to confront the leadership at Fort Garry, this time demanding the release of a Métisse who was felt to have been unjustly charged with theft. The woman was let go before her trial.

The Hudson's Bay Company had lost a great deal of face during these confrontations, and John Ballenden, the chief factor brought in to replace the disgraced Christie, was determined to re-establish the company's monopoly rights at all costs. The very opposite occurred.

Pierre-Guillaume Sayer was the son of a North West Company bourgeois and a Métis mother. He openly defied the company by purchasing merchandise from Pembina and then illegally trading the goods for furs trapped by the Indians of Lake Manitoba. In spring 1849, Ballenden ordered Sayer and three others arrested and charged with illegal trading in furs. A protest committee was immediately formed in the Red River Settlement, with Jean-Louis Riel as leader. One of his first acts was to travel to Pembina to consult with his friend Father Belcourt.

After mass on the Sunday before Sayer's trial was scheduled, Riel read a message from the popular priest declaring HBC's law invalid and urging the Métis to take up arms if necessary.

The trial was set for May 17, Ascension Thursday, in the hope that troublemakers would dutifully attend church service. But on Riel's suggestion mass was rescheduled to an earlier time from eleven to eight a.m. As the congregation departed, he stood on the steps of St. Boniface Cathedral exhorting them to "come armed and fully prepared to assert your rights!"

About four hundred Métis arrived en masse at Fort Garry. The jury could hear the sharp crack of gun volleys and the chanting—"Free Sayer! All persecution for trading in furs must end!" As the trial began, a delegation, including Jean-Louis Riel, forced its way into the courtroom and more or less took over, presenting an ultimatum—if the accused man was punished, force would be used to free him. The turmoil probably had everything to do with the verdict. As expected, Sayer was found guilty, largely on the evidence of his own son Louis, a boy of twelve, but—and it was an enormous "but"—no penalty was to be imposed. Sayer's confiscated furs were to be returned; charges against the other three accused were dropped. As a Métis juror was leaving the courtroom, he issued the *cri de joie* which would resound throughout the Northwest, "*Le commerce est libre. Vive la liberté!*" The Hudson's Bay Company had been stripped of its muscle; enforcement of its monopoly was never seriously attempted again.

Louis Riel was only five—he hadn't started school yet—when the Sayer victory exploded on his landscape. Yet there's no doubt he was deeply affected by it; in adulthood he considered his father a hero of gigantic proportions, his activism a prologue to his own life of revolution.

But as important as the victory over the Hudson's Bay Company establishment was to a young boy's perception of his world, there was a darker undercurrent to life in Red River that would profoundly mark Riel's psyche. The place was seething with bigotry and pretension.

In the English-speaking community, the first Selkirk colonists, a mixed bag of Presbyterian Scottish Highlanders, Catholic Irish and Anglican Orkneymen, had hardly stepped off the boat at York Factory in 1811 when they began fighting among themselves. The animosity continued for years, as one denomination squabbled with another.

It was the dominant Anglican clergy, however, who had the most precise and rigid idea of how they would mould the "primitive" Red River community— it was to become, as the historian Frits Pannekoek labels it, "A Little Britain in the wilderness",* with all the nineteenth-century moral baggage that implied. The Reverend William Cochran, who arrived in the Red River Settlement in 1825 and stayed until his death forty years later, was typical of this breed. He made no bones about his belief that "the dominant Race of this Continent are the English" and that the Indians and mixed-bloods would always be "immoral, capricious,

---

* *Among the increasingly wealthy English-speaking elite of Red River, aping the habits of Victorian England became a passion. Monogrammed silverware, letter seals and crystal goblets were all the rage.*

intractable, indolent, callous, prideful, wayward, extravagant, ungracious, improvident and careless." Buffalo hunting, fur trading, fishing were all pastimes of the "indolent Catholic Savages"; a pious "Christian" would dedicate his life to tilling the soil and raising his numerous offspring "in the service of the British empire."

But it was in imposing their ideas of sexual morality that these ardent, blinkered missionaries, puffed up with their own self-importance, did irreparable damage to the Red River community's social fibre.

In 1830 HBC governor George Simpson cast aside his Métis wife of many years and married his beautiful eighteen-year-old cousin. If Frances Simpson brought "an air of high-life and gaiety" to Red River, she also established a new trend—wives were to be white, schooled in British ways, fashionable in the European sense, and above all married in the Anglican church. Indian and Half-breed women wed *à la façon du pays* were suddenly out of fashion. Egged on by the clergy, and hoping to re-establish their Christian respectability, many of the HBC's retired "gentlemen" discarded their Indian wives and sent east for younger, whiter, "daintier" brides. Those mixed-blood and Indian wives who remained—some of the most influential, intelligent women in Red River—were acutely aware of the disdain in which clergy and others of the elite held them. What ensued was a poisonous atmosphere of gossip, scandal and character assassination; Pannekoek describes it as "open social warfare".

The most furious battle, which came to be known as the Ballenden scandal, erupted in the spring of 1850. Sarah Ballenden was the beautiful Half-breed wife of John Ballenden, the HBC's chief factor for the Red River District, the man who had been overwhelmed by Jean-Louis Riel and the Métis during the Sayer trial. She and a dashing British captain named Vaughan Foss somehow insulted two matrons of the Red River Settlement's upper crust. Jealous that a mixed-blood could sit higher than they on the social ladder by virtue of her husband's position, these two women set out on a campaign to spread malicious rumours. Mrs. Ballenden and Foss, they whispered, were having a passionate affair. The child she was carrying was not her husband's but the dashing captain's. (As an added twist in the sordid affair, the husband of one of these women had made sexual advances to Sarah Ballenden and she had bluntly rebuffed him.)

In June, John Ballenden left the settlement on business, which gave the two connivers an opportunity for revenge. They convinced Red River society to socially ostracize Mrs. Ballenden. Deeply hurt, she sought refuge at the home of the local judge, Adam Thom. He was convinced of her innocence and advised Captain Foss to post a notice on the front gate of Upper Fort Garry announcing that charges of defamatory conspiracy would be pressed against the two women and their husbands.

The trial was a sensation. The entire Anglican clergy—especially the notorious Reverend Cochran, who had a special personal hatred for John Ballenden—came down on the side of the gossip-mongers. But the twelve-man jury was padded with pro-Ballenden forces and the chief witness for the defence was whisked out of the settlement just before the trial began. Not unexpectedly, the proceedings resulted in a complete vindication of Sarah Ballenden and the defendants were required to pay her the then hefty sum of £400.

The scandal split the English-speaking community along racial lines—the mixed-bloods, veterans of the country, against the British ruling class—and along religious lines—Anglicans (anti-Ballenden) and Presbyterians (pro-Ballenden). Factions of each group snubbed each other socially for years.

Meanwhile, over on the east bank of the Red River, at St. Boniface, the Catholic French-speakers watched these shenanigans with incredulity and confusion. Yet they were not surprised at the boiling over of such a scandal.

For years the Métis had bristled at the bigotry growing in the English establishment. The man they despised the most was the colony's judge, Adam Thom, a Scot who had immigrated to Montreal in 1832, where he dabbled in journalism and at the same time studied law. A pious Presbyterian given to minute interpretation of the Scriptures, he was one of the chief authors of the infamous Durham report, advocating the assimilation of Canada's French-speaking population. Thom had arrived in Red River in 1839, as recorder of Rupert's Land for the general quarterly court of Assiniboia. The court was made up of the governor of Assiniboia and several prominent citizens who served as magistrates, but since Thom was the only one with any legal knowledge he dominated and was referred to as "the judge". He could speak not a word of French, never mind that three-quarters of the colony's population spoke no English, and he made no secret of his contempt for those he was supposedly administering justice to. In a letter to Governor Simpson he opined that "the French element of the population possesses only one percent of the intelligence and capacities of the Anglo-Saxon group."

Two months after their victory in the Sayer trial and less than a year before the Ballenden scandal, the Métis presented a petition to the Council of Assiniboia demanding that Thom be removed from "any charge of affairs in this colony" and threatening that the judge would be physically prevented from presiding at the general quarterly court. Governor Simpson persuaded Thom to step down from the bench for one year, although he could continue in his job as chief counsel for the HBC and the Assiniboia Council. This didn't satisfy the Métis, and another petition was presented. "We have often been called a band of savages," they wrote, "and at this time, it may be said with truth, for we are now without justice, without magistrates, and ... without councillors." They then threatened to burn Thom's house down. In June 1854, with a large pension in place, Adam Thom would sail from York Factory to return to Edinburgh.

The Métis antipathy for the magistrate was so strong that it coloured their feelings about the Ballenden scandal. Since Adam Thom sided with Mrs. Ballenden, the Métis sided with the gossip-mongers, even though the latter considered mixed-bloods of any language inferior beings.

Jean-Louis Riel was the main instigator during these political upheavals and his abhorrence of Thom and all he represented must have deeply affected his son. The boy would also come to realize that his father paid a price for his defiance of the establishment. When Simpson finally agreed to allow "respectable" Métis to sit on the Council of Assiniboia and hold other public offices, Jean-Louis, despite his good education, his influence and political experience, was never asked. He was considered by the next governor of Assiniboia, Eden Colvile, who personally detested him, as a dangerous radical. As a result, Jean-Louis lost out on government appointments that brought not only influence but wealth.

In spring 1852, Red River was inundated with non-stop rain; the Riel farm was flooded and the family was forced to take refuge at Bishop Provencher's house and the cathedral. It was several months before they could return to their land, seeding was late and the harvest was poor, so that the Riels suffered a major financial set-back. Jean-Louis, weary of farming, had wanted to start his own business again anyway—this time he would operate a grist mill on the Seine River—but found his capital dwindling. He therefore asked the Council of Assiniboia to sell him the building that had been constructed five years before for the carding operation, minus the fulling equipment, which he wouldn't need, for £15. The council agreed to do so but, perhaps in retaliation for his political activism, they refused to allow him to pay the money over time. Riel managed to borrow this sum, and £100 more, from the Hudson's Bay Company, for which he took a three-year mortgage on his land, to be paid in cash or in wheat or flour. The grist mill was in operation by 1854 and, as much as the depressed economic conditions in Red River would allow, became fairly successful. The mortgage was paid off in 1855.

The Riel family was flourishing. A new house was built near the mill to accommodate the many new babies with which the Riels had been blessed—as well as Sara, born in 1848, Marie had arrived in 1850, Octavie in 1852, Eulalie in 1853 and Charles in 1854. And Louis had started school, at first with the Grey Nuns, the same order that had been setting up a school when Jean-Louis arrived at Red River.

The establishment built for the nuns was a large, wooden, three-storey affair which came to dominate the Red River skyline almost as much as the cathedral.

Many of the young students lived in residence, and Louis Riel probably did so when he began his studies on April 1, 1853. The Grey Nuns were affectionate, enthusiastic teachers but not exactly scholarly. When the Christian Brothers arrived in Red River in December 1854, Louis Riel became one of their first students. Under their tutelage he managed to acquire the foundations of a classical education. Religion, of course, was at its heart.

Louis was a handsome child with a mop of thick brownish-auburn hair and huge saucer eyes which were nearly always serious. He was quiet and introspective, almost too thoughtful, too caring, for his age. His sister Henriette would later tell the story of how Louis developed a habit of giving his lunch away, on his way to school, to poverty-stricken Indians and then, without a word to anyone, going hungry himself. This happened so often that his mother had to ask the bishop's housekeeper to feed him. He was an attentive, eager student, and early on the priest Alexandre Taché (who became bishop after Provencher's death in 1853) marked him as a possible candidate for the priesthood. With this in mind, in September 1857, just before his thirteenth birthday, Riel was given access to the bishopric library, where he spent hours thumbing through tomes of philosophy and literature. He also began studying Latin with Father Jean-Marie-Joseph LeFloch, the same priest who had prepared Louis for his first communion and, as Riel himself pointed out, "had succeeded in teaching me the fear of God."

In spring 1858, Bishop Taché announced that Louis Riel would be awarded a full scholarship to attend one of the best colleges Quebec had to offer. Louis's mother, Julie, must have been both delighted and saddened, for as proud as she was that her eldest had been chosen, he remained the apple of her eye and she knew she would miss him desperately.

The other day I said to Marie:
Ah! If only you cared for my happiness!
For the rest of my life
I would remain your loyal servant.

Louis was not the only Red River boy honoured with an advanced education in the East. Madame Marie-Geneviève-Sophie Masson, the doyenne of a wealthy and influential Quebec family, had provided scholarships for four Métis lads who had been judged as potential priestly material. They were Joseph Nolin, Daniel McDougall, Louis Schmidt and Louis Riel. When Nolin's parents learned that funds would not be provided for Joseph's return home on holidays, they would not permit him to go. McDougall made the trip, but he was an immature boy who would suffer debilitating homesickness in Montreal. Louis Schmidt would become the closest friend of Louis Riel; indeed, in later years Schmidt would play a prominent, if sometimes dubious, role in Riel's stormy political career.

Louis Schmidt was a small-boned, fine-featured, rather frail boy. Very fair for a Métis, blond and blue-eyed, he had been born in the same year as Riel, in the far Northwest, at Lake Athabasca. His father was a fur trader for the Hudson's Bay Company, his mother a daughter of a famous Métis guide. When Louis was eight she became ill, and the family moved to Red River seeking medical attention. It was at that point that Louis began attending school at St. Boniface, where M. Taché, insisting that the family's roots must be German, arbitrarily changed his name from Laferté to Schmidt.

On June 1, 1858, the three boys stood on the steps of St. Boniface Cathedral to be blessed in their endeavours by Father LeFloch—Taché was already in

Montreal making arrangements for their sojourn there. Their chaperons were to be Sister Valade, superior of the Grey Nuns of St. Boniface, who was on her way back to Montreal to round up more recruits for her school, and an old free-man guide called Granger. They were to join a brigade of Red River carts on its way to St. Paul, Minnesota. The boys were delighted that each would be captain of his own ship. Schmidt remembered with fondness that the ox that pulled his cart was called "Lady".

As Julie Riel said goodbye to her beloved son, she must have felt a pang of sorrow, for she knew he'd likely be gone for a good half-dozen years. Yet she may not have worried quite as much as the other parents; her husband's relatives were still living in the Montreal area, including Louis's grandfather, Jean-Baptiste Riel, his uncles Baptiste and Henri and his aunts Lucie and Charlotte, and Julie knew they would comfort a homesick young man.

Even for someone as young as Louis, the trip southward along the dusty, rutted trails through the blossoming June prairie must have conjured up memories of times past. Pembina was the place Grandmère Lagimodière talked about so much, where she had arrived as a young bride. It was to Pembina that his father had travelled so often to scheme rebellion with the radical priest, Belcourt. But when the caravan of squeaking carts reached the spot, what Louis and his pals encountered was a near ghost town. Since the devastating flood of 1852, the trader Norman Kittson had moved his post some twenty miles west to the higher ground at St. Joseph, and there was little left of the once notorious home of smugglers and border banditti.

From Pembina the group travelled due south following the Red River through lonely forest country. The tripmen were terrified of attack by the Sioux, so, as soon as they were able, they veered off east onto the infrequently used but better-protected "Woods Trail". One night camp was set up at Old Crossings, near Red Lake Falls in Minnesota. There on the banks of the Red Lake River, Louis Riel unexpectedly ran into his father.

Riel senior had been away from home for over a year, seeing to the purchase of machinery for a textile mill. Jean-Louis was an emotional, uninhibited man, as was his son; neither hesitated to display the joy they felt in meeting each other. Louis Schmidt, perhaps with a twinge of envy, wrote, "The encounter of father and son was very touching." It was fortunate that Louis had the chance of hugging his father farewell, for the Riels, *père et fils*, would never see each other again.

For another twenty-eight days the caravan wound its way through the heart of Minnesota, which had become a state only a month before Riel's journey, to the capital, St. Paul. To the three green Métis lads, it must have seemed a bustling, exciting place. Although still a rowdy frontier town, it boasted a population of fourteen thousand, a magnificent city hall, several stately churches and the Winslow House, a hotel that would have been considered grand in a city five times its size. At the banks of the Mississippi were docked steamboats; some, like the *Ben Campbell* or the *Milwaukee*, were luxurious by any standard. The Red River boys had never seen anything like them before.

After a day or so of sightseeing, Sister Valade and her charges boarded a steamboat and sailed down the Mississippi to Prairie du Chien in Wisconsin. There they took a train to Chicago, travelled on to Detroit and finally into Upper Canada. Louis Schmidt was particularly impressed with Hamilton. "What a beautiful city; what a magnificent view," he wrote. The boys gobbled up the oranges Sister Valade had bought them, the first they had ever eaten. The group passed the night in Toronto at a convent and the next morning they began the last leg of the journey. On July 5, five long weeks after they had started out, they reached their destination. Once the unruly trio was handed over to someone else's care, Sister Valade breathed a sigh of relief; she later admitted that the deeper they journeyed into "civilization", the more unruly the boys had become.

In 1858 Montreal was a magical city, a city of light and darkness, of contrasts and drama. Neighbourhood streets were dark, narrow and gloomy, but the roofs of the houses, churches, and cupolas gleamed like polished silver from the over-lay of fire-proof tin. Although the city had suffered dreadful financial set-backs, particularly in the 1820s and 1830s, by the year 1858 it was enjoying the last stages of a fantastic fourteen-year boom. The St. Lawrence canal system, including the Lachine, had been built, and the channel to Quebec City had been deepened, so that Montreal had become a great seaport. It was also Canada's banking centre, its financial heart and the centre of the country's infant but already important railway web.

The ghostly wail of the rag man, the shrill steam whistle of the french-fry and popcorn vendors' carts, the chirping wagon of the rubber-aproned iceman must have seemed exotic music to the young men from Red River. But the ever-impressionable Louis Riel was overwhelmed by the number of steeples that dotted the city landscape. Churches were everywhere: the famous Notre Dame, St. Jacques Cathedral, St. Andrew's Church, Church of Notre Dame de Bon-Secours, St. Paul's.

By 1858 Montreal's population had grown to 91,000, with English-speakers still making up the majority. The Grand Trunk Railway had just announced that all the locomotives, cars and tracks needed in their epic expansion would be built in that city. The awesome Victoria Bridge, considered the engineering feat of the nineteenth century, connecting the Island of Montreal with the mainland, was just being completed. The construction of McGill University was in its final stages. The stately Palais de Justice had been finished two years before. The splendid Crystal Palace was being readied for the visit of the Prince of Wales (the future Edward VII). Indeed, the city that greeted Louis and his two school-mates was robust, rambunctious and full of self-confidence.

Louis and the others spent their first night in Montreal at the huge convent of the Grey Nuns near St. Antoine Market. There, Daniel McDougall learned that he had been assigned to the Collège de Nicolet, Louis Schmidt to St. Hyacinthe College and Louis Riel to the Collège de Montréal, run by the Sulpician order.

The Company of Priests of St. Sulpice had been founded in Paris in 1641; Sulpician missionaries had been sent to Canada sixteen years later. As a reward for their evangelist zeal, they had been designated the seigneurs of the entire island of Montreal, and had remained so until the British conquest. This meant the Gentlemen of Saint Sulpice owned large chunks of the city on which, for two hundred years, they paid no taxes. It was as landlords that they earned the money to support their schools, seminary and churches.

Among the institutions they ran was the Collège de Montréal, or *le petit séminaire*, as it was called. Founded in 1767 by a Sulpician *curé* to train young boys for the ecclesiastical life, it was also a thumbing of the nose at the British conquerors and an attempt to maintain French culture and language and the Roman Catholic faith under a Protestant regime. A grim, four-storey, T-shaped stone building, located in Montreal's lower town at the corner of St. Paul and McGill streets, it was enclosed by forbidding high walls. The so-called play-ground was nothing but a patch of dirt.

Routine at the college was strict, monotonous and spartan. Breakfast of bar-ley porridge was served very early, followed by attendance at mass and morn-ing lessons; a light lunch featuring bread and cheese was followed by more lessons, then a short recreation period; dinner was an endless diet of boiled beef—only on certain feast days was some butter, ham or meat pie served—accompanied by a Scripture or morality reading, droned forth in Latin by one of the students; the day ended with more study and more prayers. The boys were seldom allowed beyond the walls of the college so there was little contact with the outside world. Their Saturday-night treat consisted of a tepid bath.

It must have seemed a tedious and confining existence to a boy like Louis Riel, used to a warm, affectionate family and the wide-open spaces of the prairies. A letter written to his patron, Madame Masson, at New Year's 1862, gives some idea of how lonely and homesick he was even after more than three years of college life.

> Alone and far from all that is dear to a son's heart, I need not tell one such
> as you who has so tender and good a soul what I am feeling as the New

Year approaches and I think of my family's home ... as it is impossible for me to share in the joys of this wonderful day, the joys of family, I compensate by bestowing my warmest wishes....

But Riel also realized that he was privileged to be attending what was considered the finest seat of learning in Lower Canada. The alumni was a roll-call of Quebec's elite; not only had George-Étienne Cartier been educated there but so had his father and grandfather. Two men who had had a profound effect on Quebec's political renaissance during the chaotic 1830s and 1840s—the revolutionary separatist Louis-Joseph Papineau and the pragmatic reformer Louis-Hippolyte LaFontaine—were both graduates.

The curriculum which the Collège de Montréal followed would not have been out of place in seventeenth-century France. It was a thoroughly classical education based on the literature and philosophy of Greece, Rome and France. So remote was the Sulpician world from reality that newspapers were considered great corrupters and were not allowed inside the college. Such an education had produced a middle class swollen with lawyers, doctors and politicians, but few businessmen or industrialists.

Over an eight-year period, pupils were served up huge dollops of Latin, Greek, French, English, mathematics and philosophy, and only a smattering of physics, chemistry, astronomy and botany. The workload was heavy, examinations, both oral and written, were frequent, discipline was extremely strict.

Louis Riel was assigned to the second level of the eight-year program. In his first report, received on October 8, 1858, only a month after he had started his first term, he ranked twenty-fourth out of thirty-seven students in his class. Three weeks later he had jumped to thirteenth place. For a naive and ungainly boy whose early schooling at Red River had been rather sketchy—he hadn't even begun his studies until he was well into his ninth year—it was a remarkable achievement. This was especially so when his early training was compared to the quality elementary education his classmates had enjoyed as sons of Quebec's wealthy and prominent.

As he grew accustomed to his surroundings and routine, he did even better. In a Latin composition presentation he placed second in his class, tying with one Eustache Prud'homme, but several weeks later he stood first. That same Prud'homme would later write of Louis, "During his entire course of studies, he knew how to win the esteem and friendship of his companions; without doubt he was one of the quickest and best students there was: the prizes he won attest to it."

In his third and fourth years Riel consistently ranked in the top ten of his class. His teachers must have been impressed with the brilliant young scholar from the exotic Métis community of Red River. And exotic he did seem.

Prud'homme later wrote of how fascinated the students were with this living specimen of the Wild West in their midst. One can almost hear the boyish wonderment in his description.

> A young man from so far away who knew about pemmican and the tomahawk, who had seen the long hair of the Sioux, of the Blackfoot or other warriors belonging to the savage tribes of that vast region, a young man who had maybe almost been scalped; that was more than enough to pique the curiosity of his classmates, little imps of twelve to fifteen years of age. In the hours of recreation, after the excitement of the games the unruly boys were somewhat calmer, they would gather around him and their young faces bore the expression of whatever emotion he wanted to give them in the course of his story. He would tell some story about the habits and customs of his region, or a comical tale about a remarkable adventure of which he was never the victim. These were scenes of terrible prairie fires in the west, of children crushed or kidnapped by the wild horses of fearless hunters who could jump over a large river in a single bound to end their determined pursuit of ferocious animals.

That he was exceedingly popular there can be no doubt; indeed, a web of closely knit friends, some of them to become powerful politicians and wealthy businessmen, would come to Riel's aid many times in the coming turbulent years. A friend, J.O. Mousseau, wrote in 1886:

> All the students who had known and appreciated him always remained loyal friends and supported him through good times and bad. Many men can develop friendship but few have the capability to maintain it.... Riel was among those happy few who had great talent in this area.

His loyalty to friends became something of a legend. When one of his closest chums was stricken by smallpox, Louis refused to leave him, "could not be driven or torn from his side," despite the obvious danger. The dying boy's last words were thanks to the sobbing Riel kneeling at his bedside.

Louis was not much of a sports enthusiast. Instead of throwing a ball he preferred to roam around the playground, debating "the meaning of life" with certain chosen classmates. He seems not to have been discriminated against because of his mixed blood; indeed his Métis heritage gave him a special status and, if he was taunted about it, he was certainly capable of defending himself with his sharp, sarcastic tongue.

He was not an angel while at the Collège; he could be quite cantankerous. A short poem he wrote in 1861 gives a hint of this. It is a take-off on his teacher's name, Moyen, French for "method".

My inattention has made you stern.
It is true you have little faith in my work.
Surely, some kind advice would solve the problem,
But no, everything is severity! Oh really what a method [moyen].

After 1862, life at college must have improved for Riel and his schoolmates, for that year they moved from the dingy St. Paul Street residence to grand new premises on Sherbrooke Street. It was an imposing, grandiose complex. Designed in the French Provincial style, it boasted gardens, elm trees, a man-made lake, picturesque towers left over from an old fort which had stood on the site, recreation yards, a three-tier library and a magnificent chapel.

In December of 1861, the old building on St. Paul Street was requisitioned by British military authorities, even though the new college had not been completed—even the glass for the windows was missing. The boys and their teachers huddled against the cold of that long winter, trying to do their lessons with gloved hands, discovering their fingers froze anyway. Riel continued to get excellent marks, standing fourth, fifth or sixth in his class.

Several vivid strains in Riel's personality emerged during the latter years of his schooling which would amplify as he grew older. He was often moody, quick-tempered and stubborn. In arguments with his classmates and teachers, he would give little ground, insisting that his analysis was the only one possible. Recalled Mousseau, "To offer an opinion contrary to his was to irritate him. He did not understand that everyone could not share his views, so much did he believe in his personal infallibity."*

He hated deception. Mousseau recalled that "sometimes when he did happen to play ball, he would suddenly leave off the game without saying a word whenever he saw that his contemporaries were cheating."

What he was best known for in those years, however, was his tenacious defence of the underdog. He loathed bullies of any kind. Mousseau tells the following story:

> One day a student arrived from Ireland. He was big and at least eighteen years of age, he was strange and sinister looking, his arms hung strangely from his body, like handles on a basket ... all in all, poor Quinn—for that was his name—moved like someone who had experienced much bad weather and many a storm while on board ship. It did not take more than that to attract the attention of many students who teased him mercilessly, but one

---

* Dr. J.O. Mousseau wrote his memoirs in 1886, just after the Métis had been defeated in the North-West Rebellion and Riel had been hanged. His opinions of Louis as a young man may have been coloured by these events.

day Louis became very angry and yelled, "Let him alone, the poor fellow, he hasn't done anything to you. Anyway if England had made you eat as many potatoes as he has had to, you wouldn't be any more solid on your legs than poor Quinn." Riel became the ungainly boy's best, and only, friend.

During his school years Louis Riel developed a habit of writing poetry which he maintained until his death. Most of it was not meant to be published, and therefore was not polished, but it is fascinating. The writing of verse was for him a kind of catharsis, a personal diary, his creative expression, a mirror unto his soul. He wrote about everything from politics to partridges, and during his schooldays his poetry revealed a revolutionary in the making.

The assigned literature readings at college were full of parables—the Bible, Aesop in Greek, Phaedrus in Latin, La Fontaine in French. Louis excelled in belles-lettres and rhetoric, and poetry became an infatuation; he enjoyed particularly creating those clear-cut moral tales where virtue always wins over vice, where the bully always meets his nemesis. Twenty-two of these fables were found in a classroom notebook kept by Riel between 1864 and 1866, when he was a mature student just completing his college education. These are vivid tales, not subtle or ironic, but powerful in their conviction; justice is always done and sometimes retribution is awful. The first stirrings of an intense political interest are also in evidence.

"La Souris" ("The Mouse") tells of a young female mouse who attends a session of Parliament and is shocked by what she sees. Instead of dignified, thoughtful statesmen conducting the nation's business, she sees a group of squabbling, vengeful antagonists who shake their fists and shout insults at each other. Upset and scandalized, she tells her mother all about her experience. "Are these the wise and worthy men so often praised?" she asks. "What can we expect of the ordinary subjects if the leaders act in such a barbaric manner?"

Probably Riel's best-written fable, and one of his most crafted works of poetry, is "Le Chat et les Souris" ("The Cat and the Mice"). The villain of the piece is:

> A cat of fine breeding
> Very English by birth, its upbringing quite stern
> Or so it would seem, usually unperturbed,
> Like a cruel Lord, lived solely off his hunting.
> 'Twas his stock in trade. And so long as his prey
> Abounded, Sir Gallopin acted the same way
> > Always returning home,
> > Making himself at ease
> > To enjoy his rich feast.
> > Our Anglo-Saxon host
> Served in endless supply a delectable dish

> of succulent mouse flesh.
> He offered relatives and all his friends a treat
> Of the finest ground meat
> Befitting an accomplished gourmet,
> And let rowdy tom-cats rule the day....

The victims, the mice, finally decide enough is enough and meet to talk about their terrible predicament.

> Then they realized to what extent their numbers
> Once so impressive, had now horribly dwindled.
> All the remaining survivors
> Wept profusely as their sadness was rekindled.
> Those who presided could barely
> Bring the meeting to order. How could a people
> Be sent by a barbaric ruler so haughty
> And so vicious to its certain destruction!
> Can a cruel man's ambition
> Be sufficiently strong to seal a people's fate!

The mice decide that, no matter what the cost, they must stand up to their oppressor. Around midnight a terrible, bloody battle ensues. The cat is so much bigger and more powerful than the mice that many lose their lives. But they refuse to quit:

> Wildly they tear at him, they scratch and claw, they bite.

Finally the cat is blinded and makes his escape, "his tail between his legs."

> The mice, their ranks thinned, finally claim victory,
> A galling taste though not without some glory.
> They at least have the consolation, the sweet taste of revenge. They can
>   cling to the memory
> And to future generations recount the tale.
> Where our unfortunate cat is concerned,
> He lives out his life in hunger and shame.
> He dies alone and insane.
> Thus righteousness is in the end well served.*

Scholars have always assumed that the nation of mice represented French-Canadian *patriotes* and their resistance to English rule. But the people who were influential in Riel's life at the time were hardly revolutionary nationalists;

---

* Translation by Paul Savoie.

they were, for the most part, conservative-minded, busy accommodating the British and working towards Canadian Confederation. More likely the underdogs represented his people, the Métis, and their struggles with the Hudson's Bay Company at Red River, in particular his father's role in the 1849 uprising, as well as the general bigotry and elitism of the English-speaking establishment.

After so heavy and strict a study schedule, summer vacations, even in the muggy Montreal weather, must have seemed like heaven to Louis Riel and the other Red River boys. Freed from the strict regime of their schools, they could finally taste the life of bustling Montreal.

They were invited to stay at the Grey Nuns' residence, the elegant fieldstone Maison Youville, nicely secluded on Île St. Bernard at Châteauguay, with its magnificent view of the St. Lawrence at what is called Lac St. Louis. The boys spent hours scampering among the apple trees, willows and pines, always taking time out to say their prayers at the impressive Calvary atop the highest hill.*

They also spent some time with Bishop Alexandre Taché's mother at her home at Boucherville, not far from Mont-St.-Hilaire, where Riel's father had spent most of his early years. The boys particularly liked the stately woman but her brother, Joseph de la Broquerie, made a lasting impression on Riel. The old bachelor never missed mass in the morning even though it was a long walk to the parish church and back. He spent the rest of his time visiting the poor and ill of the village.

In August 1860, the boys were allowed to join the cheering throng who had come out to greet the Prince of Wales. Montreal was decked out in triumphal arches, replete with flags and bunting; a herd of brass bands was on hand to welcome the eighteen-year-old royal. He was driven in his crimson-lined carriage to the centre of the Victoria Bridge and there drove in the last rivet of the imposing new structure. Whether Louis Riel was impressed by this spectacle or not, he would, curiously, retain a soft spot for the British monarchy and its attendant pomp.

Louis Schmidt had been in hospital off and on with a bronchial infection and, although he was doing well at his studies, doctors advised that, for the sake of his health, he return to the dry climate of Red River; Daniel McDougall, who had suffered from severe homesickness, had already been sent back home. Of the four Métis boys chosen, only Louis Riel remained. After that, he spent summers either at the home of his aunt Lucie Lee and her husband John, who lived in the village of Mile End, or at the estate of Riel's patron, the wealthy and influential widow Sophie Masson, whose husband had made a fortune in the import-export business.

---

* *Louis Riel would remain a favourite with the Grey Nuns, even after he ran into serious trouble with the Canadian government. They considered him "a sincere and devoted friend."*

Louis was not the only one of the Riel family to have benefited from Madame Masson's largesse.

While in Montreal in 1857, his father, Jean-Louis, had discovered that the Massons owned a large mill which sat unused. Riel senior approached Archbishop Taché, who was in Montreal at the time, and he managed to set up a meeting. Jean-Louis convinced Madame Masson to sell him the machine, which he estimated was worth £1,000, for a mere £200.

In his encounters with the Masson family, Jean-Louis talked at length about the nationalistic aspirations of the Métis and their struggles with the Hudson's Bay Company. He made such an impression on one of the Massons' sons, Louis-François-Rodrigue, that he would become a passionate supporter of Riel junior in years to come.

It was in the elegant and refined Masson manor house in Terrebonne that Riel spent part of each summer vacation. His devotion to Madame Masson thereafter was intense. Riel's letters written to her during his years at college were profuse in their gratitude, naturally so, but they also expressed his genuine affection for Sophie and her family. His devotion is obvious in a letter written in 1862.

> ... some time ago, as I was about to take leave of you, you told me that you had never received advice from your dear parents; you then added in a motherly tone, "I hope you will not mind me giving some advice as if I was your own mother." Ah! Madam, how such affection had comforted me and will always comfort me, being as I am so far away from my beloved mother and father.

At beautiful Terrebonne, Riel would grow to feel comfortable among the rich and powerful, would learn their manners, their customs and their speech. But he was also steeped in the politics of conservatism. Sophie's late husband, Joseph Masson, with extensive British empire trade links, had been anything but a fan of Louis-Joseph Papineau and the *Parti Patriote*. Naturally his offspring adopted that political philosophy and were prominent supporters of the Parti Bleu, the followers of Louis-Hippolyte LaFontaine and his moderate reforms. One Masson son, Rodrigue, became a close friend of George Cartier and, after a long career as a member of Parliament, would serve as Lieutenant-Governor of Quebec. Although Louis was much younger, he established a close relationship with the budding lawyer at Terrebonne.

In 1863, Louis Riel, age nineteen, entered his first year of philosophy (loosely equivalent to first-year university), thereby taking another important step towards the priesthood. There is no question that this was expected of Riel, and if his teachers seemed perhaps a little hasty and somewhat overbearing in pushing young men towards the religious life, that was only what their superiors in the church demanded.

Ignace Bourget, a man who would have a profound influence during Louis Riel's eventful life, had become Bishop of Montreal in 1840. Determined to fight what he saw as the religious lethargy and indifference among Catholics under his charge, he set out to fuel a resurgence of faith in the church. Education was his essential instrument in this renaissance. Well-educated priests were needed, as many and as soon as possible, and the Sulpicians were happy to oblige. In the hundred years after 1840, the brothers trained 2,600 priests for American parishes and 5,000 for Canadian ones.

While Riel had grown up immersed in his parents' intensely emotional Catholic faith, it had been at least benign. It was during his formative teenage years with the Sulpicians that his psyche was branded with a terrifying image of God. "Medieval Catholicism" is how the novelist Clark Blaise describes the nineteenth-century Quebec church. The Almighty was seen as an omnipotent, omniscient judge, a kind of magistrate full of wrath and revenge. Terrible punishment was inflicted on even the mildest of sinners.

Riel's writings in this period reflect this view. The *tour de force* among his religious poems was a piece entitled "Incendium", written entirely in Latin. Even Riel's most severe critics acknowledge that, despite some errors, the work is a scholarly accomplishment. (It is not precisely dated but is thought to have been written in either 1865 or 1866, just after Riel had left the Collège de Montréal.) The prose-poem describes a great fire, an inferno, which devastates Montreal. Descriptions from classical literature are woven throughout: the devastation of Troy as related in the *Aeneid*, the destruction of Rome described by Tacitus in *Annales* and the eruption of Vesuvius outlined by Pliny the Younger in *Epistles*—all of which were studied in depth at the Collège. But it was likely the terrible fire which had swept Montreal in June 1852 and nearly destroyed the church of Notre Dame that caught Riel's rather morbid imagination. While he himself had not experienced the tragedy, to the Sulpicians it was a terrifying memory—they had been part of a bucket brigade wetting down the roof of the Hôtel-Dieu—and they talked about it often.

Basically "Incendium" is a poem of godly revenge. "The people ... are contrite for their sins, but too late do they, as suppliants, beg for pardon from the bottom of their hearts, weeping. God looks down upon them. But the judgement of heaven must first be fulfilled. The flames increase—a third of the city now looks like a huge funeral-pyre...."

What is unnerving about Riel's early religious poetry is the obvious satisfaction derived from the punishment of the wicked, whether they are drowned in horrible floods, or incinerated in heaven-sent flames. They are replete with self-righteous moralizing, but then what else could be expected? For the other side of the religious coin taught by the Sulpicians was that the truly repentant would be spared from the Almighty's revenge. A young student at the Collège de Montréal spent much of his time and energy repenting—attending mass, praying, studying church dicta, examining his conscience, going to confession. No wonder Riel began to think that God might be on his side.

In February 1864, when Riel was in his sixth year at college, he suffered an overwhelming emotional trauma. His beloved father, Jean-Louis, after a short and painful illness, had suddenly died. Nothing could have been more devastating to the young man exiled in Montreal.

During the years his son was in college, Jean-Louis Riel had continued to play a strong, active role in the politics of Red River; several times he had found himself once again pitted against the establishment, often to his own detriment and sometimes foolishly. "A man who put the welfare of his people before his own wealth" was the common tribute. His marriage to Julie continued to be a happy one; two more children had been born after his return from Montreal in 1858, bringing the total to nine. And his milling enterprise, although not without problems, was prospering. With all the older children doing well at school in St. Boniface and with the eldest, Louis, headed for the priesthood, the future looked rosy for the Riel family. Then, in December 1863, Jean-Louis became gravely ill.

He had been a dedicated friend of the Grey Nuns, assisting them over the years in many ways, from setting up their carding operation—the sisters were ambitious weavers—to organizing the burial of their mother superior. They were genuinely distressed by his sickness. "From the first day of the year our nursing sisters have given Mr. Louis Riel all the care possible and have remained near him day and night," their journal noted. Their efforts were futile. On January 21, 1864, the date of his twentieth wedding anniversary, with his much-loved wife Julie and all but two of his children—Louis in Montreal and the eleven-month-old Alexandre—at his side, he died. He was forty-six years old.

When the sad news finally reached Louis Riel on February 17, he was utterly desolate. He had loved his father passionately; not only had Riel senior been much admired, but he had been a tender and fun-loving father. "Dear and gentle", his son would often describe him. On February 23, 1864, Louis wrote his family:

> Dearest Mother, dear little sisters, dear little brothers:
> After I received the news that plunged me, as you can imagine, into the depths of pain, I was advised not to write immediately so as to be better in

control of myself, and not to sadden you over much. But I cannot contain myself any longer....

Riel's deep despondency at the death of his father has often been cited by biographers as the reason for the turmoil that occurred at this point in his life— his rebellion against the Collège regime, his disillusionment with the priesthood, even the onset of mental illness. Certainly his uncle John Lee thought his nephew's reaction extreme.

> That death caused him extraordinary sorrow. He was then at the Collège de Montréal, and my wife and I brought him out [to their home at Mile End] to give him consolation. [But] that death had so touched his heart that he was inconsolable. I perceived then that this profound sorrow was affecting his brain and that he was delirious. That was obvious in his exaggerations and religious eccentricities; for he threw himself into excesses of piety and spoke in language on religious matters which I found unreasonable. My wife noticed the same thing and mentioned it to me. Afterwards, he remained very melancholic; I observed that to last about a year or a year and a half, after which he became his old self again.

But Lee's recollection was written twenty years after the fact, after Riel had been hanged for treason, and when the debate over whether he had been insane and therefore should not have been put to death was raging. Lee, in supporting Riel, may have exaggerated his despondency, for there is evidence that the young man was coping quite adequately with his grief. In his letters home, Louis says as much himself: "I am beginning to regain my senses somewhat." "My health is good, thank God!" More telling, in exams written in mid-March, he managed a "very good" in philosophy and a "good" in physics and chemistry— hardly the sign of a young man out of his mind with grief. The following December, his grades were still satisfactory. As well, during this period he wrote some of his most interesting poetry, primarily fables, probably in an attempt to mitigate his sorrow. Many of these are rather morbid, dealing with death and punishment, with hypocrites and disobedient children, but they are complex and often skilful, hardly the rantings of a madman.

Yet by the end of 1864 he had made up his mind to abandon the priesthood and quit the Collège de Montréal.

There were good reasons for this monumental decision. Riel may have come to realize that his was too eccentric and strong a personality to fully accept the discipline and conformity of the priesthood. As well, bitter reality had been thrust upon him. He was now the head of a large family, his mother and eight brothers and sisters, and would be relied upon for financial support; a religious vocation would not provide the income needed. But there was a third, perhaps more compelling inducement for suddenly altering his career plans—he had fallen head over heels in love.

The Riels of Montreal were not a successful family. Louis enjoyed a warm and close relationship with his paternal grandfather but Jean-Baptiste Riel was rather old and feeble during Louis's sojourn in Montreal—he died in 1868. Uncle Baptiste was a drunk, Uncle François was out of work and Aunt Charlotte suffered an unhappy family life. Only Aunt Lucie Lee could be considered respectable and well off.

John Lee had immigrated from Kilrush, County Clare, to Montreal with his family when he was two years old. In 1849, at age twenty-two, he had married the seventeen-year-old Lucie Riel. The couple had two children; Lucie was fifteen and Matilde was thirteen when Louis Riel stayed off and on with this totally bilingual family. John Lee had been a carpenter and undertaker, and in 1864 had started a business of ship's carpenters, caulkers and sparmakers which would prove quite successful. Lee was also an alderman, a man of some influence in the community. When Riel was in Montreal as a student, the Lees lived in a one-storey house of stone on Mile End Road in the village of St. Louis du Mile-End, near the present-day Parc Jarry in Outremont. Next door lived the family of Joseph Guernon. Sometime in late 1864, Louis Riel met and fell madly in love with Guernon's eldest child, the twenty-year-old Marie-Julie.

That Marie Guernon was very pretty we know from Riel's poetry. In "My First Love" he assures her that she was so beautiful any man would remain faithful to her. His verse paints her as something of a coquette, playful and teasing.

> The other day I said to Marie:
> Ah! If only you longed for my happiness!
> For the rest of my life
> I would remain your loyal servant.
> She playfully answered
> That she did not hear me.
> And that she was much too ladylike
> To listen to such silly talk.
> Love is in fact much too fickle
> To trust its promises.
> And I fear to commit myself to
> Vows that would last too long!

But Louis seems confident about winning her over:

I detected the beginning of a smile
And I told her sweetly:
Believe that love is not fickle.
You can trust its promises.
The tender vows pledged as a token of love
Will last a very long time!

There was every reason for a young girl like Marie to fall in love with Louis Riel. Not only was he charming, with just enough Red River patois in his speech to make him seem exotic, but he was exceedingly handsome. In a photograph taken about 1866, he looks very much the dandy. He is standing in a formal pose, his hand on a book. Elegant in his frock coat and bow tie, he is clean-shaven, with his thick wavy hair, the great vanity in his life, cut rather short. Standing about five foot ten, he is slender but well built— a gift of his fur-trading, buffalo-hunting ancestors. He could be any young French Canadian of a wealthy family about to enter his profession, yet there is a slight hint of the revolutionary. It is in his eyes; they are large, deep-set, black as midnight and very intense.

Not only was Riel good-looking, but he was highly educated for his times, with good prospects for a profession and stable income. None of this mattered to Marie Guernon's parents. Once they discovered that he was a mixed-blood, from the north country—as he himself put it, a "country bumpkin"—they frowned on the match. A few verses of a song found in Riel's notebook illustrate what he was up against. The voice of Madame Guernon is heard. The fictitious Cecile is obviously Marie.

My daughter is much too well bred
To associate with a bandit.
Without question, for you
She is much too genteel

Without question, for you
She is much too genteel
Thus is it so for my Cecile
Consider yourself spurned and rejected.

And yet the Guernons were hardly upper-class society themselves. In the 1871 census, Joseph Guernon's occupation is listed as day-labourer; at other times he is called a carpenter. They and their six children lived in a single-storey house made of wood. And there is evidence that Marie herself was not well educated. Two love poems written by someone other than Riel have been found in the notebooks he kept at the time. They are so full of spelling and grammatical errors that the writer appears to have been almost illiterate, a product of poor schooling. It has been assumed that this work is Marie's, although this may be unfair as there is no conclusive proof. Still, the prospects of her marrying someone with a brighter future than young Louis Riel's at that time seem remote. It's likely her family's disapproval of her suitor stemmed from only one source—pure bigotry. The couple continued their relationship, but on the sly.

Riel's decision to give up the priesthood naturally brought him anxiety and questioning. What was he going to do with his life?

Shortly after making this decision, Riel informed the director of the Collège de Montréal that he wished to continue his studies as a day student and that he would live at the convent of the Grey Nuns, with whom he still maintained a warm friendship. Permission was reluctantly given but almost immediately Riel began breaking the rules—he paid little attention to the convent's curfew and he skipped classes. His grades began to slide. It was obvious to everyone that his heart was no longer in his studies. On March 8, 1865, after six and a half years of rigorous schooling and only four months before he would have received his baccalaureate, Louis Riel informed the college that he was quitting. While maintaining that there were no hard feelings, the director wrote a rather nasty, condescending letter to Bishop Taché at Red River.

> We have no regret for having given him his education. It is true that we would have been happier if we had been able to return to you, in his person, a good missionary. But God does not seem to have called him to that estate. I am very much afraid that the poor boy was not worthy of it. In any case it is a thousand times better that he should be an ordinary Christian than become a bad priest.

Riel would never be "an ordinary Christian", and if the director had spotted anything in his character which revealed that the "poor boy" would soon be considered a great leader of men, he mentioned not a word.

How Riel felt about giving up what for years he had considered his heaven-inspired calling is debatable. A poem included in an 1864–65 notebook entitled "Young Man Dying" has always been interpreted as a reaction to his abandonment of the priesthood. It is one of Riel's loveliest, most poignant works:

> The dark fall is nigh
> With cold winds blowing
> To bend with my sighs
> In endless droning.
> All of nature lies
> In a pall of frost
> And death's plaintive cries
> Echo my deep loss.

Withering verdure
Strewing the hedges,
Life cannot endure
Death at its edges.
And I, frozen sheaf,
Am buffed by the cold,
Single falling leaf
Unable to grab hold.

Spying leafless trees,
Wandering birds fly,
Seek a softer breeze
For their plaintive cry.
Joy was so brief!
I walk bereaved
And oppressive grief
Foreshadows my death.

O love, cherished,
Let friendship guide you.
When I've perished
To our vows be true.
At times keep vigil
Where my ashes lie.
And at my side still
Silent prayers pray.*

A lament for a lost spiritual calling? Perhaps, or merely an anguished cry after a lovers' quarrel. The courtship of Louis and Marie was hardly a smooth one, given her parents' severe disapproval. Perhaps Louis was simply expressing how pathetically lonely he felt.

After leaving college, Riel's first concern was to find a way to make a living. He must have been thinking of Red River because he attempted to find a wealthy investor to back him in the fur-trading business. At the same time he attempted, at the urging of the Masson family, to pull a few political strings.

Five years earlier, the impressionable sixteen-year-old had sat mesmerized in the Collège cathedral during year-end ceremonies. While the choir sang with great feeling, "O Canada, my land, my love," the man who had composed

---

* *Translation by Paul Savoie.*

that song, the elegant George-Étienne Cartier, had stood ramrod straight, contemplating the most recent crop of Quebec's elite in training. He gave an emotional address, promising the students a rosy future in "the great land" that was Canada.

For the next decade Cartier remained the key player in the fierce controversy over the future of a united Canada. Riel, who had become entranced with politics, and was obviously thinking of the mixed-bloods of Red River, admired the senior statesman's fervent defence of minority rights during the Confederation debates at Quebec City. It seemed natural to ask a man he considered such a hero, a fixer who was so adroit at dispensing political patronage, and also, not insignificantly, a fellow alumnus, for help in finding a paying position.

Louis's appeal to Cartier took the form of three letters written in verse form from January to April 1866. Louis knew that the statesman was a great lover of poetry and a sometime poet, and probably thought such an appeal would grab his attention.

Riel rather pretentiously flattered Cartier—the politician, he decreed, could be another Maecenas, the great Roman patron of the arts who assisted such luminaries as Virgil and Horace, by helping French-Canadian poets such as himself. After much such flattery Riel finally got to the point: he wanted a job, at the customs service, at the post office, in any bank, it didn't matter. When he received no response, he wrote a second verse-letter, more subdued in tone but just as congratulatory, heaping praise on Cartier's achievements and asking him for an interview. When he again heard nothing he wrote his third and last appeal, which is one of his best poems, entitled "Amid the Teeming Crowd". In it the young man reveals his frustration at not yet being able to find a place for himself.

> Amid the teeming crowd
> So boisterous and so loud,
> Where a man, lost in deep thought, stands out,
> Something noble in his stance,
> Eyes filled with sadness and doubt,
> He is given a furtive glance.
> And should he speak out, who will whisper:
> Brothers, pray tell, who is this stranger?
> For his presence engenders
> A vague sense of danger.
> He goes on his way under sullen skies
> Weighed down by worry,
> His heart swollen with sighs,
> His life long and dreary.*

---

* Translation by Paul Savoie.

Louis was evidently hoping that Cartier would feel sorry for him. If that was the strategy, he failed miserably, for he received no reply, not even a token acknowledgement. Riel finally did obtain a position as a law clerk. And when he walked into the law office of Laflamme Huntington and Laflamme, at 232 St. Denis Street in downtown Montreal, he walked into a very different world.

Rodolphe Laflamme's politics were as ardent as his name implied. For years he had been at the very heart of the powerful French-Canadian revival—a renewed, enthusiastic pride in the history of New France; an examination of the role of the church; and a new nationalism for Quebec. This was partly a response to the Durham report of 1839, which had contemptuously denigrated Québécois culture and advocated the assimilation of the French into English Canada. What followed was a blossoming of Quebec arts and politics that was unprecedented, and resulted in the very opposite of Durham's death sentence— on the national scene Quebec gained political power.

Laflamme had been president of the Institut Canadien, set up in 1844 as a political and cultural centre with a well-used library, reading room and lecture hall where the economic, cultural and political questions of the day were hotly debated by young French-Canadian nationalists. He had also been a founder and editor of the institute's controversial newspaper, *L'Avenir*. Riel, who for years had been cloistered in the conservative, elitist atmosphere propagated by the Sulpicians, must have experienced a shock when confronted with Laflamme's anti-establishment creed, especially its blatant anti-clericalism. But he must have been impressed, as well. Laflamme was considered a lot more than a hot-headed radical; he was highly accomplished in his profession, a skilled trial lawyer and a professor of law at McGill. And the most interesting intellects of the time—among them the politician Antoine-Aimé Dorion, the writer-editor Joseph Doutre and the historian François-Xavier Garneau—regularly visited Laflamme's office. A person who was as intellectually curious as Riel must have been deeply affected by them and their ideas.

Academics and biographers have always assumed that Riel, as the historian George Stanley states, "was not cut out to be a lawyer." He is supposed to have been a lackadaisical dreamer, unable to cope with the subtleties and formalities of law. These accusations are based entirely on one comment made by Riel's school chum, J.O. Mousseau, that "Louis, as a lawyer, would have had his office in his hat and would have received his customers on the top of Mount Royal." Given that this remark appeared in an article written twenty-odd years later, at the time of heated debate over Riel's insanity, by a man who may or may not have had contact with Riel during the period he worked for Laflamme, the assessment seems blatantly unfair. Indeed, Riel's leadership of the Red River

Rebellion was distinguished by his knowledge of the legal and constitutional process. And he must have thought his legal career was taking root because he decided he was finally in a position to marry.

Since leaving college, Louis had been living with his Aunt and Uncle Lee at Mile End, feverishly writing poetry and courting, successfully it at first seemed, the lovely Marie. On June 12, 1866, Louis and Marie-Julie signed a marriage contract, without the knowledge of her parents. The couple may have been trying to mollify the Guernons, for the agreement called for a strict separation of property, in the present and in the future. As well, Riel consented to give up any rights to a dowry from his bride's family. To no avail. The parents forbade the marriage. While there are indications that Louis fought their decision, Marie finally acceded to their wishes.

Riel was utterly devastated. Almost overnight he decided to flee Montreal. The poem he wrote just before leaving, entitled "To My Friends", while certainly revealing a deep sorrow, still has a sense of anticipation.

> I must go, the time is ripe.
> My heart is overflowing
> with joy and sadness alike
> as I ponder my leaving.
> I know I lose by going.
> I am consoled by knowing
> All the love that you have given
> Will remain a part of me....

PART II
TRIUMPH

One day ontario
Tried to invade our land.
A fine trio was spying on us:
Mair, Snow, Schultz were seeking some butter
To grease their bread at our expense:
But these miserable people
Found nothing but a scuffle.

R ed River was suffering hard times and the Riel clan was struggling; it was necessary for the eldest son and head of the household to earn some hard cash before he returned to the Northwest. According to his friend Louis Schmidt, the first place Louis Riel headed for was Chicago, and the obstreperous cabal of Quebec nationalists who had gathered there.

In 1867 Chicago was finally coming into its own as the bustling, albeit eccentric, commercial heart of America's northwest. In the seventeenth and eighteenth centuries, it had been a popular portage for French and *canadien* fur traders, many of whom settled there. Once the Indians had been subdued and the canal and railroad systems had been built, white settlers flooded in, but the French connection had taken root. It was not surprising, therefore, that nationalistic Québécois who were bent on fighting Canadian Confederation headed to this vigorous city. Among the most passionate and vociferous of these expatriate *canadiens* was the poet Louis Fréchette.

Fréchette ran in the same circles as the lawyer Laflamme, and Riel may have met him through that connection. Certainly Fréchette had already made a name for himself as an ardent Québécois nationalist. After studying law at Laval University, he opened a legal office in his home town of Lévis, but, more to his taste, he began writing hard-edged political journalism and poetry. When his views proved too radical for the conservative population of Lévis, he became disillusioned and moved to Chicago, where he founded a French-language newspaper, *L'Observateur*. To earn his living he worked as the corresponding secretary of the Illinois Central Railway's land department. Louis Schmidt says Riel lived with Fréchette there. If so, the young Métis found himself in a hive of literary creativity and rabble-rousing politics. While in Chicago, Fréchette wrote for several radical newspapers, created and directed a political comedy, composed an opera in five acts and helped found the city's first St. Jean Baptiste Society. He had already published his second book of poetry, *La Voix d'un Exilé*. In the manner of the famous political satire *Les Châtiments*, by Fréchette's great hero, Victor Hugo, these poems were satirical attacks on Canadian politicians; annexation to the United States was certainly considered preferable to Confederation. How far Louis Riel was influenced by Fréchette's ideas is not known, although the two remained mutual admirers; in 1887, after Riel's execution, Fréchette published a volume *La Légende d'un peuple* which included a long paean to "the last martyr" called "Le Gibet de Riel" ("The Gallows of Riel").

Schmidt claimed that while Riel was in Chicago, he wrote poetry in the style of the famous French poet Alphonse Lamartine, the father of romantic verse, full of melancholy, poignant despair, exalted love, communion with nature and religious ecstasy. Lamartine was also a political activist. Unfortunately none of Louis Riel's poetry has survived from this period, but events that would soon follow suggest he was very much inspired by Lamartine's life and work.

Schmidt does not say how long Riel spent in Chicago, but by the summer of 1867 he had moved farther west and a little closer to home.

The frontier town of St. Paul, Minnesota, had grown considerably since he had last seen it as an impressionable fourteen-year-old on his way to school in the east. It was now a sooty industrial city of brick and stone. The construction of the Chicago, Milwaukee and St. Paul's Railway had resulted in a flood of immigrants, mostly Europeans, both labourers and farmers. But there were still pockets of the French community at St. Anthony, situated north of Minneapolis (it would amalgamate with that city in 1873), and in a village, "Little Canada", on Lake Gervais, where settlers from Quebec and Métis freighters from Red River congregated. It was in long conversation with these people that Riel was able to immerse himself in the intricacies of Red River politics. He also became intrigued by the gruesome drama being played out in the United States at the time. But with the end of the Civil War in 1865, American annexationists advocating the take-over of Canada's Northwest

Territories were beginning to flex their muscles. Louis must have been fascinated by their arguments.

During this time he worked at a variety of jobs, most prominently at the dry-goods store owned by Edward Langevin, a rags-to-riches immigrant from Quebec.

Bishop Taché would later write that Riel "tried in the West all sorts of business, and failed to secure any success." But this was written in 1887, when Taché and the Riel family were estranged and the bishop expressed many denigrating interpretations of Louis's past. Whatever his purpose in St. Paul, Riel obviously missed his family desperately. In a letter to Julie Riel on August 10, 1867, he wrote: "You are always in my thoughts. You all know how much I love you, my good mother and my little brothers and sisters. I am sad that I cannot make you as happy as I would like."

There were likely several reasons Louis did not hurry back to Red River. He may well have been trying to establish himself in business as a trader, and he was probably trying to raise a cache of money. The Riels were facing drought and a terrible grasshopper plague that would threaten not only their family farm, but all of the Red River Settlement, and Louis may have been sending funds back to them.

Finally, the following July, Louis left St. Anthony for the Métis village of St. Joseph, which the trader Norman Kittson and the priest Georges Belcourt had established after the floods of 1852. Doing business for a St. Paul merchant, he encountered Antoine Blanc Gingras, a fur trader who would soon become a valuable ally.

On July 26, 1868, Louis finally arrived at St. Boniface for what must have been a joyous reunion. He would later comment, "It was early on a Sunday morning, before services when I saw my birthplace again. It was a beautiful day." Riel must have savoured being once again at the centre of his large, closely knit, affectionate family. His grandfather Lagimodière had died in 1855, but his grandmother Marie-Anne, although in her late eighties, remained sprightly and was still telling her stories of the early West. His mother Julie, now forty-six years old, was as warm-hearted and sympathetic as ever, but she was beginning to suffer the illness that would periodically plague her, especially during family crises. Sara Riel, the sibling to whom Louis was closest, had remained a devoted, almost fanatical Catholic and, five months before, had taken her vows as a Grey Nun missionary. Pretty eighteen-year-old Marie, who had been a bright student, was already teaching elementary school at St. Charles, but she was a pale, sickly girl, the worry of her entire family. Charles, the next eldest boy to Louis, was the unluckiest of the bunch; born on November 4, 1854, he would be pulled out of school to help support the family. The rest of the children—

Octavie, sixteen, Eulalie, fifteen, Joseph, eleven, Henriette, seven, and Alexandre, five—were either at school or working on the farm. Riel would grow particularly attached to the two youngest, who had been born while he was away.

And what must the Riels have thought of Louis? He had left Red River ten years before as a shy, simple fourteen-year-old, and returned a handsome, sophisticated young man of almost twenty-four. He was now incredibly well educated for his time and place, spoke beautiful French and was fluent in English and the classical languages. Yet he hadn't lost his deep affection for his family, and he never put on airs or was condescending towards them. His mother, in particular, must have rejoiced at the blossoming of her oldest child.

As overjoyed as he was to be home, Louis must have been shocked at the terrible troubles that afflicted the Red River Settlement. That spring the grasshoppers had arrived; so thick were the clouds of ravenous insects that as one correspondent wrote: "They penetrated into the parlours and kitchens, bed chambers and bedding, pots, pans, kettles, ovens, boots and coat pockets. One scarcely dared to open one's mouth. On the river they floated like scum, or were piled two feet deep on the banks where they rotted and stunk like carrion." They ate everything green in sight; not a stalk of wheat remained. To add to the misery, the buffalo hunt, which had been growing poorer by the year, completely failed that spring. There were few fish and the rabbits and prairie chickens simply disappeared. "I have heard of one family last week who had killed and eaten their house cat, and others in the distance have eaten their horses," the Reverend George Young wrote to a friend. In 1868, the Métis population would harvest only 1,200 bushels of wheat, compared with 15,000 the year before (and that had been a poor crop).

As a final blow—a sign of God's vengeance, some people thought—a tornado destroyed the Anglican Holy Trinity Church in the village of Winnipeg.

The Riel family had not been spared the ruin. They had harvested almost nothing in 1867, and although they had obtained an advance of seed grain from the St. Vital Executive Relief Committee, it looked as though the following year's crop would prove a disaster as well. The family's difficulties must have been doubly hard for Julie Riel. Before his death, Jean-Louis's grist mill had begun showing a profit, and his farming operation had thrived. The future had seemed so bright.

Julie had given up the mill and moved her brood from the property on the Seine River to a lot on River Road at St. Vital, some four miles south of St. Boniface on the west side of the Red River. This was land which had been owned by her brother Benjamin Lagimodière. On it, about four hundred yards from the heavily treed banks of the Red River, a traditional two-storey log house was built with a large fireplace and kitchen addition. The arrangements to purchase this new property were made by Bishop Taché; either he lent the family the money or, more likely, he was following the deathbed instructions of Riel senior, using family funds.

There were good reasons for the move. First, Julie and her young family could not operate the mill—increasing drought and shrinking markets did not bode well for a profitable business anyway—and the River Road lot with its water frontage was far better agricultural land. The Riels worked a mixed farm, growing oats, wheat, barley, peas, potatoes, cabbages, onions, carrots, cucumbers and pumpkins, and also raising livestock, a good-sized herd by Métis standards—by 1867 it included three bulls, three milk cows, five calves and five horses. In a year free of grasshoppers and drought, it provided a reasonable living. Secondly, the Grey Nuns had set up a school and chapel less than a mile away which was easy for the younger children to walk to. And perhaps most important for a lonely widow, this was a more heavily populated area and Julie could be close to her friends, the Naults, Proulx and Sauvés, as well as to the huge Lagimodière clan.

The Riels had scraped by while Louis was at school. There had been income from the farm; Marie had contributed as much of her tiny teacher's salary as she could; Charles had earned money helping his Uncle Benjamin Lagimodière operate his grist mill; and Louis had been sending funds home. Still, Julie must have heaved a sigh of relief when her eldest, now twenty-four years old, well educated and capable, finally showed up in Red River.

Louis began farming that summer and conditions did improve for the family. They turned down offers of free meat—Riel had probably brought some cash with which to buy some surplus grain stored over the years by Selkirk farmers. By the following winter the Riels had paid back the seed grain loan advanced by the relief committee.

In January 1869, Louis was able to purchase a lot of eighty-four acres adjacent to the family's property at St. Vital. The asking price was a two- or three-year-old ox of a hundred pounds, twenty-two aspen logs and one pelt. (A new contract was drawn up on June 24 which called for a cash payment of £2 payable in September, £2 on All Saints' Day, and £2 and 5 shillings on New Year's Day 1870, but it is not known whether it was honoured.)

Anticipating that white settlers would soon be gobbling up land around Red River, many Métis had begun staking claims on lots outside the area officially surveyed by the Hudson's Bay Company, which they marked by a blaze on a tree, stakes in the ground or a ploughed furrow. Sometime in 1869, Riel selected a lot on the south bank of the Seine River, in what would become the parish of Lorette, denoting it by a pile of logs shaped like a house. Other land acquisitions followed: another staked claim on the upper reaches of the Rivière Sale and, between 1870 and 1873, three more river lots, all of which had once belonged to Riel's father. Obviously Louis was intending to remain in the Red River Settlement, but farming was only what he did to earn his living. A quite different passion was about to consume him—political intrigue, which was on the boil in the Red River Settlement.

During his sojourn in St. Paul, he had chatted with mixed-blood freighters and traders about the situation in Red River. But it was his old school pal, Louis Schmidt—as boyish-looking as ever, with just the first hint of seediness evident in his demeanour—who brought him up to date.

Since his return to Red River from Montreal's St. Hyacinthe College, Schmidt had worked as a jack of all trades, mostly for the Catholic establishment. As Father Joseph-Jean-Marie Lestanc's secretary, he had copied, with his extravagantly beautiful handwriting, a Cree grammar and dictionary for the use of missionaries. He became Father Noel-Joseph Ritchot's assistant in St. Norbert parish but "difficulties" arose—Schmidt's drinking problem was already apparent—and in the fall of 1863 he travelled to Pembina, where he worked with Joseph Lemay, the customs collector. After Lemay's wife took a violent dislike to him—again probably because of his drinking—he moved on to St. Joseph, where he became acquainted with Father Alexis André, who twenty years later would play a major role in the North-West Rebellion. When that priest was asked by the American government to try to convince a group of rebellious Sioux to lay down their arms and return to their reserve, Schmidt acted as translator-secretary. The mission failed, but Schmidt always remembered the Indian chief's response: "You, Black Robe, are a man of God, you wouldn't know how to lie. However, those who sent you are not like you. They use you to lure us because they know that we trust you."

Over the next few years Schmidt performed a variety of tasks for the church: he was in charge of several caravans transporting missionary supplies to and from St. Paul; he condensed articles from Canadian and European newspapers and magazines for distribution to far-flung missionaries; and he taught school at St. Boniface, a job he loathed. All the while, he was trying to raise some cash so as to set himself up in business as a freighter. In the winter of 1868 he saw his opportunity; the American government approached him and some associates to open and run a mail route between Abercrombie, North Dakota, and Helena, the capital of Montana. But the enterprise suffered one disaster after another, until finally, during a savage blizzard in the winter of 1868, Schmidt was separated from his companions, his horse died of exhaustion, and his left foot was frozen so that several toes had to be amputated. As his biographer,

Donatien Frémont, put it, "The mail route finally had to be abandoned. Louis hobbled home again to Saint-Boniface as poor as Job."

It was therefore a rather disillusioned and bitter young man whom Louis Riel invited as a house guest in the summer of 1868. What followed were fervent, all-night conversations—and the eventual emergence of two uncompromising political activists.

What Riel soon understood from his discussions was that the endemic racism which his father had fought against with such dedication twenty years before had gained strength until it had become a treacherous current undermining the Red River Settlement. He also realized that the existence of the Métis as a people was in peril.

A bizarre scandal that had rocked Red River five years before had come close to precipitating a religious war between Catholics and Protestants, Métis and English-speaking Half-breeds. The antagonism, which had not much abated when Riel returned, could be traced directly to the preachings of one Anglican minister who was as bigoted and closed-minded as the most dedicated member of the Orange Order.

The Reverend Griffiths Owen Corbett's past was rather shady. After he had served an apprenticeship as a Scripture reader and then catechist, the Anglican Bishop of Montreal had refused to ordain him, nor was he to be assigned his own parish—probably because of the man's insufferable personality. Missionaries for Rupert's Land were in short supply, however, and Corbett was finally sent to a Red River mission in 1852. Three years later, he resigned because of poor health and low wages, but in 1858 he returned to the parish of Headingley, situated west of Fort Garry on the Assiniboine River, and immediately began sowing seeds of hatred and discontent.

Reverend Corbett despised Catholics and considered them, especially the Métis, "barbarians". In the propaganda he never ceased writing, he insisted Red River was "a Protestant Colony of a Protestant Queen". Catholics were moral degenerates out to conquer the world. He was enraged when Hudson's Bay Company governor William Mactavish married a Catholic in a splendid wedding at St. Boniface Cathedral and in subsequent years baptized his children in the Roman Catholic faith. Because the local government, the Council of Assiniboia, was evenly split between Protestant and Catholic members, Corbett felt Mactavish, who was the chairman, would tip the balance towards the "Pope of Rome". "The Papal anti-Christ" had to be stopped at all costs.

Corbett's parish was made up primarily of English-speaking Half-breeds and it was in preaching to these people that the minister did the most harm. Long subject to humiliating discrimination by other English-speakers, the Half-breeds were only too willing to believe Corbett's vicious propaganda. As the historian Frits Pannekoek puts it, "Here was assurance that as Protestants, the Half-breeds were superior to at least the Catholic Métis at Red River."

Corbett also harboured much malice towards the Hudson's Bay Company; he thought Red River should become a British crown colony with a local government, presumably out of reach of French Canadians. This too appealed to the Half-breeds.

In early December 1862, Corbett was arrested and imprisoned in the Hudson's Bay Fort Garry, charged with attempting to abort the unborn child of Maria Thomas, a young maid in his household. It was alleged that Corbett and Thomas were having an affair when she became pregnant. The abortion attempt failed and the baby was born five months later.

Bail was denied Corbett and almost immediately about 150 of his supporters arrived at the fort. They were convinced, and would remain so for years after, that the Hudson's Bay Company had trumped up the charges against their minister. They made such a clamour that the then HBC governor, Alexander Dallas, fearing a full-fledged riot would break out, agreed that Corbett could address the crowd. In an inflammatory speech, Corbett urged them to demand justice for him at all costs. They did just that, and a frightened Governor Dallas released the clergyman on bail.

The trial, which began on February 19, 1863, lasted nine days and heard sixty-one witnesses. Anglican minister John Chapman described it thus:

> What a spectacle.... Mr Corbett in one box & Maria Thomas a young girl of 16 years in the witness box, with her babe in her arms which she declares is Mr Corbett's and whose embryo life he is charged with attempting to destroy by means of medicine, instruments etc.

Corbett was found guilty and sentenced to six months in jail.

About two months later, the Half-breeds of Red River submitted a petition of 552 names, nearly all English, demanding a pardon for Corbett. When the Council of Assiniboia and the governor refused their request, they marched on Fort Garry, broke open the prison gates, overpowered the Métis jailer and freed the minister. Governor Dallas responded by appointing some twenty special constables—mostly Métis farmers and freighters who quite naturally despised the Corps Bête, as they called Corbett. They arrested the Half-breed ringleader, a teacher by the name of James Stewart. The following day, a force of twenty-seven armed English Half-breeds stormed Fort Garry and freed Stewart. Infuriated Métis volunteered to recapture Corbett and Stewart, but Governor Dallas, sensing that civil war was about to break out, wisely disbanded the posse he had assembled.

The Council of Assiniboia decided that without a strong police force, nothing could be done; the minister was allowed to remain free, and no punishment was meted out to the law-breaking English Half-breeds.

The following year Corbett finally followed the orders of his superiors and gave up his ministry, but he left a bitter legacy. He had poisoned the minds of Protestants against Catholics, English-speakers against French-speakers, and Métis against Half-breeds. And he had left the authority of the Hudson's Bay Company in shreds.

Riel must have been flabbergasted on hearing this tale; before his departure for the east, relations between Half-breeds and Métis had been amiable. But he quickly became aware of an even more sinister force that had emerged in the Red River Settlement during his absence—carpetbaggers from Ontario.

During 1857–60, two exploratory expeditions—one British, captained by John Palliser, and the other Canadian, led by the engineer S.J. Dawson and the geologist H.Y. Hind—had concluded that a portion of the Canadian prairies, including the Red River Valley, was remarkably fertile, with heavy black clay soil wonderfully suited to growing grain. Their findings encouraged a trickle of pioneers to the West. At Red River, the farmers among these new arrivals established themselves in two areas: at Kildonan among the old Selkirk settlers and at the new "all English" community, Portage la Prairie, twenty-five miles west along the Assiniboine River. A second group, the free traders, merchants and quick-buck capitalists, settled in the tiny but growing village of Winnipeg.

Most of these newcomers came from western Ontario or the Ottawa Valley, where the Loyal Order of the Orange, that clandestine society dedicated to preserving British supremacy and promoting unthinking bigotry, thrived. They were intent on two things: making a fortune for themselves from land speculation, and ensuring that the Northwest became an extension of white, Protestant Ontario. The "miserable Half-breeds"—this was Prime Minister John A. Macdonald's term, but most of the Red River Canadians shared the same sentiment—were considered mere nuisances to be exploited wherever possible.

They purported to believe in "Canada's Manifest Destiny", but they had more immediate reasons for laying claim to the Northwest. The economic advantages were obvious. Moreover, a flood of Anglo-Saxon settlers, especially from Britain, would throw off kilter the delicate balance that had momentarily been achieved between Ontario and Quebec in the new Confederation—in favour, of course, of English-speakers. For propaganda organs like Toronto's *Globe*, annexing the Northwest became a holy crusade.

The Canadian Party, as the new settlers in Red River came to be called, also detested the Hudson's Bay Company, the very symbol to them of the "backward" frontier. Their antipathy was part of the nineteenth century's general disdain for crown-granted monopolies, particularly a monopoly perceived as part of the Montreal financial mafia. But it was the political system that truly irked them—the governing body, the Council of Assiniboia, was still chosen by the HBC governors (and, needless to say, few of their kind were ever asked to sit). In the aftermath of the 1837 rebellions in Upper and Lower Canada, such an undemocratic political system was considered anathema.

But the majority of Red River residents weren't interested in being annexed to Canada. Some thought the present form of government would do just fine—although it was becoming increasingly obvious that governing such a diverse and quarrelsome community was too much for the Hudson's Bay Company. Many felt an independent crown colony connected to Britain with some degree of self-government would be ideal. "The Canadians", therefore, were not at all popular. Meetings they organized to gain support for their ideas were, according to Alexander Begg, a free trader and unofficial historian of Red River, "miserable failures ... the annexation to Canada became a by word of ridicule. The meetings held were scenes of uproarious merriment instead of orderly gatherings." The Canadians did have some supporters among the older Selkirk settlers and English Half-breeds, but they were few in number.

The Canadian Party did have one powerful instrument at its disposal. In the autumn of 1859, two entrepreneurs, William Coldwell and William Buckingham, arrived at Red River and immediately set up the settlement's first weekly, the *Nor'Wester*—it would remain the community's only newspaper for the next ten years. Coldwell and Buckingham had been connected with George Brown's *Globe*, the leading and most powerful advocate of Canadian annexation of the Northwest, and the *Nor'Wester* was nothing more than a zealous progeny of the Toronto paper. It certainly was shrill. The paper's editors never stopped harping at the Hudson's Bay Company and the Council of Assiniboia.

Still, the Canadians were so unpopular among the general populace at Red River that they would have been as lethal as a mosquito bite—if it hadn't been for their Hercules-like leader, Dr. John Christian Schultz.

There are few villains in Canada's frontier history as vivid and menacing as Dr. Schultz. He was a strikingly handsome man, with fine regular features, wavy red-gold hair and bright blue eyes. Well over six feet tall, he had the build of a circus strongman; he was supposed to have once cowed a hostile crowd by ripping a bar from a solid oak chair and threatening the rabble-rousers with it.

Schultz had been born in Loyalist country, in the town of Amherstburg, south of Windsor. Earning his tuition fees by working in the drygoods store of his half-brother Henry McKenney, and then as a sailor on barges travelling between Chicago and Buffalo, Schultz had attended Oberlin College in Ohio and later studied medicine at Queen's University and then Victoria College in Cobourg. On his graduation in 1861 he headed for the Red River Settlement, perhaps because Henry had already moved there, but he soon discovered that a doctor's practice was not a money-maker. And if John Christian Schultz had one goal in life, it was to make a fortune, any way he could, as quickly as possible. He gave up medicine and began buying valuable waterfront land and clearing it; he rapidly acquired interests in the fur trade; and, with Henry McKenney, he set up a retail supply business, an inn and a restaurant.

In 1864, he and Henry gave up on the hotel business, deciding instead to concentrate on general trade, and they erected a large new building in the village of Winnipeg to do so. In 1867 Schultz married Anne Campbell Farquharson, granddaughter of the Governor of British Guyana and daughter of a prominent fur trader. Anne was a high-spirited, headstrong woman who would play an important role in her husband's many subsequent intrigues and predicaments.

That year Schultz also bought out William Buckingham's shares in the *Nor'Wester*. This provided him with the mouthpiece he needed to promote his great obsession—the annexation of the Northwest to Canada. Schultz was a typical imperialist of the time; he genuinely believed that a Canada stretching from coast to coast was the will of God. But there was more than a little self-interest involved. He could see Red River land—including the land he had so prudently snapped up—soaring in price as immigrants streamed in. He could imagine homesteaders buying their supplies from his retail outlets—at inflated prices, of course, to compensate for the community's isolation. He dreamt of the lucrative government contracts and prestigious positions of power that would be available in a new administration, and would naturally flow to those who had paved the way for a Canadian take-over.*

As unpopular as the idea was, if all the *Nor'Wester* had advocated had been Canadian annexation, Red River inhabitants would not have been overly offended. But Schultz was an aggressive, obnoxious bigot—he despised Métis and Indians, Catholics and French-speakers in that order. As if to broadcast his racism, in 1864 he was installed as the Worshipful Master of Northern Lights Lodge—the first Masons to set up in the Northwest. Immediately his newspaper was filled with stories about the intriguing goings-on of this mysterious and, as the Catholic priests and Métis saw it, ominous cabal of bigots.

His dreams would come true. He would become Sir John Christian Schultz, Senator, Lieutenant-Governor of Manitoba, and an exceedingly wealthy man.

The *Nor'Wester* constantly published venomous editorials castigating the Hudson's Bay Company and the Council of Assiniboia. (Schultz was particularly upset when, after loudly promoting himself for months, he was not chosen to fill a vacancy on the council.) Insults against the Métis and Indians were commonplace: "The wise and prudent will be prepared to receive and benefit by them [the changes to be made when Canada assumed sovereignty] whilst the indolent and careless, like the native tribes of the country will fall back before the march of a superior intelligence" was typical.*

The year that Riel arrived back in Red River, Schultz became embroiled in a legal altercation that Louis must have watched with fascination. The doctor had a habit of quarrelling with everyone, including his half-brother, Henry McKenney.

In 1865, McKenney had been given the rather lucrative job of sheriff of Assiniboia, and shortly afterwards he announced to Schultz that he wanted to dissolve their business association. What followed was a mighty battle over assets. After years of frustrating court hearings, which included Schultz being several times found in contempt for the insults he levelled against the court system, the judge finally ruled in McKenney's favour and the doctor was ordered to pay some £300 to his half-brother. Schultz flatly refused. Since McKenney was the sheriff, he, along with two constables, went to Schultz's store to collect the debt. A free-for-all ensued. Schultz was determined to resist arrest and he was such a big, powerful man that the three adversaries had a terrible time overpowering him. Finally they tied him up with a clothesline he had on sale in his shop and bundled him off to the justice of the peace. He was charged with assault and promptly thrown in prison. The same evening fifteen "Canadians", led by the irrepressible Anne Schultz, broke into the Fort Garry jail and freed the prisoner. They all retired to the Schultz residence, where "they made a night of it". No further attempt was made to bring the doctor to justice or to collect the debt. It was one more indication to the French-Canadian community that law and order had broken down in Red River; it made them all the more frightened of Schultz and everything that he represented.

John Schultz would prove to be Riel's *bête noire*; the two men would soon be locked in a bitter struggle. When there was a level playing-field, Riel and the Métis would trounce the doctor and his friends. Only when the Anglo-Saxon

---

* *Yet, as with many vital individuals, there was another, more civilized side to Schultz. He often performed acts of kindness for Indians and Métis—Louis Schmidt said so himself. And Schultz was a dedicated naturalist. Articles he wrote on the flora of Red River were praised by the Botanical Society of Canada, and studies he made of western fortifications and the Eskimo led to his election to the Royal Society of Canada.*

financial and political establishment lined up squarely behind the Canadians were the Métis crushed.

By the summer of 1868, Winnipeg was starting to blossom. As a home-steader newly arrived from Ontario put it, "it is a smart little place with several hotels, stores etc. Buildings mostly logs, but are built with great taste." A few brick houses, grand and imposing, had sprung up here and there like preten-tious roses. The village attracted every type of entrepreneur, quick-buck artist and political adventurer. Schultz had built his retail business, drugstore and house on the west side, two blocks from the offices of the *Nor'Wester*. The Hudson's Bay Company had opened an outlet on King Street, but it was the veteran free traders, long considered the elite of Red River, who boasted the largest enterprises. Andrew McDermot was undoubtedly the most powerful among them.

An Irish Catholic, he had arrived with the second group of Selkirk settlers in 1812 at the age of twenty-three. He worked as a clerk for the Hudson's Bay Company, but soon struck out on his own as an independent fur trader and carting agent. In his store, it was said, you could get everything from "a harness strap to the horse itself." He was considered to be the epitome of a Red River soldier of fortune. As one writer put it:

> He could speak the language of the Indians better than the Indians them-selves,... he could run like a deer and endure cold like an Eskimo ... there was no better judge of men and horses in Red River, or any man who was his equal in address and accommodating qualities, in humour and shrewd-ness and the power of making money.

He was also a very wealthy man. His house, called Emerald Grove and situ-ated on the banks of the Red River, was the largest in the Settlement.

McDermot had married an English-speaking Half-breed, Sarah McNab, and the union had produced fifteen children. Their marriages within the Red River community created a vast and important network. His daughter Annie, for instance, married A.G.B. Bannatyne, one of the great characters of Red River and a rich man in his own right. With his partner, the indefatigable scribbler Alexander Begg, Bannatyne owned warehouses and stores (right next door to his father-in-law McDermot) on the east side of Winnipeg village.

McDermot, Bannatyne, Begg and other prosperous free traders had once bitterly fought the HBC's monopoly, but over the years a lucrative accommoda-tion with the fur-trading giant had evolved. And as long as money could be made, these "gentlemen" were content with HBC rule. Naturally, then, they opposed the annexation of Red River by Canada and they detested the

Canadian Party and Schultz in particular, whom they considered an arrogant, obnoxious newcomer. Having worked with Métis freighters for years, they were not as prejudiced towards the mixed-bloods as other Anglo-Saxons. Bannatyne would even become an admirer of Louis Riel's.

After the Canadians and the gentlemen traders, the third major presence in Winnipeg, the most flamboyant and outrageous, was the Americans. Deserters from the Union Army, adventurers, and wily merchants, they had congregated in Winnipeg from 1865 on. They owned the most popular bars—H.F. O'Lone's saloon and "Dutch George" Emmerling's hotel were favourite watering holes. The merchants among them were not involved in the fur trade, specializing instead in retail goods from St. Paul, so they were not at odds with the HBC.

There was no doubt in their minds that Canada's Northwest would eventually be absorbed by the United States. And since they had seen the tremendous fortunes made in booming St. Paul, they intended to be first in line when the same thing happened in Red River. However, the Americans were smarter than the Canadians; understanding the sensitivity of the Métis and others, they didn't flaunt their annexation dreams in public. But then, they believed it wasn't necessary. From the first time a Red River cart bumped over the prairies carting furs and buffalo hides to St. Paul, the economic current of the colony had flowed from north to south. The Americans believed that this pull was so great that the annexation of Canada's Northwest would happen naturally.

With such divergent and potentially dangerous political undercurrents flowing through Red River, the Métis were confused and alarmed. They still made up the majority in the colony but they were losing influence, not only because Anglo-Saxon immigrants were starting to trickle in, but because their standard of living was eroding disastrously.

By the late 1860s, the Métis sensed that they were facing an unimaginable tragedy: the buffalo were disappearing. They must have realized that they themselves had been terribly profligate; the twice-yearly expeditions had grown to ridiculous proportions and involved great waste. But Métis overhunting was not the only cause, or even the major one, of dwindling herds. Buffalo robes had become so valuable that professional hunters, Canadians and Americans, all armed with the most deadly firearms, had initiated a savage, systematic slaughter.

One of the old Half-breed plainsmen, Norbert Welsh, writing in *Maclean's* magazine in 1933, vividly describes the massacre:

> The Yankees shot more buffalo for their hides than all the Half-breeds and Indians together. Parties of Yankees used to come up to shoot for sport. Buffalo Bill once came on a trip and shot five hundred buffalo. Colonel

Cody had a contract for the Kansas Pacific Railway to supply its laborers with buffalo meat. In eighteen months he killed 4,280 buffalo.

And the United States government today stands accused of encouraging the carnage; with the herds gone, desperate Indians could be subdued and placed on reserves, and the vast plains could safely welcome homesteaders and cattle ranchers. By the 1860s, the Métis of Red River were having to range farther and farther south, and westward into Alberta, in search of the big beasts; in some years, 1868 for example, the hunt failed completely, a taste of the disaster that would soon follow.

But vanishing buffalo weren't the only threat to the Métis livelihood. In the first half of the nineteenth century the silk hat became fashionable right across Europe, and those made of felt from beaver pelts were suddenly passé. The repercussions were immediately felt across the ocean. Canada's fur trade went into sharp decline, trappers got far less for their catch, pemmican producers suffered as the demand for the product shrank. Even the legendary voyageur found himself in dire financial straits. For years the boatmen had resented the low wages and poor working conditions imposed by the Hudson's Bay Company; purposely damaging goods and outright mutiny were not uncommon. In retaliation, by the late 1860s the HBC was bypassing the brigades whenever possible.

Financial hardship hit the independent freighters, the backbone of the Métis bourgeoisie. Railroad construction slowly snaking across the northern United States and steamboats plying the rivers and lakes threatened to render the Red River cart obsolete.

Many Métis turned to full-time farming but even that was not secure. In the spring of 1868, the *Nor'Wester* had declared that "the tenure of land is precisely the same with the new-comer as it is with the Hudson's Bay Company—you hold as much as you occupy." This was a declaration that the Métis and Indian claims to lands they had held for decades was being challenged. The Métis feared the Canadian government would cave in to pressure from the land-hungry friends of Schultz.

What the Métis knew they desperately needed was a leader, one of their own, who had the confidence and sophistication to take on the white establishment.

Louis Riel seemed sent from heaven. His very name was magic, bringing back proud memories of the defiance of Jean-Louis Riel; the joyous declaration *"Le commerce est libre"* had never been forgotten. The son was now so highly educated that he could speak and write English fluently, he understood the complexity of Canadian politics and, most amazingly, for all his seemingly urbane mannerisms, he understood the Métis as a distinct people and was dedicated to their welfare.

Four months after Riel's return to Red River, word spread that a road would be constructed from Winnipeg to Lake of the Woods and scores of men would be hired on as labourers at good wages. For Métis families surviving on what little relief Bishop Taché could round up, it was wonderful news.

As early as 1857, Simon J. Dawson, a civil engineer, had been hired to map out a land and water route from Thunder Bay to Fort Garry. The Dawson Road, as it came to be called, was a tortuous undertaking: there were wagon roads planned at both ends, but the centre part, 311 miles long, would traverse lakes and rivers, with no fewer than twelve portages. By 1869, only a small part of the eastern section had been completed. Then the Canadian government suddenly saw, in the building of the 95-mile western portion from Lake of the Woods to Red River, two unique opportunities: work relief could be offered to a desperate, drought-ravaged population, and a Canadian presence would be established in the colony. The plan would backfire on both fronts.

The federal Minister of Public Works, William McDougall, who initiated the project, neglected to ask permission from the Hudson's Bay Company, even though the territory over which the road would be built was still owned by the Company. The HBC protested bitterly, but then, realizing that nothing could be done, acquiesced. Red River settlers were indignant over Canadian audacity and began to see the imported construction crew as an invading army. It didn't help that the newcomers began staking out claims for their own possession right away.

Clearing the bush and trees from the right-of-way without proper equipment was hard work—the labourers actually carried the trees on their backs. The pay was terrible—$15 a month. (There is some suggestion that the Canadian government budgeted for $18 but that someone, probably the man in charge, John A. Snow, pocketed the remaining $3.) The headquarters for the crew was located at Oak Point (also called Ste. Anne-des-Chênes), some twenty-five miles southeast of Winnipeg. Supposedly for convenience's sake, since the men were living at the site, a portion of wages was paid in vouchers to the local supply depot. It was owned by none other than Dr. John Schultz and, true to form, he charged outrageous prices. Flour that cost $18 a barrel in Schultz's store cost $15 at Fort Garry.

A few Métis were hired, but many of the jobs were given to Ontario immigrants or Americans, either deserters or recently demobbed from the U.S. Army. They were a hard-drinking, foul-mouthed lot. Thomas Scott, a six-foot-two giant from Orange Ontario, was particularly irascible. He was only on the job for two days before he demanded that he be paid his travelling expenses, never mind that that was not part of his contract. When John Snow, the construction boss, refused, Scott and his co-workers (not the Métis) went on strike. When Snow finally backed down and handed over the cash, Scott insisted that they get paid for the two days they had been off the job. This time Snow was adamant in his refusal. According to eye-witness accounts, Scott then put a gun to Snow's head while three of his cohorts grabbed the frightened man and dragged him to the bank of the Seine River. They threatened to throw him in—the river was swollen with a rapid current at the time and he probably would have drowned—but two Métis, Damase Harrison and Louis Blondeau, came to his rescue. Snow gave in and paid the troublemakers the money they demanded, but then promptly rode to Fort Garry and, before a justice of the peace, charged the four with aggravated assault. Scott and one other were found guilty and fined £4, and they lost their jobs. As he was leaving the courtroom, the defiant Scott yelled that it was a pity he hadn't thrown Snow in the drink, because, as it was, he hadn't gotten his money's worth. This contemptuous and hot-tempered man would soon play a tragic role in Red River affairs, and indeed would become a heavy cross which Louis Riel would have to bear for the rest of his life.

If the Red River inhabitants were shocked at such shenanigans, they were mortified by the behaviour of another Ontario member of Snow's road crew. The part played by the paymaster Charlie Mair in the Red River drama, as quirky a comedy of errors as found anywhere in Canadian history, also illustrates the condescension and arrogance of the incoming Canadians.

Mair was born on September 21, 1838, in Lanark, near Perth, Ontario, an area famous for its cheese. In his early education, he seems to have been imprinted on the works of Sir Walter Scott, the epitome of British manliness. Charles studied medicine at Queen's University at the same time John Schultz did, and the two men became friends. His tenure there was short; he had to rush back to Lanark to try to save his father's drygoods business. After ten years serving behind various store counters, he returned to studying medicine at Queen's, but again he didn't finish—this time politics got in his way.

The year after Confederation, Mair and four other "up-and-comers"— George Taylor Denison, William Alexander Foster, Robert Grant Haliburton and Henry James Morgan—founded the "Canada First Party", supposedly to give the young dominion a sense of national purpose, to arouse in the hearts of Canadian citizens a passion for their newly confederated nation. In fact these were arrogant young men, imperialist to the core, dedicated to spreading "superior" Anglo-Saxon values and in the process stamping out the influence of the French-speaking Roman Catholic. Native peoples were considered so inferior in the human hierarchy that they were simply not acknowledged.

The Minister of Public Works, William McDougall, felt much as they did, but, unlike them, he was in a position to do something about it.

McDougall represented the North Lanark district in the House of Commons, so Mair's family had known him for years. It was only natural that the seasoned politician should take bright young Charlie under his wing. He suggested that Mair size the situation up in Red River first-hand and report back to him. In other words, Mair's main job was as a spy. With that end in mind, a sinecure as paymaster on the Dawson Road work gang was found for him.

During a lovely fall evening in late October 1868, Charles Mair and John Snow arrived at the Red River colony, "just in time to hear the convent bells of St. Boniface sounding sweetly over the water." Mair checked into "Dutch George" Emmerling's hotel in Winnipeg village, but not for long. The next day he accepted the invitation of his old friend John Schultz, and moved into the doctor's home. Shortly after, Mair would write his brother in Perth. "The change was comfortable, I assure you, from the racket of a motley crowd of half-breeds, playing billiards and drinking, to the quiet and solid comfort of a home."

Some months before his arrival in Red River, a slim volume of Mair's called *Dreamland and Other Poems*—a collection of kitschy verse with a vaguely Keatsian flavour—had been published to great critical acclaim. Journalists had enthusiastically labelled him "The Canadian Poet" and the fame had preceded him to the village of Winnipeg. Since, as a friend once wrote, Mair was "as brimful of fun and frolic as a schoolboy" and, with his bright blue eyes, round, pudgy face and mass of brown curly hair, an attractive young bachelor, he was quickly taken up by Red River society. Among those who extended warm hospitality was the free trader and postmaster A.G.B. Bannatyne.

The Bannatyne house was large and rather grand, full of books, house plants and heavy Victorian furniture. There was available for anybody's pleasure a piano, an accordion, a flute and a melodeon. The country was still present— the entrance hall contained not only coat but also gun racks—and the atmosphere was warm and cheerful. Charlie Mair would write, "they live like princes here." There were "nuts of all kinds, coffee, port and sherry, brandy punch and cigars, concluding with whist until four o'clock a.m."

But all the time Mair was enjoying such hospitality, he was laughing under his breath. His true feelings were revealed in a series of letters he sent to his brother. Later Mair would make the excuse that this was private correspondence, yet he made no complaint when it was sent to the Perth *Courier*, nor did he object when the Toronto *Globe* picked it up.

> I received hospitalities to my heart's content and I left the place thoroughly pleased with most that I had met. There are jealousies and heart-burnings,

however. Many wealthy people are married to half-breed women, who, having no coat of arms but a "totem" to look back to, make up for the deficiency by biting at the backs of their "white" sisters. The white sisters fall back upon their whiteness, whilst the husbands meet each other with desperate courtesies and hospitalities, with a view to filthy lucre in the background. *** *

Mrs. Bannatyne, Andrew McDermott's daughter, was one of the Half-breed back-biters Mair described. She had been educated at the Grey Nuns Convent, had travelled to the United States and was used to being considered part of the *crème de la crème* of Red River. There was no way Annie Bannatyne was going to let a fat little cocky newcomer like Charlie Mair get away with such insults.

Mair usually picked up his letters every Saturday afternoon at four p.m. One day Mrs. Bannatyne asked the postal clerk, Daniel Mulligan, to let her know when Charlie showed up. Mulligan did as promised. Annie donned a large black shawl and marched off to the post office, which on that day was packed with chattering people. Spotting Mair in their midst, she grabbed him by the nose and, pulling a large horsewhip from under her shawl, she smacked him five or six good ones. "There," she scolded him, "you see how the women of Red River treat those who insult them."

Within an hour the entire settlement knew of Charlie's humiliation. Returning from his supply depot at Oak Point, John Schultz stopped at the house of an English-speaking Half-breed whose hospitality he had often enjoyed in the past. He later wrote, "much to our surprise we were refused admittance—refused in fact point blank until the young lady in charge was assured the Monsieur 'chuchacheese' [Mair] was not with us."

Riel memorialized the incident in a silly song he wrote at the time. The dog or dog-fish referred to is, of course, Charlie Mair, the "lady" Annie Bannatyne. A few verses will give the flavour:

> At the pointe de chênes [Oak Point]
> La-i-tou-trà-là
> At the pointe de chênes
> > Down there!!!

> *Chorus:*
> Hasten! Hasten!
> Little Girls
> Young ladies

---

* The asterisks indicate a portion which Mair's brother considered too strong to publish. One can only imagine the insults it must have represented.

Hasten! Hasten!
Come and enjoy yourselves tonight
Down there!!!

Let us proceed to wring
La-i-tou-trà-là
Let us then proceed to wring
the nose of this dog-fish
Down there!!!

It is a lady who shows us
La-i-tou-trà-là
It is a lady who shows us
How we should treat them
Down there!!!

Louis's song went over well—people actually sang it—because Mair had not only affronted the English-speaking mixed-bloods of Red River, he had also made plain his contempt of the Métis.

The half-breeds are the only people here who are starving. Five thousand of them have to be fed this winter, and it is their own fault, they won't farm. They will hunt buffalos, drive ox-carts 500 miles up and 500 miles back to St. Cloud, at the rate of twenty miles a day: do anything but farm.

Not only did his observations display a lack of sensitivity and knowledge of the Métis situation, most of them were blatantly untrue.

On February 25, 1869, the following letter appeared in the Montreal newspaper *Le Nouveau Monde*:

Red River, February 1, 1869
    Mr. Editor:
    Please be so good as to give me a little space in the columns of your journal, so that I too may write of Red River.
    I cannot resist that temptation since I have read the outrages which a journal of Upper Canada (the Globe) has just uttered in publishing a letter of a certain Mr. Mair, who arrived in Red River last fall. It is said this gentleman, an English Canadian, is gifted in writing verse; if such is the case I advise him strongly to cultivate his talent, for in that way his writings would make up in rhyme what they lack in common sense.
    Only a month after his arrival in this country, Mr. Mair set out to describe it and its inhabitants. He was as successful as the navigator who, passing by a league from the coast, writes in his log: "The people of this country seemed to us very accommodating."

The writer then went on to list all the mistakes of fact and exaggerations Mair had made in his descriptions of Red River. But he was most upset at Mair's careless remark that only Métis farmers had been forced to seek relief the previous winter.

> I am a half-breed myself and I say that there is nothing falser than those words. I know almost all the names of those who received help this winter, and I can assure you that they were all colours. There are some half-breeds who do not ask for charity, as there are some English, some Germans and some Scots, who receive it every week.*
>
> It was not, of course, enough for these gentlemen [Mair and company] to come to mock the distress of our country by making unfortunate people driven by hunger, work dirt cheap [on the Dawson Road crew]. They had also to spread falsehood among the outside world, to lead people to believe that the relief sent to R. R. was not needed....

The letter, signed L.R., was written by Louis Riel, and it was much more sophisticated and barbed than what the famous "Canadian poet" Charles Mair had managed. It's also interesting that Riel clearly identifies himself as a Métis, an indication that he was establishing himself as a spokesperson of the community.

Riel was scornful of Mair's eulogy of the prairies as paradise —"We passed through a most beautiful country, parts of which were perfect paradises of lakes and hills, swarming with ducks, geese, brant, and every species of game...," Charlie had written—because he realized what the poet's true motivation was—to lure to Red River as many Anglo-Saxon immigrants as possible, all of whom would be eager to snap up, at wonderfully high prices, the prime land which Mair had already staked out. From the moment he arrived in Red River, Mair had been scheming with John Snow, the road crew boss, and John Schultz to get his hands on Red River's best lots.

Oak Point, where the log-hut and mud-hut headquarters of the road crew was situated, was already an established Métis community. There was a scattering of houses, and some of the bush had been cleared in preparation for farming. The three Canadians contemptuously ignored any rights these people claimed they had to the land and began negotiating with the Indians, who had no particular claim to the area. The currency the trio often used to entice the Natives was liquor—at that time it was illegal to sell alcohol to Indians. The mixed-bloods became so incensed with these tricks that they finally grabbed Snow (and perhaps Mair, the evidence is inconclusive) and marched him to Fort

---

* *This statement is backed up by minutes of the Executive Relief Committee.*

Garry. He appeared before the courts there and was fined £10. In early 1869, Louis Riel would write,

> They [Snow *et al.*] have come here to chase us from our homeland. They assume that after fifty years of civilization, our society has borne no fruit.... instead of respecting the laws established in the colony ... they have publicly repudiated them by selling liquor to poor Indians who in turn, without authority, sold them three square miles of land that, in part, includes several of the dwellings of Oak Point Village.

In the following months Mair was forced to hire a guard at the road construction site, because "fire had lately taken place in the woods" which threatened bridges and other roadworks. The blazes were probably set by angry Métis.

By the spring of 1869, it was obvious that the Hudson's Bay Company was about to sell its vast Rupert's Land territories to the Canadian government. Actually, negotiations had been going on for years, but not very smoothly. The Canadians didn't see why they had to pay a large price for something they believed was rightfully theirs; after all, Québécois fur traders had explored and then occupied the territory long before the HBC had wandered inland. But the year after the birth of the Canadian nation, bargaining had begun in earnest. HBC brass were weary of having to administer a huge territory, including the cantankerous Red River community, and were ready to bow out; the Canadians, eager to consolidate what they envisioned as a dominion from sea to sea, were willing to accept the principle of compensation. In mid-March 1869, a deal was finally struck. The HBC would receive £300,000 cash, a token sum for such a vast acreage of land; no restrictions against the company's trading would be imposed; and an opportunity to make vast sums on land speculation would be provided—the HBC would receive one-twentieth of all township land opened for settlement and retain 45,000 acres of land around its existing trading posts. The transfer was to take place officially on December 1, 1869.

When the news of the accord reached Red River at the end of April—an announcement appeared in the hated *Nor'Wester*—most of the twelve thousand residents of Red River were indignant. Unbelievably, nobody from the dominion government, not the prime minister, a minister of the crown, a diplomat, or even a bureaucrat, no official from the Hudson's Bay Company, no representative from the British crown, had arrived to announce the transfer of sovereignty. In fact there was no official communiqué at all. As Bishop Taché would write, "The people cannot tolerate the idea of having been sold." He might have added "like cattle or slaves."

Only Schultz and company were overjoyed. A huge bonfire was lit and a

Union Jack with large letters spelling CANADA printed across it was hoisted on Schultz's flagpole.

There was even more consternation when the form of government Ottawa had planned for the colony was revealed. It was certainly not the self-governing democracy promised by Schultz and his friends. Legislation creating the government of Rupert's Land and the Northwest Territories, passed by Parliament in June 1869, set in place a lieutenant-governor with an appointed council "to make provision for the administration of justice, and generally to make, ordain, and establish all such laws, institutions and ordinances as may be necessary for peace, order and good government." Red River was to be nothing more than a dependent tied tightly to the apron strings of Mother Canada.

The Métis and other French-speaking Catholics were particularly enraged. They realized that they could easily be excluded from an appointed council, and that an Anglo-Saxon lieutenant-governor—the Minister of Public Works, William McDougall, an old friend of Charlie Mair's and the Canada First group and an Orangeman to his very core, was rumoured to have the job in his pocket—would in all likelihood favour the aggressive Canadians. Their fears were heightened when, in spring 1869, the trickle of immigrants from Ontario turned into a flood. There was such a large number by the end of May that the Victoria Day celebration became a riotous event. Horse races, games of cricket and a dance were all played out in the muddy streets of Winnipeg village. Dominion Day was even more boisterous; wrote Charlie Mair, "we celebrated by firing a number of shots out of an anvil, hoisting the ensign, and by a bonfire in the evening." The Métis watched the Canadian-sponsored celebrations with suspicious eyes.

The grasshoppers had, thank God, not returned that spring, and there was plenty of rain. Métis farmers, including Louis Riel, were kept busy in their fields trying to make up for the previous two years' devastation, and the buffalo hunters had set out prepared to travel farther than ever to find the elusive herds. Still, there was time for meetings and consultations. They went on constantly, at this church, that schoolhouse, the log homes of various Métis families. Many took place in the Catholic church at St. Norbert, organized by the sympathetic priest whose parish it was.

Father Noel-Joseph Ritchot would become to Louis Riel what Georges Belcourt had been to his father twenty years before, during the free-trade struggle. While Ritchot was not as overtly radical in his actions as Belcourt, he was a tenacious fighter for the Métis. He was also, like Belcourt, disdainful of the "cathedral priests", the Oblates gathered at St. Boniface. Ritchot was a big, burly, handsome man, with a long black beard snaking down his chest which in his fifties would turn stark white and make him look like Methuselah. He had been born in L'Assomption, Quebec, in 1825 of a modest farming family, had attended local college and had been ordained to the priesthood in 1855. He had served as a French teacher, farm instructor and *curé* before coming west in 1862.

St. Norbert Parish, to which Ritchot was assigned, was located south of St. Boniface where the Rivière Sale (La Salle since 1975) met the Red. It had early on been a gathering spot for Métis buffalo hunters, and by 1835 seventy-two families lived there. By that time they were engaged in farming part of the time on their long narrow strips of land. In 1853 a road was built connecting Fort Garry to Pembina, passing by St. Norbert, and in 1855 the little white church was constructed.

Since the parish was located on the west side of the Red River and several miles south of St. Boniface, Father Ritchot enjoyed a certain freedom from the church hierarchy. Given his quiet but very tenacious and cunning personality, he likely would have taken that liberty anyway.

Ritchot and Riel would become devoted friends and indeed brothers-in-arms. But the priest had an interesting style; he was not the least aggressive or outspoken. He was labelled by his admirers an *éminence grise*, a reputation he thoroughly enjoyed. Here was the perfect sounding-board for the imaginative but sometimes volatile young Louis Riel.

Almost from the moment he arrived back at Red River, Louis frequented the village of St. Norbert, but it wasn't just Ritchot who attracted him. Sara was teaching at the Grey Nuns' St. Norbert mission; the relationship between sister and brother had not diminished during their long separation. In September 1868, Sara wrote Louis a letter expressing her love for her brother in her usual passionate, almost hysterical, manner.

> After you left, I followed you with my eyes across the river, until at last the trees hid you from view.... Then I went to church and before God who brings sorrow and comfort, I unburdened my heart by crying tears.... I prayed to Him in a very special manner, asking Him to comfort and strengthen and bless the brother I had just kissed goodbye. It seemed to me that our Lord heard my prayers. I was confident, for I left the church full of courage and hope. Courage, my beloved Louis!

Such passionate devotion must have added another emotional, perhaps troublesome, dimension to Riel's already intense life.

In late June 1869, farmers in St. Norbert spotted Charles Mair and John Snow walking along the side of the road, parallel to the Rivière Sale, carrying a bunch of wooden sticks. Now and then they would stop to pace out lots adjacent to the road. Realizing the duo were there to stake out land, the Métis quickly gathered around them, shouting threats of what would happen to Mair and Snow if they didn't immediately quit the vicinity. The two men scurried to their horse and buggy and took off as fast they could.

In his writings, Mair indicated that he met Riel for the first time that June. It may well have been at that encounter; the Riel farm was situated just north of St. Norbert and it would take no time for Louis to arrive at the scene. The differences between the two could not have been more striking. Charlie Mair had grown pudgier and his complexion more florid since his arrival at Red River, probably from all the socializing he had indulged in; his patron, William McDougall, had already written a letter castigating him for his excessive boozing. On the other hand, the heavy farm work had made Louis Riel more muscular, more rugged. He only occasionally took a drink, usually in celebration, so there was no sign in his appearance of the dissipation that marked Mair's. Mair could hide nothing of his emotions, they bubbled over into giggles; Riel had learned already to be detached, almost sullen, when confronting the enemy. The only thing they had in common was poetic inclination, but even their verse was as different as Walter Scott's from Alphonse Lamartine's.

On July 5, a group of newly arrived English-speaking settlers were spotted by Métis horsemen at Pointe Coupée (later called Ste. Agathe), south of St. Norbert on the east side of the river. Already timber had been cut for the construction of newcomers' homes, and a well dug. The Métis were incensed and insisted that these people immediately move to English parishes. To emphasize their demands they scattered the timber and filled up the well. The frightened settlers quickly did as they were told.

That same day, at a meeting called by Jean-Baptiste Tourond and Jean-Baptiste Lépine, two of the major players in the Métis action to date, it was decided to organize a system of mounted patrols. These were to insure that "no stranger should establish himself on the lands" in the French parishes. From that moment on, Métis anger would reflect a militant face.

On July 24, a notice appeared in the *Nor'Wester* inviting all Native peoples in Red River to a mass meeting to discuss the take-over of the colony by the Canadian government. It was signed by the well-known Métis Pascal Breland and the English Half-breeds William Dease and William Hallett.

Five days later, the courthouse was filled to overflowing with curious but skeptical people. William Dease did most of the talking. Wasn't it right that the £300,000 be paid not to the Hudson's Bay Company, but to the original owners of the soil, the Indians, Métis and Half-breeds? The crowd cried out that this was indeed a fair proposition. Then, said Dease, surely armed insurrection must follow;

all property owned by the HBC, including Fort Garry, must be confiscated. The implication was that Dease would be named governor. There was shocked silence until John Bruce, a carpenter and community leader in St. Norbert, jumped up and began arguing against the second motion. Louis Riel did the same, and the meeting quickly petered out.

The Métis simply did not trust Dease and Hallett, who they believed were *agents provocateurs*. Yet both enjoyed standing in the Red River Community. Dease, who had been educated and could speak both English and French, was the son of a former chief factor of the HBC. Since 1852 he had served the Council of Assiniboia in many capacities (receiving good money for each job), and by 1869 he was justice of the peace. He was also a large land owner at Pointe Coupée. William Hallett was a Scottish Half-breed who had led the buffalo hunt for years. To the Métis, however, both men were suspect; Dease, as a councillor, most often seemed to be serving his own interests rather than the Métis community's. Hallett had been a ringleader in the violent campaign to free the Reverend Corbett from jail, and the aftertaste of that sordid affair was still sour in everyone's mouth. As well, both men had been seen in the company of the Canadians. Father Ritchot believed strongly that they were in the pocket of John Schultz—for the doctor, money spent diverting Métis wrath from the Canadian party to the Hudson's Bay Company would be well spent. In fact, events over subsequent months would confirm the Métis suspicions that Dease and Hallett were enemies, firmly established in the Canadian camp. The ill-begotten meeting did serve one purpose. As Father Ritchot said, "it put the Métis on their guard" and drew them together.

Two weeks after the meeting, another intriguing ingredient was thrown into the political stew—Oscar Malmros, the counsel whom the United States government had appointed to look after American interests at Red River, arrived in Winnipeg. The Americans were overjoyed to see him—O'Lone's saloon was full of celebration and dreams of growing rich—and the clergy and elite at St. Boniface were charmed by his gentlemanly manners and elegant French. Although Malmros maintained that he never stepped beyond his role as disinterested observer, he was in fact a spy for the U.S. government, full of intrigue and design. He was tied to the St. Paul entrepreneurs and land speculators waiting in the wings to make a fortune from what they perceived would become "the gateway to the north" and unimaginable riches. A dedicated annexationist himself, he was confident the Northwest could be wrenched away from the Canadians, if only the people of Red River could be persuaded to rebel.

Malmros began meeting with Louis Riel almost immediately upon his arrival. His impression of the Métis leader is interesting—"ambitious, quick of perception though not profound, of indomitable energy, daring, excessively suspicious of others [probably meaning himself] and of a pleasing and rather dignified address."

Over the next few months Malmros would tempt the Métis with all kinds of promises, including $25,000 from his government (which never became a reality).

Riel never seriously advocated the annexation of the Northwest to the United States; perhaps his sojourns in Chicago and St. Paul had made him realize how quickly the French language and culture would be diluted in the American melting-pot. But the presence of Malmros and other eager adventurers from south of the border was another potentially dangerous complication that he and the Métis would be forced to deal with.

On August 20, 1869, a party of a half-dozen Canadians, their wagons stacked with camping gear, hundred-link chains and sextants, trotted into Red River. They were surveyors come to divide the settlement into townships. Not one of them could speak French. All were militia officers or cadets, some of whom had brought their uniforms with them. Not only that, but their leader, Colonel John Stoughton Dennis, had been met at St. Cloud, Minnesota, the end of the railway, by none other than John Schultz, who had driven him to Red River in his fast wagon. Dennis then accepted Schultz's invitation to stay at his home. This, of course, immediately undermined his status in the Red River Settlement.

William McDougall was determined to open the prairies for mass settlement as quickly as possible. Sovereignty had not as yet been officially transferred from the Hudson's Bay Company, and Canada had no more legal right to send surveyors to Red River than to Minnesota, but he would proceed. He had hired John Stoughton Dennis, who boasted the bushiest mutton-chop whiskers in the Northwest. Born in Kingston of a United Empire Loyalist military family, Dennis had become a surveyor in 1842, but the military was his passion. He rapidly rose through the ranks of the militia until he made lieutenant-colonel. But embarrassing gaffes during a dust-up with the Fenians (those Irish-Americans dedicated to pressuring England into Irish independence) on the Niagara River in 1866 had left his military career in shambles. He was determined, through his service in Red River, to recover his reputation.

The American system of dividing the prairies into rectangular townships was chosen, with some modification: each homestead was to be 180 acres rather than 160. The system was suited for large, wheat-producing farms, which McDougall insisted would attract "the most desirable emigrants", meaning Anglo-Saxon Canadians. The farmers already settled in Rupert's Land mattered not a damn.

Who owned what land had been a source of worry for the Métis and others in the Red River Settlement for over a decade, but as Schultz and company, as well as some more sophisticated English-speakers, began driving stakes to mark their acquisitions, old settlers began to panic. While the Selkirk estate and the Hudson's Bay Company had issued titles to lots, it had been a very casual affair, the only record often being a pencilled scribble in the land books of the Company. It had always been felt that unoccupied land was free for the taking, and that purchases from the HBC were made not for a particular plot, but for the improvements made to it. A few smart operators like the trader Andrew McDermot had had their names entered against lot after lot. But most farmers had relied on the "custom of the country", had no official paper to state that they had worked a particular parcel for, say, twenty or forty years, and could, in fact, be considered mere squatters. With Dennis marking out lots completely out of joint with the contours of their land, the Métis naturally thought they were in grave danger of losing their very livelihood. They also thought that his survey plans were crazy and wouldn't work, for they ignored what the Métis considered was the most important element of farming—water.

From the beginning the Quebec-style strip farming had been adopted in Red River, by Selkirk pioneers, the English Half-breeds and the Métis. From a small river frontage with adjacent water rights, lots ran back in a ribbon four miles long; on the half fronting on the river some land was cleared and crops were grown, and some land was left as woods for building materials and firewood. The back half of the lot was usually a stretch of prairie grass. This configuration was suitable for small, mixed enterprises: the Riel family farm was a prime example. Not a lot of land was cultivated, maybe five or ten acres on which wheat and other grains and vegetables were grown; livestock were just as important, the cattle relying on access to the river for drinking water, and grazing on nutritious prairie grasses on pasture behind the cultivated acreage. These "hay privileges", as the two-mile strips were called, were seldom fenced and generally used in common by neighbouring farmers. However, there was no question in the community's mind that each household had a legal right to the strip directly behind its own farm.

Colonel Dennis had very specific instructions: he was not to disturb existing claims and holdings, and he was to survey only two or three townships on the outskirts of the colony. He did make an attempt to mollify the Red River population, running ads in the Nor'Wester that explained his mission, although that hardly pacified the Métis. He visited Governor William Mactavish, who reluctantly gave him permission to go ahead even though he thought the project "ill-conceived and dangerous". Dennis also paid a call at St. Boniface Cathedral—Bishop Taché was away attending an ecumenical council in Rome and the rather flighty Father Lestanc was in charge. Dennis pleaded with Lestanc to explain his mission to the French-speakers of Red River. The priest was all set to do what the surveyor asked, but he was then dissuaded by the Reverend Georges Dugas, director of St. Boniface College and a good friend of Louis Riel's. Dugas felt sure that Lestanc and the entire clergy were being used as pawns in the complicated chess game being played by the Canadians.

Dennis had planned to begin the survey at Oak Point, the headquarters of the Dawson Road crew, but the residents bluntly told him that "if he wished to keep a head on his shoulders" he was not to set foot in their neighbourhood. Wisely, he decided to start near the American border, ten miles west of Pembina.

For a month, Red River was calm, albeit very tense. During September, growing numbers of English-speaking settlers continued to arrive at Red River. As well, no legal documents—the "letters patent" that Dennis had promised would be issued by the Dominion government—arrived, acknowledging the land holdings of the Métis or any other long-time residents.

By October the principal meridian running north from the American border had been charted. Dennis then organized sub-parties to survey townships immediately around Red River; one base-line ran from Headingley east and south to St. Vital, where the Riel family farm was located. Along the way, it passed over the "hay privilege" owned by the prominent Métis Edouard Marion.

October 11 was a dreary day, the sky a leaden grey. André Nault, a cousin of Louis's, was tending his cattle on Marion's land when he caught sight of the surveying team. He confronted them, excitedly explaining that they were trespassing. But he spoke not a word of English and not one of them understood French. Nault galloped off, looking for help.

About an hour and a half later, sixteen Métis horsemen arrived at the Marion farm. They quickly dismounted and formed a menacing circle around the frightened Canadian surveyors. Louis Riel was calm and firm; in clear English, he ordered, "You go no further. This land belongs to M. Marion." Then Janvier Ritchot, a giant of a man, firmly clamped his foot on the surveyor's chain. The Red River Resistance had begun.

– 5 –

I am a Métis girl. How proud I am
To be a part of the Métis nation
God surely uses his generous hand
To mould each race with special attention
Though rather limited in terms of size,
The Métis already follow a clear path
To be so hated is their worthy prize
They already boast a glorious past.

It may have been convenient for Sir John A. Macdonald to appoint William McDougall the first lieutenant-governor of the Northwest Territories, but it would prove an enormous mistake, one the prime minister would come to regret.

Born near York (Toronto) in 1822, McDougall had studied law, but preferred journalism and politics. One of the leaders of the Clear Grits, the radical arm of the Reform Party, in 1850 he established the *North American* in Toronto as a propaganda vehicle to express his political views. Seven years later the newspaper amalgamated with the *Globe* and McDougall became that journal's leading political writer and a crony of George Brown's. He ran and was defeated several times, until finally in 1858 he was elected a Liberal Member of Parliament. From then on he did well in political life, holding such profitable positions as commissioner of crown lands. In 1867, he, along with Brown, succumbed to Macdonald's enticements and switched to the Conservatives. Since he had changed his mind on political matters before, McDougall thereafter was called Wandering Willie.

He had attended all three conferences leading up to Confederation, and indeed was one of the Fathers of Confederation. For years he had been the chief advocate of Canada's expansion into Rupert's Land—after all, he represented the riding of North Lanark, where the sons of small farmers were itching for greater opportunity in the Great West.

He seemed a logical choice for the job of lieutenant-governor. He was hungry for it; as the writer Joseph Kinsey Howard put it, "He had not been able to obtain, as yet, any record as an administrator. Rupert's Land would provide that. Then perhaps a title; and ultimately, why not the Prime Minister?"

And Sir John A. wanted to get rid of him. A cabinet shuffle was months overdue and to free up the Public Works portfolio would allow more room for manoeuvring, more political plums to pass out. More to the point, McDougall had developed a well-deserved reputation as a dangerous loose cannon.

A tall, heavily built man, he had luxuriant hair slicked back off a wide forehead, a great, drooping moustache, deep-set, rather cold eyes, and thick, heavy lips. Never very happy in the Conservative camp, he was morose and arrogant, and although he had some political support, mostly from Orange Ontario, he could count his friends on one hand. And he had made serious political errors in the past. While still a Liberal, he had once suggested that annexation to the United States would be one way to curb the power of French Canada. Sir John A. had rubbed his hands in glee—McDougall's gaffe had helped the Tories win the 1861 election—but it should have sounded alarm bells in the prime minister's head. As a strong anti-cleric, uncompromisingly Anglo-Saxon and rather mean-spirited, McDougall was certain to annoy the French-speakers in Canada's new territory. But then the prime minister never did take seriously the feelings of the "miserable Half-breeds".

When Sir John went to the Ottawa railway station to see McDougall off, he did, however, underline an important constraint. The transfer of the Northwest to Canada from the Hudson's Bay Company would not officially occur until December 1, 1869, two months in the future. Until that time McDougall would have no more authority in Red River than an ordinary private citizen and he must take care to act accordingly. It would have been to Macdonald's credit if he had paid more attention to an offhand remark McDougall made at the time of his appointment. Being named lieutenant-governor, he said, was rather like being crowned "king" of the Northwest.

When, at the beginning of September, news reached Red River of McDougall's appointment, an uproar ensued. The Métis in particular had already formed a bad opinion of the man. It was he, after all, who had dispatched the Dawson Road construction gang and the surveyors without a French-speaker among them. And the connection between the new lieutenant-governor and the despised "Canadian Party" was already evident: McDougall was Mair's political patron, indeed for months Charlie had been spying for him;

Schultz was an old acquaintance and had often visited McDougall on business trips to Ottawa.

More alarming details reached Red River. Three members of McDougall's governing council had already been appointed—as Riel would note, "men of whom we knew nothing"—and were travelling with him. Already the chance for Métis and other Red River settlers to play a role in the new government was narrowing.

On the same day that the Métis had stopped the surveyors at St. Norbert, William McDougall and his entourage had arrived at St. Cloud, Minnesota—the end of steel for those travelling from the East. Charlie Mair was honeymooning with his new bride, Eliza—he had married the pretty daughter of Augustus McKenney, another half-brother of John Schultz—and was on hand to greet the party. And it had all the trappings of a royal tour. With McDougall travelled Captain D.R. Cameron of the Royal Canadian Artillery, who was to organize a police force, J.A.N. Provencher, the secretary-designate to the council, and Alexander Begg (not to be confused with the historian of Red River) as customs collector. Most of these men had been personally crowned by the prime minister; McDougall's one choice was Albert Richards, a forty-six-year-old lawyer and reformer who would serve as attorney-general. As well, Cameron's wife, Emma, McDougall's three sons, a daughter and a gaggle of servants were along. Finally, there was a Dr. A.G. Jacques, an obnoxious fellow who seemed to have offended everyone he had met. He was probably included because Emma Cameron was expecting a baby.

The party was forced to sit in St. Cloud for two weeks waiting for the baggage cars packed with their personal and household effects to arrive. Back in Winnipeg, the historian Alexander Begg laughed out loud when he learned that the lieutenant-governor had brought with him a magnificent gubernatorial chair manufactured by the Jacques & Hay company—"it is said a finer article of furniture than the Throne in Ottawa—poor silly McDougall," he wrote in his diary.

Finally they were ready to continue their journey. They would travel along the Crow Wing Trail, 450 miles due north, by ox cart, accompanied by no fewer than sixty wagons piled high with their baggage.

Meanwhile, in Red River, Louis Riel spent long days making the rounds of the villages, visiting one farm after another, all the time preaching rebellion. His appeal, his inspiration, sprang from the idea now deeply embedded in the Métis psyche that they were a separate people, a nation unto themselves. "Lords of the Land" was what they had been called when as voyageurs, hunters and warriors they dominated the vast prairies. This pride of nation lay in past military victories, particularly the Battle of Seven Oaks. The voyageurs still sang what had become a national anthem written by one of their own, Pierre Falcon. One verse gives the flavour:

> Ah, would you had seen those Englishmen
> And the *Bois-brûlés* a-chasing them!
> One by one we did them destroy
> While our *Bois-brûlés* uttered shouts of joy!

The arguments that Louis Riel used to convince his "countrymen" are found in a petition to Ulysses S. Grant, the United States president, written in the fall of 1870. Although composed in the stilted language of such documents, it conveys the outrage the Métis felt at the time.

> That learning through the public press, our only medium, that we had been sold by a company of adventurers residing in London, England, with our lands, rights and liberties as so much merchandise to a foreign government; and further learning through the same medium, the press, that the Parliament of the Dominion of Canada had organized a Government for our country, as if it had jurisdiction over us, and that we were to have no voice in the Government, and that a Governor appointed to rule over us, clothed with "almost despotic power" had started from Canada en route to our country, accompanied by a band of unscrupulous and irresponsible followers, who were to form his Council, and fill other offices in the Government, and thus plunder and eat out our subsistence.

Not everyone was inspired by Riel's vision. A hard core of Métis bourgeoisie, the prosperous who were sophisticated enough to have their land titles secured with the Hudson's Bay Company, were opposed to any direct rebellious action. Even some of Riel's inner circle felt that to fight the take-over by Canada was futile and dangerous. Still, by October Riel believed he had enough support to call a public meeting.

The organization of the buffalo hunt was used as a model government and, in contrast to how the Canadians proposed to govern the Settlement, it was a most democratic process. Each parish chose two representatives who gathered at St. Norbert church on October 16 to take an oath of mutual loyalty and form what would be called the National Committee. John Bruce, a Métis, was elected president, and Louis Riel secretary. The son of Pierre Bruce, a renowned guide and voyageur for the Hudson's Bay Company, John Bruce worked as a carpenter and farmer at St. Norbert. Acting as a kind of senior statesman, he had helped various neighbours sort out legal tangles. Years older than Riel, he was.

nothing more than a figure-head; it was understood that well-educated, well-spoken Louis would be the brains behind the movement.

It was not so much a government as, in Riel's words, a "'Committee of Safety', with full power and authority to raise and equip an army to defend our country against that [McDougall's] lawless invasion." He had no trouble raising his army. Hundreds of men came forward, primarily buffalo hunters and the voyageurs of Portage La Loche, and the York and Saskatchewan boat brigades, who had just completed the work season. A captain was elected to head each brigade and Maxime Lépine, a six-foot-three leader of the buffalo hunt, was put in charge of the troops. (His brother Ambroise would later play an even bigger role.) Father Ritchot noted that each man was armed "with a musket, a revolver, a powder horn, and a bag of cartridges, with a dirk or hunting knife." It would not be an easy job keeping these tough, aggressive and deeply alienated individuals under control.

Over the next week the executive of the National Committee, as Louis Schmidt would write, "sat as it were permanently, for events became more and more grave."

On October 21, news reached St. Norbert that among the sixty carts of baggage in McDougall's caravan, slowly winding its way northward, were 350 Enfield rifles, to be used by the soon-to-be-organized police force. The Métis assumed that the Canadians would be armed with these weapons and would attempt to bring McDougall in by force.* A provocative call to war.

At the point where the public highway—the only trail leading into Fort Garry—crossed the Rivière Sale and narrowed through dense woods near the little church at St. Norbert, blockades of logs three feet high were set up. There, armed Métis guards were stationed day and night; they searched every passing traveller and his or her accompanying baggage. As well, brigades of forty mounted scouts, sharpshooters to a man, continuously patrolled the sixty-mile road from St. Norbert to Pembina.

Meanwhile, as word of the daring Métis action swept from one household to another along the Red and Assiniboine rivers, reaction was mixed. Many of the old Selkirk settlers and the prosperous trader-merchants had been outraged that Canadian sovereignty had been imposed without anyone consulting them, and if they would not join the Métis rebellion they would regard it with some sympathy. The English-speaking Half-breeds were as insecure as ever, torn between their hearts and their minds, between the Métis whom they still considered their brethren and the English elite who represented respectability.

---

* *The rumours were not quite accurate. Sensing real danger if hostile forces got their hands on the weapons, McDougall had sent the rifles to be stored at Fort Abercrombie in Dakota Territory.*

And there was still a small but articulate core among the Métis themselves who remained strongly opposed to Riel's bold initiatives. After mass on October 24, the conservatives and radicals of the French-speaking community debated on the steps of the St. Norbert church. The discussion soon grew bitter, tempers flared, and Father Ritchot, frightened that violent fighting was about to break out, reluctantly intervened. The priest was a clever political manipulator; he hinted to the conservatives that he was sympathetic to their concerns, but, he asked, wouldn't it be disastrous for everyone if Métis fought Métis? Surely, the best course for those opposed to the National Committee would be to remain neutral. As the historian George F.G. Stanley puts it: "It was cleverly done and was a good political lesson for Riel. For the most part the conservative métis remained throughout the period of the resistance simple spectators of Riel's success."

The "Canadian Party" were, of course, beside themselves. They had been totally unprepared for the Métis brazenness; that the lowly French-speakers would have the audacity to interfere with their lieutenant-governor was beyond their comprehension. Under pressure from the "Loyalists", as Schultz and company called themselves, the Council of Assiniboia summoned Riel to appear before it.

The council was in a very sticky position. While it remained the official government of the Northwest Territories until the transfer to Canada took effect, it was, with no military force or strong leadership, spineless, in fact virtually moribund.

The man in charge was William Mactavish, a tall, sandy-haired, heavily whiskered Scot who had been a long-time dedicated servant of the Hudson's Bay Company. He had joined the Company at age eighteen and spent the next twenty-four years in the gloom of York Factory, at the edge of Hudson Bay. Conscientious and devoted, he had steadily worked his way up through the ranks from clerk to chief trader to chief factor, until in 1858 he was appointed governor of Red River and Rupert's Land. Almost everybody liked him. He was honest, respected, able to see all sides in a dispute. And he had quickly developed strong links with the wealthy old families of Red River; in fact, he had married the half-breed daughter of the trader Andrew McDermot. But he loathed the job of governor. Once, when pleading with his bosses in London to be reassigned, he wrote that he'd "rather be a stoker in hell." The trouble-making Canadians, John Schultz, Charlie Mair and their friends, had a lot to do with his discomfort. He was simply not capable of wielding the heavy hand needed to cope with the intrigue and chaos they spread in Red River. This was especially true now, since Mactavish had contracted tuberculosis and was slowly dying of the disease.

On October 25, the day that Louis Riel appeared before the council, Mactavish was too ill to get out of bed; in his place sat Judge John Black. Seven other English-speaking councillors were present, but all the French except

William Dease, who was now known to be in the pocket of Schultz, had absented themselves.

Louis Riel appeared remarkably collected and self-confident for someone so young and inexperienced in political affairs. He listened politely as the councillors tried to reason with him. Surely he knew that the Métis actions were "erroneous" and "disastrous consequences" would follow? A long and rambling discussion ensued—Riel related how the Métis were satisfied with the government in place, they were frightened of "being crowded out of the country" by an influx of white settlers, they were acting in defence of their own liberty and for the good of the whole Red River. Finally, Riel left no doubt of his intentions; his people were "determined to prevent Mr. McDougall from coming into the Settlement at all hazards."

After some discussion, A.G.B. Bannatyne suggested that William Dease and another mixed-blood, Robert Goulet, recruit as many of "the more respectable of the French community" as possible to confront the rebellious Métis and persuade them to put down their arms.

While Goulet wisely refused the assignment, William Dease tried, but even with cash and other gifts in his pocket, he was so out of odour with the French-speakers that most just laughed at him. Nothing came of his attempts.

On the night of October 27, Métis from all over converged on the parish of St. Norbert; Riel's followers worried that a full-fledged riot might break out, but the meeting was a complete triumph for the young leader. The only allies of Dease were Georges Racette, a thug whom most Red River people despised, about five other Half-breeds and a half-dozen unidentified Indians. Many dozens of Métis were won over to Riel's side that night.

When the Council of Assiniboia met three days later, Judge Black reported that "Mr. Dease's mission had entirely failed in producing the desired result." The only thing to do was to send a letter to the lieutenant-governor designate, William McDougall, advising him that "for his own peace and safety and the public welfare" he should stay put in Pembina, south of the American border. Then the councillors threw up their hands in despair and never met again.

McDougall would later insist that he hadn't known of the critical situation developing at Red River. He must have been deaf and blind. His chief surveyor, John Stoughton Dennis, had written him that the Métis were "likely to prove a turbulent element" and that they had already threatened violence over the survey. McDougall chose to ignore that warning, just as he saw no significance in the presence of Elzéar Lagimodière, Riel's cousin, who had stalked in the background and watched as the luggage was loaded in St. Cloud, or the Métis horsemen who daily galloped by his caravan as it snaked north.

John Harrison O'Donnell, a physician en route to Red River, joined McDougall's party at St. Cloud. O'Donnell was well connected in St. Paul and he had been told that the new lieutenant-governor would never be permitted to enter Fort Garry. He passed this tidbit on to McDougall, who pooh-poohed it. Days later Dr. O'Donnell encountered two American businessmen who spent much time in Red River and they told him tensions were mounting there. Again he relayed the information to the lieutenant-governor, who laughingly told the doctor that there had been many "wild and contradictory" rumours. It was enough for him that his travelling companion Charlie Mair, who knew the people of Red River like the back of his hand, insisted there was nothing to this "gossip". Then, as Dr. O'Donnell wrote, "All faced the north cheerfully, as if on a pleasant outing."

The weather was gorgeous. The days were still fairly warm, the sun shimmering orange off the extravagantly coloured leaves, the prairie grasses still touched with gold. It was chilly at night and the two women on the excursion were glad they had remembered to leave unpacked their woollen capes. They laughed when Captain Cameron, his monocle carefully placed, his magnificent carved double-barrelled fowling piece in hand, managed to bag not even one of the thousands of Canada geese and ducks flocking overhead. But in a few days the weather turned abruptly cold and windy. By the time the group reached Dakota Territory, still many miles from Winnipeg, winter was in the air. It was just beginning to snow when on October 18, on the trail north of Fort Abercrombie, they unexpectedly encountered the Honourable Joseph Howe, going the other way from Red River to St. Cloud.

Howe was a wily old politician, the former premier of Nova Scotia and now the secretary of state for the provinces in Macdonald's government. He had come to St. Paul with a group of Canadian entrepreneurs to talk railway business but, since he had long been curious to see Red River—after all, it would soon be his responsibility—he had decided to spend a few days there, but as a sightseer, not an official of the government. Although he was tired from his long trip and spent much time resting in Dutch George's hotel, he quietly did the rounds of influential people, chatting with Governor Mactavish and the Reverend Lestanc, and assuring both that full political rights would quickly be granted in the Northwest Territories. He had written Riel a letter asking for an interview, but Louis refused, probably because he considered Howe merely part of the Canadian business establishment. But most of the inhabitants of Red River were courteous and warm, and Howe left convinced that trouble could be avoided if the citizens were treated with respect and care. If only William McDougall had been of the same opinion.

When Howe ran into McDougall on the trail to St. Paul, the sixty-five-year-old secretary of state was exhausted from his travels. All he could think about was seeking shelter before the blizzard got worse. He exchanged pleasantries with McDougall for a few moments and then the two parties went their separate ways. For years after, McDougall ranted about this meeting. By not warning him of the dangers at Red River, he insisted, Howe had sent him into a trap.

On the evening of October 30, the lieutenant-governor's procession finally reached Pembina. The town was much diminished since its glory days as a free-trade depot; only ten ramshackle shacks remained, most made of mud with thatched roofs, and most of these were saloons, including the Robbers Roost, the Dead Layout and the Ragged Edge. McDougall and his entourage came to a stop at the customs house. Suddenly they found themselves confronted by two Métis envoys, Janvier Ritchot, the giant who had clamped his foot on the surveyor's chain weeks before, and Louis Riel's cousin André Nault. The two men politely—McDougall would later admit as much—told the lieutenant-governor designate that they had been sent to present him with a communiqué written nine days before by the National Committee. It simply read:

Dated at St. Norbert, Red River, this 21st day of October, 1869

Sir,

The National Committee of the Métis of Red River orders William McDougall not to enter the Territory of the North West without special permission of the above-mentioned committee.

By order of the President, John Bruce.

Louis Riel, Secretary

The exact words of William McDougall's response were not recorded, but it is said they were contemptuous, insulting and racist. And, as Riel would write, the future lieutenant-governor made no attempt to find out why so many of his constituents were discontented.

McDougall did realize, however, that he was in a tricky situation. Nault and Ritchot, both burly, well-seasoned men, were just menacing enough to give him a sense of what was waiting for him across the border. "We will camp here for the night," he announced, and the procession pulled to the side of the road.

The next morning the lieutenant-governor's company set out once again, but they travelled only a very short distance—to the Hudson's Bay post a mile and a half north of the U.S. border. The man in charge promised he would make the party as comfortable as he could, although he complained that his was probably the most ill-equipped post in all the Northwest. Surely, though, the McDougall party reasoned, it would be more comfortable than the scrawny village of Pembina.

By this time McDougall had assessed his situation and mapped out a strategy. He would send his secretary, J.A.N. Provencher, as an emissary to Fort Garry. A mild-mannered young man of twenty-six, he was the nephew of the late Joseph Provencher, first bishop of Saint Boniface, whose memory was still revered by the Métis people. As Provencher was preparing to depart, Captain Cameron suddenly announced that he too would travel to Winnipeg, as he had to find a warm house for the comfort of his pregnant wife. (She would follow later.) McDougall tried to argue him out of the idea, but he had no authority over Cameron.

A more pig-headed, arrogant man would be hard to imagine. As the son-in-law of Charles Tupper, another Father of Confederation, Cameron had received the appointment for purely political reasons; Tupper had wanted to make a man out of him, and duty in the Northwest would be just the trick. He was supposed to organize a police force, but he could already see himself as future Minister of Militia. The historian Alexander Begg described him beautifully: "A natural ass ... and one no more fitted to be a member of the Council than a real live donkey."

As Cameron had to arrange the half-ton of luggage he was taking with him in wagons, Provencher didn't wait but started out alone. He noticed that mounted scouts were following him all the way. Early the next morning, he was stopped at the Métis barricades at St. Norbert by some thirty to forty armed guards. Nearby a virtual army camp for two hundred men had sprung up; Father Ritchot had thrown open his own stores of supplies after extracting a promise from the Métis soldiers that his chickens wouldn't be harmed. Provencher was escorted into Ritchot's residence. It was only a few moments before services for All Saints' Day were to begin, and Provencher was invited to attend mass. He told his friends later that he had never prayed with such fervor as he did that morning. Later he met with Riel, John Bruce and other Métis and carefully explained the Canadian government's position and then listened to their side of the story. He was genuinely sympathetic and Riel finally agreed to release him. But he was ordered to return to Pembina under armed guard.

Provencher was just leaving when the redoubtable Captain Cameron drove up in his surrey. "Take down that *blawsted* fence!" he yelled. When nobody obeyed his command, he whipped his high-spirited horses, urging them across the barricades. Luckily for him two Métis guards grabbed the horses' bridles, bringing the animals to a halt. Cameron was taken to Ritchot's rectory, then serving as the Métis strategic command. There, according to Louis Schmidt's memoirs, the captain was treated with politeness he didn't deserve and given "a bumper glass of whisky which helped settle him down." Under military guard, both he and Provencher were escorted back across the border to Pembina, but Cameron's luggage was confiscated.

Meanwhile, at exactly the same time, some fifty armed soldiers galloped into the Hudson's Bay post north of Pembina where McDougall and friends had been lodged for a day. The first thing the Métis did was search out William Hallett, the Half-breed who had attempted to coerce them into rebellion at the trumped-up meeting held the previous July. Since that time he had shown his true loyalty, directing Canadians through the Métis lines and acting as a guide for McDougall. The Métis tied the enraged man to a wagon wheel.

Ambroise Lépine, the Métis's adjutant-general, then ordered the shaken McDougall and his entourage to return across the border. Stiffening his back, the would-be lieutenant-governor produced his commission and, in an officious manner, proceeded to explain each clause in detail. When this failed to impress Lépine, McDougall finally demanded to know who had issued such a ridiculous order. Lépine merely replied, "The government." The next morning McDougall and company left the post before breakfast and returned to "wretched" Pembina. In their haste they left behind most of their baggage, but Lépine considerately had it sent to them the next day.

McDougall had rented a residence befitting his station at Silver Heights, near Fort Garry. Where he and his children ended up was in a log cabin owned by a Half-breed, Michael Hayden. Between the McDougalls and the Haydens, eighteen people lived in a house which measured twenty feet by twenty. Desperate for privacy, the lieutenant-governor-in-waiting partitioned his share of the main floor with canvas sheets, but it didn't help much. The racket was unbearable.

Provencher, the secretary, became a paying guest at the home of Joe Rolette, Jr., and Albert Richards, the attorney-general, shared a one-room cabin with Joe's father. Captain Cameron installed his bride in a sod hut—he kept pointing out to everybody that she was the daughter of a Cabinet minister, as if that mattered to the citizens of Pembina. Because the Camerons' baggage had been confiscated by the Métis of St. Norbert, Emma had no choice but to accept the charity of an old Chipewyan Half-breed who offered her a tattered wool coat.

It wasn't just the inadequate toilet facilities, cramped space, restricted diets or muddy streets that made life so uncomfortable for the McDougall group. They existed under the watchful eye of allies of the Métis—the Rolettes, the Caviliers, the Gingras and the most devious and flamboyant of the American pro-annexationists, Enos Stutsman. That Stutsman was a speculator *par excellence* was not what made him unusual; he had been born without any legs. His ability to ride a horse turned him into a legend in the West.

In a short time a separate log house was constructed for the lieutenant-governor's family—at a cost of £90, to be paid by the Dominion government—but still McDougall chafed under forced exile. As a *St. Paul Press* reporter put it, "A

King without a Kingdom is said to be poorer than a peasant. And I can assure you that a live Governor with a full complement of officials and menials from Attorney-General down to cooks and scullions without one poor foot of territory is a spectacle sufficiently sad to move the hardest heart." The "king" finally wired the prime minister demanding that 1,500 Canadian soldiers be dispatched, 500 of them to travel via the United States where they would pick up the guns left at Fort Abercrombie. The rest were to proceed over the Canadian Shield in the spring. And he added, "But for Heaven's sakes don't send us any more Captains of the Royal Artillery with glass eyes." (Cameron wore a monocle.)

While McDougall was cooling his heels at Pembina, the Métis accomplished a most daring act—they occupied Fort Garry, and performed a bloodless coup in the process.

The huge stone quadrangle, surrounded by walls fifteen feet high and protected by ten bastions mounted with six-pounder cannon, was the strategic centre of the Red River Settlement. Since all roads radiated from this point, it was understood that whoever controlled Fort Garry controlled all of Rupert's Land.

Riel had heard rumours that Schultz and company were poised to take over the fort, and that made him very nervous.* With 390 "Brown Bess" muskets at the fort, and a possible 300 more rifles from McDougall's cache, the Canadians would be well armed indeed. But there was another reason for considering such a bold move. Four hundred men were now listed on the muster role of the Métis army, and if they were to remain engaged, food, clothing and some cash would have to be found for them. Fort Garry had in storage what seemed like a boundless supply—some £100,000 worth of pemmican and other provisions.

On the morning of November 2, Riel and Father Ritchot erected a wooden cross next to the barrier at St. Norbert on which was carved *Digitus Dei est hic* (God's finger is here). Falling to their knees, all present were led in prayer by the serene priest; there was no doubt in their minds that theirs was a mission blessed. Leaving a small guard to man the barricades, the Métis set off in groups under cover of the trees on the south bank of the Assiniboine River.

François Marion was the first to enter, through the back door of the fort. He nonchalantly looked around and, not spotting danger, he waved his handkerchief. Twenty armed men led by André Nault arrived immediately and quietly took possession of the Hudson's Bay Company headquarters. Within fifteen minutes

---

* *The rumours were true. James Mulligan, chief of police, had urged Dr. William Cowan, chief factor for Fort Garry, to call out three hundred special constables who had once formed a home guard. And he suggested the Canadians would provide the leadership.*

another one hundred soldiers had marched three abreast into the quadrangle. These men were organized as sentries guarding the gates, walls and bastions.

Governor Mactavish was confined to his bed and the man in charge was Dr. William Cowan.

"What is your business here?" Cowan demanded.

"We've come to guard the fort," responded Riel.

"Against whom?" asked Cowan.

"Against a danger which I have reason to believe threatens it, but which I cannot explain to you at present."

Riel then assured Cowan that his men would not molest any individual or disturb private property. And he promised that any provisions taken would be carefully recorded; eventually the HBC would be compensated by the National Committee.

Mactavish and Cowan would later be accused of too easily acquiescing, even encouraging, the Métis invasion of Fort Garry, but with no armed police force at the ready there was little else they could do.

To provide offices and a council chamber, a large house facing onto the Assiniboine River that had once been the governor's residence was commandeered. (Mactavish had moved into a new, stately home located at the northwest corner of the fort.) Another building, called Bachelor's Hall, was used as lodging for the sentries. Interestingly, Riel himself did not take advantage of the comfortable accommodation at the fort. He moved in with Henri Coutu, a friend and relative by marriage who owned a butcher shop on King Street in Winnipeg. Louis didn't want to appear as though he was deposing William Mactavish. The governor was still to be treated as head of government; the Métis were merely guarding the fort, for the good of the community as a whole.

The Métis now totally dominated the Red River Settlement. But Riel was politically sophisticated enough to realize the dangers of relying on a military occupation. He knew he would have to prove to the Canadian government that he had wide support in Red River, which meant fighting for the hearts and minds of the English-speaking community.

The first step was to set down clearly what the Métis intended. Riel and his executive worked hard to write a proclamation that was friendly but carefully stated. On November 6 it was completed and a messenger was dispatched to have posters printed at the only press in the Settlement, the *Nor'Wester*. The newspaper was now owned by the dentist Walter Bown, an Ontario Orangeman and a good friend of Schultz. He took one look at the announcement and, insisting that he would have to seek the advice of his friends, ran out of his office. On his return a half-hour later, he flatly refused to co-operate with "the rebels". The Métis simply responded by locking Bown in his cupboard and calling in friendly typesetters. It gave Schultz and his friends a taste of who was now boss and they were outraged.

On November 9, one week after the occupation of Fort Garry, the following proclamation appeared throughout Red River:

> The President and Representatives of the French-speaking population of Rupert's Land in council (the Invaders of our rights being now expelled) already aware of your sympathy, do extend the hand of friendship to you, our friendly fellow inhabitants; and in so doing invite you to send twelve Representatives [one each from ten parishes, and two from the town of Winnipeg] in order to form one body with the above council, consisting of twelve members, to consider the present political state of the country, and to adopt such measures as may be deemed best for the future welfare of the same.

Over the next week Riel and his associates made the rounds of the English-speaking parishes. In many instances the Schultz group had been there before them, planting vicious gossip and predicting that the English would snub the French invitation and not send one delegate to the convention. Certainly, the Selkirk farmers and the Half-breeds did not hesitate to express their resentment at what they called Riel's "highhandedness". But Louis could offer interesting enticements to the English. Political equality with the French was proposed, even though the French population was in the majority. As well, the English had become intrigued with the articulate, clever young Métis. And they had nothing whatsoever to lose. In the end, every parish agreed to send delegates.

On the morning of November 16, 150 armed Métis ringed the courthouse situated just outside Fort Garry. Riel thought the guards necessary, but he also realized they might offend. To counter this, he planned a sensational welcome. Once a sentry spotted the English delegation approaching, the clatter of gunshot and the boom of cannon—twenty-four salutes, two for each delegate—rang out.

It got the meeting off on exactly the wrong foot. The English-speakers to a man regarded the outburst not as a warm welcome, but as an arrogant show of force. As Henry Prince, the Saulteaux chief who had been elected from St. Peter's parish, said, "When we hold a council of peace, we go without our guns."

And Riel had not properly prepared for the session. He had not formulated an agenda, there was no concrete plan of action and John Bruce, who was acting as chairman, was not skilled in parliamentary debate. Very quickly the meeting floundered and became a sparring-match, primarily between Louis Riel and the only other man in the room to match his education and intelligence—the thirty-four-year-old Half-breed James Ross.

Ross was one of a huge brood of children parented by Alexander Ross, the famous historian and explorer, and his wife, an Okanagan Indian princess. Born in 1835 in Red River, James had been sent east for his schooling, obtained an arts degree and returned with his Canadian bride in 1858. Two years later he became co-editor of the *Nor'Wester*, associated with the Canadians, Schultz in particular. And he became heavily involved in the sordid Corbett affair—he believed the Hudson's Bay Company was persecuting the minister. By 1864, at the request of Governor Mactavish, Ross had been deprived of his lucrative jobs as postmaster and sheriff. He felt his influence in the Red River Settlement had diminished so much that he returned to Upper Canada. In Toronto he completed a Master's degree, began articling in a law office and became a lead writer and reporter for Brown's *Globe*. It was William McDougall who talked him into returning to the West: a well-educated, clever and bilingual young man like himself would have a great future there, promised the lieutenant-governor-to-be. Ross arrived in Winnipeg in the summer of 1869 with plans to set up his own newspaper, the *Red River Pioneer*.

Given his education and family background, James Ross naturally assumed the leadership of the Red River English Half-breeds, and yet he never inspired his followers the way Riel did. He was not a dynamic speaker, he too often vacillated on important issues, and, perhaps most damaging, he drank too much. As events unfolded, a streak of bitterness developed in his character which many attributed to his growing jealousy over Riel's prestige.

In the courthouse council chambers, the two sides, French and English, argued endlessly back and forth. The English protested against the Métis militarism, their seizure of the fort, their ejection of McDougall from "Canadian" soil. The Métis replied that it had always been their custom to take up arms against the enemy. "As the Indian war parties have been repulsed so Mr. McDougall will be."

Nevertheless a consensus was slowly evolving. Then, out of the blue, J.J. Hargrave, Mactavish's secretary, appeared with a sealed letter from the governor which he demanded be read immediately. Riel had a pretty good idea what was in it and refused. The English insisted. Finally, after a couple of hours of meaningless debate, the Métis leader gave in.

Actually, Mactavish had been most reluctant to put his name to such a document. He thought the Métis could be won over by persuasion and he realized that the moment he labelled their actions an insurrection, they would have to desist or become outlaws. But McDougall, waiting impatiently in Pembina, kept putting pressure on him to condemn the rebels. And Schultz's group had got up a petition demanding the same thing. When Governor Mactavish finally acquiesced, he went all the way, insisting that the Métis had committed unlawful acts;

they were to lay down their arms and leave Fort Garry immediately "under the pains and penalties of law."

James Ross responded immediately. No further debate should follow, he insisted, because what the Métis were engaged in was sedition, pure and simple. Riel jumped to his feet and gave one of those emotional, perceptive, dead-on speeches that he was quickly becoming famous for. He used the few words of optimism in Mactavish's statement—"You are dealing with a crisis out of which may come incalculable good"—for his own end. In a dramatic, emphatic voice, he said:

> ... we are true to our native land. We are protecting it against the dangers that threaten it. We wish the people of Red River to be a free people. Let us help one another. We are all brothers and relations, says Mr. Ross, and it is true. Let us not separate. See what Mr. Mactavish says. He says that out of this meeting and its decision may come incalculable good. Let us unite. The evil that he fears will not take place. See how he speaks. Is it surprising? His children are half-breeds like ourselves.

So persuasive was Riel that the English delegates agreed to meet again the next day.

But it was another session of verbal wrangling, frustrating for everybody. Much time was spent by James Ross justifying his association with Schultz and company, and by Riel, in response, trying to cajole him through flattery. "Rather than hindering us from offering an energetic resistance to him [McDougall], why does he not allow himself to speak with his eloquent voice in the name of the love which he bears to the country of his birth...?"

After several more hours of argument the delegates were exhausted and agreed to adjourn for four days; the quarterly session of court was scheduled to sit and the judges needed their courtroom back anyway. Back at the courthouse again on November 22 and 23, the increasingly impatient delegates heard more fruitless arguing, primarily by Ross and Riel.

Riel realized that the dickering could not continue indefinitely. A daring and novel plan of action was needed and this was worked out at a secret meeting of the Métis and their supporters held the night of November 23. Probably the American consul, Oscar Malmros, and the speculator Enos Stutsman, both of whom were in town that day, and the clerics Ritchot and Dugas, participated in the discussions, but Riel was the chief architect. And it was a brilliant strategy. A provisional government would replace the near-dead Council of Assiniboia. By this one act, the political machinery needed to negotiate with the Canadian government would be put in place. Schultz and company's argument that

McDougall was the only practical alternative to the Hudson's Bay Company administration would be demolished.

Much to Riel's amazement, many of the Métis delegates were fiercely opposed to his plan. "It is incredible what misgivings I had to overcome in them," he would later write. They were frightened that they would be seen as traitors to the queen. Riel wrestled with them all night. Establishing a provisional government, he argued, was not meant to usurp the authority of the British monarchy—"If the Queen knew what we wanted, she would listen to us," he argued. It was simply a temporary affair, its main purpose to negotiate the terms by which Red River would enter Canada. Through sheer perseverance Riel persuaded his reluctant compatriots to agree to his bold scheme.

Early the next morning, to give concrete action to their plans, Métis soldiers walked into the Hudson's Bay Company office and confiscated all bookkeeping accounts, including cash, correspondence and other papers belonging to the Council of Assiniboia. They also seized the contentious land registry journals. These contained the deeds to over half the farms in the Settlement and, had they been destroyed, chaos would have resulted. This, more than almost any other act, caused bad feelings on the part of the English. Still, everybody understood that, after two hundred years, the HBC control of Rupert's Land had abruptly ended.

When the English delegates showed up for the convention later that morning, they were shocked to find more Métis guards milling about than ever. Word spread that Governor Mactavish, Dr. Cowan and other HBC staff would not be allowed outside Fort Garry walls that day. Worried about their own safety, many of the English-speakers considered not attending the meeting, but finally, after much reassurance by Riel, they entered the courthouse. James Ross immediately demanded: What exactly were the French plans?

Riel's answer was clever:

> You know perfectly well what we want. We want what every French parish wants. And they want to form a provisional government for our protection and to treat with Canada. We invite you to join in it in all sincerity. This government will be made up equally of French and English. And it will be only provisional in nature.

His announcement stunned the English side. They were totally unprepared for such a bold move. Ross asked for an adjournment to consider Riel's proposal.

December 1 was an unusually mild and pleasant day (by evening the thermometer would plunge). The French delegates waited to resume the convention at the courthouse at the appointed time, but the English were too busy and excited to attend; the proclamation signed by the queen declaring Rupert's Land officially part of Canada had apparently arrived. Surely now William McDougall would be proclaimed lieutenant-governor without any more trouble.

The English delegates finally showed up and the meeting began. What demands did the Métis want to make of McDougall, James Ross asked, now that he was officially the government at Red River? The French delegation asked for an adjournment. Two hours later they returned with a remarkable document.

The List of Rights was politically sophisticated—so much so that historians have suggested twenty-five-year-old Louis Riel could not possibly have written it; they claimed it must have been Malmros and Stutsman, or the priests Ritchot and Dugas, who were the true authors. While it's true that these people probably contributed, it was Riel who had the legal and political knowledge to formalize the provisions under which Red River would enter Canada. Everyone's rights—English-speakers, old settlers and new arrivals, Half-breeds, Americans, Métis, Indians—were protected. It would be a totally bilingual community. Most important, perhaps, it was not a document of submission or surrender, but the demand of an equal people entering Confederation, as Riel would point out, much as the citizens of Nova Scotia or New Brunswick had.

LIST OF RIGHTS

1. That the people have the right to elect their own Legislature.

2. That the Legislature have the power to pass all laws local to the Territory over the veto of the Executive by a two-thirds vote.

3. That no action of the Dominion Parliament (local to the Territory) be binding on the people until sanctioned by the Legislature of the Territory.

4. That all sheriffs, magistrates, constables, school commissioners, etc., be elected by the people.

5. A free homestead and pre-emption land law.

6. That a portion of the public lands be appropriated to the benefit of schools, the building of bridges, roads, and public buildings.

7. That it be guaranteed to connect Winnipeg by rail, with the nearest line of railroad, within a term of five years; the land grant to be subject to the Local Legislature.

8. That for the term of four years all military, civil, and municipal expenses be paid out of the Dominion funds.

9. That the military be composed of the inhabitants now existing in the Territory.

10. That the English and French languages be common in the Legislature and Courts, and that all public documents and acts of the legislature be published in both languages.

11. That the Judge of the Supreme Court speak the English and French languages.

12. That Treaties be concluded and ratified between the Dominion Government and the several tribes of Indians in the Territory to ensure peace on the frontier.

13. That we have a fair and full representation in the Canadian Parliament.

14. That all privileges, customs and usages existing at the time of the transfer be respected.

The List of Rights was generous to the minority English-speakers, and the delegates readily accepted it. Riel and his people were overjoyed, but a snag quickly developed. The Métis were insistent on sending a deputation to negotiate with the executive party in Pembina. If McDougall did not have the authority to accept the List of Rights, he must obtain the necessary consent from Ottawa before entering Red River as the lieutenant-governor. The English-speakers were adamant that McDougall be allowed admittance at once. For the first time during the long days of negotiations, Riel lost his temper. His face flushed with anger, he jeered at the delegates, "Go, return peacefully to your farms. Stay in the arms of your wives. Give this example to your children. But watch us act. We are going ahead to work and obtain the guarantee of our rights and yours. You will come to share them in the end."

Riel's strenuous efforts to unite the Red River colony had failed, not because of any lack of will on his part—indeed, he had been courageous and remarkably innovative in his attempt—but because working against him were the Canadians, including the would-be lieutenant-governor. And as these people saw a possibility of accord growing among the Red River population, they became more devious, more determined in their plotting.

– 6 –

We stormed Schultz's house and we cornered them,
His forty-eight men faithful at his side.
The sun with its resplendent diadem,
On December 7th at eventide,
Watched over us until we had won.
Schultz finally gave up, laid down his arms.
December the 8th was a glorious morn.
A kneeling race lifts its triumphant arms.

Charlie Mair, John Schultz and friends considered Riel's audacious performance nothing less than sedition. They had armed themselves and were quite eager to fight the rebellious Métis. But they weren't having an easy time of it.

Charlie Mair and his wife, Eliza, had actually been imprisoned by the Métis at St. Norbert for a few days. When they were released, they moved into John Schultz's house, but Charlie had to keep a low profile, for fear the Métis might corner him again.

Schultz was so unpopular among the English-speaking old-timers in the Settlement that he had little success in scrounging up recruits. What was needed was an incident so outrageously impudent on the part of the Half-breeds that the English would surely rally to his side. He didn't have long to wait.

Back in mid-November, a shipment of twenty tons of pork and other supplies for use over the winter by the survey crew and road construction gangs had arrived in Red River. Arrangements had been made for the "government pork", as it came to be called, to be consigned to Schultz for storage in his large warehouse. A few days later, Riel, on his way home to his lodging at Coutu's butcher shop, had noticed barrels being loaded into wagons at the back of the Schultz establishment. Surmising, correctly as it turned out, that the food-stuffs were being sent to the English settlement at Portage la Prairie as rations for armed men loyal to the Canadians, Riel had immediately ordered Métis soldiers to surround the warehouse and guard the precious pork. Schultz had gone running to Riel, armed with invoices and an offer to pay any amount demanded. The Métis leader had merely scoffed at him. As Alexander Begg noted in his diary, the offer was "a subterfuge on the part of Dr. Schultz." Métis guns had remained trained on the doctor's home and business day and night, to "protect" the pork, it was explained.

Schultz knew what the real danger to his dreams of wealth and power was—if the Canadian government perceived that a united front of opposition had cemented in the Red River Settlement it might sideline its plans to take over the West. It was important, therefore, to ferment conflict and discontent whenever possible. Schultz saw his big chance when A.G.B. Bannatyne, the wealthy Winnipeg merchant whose wife had horse-whipped Mair, called a community meeting in Winnipeg for the evening of November 26.

The fire-engine house on Post Office Road was jammed with curious spectators, many of them armed. The American traders were well represented. The Half-breeds, led by James Ross, were on hand, as were the Selkirk old-timers. John Schultz had gathered a delegation of recently arrived homesteaders from Ontario, and a few surveyors and road-gang crew. Louis Riel was there with his supporters. But it was the Métis leader, not Schultz, who received warm applause, even a standing ovation. One of the issues debated was a compromise which the good-natured Bannatyne had devised. The settlers, he proposed, should unite under a strong executive council acting in the name of the Hudson's Bay Company which could negotiate with Canada. Few understood what the difference was between Bannatyne's executive and Riel's provisional government, but the question was argued throughout a long and rowdy night. Bannatyne expected a riot to break out, and fireworks did finally explode when the vote was called. Who would be considered eligible? Since most of Schultz's supporters had recently arrived in the settlement, he insisted that only a week's residency be required. He was soundly defeated and the meeting broke up in an uproar.

The next day the ever-patient Bannatyne called another session, this time only of Winnipeg householders. Schultz tried the same trick, but again he was rebuffed by those voting.

Schultz could lick the many wounds to his dignity with some calm, however, because he was sure he would soon have his revenge. Once William

McDougall was safely ensconced in his magnificent gubernatorial chair in the council chambers at Fort Garry, the rowdy Métis and the perverse older settlers would have to do his, and by extension Schultz's, bidding.

Despite the censoring of all incoming and out-going mail by Riel's government, the Schultz faction, using Indian and Half-breed runners—Schultz had a habit of keeping a number of Native people on his payroll as his special agents—was able to keep in contact with McDougall. They even put pressure on him to proclaim his rule before the official date of December 1, but he wisely refused. As he wrote to Ottawa, the Métis leaders "understand perfectly that I have no legal authority to act or to command obedience until the Queen's proclamation is issued."

Many times a day, the would-be lieutenant-governor, stuck in miserable little Pembina for weeks now, would scan the horizons hoping to spot a messenger galloping towards him carrying the most precious of documents—the queen's royal proclamation decreeing that the Northwest Territories and Rupert's Land were now part of Canada.

What McDougall did not know, to his great detriment, was that Ottawa had received the news of resistance at Red River with utter dismay. Indeed, Sir John A. flatly refused to have anything to do with the mess. A solution was quickly found. As historian Donald Creighton put it: "Canada could refuse to accept the transfer until peace was restored, and the whole responsibility could be flung back to the imperial government and the Hudson's Bay Company. It was the one neat, quick way out." For reasons unknown, the prime minister's office foolishly sent the letter informing McDougall of the delayed transfer by regular post, which took sixteen days, rather than by a special messenger, who might have got it there in six or seven days.

By November 30, the documents officially decreeing the incorporation of the Northwest and Rupert's Land into Canada had not reached Pembina, but neither had news that the deal was off. McDougall logically thought that if the transfer had gone ahead as planned, no government would exist unless he proclaimed Canada's rule. He must make a dramatic gesture on Canadian soil; otherwise, the Métis might legally step in and set up a legitimate administration. There was nothing to do but write his own "letters of Royal patent under the great seal of Canada," proclaiming his own appointment as lieutenant-governor. The queen's signature would simply have to be forged.

The evening of December 1 was bitterly cold and snowy, the temperature dropping to minus 20 degrees F. The residents of the Red River Valley, including the Métis patrols, knew enough to snuggle themselves before their fires. But in Pembina William McDougall and six assistants, as well as two hunting dogs, bundled into sleighs and drove the mercifully short distance across the border to the deserted Hudson's Bay post. What they did when they got there has best been told by the American writer Joseph Kinsey Howard. The detail may be somewhat apocryphal but it wonderfully describes one of the most bizarre incidents in Canadian history.

> McDougall fumbled with his heavy overcoat, found a Dominion flag, handed it to an aide. The latter held it with some difficulty, for the gale tugged at it incessantly and whipped it across his stinging face.
>
> McDougall stepped into the center of the circle, wrestled again with his coat and drew out a sheet of parchment. A man stepped forward with a lantern and the others moved in to shield their chief from the icy wind.
>
> The parchment scroll was hard to hold through the big fur mittens, and in spite of them McDougall's hands shook with the cold. He fumbled the sheet, lost his place, reread; but somehow ... got through it, shouting his forged proclamation in the heedless wind.
>
> He then high-tailed it back to his log cabin in Pembina.

This was the document that had arrived in Red River—Schultz had plastered his front door with copies—the day Riel had almost succeeded in forging a provisional government representing both English and French, before the announcement that the transfer of the Northwest to Canada was a *fait accompli* had made short work of his efforts. Interestingly, only Louis had suspected that there was something wrong with the proclamation, that it might be a phony.

At the same time as he had crowned himself lieutenant-governor, McDougall had issued a second edict that came close to effecting a bloody civil war. He named the government surveyor, Colonel Dennis, "conservator of peace", an ironic title since the intention was to crush the Métis defiance. Dennis was authorized to raise an armed force sufficient to "attack, arrest, disarm, or disperse the said armed force ... to assault, fire upon, pull down, or break into any fort, house, stronghold." Later McDougall would claim that he hadn't meant that Dennis should wage war on the French; he was simply giving his "lieutenant" the necessary tools to cool down the rebellion.

Colonel Dennis started out early on December 1, as the temperature dropped to minus 23 degrees. By five a.m. he had reached the Assiniboine River, and shortly after he sat thawing out by the kitchen fire in William Hallett's farmhouse. They were soon joined by James McKay and Robert Tait, both prominent men in the Red River community and both sympathetic to the Canadians led by Schultz. McKay and Tait said they were fearful of the violence that would flare if Dennis went ahead with his plans to raise an army and attack Fort Garry. Hallett, who had been released from Métis custody only a few weeks before, had no such qualms. He assured the colonel that the English-speakers would flock to his cause and gladly take up arms. By the time they left for Winnipeg, William Dease had joined the group, and he bragged to Dennis that he could easily muster over ninety armed Métis. Riel's force numbered only three hundred at the very most, he assured the colonel.

In Winnipeg, Dennis dropped into the *Nor'Wester* office and had the false royal proclamation naming McDougall lieutenant-governor printed off to be distributed throughout the Settlement. He could see at once that the situation in the village was tense—the Métis were still guarding Schultz's warehouse and the government pork. Nevertheless, after chatting with the doctor and several other Canadians he became convinced that the English-speakers were eager for a fight. He issued a general call to arms.

Dennis was sure that the Métis planned to occupy the abandoned Stone Fort twenty miles north of Fort Garry—an incorrect assumption, as it turned out—and he decided to set up his military headquarters there. He had hired an English Half-breed, Joseph Monkman, at ten shillings a day to recruit Indians from the parishes east of Red River. Monkman was successful, and the first seventy volunteers for Dennis's proposed army appeared at the Stone Fort the day after the colonel arrived. These were Saulteaux from the parish of St. Peter, led by Chief Henry Prince. From the time of the Seven Oaks massacre, when the tribe had sided with Lord Selkirk against the Métis, relations between the Saulteaux and mixed-bloods had hardly been friendly, and the Indians were ready to side with the establishment again. Dennis used Prince's men to garrison the fort. He then began plotting an alliance with a much more dangerous group of warriors.

John Schultz, through the infamous Georges Racette, had established contact with the Sioux, the long-time bitter enemy of the Métis; many had been paid by him for services which sometimes bordered on the illegal. Schultz had no trouble interesting Sioux warriors in Dennis's campaign, and rumours that they were about to attack Fort Garry terrorized the settlement for weeks. The townspeople in Winnipeg were so frightened that they formed a militia of their own; twenty-four people signed up.

Nothing could have been more infuriating to the French Half-breeds than Dennis's attempt to stir up the Indians. When Ottawa heard, through the outraged American press, that the colonel was planning to arm and train the Sioux, an uproar ensued. Sir John A. in particular was appalled. The last thing he wanted was a ferocious Indian war.

Dennis meanwhile set about his main task, which was establishing a militia from among the English-speaking settlers. At Portage la Prairie he could count on his surveying crew, the men who had worked for him, and the road construction gang. In several parishes he was supported by the Protestant clergy, many of them violently anti-Catholic and anti-French, who urged their flock to take up arms. But it was in Winnipeg village that the most aggressive contingent, about forty-five Canadians including, of course, Schultz and Mair, were itching for a fight.

By December 5, about 380 Indians, Half-breeds and Canadians had signed up and been organized into eight divisions, and some had begun drilling exercises in the Stone Fort quadrangle. But this was not what Dennis had anticipated, nor what he had been so assuredly promised by the Canadians. He had only two hundred guns, many of them old and dysfunctional, and more important, almost all the long-time English-speaking settlers refused point blank to have anything to do with his "inglorious schemes". The old-timers were still smarting from the Canadian government's failure to consult them about the transfer. They were certainly not going to take up arms against a people they had lived beside peacefully for almost sixty years.

When word started filtering in to Fort Garry of these events, the Métis naturally concluded that Dennis intended to wage war on them. Riel had acted swiftly and decisively. On December 2, he had shut down the *Nor'Wester*—it must have felt good to silence that whining voice—and James Ross's *Red River Pioneer*. And he had confiscated all weapons and ammunition on sale in Winnipeg shops.

Two days later his soldiers watched anxiously as the John Schultz contingent busily organized sleighs and horses to transport them the twenty miles from Winnipeg to the Stone Fort. But when they got there, Dennis told them he was not ready to attack the French. "Go back to your homes and stay there until otherwise instructed," he ordered. "In the meantime do not in any way provoke the French Half-breeds." Schultz was beginning to think his general a touch cowardly; certainly he had no intention of obeying his orders.

Schultz's Winnipeg establishment consisted of a large log building which was a store and residence combined, an unfinished brick house, a drugstore and a flagpole, all situated in a cluster on the south side of the village, close to Fort Garry. On Saturday December 4, the doctor was seen loading his furniture and household effects into several wagons. Shortly after, various sympathizers, luggage in hand, began arriving at his house, until finally forty-five men, some with their wives and children, were holed up there. Each man was armed and four hundred rounds of ammunition were distributed. By late evening the windows and door were barricaded. It then occurred to the Métis guards that the house had been turned into a fortress—Fort Schultz, as it was immediately christened. It's unclear what Schultz and the others thought they could accomplish; they might have reasoned that their action would pressure Colonel Dennis into attacking Fort Garry and liberating Winnipeg. But it wasn't long before bad news arrived from the Stone Fort; Dennis had not succeeded in rounding up a force large enough to come to their rescue. He realized Riel could call on six hundred Métis, many of whom were highly skilled sharpshooters. "You speak of enthusiasm," Dennis wrote. "I have not seen it yet with anybody but Prince's men [the Saulteaux]."

Riel kept insisting the Métis did not plan to harm anyone, but he called up another hundred armed men. This probably discouraged Schultz from carrying out what he had been itching to do for three days—run the Canadian-stamped Union Jack up the pole next to his drug store.

On Monday December 6, the infuriated Métis guards caught sight of guns pointed at them through the windows of Fort Schultz, supposedly covering the escape of two of the agitators, Alexander McArthur and Thomas Scott. Both men were quickly caught and arrested. The Métis wanted them, not so much because of the foolish show of bravado by the Canadians, but because a tip had been received that they were plotting to assassinate Louis Riel. Although they were probably just making a run for Colonel Dennis at the Stone Fort, there was reason to fear the warning might be true. Scott was the loudmouth who had run afoul of the law when he assaulted his boss, John Snow, of the Dawson Road work crew. He had subsequently found a job as a bartender in O'Lone's saloon in Winnipeg, a favourite watering hole for Riel's guards. There, the Métis believed, Scott listened to every word they said, and reported back to Schultz. He never lost an opportunity to make a racist remark, he hated the "depraved half-breeds", and he had once accosted Riel on the streets of Winnipeg, screaming obscenities at him and almost striking him. Now the arrogant Scott was under lock and key in the prison at Fort Garry.

The first days of December were unseasonably sunny and mild. The Métis guards whiled away their time competing in foot races and weaving long yarns about their days as buffalo hunters or voyageurs, but the nights were cold, and they were growing bored with the incessant watch. Riel probably wouldn't have acted on their complaints if the details of Colonel Dennis's commission hadn't finally surfaced, with its command to "attack, arrest, disarm or disperse" the Métis, as well as burning down their homes and businesses. Riel summoned his soldiers for review, read the infuriating document to them, then ripped it up and threw it in the snow.

On December 7, three hundred armed Métis soldiers surrounded Schultz's establishment. Two cannons wheeled from Fort Garry were trained directly on the house. An excited A.G.B. Bannatyne ran over and pleaded to mediate. Riel consented, but Bannatyne, at first, had little luck. Even though the Canadians had run out of water, food and fuel, the foolish Schultz was still demanding the Métis agree to a long list of conditions before he and his followers would give up; Riel wanted nothing less than unconditional surrender. He finally sent Bannatyne into Schultz's house, with the following "agreement".*

> Dr. Schultz and his men are hereby ordered to give up their arms and surrender themselves. Their lives will be spared should they comply. In case of refusal all the English Half-breeds and other natives women and children are at liberty to depart unmolested.

The Canadians were given fifteen minutes to sign the document and surrender before the assault began. It was John O'Donnell, the doctor who had travelled from Minnesota with William McDougall's party, who blinked first. He realized that Schultz had stupidly manoeuvred them into an impossible corner. They were trapped, and to avoid unthinkable bloodshed, they would have to surrender. He stepped forward and signed the "agreement"; forty-four others, including John Schultz, immediately followed. Only Charlie Mair refused, demanding that they fight to the death. But as his cohorts filed out at gunpoint, he had no alternative but to sheepishly fall in line.

Riel had no intention of incarcerating the women or children, but the wives of Mair, Schultz and O'Donnell insisted on accompanying their husbands. Eliza Mair burst into tears and Anne Schultz fainted—she was gravely ill, "deathly pale" as Bannatyne reported. A humiliated and infuriated John Schultz bundled her into a cutter and, drawing it by hand, joined what must have been a pathetic procession. The prisoners were marched along Main Street between rows of alert soldiers, their rifles poised, to nearby Fort Garry and the waiting prison cells. As the last entered through the huge gates, the Métis guards let loose into the dark night a barrage of gunfire, a terrifying *feu de joie* which enraged the mortified Canadians even more.

---

* *Louis Schmidt, in his memoirs, has a different version of this event. He says that Riel ordered his adjutant-general, Ambroise Lépine, to summon the besieged to surrender. Continues Schmidt: "Lépine did not hesitate but stalwart Morin (Baptiste) who did not think it reasonable to send one man alone into this dangerous situation, offered to accompany him. It was a solemn tragic moment. Would our men come out alive? At last, a few interminable minutes, the capitulation was signed, the men were disarmed and conducted inside the walls of the fort."*

It is interesting to speculate as to what would have happened if Schultz and company had not surrendered. Given Riel's deep aversion to violence, it's possible that he might not have attacked that day. Perhaps a peaceful agreement might have been negotiated by someone like Dennis; or just as likely some provocation, some offhand remark, a misunderstood signal, would have initiated a bloody shoot-out. And given the superior fire-power of the Métis, their expertise with guns, their better positioning, the Canadians would have been massacred.

Two days after the surrender of Fort Schultz, Colonel Dennis issued a peace proclamation, ordering everyone to "cease further action under the appeal to arms made by me." He then disguised himself as an Indian woman and walked for four days in heavy snow before he finally reached William McDougall, still cooling his heels in Pembina. On hearing this news, the Canadians, packed in their grim Fort Garry jail cells, were infuriated and frightened at thus being abandoned by their "general".

The day after Fort Schultz was taken, December 8, Louis Riel finally proclaimed a provisional government for the Northwest Territories—if the English wouldn't co-operate, the French would go it alone.

All through the previous night, Riel's old schoolfriend from Montreal, Father Georges Dugas, with the help of Father Ritchot, had sat in a small room at St. Boniface College, setting down the principles that would provide the legitimacy, the legality, for Riel's government. Called the Declaration of the People of Rupert's Land, it was an amalgam of ideas which the two priests and the Métis leader had been tossing about for weeks. Echoes of the Declaration of Independence which had justified the American Revolution sounded throughout, but so did the ideas of the French political theorist Jean-Baptiste Du Voisin, a strong Catholic as well as avid monarchist. Du Voisin in turn had been influenced by the English philosopher Thomas Hobbes, who wrote, "The obligation of subjects to the sovereign, is understood to last as long, and no longer, than the power lasteth, by which he is able to protect them."

The Métis case for the legitimacy of their provisional government reflected that philosophy:*

> Whereas, It is admitted by all men as a fundamental principle that the public authority commands the obedience and respect of its subjects. It is also admitted that a people, when it has no Government, is free to adopt one form of Government in preference to another to give or to refuse allegiance to that which is proposed.

---

* For the complete Declaration of the People of Rupert's Land see Addendum One, page 449.

Riel and his supporters argued that the Hudson's Bay Company administration, in abandoning Rupert's Land without consulting the people who lived there, had dissolved the obligation of those people to be loyal to the HBC or to its imposed successor. Without a legitimate authority in place, the Métis were free to choose their own government. And they would not give their allegiance to Canada because it intended to impose a "despotic" form of administration. "We have but acted conformably to that sacred right which commands every citizen to offer energetic opposition to prevent his country being enslaved."

The declaration gave November 24, 1869, as the date the provisional government had been established, the very day that the Hudson's Bay Company had signed the documents transferring the Northwest to Canada. It was obvious that Riel thought that he and his allies were filling a vacuum created by the HBC's abdication of political power. When the declaration was written, the Red River community, including the Métis, still believed that McDougall's proclamation was genuine. When, in mid-December, it was finally revealed as bogus, Riel's arguments that his provisional government was perfectly legitimate took on more force.

The prime minister himself had enunciated the same arguments. In a letter to William McDougall, warning him not to be too hasty in assuming authority, Sir John A. wrote that if the Hudson's Bay Company's sovereignty was preempted prematurely by McDougall, "...it is quite open, by the law of nations, for the inhabitants to form a government ex necessitate for the protection of life and property." Like Riel, Sir John A. seems to have been influenced by that crusty old "modernist" of the seventeenth century, Thomas Hobbes.

On Friday, December 10, after high mass at St. Boniface, Louis Riel announced that one and all were invited to celebrate the creation of the provisional government that day. It was still remarkably mild weather; patches of fog floated up from the river like happy ghosts as the ceremony got under way at three that afternoon. Fort Garry's quadrangle was packed with people. The St. Boniface Boys' Bugle Band, under the baton of Father Dugas, blasted out various old French folk tunes and hymns. A prayer was intoned by Father Ritchot and a new flag—a fleur-de-lis and a shamrock on a stark white background—was hoisted up the pole. As the wind grabbed the new symbol of independence, the band struck up another tune, the crowd shouted in joy and volleys of gunfire blasted. A huge kettle filled with liquor, a goblet at the side, was hauled out and everyone present toasted the realization of the Métis dream. This was followed by three cheers, one for the provisional government, one for Riel and the other leaders and one for the brass band. Then three groans, all for the deposed police chief, James Mulligan, sitting gloomily in the Fort Garry jail. It was not only Mulligan who watched the proceedings through the iron grille; Schultz, Mair and the others could hardly endure this final indignity.

What people talked about afterwards, however, was Louis Riel's speech. Much of what he said has been lost to history, except that he exhorted the Métis to remember that they were still loyal to the British crown, and he did so in three languages, French, English and Cree. At twenty-five years old, he had evolved into a strikingly charismatic leader, energetic, eloquent and passionate. As his friend Louis Schmidt would later write, "Riel was a born orator. His character predisposed him to that. By nature enthusiastic and a little exalted, his speeches made a great impression on crowds."

The photograph taken of the provisional government at the time shows maturity already etched on Riel's round face. His hair is glossy and thick, worn long, he sports a well-trimmed moustache and he is dressed like any politician of his day—a winged collar, a well-fitting jacket and vest. But all the councillors in the picture are dressed thus—no sign of the buffalo hunter here. Riel is placed emphatically in the middle, although the others surrounding him—including John Bruce, the president of the provisional government, who seems to have been cast to one side—are seated or standing in an informal, relaxed manner. The tavern owner, H.F. O'Lone, is resting his arm on Louis's knee—an indication, perhaps, of the democratic nature of Riel's administration.

Seventeen days after the flag-raising ceremony, it was announced that John Bruce was stepping down as president. In mid-December he had become seriously ill, close to death, and this provided an excuse for his retirement. The Métis considered that he had made a real contribution—Riel would write of "his modesty, the natural moderation of his character and the justness of his judgement"—but Bruce was resentful and in time would turn violently against Riel and Lépine.

With Bruce's retirement, the provisional government was reorganized. To nobody's surprise, Louis Riel was elected president by the twelve representatives. And a new body, a military council, was set up, with Riel as commander-in-chief. From then on, he sometimes signed his letters *Commandant en chef*, or Commander at Fort Garry. It was an indication of how powerful he had become, how idolized he was by the Métis.

His executive was a very mixed bag. François Dauphinais, a fifty-four-year-old fur trader from St. François-Xavier, considered a moderate, was named vice-president. Riel's old friend Louis Schmidt was chosen secretary. Ambroise Lépine (brother of Maxime), the man selected to be adjutant-general in charge of the military, was a legendary figure on the prairies. He was the grandson of Alexander Henry, the famous explorer and wintering partner of the North West Company. His father, Jean-Baptiste, had been born in Quebec and owned a rather large river-lot farm at Ste. Agathe. Ambroise Lépine had been educated at St. Boniface College and now made his living by farming, carting and buffalo hunting. He was a strikingly handsome man. The Reverend Robert MacBeth described him thus: "He was one of the finest specimens of physical manhood I ever saw. Six feet two in his moccasins and built in splendid proportions, straight as a pine, and a leader of acknowledged prowess on the plains, Lépine had all the natural accessories of a soldier of fortune."

Louis Schmidt was equally ebullient in his praise of Ambroise. "Lépine was the exact opposite of Riel," he wrote. "Cold, practical, he never lost control. He personified courage and gallantry. Gifted with a fine presence and extraordinary physical strength, he was born to command and he became, quite naturally, a leader to the soldiers of the revolution."

Lépine was the one man who might have challenged Riel for the leadership of the Métis, but he lacked Louis's political savvy, his oratorical skills, his driven, obsessive vision, his ambition. He was content to serve under the younger man, whom he admired beyond question for his entire life.

The third person (selected by Riel) to serve on the executive, the treasurer, was William Bernard O'Donoghue, a tall, thin-faced man with silky blond hair and fine, small hands. One unsympathetic Toronto *Globe* reporter wrote that he had "a cringing, cunning way with him, which at once suggested to my mind my old acquaintance Uriah Heap." The pejorative stuck; his enemies thereafter called him Uriah.

No question that O'Donoghue had a profound effect on Louis Riel, that for a time he was his right-hand man. The intellectual, urbane Riel likely had more in common with the quick-witted, well-educated O'Donoghue than he had with an old plains hunter like Lépine. The two men developed an intense love-hate relationship that was forged during the battles over political theories that raged during those months.

Irish-born O'Donoghue was twenty-six, a year older than Riel and old enough to have some memory of the terrible potato famine and the rebellion of 1848. After immigrating to New York at sixteen, he somehow managed to finish his schooling, and he was teaching at Port Huron, Michigan, when in 1868 he met Bishop Vital-Justin Grandin, who was on his way to Red River. O'Donoghue was fluent in French and the bishop offered him a job as professor of mathematics at St. Boniface College, which he accepted. Within a few months he decided to become an Oblate priest, but gave it up to join Riel's rebellion. The shamrock on the provisional government flag was a courtesy to him and all the other Irish Americans in Red River who supported the cause. And yet the Métis never quite trusted him. Schmidt would write, "O'Donoghue was coldness itself although his Irish blood boiled continually in his breast. That blood rose to his face when things did not go as he wished."

Although there's no question that O'Donoghue was an Irish patriot and believed passionately that British rule in that country must end, there is little evidence that he had strong Fenian connections when he first met Riel. And although he was very much in favour of the American annexation of the Northwest, he realized that if Canada agreed to negotiate adequate terms, Riel would deliver the Northwest into Confederation. But O'Donoghue stood for a choice that the Métis could consider if all else failed, a formidable negotiating weapon—the annexation of the Canadian West by the United States—which they would use effectively against Ottawa.

With the government structure in place, Riel and his council faced the difficult task of governing. At first, money was a very real problem. The Métis army was being provisioned through the Hudson's Bay Company stores; pemmican, clothing and ammunition had been distributed, despite Governor Mactavish's protests. But this was hardly enough to support a full-fledged government; what was needed was hard cash.

On December 16, Riel asked Mactavish, still operating as the HBC's chief factor, for a loan of £1,000. Mactavish flatly refused. Louis tried again on December 20, explaining that the American consul, Oscar Malmros, was promising that the United States government would come to Riel's aid to the tune of $25,000. While he didn't want to take help from foreigners, especially foreigners who were eager to gobble up the Northwest Territories, what else could he do? Mactavish was not persuaded by his arguments.

Two days later Riel and O'Donoghue, this time with a guard of men showing fixed bayonets, walked into the HBC offices and again pleaded for a loan. Again Mactavish turned them down. At that point, the bookkeeper, John M. McTavish (no relation to William Mactavish), was rounded up by the Métis soldiers and a key to the safe was found in his pocket. O'Donoghue counted the money, £1090 in cash and promissory notes, just the amount Riel had asked to borrow.

The provisional government did a remarkably good job in maintaining peace and good order in the Red River community. During the Christmas holidays Riel prohibited the sale of liquor. Merchants such as Bannatyne and McDermot complained vehemently about this but, despite the hundreds of restless Métis under arms, no one in the Settlement was attacked, no one was robbed.

Yet Riel realized that his government represented only "a section of the people of the country." To impress Canada, the support of the English-speaking community would have to be garnered. A.G.B. Bannatyne was talked into keeping his position in the provisional government as postmaster. And Riel made several visits to English parishes offering equal representation in his administration to Scots and English Half-breeds. Most people he spoke to were not antagonistic, nor were they eager to join his revolution; most had decided to wait to see what hand Canada would play next.

On Christmas Eve, Louis, his mother and brothers and sisters attended midnight mass at St. Boniface Cathedral. Riel was amazed that so few men were present; most of the Métis soldiers, having been paid from the "borrowed" HBC funds that day, were at Dutch George's celebrating the holiday by getting drunk. (Perhaps if Riel had not prohibited the merchants from selling liquor, the men might at least have partied at home.)

Immediately after Christmas, Riel was suddenly besieged by a stream of visitors from Canada, and among the strangest of these encounters was with Charles Tupper. Tupper was a physician from Nova Scotia who was just beginning a long, eventful political career—he had been elected to the House of Commons in 1867—which would lead to a sojourn in the prime minister's office, albeit a very short one, in 1896.

Tupper had sat in Ottawa stewing about his pregnant daughter, Emma, the wife of the unfortunate Captain Cameron. He was a big, robust man, and decided to journey the 1,200 miles to fetch her. He was travelling north from St. Cloud to Pembina when he ran into William McDougall, J. Stoughton Dennis and their entourage proceeding in the opposite direction. McDougall had finally realized that his ambition to be lieutenant-governor of the Northwest Territories was dead. A week before, he had left Pembina to return to Ottawa and a political career that was now a complete shambles. He was without his gubernatorial chair. It and the other furniture for his "Silver Heights" mansion, prematurely shipped to Red River, were now in storage at Fort Garry.

Captain and Mrs. Cameron were still stuck in Pembina, however. When Tupper finally found them in their miserable sod hut, he promised he would make a quick trip to Fort Garry to retrieve their baggage. They were not wealthy people, and all their worldly goods had been confiscated during their run-in with the Métis guards at St. Norbert.

He bribed a young Half-breed to guide him and the pair set out north. The weather couldn't have been worse: the trail was packed with four feet of snow, the temperature had dropped to 30 degrees below zero, and a haunting ice fog enveloped them. The first night was spent at the cabin of a Métis farmer who "greeted us cordially, and who provided venison and tea with biscuits." The second day they reached St. Norbert, where Tupper hoped to encounter Father Ritchot, not knowing the priest was with Riel at Fort Garry. Tupper did meet Louis's sister, Sara Riel, still living at the Grey Nuns convent. The two took an immediate liking to each other. A warm, spontaneous friendship was struck, so much so that Tupper would continue to correspond with Sister Sara until her death. She provided him with an introductory letter that gave him access across the St. Norbert barricades, and at Fort Garry he was courteously received by Louis Riel. Although Riel would not permit Tupper to circulate freely in Winnipeg, he did return his daughter's possessions. The Nova Scotian seemed amazed that "nothing at all had been taken."

Although Tupper did not condone the Métis rebellion—he was particularly fearful of the American influence—he was impressed with the young president and told his colleagues in Ottawa so.

But Tupper was a mere digression. At the same time as Sir John A. Macdonald had postponed the transfer of the Northwest to Canada, he had done something he should have done months before—appointed two representatives to travel to Red River and convey to the residents the friendly and wholesome intentions of the Canadian government. On Christmas Day Riel had been informed that the two emissaries had reached Pembina. The long-awaited negotiations were about to begin.

Macdonald looked for men who he thought knew the French at Red River well and would be well received by them. The Very Reverend Jean-Baptiste Thibault seemed a perfect choice. He had served as a missionary in the Northwest for thirty-six years; it was he who had baptized Louis Schmidt. For years he had been the parish priest to the buffalo hunters at White Horse Plains, and when his health began to deteriorate, he taught at St. Boniface College until he retired to his native Quebec in 1868. Macdonald might have had second thoughts about the priest if he had known the reason Thibault was so adored by the Métis. Like his fellow cleric Georges Belcourt, he most often took their side in disputes with the Hudson's Bay Company and the church hierarchy.

The other envoy selected was Colonel Charles de Salaberry. Born of a distinguished military family—his father was the hero of the 1813 victory over the Americans at Châteauguay—Salaberry had been the quartermaster of a Canadian expedition which had explored the prairies in 1857. He was charming and affable, a man the Métis very much liked, but he was not quick or cunning.

Thibault and de Salaberry were armed with various letters of good intention from politicians, including one from Howe disowning the "acts of folly and indiscretion which had been committed by persons purporting to represent the Dominion", meaning McDougall, and an amnesty for those who would lay down their arms and desist from further "illegal action".

The two emissaries were shocked at the suspicion and distrust with which they were greeted by the Métis when they finally reached Pembina on Christmas Day. Riel was prevailed upon by priests at St. Boniface to grant Frère Thibault a safe-conduct pass, and after spending the night at St. Norbert he arrived at Red River on December 26. De Salaberry was advised for his own safety to remain south of the border; Riel thought he was carrying cash bribes— an unfounded suspicion as it turned out. Finally Louis relented and on January 6 an armed guard accompanied the colonel to Fort Garry.

As soon as Riel talked with Thibault and de Salaberry, he realized that the two men had travelled a long way for nothing. They had no authority, no power; they were merely "goodwill ambassadors". Riel made it clear that he would take seriously only those officially accredited to negotiate directly the terms of transfer with Canada. Despite their obvious lack of power, Riel remained leery of the harm these two envoys' propaganda might do. While remaining polite and even diffident towards them, he had them placed under casual house arrest in the Bishop's Palace at St. Boniface and confiscated their documents, including the governor-general's amnesty.

De Salaberry would later claim that he "had been a prisoner throughout", but his two-and-half-month incarceration mustn't have been too onerous. He was allowed to dine at the home of A.G.B. Bannatyne, enjoying the same kind of hospitality Charlie Mair had abused only a year before; he rehearsed the boys' bugle band at St. Boniface College; he visited the post office in Winnipeg daily for his mail.

On January 13, the two envoys were invited to appear before the council of the provisional government. Father Thibault rattled on in his best sermonizing style about the good intentions of the dominion government. As one observer put it, "some explanation and compliments were exchanged, after which the very Reverend gentleman and his associate were politely bowed out and lost sight of."

Actually the old missionary had already seen the justice of the Métis cause. He had been delighted to meet with his former colleagues at St. Boniface College; it had taken only three days for the priests Giroux and Dugas to convert him. He soon became an effective weapon in Riel's cause. But by that time a third envoy appointed by the prime minister had arrived in Red River, and he was a bird of a very different feather.

It had occurred to Sir John A. Macdonald that since many French Half-breeds remained stubbornly loyal to the Hudson's Bay Company, revitalizing the HBC administration at Red River might possibly solve the messy problem of the Half-breed insurgency. He had approached George Stephen of the Bank of Montreal, who had pointed him in the direction of his cousin, the astute Donald A. Smith, the chief factor of the HBC's Montreal district.

Although Smith had never been to the Northwest before, his roots were tangled deep in the fur trade. Born in 1820, in the little trading town of Forres in northeastern Scotland, he had started his working life as a town clerk, a dull and unpromising job. Fortunately for him, his uncle John Stuart had arrived home on leave after years of service in the Northwest fur trade—he had been second in command of Simon Fraser's famous exploration to the mouth of the river which now bears Fraser's name. Stuart had written his young nephew an introduction to George Simpson, the HBC's top man overseas, and Donald Smith had set out for Canada.

He was hired on as an apprentice clerk at Lachine, Quebec, counting "stinking" muskrat skins, as he once put it. For obscure reasons—it may have had something to do with a flirtation between Smith and the young and pretty Mrs. Simpson—he was banished to the outpost of Tadoussac on the St. Lawrence, where he spent seven unhappy years. The HBC was in the process of trying to revive its Labrador district, and in 1848 Smith was given a chance to prove himself there. In this bleak part of the world, he set out to educate himself, reading deeply in the arts, sciences and philosophy. He also, as the writer and historian Peter C. Newman puts it, "developed the cold insensibility that allowed him to betray political and business associates at will. The pressures that made him one of the most frigid, class-conscious aristocrats of this era had their origins here...."

Smith married Isabella Hardisty, a charming Métisse who was the daughter of the chief trader of Labrador, Richard Hardisty. (There was a touch of scandal about the lovely Isabella; she had been married, *à la façon du pays*, to a fur trader, but the union had proved a disaster and her father had encouraged its end.) In 1853 Smith succeeded his father-in-law, who was retiring, as the chief of the Labrador district. Although his post was geographically isolated, he was not out of touch with the powers of the Hudson's Bay Company or Canada's business establishment. Leave was spent in London, England, or Montreal, cultivating important people—he was especially friendly with George-Étienne Cartier—and latching onto financial opportunities. Early on he had convinced his HBC "servants" that their savings would grow in a far more interesting way under his management than if left with the company's pension fund. His investments in securities and mortgages proved so successful that eventually he came to represent a sizeable block of stock in the Bank of Montreal. By 1869, when he was promoted to the position of chief factor, Montreal District, he was well on his way to becoming a very rich man.

When Sir John A. made him the government's negotiator, the "special commissioner" charged with sorting out the Red River mess, he was almost fifty years old; his sandy hair, rust-coloured beard and thick red eyebrows were greying. Yet he was only at the beginning of his astonishing career. Waiting for him were a seat in the House of Commons, governorship of the HBC, elevation to the peerage as Lord Strathcona, and, as founder and backer of the Canadian Pacific Railway, a place among the most powerful of North America's financial magnates. He was cunning, astute and bloody-minded. He seldom displayed any emotions and therefore was a great master at manipulating events. He would prove a difficult adversary for the volatile, passionate Louis Riel. Louis Schmidt had his number when he called him "an old trickster".

As boss of the Hudson's Bay Company, Smith and his companion, his brother-in-law Richard Hardisty, had no difficulty passing through the Métis barriers at St. Norbert when they arrived on December 27, 1869. Riel confronted Smith at the gates of Fort Garry, and the two men sat down to talk at once. Smith said he was there to help out Governor Mactavish, growing weaker from his tuberculosis by the day, but he also hinted that he had important Canadian government business to discuss with Riel. The Métis leader extracted a promise from Smith that he would do nothing to undermine the provisional government, an oath which Smith had no intention of honouring. In return for his pledge, Riel permitted him entry to Fort Garry and access to the HBC officers.

Louis might not have been so lenient towards Smith if he had known more about the man.

Donald Smith was the ultimate land speculator. Over the next couple of years, he would gobble up Red River lots until he owned ten thousand acres of valuable land, double what John Schultz could get his hands on. He was also the largest shareholder in the Hudson's Bay Company. When, after the news that the HBC was handing over Rupert's Land to Canada, the company stock nose-dived, Smith quietly began to buy up as much as he could. While the £300,000 compensation paid to the HBC by the Canadian government was indeed a paltry sum, Smith realized that the enormous land holdings granted as part of the deal could make the Company, and him, rich. Immigration, of course, was the key, and only control by the Canadian government could guarantee that. In other words, Smith's interests and the Canadian government's interests were identical—to get rid of Riel and the rowdy Half-breeds as expeditiously as possible. As Macdonald wrote, "It is hoped here that while Mssrs Thibault & de Salaberry are acting upon the French half breeds, Mr. Smith will be able to strengthen, encourage and organize the English & Scotch half breeds & the whites who are loyal to Canada...."

And the prime minister had provided his "special commissioner" with the means to achieve this end. What Riel may have suspected but didn't know for sure was that Smith had been given *carte blanche* to bribe the Métis and Half-breeds while attempting to pry their loyalty away from Riel. The effect of this was immediately evident.

Although Donald Smith was confined by Riel's orders to Fort Garry proper—he stayed at the home of Dr. Cowan, acting head of the HBC—he was allowed visitors, and the hoi polloi streamed in. Both Smith and his wife had Métis and Half-breed relatives in Red River—the famous Cuthbert Grant had been a distant cousin of his—which made him all the more popular. Through these contacts, and the Hudson's Bay Company officers, he gained the information necessary to pinpoint those Métis who could be bought off with cash or job offers with the company. In a couple of months he would hand out £500 in such bribes. Almost immediately, support for Riel and his provisional government began to crumble. As Louis Schmidt wrote, "It was [at this time] that the true patriots were to be recognized, and the well-tried men."

The next six weeks would be a frustrating, difficult time for the young Métis leader; all the political skills of manipulation and appeasement which he had recently cultivated would be brought into play. He would succeed in the end, but not without enormous cost to his physical and emotional well-being.

While others were enjoying New Year's Day horse races in Winnipeg, Riel travelled to Ste. Anne-des-Chênes (Oak Point) to confront his cousin Charles Nolin, a prosperous farmer and entrepreneur. Although Nolin had been elected a councillor in the provisional government, he had walked out of a meeting in a huff on December 24 and was now fomenting opposition to Riel, plying Smith's bribe money. Nolin was an opportunist, full of intrigue and duplicity, who eventually would be despised by the Métis. But in 1870 he had influence with his compatriots, and Riel knew he would use it to further his own ends. Riel would repeatedly try to win over his cousin, without much success. The Nolin family—there were five brothers—had a reputation for violence. And as events heated up in Red River, Riel became terrified that they were planning his assassination. One night, Louis was dining with Augustin Nolin when he saw a shadow pass outside the window. He threw down his knife and fork and, choking on his food, called out that he was about to be murdered. Nolin yelled to Louis, "You'll never be killed in my house," then ran out with his gun to see if he could find the intruder, but he had disappeared. Shortly after, forty Métis soldiers arrived to accompany the shaken Riel back to Fort Garry. It was later discovered that the man Riel had seen was a trader from Pembina, merely passing by Nolin's house. Charles would use this incident to illustrate how neurotic Riel was; but in fact, events in the immediate future would indicate that Louis had every reason to be suspicious of the Nolins.

As Riel's support flagged, the internal workings of his administration and his militia operation weakened. The jail-break of Sunday January 9 was a case in point.

The Canadians who had been smoked out of "Fort Schultz", and others taken captive, had recently been moved from Fort Garry to a common jail outside the walls, where six cells held forty prisoners. Their imprisonment remained a sore point for the English community. Attempting to appease them, Riel had announced that any prisoner who would take an oath of allegiance to his government, or promise to move out of the country, would be released. Nine had taken up his offer, but the hard-core Loyalists, Schultz and Mair included, adamantly refused to obey Riel, or any "damned half-breed" for that matter.

For days a few of these prisoners had worked with their penknives to whittle away at the wooden casings of two windows. While the Métis sentries were changing, the bars on the windows were removed and several prisoners managed to crawl to their freedom. While others deliberately distracted the guards' attention by creating a racket, another eight escaped.

Five were caught the next day. It was bitterly cold and without coats and mittens they had suffered terribly, but the fiasco had made the Métis military look gauche and incompetent. Lépine was furious when he found out. Of the seven who had escaped, two were the most reviled enemies, Charlie Mair and Thomas Scott. Mair had taken refuge in the Winnipeg house of William Drevers, where Eliza was staying. After fortifying himself with a shot of whisky and kissing his wife goodbye, he borrowed some warm clothing and a sleigh and pony, and headed for the English community of Portage la Prairie. Eliza was determined not to be left behind; the Métis might come looking for her. Dressed as a Half-breed, she eluded the Métis patrols, and in ten hours joined her husband. Scott and two confrères tried to steal some horses in Winnipeg, but they failed and had to walk the ten miles to Headingley, where they found "sympathy and shelter". Scott would eventually join Mair and others at Portage. Riel knew the formation of this cabal would mean deep trouble for him and his government.

During those confusing days, Louis also had to contend with growing pressure from the Americans promoting the annexation of the Northwest to the United States. As if the manipulation of the suave Malmros, the clever Stutsman and the cunning O'Donoghue were not enough, the one newspaper now published at Red River turned out to be a blow-hard Yankee-booster.

Riel had not allowed the *Nor'Wester* and the *Red River Pioneer* to re-open after he had closed them down in early December. But he realized the community badly needed a voice. After Stutsman and journalist Major Henri M. Robinson assured him that they would support the views of the provisional government, Riel gave them permission to establish a newspaper. For £550, they purchased the presses and type of the *Red River Pioneer*. The first issue of the new paper appeared on January 7, 1870, under the banner of the *New Nation*, obviously a sop to the Métis revolutionaries. The historian Alexander Begg, like many old settlers, didn't like it one bit. "The name is not appropriate nor the annexation of the Canadian West to the States sentiments contained in the sheet wise or right," he wrote in his diary.

Since Riel had no control over the paper's editorial policies, there was nothing he could do but suppress it, and this was not an option for several reasons. On all issues except American annexation, the *New Nation* did support the provisional government. And Louis was keenly aware by that time that a show of support for an American take-over, even if it was mostly hot air, would serve as a potent tool when he negotiated with the Canadian government. Still, with the English community, and some French, complaining bitterly, he was forced to chastise the editor several times. It was another major complication for the already nervous commandant.

What irritated Louis the most, however, was the serious split in his council. Many of the Métis councillors resented O'Donoghue and his constant carping on American annexation. (There had been charges that O'Donoghue had actually censored Riel's mail, which infuriated the Métis leader.) And they thought the *New Nation* should be vigorously censored. Riel was upset that many of his inner circle were becoming too friendly with Donald Smith and his always-open money-belt.

Then there occurred a most humiliating episode, which sent signals through the Red River Settlement that Riel was losing control, not only of the Métis population but of his entire rebellion.

Having been warned that the official documents of Thibault and de Salaberry had been confiscated by Riel's men, Donald Smith took the precaution of leaving his in the care of McDougall's former secretary, J.A.N. Provencher, still in Pembina. Riel had no idea if Smith had the power he claimed he had to act on behalf of the Canadian government, and kept asking for his credentials. Smith, on his side, wanted to avoid any recognition by the provisional government, for that might legitimize Riel's regime. Finally it was agreed that Richard Hardisty, Smith's brother-in-law, who had accompanied him to Red River, would retrieve the documents. Riel assigned two Métis guides to accompany Hardisty with the idea of seizing the papers. But the Smith sympathizers completely outsmarted Riel's forces. HBC governor Mactavish tipped off three Half-breeds in the pay of Smith, and one of them, Pierre Léveillé, managed to get his hands on Smith's papers before the Métis guides. When Riel rode to St. Norbert to meet Hardisty and take possession of the papers, he found himself staring down the barrel of a pistol. Schmidt would later write that Léveillé would have fired if a companion hadn't held him back. Father Ritchot was shoved aside and told "not to interfere any further with matters unconnected with his spiritual duties." Riel rode back with the party and watched with red-faced embarrassment as Hardisty handed Smith his papers.

There were immediate repercussions. As Schmidt recalled,

> the excitement in the Fort was great when it was seen that Riel had not car-
> ried out his design. It was a humiliating check for us, and it was only by a
> narrow margin that our adversaries missed paying dearly for their resistance
> ... a sullen resentment simmered in the bosoms of those concerned, and it
> would not have taken a great deal to have made it break out.

Frightened of possible bloody conflict, Riel had no alternative but to agree
to what Smith had been demanding—a public meeting at which he could present his commission. If ever there was a battle of David versus Goliath, this
would be it.

Riel's father, Jean-Louis, probably taken around 1850, when he was 33 years old.

Louis Riel's beloved mother, Julie Lagimodière.

Henriette Riel. Louis's favourite sister was sixteen years younger than he was.

The earliest photo of Louis Riel,
at about age 14.

Riel as a twenty-two-year-old law clerk in
Montreal, just before he left for the West in 1866.

Riel as a young revolutionary at the time of the
Red River Resistance, 1869–70.

Louis Riel at the time he was elected to
Parliament, *ca* 1873–74.

Rodolfe Laflamme, Montreal intellectual, lawyer and politician, 1870. Riel had worked as a clerk in his law office.

Father Noel Joseph Ritchot, the parish priest at St. Norbert's and a close ally of Riel's during the Red River Resistance. In his role as the chief negotiator with the Canadian government, he was considered as tenacious as a bull dog.

Louis Riel and his chief advisers, 1869. *Top row:* Charles Larocque, Pierre Delorme, Thomas Bunn, Xavier Pagée, Ambroise Lépine, Baptiste Tourond, Thomas Spence. *Middle row:* Pierre Pointras, John Bruce, Louis Riel, W.B. O'Donoghue, François Dauphinais. *Front row:* H.F. O'Lone, Paul Proulx.

Thomas Scott, the trouble-making Orangeman who was condemned to death by a Métis court martial. He was to become Riel's cross to bear.

Below: John Christian Schultz. Medical doctor, merchant, land speculator, he was Riel's sworn enemy.

Above: Ambroise Lépine, the adjutant-general of the provisional government, 1869–70.

William Bernard O'Donoghue, the secretary in the provincial government. An Irish immigrant, he would eventually turn against Riel and seek the help of the Fenians to invade Manitoba.

John "Mutton-chops" Dennis was the boss of the survey that sparked the Red River Resistance. He unsuccessfully tried to raise a force of "Canadians" against the Métis.

Charles Mair, the "Canadian poet", was John Schultz's sidekick and a member of the "Canada First" group, dedicated to opening the West to settlement.

Donald Smith, the senior officer of the Hudson's Bay Company in Canada, and Riel's chief adversary.

Below: Garnet Joseph Wolseley, commander of the Red River Expeditionary Force, 1870.

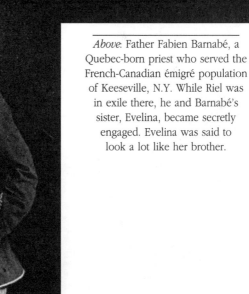

Above: Father Fabien Barnabé, a Quebec-born priest who served the French-Canadian émigré population of Keeseville, N.Y. While Riel was in exile there, he and Barnabé's sister, Evelina, became secretly engaged. Evelina was said to look a lot like her brother.

Bishop Alexandre-Antonin Taché, who ruled
the French community at Red River with a
"velvet fist". Although Taché was Riel's great
benefactor for many years, the two men
would later become estranged.

Members of the Red River Expeditionary
Force, 1870.

Some of the Métis and Indian population at Fort Garry, *ca* 1868, with a typical Red River cart.

- 7 -

Grant me righteousness in everything I do
That I may always behave in honesty.
Explain the meaning of the Scriptures
Through those who hold your authority.

When he agreed to Donald Smith's request for a public meeting, Louis Riel knew that he himself had a great deal to lose. The big Scot, after all, was twenty-five years older and far more experienced at handling people. If Smith took control of the proceedings, it would be he and not Louis who would pilot the negotiations with Canada. The provisional government would be rendered superfluous. Riel also realized there was real danger of a riot breaking out, or even civil war. Still, he decided to chance it, believing that, in the end, his Red River people would rally around him. He chose January 19 as the date, and doubled the number of Métis guards on duty.

It was a sharp, frigid day, ice crystals shimmering in the wan yellow sun, temperature minus 20 at eight a.m. and dropping, and yet, enveloped in buffalo coats or huge blanket *capotes*, bundled into horse- or dog-drawn sleighs that glided across the hard-crusted prairie squeaking like an unearthly choir, they travelled from all over—from the English Half-breed parish of Headingley in the far west to the French Ste. Anne-des-Chênes in the east. So many people came that no building was large enough to accommodate them. They would stand outside in the bitter cold, stamping their feet, clapping their mittened hands, pulling their otter hats or woollen hoods tighter around their red faces, lighting small fires to warm themselves by, and listen for five hours as Donald Smith waved Ottawa's olive branch.

They congregated inside Fort Garry's walls, in front of the square wooden hall where HBC officers and clerks resided. At the front of this building, overlooking the square, was a small veranda, and it was here the main players assembled: Donald Smith, formidable with his great red eyebrows, clear speaking voice and commanding presence; Louis Riel, a little heftier than he had been when he first arrived at Red River, some of his urbanity now given way to a frontier ruggedness. Beside them were the sour-looking Anglican Bishop Machray, and Riel's mentor, Father Ritchot, as well as various members of the French council.

As soon as the meeting was called to order, Riel nominated the respected English Half-breed Thomas Bunn as chairman, and Judge John Black was appointed secretary. Riel himself was named translator. By all accounts he performed this difficult duty with accuracy and speed, but to mouth the words of Donald Smith hour after hour without being able to once intervene, without being able to express his heartfelt disapproval, must have been exceedingly hard on him.

Smith began by complaining about the Métis flag, with its shamrock and fleur-de-lis, flapping overhead, but he quickly sensed that the gathering would not tolerate this interference, and he dropped the matter. He then read his letter of commission from Joseph Howe, the secretary of state for the provinces. In vague language, Howe had told Smith to win the Red River Settlement over to Canada, taking "such steps as after consultation, may seem most expedient."

When he had finished, a small but potentially dangerous skirmish broke out. Smith asked that the official letters of the other two ambassadors sent by Canada, Thibault and de Salaberry, be brought forward. Riel refused, but after sharp debate the assembly voted against him. O'Donoghue was sent to fetch the documents; then the meeting promptly forgot about them and they never again became an issue.

It may have been that the proceedings were already growing rather monotonous, especially with the temperature dropping to minus 25 and a biting wind coming up. Still Smith continued to read—in particular, verbose correspondence from Governor-General Sir John Young, reiterating that the queen was upset at the rebellion and that Her Majesty was willing to listen to her subjects' complaints.

Just as the meeting was closing, John Burke, an English Half-breed and one of Smith's sympathizers, yelled out, "Release the prisoners," referring to those Canadians captured at "Fort Schultz" who were still in jail.

"Not yet," Riel replied, as steadily as he could.

"Yes, yes, they must be released," yelled the Smith faction in unison.

It was a dangerous few minutes; many in that crowd would have gladly joined in if a riot had erupted right then. But Riel still had his loyal armed guard and they pushed menacingly forward. The hecklers shut their mouths and the meeting was adjourned until the next morning at ten a.m.

Smith assumed that he had won this round hands down, but in reality something else was happening. The priests—Ritchot, Lestanc and Thibault, the last the envoy Sir John A. had personally selected—were appalled at Smith's behaviour, especially his never-ending tricks of bribery. They believed he was inciting violence within the Métis community, and they set out to weaken his influence. Quietly they talked to the influential families, the Nolins and Léveillés among them, reminding them how much young Riel had already accomplished, how much they had to lose. By the next morning the atmosphere was decidedly different, but the Smith contingent probably didn't realize it.

While the weather was not quite as cold, it was still horribly uncomfortable standing outside. Yet there arrived at Fort Garry gate a wonderful parade—brightly painted horse-drawn *carioles* or sleighs pulled by teams of dogs, each wearing its own blanket artistically decorated with beadwork of flowers and a fancy, colourful harness. This day a few more Métis and Indian wives, wrapped in thick black woollen capes, came to watch the proceedings.

The meeting started at noon on a rather sour note; Judge Black, miffed over a sharp exchange he had suffered with Riel the previous day, refused to serve as secretary, but the easy-going A.G.B. Bannatyne quickly stepped in. Then the mood abruptly changed; as someone said, you could taste the good-will in the air. The Reverend Henry Cockran joined the platform group, translating from English into Cree, which greatly pleased the Indians in the crowd. John Burke apologized for his outburst the day before; demanding the prisoners' release had been "sentiments not his own, but were put to him by another party to say." Father Lestanc then stepped forward and pleaded, "We have been good friends to this day in the whole Settlement; and I want to certify here that we will be good friends tonight." The entire gathering erupted into applause.

Smith began by reading more long-winded letters and documents pleading the case for Canada. He must have sensed that he was losing the attention of the crowd—for one thing, it was growing decidedly windier by the minute—for he finally made a personal statement.

To loud applause he dissociated himself from the bumbler William McDougall; he reminded everybody that he had relatives in Red River; he admitted that, yes, he was an employee of the Hudson's Bay Company, but he would resign instantly if it would help the cause of Red River. He concluded, "I sincerely hope that my humble efforts may in some measure contribute to bring about peaceably, union and entire accord among all classes of the people of this land." Cheers followed this, but as he began reading yet another interminably long document, he probably sensed that loyalties had shifted away from him. The crowd began to realize that although nice-sounding words were flowing rapidly from Smith's mouth, he was proposing almost no concrete suggestions to solve the dilemma of Red River's entrance into Confederation.

Louis Riel, more self-confident on this day, must have detected the same thing, for he got up and proposed something that he had long desired—that a Convention of Forty be assembled of twenty elected representatives from the English population and twenty from the French. He concluded the meeting with a speech of conciliation to the people of Red River, and yet his usual defiance was there.

> I came here with fears. We are not yet enemies [loud cheers] but we came very near being so. As soon as we understood each other, we joined in demanding what our English fellow subjects in common with us believe to be our just rights [loud cheers]. I am not afraid to say our rights; for we all have rights [renewed cheers]. We claim no half rights, mind you, but all the rights we are entitled to. Those rights will be set forth by our representatives, and, what is more, gentlemen, we will get them [loud cheers].

Smith's mission, as the prime minister had written, "to make arrangements for the dispersion of the Insurgents, and the dissolution of their committee", had not succeeded; Riel was now in a position to gain control once again. As a good-will gesture, he ordered most of the Métis guards to disarm and return to their homes.

But it would not have been in keeping with Red River's long history of racial bickering and back-stabbing if the elections had gone off without incident. In the village of Winnipeg, the Americans packed the fire-engine house and elected Alfred Scott, a clerk in Henry McKenney's store, over the fur trader and mediator A.G.B. Bannatyne. Despite the efforts of Bannatyne's friends, who were outraged, claiming they hadn't known about the meeting, the decision stuck.

In the French community, a nasty battle between Louis Riel and Charles Nolin was shaping up. Despite the efforts of fathers Lestanc and Thibault to bring Nolin into line, he had remained the hub of an anti-Riel movement among the Métis. Although Riel's forces won seventeen of the twenty places— O'Donoghue, Louis Schmidt and Louis himself were all readily re-elected—the Nolin forces captured three seats. Riel was furious. He had wanted to present a solid front of French-speakers to the convention; as it was, if the twenty English delegates plus the three-man Nolin contigent managed to stick together, they could easily defeat Riel's proposals.

The convention was to convene on January 25, 1870, but was delayed a day because of a blinding snowstorm. When it finally sat at eleven the next morning, Riel was determined to be conciliatory. He proposed that Judge John Black, a man he did not like at all, be elected chairman. It was a move he would soon regret. Black was a supercilious, pompous man, adept at deploying ridicule and mockery in debate. He would treat many of Riel's ideas with contempt.

Louis Schmidt was appointed secretary for the French and William Coldwell for the English. James Ross would serve as translator from French to English, and Riel from English to French. As a first order of business, Donald Smith was asked to again read his papers of commission. Afterwards, as the meeting adjourned, the delegates shook hands and patted each other on the back. Someone noticed that the United States flag in front of O'Lone's Saloon had been lowered—a symbol, they all assumed, that the American influence was weakening.

That evening the Mactavish Fire Company gave a fancy-dress ball in Winnipeg which many of the English upper crust attended. Donald Smith was there and, as the music played on, he noticed the party-goers were not as obsequious towards him as they usually were. His popularity was on the wane and he was more than a little hurt.

At the second session of the convention, Riel was again in a conciliatory frame of mind. When it was suggested that the List of Rights that had been drawn up in December should be discarded because it hadn't been adequately debated, Louis acquiesced. He was selected to sit on a committee charged with drawing up a new Bill of Rights, along with Louis Schmidt, Charles Nolin, James Ross, Thomas Bunn and Dr. Curtis Bird.

The six hammered out the testament in just two days. It was much like the old List of Rights: bilingualism was emphasized, as was protection of the customs and lands of the long-time residents of the Northwest, but the authors also included new points—the form of democracy that would be implemented immediately and in the future, the payment for schools and bridges, the setting up of a militia.* It took four days for the Convention delegates to discuss the document point by point, but they did so calmly and rationally. When agreement was finally reached, it was suggested that Donald Smith be invited to the next day's meeting to comment. At that point the camaraderie and good-natured quipping that had so far dominated the meeting abruptly ended. Louis Riel stood up and objected to Smith's intervention at that time; he had other business he wanted to deal with before the Canadian representative was involved.

All during the week of meetings there had been a basic assumption which had moulded the deliberations—that the Red River Settlement would enter Canada as a territory. Suddenly, Riel was insisting that provincial status was necessary. He had abruptly returned to the Métis rationale for taking over Red River

---

For the complete Bill of Rights see Addendum One, page 449.

in the first place—the need for a legitimate, self-assured government, with a deep understanding of the value of its people and land, negotiating the best possible terms for its entry into the Canadian Confederation. Riel particularly wanted the control over public lands that provincial status would bring; it was, after all, the loss of their land that the Métis, quite rightly as it turned out, feared the most.

The objections from the English side were loud and vehement. Riel's old bugbear, the English Half-breed James Ross, was in fighting form, arguing that the small community simply was not ready to become a province; it would get stuck with too much responsibility and too many bills.

When the vote was finally put to the assembly, it was defeated 24 to 15 (the chair did not vote). Riel's worst fears came to pass—Nolin's supporters lined up with the English, and they were obviously prepared to do so again. Still, Louis didn't give up. Before the Bill of Rights was presented to Donald Smith, he insisted, he had another resolution he wanted the convention to consider—that the bargain struck between the Hudson's Bay Company and the dominion government for the take-over of Rupert's Land be declared null and void. The people living in the country should carry out the negotiations, he maintained, not some foreign power.

This proposal was belittled even more than the idea of provincial status. Judge Black, the supposed neutral chairman, had a field day with his sarcasm, and laughter rang out again and again during his remarks. The proposal was easily defeated, 23 to 16.

It was all too much for the young Métis leader. He began pacing up and down in the drafty courtroom, and finally could no longer restrain himself. He blurted out: "The devil take it; we must win. The vote may go as it likes; but the measure which has now been defeated must be carried. It is a shame to have lost it; and it was a greater shame because it was lost by those traitors." Riel then pointed at the Métis who had voted against him.

Nolin jumped up, indignant, furious, and yelled: "I was not sent here, Mr. Riel, to vote at your dictation. I came here to vote according to my conscience...."

Riel hesitated, trying to get his emotions under control. Then, in a calm but emphatic voice, he replied: "While I say this matter must be carried, I do not wish to speak disrespectfully to the Convention. But I say it will be carried at a subsequent stage. You must remember that there is [already] a provisional government, and though this measure has been lost by the voice of the Convention, I have friends enough, who are determined to add it to the list, on their own responsibility." And turning to the French side of the convention, he spat out, "As for you, Charles Nolin, Tom Harrison and George Klyne—two of you relatives of my own—as for you, your influence as public men is finished in this country!" And Louis Riel was quite right. Nolin, in particular, would soon be denounced by the entire Métis community.

In a show of defiance and bravado, Riel's supporters ran up a larger version of the provisional government flag.

As the recorder or judge for the Council of Assiniboia, Black was in reality an agent for the Hudson's Bay Company. His high-handed performance during the sessions of the convention, coupled with Smith's deceitful tactics in wooing the Red River Settlement, convinced the Métis that the HBC was indeed the enemy. They were positive that the Company brass were handing out jobs merely to pry support away from their side. Riel grew increasingly more resentful, and the defeat of his motions at the convention was the final straw. He placed an armed guard at the door of Governor Mactavish's residence. Since the man was near death, it seemed a particularly insensitive thing to do. Riel also harangued the chief factor and magistrate, Dr. William Cowan, who later claimed—though the Métis always denied it—that he was warned that he would be shot if within twenty minutes if he did not swear allegiance to the provisional government. He refused and was imprisoned in a small room with the Half-breed William Hallett, who had once again been captured by Métis guards.

A.G.B. Bannatyne refused to believe that Riel would give in to his wounded pride in such a bizarre manner. He marched into Louis's office and demanded to see Mactavish and Cowan. Riel not only flatly refused, but he told Bannatyne to vacate Fort Garry at once. Now it was the turn of the fur trader to whimper over his wounded pride. After all, among the English he had been the most tolerant and accommodating of the Métis cause.

That evening Bannatyne dined with Colonel de Salaberry, all the time lamenting the turn events had taken. Finally, well fortified with brandy, he declared that he was going to see Mactavish "some way or another". Making his way to Fort Garry, he scrambled up the southern wall. Just as he made it to the top, a young Métis guard spotted him and threw a stick at him. Bannatyne jumped back, but not before his precious revolver and snuffbox had dropped on the other side of the wall. He then decided to wait outside Henri Coutu's butcher shop until the Métis leader arrived for the night. Spotting Riel, Bannatyne marched in and began chiding him. Riel finally lost patience and warned the trader not to go near the fort or he would be taken prisoner.

The next morning, Bannatyne and his brother-in-law Henry McDermot decided they must at least meet with Mrs. Mactavish to comfort her. They accomplished their mission, but on their way home Riel, rushing from church, accosted them. How dare they disobey his orders, he demanded. He then had the astonished Bannatyne arrested on the spot.

It was all done in a fit of pique—Bannatyne, Cowan and Mactavish would be released in a few days—but it was an indication of how frustrated, even desperate, Riel had become. And how determined.

Riel and his advisers had decided that the traitor Charles Nolin should be imprisoned, and a posse of twelve soldiers were sent out to Ste. Anne-des-Chênes to arrest him. Two of these arrived at the Nolin residence in advance, only to discover armed vigilantes waiting for them.

The Nolin brothers were eager for a fight. The youngest, Duncan, fired at the head of one of the guards, but fortunately the pistol didn't go off. In response, the other Métis soldier levelled his carbine, but it too misfired. Violence between the two French factions had only narrowly been averted. "It was the hand of God," wrote Father Giroux. It was also a sobering experience for everyone involved. Charles Nolin must have sensed that the French community was turning against him, for from that time on he would play a much less belligerent role in the political events of Red River.

With all the Riel-inspired manhandling going on, the English delegates considered not returning to the next convention session, scheduled for February 7, but after a meeting at Dr. Bird's house the more reasonable among them prevailed and they decided to continue.

The session turned into the last great sparring match between Louis Riel and Donald Smith. The Métis leader was sure Smith did not have the power to guarantee Canadian acceptance of the Bill of Rights and he was determined to make the other delegates aware of this inadequacy. Riel was not satisfied, he said, "with what Mr. Smith thinks but what he can guarantee.... I want some certainty and not merely an expression of opinion on what we desire. We are now in a position to make demands. How far is the Commissioner in a position to guarantee them?"

Smith parried Riel's bull's-eye thrusts as best he could, but in the end the Métis leader emerged the clear winner. It became all too obvious that the Canadian commissioner, although he agreed that almost every demand was reasonable, had little power to decide anything of importance on behalf of the Canadian government. Finally, in desperation, Smith suggested that the assembly appoint their own negotiators to deal with Sir John A. and his administration. That was exactly what Riel had been hoping for all along.

But the Métis leader was set on yet another victory. He would reopen the tricky question of provisional government. To whom would their negotiators be responsible if a governing body was not in place to accredit them? And just as important, who would govern the Red River Settlement while the deal with Canada was being hammered out? His logic seemed irrefutable, but several English delegates hung back, afraid of such a revolutionary step. The debate, although not acrimonious, dragged on for two more days. Finally, to break the deadlock, it was suggested that a formal delegation of two English and two French be sent to ask the ailing governor what he thought.

Pale and terribly weak from his illness, despondent over the turmoil in Red River, Mactavish partially sat up in his sickbed and managed to growl, "Form a government, for God's sake, and restore peace and order in the Settlement."

His few words were all that was needed to unite the Red River Settlement behind Riel's proposal. Yet another committee was set up, to draft a constitution, and on February 10 its recommendations were submitted to the Convention. What it suggested was an elected council of twenty-four, twelve English and twelve French, and an executive made up of a president, English and French secretaries and a treasurer.

The Métis representatives were determined that no one but Riel would be considered for the presidency. When some of the English began making other noises—some insisted they would have to go back and consult their constituents—it was Louis who came to his own defence. If the English wouldn't act to establish the government with him as the head, the French were willing to go it alone, he warned. Then, in a passionate outburst, he exclaimed, "On my life I will say so, if the prejudices of your people are to prevail, they may do so, but it will be in my blood!" It was as though his father was egging him on from the grave, reminding him of the years of struggling against English bigotry, English dominance.

When the motion accepting the provisional government with Riel as president was finally put to the convention, not one dissenting voice was heard. Three people did abstain, however, including the arrogant Judge Black.

It was ten p.m. by the time the vote was taken, a windy, snowy night—which didn't matter one bit. The moment the convention's success was made public, people streamed into the streets of Winnipeg, cannon boomed from Fort Garry, delighted Métis guards shot their firearms into the heavens. And then a miracle—high in the sky a magnificent display of fireworks magically unfolded. It was a wonderful spectacle, and a delicious irony—for these were the very same explosives which John Schultz had collected to celebrate William McDougall's grand entry into the Red River Settlement. Louis Schmidt would later write, "That was one of the rare good moments that we enjoyed in the Fort."

Meanwhile an all-night drunk got under way in Winnipeg. Revellers hooted and sang the hours away, as they circled from O'Lone's saloon to Dutch George's Hotel to Monchamps's Public House. Louis Riel was not among them; he loathed such debauches. He would mark the occasion in his own, quiet way.

Immediately after the convention deliberations ended, he kept a promise and released Governor Mactavish, Dr. Cowan and A.G.B. Bannatyne from prison. So overjoyed was he with the turn of events that the good-natured Bannatyne quickly forgave the Métis leader. Indeed, the two men celebrated the provisional government together at midnight, sharing a "good horn of brandy".

But the euphoria would soon vanish. Dark clouds were once again massing on Red River's horizon.

On February 12, two days after the official establishment of the provisional government, *le président* undertook to carry out one of the important promises he had made. He arranged to release the thirty-six prisoners, mostly Canadians, still languishing in the Fort Garry jail. With almost the entire Red River community now supporting his administration, Riel saw no danger in the release of a few loudmouths. Still, he required them all to sign an oath not to attempt a *coup d'état.* The process was rather slow because several of the prisoners refused to sign the pledge; they mistakenly thought they would be required to take up arms for the provisional government if circumstances warranted it, and they obviously didn't understand how representative of Red River Riel's administration now was. But by the end of the day, sixteen had signed the oath and had been released.

There's no question that the others would have been released the next day if Riel hadn't heard some startling news—a gang of armed Canadians led by Major Charles Boulton was marching to attack Fort Garry.

When, five weeks before, Charlie Mair and Thomas Scott had eluded their Métis guards and escaped from the courthouse prison, they had hurried to the English community of Portage la Prairie, some sixty miles west of Fort Garry. It was fast becoming a Canadian enclave. The Reverend Cochran had established a mission there in 1851 and since it was situated on the vast and fertile Portage plains, it had since attracted ambitious farmers, mostly from Upper Canada.

Two years before, one Thomas Spence had led a separatist movement attempting to secede from Hudson's Bay Company rule. A petition had been sent to the queen pleading for the formation of the "Republic of Manitobah" with a democratically elected government. Nothing much had come of it, but Portage la Prairie remained a hotbed of dissidence. It was here that most of the workers on Snow's road gang and Dennis's surveying team had gone to spend the winter.

The community's leading light was Major Charles Arkoll Boulton, who had come to Red River the year before as second in command on the surveying team. Son of a lawyer and militia officer, Charles Boulton had been educated at

Upper Canada College and through his family had strong connections to the military and political elite of Upper Canada. At age sixteen, he had donned a too-large army uniform provided by a retired officer, borrowed his father's horse and wagon and persuaded a friend to play the bagpipes. Thus equipped, he had paraded through little towns around Peterborough, eventually recruiting some twenty young men, which was all that was needed to obtain his commission in the British Army's 100th Regiment.

After ten years of service in Europe and Africa, during which he saw not one day of actual combat, he sold his commission and was subsequently named a major in the 46th Battalion of Militia in Ontario. His was not a wealthy family, however, and in 1869 he decided he'd head west to make his fortune.

Boulton, now aged twenty-eight, had been embroiled in the intrigues of the Canadians from the moment he arrived at Red River in July of 1869. His way of seeing things was identical to theirs: that those of British origin were far superior to everyone else was as natural a philosophy for him as breathing.

He was one of those who had helped plaster McDougall's phony royal declaration all over Winnipeg; he had made the rounds of the parishes trying to drum up recruits for Dennis's ill-fated venture; and he had organized those would-be insurgents who had holed up in Schultz's store waiting for Dennis to attack the French at Fort Garry.

Once Charlie Mair arrived in Portage la Prairie, he set out to persuade Boulton to raise another force; after all, the major had many years of experience in the military, didn't he? Canadians languishing in the Fort Garry jail simply had to be freed, Mair said; it was up to Major Boulton to do his duty.

Of all of Riel's opponents, Boulton was the one who wore a sheen of respectability—so much so that he began to win converts among the English-speaking settlers. Thomas Scott was there, as well, to incite their imaginations with tales of his gruesome imprisonment and his brave escape—most of which were totally untrue. Riel was certainly alarmed at Boulton's influence, and this was one reason why he had begun, as soon as he thought it safe, to make the goodwill gesture of releasing the Canadians still in prison.

Major Boulton was cautious about the wild schemes being hatched by the hotheads in his midst, but unbeknownst to him a band of Canadians, stirred up by the rash Thomas Scott and Charlie Mair, were secretly meeting each night. On February 9, they announced that they were ready to march on Fort Garry and free the prisoners. Whether their commander would join them was up to him.

Boulton realized that his was a ragtag army of about sixty—most were farmers with no military training, many were armed only with oak clubs, and no supplies of food, ammunition or fuel had been laid in. In his memoirs* he claims that he pleaded with the likes of Mair and Scott to give up their hare-brained schemes but they wouldn't listen to him—"when I discovered they were determined to go, I felt it my duty to accompany them, and endeavour to keep them to the legitimate object for which they had organized," he later recounted. The plan was to reach Fort Garry at daybreak, when, they reasoned, there'd be few guards about and in no time they could scale the walls of the fort and free the prisoners.

After a "good, hefty dinner" on February 10, the men left Portage la Prairie at six p.m. and "marched merrily along the frozen snow for about six hours without rest" until they reached Headingley, about fifteen miles from Winnipeg. By this time Boulton had cheered up. More men had joined them at Poplar Point and High Bluff, so that now they numbered over a hundred. They were preparing to continue their march towards Fort Garry when a blizzard descended on the Red River Valley. Boulton and his men were stuck for forty-eight hours.

They were billeted in the homes of some settlers and at the Anglican church, where the Reverend J. Carrie greatly encouraged them in their plans for attack. The two Headingley delegates to the convention tried to talk them out of their mad-hatter's scheme, but men like Mair and Scott cared not a fig if the convention was a democratically elected body and the provisional government a result of its deliberations. The very idea that a "depraved half-breed" had been named president was anathema to them. They would proceed, no matter what the consequences.

As soon as the storm eased a little, an influential Half-breed settler, William Gaddy, was sent to William Dease with a message to root out any anti-Riel Métis who might support them. John Taylor was dispatched to John Schultz, for of course the doctor would play an important role in any uprising against Riel and the Métis.

Schultz had not been among the group of Canadians who had made their escape on the cold night of January 9. He hadn't even been in the courthouse jail. Because he was considered enemy number one by the Métis, he had been detained inside Fort Garry's walls, in a large two-storey building. Despite what he would later claim, Schultz's imprisonment had not been an entirely grim experience. His wife, Anne, was allowed to visit him every day, bringing newspapers and books, freshly washed underwear and full-course meals of roast beef and apple brown betty. In fact, it was in his favourite pudding that she hid the penknife he asked for.

---

* Boulton's Reminiscences of the North-West Rebellions, *published in 1886, is a self-serving memoir full of half-truths and ridiculous interpretations. It has been used by many historians as a legitimate account of the Red River Rebellion.*

Whenever his guards weren't looking, Schultz would work away at cutting his buffalo robe into long strips, the shaggy hair hiding his handiwork when necessary. He conscientiously braided the strips into a heavy rope and then asked Anne to deliver one more pudding, this time with a small gimlet tucked inside.

On the frosty night of January 23, Schultz was finally ready to make his getaway. He screwed the gimlet into the window sash, tied the buffalo-skin braid to it and using it as a rope, he clambered out the window. Hand over hand, he carefully began his descent down the side of the building. Then the gimlet pulled loose, and suddenly Schultz, all six foot four, 250 pounds of him, tumbled two storeys to a snowbank below. He didn't break his leg but he badly twisted it, so much so that he would thereafter walk with a limp.

His injured limb dragging behind him, he hobbled to the walls of Fort Garry. Fortunately for him, it was so cold and so late at night that there were few sentries about. Finding some boxes piled against the wall, Schultz managed after several tries to drag himself up on them and then climb over.

The temperature had dropped to minus 25 and he was dressed only in a light topcoat, but the big man staggered on, nearly blinded by the snowdrifts, his feet frost-bitten. Finally he reached Kildonan, and only managed to pound on the door of Robert MacBeth before he collapsed.

MacBeth had no great love of Schultz—he had sat on the Council of Assiniboia when the doctor was daily ranting against it and the HBC in the pages of the *Nor'Wester*—but he also knew he couldn't turn his back on this pathetic apparition, "thinly clad, tall, haggard and gaunt," which had fallen into his arms. For two days, he hid Schultz in his attic.

Riel and Lépine had been furious that the man they despised so much, the man they blamed for the entire Red River turmoil, should escape. The tongue-lashing the Métis guards suffered that day would leave emotional scars for a long time to come. They were ordered, no matter what the weather, to comb the Red River Valley, and when they found Schultz they were to shoot him dead. For days they searched the homes and business establishments of the doctor's friends and associates, but they neglected MacBeth's house, perhaps because he was considered an ally.

MacBeth secretly arranged transportation for the injured doctor, and two days later he was taken by sled to the Stone Fort. As soon as he was able, Schultz moved into a house in the English parish of St. Andrew, north of Fort Garry on the east side of the Red River. And it was there that he began to assemble his troops—some Sioux, the Saulteaux of St. Paul's and the English Half-breeds of St. Andrew's. Because their long-time enemies, the Sioux, were involved, Riel and his Métis considered Schultz's army more of a threat than Boulton's.

It was all part of a planned three-pronged attack: the Portage party was to move on Fort Garry from the west, Schultz was to sneak down from the north and Dease, who would command only a small group of anti-Riel Métis, was to march from the south. The strategy called for Dease's men to surround the homes and then threaten the wives and children in nearby French parishes. This would surely lure the Métis soldiers from Fort Garry, they determined.

The plan collapsed when the messenger to Dease, William Gaddy, and five others in his party were captured by Riel's soldiers in Dease's home at Pointe Coupée. Gaddy was almost executed on the spot by the enraged guards, but Lépine stepped in and ordered him brought to Fort Garry as a prisoner. Dease himself escaped through the back window of his house.

On the night of February 14, Major Boulton's flock resumed their march east and south; fortunately for them, although it was cold, it was a clear, moonlit night. They planned to reach Winnipeg the next morning.

The Métis surveillance network had been reporting details of the march to Riel and his adjutant-general, Lépine. The Métis soldiers, who only a few days previously had finally been able to return to their homes, rearmed themselves and regrouped, although Riel kept reassuring everyone that this was purely an army of defence—no aggression would be tolerated. Still, all of Winnipeg was terrified. There was little activity on the streets, shops remained shuttered, even O'Lone's bar was remarkably quiet.

Some of the Portage la Prairie contingent were walking, others travelled by sleigh mounted with long ladders with which to scale the walls of Fort Garry.

From the fort's turrets Métis soldiers were watching their every move. Riel had great difficulty in restraining his men that night; they desperately wanted to attack but he knew the Canadians, chilled to the bone, and poorly armed, could hardly defend themselves. A Métis assault would mean a massacre. The Canadians were unaware of all this, and they wasted no time in going after the Métis leader. While he was at Fort Garry curbing his soldiers' aggression, Scott and Boulton broke into Henri Coutu's place and, in their mad search for Riel, ransacked it. Scott boasted loudly that when the "Métis scoundrel" was finally found, he himself would gladly shoot him.

Although they were now very close to Fort Garry, the Canadians planned not to attack right away, but to first march to Kildonan and team up with Schultz's contingent.

Schultz had been delighted when news of the offensive came. At last he and his men, now numbering about three hundred, would see action. They had uncovered an old cannon from the Stone Fort with which they planned to smash the walls of Fort Garry—never mind that thirteen heavier weapons would be looking down on them from the turrets. As they marched along, their pathetic cannon hauled by four oxen, they sang out in the crisp winter air:

> Hey, Riel, are ye waking yet,
> Or are your drums a-beating yet,
> If ye're nae waking, we'll nae wait,
> For we'll take the fort this morning.

Even their bravado could not hide the reality of their situation: they were poorly armed, most didn't have horses, many weren't even dressed properly and they hadn't had enough to eat for days. They were hardly a match for the six-hundred-strong, well-disciplined Métis army, each soldier mounted, each a crack shot and each with plenty of ammunition.

The forces of Schultz and Boulton finally met at Middle Church, in the parish of St. Paul's north of Fort Garry, and continued to Kildonan. There the schoolhouse was made their military centre of operation; the Union Jack was hoisted up the flagpole. The soldiers were billeted in private homes and in the Presbyterian church of Reverend Black. But the old Selkirk settlers realized what a foolhardy, potentially tragic drama was about to unfold, and many tried to talk the rash Canadians into laying down their arms. Most of Riel's prisoners had already been released, and the others would follow in a matter of hours, they pointed out. Still, the debate raged, with Thomas Scott calling anyone who wanted to give up "bloody cowards". It was inevitable that tragedy would strike.

Norbert Parisien was a mentally handicapped Métis in his early fifties who made a little money every day splitting firewood for the residents of Winnipeg. He was simple-minded, rather silly and easily influenced. The Métis believed that the Canadians had co-opted him and that he was spying on their behalf.

On February 15, he was on his way home when he decided he'd see what was going on in the village of Kildonan. The Canadians arrested him because—a sad irony for Parisien—they too believed he was a spy, but, of course, on behalf of the French. He was imprisoned in the schoolhouse. The next morning at about ten o'clock, on his way back from the outhouse, he escaped and, stealing a double-barrelled rifle from a sleigh, ran to the riverbank to hide among the trees.

John Sutherland, a prominent Scottish settler, had just returned to his farm across the river from Kildonan. He had been at Fort Garry during the previous two days, as part of a citizens' group which had successfully pressured Riel into releasing the remaining prisoners. Now safely at his home, Sutherland was anxious to inform the insurgents of the progress made, and told his son, Hugh, "Ride as fast as you can across the river to Major Boulton and Dr. Schultz, and tell them that all the prisoners are to be set free!" Young Sutherland was galloping across the frozen Red River when he suddenly encountered the badly frightened fugitive running towards him. Norbert Parisien believed Sutherland was one of the Canadian guards chasing him. He raised his rifle and fired, and a bullet lodged in Hugh's wrist. The young man was just falling from his horse when the Métis fired again. This time Sutherland was struck in the chest.

Meanwhile, Parisien's pursuers had arrived on the scene. Two of them carried Sutherland to Reverend Black's house nearby, where Schultz and another doctor would treat him. The others went after the Métis. Thomas Scott was particularly vicious; he struck Parisien on the head with an axe. The others joined in beating him again and again, venting their hatred of the French, the Catholics, the Half-breeds. Parisien's own l'Assomption sash was tied around his neck and he was dragged over the ice, a river of blood snaking behind. Finally, Reverend Black and Major Boulton came to the riverbank and ordered Scott and the others to desist.

The next morning, February 17, twenty-one-year-old Hugh Sutherland died, but not before he had begged that Norbert Parisien not be punished. "The poor simple fellow was too frightened to know what he was doing," he pleaded. A month and a half later, the Métis himself would succumb to his wounds.

These, the first fatalities of the Red River Rebellion, were entirely the fault of the reckless Canadians. Sadly, as the debate over Louis Riel and his "rough" justice has raged for over a century, the tragedy of the young Scot and the mentally handicapped Métis has been mostly forgotten.

It did have a sobering influence in Kildonan; Charlie Mair would write that "a panic began." Young Sutherland's mother and other women were "crying and beseeching the men from the lower parishes to separate or they would all be murdered, kneeling and clasping them around their legs and imploring, and they and the clergy urging Boulton and his men from Portage not to start a civil war." Then word arrived from the president himself.

During the day Riel had received word of the death of Sutherland. Louis was horrified; he was not much older than Hugh and had known him in his younger years.

Other upsetting news arrived shortly after—the English parishes would no longer recognize his provisional government. Riel could see all his accomplishments collapsing. He immediately sent a plea to the Canadians at Kildonan. The English is awkward, but it was likely written in great haste.

Fellow Countrymen,

Mr. Norquay came this morning with a message & even [though] he has been delayed he will reach you time enough to tell you that for my part I understand that war, horrible civil war, is the destruction of this country. And Schultz will laugh at us all if after all he escapes. We are ready to meet any party. But peace our British rights we want before all. Gentlemen, the prisoners are out, they have sworn to keep peace. We have taken the responsibility of our past acts. Mr. William McTavish [*sic*] has asked you for the sake of God to form and complete the provisional government. Your representatives have joined us on that ground. Who will now come and destroy the Red River Settlement?

I am your humble,

poor, fair & confident

public servant

L. Riel

The half-conciliatory, half-threatening message was all that was needed. Most of the Canadians decided to go home. But how to do so without looking like dogs with their tails between their legs? One of their number, Michael Power, insisted, "We had come down like brave men and we should go back like brave men, in a body."

Boulton claimed he tried to discourage this but somehow he didn't order them disbanded, somehow he ended up leading a contingent of forty-eight armed men who were intent on passing right in front of Fort Garry. How they expected the Métis guards to react is hard to imagine. Hourly reports had been arriving that more and more armed insurgents were collecting at Kildonan. Riel had been warned that he was a target for assassination. He and his men were in a state of panic. The *New Nation* reported the scene at Fort Garry thus:

> Men were gathering in hot haste. Cannons mounted, grape and cannister laid in order. Five hundred men and more, we are informed, were told off to man the bastions, ramparts, etc. Shot and shell were piled around promiscuously. Everything that could be done, was done to make a bold stand to strike terror into the hearts of les anglais.*

One hundred armed soldiers were sent to guard St. Boniface Cathedral; it was felt that the heavily treed banks of the Red and Seine rivers would provide perfect cover for the attackers.

In Winnipeg, O'Donoghue and several Métis soldiers searched the shops for weapons and ammunition; all available horses were rounded up. Bannatyne refused to hand over the key to his storehouse, but the door was torn down "and such a clean sweep made of its contents that not a solitary keg was left to the disgusted proprietor."

At eleven o'clock on the morning of February 18, a column of armed men were spotted by the Métis patrol approaching Fort Garry; they were struggling along in single file, following in each other's footsteps through the waist-deep snow. Lépine

---

* *Neither side liked the the* New Nation*'s coverage of events—Riel had the February 18 issue confiscated—which probably indicates it was a fairly accurate account.*

and O'Donoghue, surrounded by Métis cavalry, galloped out the north gate and plunged through the snowdrifts towards the now dead-still Canadians.

The citizens of Winnipeg expected a shoot-out; as Begg wrote, "People in town crowded every available spot overlooking the prairies. Faces thronged windows. Wood piles and fences were crowded with sight-seekers, all expecting to behold a miniature battle." They were disappointed. Boulton had given orders that no one, "on no account", was to fire. Whether because they were obeying their commander, or because they knew they were vastly out-gunned, the Canadians simply gave up. Protesting their innocence, claiming aggression was the last thing on their minds, they were led away to Fort Garry. Only days after they had been emptied, the jail cells were full again.

The Canadians always claimed that a message had been received from Riel promising them safe passage; the capture of his men, Boulton would write, "was to strike terror in the hearts of the people, and to more firmly fix himself as the autocrat of the country." But the memoirs of the English Half-breed George William Sanderson, who was part of Boulton's group, say something different, and with their lack of boasting they have a ring of authenticity about them:

> Riel had sent word that we should follow the road and if we had any arms we should keep them to ourselves and not make any show of them. There is no doubt everything would have been alright had we followed the road as we were bid.
>
> When we got to the place near Fort Garry where the road made a detour we halted for awhile and had a council. Some of the men from eastern Canada wanted to show off and defy Riel's orders. They wanted to go straight across the forbidden ground....
>
> The young fellow named [Thomas] Scott swore and said we were a bunch of cowards. At that the Pochas, father and sons took offence, Suza was going to slap him but the old [man] stopped him and said, "let him alone and perhaps he will yet find out that the little French ... are not afraid of him, come captain, we will pass by the fort,["] off we started again I will not say we marched, we were all walking any way we could, the snow was deep.

As they approached the fort, a dozen men on horseback shot out of the gate "like arrows" and rode towards them. Old Mr. Pocha walked up to one of the Métis and said in French, "Good day, what do you want?" The man answered, "Our leader, Louis Riel, and his officers wish you all to come into the fort and have dinner with them."

The Canadians found this suggestion, as Sanderson put it, "very acceptable, we wouldn't dream of refusing such an invitation as we had not had too much to eat since we left home."

They were all ushered into the fort and kept prisoners for more than a month.

Some of the Métis soldiers may have been in a mood to joke a little with the prisoners, but Riel and his military council were not. They had run out of patience. Five of the ringleaders, Major Boulton, Thomas Scott, Murdoch McLeod, George Parker and John Taylor—the only delegate to the convention who had turned against Riel—were sentenced by tribunal to be shot at midnight.

In a farmhouse near Kildonan, the mother of young Hugh, who had died the day before, had been overcome by grief. When news came of the impending executions, the stricken woman managed to get out of her bed and, with the help of her husband, travel to Fort Garry. She met Riel in the council chambers. "There's been too much bloodshed already," she pleaded. "There must not be any more."

"Those men are guilty of the death of your son, a man born of the soil of this country," Louis responded. "They must pay for their crimes." But it would not have been in character for Riel to ignore the woman's pleas—his family and the Sutherlands had been friends for years; Mrs. Sutherland had been particularly fond of Louis when he was a boy. He agreed that the death sentence of three of the condemned men would be lifted, but Boulton, who was the leader and therefore responsible, must suffer. "Indians have been raised and the homes of our men threatened," he reminded her. He did, however, give the major a reprieve until noon the next day.

When Boulton was informed of Riel's decision, he called for a basin of water and a towel with which to wash his face and hands. Then he asked for a glass of wine to warm him, lest his shivering in the cold of the execution grounds be mistaken for cowardice.

Over the next hours, a steady flow of supplicants appeared at Riel's door, but Louis remained firm: Boulton must die at noon the next day.

But the whole thing was probably a charade. There's evidence that Riel, who hated bloodshed of any kind, had no intention of having Boulton shot. He was using the threat of execution to coerce the English into participating in the provincial government. All he needed was for Donald Smith, the heavy-handed Canadian commissioner, to bow in.

In his self-serving report, Donald Smith credits his powers of persuasion with changing Riel's mind about Boulton's execution. In reality, Louis was using Smith as a pawn. After playing with him for twenty or so minutes, Riel said he would save Boulton's life; all Smith had to do was mount a campaign to pressure the English into joining the provisional government. The Canadian commissioner agreed. Over the next days, he travelled in the frigid weather from one parish to another, holding public meetings, reassuring the English-speakers. Slowly they fell into line—by February 21, St. Andrew, St. John, St. Paul and St. James had all elected representatives to the provisional government. By February 26 all the English- and French-speaking parishes had done the same thing.

But events had not turned entirely in Riel's favour. Riel's two worst enemies, Charlie Mair and John Schultz, were still at large. Métis scouts by the dozens were patrolling the Red River Valley with strict orders that John Schultz was to be shot on sight. For days they travelled the trails, the blankets of their horses spots of bloody red on the vast white prairie. But it was to no avail. Both men had disappeared, seemingly into thin air.

After the Canadian troops had decided to disband at Kildonan, Mair had been smart enough not to follow Boulton and company as they made their way towards Fort Garry. Charlie had fled to Portage la Prairie, arriving on February 17. Word quickly got back that he was a marked man. On February 22, leaving Eliza, his wife, with friends, he bundled himself into a dogsled and took off with John J. Setter, a long-time settler, and two Half-breed guides.

Meanwhile, John Schultz had fled east, accompanied by his trusty guide, the Scottish Half-breed Joseph Monkman and a young friend, G.D. McVicar. When Schultz's party crossed Lake Winnipeg it was 30 below; by the time they got to Duluth, Minnesota, twenty-four days later, they had "travelled through Hell". Schultz's health was permanently damaged.

By separate routes, both Schultz and Mair endured the long, torturous journey to the United States, suffering fierce blizzards, snow-blindness, and near starvation. But both made it, and on a warm afternoon in early April, on a street corner in St. Paul, the two men ran into each other. They were overjoyed. Before travelling back to eastern Canada, they would have an opportunity to plot revenge, for their experiences had made them more determined than ever to overthrow the Métis-inspired provisional government.

On February 24, several Grey Nun sisters (likely including Sara Riel) and fathers Ritchot and Lestanc were seen entering Henri Coutu's house. Julie Riel also arrived, a suitcase in hand. Word quickly spread that Louis was suffering from a severe case of what was called "brain fever". It may have been a bad case of flu; it took only three days of his mother's nursing for him to be well enough to walk around a little and perform some duties of state. Or, given the anxiety of those close to him, it may have been more serious, a form of mental breakdown. After all, he had been under incredible strain for months. The escape of two such mortal enemies as Schultz and Mair may have been the last straw. Riel, with his political savvy, could foresee the damage the two men could do to his cause in the East. If this was the case, he was remarkably prescient.

– 8 –

My dealings with Canada
Have always been righteous
Honesty
Was my guide: my signature sealed the pact.
I hoped it would be respected.
Now it's abrogated, a free-for-all.
Nothing left but a scrawl.

It wasn't long before Charlie Mair and John Schultz were handed the ammunition they needed to mobilize their forces of revenge.

Among the forty-eight men who had been rounded up with Major Boulton and imprisoned at Fort Garry was the obnoxious Thomas Scott. The Métis despised him; he was the quintessential Orangeman, and he was foul-mouthed, bigoted and outrageously abusive in his never-ending heckling of the "damned depraved half-breed".

His background naturally led him to form such opinions. Born in 1842 in Clandeboye, County Down, of tenant farmers on Lord Dufferin's vast estate, he quickly acquired a deep-seated hatred and contempt for the Catholics of Southern Ireland. In about 1863, he immigrated to Canada, settling in Hastings County, not far from where McDougall and Mair hailed from, and quickly joined the militia.

From the moment he arrived in Red River in 1868, he had been a trouble-maker. Six-foot-two, he was a thin, wiry, strong young man, with a violent temper and a penchant for using his fists at the slightest provocation. It was he who had led the strike of the Dawson Road crew gang and had almost drowned his boss, John Snow. He had been found guilty of assault, fined and fired from his job. After that he had wandered around Winnipeg, working as a labourer and bartender. An unrelenting boozer—one of his acquaintances said he somehow was able to stay "half-drunk" even while in jail—he ended up in one brawl after another. Soon he was serving as a henchman for John Schultz, whom he admired as much as his real hero, the "Iron Duke" of Wellington.

The Irishman became deeply embroiled in the intrigues of the Canadian party. Among those who holed up at "Fort Schultz", he was one of the two men who attempted to make a break for it, only to be arrested and imprisoned by Métis guards. It was thought at the time that he was the chief player in a plot to assassinate Riel. He certainly had a deep, almost psychotic hatred of the Métis leader, perhaps because Louis did not conform to Scott's stereotype of a Half-breed as stupid, dirty and duplicitous. Once, on the streets of Winnipeg, he had accosted Riel, hurling racial slurs at him. Only the intervention of Métis guards had prevented the drunken Irishman from assaulting their leader.

After escaping from prison on January 9, 1870, and fleeing to Portage la Prairie, he was among the most eager soldiers of Boulton's army and certainly one of the most violent. It was Scott who whacked Norbert Parisien on the head with an axe after Hugh Sutherland's tragic shooting, and who beat the simple-minded Métis so viciously that he died from his wounds weeks later.

The members of Boulton's army who had been arrested were all locked in one big room in the clerk's mess within Fort Garry. George William Sanderson recalled that he and the others were not treated so badly; their rations were the same as their guards', except that the Métis got a little sugar in their tea. The one thing that was truly annoying about their imprisonment was the conduct of one of their own—Thomas Scott. "We would have been quite comfortable had it not been for that man Scott making such a racket, he would kick the board partition, yell and curse and was most impudent to the guard."

Sanderson claimed that "Scott was so obnoxious and made so much trouble that some of our men asked the guard to have him removed." Scott's only weapon against his captors was the obscene insults, full of racist hatred, that he let fly night and day.* He would have each and every one of them hanged as soon as he was free, he often threatened. Henri Woodington, another of Boulton's men, recorded in his diary that Scott was "very violent and abusive in his actions and language, annoying

---

* *In his account of events, the Reverend George Young, a Methodist minister, claimed that Scott had diarrhea and that the Métis guards were slow in serving his needs, but to verbally abuse someone with racial attacks seems an odd way to seek help.*

and insulting the guards and even abusing the President. He vowed that if ever he got out he would shoot the President."

On March 1, Scott and Murdoch McLeod forced the door of their cell and jumped two guards, shouting that the other prisoners should do the same. Other Métis quickly arrived, strong-arming the two men into submission. But this outrage by Scott was the last straw. The guards dragged the big man, cursing and screaming, into the courtyard, and were just starting to beat him when a member of the provisional government heard the noise and intervened. Scott's brush with death—the soldiers were so enraged that that's what their beating probably would have led to—didn't improve his conduct one iota. He continued his fanatical, and rather ridiculous, ranting.

The guards remained resentful and bitter about the endless abuse they suffered from Scott's tongue and Louis Riel decided that he had better talk to the man. Sanderson was listening through a peephole in the wall and he remembered the encounter this way:

> When Riel came in, Scott says, "Where are my papers?" Riel answered, "I do not know anything about your papers, what sort of papers did you have?" Scott then cursed, "You God damn son of a bitch, I will have my papers in spite of you." He was awfully mad. Riel answered, very quietly, "That's no way to speak to a human being, a man like you coming from a civilized part of the country should know better than use such language, you will all get your papers and letters back before you leave here."

Paul Proulx, a member of Riel's council, adds another dimension to the incident illustrating how Louis tried to avoid the penalty of death:

> The Métis said to Riel that if Scott was not executed, they would shoot him. Riel went to warn Scott, who sneeringly said: "The Métis are a pack of cowards. They will never dare shoot me." Then Riel asked him again, "Ask me anything at all for a punishment." "I want nothing," Scott retorted, "you are nothing but cowards."

Finally everyone's patience was exhausted. On March 3, Thomas Scott was court-martialled for treason.

The trial took place in Fort Garry council chambers in the early evening. The adjutant-general, Ambroise Lépine, was the presiding officer; the others, appointed by Riel, were Janvier Ritchot, the big man who months before had clamped his foot on the surveyor's chain; André Nault, a relative of the Riel family; Joseph Delorme; Elzéar Lagimodière, Riel's cousin; Elzéar Goulet; and Baptiste Lépine. The clerk of the court who would take the oath from each witness was Joseph Nolin, who years before had been selected by Bishop Taché to attend school in Quebec along with Riel and Louis Schmidt but whose parents had forbidden him to go.

In the preliminary stages, Thomas Scott was not present. Several witnesses were called to testify. Under oath, they told how Scott had rebelled against the provisional government, how he had assaulted the Métis leader, how he had attacked a captain of the guard, how, while searching Henri Coutu's butcher shop, he had threatened to kill Riel. Louis himself gave evidence regarding these events, but he also pleaded with the military tribunal to show mercy to the prisoner. At that point Scott was brought into the courtroom.

Joseph Nolin was asked to read the charges against the prisoner, but he excused himself, saying he could not properly make out his notes. Riel then stepped in and in clear English explained the proceedings to Scott. It is not known whether the accused was allowed to call his own witnesses or question those of the prosecution. Finally, Janvier Ritchot moved that the death sentence be invoked. André Nault seconded the motion and both Goulet and Delorme backed him. Baptiste Lépine was opposed to so drastic a punishment, and Elzéar Lagimodière thought exiling him from "the country" would be sufficient. The judge, Ambroise Lépine, ruled that since the vote was four to two, the accused must face a firing squad. Scott, not understanding a word, looked desperately from one speaker to another. Finally, Riel, who had not had a vote, translated the decision and the prisoner was led back to his cell in chains.

All through the night and during the next morning the English-speaking community tried to save Thomas Scott's life. The Methodist minister called in by Riel to minister to the condemned pleaded with the Métis leader. So did Donald Smith and Father Lestanc. If Riel could be humane in the case of Boulton, the man in command of the insurrection and therefore responsible for it, surely *le Président* could forgive this rather impetuous and stupid foot soldier. But it was all to no avail. This time, under great pressure from the Métis guards, Riel would not relent.

At noon on March 4, Goulet and Nault went to Scott's cell to escort him to the courtyard of Fort Garry. Permission was given for the condemned man to bid goodbye to the other prisoners. He did so, and with the Reverend George Young whispered a short prayer. A piece of white cloth was tied around his eyes, and then he was led away, the minister placing his arm around Scott's shoulders to keep him from stumbling. "This is horrible. This is cold-blooded murder!" Scott suddenly sobbed, as if the awful truth of his predicament had finally dawned on him. The Métis too may have had second thoughts at that moment, but O'Donoghue, who was standing nearby, only said, "It is very far gone."

Scott knelt on the snowy ground. Rifles were raised. André Nault gave the signal—a handkerchief dropped from one hand to another. All six executioners fired, but only two or three bullets—the number is in dispute—struck Scott. He sank to the ground in a pool of his own blood, but he was still alive, and the spectators heard a ghastly moan. François Guillemette then stepped forward with a revolver and, with a bullet to the head, put the man out of his misery.

Riel had stood among his people, watching the ghastly proceedings. When it was over, he barked that the crowd should disperse. Then he ordered that Thomas Scott's body be placed in a rough wooden casket. Reverend Young pleaded with the Métis leader to hand it over for burial in the Presbyterian cemetery. Riel refused, believing quite rightly that the grave would become a shrine for Orangemen worshipping their first real martyr in Canada. Scott's body then seems to have disappeared.*

In his memoirs, George William Sanderson has an interesting interpretation of Scott's death. He and the other forty-six prisoners felt bad about it, but, as Sanderson put it, "There is no doubt that he [Scott] would have been spared and let out when we were, had he behaved himself."

Almost every historian over the years has condemned the execution of Thomas Scott as being without any legal foundation, a summary, vicious act. But the Métis and Riel believed the government was a legitimate one, invested with the power to mete out justice and impose the death penalty if need be. As far as they were concerned, they had carried on a trial in a proper fashion with sworn statements by witnesses and deliberation by senior members of the Métis community. The American consul who had replaced Malmros, James Taylor, understood the rationale. He wrote: "There is much evidence that Riel firmly believed the execution necessary not only to prevent bloodshed within the walls of the prison itself but to check further attempts at insurrection with the possible contingency of an Indian war. 'I take a life to save lives,' was his reply to an appeal for mercy."

Perhaps Louis's brother Joseph, in a letter dated May 9, 1887, to the

---

* *For years incredible rumours circulated about Scott's fate. Some claimed he had not died before the firing squad, but had been buried alive in his coffin. Others insisted his body had been hacked to pieces by the "savage half-breed". The Métis have their own myths, the most prominent being that Scott was not killed at all, but allowed to escape to the United States, never to be heard from again. The most colourful, and the one that probably comes closest to the truth, is that Elzéar Lagimodière and Elzéar Goulet dressed the body in a Métis outfit, sat it between them in a sled and then drove at midnight to the river, where "the fishes soon had a feast".*

American author W.F. Bryant, places the tragedy in the right context.

> Let anyone put himself in the place of those chiefs and of the young man of
> 25 years, called by his nation to the presidency of a government at its most
> critical moment; let them consider all the circumstances; and the irritating
> opposition made to them; and he will be astonished that they exercised so
> much clemency.

The reaction in Ontario was overwhelming. Thomas Scott became an instant
symbol—the up-standing, courageous young British loyalist toiling to civilize the
West on behalf of the Canadian people, cut down in his youth by savages. His
martyrdom was just what John Schultz and Charlie Mair needed to spread their
propaganda of hatred and bigotry. In April the Toronto *Globe* carried a story
about an Orange Lodge meeting including the following resolution:

> Whereas Brother Thomas Scott, a member of our Order was cruelly mur-
> dered by the enemies of our Queen, country and religion, there be it
> resolved ... we, the members of L.O.L. No. 404 call upon the Government to
> avenge his death, pledging ourselves to assist in rescuing Red River
> Territory from those who have turned it over to Popery, and bring to justice
> the murderers of our countrymen.

It was a typical reaction of Orange Ontario to an event they knew almost
nothing about. In the Red River Settlement, on the other hand, Scott's death
caused only a momentary upset. On March 4, Alexander Begg reported that "A
deep gloom has settled over the settlement on account of this deed." Yet by the
following day he was chatting about the weather and the mail. More telling, just
five days after the execution, the first session of the provisional government
opened without a hitch.

The day was sunny and clear, although the sharpness of winter was still in
the wind. The elected representatives, seated in the Fort Garry council chambers, heard a conciliatory and soft-spoken Riel tell them, "The people generally
now have, for the first time in the history of this land, a voice in the direction of
public affairs." And he was right; democracy had finally come to Canada's
Northwest. Not a word was mentioned about the fate of the unfortunate Scott;
there was hardly a hint of the Boulton uprising. Yet as the session closed with
the English- and French-speakers warmly shaking each others' hands, Riel
steeled himself to face yet another difficult situation—for him, a particularly
thorny problem—the return to Red River of the formidable Alexandre Taché.

No one had more influence among the French-speaking population than
Bishop Taché. By the time of the Red River Rebellion, he was forty-six years old

and had served more than half of his life as a missionary in the Northwest. By 1869 he was rather corpulent, with a pudgy face which sported round gold-rimmed glasses, but behind that cherubic choirboy façade was a man who was long used to being obeyed.

Although he had been born into a family with roots deep in Quebec's establishment, Taché's early life had not been easy. His father had established several businesses, all of which had failed, and by 1825 he had taken a job as the manager of a large seigneurie at Rivière-du-Loup. He died soon after, leaving his wife with five children, the eldest only six years old.

Louise Taché—Riel and Schmidt had spent part of their summer holidays with her during their schooldays in Montreal—had been left in a difficult financial position, but she was a strong-willed woman who managed to provide her three sons with an excellent education, so that one became a lawyer, another an influential politician and her youngest a priest.

In 1841 Madame Taché became seriously ill, and Alexandre made a vow to God that if his mother recovered, he'd devote his life to converting the pagan Indians. Louise Taché lived another twenty-six years and her son entered the seminary of the Oblate Order of Marie Immaculate. Taché's first mission was to Île-à-la-Crosse, twenty-five years after Louis Riel's father had been born there. In his search to "civilize and save souls", Taché travelled far and wide, to Lac La Ronge, Reindeer Lake and even Lake Athabasca.

In 1853, Bishop Provencher died and the energetic, robust Taché was chosen to replace him over an older, more experienced missionary. Ensconced at St. Boniface in the drafty but comfortable stone rectory with the rather grandiose name of Bishop's Palace, he quickly became one of the most influential men in Red River. In 1858, he was sworn in as a member of the Council of Assiniboia, the governing body of the Settlement, and among his duties was to hand out patronage positions. Quickly the French parishes of Red River became Taché's fiefdom, which he ruled with a velvet fist.

He was considered an able administrator, especially where money was concerned, a talent which benefited him personally. He became a wealthy man—in Quebec he was known as the "millionaire priest"—through the accumulation of choice farm acreage. He was always urging his parishioners to stake out their lots, because without land, he insisted quite correctly, "our goose is cooked."

As a member of the governing body, Taché was very much part of Red River's elite; it was the prosperous bourgeoisie among his parishioners whom he associated most with. He was also part of the old Hudson's Bay Company clique—Governor Mactavish was among his closest friends. Taché's philosophy naturally reflected his alliances. As paternalistic and undemocratic as the HBC rule was, he always defended it. He was thus very concerned about the annexation of the Northwest to Canada. He could see that a flood of Protestant immigrants from Ontario would, as the historian W.L. Morton puts it, expose his "hitherto sheltered charges to the pressures and temptations of a secular, commercial and callous Anglo-Saxon civilization," not to mention the worry that his own mighty influence would be considerably diminished.

Bishop Taché had been scheduled to travel east in the fall of 1869 to attend an ecumenical council in Rome, but after the Métis run-in with Dennis's surveyors, he had begun thinking of leaving several months earlier to engage in some political lobbying. His old friend William Mactavish told him he'd be wasting his time. "I have just returned from Ottawa," he wrote, "and although I have been for forty years in the country, and Governor for fifteen years, I have not been able to cause any of my recommendations to be accepted by the government...." Taché decided to go anyway. Not surprisingly, he, too, was summarily dismissed.

When he reached Ottawa in July, he immediately contacted George-Étienne Cartier—the Cartier and Taché families had been friends for years—warning the deputy prime minister of the dangerous political unrest in Red River. Cartier responded curtly, "I am much better informed on this subject than you are and I am not in need of any information." Taché was "hurt to the quick" by this slight, but tried again. In a letter to Cartier dated October 7, 1869, he wrote, "I have always feared the entrance of the Northwest into Confederation, because I have always believed that the French-Canadian element would be sacrificed; but I tell you frankly it had never occurred to me that our rights would be so quickly and so completely forgotten." Again nothing came of his plea; "Cartier rather snubbed Bishop Taché when he was here on his way to Rome," Sir John A. Macdonald would later admit.

Smarting under such cavalier treatment, Taché had set sail on October 16, 1869, reaching the Vatican two and a half weeks later. But he had only settled in when he received a telegram from the prime minister's office: the political situation in Red River had unhappily deteriorated. Would he quickly return as "his influence will be quite sufficient to put an end to the troubles."

By February 10, 1870, he was in Ottawa sitting in the governor-general's elegant office, being courted by Prime Minister Macdonald, Deputy Prime Minister Cartier, and Secretary of State Joseph Howe. When the conversation ended, Taché believed that everything had been solved: there was to be a general amnesty for all those involved in the rebellion; and the government would not only meet with, but pay all the expenses of, the negotiators chosen by the Red River people. The promises were verbal; nothing specific in regard to the amnesty was committed to paper. Taché's naivety in dealing with political animals such as Macdonald and Cartier would soon cause him great heartache.

On March 8, the bishop arrived at St. Norbert. He spent the evening being brought up to date by Father Ritchot, and the next day he travelled on to St. Boniface, where two hundred people were waiting to greet him at the cathedral. Louis Riel was not among them.

The relationship between the bishop and the revolutionary was a complex, often difficult one. It had been Taché, of course, who had made possible Louis's education in Quebec, and Riel would remain grateful for the opportunity. He would later write, "There is probably no one who has received more affection from his bishop than I from you." But Louis had not returned from the Montreal seminary wearing a cassock, and Taché had been disappointed. Observing the young man in the early stages of the Red River resistance, he was concerned about his "impetuous character"; the bishop remembered another dreamer and revolutionary full of hare-brained schemes—Louis Riel's father.

In a few years Taché and Riel were to become deeply estranged. The bishop would say of Louis that "he was a miserable madman and a lunatic," that he was "brain dead." Riel would criticize the bishop (archbishop by that time) for his involvement in suspect land deals. "I have seen him surrounded by his great property, the property of a widow." Only when he was close to death did Riel attempt a reconciliation with his childhood mentor.

In March 1870, however, Louis was in a dilemma. Word had reached the Red River community that Taché had been named a commissioner by the Canadian government. Did that mean that the bishop had the power to determine the conditions under which the Northwest would enter Canada? Riel knew very well how profound was Taché's influence among the Métis. If he disapproved of the provisional government and the Bill of Rights, all of the preceding months' struggle would be for naught. Riel had to illustrate that he was still in command. He ordered a guard of twenty Métis soldiers posted at the door of the Bishop's Palace. And to prevent another reactionary cabal from grabbing the bishop's ear, Riel had the four men he considered the most destructive troublemakers—Charles Nolin, Salomon Hamelin, John Grant and Angus McKay—arrested and jailed.

The bishop was most annoyed, and the guards placed at his door were the least of it. It was the support that his own priests had given the insurrection that upset him the most. In fact this was the latest manifestation of a long and irritating struggle among the Roman Catholic clergy of Red River over the involvement of the religious in the secular. The Oblates were very much opposed to mixing in daily affairs, believing that spiritual matters were their only concern. Others, like Georges Belcourt, identified closely with the Métis, accompanying them on their buffalo hunts and siding with them in their disputes with the church or Hudson's Bay Company. All during the resistance there happened to be a large number of these secular priests in Red River—Ritchot, Giroux and Dugas had all played important roles in the recent struggles, while only the rather ineffectual Lestanc and nondescript Joachim-Albert Allard represented the Oblates.

Taché scolded his subordinates—they hadn't even been dutiful in corresponding with him while he was in Europe. He then forbade fathers Giroux and Allard to continue serving as chaplains to the provisional government.

The bishop did not approve of Riel's rebellion—if only he, with his sense of compromise and propriety, had not left the Red River Settlement, he thought, all would have been well—but he had served in the West long enough to know that there was a limit to how far he could impose his authority on his parishioners. The Métis had rebelled against the church in the past. He would have to accept that the provisional government was a *fait accompli*. And after two days of consultation with Thibault and de Salaberry, among others, he began to understand how serious were the Métis grievances. He wrote to Howe two days after he arrived home, "I am most of all astonished at my own ignorance of the real state of affairs during my stay in Ottawa. The sight of the evils which weigh our people down, and the dread of still greater evils, which, it may be, threaten them, cause one's heart to bleed." Reconciliation with Riel must be undertaken.

On Friday March 11, 1870, a meeting took place in Riel's office in Fort Garry. Ambroise Lépine was there, as was O'Donoghue. The bishop smiled with the complacency of a Cheshire cat. Everything was in his pocket, he assured them: the Canadian government had promised amnesty for everyone; their negotiators would be welcomed with open arms. When he had reached St. Paul on his journey home and had read in the local newspapers about the provisional government's Bill of Rights, he had telegraphed the news to Joseph Howe, who had responded immediately, "Proposals in general satisfactory, have delegates come here to arrange details." That was all Riel and Lépine needed to hear to be won over.* That night the guards at the Bishop's Palace were removed.

The next Sunday, St. Boniface Cathedral was packed with worshippers as Bishop Taché preached his first sermon. His plea for peace and unity was so heartfelt—"I love all Catholics and Protestants. All must work in harmony," he exclaimed—that there was hardly a dry eye among the congregation. Riel was among those who "profusely shed tears".

---

* O'Donoghue was another matter. He was disgusted with Riel when the latter told the bishop he had never had any intention of rebelling against the British crown, and pledged support for the queen.

Now that a reconciliation, at least a superficial one, had been effected with Bishop Taché, Riel and his council could get down to the most serious business facing them—negotiating the entry of the Northwest into the Canadian Confederation. Over a month before, at the final session of the Convention of Forty, Riel had nominated three candidates as negotiators, and the delegates had voted to accept them. Alfred H. Scott, a barkeeper in O'Lone's Saloon and a clerk in Henry McKenny's store, had been chosen to represent the Americans. Something of a drifter and drunk, and definitely in favour of American annexation, he proved an odd choice, playing almost no role in the deliberations and preferring instead to bend his elbow at the Ottawa saloons. Judge Black was to oversee the interests of the English-speakers. He too didn't put much energy into the job; he was far too open to compromise, accepting anything the Canadian politicians put forward. It was left to the French representative, Father Ritchot, to fight for Red River. He would prove a tough and capable negotiator, a bulldog with a bone in his mouth.

There remained the question of what was to be negotiated. A Bill of Rights had been accepted by the Convention of Forty in February 1870, but it was now understood that that body had had no more legal status than any mass meeting held at Red River. The provisional government, as a legal entity, would have to pass a new Bill of Rights. In spirit it remained the same as the previous document, except that the Métis leader took the opportunity to redraft and add some items he thought were particularly important. The Northwest was to enter Confederation as a province called Assiniboia, the new lieutenant-governor would be bilingual, and there would be an amnesty for all who took part in the Red River resistance. This third Bill of Rights was accepted by the provisional council as the basis for negotiating with the Canadian government. But then a sleight-of-hand occurred; it's unclear how it happened, although Bishop Taché was certainly instrumental in it. By the time the negotiators got to Ottawa another clause had been added, and it was a contentious one. Schools would be run by religious orders, and tax money would be distributed to various denominations according to population size. This was at a time when a fierce debate raged about the value of religious as opposed to secular schools, and the secret inclusion of that proviso caused some bitterness in later years. Nevertheless, in the early spring of 1870 there were high hopes the odd trio of negotiators would meet with success.

On March 23, despite a late snowstorm that suddenly swept down the valley, Father Ritchot and de Salaberry, who was at last leaving Red River, bundled into ox-driven carts and headed south over the muddy rutted trails. At Pointe Coupée they teamed up with Alfred Scott and continued on. The next day Judge Black and the luckless Major Boulton, who had just days before been released from jail, started out. The entire group met on March 25 in Pembina and from there went by train to Ottawa. Their business would take many weeks. All the people of Red River could do was wait patiently for news.

Meanwhile, after months of chaos, the Settlement was at last enjoying some tranquillity. As Alexander Begg wrote in his diary, "Everything is working harmoniously and there is every prospect of peace and a return of confidence among the settlers."* By March 24 every one of the prisoners had been released. And an attempt had been made to appease the Indians.

The Saulteaux were furious that their long-time rivals had been allowed to occupy Fort Garry for so long. It seemed to them that this was merely an opportunity for the Métis to steal from the Hudson's Bay Company stores. Chief Henri Prince bitterly remarked that if an Indian stole an axe or an old blanket, he was severely punished, but that the French had been allowed to plunder wholesale all winter. If the Half-breeds had not vacated the fort by spring, he insisted, they would be attacked.

On March 23 the provisional government printed a declaration ensuring that Native interests would be protected in negotiations with Canada. Armed with this document, Bishop Taché and the Anglican Bishop Machray travelled to the northern parishes of St. Peter's and St. Andrew's to listen to the grievances of the Saulteaux and some Sioux and to try to reassure them. Chief Prince and his band remained bitter and angry, but the threat of Indian attack subsided. Another fear that had nagged at the Red River Settlement for months had eased.

But it was the Saint Patrick's Day celebrations that truly set the tone of reconciliation. The day was warm and sunny, the first real hint that spring was on its way. Cannon boomed from Fort Garry and all morning the bells of St. Boniface merrily chimed away. Bishop Taché even preached his sermon that morning in English, in honour of the Irish.

In the evening, a formal dinner was held in Government House in Fort Garry, with an elegantly dressed Louis Riel as official host. The St. Boniface Boys' Bugle Band serenaded the guests, who included members of the provisional government, the clergy and their wives. Many speeches were given and toasts proposed. As Alexander Begg reported, "The evening passed off pleasantly and without any discord."

Historians have traditionally given Bishop Taché credit for this return to normalcy. More likely it was Riel's belief that negotiations with the Canadian government were finally on the right track. As Louis Schmidt would write, "It has been claimed that the preservation of the Red River ... was almost sole responsibility of Mgr. Taché.... This is an exaggeration. Without any doubt, Mgr. Taché had given advice and his counsels were taken to heart. But His Excellency was preaching to souls already converted. No, by all means, let us not take away from Riel the credit that is his just due."

A formal portrait of *le président* taken sometime during the spring of 1870 by a St. Paul photographer, C.A. Zimmerman, reveals a very distinguished Riel. He is dressed in ceremonial attire, a well-tailored frock coat, a beautifully tied bow at his throat. He sports a nicely trimmed beard; his thick wavy hair has somehow been tamed. Indeed, he looks very much like a Father of Confederation.

And he could now bask, at least for a while, in his success. The political quilt that he had so carefully stitched together seemed suddenly a work of art. With no text to guide him, he had accomplished for the Métis what few other Native people in North America had managed—a near bloodless resistance to an authority bent on denying them their rights. A telling testimony to Riel's remarkable accomplishment was given by a Captain W.F. Butler, who visited the Red River Settlement that spring. Butler was hardly a friend of the Métis; in fact he had nothing but contempt for anybody who wasn't of British stock. But he said of Riel:

> It is almost refreshing to notice the ability, the energy, the determination which up to this point has characterized all the movements of the originator and mainspring of the movement, M. Louis Riel. One hates so much to see a thing bungled that even resistance, although it borders upon rebellion, becomes respectable when it is carried out with courage, energy and decision.

What impressed people like Butler was that Riel seemed to have single-handedly defeated what they regarded as the most dangerous threat to Canadian nationalism—the annexation of the Northwest by the United States.

The Americans had been part of Riel's inner circle because they were the only group among the English-speakers who wholeheartedly supported his initiatives. While Canadians were taking up arms against his government, he badly needed their endorsement. But he had no intention of encouraging U.S. annexation. Once things were quiet in Red River, he didn't hesitate to silence the shrill American voice.

Actually the Americans, with their boastful propaganda and political intrigue, had a tendency to shoot themselves in the foot anyway. On March 16, 1870, the U.S. consul, Oscar Malmros, shocked the Red River community by announcing that he was leaving that very day. He had been called back to Washington "on his own business", he said, but it quickly became known that in truth the State Department had allowed his unedited dispatches to be published in pamphlet form, and that they showed he was anything but the "neutral statesman" he had claimed to be. Before he left he named Major Henri M. Robinson as his replacement, but Robinson himself was soon in hot water as well.

Robinson was the American journalist who, with Riel's approval, had begun the *New Nation*, the only newspaper still publishing in the Red River Settlement.

Since the first edition had appeared on January 7, 1870, it had irritated many in the community, so much so that readers by the score sent it back to the editor scribbled over "with some pretty hard writing", as Alexander Begg put it. Calling it the *New Damnation* was the favourite insult.

It wasn't just its pro-American annexation stance that exasperated people, although that was bad enough. It had a tone of ridicule to it, "too flippant a nature", as Begg described it, and often belittled important events. Riel himself grew sick of its impertinence and increasingly interfered with its publication. When Scott was executed on March 4, Riel refused to allow the edition intended for outside distribution released until he had censored the story. Finally, on March 18, after Bishop Taché had spoken to the council of the provisional government, Riel wrote Robinson, "Dear Major, Don't you issue the New Nation of the day without I see it, if you please. It is always important to be very right. Yours Louis Riel." Robinson felt he could no longer tolerate such interference and he resigned.

Riel soon found another editor. Thomas Spence, the only Canadian to serve as a delegate to the Convention of Forty, was to be paid £40 a quarter to do the job. But the American refused to hand over the keys to the printing office, insisting he wanted to make sure he wouldn't be stuck with the newspaper's outstanding bills.

Robinson and the provisional government continued wrangling until Riel finally took the matter in hand. An armed guard escorted the major into Fort Garry and after only a few hours "an understanding" was arrived at. Robinson handed over the keys.

On April 2, Spence published his first edition, which was remarkably pro-British (and not nearly as lively or interesting as Robinson's paper). The mocking American voice had been silenced.

In Riel's inner circle, it was William O'Donoghue who was most passionately devoted to American annexation. Riel rather liked the man; he was nervy, clever and energetic, performing his job as treasurer of the provisional government with diligence. Finally, however, the Métis leader had to rein O'Donoghue in, in what turned out to be one of the most curious struggles of the Red River resistance.

On March 25, 1870, the provisional government's flag was found lying on the ground, having been cut down by someone during the night. It had become an important symbol of independence to Métis supporters and a few days later it was hoisted again. But Riel became determined, for the sake of the negotiations going on in Ottawa, to make a dramatic and visual act of allegiance to the British crown. Bishop Taché had asked that the Union Jack be raised in place of the shamrock and fleur-de-lis and Louis, probably reluctantly, agreed. O'Donoghue fought furiously against it for weeks but finally, on April 20, Riel gave the order to hoist the British flag. That same morning the Irishman marched into Fort Garry and demanded the Métis sentries take it down. Riel was furious, ordered it back up and assigned André Nault to shoot his treasurer or anyone else who tried to fool with it again.

But it was not in O'Donoghue's nature to give up. He was livid that the very symbol of the revolution could so easily be dismissed on a whim of a Catholic prelate. He and his followers dug up the flagpole in front of Schultz's business, carried it into Fort Garry and planted it in front of the governor's house. Once again the Métis symbol of independence flapped overhead, not far from the Union Jack. Riel wisely let both flags fly.

The "flag wars" became something of a joke among Red River's citizenry. Alexander Begg's wife, Katherine, hoisted up one of her colourful shawls on the flagpole in front of their house. Someone at Fort Garry spotted it and a Métis guard was sent running to investigate. He found the portly Mrs. Begg in tears— from laughing so hard. It was an indication that life was slowly getting back to normal in the Red River Settlement. All that was needed was for the Hudson's Bay Company to resume business.

Commercial activity in the Settlement had all but ceased over the months of chaos. The Métis had continually nibbled at the Company's supplies, and in retaliation Governor Mactavish had refused to issue any more bills of exchange, the basic currency then used in the Northwest. As well, the HBC's general store remained closed to the public. As spring approached, farmers, voyageurs and tripmen all needed supplies, and the provisional government badly needed cash to function. Something had to be done to get business going again.

On March 28, Riel presented Mactavish with a proposal. The HBC would recognize the provisional government and lend it £3,000; if negotiations with Canada failed another £2,000 would be provided. As well, some £4,000 worth of provisions and supplies "for the support of the present military force" would be provided by the Company. Mactavish balked at Riel's demands but very quickly acceded, for Riel held the important bargaining chip. Métis and some Indians across the Northwest were waiting to do his bidding; one word from him, and scores of HBC posts would be looted of their furs.

Mactavish agreed to lend the money, issue new bills of exchange and, to a chorus of thank yous from the housewives of Red River, open the general store. On his part, Riel had Louis Schmidt draw up a circular letter to the Métis of the plains, outlining the actions of the provisional government and pleading for law and order.

On April 9, the president announced that civil rule had returned to the Red River Settlement: the barriers on roads would be removed, mail would no longer be censored and an amnesty for all who would submit to the provisional government would be granted. The announcement, called "To People of the

North-West", reads more like a song of victory than an official declaration. A paragraph gives the flavour:

> HAPPY country, to have escaped many misfortunes that were prepared for her! In seeing her children on the point of a war, she recollects the old friendship which used to bind us, and by the ties of the same patriotism she has re-united them again for the sake of preserving their lives, their liberties, and their happiness.

With the arrival of April came unusually pleasant weather. The sun shone most of the time, the breezes were wonderfully warm, the snow rapidly disappeared, but like all good things that came to the Red River Valley, there was an ugly side effect. The ice broke up very quickly and the Red and Assiniboine rivers began to swell. The threat of floods worried the Settlement for weeks—a couple of bridges were washed out, John Inkster's mill collapsed and the mailman, not realizing how thin the ice was, fell into the river, taking all his parcel bags with him. Fortunately he was spotted by some passers-by and hauled out just in time.

Still, the lovely spring that year was enjoyed by all. The Scottish settlers who had been wintering with their herds of cattle out on the prairie returned sooner than normal. Farmers began preparing for a possible early seeding. And the Métis soldiers became eager to get on with their lives as farmers, tripmen in the Red River cart caravans and voyageurs—the winterers would be returning soon with their bounty of furs, which would have to be carried to York Factory on Hudson Bay.

During those lovely April days even the president of the provisional government seemed relaxed, enjoying life a little. Louis had finally moved from Henri Coutu's butcher shop into more appropriate accommodation in Fort Garry. William McDougall's furniture, left behind when he returned in disgrace to the East, was unpacked and set up in Riel's living quarters. His enemies all criticized him for this—he was "putting on too much style," they said—but Riel was a man with a highly developed aesthetic sense and he must have enjoyed his brief taste of luxury.

Now he could properly receive important guests—American businessmen, for example. On April 24 an important party of railway men arrived, led by William Rainey Marshall, the former governor of Minnesota and the founder of the St. Paul *Daily Press*. They were agents of the daring American tycoon Jay Cooke, who had recently underwritten the construction of the Northern Pacific Railway. Cooke was considering running a line to Winnipeg from St. Paul, and Marshall was there to explore this possibility, which depended in part on the political situation. Was there any chance that, with a little help in the form of money or Fenian mercenaries, Red River might embrace the United States?

Marshall found the Red River Settlement unpleasantly peaceful and the senti-ment pro-Canadian, and the Northern Pacific branch line was not constructed. What is interesting about this episode, however, is the description of Louis Riel written by one of Marshall's party, N.P. Langford:

> Riel ... has a fine physique, of active temperament, a great worker, and I think is able to endure a great deal. He is a large man, with a high forehead (not broad) of very winning persuasive manners; and in his whole bearing, energy and ready decision are prominent characteristics;—and in this fact, lies his great powers—for I should not give him credit for great profundity, yet he is sagacious, and I think thoroughly patriotic and no less thoroughly incorruptible. In his intercourse with us, he was very diplomatic and non-committal. Yet there was nothing offensive in this, but rather it appeared to me to be a merit in him.

On May 4, the long-awaited steamship *International* finally steamed up the Red River from Georgetown, Minnesota, and in its cargo were two dispatches from the Red River negotiators. There was shocking news. When Father Ritchot and Alfred Scott had reached Ontario, they had been arrested like common criminals and charged with abetting murder. The arrests had been set up by those seemingly irrepressible forces of darkness, John Schultz and Charlie Mair.

After Schultz and Mair had run into each other in St. Paul, after their har-rowing escapes from Red River, both men had sent telegrams to family and friends in Ontario, relating, in vivid, exaggerated terms, what had happened to them. Among those contacted was Charlie's old friend George T. Denison, leader of that secret and insidious men's club of patriots called "Canada First".

Denison had been disappointed that neither McDougall's failure to establish himself at Red River, nor the imprisonment of Schultz, Mair and others, had caused much of an uproar. The Ontario and Quebec public seemed to think that the would-be lieutenant-governor and the Canadians deserved what they got. The execution of Thomas Scott changed all that. Denison used "the murder of the brave young Orangeman" mercilessly. Toronto's *Daily Telegraph*, owned by one of the Canada First supporters, went into mourning for Scott; other Ontario newspapers jumped on the bandwagon. The propaganda spewed forth, painting a picture of events in Red River so false and twisted it was breath-taking. But it worked. When Schultz and Mair finally arrived in Toronto on April 7, 1870, a huge crowd was waiting impatiently at the railway station to greet them. The two "refugees" were cheered as "great patriots" all the way to the Queen's Hotel.

That night a rally had been organized by the Canada First movement, and it was successful beyond their wildest dreams. The St. Lawrence Town Hall proved much too small for the crowd, so the gathering had to move down the street. Eventually five thousand people crowded into the square in front of City Hall. Of all the outrageous versions of events dreamed up by the speakers, none was so ridiculous as the mayor's. S.B. Harman, gesturing at Schultz and Mair, who were sitting on the platform nearby, assured the excited crowd that the names "of those gallant men who stood up for British supremacy in Red River ... would live in history, and be handed down side by side with those who led the gallant charge at Balaklava to uphold the dignity of Great Britain against the greatest odds that could be brought against them." That this was entirely overblown—surrendering to the Métis at Fort Schultz without a fight was hardly leading a "gallant charge"—mattered not at all to His Worship or any of the cheering crowd. But it was Schultz, all handsome, six foot two of him, who told the most fabulous stories and stole the show that night. The situation at Fort Garry was simple, he said—"the Fenian flag floated from its flag staff. The rebels hold high revelry within its walls, and Canadians lay in dungeons within." He concluded to great cheering, "It was from Ontario this movement to add Red River to the Dominion commenced; it was in Ontario this expression of indignation was expressed; and it was to Ontario the Territory properly belonged." The rights of the Indians, Métis and others who regarded Red River as their home were considered not at all.

The rally was judged such a success that immediately plans were made for similar "indignation meetings" in towns throughout Orange Ontario. Handbills and posters screaming RED RIVER OUTRAGE—A ROPE FOR THE MURDERER RIEL were plastered everywhere. And with each appearance, Schultz became more adept at whipping up the crowds. He would hold up a piece of rope and rant: "This is what was used to bind the wrist of poor murdered Scott whose only crime was loyalty to his Queen and devotion to his country." Later, little bottles of what was purported to be Thomas Scott's blood became part of his extravaganza.

Charlie Mair was not as forceful a speaker as Schultz, but he could be more descriptive. His favourite speech featured the supposedly vermin-infested cell he had suffered at Fort Garry, much like the Black Hole of Calcutta, he insisted. The Canada First propaganda machine, propelled by Schultz and Mair, quickly produced results.

Meanwhile, a Canada First deputation had made its way to Ottawa. The mission was simple: Red River's negotiators represented those "who have robbed, imprisoned and murdered loyal Canadians"; they must not be received by the dominion government, amnesty for the rebels must not be granted. Much to their surprise, the emissaries were given a chilly reception by Sir John A. Macdonald. The wily old politician knew that while Orange Ontario might cry out for revenge, Quebec felt quite differently. In fact his Cabinet was divided on the issue, with George-Étienne Cartier threatening to quit if anything drastic was done.

Given a brush-off by Macdonald, Schultz and company decided to act on their own. Thomas Scott's brother, Hugh, and William Foster, another member of the Canada First group, went to the police magistrate in Toronto and applied for a warrant charging Father Ritchot and Alfred Scott with aiding and abetting the murder of Thomas Scott. This was granted and then sent on to the Ottawa police department.

Meanwhile the Red River negotiators and their companions had been travelling by train eastward through the United States. Father Ritchot had been optimistic about his mission; the fish would either swim into his net or be guided by Providence, he wrote. But along the line word reached them of the fanatical campaign being waged against the Métis. It was rumoured that a mob was ready to lynch both Ritchot and Alfred Scott as soon as they set foot on Ontario soil. On the advice of the Canadian government, the men changed their route. Separating from Judge Black and the others, Ritchot and Alfred Scott circumvented Toronto, arriving in Ogdensburg, New York, directly south of Ottawa. There they were met by a Canadian Secret Service agent who accompanied them by private coach to the capital.

The day after he arrived in Ottawa, Ritchot paid George Cartier a visit at Parliament Hill. The politician was most congenial and assured the priest that "the members of the government would not pay attention to the outcries of a class of men who only sought to cause trouble for the government." However, Cartier did suggest that they hold off talks for a few days until Judge Black arrived. The clamour over Thomas Scott would have died down by then, Cartier assured him.

But Ritchot was not reassured—and with very good reason. The next day Alfred Scott was arrested and jailed and the priest learned that the Ottawa police were looking for him also. He quickly gave himself up. The necessary bail was raised and the two negotiators from Red River were arraigned before Judge Thomas Galt. He immediately ruled that the Toronto magistrate had no jurisdiction in Ottawa and dismissed the charges. But Hugh Scott was waiting in the wings. With the help of Canada First, he had travelled to Ottawa and sworn out a new warrant. Before they even got out of the courtroom, Ritchot and Alfred Scott were arrested again. The two men were taken to the police station, where they stayed in custody for the good part of the day, until they were escorted back to their lodgings. There they remained under guard, in a kind of house arrest.

By this time Father Ritchot was outraged. He wrote an indignant, strongly worded letter to Governor-General Sir John Young protesting the violation of his diplomatic immunity as a negotiator for the government of Assiniboia. But about all the authorities could do was provide the two envoys with a lawyer.

Negotiations went on behind the scenes, though, and when the case came to trial on April 23, twelve days after Ritchot and Scott had arrived in Ottawa, the judge immediately dismissed the charges for lack of evidence.

When they stepped outside the courthouse, a huge crowd of well-wishers, including several members of Parliament, gave them a rousing cheer. Alfred Scott enjoyed it all, and took off with several sympathizers for the nearest pub. But the priest refused to join the celebration. He went back to his room at the Episcopal Palace alone, and there nursed his wounded pride.

Before they had arrived in Ottawa, Prime Minister Macdonald had written of the Red River delegation, "If we once get them here we will easily deal with them." And that obviously was the mode of operation with Ritchot and Alfred Scott; the discussions were to be informal, private. The idea of official status would have to be avoided. The two elegant politicians, Macdonald and Cartier, were polite, indeed charming, towards their guests from the "primitive country". But weeks had gone by and negotiations hadn't even started. Ritchot was growing impatient. Finally, in a meeting at George Cartier's house on April 25, the priest demanded that he and the other two negotiators be given formal recognition by the Canadian government. This was an important principle for Ritchot, because such ambassadorial status would stamp the provisional government as legitimate, and as such would offer a rationalization for the trial of Thomas Scott. As Macdonald and Cartier smiled and mouthed pleasantries, Ritchot would not be put off his task: Where was the amnesty promised to Bishop Taché, he demanded. Moreover, he was giving notice that he would accept nothing less than provincial status for the Red River Settlement. The suave and sophisticated politicians looked aghast. Macdonald had written two months before, "Everything looks well for a delegation coming to Ottawa, including the redoubtable Riel. If we once get him here, he is a gone coon." Riel's representative, the prime minister soon found out, was anything but a "gone coon".

Ritchot was promised that formal recognition would come in a letter from Joseph Howe that evening. The priest accepted this and the two parties began negotiating that afternoon. Judge Black was willing to capitulate to the Canadian politicians on every point; Father Ritchot certainly was not. Over the next three days he bargained hard for what he believed were the rights of the Métis people. But he was also forced to compromise, altering many of the clauses in the provisional government's Bill of Rights. Finally, an agreement began to take shape.

The Red River Settlement would enter Confederation as a province, but one much reduced in size. Rupert's Land and the Northwest Territories would have created a political entity larger than either Quebec or Ontario, which meant that its 15,000 inhabitants would control vast wealth in resources. Macdonald understood well the political backlash that would produce. Manitoba, as the new province would be called, on a suggestion from Ritchot,* would be hardly bigger than the present District of Assiniboia, the country within sixty miles of Fort Garry. Still, it would have a government responsible to the people of Red River, and that was a big step forward.

Riel had insisted on provincial status because, under Section 92 of the British North America Act, the provinces of Canada controlled their own lands and forests; this, he thought, would ensure that Métis land claims were protected. But Sir John A. flatly refused to hand over ownership of the vast prairies to the new provincial government. He envisioned settlers streaming into the west by the millions, a railway would have to be constructed, and a Homestead Act passed by Parliament, which the dominion government would use to control the lands of the vast Northwest. Again a compromise was worked out. It was agreed that the citizens of Red River would keep the property then in their possession, whether money had been exchanged with the Hudson's Bay Company or not, and, more radically, 1.4 million acres of land in the new province would be set aside for the children of Half-breed families in recognition of their share of Indian title. Ritchot thought that the land should be chosen in several large blocks around the French parishes, where lots would be parcelled out to heads of mixed-blood families for their children. This was to be done as expeditiously as possible. It was an attempt to preserve the Métis nation and its way of life without resorting to the kind of reserve system that had been foisted on the Indians.

But when the Manitoba Bill, as it was called, was presented to the House of Commons on May 2, it had been changed dramatically under pressure from the British government. The frontiers of the province had been altered to include the troublesome English stronghold of Portage la Prairie. Of more significance, although the amount of land to be reserved for Half-breed children remained the same, there was no reference to the timing or method of distribution, except to say that it would be left to the lieutenant-governor to decide. Ritchot didn't like the changes one bit, but Macdonald assured him that mechanisms would be set up to ensure that the original ideas on the way the land should be distributed were adhered to. Trust me, the prime minister said. Ritchot did, and thereby made the worst mistake of his life. As historian D.N. Sprague has concluded, from the beginning "he [Macdonald] intended to subvert the agreements

---

* *In a letter to Ritchot, Louis Riel had suggested that either Manitoba or Nord-Ouest (Northwest) be used; the Métis did not much like Assiniboia because of its association with the HBC administration.*

reached with the delegates while at the same time attempt to convince them, and London, that all was well."

Ritchot was in the visitors' gallery of the House of Commons during the final debate on the Manitoba Bill. He was an exotic sight, this big burly priest, with his fierce black beard curling down his chest, his years of experience in the harsh Northwest imprinted on his face. As he listened to the often furious debate, he could feel some pride of accomplishment. On May 9, the Bill passed third reading in the House of Commons by an overwhelming vote of 120 to 11. Three days later it received royal assent. Red River was now the province of Manitoba, with its own government and the right to elect senators and members to the House of Commons. The Métis land claim issue was now settled, and quite well, he thought. Moreover, bilingualism was now an official fact, and Catholics and Protestants had been given the right to run their own schools. The monies promised by the dominion government for such things as roads were generous.

On June 17, a warm, rainy day, Ritchot arrived back in Red River via the steamer *International*. A huge crowd of eager people had gathered at the docks to greet him, including Louis Riel. For weeks, the Métis leader had been anxiously awaiting the negotiator. Louis already knew the details of the Manitoba Bill, which had been telegraphed almost a month before. It had seemed quite reasonable except for one glaring omission—there had been no mention of a general amnesty for leaders of the rebellion.

Ritchot reassured Louis at once, explaining exactly what had happened during his month-and-a-half stay in Ottawa.

Right from the beginning of the negotiations, Ritchot had made it very clear that an amnesty was a *sine qua non* of any agreement. Cartier and Macdonald had explained to the priest that since the Canadian government had no legal authority in Red River at the time of the resistance, it was not up to them to grant an amnesty. The queen would have to deal with the problem. But, they insisted, they were in a position to know Britain's thinking on the matter and they were sure an amnesty would be granted immediately following the passage of the bill creating the province of Manitoba. Written evidence was certainly not needed; their word was guarantee enough.

The governor-general, Sir John Young, reminded Ritchot that an amnesty had already been provided—a royal proclamation of December 6, 1869, had promised dispensation to all who laid down their arms. Could he not accept that and not cause the government political embarrassment by insisting on a new document? Ritchot was not totally convinced and he kept nagging at the Canadian negotiators—did that mean all actions after December 6 (although he didn't specially mention it, he was thinking of the shooting of Thomas Scott) would be covered by the proclamation? Even if the citizens had not laid down their arms, as the proclamation had demanded?

Even after the Manitoba Bill had passed, Ritchot kept on and on about the amnesty, nearly driving Cartier to distraction; even during a formal, black-tie dinner, he would not let the matter drop. Finally, on May 19, he had a long audience with the governor-general, and what followed is best described in his words:

> His Excellency told us that the Proclamation of December 8 is enough to assure us that a general amnesty is going to be proclaimed immediately, that it is not necessary to give another guarantee in writing. I remarked to him again that that proclamation was dated December 6, 1869, and it could happen that it would not be sufficient and not include events that had taken place since. His Excellency assured me that that it would suffice, that moreover, Her Majesty was going to proclaim a general amnesty immediately, that we could set out for Manitoba, that the amnesty would arrive before us.

At the request of the Canadian politicians, Ritchot and the other two delegates signed a petition to the queen requesting the amnesty promised by the Canadian government. A mere formality, Cartier said; Sir John Young would be delighted to support his request.

When Ritchot reached Red River, he was not surprised that the royal decree had not yet arrived; he had realized that it would take longer than the governor-general had estimated. But Ritchot had been promised that it would be in place before the new lieutenant-governor of Manitoba arrived.

Riel's worries were calmed by Ritchot's explanation but he had heard another unsettling rumour—that an army of "blood-thirsty Orangemen" were on their way to put down the revolution. As early as April 19 he had written to Ritchot, then in Ottawa, "Without setting too much store to it, I have received a letter saying that 150 boats destined to serve on lake Superior, were acquired by Canada, in order, it would seem, to send troops to us." Ritchot replied that yes, Canadian troops had left Toronto for the West on May 21 under the command of Colonel Garnet Wolseley, but it was an entirely friendly expedition, merely, as the prime minister had said, to act as a "police force" to pacify the Indians and serve as a show of might for the American annexationists.

The Métis leader was reassured by all that the priest had told him. He ordered a twenty-one-gun salute in honour of Father Ritchot's great achievement. (Neither Judge Black nor Alfred Scott had returned to Red River. Black had gone to live permanently in Scotland and Scott was testing the saloons of New York City.)

One week after Father Ritchot returned to Red River, the legislative assembly of Assiniboia met and Louis Schmidt moved that "the Legislative Assembly of this country do now, in the name of the people, accept the Manitoba Act." It was passed unanimously to great cheers.

Ritchot had brought other news that made Riel feel confident. At one point in the negotiations, the priest had asked Cartier, the acting prime minister as Macdonald was very ill, "Who was to govern the country pending the arrival of the lieutenant-governor?" Cartier had abruptly answered, "Let Mr. Riel continue to maintain order and govern the country, as he has done up to the present moment." Surely that was recognition of all that the young Métis leader had accomplished.

Riel could now think of his own future. He had always known that his position of power would come to an end; "I would give up my place willingly and joyfully as President as soon as the proper governor comes," he had told the *New Nation*. But at twenty-six years old, surely he had shown that he had a remarkable talent for statesmanship; surely a long and distinguished career as a politician awaited him—perhaps a seat in the provincial legislature, then the House of Commons in Ottawa.

Bishop Taché was not nearly as enthusiastic about Ritchot's news as others in the Red River Settlement. He had spotted a major contradiction: after his discussions with the prime minister and governor-general in February 1870, he had firmly believed that he had been given the power to promise an amnesty on behalf of the Canadian government. Why had Father Ritchot been told that only the British crown could offer such dispensation? The thorny question of amnesty had to be nailed down, put on paper. Barely had the celebrations quieted down when the bishop left for Ottawa.

His first visit was to Cartier, who reaffirmed everything that Ritchot had said. "We are waiting for the [royal] proclamation every day, and if you remain for a few weeks, it will arrive before you leave," he promised.

Cartier, as Minister of Militia, was on his way to inspect the troops at Camp Niagara, and he invited Taché to accompany him so he could introduce him first hand to the governor-general, who would also be there. That would give the bishop a chance to talk to Sir John Young, Cartier promised.

They travelled south to Prescott and then took the steamer bound for Toronto. But when they got to Kingston, they received startling news. Charlie Mair, John Schultz and the other Canada First members were planning another huge rally in St. Lawrence Hall, against Cartier and "the traitor Bishop Taché". Placards had sprung up all over Toronto. Their inflammatory messages were displayed in huge type: "SHALL FRENCH REBELS RULE OUR DOMINION?" "MEN OF ORANGE, SHALL SCOTT'S BLOOD CRY IN VAIN FOR VENGEANCE!" Canada First leader George Denison had threatened that his gang would take over the armoury that night and that "if anyone in Toronto wanted to fight it out, we were ready to fight it out on the streets." Asked whether he would really resort to violent revolution, he retorted in the usual apocalyptic rhetoric of that cabal, "A half a continent is at stake, and it is a stake worth fighting for."

Immediately Bishop Taché changed his plans; he would travel to Buffalo, bypassing Toronto, and thereby avoid embarrassing Cartier. But when he finally met with Sir John Young in Hamilton, the governor-general's manner was cold to the point of rudeness. When Taché asked him about the promised amnesty, he abruptly replied, "Here is my proclamation on December 6, it covers the whole case." What Taché didn't know was that the governor-general was lying, and had been from the beginning of the negotiations with Ritchot. Attached to a petition to Her Majesty from the Canada First group opposing any pardon for Riel or the other Métis leaders was a memorandum from Sir John Young. In it, he wrote that an amnesty would be "injudicious, impolitic and dangerous". Scott, he added, had been "led out and murdered in cold blood."

Young concluded his short interview with the bishop by telling him to speak to Cartier on the matter, as "he knows my views". But Cartier didn't know His Excellency's views and sadly informed Taché that he could do nothing more for him.

Meanwhile, back in Red River, the optimism that had happily enveloped the community on Ritchot's return had evaporated. Everyone's nerves seemed to be on edge. The weather was hot and dry, and the grasshoppers had again descended. The Americans, realizing their dreams of annexation were over, seemed desperate to celebrate Independence Day. On July 4, George Emmerling decorated the front of his hotel with green branches and H.F. O'Lone somehow got his hands on one of Fort Garry's cannon. All day long, it boomed. The holiday-makers kept shooting off their guns, and with each hour they became more and more drunk. The owner of Lennon's Saloon finally announced that he himself would like to hang Louis Riel for "selling the Americans down the drain".

The Métis leader suddenly seemed to have enemies everywhere. The Canadians had been quiet ever since the execution of Thomas Scott but now there were threats that soon martial law would be declared, "followed by the hanging of a few of the French party". Even some of the French-speakers started to grumble about Riel's leadership.

Even more troublesome, as the weeks slowly slipped by the royal proclamation decreeing the amnesty had not arrived, nor had Bishop Taché telegraphed word of success. And then there were the persistent reports about the army heading west. Unfortunately, they were all true.

Right from the beginning of the Red River resistance, the dominion government had considered deploying troops to smother the rebellion. William McDougall had advocated it. Sir John A. Macdonald wrote: "These impulsive half-breeds have got spoilt by this *émeute* [rioting] and must be kept down by a strong hand until they are swamped by the influx of the settlers." But it was obvious that the United States would not allow Canadian soldiers or their equipment to travel through American territory, and it was unthinkable to send an expedition overland in the middle of winter.

Macdonald was determined that the military force would include British regulars as well as Canadian militia. Not only did the Brits have more experience in warfare, but he thought soldiers of Her Majesty would intimidate the Half-breeds more than a batch of green Canadian volunteers, and an Imperial force might also convince the Americans that their ambition to annex the Canadian West was dead. There was only one problem with Sir John A.'s plan: the British wouldn't participate. They felt terrorizing the Natives would anger the Americans, with whom they were trying to patch up relations. After the pressure from Schultz and the Canada First movement became unbearable, Macdonald pushed harder. The colonial secretary, Lord Granville, finally agreed that four hundred British soldiers could be included in the force as long as "reasonable terms" were granted to the "Roman Catholic" settlers. This was a major reason Macdonald and Cartier had been so eager to negotiate with Ritchot and so ready to promise him anything, including a full amnesty.

Colonel Garnet Wolseley, the Ulsterman chosen to lead the Red River Expedition, was, at thirty-seven, young for such responsibility. But he had already served with the British Army in India, Crimea and China. In 1861 he was sent to Canada as assistant quartermaster-general, and was promoted to deputy quartermaster in 1865.

Wolseley was a typical British imperialist; anyone with Native blood was a "savage". His distorted perception of Louis Riel was indicative of his entire misinterpretation of his mission. When he wrote later about the expedition, his profile of the Métis leader included these fabrications:

> Instead of [becoming a priest], he [Riel] became a clerk in a shop at St Paul Minnesota, where he resided for a few years and was eventually dismissed for dishonesty. His prospects being thus under a cloud, he returned to the neighbourhood of Fort Garry and lived in the greatest poverty with his mother. So indigent were their circumstances, that finding himself succeeding in his rôle of demagogue, and considering it necessary to be the possessor of a black cloth coat, he was obliged to sell his mother's only cow to procure the money required for that purpose.

Wolseley's army was made up of 1,200 soldiers—hardly the small "police force" the prime minister had talked about. One-third were regular troops from the imperial garrison and two-thirds, 800 men, were two garrisons of Canadian militia, one from Ontario and one from Quebec. Charged up by the propaganda of Schultz and company, young Orangemen rushed to join the Ontario contingent, and when the Quebec garrison was slow to find volunteers, they filled those positions as well. Practically to a man, they were bigoted, ignorant and belligerent. Having never before seen combat of any kind, they were itching for a fight and the medals to pin on their chests that were sure to follow. Much was written by these people after the expedition was over, mostly in an attempt to appear heroes in what was an entirely inglorious campaign. A typical version of events was this one by "An Officer of the Force", published in *The Manitoban* in 1892.

> They [the soldiers] were prompted by a desire to protect the rights and liberty of the loyal people of Red River settlement, and to restore the Union Jack to its proper place over the walls of Fort Garry. In accomplishing this, they expected to meet in honorable combat, the scoundrels, who insulted our flag, robbed and plundered our fallen subjects, and hunted like wild beasts, the sturdy English-speaking pioneers who composed the bones and sinews of the settlement, and lastly without provocation, dyed their hands in the most diabolical butchery of a fellow being tortured in a manner that Nena Tahile in his palmiest days could never think of.

The racism and perversion of the truth were remarkable given that the force had been referred to over and over again by Ottawa politicians as "a friendly expedition to insure the safety of the Red River Settlement." If it was any compensation to the "cold-blooded murderers" and "primitive savages" they had come to fight, these soldiers endured one of the most excruciating marches in the history of the Canadian military. From Fort William the army travelled west over what was supposed to be the first portion of the Dawson Road. But fires and rain had washed it away; it would take three weeks of back-breaking, dawn-to-dusk labour to clear the fallen timber. Even though special boats had been requisitioned or built for the expedition, the journey over the waterways of the Rainy Lake and Lake of the Woods regions was agony. There were fifty portages, many of them miles long. The boats, the cannon, the ammunition, the two-hundred-pound barrels of salt pork, all had to be carried on the backs of the men. They became bogged down in the thick mud of the black muskeg, they dripped with sweat as they carried their burdens over rocky outcrops. Little food, infuriating mosquitoes and temperatures that soared to over 100 degrees added to their woes.

O'Donoghue and the Americans at Red River—in particular Alfred Scott, back from New York—wanted to send a two-man delegation to meet the expedition at the entrance to Lake Winnipeg to demand that the proclamation of amnesty be produced. If the answer was not satisfactory, guerrilla warfare would follow. With marksmen placed in strategic spots, the Métis could destroy a force of Canadians and Brits who had no experience whatsoever of the wilderness. At first Riel was tempted, especially since the long-promised amnesty had not arrived, but Bishop Taché talked him out of it. According to Riel, he insisted, "Do not do that. I give you my word of honour that a general amnesty will be proclaimed before the installation of any Canadian Lieutenant-Governor here." It was at that point, June 28, that the bishop decided to make the journey to Ottawa to make good on his word.

On July 22 a proclamation sent by Colonel Wolseley at the start of his trek arrived in Red River. He once again promised that the expedition was entirely devoted to peace. "The force which I have the honour of commanding," he wrote, "will enter your Province representing no party, either in religion or politics and will afford equal protection to the lives and property of all races and of all creeds.

"Strictest order and discipline will be maintained and private property will be carefully respected."

Riel supervised the printing of the document and had it distributed everywhere in the Settlement. He asked the various parishes to get together and plan the ceremony of greeting for the new lieutenant-governor, expected any day. There was to be a huge bonfire, speeches by Riel—he'd already begun work on his—Taché, Bannatyne and others, a splendid banquet, a special interdenominational church service.

Riel had given permission for the Canadian government to hire labourers to clear the debris that made the Red River end of the Dawson Road impassable. And he had sent four boatloads of Métis to help guide the troops and clear the road to the Winnipeg River. The word these men sent back caused the entire Red River Valley to shudder.

Around the campfires at night, the Canadian soldiers talked of little but revenge. The ninety-two-day nightmare they had just experienced had only exacerbated the itching for blood that these soldiers already felt; such misery could only find relief in the bashing of a few "savage heads".

On August 23, Bishop Taché finally arrived back at Red River. No, he told the expectant crowd gathered around him, he did not have a piece of paper on which a pardon was carefully spelled out. But an amnesty was on its way, he insisted. Sir John Young had told him so. And the lieutenant-governor would be here long before Wolseley's expedition arrived. Riel was astonished at the naivety and would later write, "I would not even reply." For by then the Canadian soldiers were camped only twenty miles away, at the Stone Fort.

That night it rained so hard and the wind struck with such force that the expedition's tents were flattened, and every man was soaked to the skin. When reveille sounded at three a.m., the fires they managed to light were just enough to provide each man a gulp of tea. The 60th Rifles were first in action. Boats carried them downriver to two and a half miles north of Fort Garry. Then everything had to be loaded into carts and pulled by a "few wretched ponies". The exhausted men strained against the carts, pushing them along the trail, waist-deep in "thick, slippery black mud". In the mist they could barely make out the twin towers of St. Boniface, the farmhouses, the windmills, the huddle that was the village of Winnipeg, but they were surprised and disappointed. They had expected to be greeted like a liberating force, with flags flying and bands playing, no matter what the weather. But hardly anybody, not even the newly arrived Canadian settlers, stuck their heads out of their houses to welcome them. Captain Redvers Buller, a member of Wolseley's staff, wrote in his diary: "We were enthusiastically greeted by one half-naked Indian, very drunk." The few settlers they did encounter told them Riel and the Métis soldiers were lodged at Fort Garry, ready to shoot it out.

The previous evening, Riel had met with his council as well as Joseph Dubuc, an old schoolfriend who had arrived that summer. He had told the group that his ministers should not leave their posts until the troops had taken possession of the fort. "More than ever," he said, "it is important that our men leave in an orderly manner." At that point he decided to reconnoitre the situation himself. Four men, armed and mounted on horseback, went with him.

In the pelting rain they could barely make out their way, and they held each others' hands so as not to get lost. In the vicinity of Seven Oaks, the very spot where years before the Métis had won their decisive victory over Governor Semple, they saw the dim lights of Colonel Wolseley's camp. The group approached a little closer, but the horses kept snorting as if on alert. Afraid they'd be spotted, they turned back, arriving at the fort at one a.m.

Riel ordered all the Métis still lodging at Fort Garry to gather everything they owned and carry it to safety. Louis Schmidt bundled up the official papers and took them into hiding. Then, as Riel would later write,

> I took off my wet overcoat and my shoes, threw two heavy blankets on my back, wrapped myself up in them and went to bed; I slept for about three quarters of an hour. When I got up, it was beginning to dawn. The rain had not abated. About eight o'clock a breakfast of cold meats was served to me: I was hungry: I ate well, but the cold and the lack of sleep had undoubtedly indisposed me too much: I felt it soon after breakfast.

Very shortly after, an English settler, James G. Stewart, arrived full speed on horseback, shouting, "For the love of God save yourself. The troops are only two miles from here and the soldiers speak of nothing but massacring you and your companions."

The Métis leader quickly made sure the fort was evacuated. Standing in the square as the wind and rain whipped through it, Louis Riel must have felt a stab of regret. Was his brief fling with power now over? Was this the end of it all? He looked around one last time and then, with O'Donoghue, he hurried out the south entrance.

The troops arrived at that very moment. As Captain Buller described it, "Finding the back door shut we marched around to the front one which we found open. We formed a line, fired 21 guns, presented arms, gave three cheers for the Queen, and stood at ease in the rain and so ended the attack and capture of Fort Garry."

What Buller and the others didn't know was that *le président* was watching the whole performance. Riel would later recall:

> I remained in view, I was small. I did not wish to stand in his [Wolseley's] way. But as I knew that he had good eyes, I said to myself: "I will stay at a distance where I may be seen and if he wants to have me, he may come." ... I was about 300 yards ahead of him. While he was saying that Riel's bandits had fled, Riel was standing beside him.

PART III
EXILE

– 9 –

You glide above my humble retreat
You have sheltered me proud American eagle!
Hail! In your rapid expansion, glory to your noble leader.
The ill-fated receive your hospitality!
But the setbacks only excite my courage!
Trembling in the calm where I walk secure
I will summon up the pride to suffer the insults.

After Wolseley's "victory" ceremonies, Riel and O'Donoghue crossed the Red River to St. Boniface. Bishop Taché, standing on the veranda of his rectory, saw the two men approaching fast on horseback through the rain.
"You have left the fort?" he yelled at them.

"Yes, we have fled for our lives, because it appears we have been deceived," Riel answered back.

A short conversation followed during which Riel, in a most respectful way, made it clear that he was disillusioned with the bishop's gullibility. He didn't say it directly to Taché, but he told others, "It is you, Monseigneur, who will cause us to hang."

Louis made a quick stop at St. Vital to say goodbye to his distraught mother and brothers and sisters. Julie had been enormously proud of, if not a little overawed by, her son's accomplishments. Now suddenly, this, her most beloved child, was in grave danger.

Ambroise Lépine joined Riel and O'Donoghue and the fugitives began their journey southwards to the American border.

During that first night, the three were so exhausted that they slept deeply, unaware that their horses had wandered away. They then had to make their way painfully and slowly on foot. The main trail to Pembina would soon be thick with Canadian soldiers, they thought, so they decided to cross the Red River and continue their journey on a well-hidden path on the west side. Taking off pieces of clothing, including Lépine's L'Assomption sash, they tied together several fenceposts which they had uprooted and created a makeshift raft. This got them across all right, but Louis lost one of his shoes. He had to endure the remainder of the journey—thirty miles or so—barefoot.

Tired, famished and soaked to the skin, they managed to reach Pembina, where O'Donoghue and Lépine planned to stay, but Riel, afraid for his life, decided to push on, though he happily accepted a warm meal and a pair of shoes. Antoine Gladu, a relative of the Winnipeg butcher who had put Riel up during the Red River resistance, volunteered to guide him through the heavily wooded country west of Pembina.

On August 28, they finally reached what was considered a safe haven—the little Métis community of St. Joseph where Jean-Marie LeFloch was parish priest. It was Father LeFloch who had prepared the young Louis for his first communion and taught him Greek and Latin in preparation for his education in the East. Riel felt secure with him. Exhausted, worried, he collapsed into bed.

The next day he wrote his friend Joseph Dubuc in St. Boniface. Anxiously asking for news of everything that had happened, Louis was obviously very upset. "Pray for me, we have been betrayed!!!!" Foremost in his mind was the well-being of his three younger brothers, who he may have thought were in danger from Wolseley's soldiers. If Dubuc should see Alexandre, "my little pet," Riel begged, "embrace him for me."

Word quickly reached Sara Riel at the St. Norbert convent that Louis was safe, and she was able to reassure her worried mother. Julie prayed day and night for her beloved son. "My poor boy—my little Louis. He is everything to me, he is my life," she told Sara.

She had every reason to be concerned. She had seen soldiers beating the bushes in the woods around St. Vital, carrying a rope to hang Riel if they should find him. Colonel Wolseley's first proclamation was an outrage. He praised his soldiers for their great "fortitude" and called the Métis "the banditti who recently oppressed Her Majesty's loyal subjects in Red River". Never mind that Riel had been asked by Cartier to continue governing the community until the lieutenant-governor arrived; never mind that Wolseley's purported mission was "to afford equal protection to lives and property of all races and of all creeds".

What Wolseley's troops had wanted was a good fight and sweet revenge. Now their gruelling trip seemed for naught. As Redvers Buller put it, "It does so disgust one to have come all this way for the band to play God save the Queen." Excitement of some kind had to be manufactured.

The looting began immediately. In Fort Garry the soldiers found Riel's breakfast on the table "warm and half-eaten", and for some reason that infuriated them. They began to plunder systematically: anything they considered of value they kept, everything else they destroyed. Buller, for example, grabbed some "elegant" writing paper that *le président* had used. Only when it was explained that it was mostly the Hudson's Bay Company's property they were demolishing did they cease.

O'Lone's, Dutch George's and Monchamps's saloons quickly filled up with the swaggering soldiers and the voyageurs who had made the long trip possible. An orgy of debauchery and violence got under way. On the streets of Winnipeg, intoxicated soldiers fought drunken Indians and Half-breeds with knives. There was "rolling and fighting in the many mudholes of Winnipeg", as the shocked Reverend Young put it, until the gutters were full of vomit and blood. In three days all the pubs had been drunk dry and more whisky had to be transported by cart from Pembina.

Ten days after the soldiers descended on Red River, Lieutenant-Governor Adams G. Archibald arrived to establish a civilian government and set up a police force. Although he was an honourable man, sympathetic to the Métis, it took him a long time to assert order. For what very quickly developed was a *de facto* parallel government more powerful and driven than his administration.

On September 18, Lodge 1307 of the Loyal Order of the Orange was established at Winnipeg, and it became the effective ruling authority in Red River. Canadians already living in the Settlement, the soldiers recently demobilized and new arrivals flooding in from Orange Ontario formed its nucleus; when John Schultz returned, he became the ruling power. They were bent on one thing—revenge against the hated Catholic French-speakers. A virtual reign of terror descended.

The frightened Métis locked themselves in their homes, rarely venturing out except in groups. But the harassment, often brutal, of these people was unrelenting. Homes were searched and ransacked; Half-breeds and Métis were hunted down like animals; young girls were stripped naked, made to dance in front of drunken gangs and then raped.*

Elzéar Goulet was an American citizen, a member of the Métis bourgeoisie

---

* Standard histories seldom refer to this unsavoury crime against the civilian population because there is "little documentary evidence". But one of the few historians entirely sympathetic to the Métis cause, Auguste de Tremaudan, claims he was told by many "old-timers" about such rapes.

in Pembina who was well liked and respected by the old settlers of Red River because he had intervened to prevent several violent attacks against them by Sioux. He had come to Red River in 1869 to assist in the resistance, and he had been a member of the court martial which had condemned Thomas Scott to death for treason.

On September 13, Goulet was on his way to pick up his mail in Winnipeg when he was spotted by one of Schultz's long-time supporters who had been imprisoned by the Riel forces. This man, a friend and two Ontario soldiers went after Goulet, shouting, "Lynch him, lynch him." The thirty-four-year-old man ran to the Red River and, in a desperate attempt to make it to the other side, jumped in and began swimming. His pursuers began lobbing rocks at him until one hit him on the head, knocking him unconscious. He soon disappeared beneath the water. An inquest was held into the death, and subpoenas for two of Goulet's attackers were issued, but no arrests were ever made. In a final brutality, his seventeen-year-old daughter, Laurette, was later raped by Canadian soldiers.

Soon the "peaceful expedition" claimed other victims. François Guillemette, the man who had administered the final *coup de grâce* to Scott, was also identified by vengeful Ontario volunteers. He fled to Pembina, but within a week his badly beaten body was found in a field. Bob O'Lone was knifed to death during a drunken brawl in his own saloon. James Tanner, a Protestant Half-breed, died after falling from his horse; a group of drunken "ex-soldiers" had shot at the animal's feet. Father François-Xavier Kavanagh, a young priest at White Horse Plains, was wounded by a trigger-happy Canadian. Baptiste Lépine, one of Ambroise's brothers, was murdered in mysterious circumstances. Finally André Nault, Riel's cousin who had intercepted the Dawson Road surveying team, was chased to Pembina by malicious Canadians bent on murder. They overtook him, repeatedly stuck him with their bayonets and left him for dead on the prairie. Fortunately he survived the attack.

War was being waged on Bishop Taché himself. Repeated threats to invade his residence, burn down his cathedral and murder him had terrified him and his parishioners. The bishop wrote angry letters to various Ottawa politicians, expressing his outrage. George-Étienne Cartier responded:

> I cannot help but see from your last letter how much your good heart is bleeding with sorrow since the arrival of the military expedition. Wolseley's stupid proclamation, the murder of Goulet and other facts and circumstances must have been more than enough to fill your soul with sadness. You must have seen from the papers of Montreal and elsewhere how much Wolseley has been blamed for his proclamation. We have let them know in England what we think of it.

Cartier may have been genuinely sympathetic, but he was also admitting that anarchy did indeed reign in Red River and there was little Ottawa was prepared to do about it. The protest to the British government about Wolseley's command obviously meant little, for on his return east the colonel was given a hero's welcome and rapidly promoted; by 1895 he was commander-in-chief of the British Army. In comparison to the chaos the expedition left in its wake, Riel's ten-month administration had been a model of order, fairness and control.

Louis himself was in the utmost danger. Wolseley had written in his diary: "Hope Riel will have bolted, for although I should like to hang him from the highest tree in the place, I have such a horror of rebels and vermin of his kidney that my treatment of him might not be approved by the civil powers."

The colonel may have had some inkling that he was transgressing the "peaceful" purpose of his mission, but there was someone else who was able to stamp his vindictiveness with legality—Riel's old sparring partner, Donald Smith.

Smith had returned to Montreal in March 1870 to find himself a hero, admired for his "untiring and unselfish effort in pacifying the rebels". He was soon promoted by the Hudson's Bay Company to president of its northern department, and by July he was back in the West. For the eight days between the time Wolseley's expedition descended and Lieutenant-Governor Adams Archibald arrived, Smith was the government at Red River. He achieved two important things: he closed the pubs at night and he signed a warrant for the arrest of Louis Riel (as well as Ambroise Lépine and William O'Donoghue). When John Schultz's father-in-law, James Farquharson, put up an award of £20, the hunt was on.

In several letters written at the time, Louis mentions his fear that he will be murdered by Schultz's supporters; on September 9 he complained to Bishop Taché, "For the last seven or eight days, the assassins surround the places where I spend the night." Whether his anxiety was founded on specific information or a general idea of what Wolseley's soldiers were capable of is not known. But everyone from his sister Sara to Bishop Taché warned him not to return to Red River. He did, however, three weeks after he had fled from Fort Garry, but only for a few days and in great secrecy.

It was the murder of Elzéar Goulet that galvanized the Métis leaders into action. Goulet had been a close friend of them all, a special favourite of Louis's, and they were outraged by his death. Riel and O'Donoghue travelled to Pointe-à-Michel, only a mile from St. Joseph, on the American side of the border, where Ambroise Lépine was hiding out. After some discussion, it was decided that a conference would be held at Father Ritchot's rectory at St. Norbert. It was here the national committee had been formed in the fall of 1869, and the Red River resistance born; perhaps the memory of their success would give them courage.

Under cover of darkness, Riel carefully made his way north on horse-back across the border to St. Norbert. There in Father Ritchot's rectory, he met with forty of his fellow Métis activists. After a night of deliberation and several days in committee, a "Memorial of the people of Rupert's Land and North-West" to Ulysses S. Grant, President of the United States, was drafted. It was a chronological detailing of the main events of the Red River resistance from the Métis point of view. It was also, though written in the stilted language of such a document, a *cri de coeur* against the injustices they were enduring:

> That not a single pledge given by the English and Canadian Government to our people, and to the Government of the United States, has been kept or performed, but on the contrary, each and every one as set forth in this memorial, has been ruthlessly and revengefully violated and trampled upon.

The American president was asked to investigate "such unwarranted outrages and unpardonable perfidy" and intervene with the British monarch on their behalf.

For most of the time the memorial was being thrashed out, the debate had gone smoothly. Suddenly, O'Donoghue was insisting that American annexation of the Northwest was the only way that the Métis would ever enjoy full status as citizens. During his short stay at St. Joseph, Riel had seen that the Half-breeds were certainly no better off in the United States. He answered O'Donoghue: there was nothing wrong with the Manitoba Act passed by the Canadian Parliament the previous May; the amnesty would soon be granted, Bishop Taché and Father Ritchot were still certain. O'Donoghue continued to argue, ridiculing Riel's naivety. Perhaps because many of his loyal followers were becoming more and more sympathetic to O'Donoghue's way of thinking, Riel lashed out at his former friend. His face beet-red with anger, he yelled that O'Donoghue had only been of value during the troubles because of "your Goddamn tongue". It was a bitter argument, and the two men were not on speaking terms when they parted.

Before leaving, Riel was able to spend a little time with his family, including his adoring sister Sara. He learned that she had been transferred from the St. Norbert convent back to the safety of the St. Boniface mother house, where she tended the ill in the hospital, taught and was "in charge of mending linen for the community".

Reluctantly, and only at the urging of all his close associates, Riel returned to the United States. He would spend the next seven months in the St. Joseph–Pembina area of what was then Dakota Territory.

St. Joseph* was the small village that Father Belcourt, the old friend and ally of Louis's father, had founded in 1851 after the Métis had been flooded out of their homes near Pembina. It was located forty miles west, on a higher elevation, nestled against the Pembina Mountains. Although it had once been an important centre for nomad buffalo-hunters, with a population of 1,200 people, by the time Riel arrived in 1870 all that remained was a handful of families living in thatched-roof log huts scattered along the Pembina River.

Most of the villagers worked for Antoine Blanc Gingras, a "large, jolly, fat" American who liked to sing patriotic Métis songs. He had built his impressive oak and cedar trading post in a secluded wooded area near the river in 1843–44, and had built up a thriving trade, plying carts full of furs, pemmican and, most profitably, whisky for the Indians, to and from St. Paul. He had supported the Métis cause during the Red River resistance, and while he was in exile at St. Joseph Riel had been a frequent visitor to his establishment. Gingras may have given him money, for Louis was beginning his long years of living off the charity of others.

At first Riel's fear of assassination forced him to be constantly on the move. But by November he had settled at Pointe-à-Michel, a tiny enclave of Métis farmhouses on the banks of the Pembina River. This was where the farm of Charles Grant was situated, and Louis probably lived in a log house on his property. A prosperous farmer and merchant, Charles was the son of the famous Cuthbert Grant and a confidant of Father Belcourt's. He had also been a close friend of Riel's father.

Louis's nineteen-year-old sister, Marie, came to tend house for her brother and teach the local children the rudiments of reading and writing. Later, sixteen-year-old Charles Riel joined them.

During the fall of 1870, Riel worked in the fields, harvesting. Ambroise Lépine's wife had visited Louis and, after returning to St. Boniface, reported her findings to the Riel family. Sara wrote, "I was sorry to hear that you were obliged to cut hay yourself. She [Madame Lépine] said your hands were sore.... Poor Louis, I wish to see a future for you in which the days are more secure, more agreeable."

It was a time of great anxiety for Riel, but also of intense inner reflection. During his walks through the grassy woodland edges at Pointe-à-Michel, he must have encountered the erratic gray partridge, because he wrote a song about the birds. Theirs, he thought, was a blessed existence:

> I hear the joyful partridge
> It is her time of love.
> She is gay. She is happy.

---

* *By 1871 there were so few Métis left and so many Scandinavian settlers arriving that St. Joseph was rechristened Walhalla, the name it bears to this day.*

> She applauds the beautiful day.
> I hear the rustle of her wing.
> Slow, striking, bending, beating, all aflutter
> She beats her wings
> And dances a greeting to her scurrying lover.

The partridge's innocent and reckless life is abruptly ended when suddenly a hunter with "cruel hands" arrives. Louis's symbolism is obvious: the partridges represent the Métis, the hunter the Canadian soldiers.

In Riel's need to find emotional respite from the almost incomprehensible injustices being perpetrated against him and his fellow Métis, two major themes emerged during that troubled fall which would grow more deeply felt in future years. First was his Roman Catholicism, which was beginning to show signs of the personal and peculiar religion he would later evolve. "To My Good Angel" was one of the first of his personal religious poems—these would grow more intense as the years passed.

> Oh! An angel of heaven walks here
> Who never ceases to guide me.
> Oh! It is to him that my soul calls
> At every instant. But especially when bitterness
> Fills the cup from which I drink,
> Angel from heaven, my good guardian angel
> Come to me, come! In the midst of adversity
> Who will support me if not you?
> Ah! I am always with you.

Riel's other shield from a reality he found hard to bear was his glorification of Quebec as a sanctuary for the Métis people, a kind of Utopia. He may also have been remembering with longing his golden time as a student in Montreal. His poem "O Québec" reflects this idealized view of history:

> Québec, our motherland,
> You were the precious love of our forebears.
> I will cherish all my days
> Your lovely name, pronouncing it always.
> Québec, beloved home,
> Never forget your many Métis sons
> By Manitoba shunned,
> Their support for you remains as ever strong.*

---

* Translation by Paul Savoie.

On November 7, 1870, a letter was sent to Louis Riel from citizens of St. Vital asking him to stand as a candidate in the first elections for the legislative assembly of Manitoba. Other invitations quickly arrived from St. Norbert and Pointe-Coupée. Riel turned all the requests down. He had received word that Cartier did not want him involved in active politics for the time being, and although it probably caused him great pain, he accepted the elder statesman's advice.

Cartier, to whom four years before Riel had sent long poems asking for a job, was still considered a hero by most Métis. The elegant "Silver Fox" personified the vision of a "noble" Quebec which Riel had so eloquently expressed. And, of course, they were still hoping the influential politician would come through with an amnesty for the Red River insurgents.

It was pointed out to Riel that the leaders of the 1837 Rebellion, including Cartier, had waited out a three-year voluntary exile and then returned to Quebec politics without a blot on their records. Louis felt he had no alternative but to decline the many "kind" petitions to rejoin the political fray and watch the historical events from his isolated exile in Pointe-à-Michel.

The election held on December 30 was a triumph for the Métis and the old settlers. At least half of those elected had been activists during the Red River resistance, including the two secretaries, Louis Schmidt and Thomas Bunn. The riding of St. Vital, where Riel would have been a candidate in other circumstances, was won by André Beauchemin, one of his greatest supporters. Best of all, John Schultz was soundly defeated, by none other than the Hudson's Bay Company's Donald Smith.

At first Riel was overjoyed at the news. Writing to Bishop Taché on January 18, 1871, he could not contain his excitement. He crowed: "God has not turned away his kindness from us. Instead of McDougall, Monsieur Archibald! Instead of wicked enemies of the country, a good number of honest people, our friends! Instead of a Schultz rejoicing in his secret schemes, a schultz full of resentment, degradation, contempt...."

But the euphoria did not last long. The former president soon became depressed and bitter. His old comrade-in-arms, Louis Schmidt, understood precisely the reason for his melancholy. "Poor friend," he wrote of Louis, "how sorry we felt to see him in exile far removed and a useless spectator of the great events taking place in his beloved country."

Riel's brief falling-out with his old friend Joseph Dubuc was indicative of his testy mood. Although four years older, Dubuc had been a great chum of his at the Collège de Montréal. He had been called to the bar in 1869, and Louis had kept writing to him, pleading with him to consider a career at St. Boniface. Dubuc had finally decided to take his friend's advice, and had travelled with

Ritchot when the priest had returned to Red River the previous June. Riel had been delighted to see him, feeling he now had a soulmate to share his inner thoughts and aspirations; Dubuc, his "great dear friend", was the first person he communicated with after he fled to St. Joseph.

In October Joseph Dubuc paid Riel a visit at Pointe-à-Michel, and it may have been he who broke the news that Cartier wanted Louis to stay out of politics. At any rate, something was said about the election that offended Riel.

Dubuc kept apologizing—"I regret that I caused you pain during my last visit. However, you promised your sentiments towards me would not change," he wrote in December—and Riel kept issuing assurances in reply—"I promise you nothing will change between us." Yet obviously Riel had felt hurt, because by mid-January his letters to his old schoolmate had stopped. "I would prefer to have something more substantial than your silence," Dubuc scolded in a letter of February 10. Riel's sister Sara wrote on February 5, 1871: "Mr. Dubuc ... suffers from your silence, by the way. He is afraid he demeaned you during his last visit to St. Joseph in regard to the elections. Your silence confirms his fears.... He is very sensitive, and was so upset that he could hardly speak. He loves you very much ... write to him please."

Joseph Dubuc, a newcomer, an outsider, had been elected by acclamation in the riding of Baie-St.-Paul and had been named secretary in the first legislative council. Perhaps Riel could sense that his friend was beginning a long and distinguished career (he would become speaker of the legislative assembly, hold a seat in the House of Commons, and have a stint as chief justice of the court of King's Bench) while he, Louis, who had in effect set the stage for such success, would likely never be rewarded for it.

Or Louis may simply have been too ill to write. At the end of the first week in February he caught a cold that went immediately to his chest. This quickly developed into what was probably rheumatic fever; his temperature soared and the joints of his arms and legs became red, swollen and painful. On top of that he was deeply depressed. He was still terrified of assassins; Dubuc had written him in mid-January to beware. Charles Nault had been told that an "Indian in your [Riel's] neighbourhood is to be paid to poison you." There was still no word on the long-promised amnesty, and important political events were fermenting without him.

By February 16, 1871, Louis's condition was so serious that his sister Marie, who was ill herself, and his brother Charles began to panic. A message was sent to their eldest sister, but Louis insisted that his mother not be told of his condition lest she worry too much. Sara's letter in response, written on February 20, is a vivid illustration of the intense emotional relationships among the various members of the Riel family.

Ah, dear Louis, forgive me for going against your wishes.... [The messenger] told me your sickness had become serious and that our dear little sister could succumb to fatigue and above all, to the pain of watching you suffer without being able to help you. This made me decide to tell Mamma. I trembled when I announced it to her, because she is so sensitive when it comes to you.... At last I made up my mind to tell her. The pallor in her face and the trembling that seized her, revealed the emotions gripping her from within.

When Sara broke the news of Louis's illness to the other children, their reaction bordered on hysteria. Eighteen-year-old Octavie, still studying at the Grey Nuns' boarding school with her sisters, "cried and sobbed ... she cannot hear her brother's name without getting upset and starting to cry."

Julie Riel made the trip to Pointe-à-Michel and slowly nursed her two children back to health. By March Louis was back on his feet again, although his legs and arms remained weak.

He had already decided that the political situation had calmed down enough that he could return to his home in St. Vital. On April 4, he wrote Joseph Dubuc telling him that unless he was was prevented by the bad roads and Father LeFloch worrying about his weakened condition, he would be home for Easter. "Waiting too long will do me harm," he wrote, "for I wish to begin my spring seeding as soon as possible." He was still responsible for the support of his large family, and this weighed heavily on him. But Dubuc replied with a letter urging caution. At the beginning of May, many of the Ontario militia would be demobilized, and they might still be looking for a fight. "If you come be careful of the roads," he warned. Finally, on May 3, 1871, Riel arrived at St. Vital.

Very quickly the crowds started gathering at the family's small white house; day and night the place was packed with relatives, friends, including some former enemies—Louis was even reconciled with his maverick cousin Charles Nolin. It was a belated celebration for a "great patriot" and the "true leader of Manitoba's destiny".

Louis remained quietly in the background for most of that summer. He was still afraid for his life, especially since his old *bête noire*, John Schultz, had started a new campaign to have "the guilty party pay for the death of poor Thomas Scott". Although Schultz had been defeated in the provincial election, the first election for Manitoba's federal House of Commons seats, held on March 12, 1871, had proved a disaster. The Ontario Party, as the "Canadians" were now called, was determined never to suffer embarrassment again. Through bribery, bullying and more subtle intimidation, "an orgy of brawling", as one historian put it, they ensured that three of the four seats went to anti-Riel English. John Schultz was one of those elected. He was also awarded compensation for losses during the Red River resistance—he asked for a whopping $65,000, $10,000 for his suffering in prison.

The Métis hummed a little song that fall that expressed their bitterness:

> To John Schultz, honour and money, aplenty;
> To friend fools, scaffolds or pockets empty.

Many of the Ontario soldiers had decided to remain permanently in Red River, mainly because they had been rewarded for their "valiant service" with 160-acre land grants. Some were still determined to have Riel's head, and continually threatened to issue warrants for the arrest of the Métis leaders.

But there were other reasons Louis Riel kept out of the limelight. He was working hard to make the farm a viable operation. And he was dealing with family crises. Chief among these was Sister Sara's announcement that she was about to make a grave sacrifice: the first St. Boniface girl to become a nun, now she would be the first Métisse to become a missionary.

When her beloved Louis was forced to flee to St. Joseph, Sara had become obsessed with the idea of exile. "I want to follow in the footsteps of my brother," she repeated so often it was like a mantra. Finally, she made what she considered a pact with God: if she withdrew from society and the family she loved so much, then Louis would be returned to his people.

When Riel arrived at St. Vital, Sister Sara concluded that God's half of the bargain had been met; now it was her turn to fulfil the other half. She announced that she was joining a group of missionaries headed for Ile-à-la-Crosse, the very place her father had been born fifty-four years before. While still on the difficult journey, she wrote, "The more I endure, and undergo hardships and misery, the more I feel that my sacrifice has been accepted and the conditions have been met."

All summer Riel refused requests for interviews from American journalists, and he not too politely declined to meet people he thought were politically dangerous, such as Alfred Scott, one of the three Red River negotiators. However, by September he felt secure enough to make a public appearance. He was among the crowd gathered in St. Boniface Cathedral to celebrate Alexandre Taché's investiture as Archbishop of St. Boniface. And on September 28, 1871, a meeting of Métis leaders was held at the St. Vital house of Riel's mother to discuss the dominion government's record of broken promises. Louis was back in the business of activist politics.

There was a lot to complain about: the amnesty was still nowhere in sight, and the distribution of land to Métis families promised under the Manitoba Act was already running into problems. Most of the discussion, however, revolved around the seemingly mad exploits of the fiery Irishman and one-time ally—William O'Donoghue.

O'Donoghue had been an exceedingly busy man since the meeting at St. Norbert almost a year before, when the Memorial had been written to President Grant. At the time O'Donoghue had seemed the logical choice to present it in Washington. He had headed first to Pembina, where, with the help of Enos Stutsman, he had reworked the document and added to it so that it sounded very much as though the Métis were in favour of annexation. O'Donoghue had then gone to St. Paul, where he was fêted as a hero so enthusiastically that he didn't press on to the American capital until December. When he did get there, he found prominent annexationists working on his behalf. On December 28, 1870, he had his audience with the president. Grant received him "very kindly" and listened carefully, but it was soon obvious that he wasn't convinced that the majority of Red River people, even the French-speakers, were in favour of union with the United States.

This didn't discourage O'Donoghue. He was confident that the Métis were so oppressed under the Canadian regime that they would rise up once again, if only they had the opportunity. Overtures from the United States then would surely be welcome.

By April 1871, O'Donoghue was in New York presenting his case to the Council of Fenian Brotherhood. But the Brotherhood was leery. In recent years, organized raids across the Canadian border had all turned into fiascos. They were sympathetic to O'Donoghue, but offered him "only prayers" instead of the arms, men and money he needed.

O'Donoghue almost gave up, but when he returned to the West he discovered even more outrageous acts of intimidation had been perpetuated by the Canadians on the French-speaking population. He again became convinced that an armed invasion organized from Pembina would prove successful. This time, he was sure, disenchanted Métis would join his "expeditionary force" by the hundreds. He knew Riel would not approve, but he now considered Louis a coward and a traitor. He had told him so when they had met at Pointe-à-Michel months before—O'Donoghue had been so angry at the passivity of his former chief that he had slapped him in the face.

O'Donoghue again pleaded with the Fenians for help. Again he was turned down, but this time General John O'Neill, the president of the organization, decided to join the cause, and recruited General J.J. Donnelly and Colonel Thomas Curley. For their invasion of Manitoba they had access to four hundred Springfield rifles, which they planned to bring west.

Over the next few months the Fenians made the rounds of the dusty towns of Minnesota and Dakota, attempting to drum up support. Although their speeches were fiery, their logic, they thought, overwhelming, precious few dollars were dropped in the collection plates and few recruits rushed to pledge their allegiance to the green flag—not even the two thousand or so Irish navvies recently laid off their railway construction jobs were interested.

Meanwhile, in Pembina, O'Donoghue drafted his constitution for the Republic of Rupert's Land. He himself would hold the following posts: president, commander-in-chief of the military and chief justice.

News of such a loud campaign quickly reached Red River. Lieutenant-Governor Archibald knew well the Fenians' reputation for audacity and violence. He realized that the Métis were seething with anger, the English Half-breeds at best indifferent and many of the old settlers resentful. He also knew that Winnipeg's small force of police and militia would be no match for a large, well-equipped army. If the French-speakers joined the Fenian force, Manitoba would certainly be lost to the Americans.

Archibald naturally wanted to take the temper of the French parishes, and to this end he queried members of Red River's establishment. He was told that the only man who could influence the Métis was Louis Riel. And the way to get to Riel was through his good friend and mentor, Noel-Joseph Ritchot.

Father Ritchot, who seemed to have emerged from political quietude at the same time as Riel, pointed out to the lieutenant-governor that the long-promised amnesty had still not materialized. How could the Métis be expected to pledge loyalty to such an insensitive government? And would Louis Riel's life not be in jeopardy if he were to come forward to lead the Métis? The lieutenant-governor assured him that Mr. Riel "need be under [no] apprehension that his liberty shall be interfered with in any way." This was certainly a hint that amnesty was inching closer.

Before he left on a trip to Ottawa, Archbishop Taché had talked directly to Riel. The Métis leader was in a quandary because of the amnesty question, but according to Taché he responded:

> You know perfectly well that my life is not safe. I may go to the front and fight against the Fenians, and I am sure to be killed by those behind me. So I am at a loss ... what I can do? But you can rest assured there is not the slightest danger of me or any one of my friends going with the Fenians. We dislike the Fenians, for they are condemned by our church, and you may be assured I will have nothing to do with them.

Six days after this encounter, on September 28, the meeting of Métis leaders was held at Madame Riel's house. This was followed by another session on October 4. Once again Riel emerged as the foremost leader, and he insisted on a united show of support for Archibald's regime. Historian Phillipe Mailhot writes of his motives, "the Rielites hoped that a visible demonstration of Imperial loyalty would refute the often hurled charges of treason and perhaps hasten the promulgation of the expected amnesty." The Métis leaders decided to send out scouts to determine just how big O'Donoghue's force was. Were the rumours of nine hundred well-armed former Civil War soldiers really true?

As fall approached, O'Donoghue and his Fenian friends began to worry about cold weather setting in. Ready or not, they must proceed immediately. On October 5, in the early hours of the morning, the invading army assembled at Pembina to march across the border. It consisted of O'Donoghue, the three Fenian officers and thirty-five ragtag soldiers. They first occupied the Hudson's Bay Company post just across the border—the same place William McDougall had howled his phony imperial declaration into the wind. This wasn't exactly a difficult manoeuvre, as there was only one person, the chief trader, in the fort.

O'Donoghue's army remained there, waiting for the cloud of dust that would signal the approach of the hundreds of Métis sharpshooters they expected would join them. Hours went by but the only soldiers to appear on the horizon were a rather bored-looking company of United States Infantry commanded by Captain Lloyd Wheaton. The Fenians scattered on the prairie but most were rounded up and escorted to jail in Pembina. All the Fenian commanders were captured except O'Donoghue. Three hours later he ran into a group of Métis horsemen, all former cohorts of his. To O'Donoghue's surprise, they were anything but friendly. They marched him back across the border to Pembina and delivered him to the U.S. Army.*

Red River did not learn of the rout of the Fenians until several days later. Meanwhile, on October 4, the lieutenant-governor had issued a proclamation calling on recruits "irrespective of race or religion, or of past difficulties", to fight the Fenians. About eight hundred men from all over the Red River Settlement had presented themselves.

---

* *O'Donoghue and the other Fenians were kept in jail for only a few days. The civil court in Pembina decided there was no evidence crimes had been committed on U.S. soil, and those that occurred in Canada were beyond their jurisdiction. O'Donoghue decided to stay in the United States and soon got a job as a schoolteacher in Rosemount, Minnesota. On March 16, 1878, he died of tuberculosis. He was writing letters in support of his political activism until the very end.*

On October 5, at the moment Captain Wheaton was rounding up O'Donoghue's friends, the Métis council agreed, twelve votes to one,* to organize an armed force to join Archibald's defence. The next day it was agreed that meetings would be held at all the French communities—St. Boniface, Ste. Anne-des-Chênes, Ste. Agathe, Pointe-Coupée, St. Norbert, St. Vital. This was quickly done and every parish agreed to support the government. At that point O'Donoghue's vision of a Métis uprising was about to collapse; Manitoba as a Canadian province was saved.

Archibald wrote a note of thanks, and on the afternoon of Sunday October 8 he crossed the Red River to St. Boniface to review the Métis troops. As he rode up, the soldiers, dressed in their blue *capotes*, fired their customary salute. The lieutenant-governor dismounted and was introduced to the Métis commanders. Ambroise Lépine and Pierre Parenteau were introduced by name; Louis Riel was not, but there is no question that Archibald knew who he was. The lieutenant-governor then shook the hands of all three men. He thanked them for their loyalty and requested that mounted guards be sent to the border near St. Joseph to ensure that no stray Fenians were about. One hundred and fifty guards were dispatched the next morning.

The results of this dramatic scene were not at all what Archibald or Riel had anticipated. Salt had been rubbed in an old wound. A howl of rage issued forth from Orangemen across the land; how dare Her Majesty's representative actually grasp the "bloody hands" of Riel and Lépine? The Ontario press lambasted the lieutenant-governor for his compliancy and Prime Minister Macdonald said he was "embarrassed" that Riel had been publicly recognized. Instead of receiving gratitude for their loyal devotion to the Canadian government, the Métis were accused of abetting the Fenian cause. And for Riel, with these false accusations came the label of traitor. The long-promised amnesty receded even further into the background.

On a mild winter evening, December 8, 1871, Louis travelled from his house in St. Vital to St. Boniface. He had been asked by Joseph Royal, a lawyer who had came west with Joseph Dubuc and established the French-language newspaper *Le Métis*, to attend a founding meeting of the local chapter of the St. Jean Baptiste Society. Louis's mother, Julie, and his sister Marie were at home. At about nine o'clock, the two women heard a loud banging, their front door burst open and a gang of ten to fifteen English thugs, most of them drunk, all armed "from head to foot", burst in. Yelling that they had a warrant for Louis Riel's

---

* *Baptiste Tourond had been physically assaulted by Canadian troops in Winnipeg and he could not bring himself to vote for anything but neutrality.*

arrest, they ransacked the little house searching for him—a framed picture of Jesus in the Garden of Gethsemane, a favourite of Marie's, was taken from the wall and smashed. Finally, one of the men pointed his revolver at Marie's head, made a racist, insulting remark, and then demanded to know where her brother was. She wouldn't tell him, and he barked, "I promise I will kill him this very night if I have to go to every house in this parish."

The men galloped away just as Janvier Ritchot and Paul Proulx arrived, but they did not get a close enough glimpse of the intruders to identify them. Riel was immediately sent for and accompanied home by an armed guard. A protest was quickly dispatched to Lieutenant-Governor Archibald, but although the Riel family claimed neighbours had witnessed the event and therefore could identify the culprits, they were never apprehended.

Riel's life was again in grave danger, and again he would have to consider exile. So many powerful people wanted him to go, including the lieutenant-governor, who was alarmed that the Métis had pledged to protect Louis no matter what. One of the obnoxious Orangemen trying to serve a warrant on Riel could ignite a bloody civil war.

Joseph Royal, who had been Cartier's law clerk, had been told by his old boss that he felt it would be best for Riel to leave the country again. When Archbishop Taché heard this he became very angry. For months he had tried to cajole the Ottawa politicians into making good on their promises to him and Father Ritchot to procure an amnesty. There was not only Riel's and Lépine's safety to worry about, but his own prestige, which had been greatly tarnished. In May 1871, he had written a telling letter to George-Étienne Cartier:

> I have spared neither pains nor fatigue, nor expense, nor humiliation to re-establish order and peace, and it has come to this, that I am to receive from my people the cruel reproach that I have shamefully deceived them.... It is bad enough to be reviled by one's enemies; I cannot suffer that my people should suspect me of having betrayed them....

When a satisfactory response was not forthcoming, the archbishop decided to personally confront Cartier and Macdonald. In mid-September, in the middle of the Fenian invasion crisis, he set off on the long journey to Ottawa. His meetings with the politicians were a rude awakening. While Sir John A. did not in any way deny that he had promised amnesty for Riel and the others, he bluntly told Taché that it would not be forthcoming, at least in the immediate future. His government was facing an election the next year, the Tories were weak, and the amnesty issue just might kill them in Ontario. On the other hand, if they arrested Riel and Lépine and tried them for murder, the Tories would likely go down in Quebec.

The prime minister and Cartier had something else on their minds, something quite different. Could Archbishop Taché not be persuaded to use his influence to convince Riel to disappear for a year? Cartier suggested that if the controversy over Riel and Scott's death died down, there would be "a larger support in the elections, and ... thus [we would] be better able to procure amnesty." As usual, the archbishop could see the logic of Cartier's thinking, but he knew it would not be an easy job selling it to Riel or his other parishioners. He told Cartier, "You must remember that this man is poor; his mother is a widow with four young girls and three young boys, and she has no means of support especially when her eldest son is away." (The rumours, including newspaper reports, charging that Riel had personally enriched himself from Hudson's Bay Company stores were obviously mere fabrication. Probably Macdonald and Cartier did not bother to work out the significance of this—if this story was untrue, how many other charges levelled against the Métis leader were also false?) The prime minister quickly responded by sending Taché a bank draft for $1,000 for the Métis leader, suggesting that since Riel was irresponsible, it should be handed to him in dribs and drabs over twelve months.

In February 1872, Riel had a secret meeting with the archbishop in the waning light of the late afternoon in the little chapel at St. Vital. Louis was naturally not pleased when Taché broke the news—"I know the sacrifice I'm asking," the archbishop said. Why should he, Louis, endure another exile to save a party that had presented him with nothing but broken promises? And he thought the government owed him a lot more money. He had administered Red River as president for a full two months before the troops arrived; he had suffered insult and damage from the occupying force; his life had been repeatedly threatened. The sum being offered was simply not sufficient. The archbishop asked Donald Smith of the Hudson's Bay Company to make a donation. Smith had never liked Riel, may have even been envious of the younger man, and was not unhappy to get rid of him. He threw another £600 into the pot.

Riel reluctantly agreed to accept what he realized was nothing more than a bribe. And Lépine, who was also part of the deal, reluctantly followed his lead. They were simply in too much danger—news had reached Red River that posed the biggest threat to Louis's life so far.

The Liberal Party of Ontario, in opposition at the time, knew a juicy election issue when they saw one, and they refused to allow the controversy over the execution of Thomas Scott to die. Their leader, Edward Blake, had tried to ram a motion through the legislature demanding that the "murderers" be brought to justice. He personally would offer a reward of $5,000 for the capture of Riel and Lépine, although he knew as well as everyone else that Scott's death in Rupert's

Land was none of Ontario's business. The motion was defeated but an election was looming, and the Liberals, campaigning on the issue of vengeance against Riel, might very well be victorious. With Blake in power, the $5,000 blood money could become a reality.

On February 23, 1872, under cover of darkness, Louis Riel and Ambroise Lépine made their way towards the U.S. border. They travelled by private carriage, guarded by several Métis sharpshooters. After a brief stop at St. Joseph, probably to say hello to Father LeFloch, they continued on to St. Paul. Fortunately the weather was clear, although it was hard going through the crusted snow. They reached the city on March 2 and booked into the Montreal House on Minnesota Road, a traditional gathering place for Métis tripmen.

St. Paul was enjoying the last phase of a boom which had started when Riel had lived there last in 1868. Flour mills had been built. Other industries had followed, giving St. Paul a decidedly factory-town flavour. Although the red lights were still burning brightly in one district, the sanitary conditions were appalling and the streets were thick with mud, the frontier image was slowly disappearing. There were elegant streetlights, the St. Paul Street Railway, which was pulled by horses, had just begun operation, and the St. Paul Opera House was in full swing.

Riel and Lépine's hotel was located just around the corner from a new and "quite extensive" reading room installed by the YMCA. The two probably didn't take advantage of these delights, for during their sojourn in St. Paul they were resentful, depressed and, worst of all, constantly afraid for their lives.

Ambroise Lépine, who had never lived in a city before, had nothing to do and was bored. But Louis had received a request from Rodrigue Masson, now a member of Parliament, asking that he write an account of Thomas Scott's execution and the events during the Red River resistance. Riel had brought a stack of documents to help him in this endeavour.

But just a week after they arrived, they were shocked when they spotted the towering figure of John Schultz, and his sidekick, the dentist Walter Bown, lurking outside their hotel. Riel knew that Schultz had never gotten over the humiliation he had suffered during the Red River resistance, that he had become deeply, almost psychotically obsessed with revenge. A conspiracy was obviously in the works, and in a few days Riel and Lépine found out what it was.

William Devlin, a young carter formerly of Red River but now living in St. Paul, was handed a card on March 17, asking him to meet John Schultz at the Merchant's Hotel. He did so and the doctor quickly got to the point. "There is an opportunity for you to make some money," he told Devlin. "I want some papers that are in Riel's trunk at his boarding house. Now, if you go to his room, take from his trunk those papers and deliver them to me, I will give you

$50 down, and $1,000 will be paid by the Government of Ontario." Devlin talked to his friend John Mager, also a Red River boy, about the proposition. Both, however, decided they would not deceive the Métis leader, even for so fantastic an amount of money. The young men went to the police station, swore out an affidavit before a magistrate and took it to Riel. It was suggested that charges be laid, but Louis refused, frightened the publicity would put him and Lépine in even more danger.

He had every reason to be worried. On March 9, the Ontario government, now controlled by Blake and the Liberals, had officially announced the $5,000 award for his capture—an incredible amount of money when the average working man made less than $500 a year. Riel went into virtual seclusion, seldom daring to go out at night, using a false name, Louis Bissonette, to hide his identity. It was not a pleasant existence. On April 16, he wrote a letter to his mother in which his ennui was obvious: "Don't worry about us. We are in good enough health. Monsieur Lépine is frightfully bored, me, I am not bored, neither am I without boredom. I am between the two, between joy and sorrow. I don't relish joy, but I don't wish sorrow."

The news from home made them even more anxious. Lieutenant-Governor Archibald, who had been most sympathetic to the Métis, had announced he was taking early retirement. The "bloody" handshake with the Métis leader had met with grave criticism in Ottawa and London; but since he was a devoted Tory, he was being forced out gently. The Ontario faction greeted this "victory" with joyous celebration. Schultz put up money to construct elaborate lifelike effigies of Riel and Archibald. These were burned in the streets of Winnipeg to great cheers from the "loyalists". And not long before this display, two of Schultz's supporters had attacked Pierre Léveillé, André Nault and Maxime Lépine (Ambroise's brother). Nault was grabbed by the throat and his life threatened. As a parting shot, Archibald wrote to his superiors, "It is a crying shame that the half-breeds have been ignored. It will result in trouble and is most unjust."

On April 28, a fire broke out near the Montreal House. Riel and Lépine went to watch and happened to stand behind two men deep in conversation, a most interesting conversation. They were carefully plotting the murder of Louis Riel for the $5,000 reward being offered by the Ontario government.

This incident so frightened the two Métis that they packed their belongings and fled to the small town of Breckenridge, about 185 miles west of St. Paul, on the Dakota border. But even in this remote area they were tracked down. Late in the night on April 30, Riel happened to glance out his window and spotted two suspicious-looking characters standing at the door of the hotel. He and Lépine fled out the back. It was later discovered that the two men had been hired by Schultz to kill Riel as he came out of the hotel.

By now Ambroise Lépine had had enough. His wife's letters were causing him great anxiety—the crop was late in being seeded, one of the cows had died, the children were sick and they cried every time his name was mentioned. More important, he felt he would be safer in Red River, where Métis guards were available to protect him, than in a dark, gritty city. Lépine went back to his farm near St. Boniface and Louis returned to St. Paul. He moved into the home of a grocer, Louis Demeules, for whom he had worked for a time four years before. "It seems to me I should feel a little less anxiety here," he wrote Archbishop Taché.

Without Lépine, Riel was even more despondent. Since his memorandum of the Red River resistance written for Masson had been completed, he found himself at loose ends. Only the correspondence from home, from Archbishop Taché, from his friends—including Joseph Dubuc, who always sent long, newsy epistles which Riel loved—and from his family sustained him. A letter dated April 30, 1872, from Marie, Louis's twenty-two-year-old sister, gives a vivid picture of how the Riel family was coping and must have made Louis homesick. She wrote,

> Dear brother, never fear that we might be forgetting you.... It is true there is always a lot of work to be done, but our first concern is to make your exile less difficult—it is always in our minds, our speech, and also in our actions, because when you love someone, as we love you, you take every means to prove your affection.

Marie went on to describe the well-being of the various members of the extended family. As to the farm:

> We have not had, thanks to Divine Providence, any mishaps with the animals. Our little brothers take very good care of the milking and the three cows had their calves without difficulty. Fens gave birth to a nice little colt, a male. I can assure you that Joseph kept a careful watch for two weeks; he would get up three or four times during the night....
>
> Now I will tell you what we are thinking of sowing—10 kegs of wheat and barley, eight of peas, 12 barrels of potatoes, cabbages, lots of them, to make the garden as large as we can. Joseph Suavé will be doing the sowing. We are preparing to have the house covered and [to get a shed built.]

Riel was worried about the farm—he desperately wanted to make a go of it—but he hinted to his mother in a letter of May 17, 1872, that another matter of economic importance was weighing on his mind. When he had first returned to Red River, he had laid claim to a piece of property near Lake Manitoba. Now the government was talking about building a canal between the Red and

Saskatchewan river systems, in the vicinity of Riel's lot. The land could become valuable indeed, and he urged his mother to have one of his cousins plant barley where it would be conspicuous, to mark it as staked property.

Riel's letter home is indicative of the kind of affection and responsiblity he felt towards his family, which would last his entire life.

> Alexandre, I thank you, my dear little brother, for your small letter. I am proud of Meunier [nickname for Louis's eighteen-year-old brother Charles]. Marie tells me he is a good boy. And for Joseph tell him not to drive his little colt to death. I have no news to tell you. Give my regards to our friends and relatives. Tell them that the longer I am absent from Red River, the more my love has grown for it. Really, no one knows the anxiety I have gone through.
>
> Tell M. Lépine to write to me. He worries me very much.

There was one seductive idea that teased and sustained Louis during these months in exile. Before he had left Red River, Joseph Dubuc had talked to him about running in the next federal election, which would likely be held in the summer of 1872. The subject had been brought up again in a letter in April from Dubuc. "The voters of Provencher riding want you, and will elect you," his old friend had promised. Since the Liberals were considered friends of Schultz and his group, it was naturally assumed that Riel would stand for the Conservatives. Dubuc had already talked to Father Ritchot and the priest was also eager for Riel to run. By May, Louis had made up his mind. He wrote to Dubuc on May 17, "As for me, I am serious. And I repeat to you that I wish to be elected to the House of Commons and the provincial house, if there is no federal law opposing it." The two friends had plotted an interesting strategy: Riel was to be elected as a federal member of Parliament and then a seat would be made available for him in the provincial legislature (participation in both provincial and dominion parliaments was not unheard of in those days). After that, his goal was to be named premier of Manitoba. Then certainly Sir John A. would find himself over a barrel: he must grant an amnesty, or go against a democratically elected Parliament and a democratically elected premier with a price on his head.

Riel's letters and those he received were soon full of election news. He still had doubts about his candidacy and revealed these to Joseph Dubuc. This somehow wounded Dubuc, and Louis wrote on June 18 apologizing. It's an interesting letter because it indicates the very close relationship Louis was able to sustain with another man.

> I received your kind letter and I begin with what preoccupies me most. Have I hurt your feelings? It seems to me that it was understood between

us, by our friendship and in every other way, that neither you nor I was responsible for the difficult circumstances in which we found ourselves. Consequently, it was also understood that our intellects and hearts were in perfect accord, that we would never reproach each other, nor even think of a rebuke.

Riel had heard that the Conservative Party was trying desperately to persuade Dubuc to run for Parliament, but that the lawyer eschewed any such ambition. The prominent Métis Joseph Lemay was thinking of running but he too made it clear he would step aside for his *président*. Louis was obviously elated at being part of the political fray once again. He wrote to his chum Louis Schmidt, "Mr. Lépine will tell you if I like our dear Politics, if I have it at heart. Yes! God willing, we will not lose all...."

In June Riel moved to his old haunts in St. Joseph, which enabled him to make frequent trips to Red River. The support expressed for Louis was overwhelming; the Métis would need a strong, powerful voice in Parliament to push for what they thought were rights designated by the Manitoba Act—already the government seemed to be reneging on their land claims. Riel decided to return to St. Vital and run in the next election.

Manitoba, by this time, had been carved into four federal ridings: Marquette, northwest of Winnipeg, where White Horse Plains was situated; Selkirk on the northeast, which contained Winnipeg and many of the English-speakers; Lisgar, a mixed community to the southwest; and Provencher, which stretched southeast and included most of the French parishes. The total population of Manitoba was about 12,000, of which forty-eight percent were Métis, thirty-four percent English-speaking Half-breeds, thirteen percent whites, mostly of British and American origin, and five percent Indians.

Louis ran in Provencher, and his opponent was an Irish Catholic with a fiery temper who was fluent in English, French and Spanish. Henry J. Clarke's colourful history included prospecting for gold in California, making a name for himself as a radical journalist, working as a criminal lawyer in Montreal and fighting in the Canadian militia during the Fenian raids of 1866. He had come west to help inaugurate the province of Manitoba, having been named the first attorney-general. Clarke felt that he had been good to the Métis population and it was time he was rewarded for his patronage. Ironically, he was a remarkably unpopular man, disliked by almost everyone in the community.

Once Riel decided to run, Clarke had no hope of winning, and some of the French establishment, including Dubuc and Royal, tried to talk him out of letting his name stand for the nomination. But the more he was opposed, the more he dug his heels in.

On the cool evening of August 18, 1872, Riel and Clarke debated against each other in a crowded schoolroom in St. Norbert. Clarke insisted that Riel would be a terrible member of Parliament because he was so out of favour with the ruling elite. "He'll be shot if he goes to Ottawa," he shouted. "How will that do any of you any good?" Clarke's fuse was very short, and he ended up berating his opponent in near-racist terms which, of course, did nothing for his own reputation among the mixed-bloods. Louis remained, as *Le Métis* put it, "calm and very dignified".

As the campaign continued and Clarke realized his chances were growing slimmer by the day, he became exceedingly bitter, even violent. In the end he challenged Riel to a duel, an invitation Louis wisely turned down.

In August shocking news reached Red River. Quebec went to the polls weeks earlier in the federal election than Manitoba did, and George-Étienne Cartier had been defeated in his riding. Many factors had played against the old Quebec statesman: the great depression of the 1870s was just beginning but already its effects were being felt on Quebec's fragile economy, and, more significantly, a powerful coalition of "nationalists" had lined up against him.

Macdonald was frantic at the thought of losing his deputy prime minister and his Quebec lieutenant. He frantically sent a coded telegram to Archibald—"get Sir George elected in your province." Informants had reported to the prime minister that Riel would easily win the riding of Provencher, and the wily politician realized he must not be indebted to the rebel, so he added a few lines—"do not however allow your late [provisional] President to resign in his favour. That would make mischief in Ontario."

But Archibald knew something that Macdonald didn't: Provencher was the only riding in Manitoba considered a safe bet. The lieutenant-governor had thought the idea of Riel running was "mad"; that he would be either "expelled or shot". Here was a golden opportunity to get rid of the troublesome rebel while gaining the services of one of the most influential politicians in Ottawa. He summoned Archbishop Taché.

Taché hadn't been happy about Louis's return to the political stage, though he was already too far in disfavour with his parishioners to attempt to prevent it. But if Louis stepped aside for Cartier, then surely the Tories would be deeply beholden to him and an amnesty would quickly follow.

Told again that he must sacrifice for the sake of the Conservative Party and the public peace, Louis did not put up much of a fight. He insisted that Cartier must promise to see that the lands allocated to the Métis by the Manitoba Act became a reality. That was all; he didn't even mention the amnesty. Sir John A. wired: "Sir George will do all he can to meet the wishes of the parties." Taché and almost everyone else believed that included amnesty.

On September 14, the names of Louis Riel and Henry Clarke were put forward as candidates for the federal riding of Provencher; both men declined the nomination (Clarke had been strong-armed into doing so by Archibald). Cartier was then nominated, and since no one else came forward he won the election by acclamation. A telegram of congratulations signed by Louis Riel, Ambroise Lépine, Joseph Dubuc and Joseph Royal was sent to Sir George: "Your election in our Country is by acclamation and have reason to hope in the success of the cause trusted into your hands."

There was hardly a soul in the French parishes of Red River who did not believe that "the cause" included amnesty for Louis Riel and Ambroise Lépine.

The golden fall was a time of relative calm for Riel. Red River was not enjoying its best harvest; the spring, and therefore seeding, had come very late, and the summer had been dry with a return of the infernal grasshoppers. Louis and his brothers salvaged as much as they could of their crop. Much time was spent in dealing with the problems of the Métis and land claims, which were growing more acute every day.

Louis waited patiently, expecting that at any moment Cartier would send word that he had at last made good on his word to secure the amnesty. What he didn't know was that Sir George was in London seeking treatment for Bright's disease (a disease of the kidneys often linked with diabetes). He was mortally ill and not in a position to do a thing for his constituents, never mind unravel the knotty problems of the Métis leader and his people.

That December the Riel family was shaken by news they received from Île-à-la-Crosse. Sara Riel had come very close to death.

Her eight-hundred-mile journey by boat and ox cart in the summer of 1871, from Red River to her missionary station at Île-à-la-Crosse, had been exceedingly strenuous. It had taken sixty-eight days; the sun had shone day after day in one of the hottest Julys anybody could remember. As Sara described it, "The oxen gasped, their tongues hung out from fatigue and heat. Blows, cries, nothing could budge them." The mosquitoes were terrible, snakes seemed to be sunning themselves on every rock and sometimes a couple of cups of duck soup was the nuns' only meal for the entire day.

When they finally reached the mission, life was even more difficult and full of deprivation than Sara had imagined. The work was never-ending, the Indian children hard to teach. Letters were few and far between and the news that arrived in *Le Métis* was months out of date. She became horribly homesick. A letter home gives an indication of life's hardships at this missionary outpost:

> Dear Mamma, a word about the mission, all is swamped at Île-à-la-Crosse
> we harvested almost nothing, our garden is miserable except for the lettuce

seeds Mamma sent which we have eaten all summer, all the Sisters and others call it "maman's salad", ... our potatoes are beautiful, but God only knows whether we'll have barley or grain ... it has rained all summer, ... the hay is drowned ... we will have no butter or milk or meat next winter....

On November 27, 1872, Sara had just finished teaching a singing class when "her lungs commenced to hemorrhage". It was likely a severe case of pneumonia. By the evening her condition had deteriorated, she was in great pain and she couldn't speak. At last a priest administered extreme unction. As Sara later wrote, "'Goodbye, God of the Eucharist,' I said in my heart, Goodbye, God of the Eucharist, friendly companion of my exile. In a few moments you may be my judge. Grant me your mercy."

One of the priests at the mission was devoted to a nun, Marguerite-Marie Alacoque, who had lived in seventeenth-century France and had been the inspiration for the cult of the Sacred Heart of Jesus, founded in 1864. She had experienced numerous visitations during which Jesus revealed his heart, "sometimes burning as a furnace, sometimes torn and bleeding from the sins of mankind."

Sara began to pray to Marguerite-Marie and was immediately cured.

> I asked for my clothes. The sisters hesitated. I insisted but they dared not give them to me. They thought I was dying and did not know what I was saying. At last they yielded and brought me my dress. I got up.
> All this time I repeated over and over again: "I believe, I believe." My Sister Superior helped me dress and I could feel her trembling all over.... From death I had passed instantly into life....

Religion for the Riels was nothing if not dramatic.

The next day Sara was back at her chores. To show her gratitude, she took the name of Marguerite-Marie. "I ought to bury my name with my life under the cold snow of the cemetery and ought no longer to be known or to live on except in the memory of a mother, of a brother and of a family who love me tenderly." Her family, including Louis, seemed confused about this, and often called her by both names, Sara and Marguerite-Marie.

On December 3, 1872, yet another attempt was made to arrest Louis Riel. Not much came of it but once again he was forced into hiding. Two years after he had been named president of the provisional government, he was still not free to walk about his home town without fear of being accosted, and he was sick of it. He asked Ambroise Lépine to co-author a long appeal outlining the main events of the Red River resistance from the Métis point of view. This they quickly sent to the newly arrived lieutenant-governor, Alexander Morris, for they had received reports that he was not nearly as sympathetic to the Métis cause as his predecessor, Adams Archibald, had been.

Alexander Morris had once been Sir John A. Macdonald's law clerk, and afterwards had gone on to win elections at the provincial and federal levels, ending up as Minister of Internal Revenue in the Conservative Cabinet of 1869. He was an intimate of Sir John A.'s and was an imperialist for the business class, much as the prime minister was: the West must be opened as quickly as possible to settlers, and if they happened to be almost all English-speaking Protestants, well, that was a matter of expediency. Problems such as Métis land claims or Riel's amnesty were to be treated as nuisances—if one didn't bother with them they would go away. Historians D.N. Sprague and Phillipe R. Mailhot write that Morris "proved much more successful [than Archibald] at playing the game of calculated delay while at the same time giving pleasant assurances that all was proceeding in a spirit of liberal generosity." Morris didn't even acknowledge Riel and Lépine's appeal; he merely sent it on to Ottawa.

On January 25, 1873, tragedy struck the Riel family. After a terrible night of convulsions and high fever, Louis's second sister, Marie, died from influenza. She was only twenty-two. Perhaps because her health had been fragile since childhood, Marie had been considered the delicate one, the "precious" one. It was she who had never failed to donate her tiny salary as a schoolteacher to her family, who had always looked after her younger siblings, who had gone to St. Joseph to care for her sick brother. The family mourned her deeply, her mother suffering terrible headaches for years after her death.

Writing to break the dreadful news to Sara, Louis lamented: "Oh! I wish to be near you to help you, crying with you, during the first moment of cruel anxiety and real pain. I am consoled over your absence because I am a Christian and I know you will submit to the will of God."

During March and April, Riel immersed himself in a religious retreat at St. Boniface. It was something he had been planning to do since he himself had taken ill in St. Joseph. Marie's death probably spurred him on but Sara was a catalyst as well. Off and on for years she had urged her brother to consider entering the religious life, and on March 9 she wrote, "Without thinking, I don't know why, I catch myself saying ... O Lord, see to it that my beloved brother steps up to the altar. Why this prayer? God only knows. I do not intend to upset you." A week later Louis began the retreat to consider his vocation. To Sara's disappointment, he emerged convinced that the life of a priest was not for him.

Writing to Archbishop Taché two years later, Louis remembered another reason for his spiritual quest. Before he left the Collège de Montréal, he wrote, he had promised to remain in secular life for only ten years before he "gave himself up to God". During his illness in St. Joseph, he had been reminded of his vow. He now wanted to be freed from it, and emerging from his retreat, he prayed to God:

> I love the world; I want to pass my life there ... I beg You, give me as a lay-man the circumstances, the opportunity and Your help so that throughout my life even to the last breath I earn You more glory, I serve religion more, I save more souls from hell and deliver more from purgatory, I work more effectively for the good of society, I sanctify myself more than I could in the ecclesiastical state....

Writing to his sister the following July, Louis hinted at something else he was thinking about: "But listen, I have a favour to ask. Pray that I may soon establish myself at home. Ask God to grant me the grace to choose a pious and holy mate...."

In the same letter he related a dramatic spiritual cartharsis that he had undergone in June 1873. (In years to come, every time someone close to him died, he would have a similar experience.) He was on his way to Pointe-à-Grouette, but when he reached the Rivière Sale he suddenly felt very weak and decided to spend the night at the St. Norbert convent, where Sara had served so long. Father Ritchot was absent, so Louis did not indulge in his usual habit of staying up half the night and chatting. As he related to Sara:

> I went to bed at nine, left my lamp dim, and tried to sleep. But, impossible. Oh! If you only knew how often I have seen you during my sleepless nights, and also the one whom we will always regret [the dead Marie]. I was also seeing our dear father. No doubt that during the night, those who love me the most came to me, despite the grave and the distance, so they might prepare me for the happiness I was soon to have. I didn't sleep at all; and I was continuously having visions. I was so moved that I could not pray without tears coming to my eyes.

Louis got up at six o'clock, and was invited to breakfast by Sister Ste. Thérèse, an old friend of the family. Riel told her about his dreams. His narrative continues:

> "Well!" she said (the emotion changed her kind face and she cried). "Well," she said, "I have a treasure to give you which I have kept for you for nine years. I have often before seen you suffer. But I thought that there would be a time when you would need even more the succour which has been reserved for you.
> "You know," she continued, "that I was present at your father's last

moments. When I saw that he was about to die, I thought of you. After he had blessed the whole family, and you at the same time, it was no doubt God who pushed me to go and throw myself at his knees. And I said to him: 'before you die, please give me a special benediction for your child who is in Canada,' so that I could pass on this blessing to him in your name."

Louis knelt in prayer while she blessed him in his father's name.

Riel was exalted by this "gift" and he interpreted it as an affirmation of his decision to seek a secular life. He felt ready now to re-enter politics. He would not have to wait long. On May 20, 1873, Sir George-Étienne Cartier died in London. The riding of Provencher was up for grabs once again.

– 10 –

Those of homeland dispossessed
Though with many friendships blessed
May receive the gift of tenderness
And yet feel a profound sadness.
Friends, forgive me if my sorrow
Grieves your feeling hearts....

Early in June 1873, Riel began campaigning for the by-election called for the fall, making the rounds of the French parishes of Ste. Agathe, St. Vital and St. Charles, sitting for hours in little farmhouses, dreaming with his constituents of a more prosperous future. The more he talked to people, the more confident he became. Almost everybody supported him; even the old English-speaking settlers and merchants were kindly disposed. Robert Cunningham, the MP for Marquette, had telegraphed that Louis should be a candidate; his old ally during the Red River resistance, A.G.B. Bannatyne, promised to campaign for him at Oak Point (Ste. Anne-des-Chênes); even Donald A. Smith of the Hudson's Bay Company, now the member for Selkirk, was said to be backing him. In July a formal invitation to run was issued by the cream of Red River's French-speaking intelligentsia. By August, it looked as though he'd be handed the seat by acclamation.

And yet he must have had a premonition that, as always in his eventful life, his well-being would be short-lived, that dark clouds were once again gathering. He wrote a sombre verse that July on a theme that would come to haunt him more and more.

Death will come as a thief.
In that very moment when my heart

Worried by sickness
Still hopes to come back to life.
Death will come. But when I recognize her,
Trembling all over between her icy hands,
I will then glimpse the web of my thoughts.
Will I then be freed from her?
A little time, only to regain
Composure, so that I may better execute the last sigh
That will seal my fate.
Can you spare me only one moment, o death?...*

There was still strong opposition to Riel from John Schultz and the Orangemen of Ontario, but this time the *agent provocateur* was Henry Clarke, the man who had fought bitterly with Riel during the election campaign the previous year, before Cartier stepped in. With the antagonistic English Half-breed William Dease, he tried to drum up opposition to Louis, but to no avail. Finally the two attempted to hold a meeting of voters without the Métis chief. It ended in a show of strength for Riel and public embarrassment for the Canadians. Nonetheless, for an ambitious, arrogant man like Clarke, there was more than one way to skin a cat.

On September 4, 1873, the Winnipeg office of lawyer and member of the legislative assembly Francis Evans Cornish was a beehive of activity. In attendance were Henry Clarke, Cornish himself and several other prominent Schultz supporters. Now, not only did the Canadians have an attorney-general, Clarke himself, who was determined to see Riel and Ambroise Lépine imprisoned for the murder of Thomas Scott, but they had found someone who was prepared to swear out the necessary information against the two Métis. He was William Farmer, of Headingley, who, as a member of Major Boulton's force, had been imprisoned for five weeks. He maintained a passionate and unrelenting hatred for Riel. With this cabal was John Harrison O'Donnell, the doctor who had travelled with would-be Lieutenant-governor William McDougall on his journey through the prairies in the autumn of 1869. O'Donnell had been named a justice of the peace, and he was being asked to sign arrest warrants for Riel and Lépine. The doctor pleaded, "Can't you find someone else? This will ruin me in my practice in St. Boniface." More pressure was applied and, to his ever-lasting regret, O'Donnell signed.

That very night, the warrants were handed over to two policemen, John Kerr and John Ingraham, who set out with a translator, Léon Dupont, to arrest

---

* *Translation by Wilfrid Dubé.*

the two Métis leaders. By the time they had crossed the Red River and made their way to St. Vital, it was raining hard. They became bogged down in the mud and as night fell they took refuge in a barn owned by a French-speaking farmer. They later suspected this man had warned Riel of their approach, for by the time they got to Louis's house, he had fled. In fact, it was A.G.B. Bannatyne who had tipped him off.

Just as the search of Madame Riel's small house was completed, Constable Kerr noted a small opening in the ceiling covered by a trap-door. He was hoisted up through it by the others to the little attic. Kerr began stamping about; his foot got caught between the joists, he slipped and went crashing down onto a four-poster bed beneath, bringing the entire ceiling down with him. Riel's sisters, Octavie and Eulalie, were by this time in tears. Kerr mumbled that he would pay for the damages, and left the women to clean up the mess.

Lépine was not as lucky as Riel. The officers found him at home and took him to Fort Garry, clearing a path through a crowd of angry Métis. It took a whole month before the charges against Lépine were articulated and all that time he remained in prison; then on October 14, Judge Louis Bétournay finally ordered him to stand trial for murder.

The entire French-speaking community was in an uproar; *Le Métis* howled its objection and a mass meeting was held on September 22. Joseph Dubuc offered to resign his seat in the provincial legislature as a gesture of protest. A furious deputation was sent to intervene with the lieutenant-governor, but Morris's true colours were beginning to show; he would promise nothing. Next to outright civil war there was little the Métis community could do.

Meanwhile, the hunt for Riel continued day and night. The homes of his relatives were repeatedly searched, as were those of Robert Cunningham, A.G.B. Bannatyne and Father Ritchot. Much to the frustration of the Canadians, he was never found. He was hiding in the woods at Vermette's Point, across the river from St. Norbert, and would remain there for a month and a half. Using the earthy language of the *canadien* folk song, Riel expressed his indignation:

> For sustenance
> I have a bit of fruit.
> The hard earth greets me
> Every night as
> I lie down in the cold.
> Sad and alone in the woods.
> The wind I hear always murmuring.
> It seems to me your voice.

My beloved country!
It seem to me your voice.
My adorable sweetheart!

The day I find
Is not so long.
Though I experience
The most profound
Sorrow. Yet my soul is charmed
When from the sun that shimmers
I see a wreath of flames.
This crown, it shines for you
My beloved country.
This crown, it shines for you
My adorable sweetheart.*

This forty-five-day sojourn in the "wilderness" was an experience that profoundly affected Louis Riel for the rest of his life. Joseph Dubuc was reminded of the biblical King David's ordeal when he hid from the Philistines in the cave of Adullam, and Louis was so impressed with this image that he would eventually call himself Louis "David" Riel.

On October 13, about five hundred Métis gathered at the St. Norbert farm of Baptiste Tourond. They were armed and determined that no one but Riel would be nominated in the by-election for Provencher riding. Quickly Pierre Delorme put forward Riel's name, and it was seconded by many in attendance, including A.G.B. Bannantyne and Charles Nolin.

Just as the deliberations were concluding, a group of Schultz supporters walked into the assembly, sure that Riel would be there. What they encountered instead were belligerent men hungry to fight it out right then. Someone moved that nominations be continued—everyone expected that the name of Clarke would be shouted out—but there was only silence. The Canadians muttered a few oaths under their breath and then retreated. Since there were no Liberals who dared run in Provencher, Riel was elected by acclamation.

The House of Commons was scheduled to convene three days after Riel's election. It was decided that the member for Provencher should leave for the East immediately, where he could take "his due place" and present his and Lépine's case to the nation. Money for the trip needed to be raised and almost all the French-speaking establishment chipped in, as did some of the English. Archbishop Taché donated $100 to assist Julie Riel while Louis was away.

By October 21 all was ready. The voyage was far different from the one

---

Translation by Wilfrid Dubé

Louis had taken fifteen years before, when he had travelled as a young teenager to school in the East. There were no caravans of Métis carts; Riel was accompanied by two bodyguards, Maxime Lépine and Quintal Pagé. They travelled on horseback south to Moorhead in Minnesota (thereby avoiding St. Paul, which was thought to be too dangerous for Riel), and then covered the short distance to Glyndon, which was a stop on the Northern Pacific line. There Riel was joined by Joseph Tassé, a twenty-five-year-old Quebec journalist who was returning to Montreal and had volunteered to accompany the Métis leader. By train and boat they travelled through the United States, then up into Quebec.

Riel was met in Montreal by Honoré Mercier, a thirty-three-year-old lawyer and journalist who for several years had been the chief cheerleader of the Métis cause in Quebec. Although initially a political ally of Cartier's, Mercier had become increasingly nationalist in his thinking; eventually he would be considered a father of Quebec separatism. He was utterly charmed by the Métis leader and introduced Louis to Alphonse Desjardins, a lawyer and editor of *Le Nouveau Monde*. This was the newspaper that had served as a mouthpiece for the major players in the Red River resistance. Georges Dugas, the *abbé* of St. Boniface College, wrote often for the paper; the letters written by Riel himself ridiculing the poet Charlie Mair had appeared in its columns. Desjardins would have an important, but not altogether salutary, influence on Riel.

Mercier and Desjardins thought Riel should immediately take his seat in the House of Commons, and the three travelled to Ottawa for that purpose, staying at the home of a friend in Hull. But just at the moment they were to cross the Ottawa River and head for the imposing new Parliament Buildings, looming grey and formidable in the mist, Riel lost his nerve. Desperate men hungry for the $5,000 reward offered by Ontario would surely be lurking there to nab him.

By this time he was emotionally and physically exhausted; his nerve-racking sojourn in the Red River woods and the long trip east had taken their toll. His friends realized that he needed time to rest if he was not to become seriously ill. The tranquil retreat of the Oblate Fathers on Lake Champlain in Plattsburgh, New York, only seventy miles from the Canadian border, seemed the perfect place.

After he had settled in—by now it was late November 1873—Riel did seem able to relax a little. He received visitors, and he began another account of the Red River resistance, a long, detailed article of the events as he saw them, concluding with an unhappy sentiment: "The Canadian Confederation ... is for Manitoba and the Northwest a fraud and a deceit." What the Métis wanted and deserved was an immediate amnesty.

Despite this productive work, Louis continued to feel unwell. Henriette Pierrotte, the housekeeper at the Oblates' retreat, later wrote Julie Riel that her son "was very lonely and I would go to see him in his room to cheer him up and pass the time ... he would always talk about his folks, his mother and his little sister, Henriette."

In the first week in December, Riel took a short trip to the small town of Keeseville, New York, the home of Father Fabien Barnabé, who would become utterly dedicated to the Métis leader and his cause.

Barnabé had been born on June 3, 1838, near the town of L'Assomption, Quebec, one of six children. His home parish bordered on Terrebonne and the Barnabé family knew Riel's patrons, the Massons, but it's unclear whether Fabien had previously met Riel through them, or simply had heard about him. Barnabé's father was a blacksmith, but his uncle farmed on considerable acreage in the seigneurie of Saint Sulpice, and Fabien followed his example. An intense dream repeated over and over convinced him that he had another vocation, and in Montreal in 1861 he was ordained a priest. For several years after, he served in the diocese of Montreal, but in 1870 he was named pastor of St. John's Church in Keeseville, a lumber town where a large number of expatriate French Canadians had settled. The priest was a thin, bird-like man who for most of his life was in delicate health; tuberculosis would kill him at age forty-four. A newspaper report described him as "a man of a vivacious disposition, but always amiable, sincere and truthful."

Barnabé lived with his mother and his sister, Evelina. Riel may not have met Evelina Barnabé on this first trip—he doesn't mention her in his letters—but she would eventually become an important person in his life.

At Keeseville Riel's talent for making instant yet profound friendships was again demonstrated. Father Barnabé and his family became devoted to him. Louis wrote home:

> They have been very attentive towards me. During our talks, I made known to him my anxiety, my worry about all of you. And yesterday evening, seeing that I was writing you, Monsieur curé Barnabé returned with three scapulars, one for Maman, one for Octavie, one for Eulalie. A beautiful little heart for my dear little sister Henriette. Reliquaries for my little brothers....

Barnabé didn't hesitate in pouring out his affection for Riel. "I have decided to write to you to tell you just how lively is the memory of your visit," he wrote in January. "Scarcely a day passes by without your name receiving an honourable mention. We think of you, we talk about you, we feel for you as one would for a devoted friend, a loved brother. You are one of the family." The Barnabé home would become a welcome and much-needed retreat for Riel over the next few years.

On January 8, 1874, Riel succeeded in obtaining an audience with the formidable Bishop of Montreal, Ignace Bourget. The meeting was the beginning of one of those intense symbolic relationships that so often marked Riel's life; this one would lead to a strange, consuming spiritualism and eventually to emotional upheaval.

Bishop Bourget's fiefdom was the very heart of Roman Catholicism in Canada, the huge diocese of Montreal. A man of great energy and power, the bishop was also profoundly conservative, with deep authoritarian instincts that, in a curious, perverse way, Louis Riel at this point seemed to hunger for. Lost in limbo, he seemed to crave a strong and prestigious authority figure to give his political mission legitimacy. Bishop Bourget, with his rigid belief in papal infallibility, filled the bill exactly.

A tall, heavy-set, handsome man who seemed perpetually weary of the world, Bourget had spent thirty-three of his seventy-five years as Bishop of Montreal. One of the most significant things he had done was to import French religious orders—the Oblates, the Pères, Frères and Soeurs de Sainte-Croix, the Dames du Sacré-Coeur and the Jesuits, who returned to Canada eighty years after they had been banished by the British government—whose members played increasingly important roles in schools and colleges, hospitals and other charitable organizations. Through them, the Roman Catholic church had greatly tightened its hold on all aspects of Montreal life.

Bourget had been familiar with the Riel family for years—as long ago as 1843 he had lent Riel's father the money for his trip to Rainy River. The bishop closely supervised the Sulpicians, and must have kept his eye on young Riel during his time at the Collège de Montréal, hoping Louis might be the first Red River Métis to be ordained a priest. The bishop often passed on his blessings to Riel through various clergy they knew in common. Certainly, the Métis leader admired the tall, stately bishop. Completely devoted to the papal cult, Bourget would instruct, in a famous edict, "Let each say in his heart: I hear my *curé*, the *curé* hears the bishop, and the Pope hears Our Lord Jesus Christ." Between 1868 and 1870, he raised a force of mercenaries in his diocese which was sent to defend the papal state against Garibaldi. Huge, cheering crowds gathered in Montreal to wish bon voyage to the Zouaves, as these soldiers were called, and although they never actually engaged in battle, they became effective propaganda instruments for a papal revival. In several of his poems Riel lavished great praise on the Zouaves, an indication that he was becoming fascinated by the ultramontane movement inspired by Bishop Bourget.

Riel visited Bourget at the Hôtel-Dieu, where the prelate had gone to recuperate from a cold. Louis was very concerned about his own physical and emotional state—he felt close to collapse—and he fell to his knees in front of the bishop's hospital bed, pleading with Bourget to help him. "Arise, arise, you are going to recover your health. Do what your doctor prescribes. I bless the medicines that are given to you," Bourget replied.

After returning to Plattsburgh, Louis assured Bourget that he had performed the novena which the bishop had urged he make. "I made two visits to the Blessed Sacrament and I said the rosary twice. I have done the same thing every day since then. In addition I listen to Mass and I say six Pater and six Ave in the presence of our Lord. I say some invocations, the Veni Sancte and the Sub Tuum. Yesterday I recited the Prayer for the Relief of the Sick...." He was, he added, feeling "more tranquil." One would hope so.

In mid-January Louis decided he was well enough to return to Montreal. He stayed with Lucie and John Lee and there, under his aunt's care, he grew stronger. (One wonders if he met his old flame, Marie-Julie Guernon, or any of her family while he was in the neighbourhood. Her father had died by this time, but she had not married yet and was living in the family home. Much notoriety had come Louis's way since their engagement had been broken seven years before, and her mother regularly thanked God that she had put a stop to the affair.)

By the end of January Riel had accepted an invitation from Alphonse Desjardins, the editor of the *Nouveau Monde*, to move into his spacious house on Dorchester Street just behind the Bishop's Palace. Louis was assured that no one would think of looking for him there, and as the Desjardins residence was a meeting place for intellectuals and activists, he might garner a deeper understanding of the complex machinations of political life. It was after all an extremely interesting time, for Ottawa had been in an uproar for months. The Pacific Scandal had just exploded on an unsuspecting Canadian public.

In the parliamentary session two years before, in the spring of 1872, the Tories had introduced two pieces of legislation that would prove of paramount importance to the young province of Manitoba. The Dominion Lands Act granted free homesteads to settlers on the prairies and paved the way for a flood of immigrants—almost all Anglo-Saxon Protestants—to sweep over the prairies. The second legislation involved the transcontinental railway that would make it possible for masses of these pioneers to travel to the frontier. It called for the completion of the rail line from the Pacific to somewhere near Lake Nipissing in ten years. The company building it was to receive fifty million acres of free land and $30 million in federal grants.

Two competing syndicates vied to take on the great venture. A Toronto group, headed by the prime minister's old friend David Macpherson, was one; Sir Hugh Allan, founder of the Allan Line of steamships, centred in Montreal, was the other. Sir John A., fearing a charge of cronyism if he chose Macpherson, and attracted to the American capital which would be needed to build the road and which would be available to Allan, selected the Montreal group. Meanwhile, the election had been held which ended in the Tory majority being much reduced and Cartier losing his seat in Montreal. (It was at that point, in 1872, that Louis Riel had graciously stepped aside and allowed the Quebec politician to be elected by acclamation in riding of Provencher.)

In the spring of 1873, Sir John A. was well satisfied with what his government had accomplished: the Canadian Pacific Railway had been founded, the route it would follow was under survey and prosperity reigned across the nation. A month later his complacency was completely shattered.

On April 2, 1873, Liberal member L.S. Huntington rose in the House and charged that Sir Hugh Allan had given some $360,000 to the Conservative campaign in the election of the previous year. Much of the money had come from Allan's American associates. The debate that followed was one of the most vicious in Canadian history. Among the many unsavoury facts that emerged was the revelation that the Liberals had obtained much of their information from letters stolen from the office of Sir Hugh's lawyer. Be that as it might, there was no doubt that Cartier and Macdonald had begged for the money from Allan and his associates to bolster flagging Tory campaigns in Ontario and Quebec. Neither politican had personally gained financially from these donations, nor did they know that the funds came from Americans. It didn't matter. The entire nation was shocked at the scandalous revelations.

The Conservative majority in the House had depended on a number of independents who had long backed the party. By October this support had started to melt away. On November 5, 1873, Macdonald announced to a stunned House of Commons that his government had resigned.

Liberal Alexander Mackenzie, a careful and stubborn Scot, was named the new prime minister; Edward Blake, the man who had offered the $5,000 reward for the capture of Riel and Lépine, would be a major player in his administration. Louis arrived in the East only days after the Liberals had assumed power, and Blake's prominence was likely one reason he was not eager to take his seat in the Commons.

Not unexpectedly, on January 7, 1874, Prime Minister Mackenzie prorogued Parliament, calling a general election for February 13.

The Liberals were desperately hoping that Riel would not run, and to that end they telegraphed Lieutenant-Governor Morris asking him to plead with Archbishop Taché to stop Riel. Taché was indignant that once again he had been asked to do such dirty work, especially as there was not even a hint of the long-promised amnesty. In a testy letter to Antoine Dorion, the chief Quebec minister in the Liberal government, he sarcastically replied: "This man [Riel] is within two or three hours' journey of Montreal, and an eight days' journey from me, and I am to take steps to induce him to hide himself and to continue with his family in misery! What is to be offered to Mr. Riel as a recompense for the sacrifices which he is called upon to make? Misery, exile or a jail if he returns to his native land...." The archbishop flatly refused to intervene.

Riel, meanwhile, had received a pile of letters and telegrams from supporters insisting that he run again in Provencher. *Le Métis* strongly supported him. He quickly made up his mind to let his name stand, and this time, if elected, he resolved to take his place in the House of Commons—even if the threat of assassination remained very real. A plan was carefully worked out that Riel would be assigned the seat next to Alphonse Desjardins, a man with great prestige in the Commons. This, it was thought, would be a "diplomatic move to quiet the brawlers from Upper Canada".

The election campaign would have to be conducted without him—he was too fearful of arrest to return to Red River—and this time he would not breeze in by acclamation. Another Métis from a well-known family, Joseph Hamelin, was running for the Liberals against him. However, despite his absence, Riel won by 195 votes to 68.

Nation-wide, the Liberals badly defeated Macdonald's Tories, winning a commanding majority of 70 in a 206-seat House of Commons. Prime Minister Mackenzie had campaigned partly on an anti-Riel platform, daily thundering that Macdonald had deliberately promised the Métis an amnesty, something he would not permit. Riel's friends advised him to seek some sort of compromise with the Liberals. After the election, Louis travelled to Ottawa and then wrote Antoine Dorion, asking for a meeting. Dorion promptly refused. What would John Schultz, the Liberal member for Lisgar, think if his party leaders were caught negotiating with the hated Métis leader?

As the new members arrived for the opening of Parliament during the last week in March 1874, Ottawa was all abuzz. Would Riel show up in the House of Commons to take his seat? Rumours abounded that he was hiding in Ottawa and that an army of Métis sharpshooters intended to guard him as he took his seat in Parliament—everyone could picture them in their otter-skin hats, L'Assomption sashes and beaded moccasins, riding menacingly into the capital. At every elegant dinner party, during political wives' at-homes, over brandy at the Russell House hotel, the topic under discussion was the same. And John Schultz, recently returned from Manitoba, was the centre of attention. It was he, after all, who never stopped reminding people that $5,000 was the handsome reward being offered for the capture of the Métis revolutionary. In fact, the entire city of Ottawa was swarming with detectives, both policemen and privately hired, all armed with warrants for Riel's arrest.

March 26, 1874, was a bitterly cold day and the citizens of Ottawa wrapped their winter coats around themselves as they huddled against the wind, many heading for the Parliament Buildings and the opening of the legislature. Alphonse Desjardins and yet another of Louis's old school pals, Jean-Baptiste-Romauld Fiset, a medical doctor and member for Rimouski, travelled with the Métis leader from Hull to the new Parliament Buildings. Riel was thrilled with the magnificent architecture. In the fashionable Gothic Revival style, the buildings were intricate and symmetrical in design, replete with ornate gates, fancy domes, stone sculpture.

Once inside the lobby, Riel mingled with the crowd including members of Parliament, their wives and families, the elite of the business establishment. No one recognized the heavily bearded, elegantly dressed young politician. Years later he would tell a reporter that he had moved "about in the lobbies like any other member and I did not make any effort to keep out of the way. I just acted in an ordinary manner." But casual socializing was one thing; it was also necessary to legitimize his place in Parliament.

At just past one—only a few of the bureaucrats had returned from lunch— Riel and Fiset walked into the chief clerk's office. Alfred Patrick had been around for a long time, and had witnessed storm after political storm. He was polite but blasé when Fiset said he had with him a new member who would like to register. The clerk administered the oath of office and Riel quietly responded, "I do swear that I will be faithful and bear true allegiance to Her Majesty Queen Victoria." The register was then pushed in front of the MP to be signed. Only when Alfred Patrick saw the large, bold signature did he look up in amazement. Louis was just going out the door, but he turned and politely bowed to the chief clerk. Patrick then ran down the hall to inform the astonished Minister of Justice. All the clerk could remember about the famous revolutionary was that he had "a heavy whisker, not exactly black".

As word spread of Riel's brazen act, Ottawa spun into an uproar; as one writer put it: "Had Banquo's far-famed ghost suddenly appeared in the Senate or House of Commons, the members could hardly have been more surprised...." The authorities were sure that massive demonstrations like those Schultz and company had provoked three years before in Toronto were being organized. And of course the French would retaliate. Extra constables were ordered out on the streets, the militia was called up to guard the armouries against attack.

That evening the visitors' gallery was packed. Lady Dufferin, the wife of the Governor-General, brought her entire dinner party to watch the spectacle. They were all most disappointed, for Riel did not show up. Knowing that an army of police officers would be stationed at every entrance waiting to arrest him, he had fled back to Hull.

But Riel continued to be a presence in the House of Commons that evening. Two long-time supporters, Rodrigue Masson, the son of Louis's schooldays patron, and Joseph-Alfred Mousseau, a journalist and future premier of Quebec (whose brother J.O. Mousseau was one of Louis's innumerable devoted class-mates), both gave elegant speeches in defence of Riel and the Red River resistance. Mousseau ended by moving a motion calling for a full amnesty for the Métis leaders. But in this Parliament the forces of Orange Ontario were large and powerful; the motion was quickly defeated. Mackenzie Bowell, a grand master of the North Hastings Orange Lodge, a future prime minister of Canada and a man about as bigoted as they came, insisted that Riel's exact legal status be established. The House then adjourned.

The next day when Parliament resumed, Henry Clarke, the attorney-general of Manitoba and Louis's bitter enemy in previous elections, suddenly appeared bearing the indictment against Riel for the murder of Thomas Scott. "He is nothing less than a fugitive from justice," Clarke announced to the assembly. He was not asked, nor did he volunteer, the reason for his deep personal antipathy to the Métis leader. Mackenzie Bowell then insisted that Riel be ordered to attend the House session the next day. The member of Parliament from Selkirk, John Schultz, must have smiled at this, for it was a delicious Catch-22: if Louis didn't take his seat he would be expelled; if he did attend he would be arrested.

On April 2, the visitors' gallery was full to overflowing again. The curious spectators scanned each honourable member carefully; many carried rotogravure pictures of Louis Riel which they were planning to use to identify the celebrity. But Riel did not appear. Everybody was disappointed when the House was simply adjourned for a week.

Public rallies supporting the Métis leader were organized in Ottawa and throughout Quebec. The French-Canadian members, no matter what their political affiliation, appeared together in a show of solidarity. But everyone advised Louis not to return to the Commons until the matter of amnesty was resolved. The Orange faction had sniffed blood, and no logic or compassion would get in the way of their tracking and dispatching their prey.

When Parliament reconvened, the seat beside Desjardins was empty. Mackenzie Bowell promptly put forth a motion that "Louis Riel, having fled from justice and having failed to obey an Order of this House that he should attend in his place, Thursday, 9th day of April, 1874, be expelled by this House." John Schultz could hardly wait to second the motion. It was passed 124 votes for, 68 against.

It was a devastating blow for Riel, and yet his supporters were far from pessimistic. For along with his expulsion, the politicians had agreed to set up a select committee of Parliament to hear evidence relating to the amnesty. Here finally was a chance to put forward a strong and public defence for Riel and the Métis people as a whole.

As it was, the other side of the story was at last slowly seeping out to Canadians. The long memoir Riel had written at the Oblate retreat in New York had been printed in *Le Nouveau Monde* in February and had excited much debate. Then in early April Archbishop Taché had dropped a bombshell—he had finally carried out his threat to expose the duplicity of the Tory politicians. His pamphlet, called "The Amnesty," had detailed all the promises that had been made by Sir John A. Macdonald, Sir George-Étienne Cartier and others. Because the essay was well reasoned, and Taché was after all an archbishop, the pamphlet's publication had stirred up a hornet's nest of controversy. It was one of the reasons why the select committee had been set up.

Actually the Catholic clergy of Red River had never lagged in their determination to obtain an amnesty for Riel and Lépine. A barrage of letters, documents and petitions from Taché and others was constantly arriving on the desks of beleaguered politicians and bureaucrats.

In the spring of 1873, Father Ritchot, who had steered the negotiations for the Manitoba Bill and who knew more about Macdonald's double dealings than anyone, had journeyed to the capital and stayed for close to five months, once again displaying the bulldog tenacity that he had become famous for. He had had the help of Rodrigue Masson, who was so devoted to Louis Riel by this time that he had refused a Cabinet post in Macdonald's government because he believed the prime minister was lying about the amnesty. Although Macdonald had smiled and assured Ritchot and Masson that absolution was on its way, nothing had happened. What Ritchot and Masson couldn't know was that Sir John was once again conniving behind their backs. The Pacific Scandal had just erupted; if it had been politically inexpedient to grant an amnesty before, now it would be political suicide. What the prime minister intended to do was to absolve everyone who had participated in the Red River resistance *except* those involved in Thomas Scott's death. Ironically, Macdonald had no intention of actually trying Riel for murder; he thought that a trial in a Manitoba court would bring either acquittal or a hung jury. The better thing, he believed, was to isolate "the firebrand" from the Métis community, so that he would be driven from, or flee, the country of his birth.

But now, a year later, the select committee would provide an appropriate stage for Ritchot and others to tell the truth about the amnesty. They intended to take every advantage of the opportunity.

The committee heard twenty-one witnesses in thirty-seven days of testimony—Archbishop Taché himself would give twenty-four hours of evidence. At one point, Taché exclaimed with great effect that what the English from Ontario wanted most was to wipe out or banish from their homeland the Métis, or, as he put it, his "*noirs protégés*". Dramatic testimony like Taché's, as well as the mountain of letters, documents and diaries, particularly those of Father Ritchot and the late Cartier, made it clear that amnesty had most definitely been promised, and not once but many times. Former Prime Minister Macdonald dismissed the accusations by insisting that he had never officially recognized Father Ritchot or the other delegates from Red River during the Manitoba Act negotiations, so how could any promise of amnesty have had official status? It was a specious argument. Archbishop Taché put it bluntly in a letter home: "Rt. Hon. John A. Macdonald lied (excuse the word) like a trooper."

The committee members included both friends and enemies: Rodrigue Masson and Donald Smith (now somewhat sympathetic to the Métis cause since many French-speakers lived in his riding) served, but so did the fervent Orangemen Edward Blake and Mackenzie Bowell. They obviously argued fiercely among themselves, because their report contained no recommendations; it was a mere compilation of facts. It would be left to Parliament "to consider whether under the circumstances stated, any other steps shall be taken." Still, the evidence seemed so overwhelming that Riel's supporters felt sure that an amnesty would have to be granted.

The publicity engendered by the select committee was amazing. Ontario newspapers covered the hearings in great depth, though they often twisted the evidence to prove their own political points; the Quebec press was also fascinated and printed some of the testimony verbatim. It was exactly what the Riel supporters had wanted, yet there was an unfortunate side effect. Louis was so much in the limelight that fears for his life increased. It was decided that he wasn't safe even in Montreal. He would travel west again.

The journey by train was uneventful but long and tiring for Riel, especially since he was so conscious of the never-ending possibility of being kidnapped or even assassinated. He arrived in St. Paul safely, however, on May 19, 1874.

Alexandre Dubeau, a French-Canadian carpenter who lived with his wife in "a pretty little cottage", had invited Louis to stay with him. But as usual during his exiles in that city, he was at loose ends. He visited Uncle François Riel in Minneapolis, tried to catch up on news of Manitoba and wrote long letters. And, despite everything, he tried to keep up his spirits. News had reached him of the sensational evidence produced at hearings into his amnesty, and for the first time in years he had real hope that soon he would be free to live his life in peace.

At the same time the news he received about his beloved Manitoba was truly alarming. In fact, the effects of the stampede of homesteaders, almost all English-speaking Protestants, were beginning to change the fundamental character of the Red River Settlement. A bill had been introduced which would redistribute the ridings so that the French-speakers would lose provincial seats. Lieutenant-Governor Morris had grabbed more and more power, so that the legislature had little control over the executive, where most laws were initiated. And Winnipeg, now a booming town of two thousand, had just been incorporated, and the mayor-elect was Francis Evans Cornish, the very man who had plotted with Clarke and others for the arrest of Riel and Lépine. Perhaps if prosperity had arrived as well, these changes would not have seemed so ominous. But much of the Métis population were growing poorer by the year. The buffalo had almost disappeared, and grasshoppers had savaged the last two harvests.

The Riel family had not been spared. In a letter written to Louis that spring, his old friend, the St. Norbert merchant Joseph Lemay, informed him that the Riel family was living off the credit he allowed them at his store. He described conditions at Red River:

> The times are exceedingly difficult. Not only is the hay scarce, it is also difficult to sell since the winter was so long. Wood is selling at a fairly good price. Money is, as our people put it, "shy".
>
> I am telling you that our people are getting on with pain and misery. I hope that things will go better soon. And amnesty, promised for so long, desired and waited for with impatience, will soon come, restoring courage to our brave people. Hope bolsters us in the midst of these hardships.

The dire financial condition of his family was a constant, nagging worry for Riel. In 1873 he had tried to sell parcels of the land he owned in St. Boniface, St. Vital and Ste. Agathe, but his mother, thinking this might mean he would never come back, had objected. In August of that year, he finally did sell a lot to A.G.B. Bannatyne for £30. ("He [Father Dugas] told me how fairly you have given the bargain," Louis wrote to the kind-hearted old trader.) In the spring of 1874 the Riels were hard up again, and he had to ask his friends in Montreal for help. In mid-May Dr. E.P. Lachapelle, another of Riel's classmates and a long-time supporter in Quebec, arranged to have $100 sent to Julie Riel in St. Vital.

Louis's sojourn in St. Paul came to an abrupt end. Since his arrival in the city, he had suspected that his mail was being tampered with at the post office; an informer told him that he was being watched; and finally the ubiquitous John Schultz was spotted in the town of Moorhead, not far away, and it was suspected that once again he was plotting to kidnap the Métis leader. By the end of May, Louis was travelling east again on the Northern Pacific Railway.

By June he was back in Keeseville, New York, enjoying the warm hospitality of the Barnabé family. Certainly by now he had met Father Fabien's charming sister. Marie-Elizabeth-Evelina was twenty-three, six years younger than Louis, and the baby of her family. She was blonde and blue-eyed, very slight and finely featured. She was also a musician of some accomplishment—she played the organ in her brother's church. A quiet but fun-loving young woman, she seems to have developed a crush on Louis the first moment she met him. A photograph taken of Riel in 1873 in Keeseville shows why. He is still remarkably handsome, dressed very stylishly, his heavy, thick dark hair slicked back, his beard moderate and nicely trimmed. There is a bit of an enigma in his smile.

This interlude must have been a wonderful respite from the turbulence Riel had experienced for the previous six years. He had every reason to hope that amnesty would quickly come, Evelina was lovely and intriguing, and in the town of Keeseville he was treated as a hero.

Keeseville would not have seemed out of place in a quaint landscape by Turner. The Au Sable River, tumbling down from the Adirondack slopes on its way to Lake Champlain, snaked through the village, the two halves of which were connected by a charming stone-arch bridge. Its banks were lined with the squat sandstone factories—saw mills, grist mills, foundry, forges, brewery, furniture and nail factories— which had transformed the village into a bustling place in the 1870s. Fortunes had been made quickly and the wealth was magnificently displayed in the elegant mansions. There were plenty of workers' cottages, of course, where life was hardly grand. And since the saloon in the Adirondack Hotel was so popular, propriety had to be maintained. There were "seven houses of religion" to minister to the four thousand souls of Keeseville, including Father Barnabé's St. Jean de Baptiste Church.

St. Jean's sat on a high plateau in a clump of evergreens, appropriately distant from the town's grimy industrial heart. The rectory across the street was most attractive—a large white-frame, three-storey building with several balconies jutting from the second floor, and a porch that wound its way around the entire house. Riel was particularly comfortable here since he was given a large corner bedroom with a veranda overlooking a huge lilac bush. He stayed there off and on during the summer of 1874, long enough to get to know Evelina rather well. As he did about almost everything that mattered to him personally, he wrote about her in verse. The following is an interesting piece because it reveals not only Evelina's character but what Riel revered in a young woman. (The title of the book referred to is not known.)

> By giving me this little book
> You share with me the conversations
> Which intoxicate your heart.
> And you want them to be mine.
> You have given me a gift that I like
> And I will keep it a long time.
> This gift will take the place
> Of your thoughts and pretty songs....

More than once, I have seen you
Reading and praying this book in hand.
Beholding you, my soul was moved
And told itself: This pretty little book
Is inspired with great divine love!
Otherwise could the face
Of the one who is reading it
Be made lovelier by such a smile.

When you sing to distract yourself
Or converse for a moment,
When your lips wish to be silent,
I tell myself, gazing at you:
This pure and angelic peace
That shines in her
Comes from the reading of this book
Which inspires such complete calm.*

Whether Louis ever sent Evelina the poem has not been revealed.

The village of Keeseville was only one of many "little Canadas" dotting the landscape of New York State and New England. They were meccas for a massive influx of French Canadians. Hundreds of thousands of them had left the small farms of Quebec for good wages in the growing industrial towns south of the border. As the numbers mounted, the clergy were forced to follow them. Thus priests like Fabien Barnabé would spend the vast part of their professional lives "in exile". There was a network of these clergy in Upper New York State and throughout New England, and it was through this connection that Louis Riel became a kind of itinerant political activist. Several times over a two-year period, he would make the rounds of the little towns—Plattsburgh, Keeseville and Albany in New York State, Suncook and Nashua in New Hampshire, Worcester, Massachusetts (which became the focal point for French-Canadian political activism), and Woonsocket, Rhode Island. In each place he would give passionate speeches on the plight of the Métis in the Northwest. He found his audience most receptive—many were deeply alienated already by Quebec's economic and political inequities. The young journalist Frédéric Houde, who lived in Worcester, covered one of these rallies. He reported:

> One could not speak with more good sense, aptness, tact and wisdom all at once. M. Riel is not a speaker who looks for big words or high-flown sentences; he aims straight for his goal and most certainly reaches it. He expresses

---

* Translation by Wilfrid Dubé.

himself plainly and with ease. Simply put he is pleasant and interesting to listen to. When he began to speak about the mission of the French-Canadian race, his voice was calm and his face unemotional, until both became suddenly remarkably animated. One could see that conviction possessed him, that emotion overcame him because the subject stirred his French-Canadian and Catholic heart.

In a letter written to his mother on July 20, 1874, Riel gives a sense of the excitement he felt: "Everyone is for us—wherever I go.... There was a meeting of French Canadians here, yesterday. They passed the most sympathetic resolutions for the Métis, especially for those being persecuted. I had to go to their meeting. They applauded. They demonstrated a generous affection for all of us."

In fact, Louis was becoming a hero of almost mythical proportions among the émigrés. But despite such adulation, by August he was back in Montreal again, for he had urgent business to attend to. He was facing another federal election.

His expulsion from the House of Commons in February made necessary a by-election in the riding of Provencher. The Liberal government kept delaying the announcement of the date, probably in the hope that the problem of Riel would somehow go away. Riel himself knew what he wanted. In a telegram in English to M.A. Girard and Joseph Dubuc on July 13, he pleaded: "Please re-elect me in Provencher, our cause is stronger than ever.... Want amnesty, responsible government." He probably acted so promptly because he had heard rumours that several former supporters in Red River were turning against him. These included Joseph Royal, the lawyer and journalist who sat in the legislative assembly, Marc-Amable Girard, also a lawyer and MLA, and, most seriously, the archbishop. Taché felt that Riel should wait until the amnesty question was resolved before he became politically active again. His reluctance to approve Riel's nomination deeply hurt Louis. But those having doubts about his candidacy did have a point. It was important in such turbulent times, they insisted, to elect someone who could actually take his place in the House of Commons. Still, there were plenty of people who wanted Riel to stand for election. They argued that if for a third time the voters decisively showed their approval, this would put even more pressure on the government to grant amnesty. His friends in Montreal urged him to run—Dr. Lachapelle sent a postal order for $50 to pay the election deposit and Rodrigue Masson actually travelled to Red River in August to drum up support. For them it was not only the survival of the Métis people that was at stake but French-Canadian culture and power—Riel's election came to symbolize the very struggle for equality between Protestant Ontario and Catholic Quebec. As well, many in Red River remained utterly loyal. Louis's old friend Joseph Dubuc, now the attorney-general in the Manitoba government, was still firmly in his camp, as were the priests Ritchot and Dugas and, most important, almost all the ordinary people living in Provencher.

The nomination meeting was held on September 3. Once again Pierre Delorme's large house in St. Norbert was filled to capacity. When the nominations were called there was not a word from any of those who had opposed Riel; they had taken the temperature of the electorate and quickly realized they would have no chance. And since no one from another party was running, Louis was elected for the third straight time.

In absentia, of course. Riel, still too frightened of arrest to return to Manitoba, heard the news of his acclamation in Montreal. This time he would make no attempt to take his House of Commons seat. Another strategy had been developed—he would meet with influential people and urge them to put pressure on the government to grant him amnesty. He began by visiting his old teacher of Latin and Greek, Father LaFlèche, who was now Bishop of Trois-Rivières. LaFlèche was an ultramontane conservative and was in agreement with much of what Louis said, so this was not a difficult encounter. But Riel knew he would have to approach those sympathetic to the Liberal administration if any concrete progress was to be made. To this end, he travelled to St. Hyacinthe to meet with Bishop Charles Larocque, and to Quebec City, where he obtained an audience with Archbishop Taschereau. Both prelates were known to have Liberal leanings. On his way back to Montreal, Riel dropped in on one of the most promising of the young Liberal MPs, Wilfrid Laurier.* Laurier later said he had not been impressed with the Métis leader, that he thought him a "monomaniac". The future Prime Minister of Canada did not give a reason for his assessment, and certainly there were few similar opinions expressed at the time.

As October neared, Riel's thoughts turned more and more to his family and friends in Manitoba. For one thing, Ambroise Lépine was finally being tried for the murder of Thomas Scott, and Riel had never stopped brooding about him. He wrote:

> Lépine, why is your brow covered with worries?
> You know the bonds which hold us together
> Are supposed to be a comfort one to the other.
> For my part also, when my expression seems
> Dreamy, speak to me. Exile is a state
> Which spills an abundance of sorrow on each day
> That passes. But undeserved sadness
> Must not affect our daily existence.

---

* There has been a debate among Laurier's biographers and historians over the date of this meeting—some claim it took place in 1874, others 1877. The earlier time is the more logical.

Lépine's trial had been postponed on several occasions because the two presiding judges in Manitoba refused to rule on whether their court could try a crime that had occurred before Canada and its judicial system had gained jurisdiction in Rupert's Land. E.B. Wood was finally appointed chief justice, however, and he agreed to preside over the proceedings.

At first, things looked good for the defence. The prosecutors, Francis Cornish and Stewart Macdonald, although Orangemen, were not considered very skilled, especially compared to the defence team. Joseph Royal of Red River was bolstered by Riel's old schoolmate Joseph-Adolphe Chapleau of Montreal.

Chapleau had been born in lowly circumstances—his father was a stonecutter—but his education, like Riel's, had been sponsored by the Masson family, and he had remained close friends with the son, Rodrigue Masson. Chapleau was not only a high-profile politician—he would serve as premier of Quebec from 1879 to 1882—but also a talented and highly respected criminal lawyer. The trial would be bilingual, conducted in English and French depending on the language of the witness. And the jury was divided exactly between English- and French-speakers, most of whom were known to be somewhat sympathetic to the Métis cause.

But early on, something began to go very wrong. The trial was conducted with little concern for normal rules of evidence. Chapleau and Royal's tactics seemed blunt and off the mark; they spent little time cross-examining the crown's witnesses. And they left unchallenged evidence that should never have been allowed in a court of law. Riel came to believe that Chapleau had concluded it was politically unwise to wage a truly strong defence and that he had softened his approach.

The prosecutors called a number of Canadians who had been imprisoned during the Red River resistance, but since they had not been involved in Scott's actual court martial or even seen the execution, they contributed little except a venting of spleen. Ironically, the crown's case rested on the testimony of three Métis. Joseph Nolin, who had served as clerk of the court martial and had taken oaths from the witnesses, testified only that Lépine had served as president of the proceedings. François Charette claimed that Lépine had handed Guillemette the revolver which had delivered the *coup de grâce* to Scott. And then there was John Bruce. He was the man who had served as president in the early months of the provisional government. After he had been shunted aside, he had turned against Riel and his followers; the trial provided a great opportunity for revenge. He claimed that Lépine had told him days before the execution of Scott, "We will release the prisoners before long, but we will put a couple to death before releasing them...." He was so obviously biased against Lépine that his testimony should not have had much effect, except that the cross-examination by Lépine's lawyers was very weak.

As the three-week trial wore on, the defence was able to establish that Lépine had not voted for the verdict of death and that most of the crown's witnesses had not seen him in the Fort Garry courtyard during the execution. Their case revolved around three other arguments. First, the Manitoba Act was not retroactive and therefore the Canadian court had no jurisdiction to try a crime that had allegedly been committed before Rupert's Land became part of Canada. However, Chief Justice Wood ruled against this defence in a judgement that at best could be called fuzzy. As one historian put it, its "wordiness showed only how embarrassed he had been."

The second plank of the accused's case rested on the repeated promises of Macdonald and Cartier to grant an amnesty for Lépine and Riel. But Mr. Justice Wood would not allow letters or papers of the two important politicians to be presented as evidence, so that defence quickly went out the window.

The last argument was that the court martial had been a function of a legitimate government and therefore Lépine, acting as its servant, could not be guilty of any crime. But what this did was tie the accused man's guilt or innocence to the belief of each juror that Riel's provisional government had indeed been a legal one.

It was perhaps not surprising, but still a terrible shock, when the jury delivered a guilty verdict. Chief Justice Wood immediately sentenced Lépine to death by hanging.

Louis Riel was, of course, devastated when the news reached him. In a letter written that November to a nun, probably Sister Catherine-Aurélie of St. Hyacinthe, the founder of the Precious Blood order, he laments, "one of my devoted friends, the one who has helped me the most in my work, has just been sentenced to death.... He is certainly not guilty. It was a time of war, when M. Lépine, acting under the orders of a just government had this enemy, who had been found guilty by a formal war council, executed...."

Riel worried about Lépine himself. The big man was suffering terribly in prison; he was kept in shackles, fed on bread and water, and he was ill. But Louis also understood that his own future was in great peril. His major accomplishment—the formation of the provisional government—had been denigrated. If a twelve-man jury in Manitoba would not accept it as a legal body, how could the rest of the country respond differently?

In mid-November, Riel made a quick trip to St. Paul. The reasons for it are unknown except that Father Barnabé, in a letter of November 14, 1874, alludes to something mysterious—"everyone thinks you are in Minnesota organizing an expedition. I let them talk." Father Évariste Richer, the priest at Suncook, New Hampshire, also hinted at secret plots in a letter of December 31, 1874—"You should write Father Primeau [of Worcester, Riel's confessor in New England] but do not tell him of the plan. I hope you will find the means this coming year to make the cause triumphant." A year later, Louis would attempt to raise a military force in Minnesota to invade Manitoba; perhaps this was a preliminary scouting foray. Whatever the case, he stayed only a few days in St. Paul. From there he travelled to Chicago, stopping just long enough to send off a letter to Bishop Bourget: "with God's grace, I will always remember with gratitude the life-giving words you spoke over me last January 8 at the Hôtel-Dieu." By the end of November he was travelling back to the eastern United States.

In Worcester and Suncook he attended rallies to protest the Lépine verdict, and then he dropped in on the Barnabés in Keeseville for a few days. The priest had managed to raise over $170 for expenses, and Louis was very grateful to him. Barnabé had also made arrangements for Riel to visit Washington, and by the second week in December he was on his way.

Actually this was his second trip to the capital; he had briefly visited the city the previous July, and at that point had met Edmond Mallet, another of the important friends in Riel's life. Two years older than Louis, he had been born in Montreal, but his family had migrated to the town of Oswego in upstate New York when he was only four. He had fought for the Union in the American Civil War so valiantly that he was promoted to major. When Riel first met him, in 1873, he was working as a clerk in the treasury department. But three years later he would be made a special agent to the Natives of the district of Puget Sound, in the state of Washington, and eventually would be named Inspector-General of Indian Affairs. His jobs were a reflection of his deep and genuine appreciation of Native culture and language, which he studied his entire life.

Because he knew many important people in Washington—he was supposed to be a friend of President Grant's—Mallet was considered an unofficial ambassador for the Francophone community in the eastern United States. In 1866, at age twenty-four, he had returned to his native Montreal and experienced a kind of epiphany. He found he had lost his heritage—his language, culture and religion—and he set out to rediscover his roots. In the process he became a leader of the French émigré community.

Like so many people before him, Edmond Mallet developed an immediate and lifelong attachment to Louis Riel, remaining one of his most vociferous and energetic defenders. Louis would stay at the Mallet house at 510 9th NW whenever he was in Washington, and became very attached to the family, especially the three young sons. It's not clear what he did in the capital in December of 1874, but he and Mallet probably talked about how they could get American political support for Louis's cause.

In January 1875 Riel was back touring the "little Canadas" of New England again, trying his best to whip up support for Lépine. He was in Suncook with his old friend Father Évariste Richer, who had once served at Louis's old stomping grounds of St. Joseph, when news arrived that Lépine's life had been saved. Only four days before his execution, the governor-general had commuted the death sentence.

"The sound of Lépine's and Nault's* chains have aroused the sympathies of every French Canadian and every Catholic," Riel thundered, and he was right. The Quebec population had been utterly shocked at the Lépine verdict and were determined the death sentence would not be carried out. The press howled for leniency. Petitions, letters and requests for interviews flooded into Prime Minister Alexander Mackenzie's office daily, reminding him that he was in a difficult hole—if he granted Lépine amnesty he would insult Ontario, the province he relied on most for support; if he didn't, Quebec would never forgive him. Finally he found a way to wiggle out of making a decision. As his predecessor Macdonald had done before him, he simply passed the hot potato over to the queen. "This is the most thorny business I have ever had to deal with thanks to the imbecility of almost everyone who has hitherto meddled with it," declared Governor-General Lord Dufferin. He did not pay much heed to the mountain of evidence that had been brought forward during the select committee hearings the previous spring, but he was impressed that the Métis had taken up arms to defend Manitoba against the Fenian raids. So, God-like, he declared that Lépine's life would be spared. However, the big Métis was sentenced to two years' imprisonment (he had already spent a few months in jail, so his release date was set at October 26, 1876) and his political rights were permanently revoked.

But it wasn't only Lépine's life the governor-general was toying with. The future of everyone involved in the Red River resistance would finally be determined. On February 11, 1875, the prime minister stood up in the House and proposed a historic motion. There would be unconditional pardon for

---

Riel's cousin André Nault had been arrested after a terrific battle with the police. But his trial for murder had resulted in a hung jury, so he had been freed. Riel's uncle Elzéar Lagimodière had also been charged but had never been brought to trial.

everyone—except Louis Riel.* He would get his amnesty but he would also be banished from Canada for five years.

Riel's friends were relieved that he would no longer be hunted down like a mad fox, that or hanged. But not to live in his beloved Manitoba, not to be involved in the politics that again seethed there, was like facing slow death.

As usual, Riel expressed his deepest emotions in verse. "Those of Homeland Dispossessed" is one of his most poignant pieces:

> Those of homeland dispossessed
> Though with many friendships blessed
> May receive the gift of tenderness
> And yet feel a profound sadness.
> Friends, forgive me if my sorrow
> Grieves your feeling hearts. But please know
> With each passing hour my thoughts soar.
> I fly a great distance afar
> To the place of my birth. I see
> Though I have been forced to flee;
> I imagine my father's home.
> In my rapture my eyes can hold
> Onto my mother's warm stare.
> My brothers and sisters are there.
> I am at my father's knees.
> Crouched and in tears I hear him pray.
> On my brow now his open palm
> His blessing a soothing balm,
> Filling me with light's purity.
> These moments give me ecstasy.
> But as I relive them I feel
> A sense of loss and my heart reels
> With sadness. For this I thank God
> Who makes our birthplace so precious.
> Let me die there. Let my heart go....
>
> Remember, you who languish so
> In exile. This is the sorrow
> The world to every man bequeaths.**

---

* *Ambroise Lépine was offered release from prison on condition that he spend five years in exile and not engage in political activity during that time. Lépine refused to sign the release form and so served his full penitentiary term, to October 26, 1876. O'Donoghue was banished forever, but he was already settled in the United States.*
** *Translation by Paul Savoie.*

I am mad in the eyes of the world
Everyone laughs at me.
I put my trust and my faith
In my God.

L ife might have been different for Louis Riel. With an unconditional amnesty he would have taken his place among the ruling elite of Red River. He likely would have increased the family's land holdings and taken advantage, like everyone else, of the imminent boom in Winnipeg. He would have been a source of pride to his mother and looked after the education of his siblings, seeing that his sisters married well and his brothers got decent jobs. He might have married the "pious and holy" mate he was looking for, and produced children who continued his life's work, much as he had done his father's. His political career likely would have thrived; with his natural aptitude, a stint as member of Parliament might have turned into a Cabinet position. Given his passionate concern for his own people, he could have served as Premier of Manitoba and then—who knows?—he might have tried for the highest office in the land.

But he was exiled. It wasn't just that he would miss his family, or that he would remain poverty-stricken, reduced to living off hand-outs. More, he well understood that a unique accomplishment in North America—the establishment of a society in which the Native peoples could have some say and maybe even prosper—had been crushed. And the interlopers, John Schultz's cabal, who cared only about the fortunes to be made in Red River and nothing for its tradition, now had their revenge and were laughing out loud. If, over the next few years, Riel suffered great emotional exhaustion and turmoil, what else could have been expected?

After his exile, neither Louis nor his friends gave up the struggle. The reaction of Father Godfroy Lamarche, canon of the Cathedral of Montreal and a dedicated ultramontane, was typical. Writing on February 28, 1875, he tried to bolster Louis's courage. "You are the true champion. The time will be not long coming when you will triumph through the Manitoba Act. It will require patience and wisdom."

Over the next year, Louis would spend most of the time roaming around New England and Upper New York State, visiting the priests who were now his close friends and supporters. He still gave his ardent speeches, but something had gone sour for him—the French-Canadian émigrés were not what he had thought.

Their reputation said everything: the "Chinese of New England" was what they were called, willing to work long hours for low wages in terrible conditions. Whole families lived in a kind of voluntary serfdom.

Riel's objective was to convince these people to give up their gloomy life in factories and migrate west to the healthy, wide-open prairies. They might provide a counterbalance to the Anglo-Saxon immigrants flooding into Manitoba, he reasoned. At first his audiences seemed enthusiastic about the idea, but the flood he had expected had not turned into even a trickle. He came to realize that they preferred a life of drudgery in a dark factory, where at least they were together and not far from their birthplace, to risking an isolated and chancy existence as prairie homesteaders. Riel mocked such cowardice. A satirical poem written during his time in the eastern United States, called "In the Great Republic", is Louis at his most humorous and sarcastic. It's a long piece, but a selection of verses gives the flavour:

> In the great republic
> I'm there to make money.
> Pardon me if I think
> That I'm quite good at it.
> Now I'm deadly serious
> About comfort and gain.
> How I find work tedious,
> Like a real Canadian!
>
> I'll never work the soil
> Like a bloody farmer
> Buried by sweaty toil,
> A brutish commoner.
> I'd rather clean the works
> Of a clanking machine

Or pose like dainty clerks,
A docile Canadian....

When at church on Sunday
Wearing my tailored clothes,
Hair well groomed and curly,
I assume my Sunday pose.
But when they take collection
I keep a well-clenched hand,
Head bent in contrition
A devout Canadian....

When death's on patrol,
And muffled drums are rolled,
The devil I'll cajole
While hiding in my hole.
And then I'll beat my breast
All the way to heaven.
I'll pass the Judgement test.
God loves a Canadian.*

During his sojourn in New England, Riel continued to put pressure on the higher echelon of the Quebec church to intercede on his behalf, but the only prelate who enthusiastically answered his call was the Bishop of Montreal.

Ignace Bourget was almost at the end of his tenure; the following year, 1876, would finally see him retire at age seventy-seven. His reign had changed the nature of Quebec society; the church was now a dominant player, but it had been a long and exhausting struggle. He had won battles and lost them, but he was satisfied that his heart-felt ultramontanism now coloured the daily lives of the faithful. It had certainly had a profound effect on Louis Riel's thinking.

Ultramontanism had begun in Europe during the French Revolution. The conservative-minded, craving a return to a world devoid of "free-thinkers", liberals, socialists and anarchists, where the hierarchy of society was firmly set and the working class showed deference and knew their place, looked "across the mountain" to Rome and the Pope for stability. This nostalgia eventually hardened into an ultra-Catholic dogmatism that insisted on the supremacy of the church over the civil state and would brook no dallying with modern thought or, for that matter, any ideas that did not originate with, or were not approved by, the Pope. It turned into a cult of the passionately devoted, and the dangerously closed-minded.

Translation by Paul Savoie.

In Canada, ultramontanism took on an added twist. In a society desperate to preserve its language and traditions, Roman Catholicism could serve as a bulwark against the onslaught of the dominant English culture. It would have to be a united, powerful and all-intrusive religion to accomplish such a feat. Education, hospitals, libraries, benevolent funds, even the rituals of marriage and death—every aspect of life was to be controlled by the clergy. The parish priest would preach to his flock on which political candidate would best serve the church—almost always the Conservative was named—and in the confessional he felt free to chastise a penitent who hadn't voted correctly. Ultramontanism seeped into Quebec society and would remain a force until the late 1950s, when the Quiet Revolution and the council of Vatican II finally undermined its ideology.

Paradoxically, ultramontanism was a bust as a political movement. In 1871 a group of its most prominent advocates prepared a political manifesto called the "Catholic Programme" which linked Catholicism with the Conservative Party, "the defender of social authority". But Archbishop Taschereau of Quebec, who had liberal leanings and the backing of those involved in the anti-clerical *Parti rouge*, and people like Riel's old employer, the lawyer Rodolphe Laflamme, denounced the "programme", pointing out that it had been issued without the consent of the bishops. In the provincial election of June 1871, the ultramontane candidate won only one seat. By 1896, after the bitter and passionate debate over Riel's execution, the Conservatives were a spent force in Quebec at both the federal and provincial level.

The "Catholic Programme" had been formulated in the home of Alphonse Desjardins. Indeed, all of Louis Riel's supporters and friends in Quebec during this period—Honoré Mercier, Rodrigue Masson, to some degree Joseph-Adolphe Chapleau, and in Red River, Joseph Royal—were devoted to ultramontanism. Naturally they would embrace Riel; the preservation of the French-Canadian state was a most important part of their creed. Louis, as a Métis, was not only an exotic to them, but was seen as a possible rejuvenator of French-Canadian culture, which they hoped would take on new vitality in the young and idealized society of the Great West. In their letters, the idea of Riel possessing a "sacred mission" was mentioned repeatedly. On June 7, 1875, for example, Alphonse Desjardins wrote to Louis, "Some better days are no doubt in store for you. Save your vitality for those days, so that you may accomplish the mission which Providence has reserved for you...."

But it was Bishop Bourget who set Riel firmly in his conviction that he was predestined by God to lead the Métis to a new Utopia. On July 6, 1875, Riel wrote the bishop, "I come and throw myself humbly at your feet to assure you that I want to spend my life in the dust at God's feet, humble in heart and body." The letter that Bourget sent in return became so symbolic, so important, to Louis that he carried it, ragged and worn, in his breast pocket to the end of his life.

July 14, 1875

Montreal

Dear Mr. Riel,

I received your letter of the sixth yesterday which has deeply touched me for this letter is proof that you are driven by very good feelings and yet you are inwardly tormented by an inclination *je ne sais quoi* that makes it difficult for you to keep to that path of obedience which you walk, [yet] you don't want to leave it, no matter what happens.

Also I have a deep conviction that you will be rewarded in this world, and sooner than you expect, for the inner sacrifices you have made which are a thousand times more painful than sacrifices of material and visible things. But God who has up until the present directed you and assisted you will not abandon you in your most difficult of struggles, *for He has given you a mission which you must accomplish step by step [and] with the Grace of God you must persevere on the path that has been laid out for you* [italics added]. That is to say, that you must give up everything that is yours: you must wish ardently to serve God and to procure the greatest Glory in the name of God; you must work without ceasing for the honour of religion; for the salvation of souls and the good of society; finally you will sanctify yourself by fervently wishing for the sanctification of others.

I have, as you asked me, offered your letter to God, praying to Him that you be confirmed in your noble aspirations and that He help you to persevere until the end. May your faith be alive and healthy so that you never back away from the difficulties that life presents to us in all its aspects.

Take care of your health and follow your doctor's orders, confide in divine Providence and believe that nothing happens in this world without His order or His permission. Prepare yourself for coming events by remaining unalterably calm. I bless you and remain your very humble and obedient servant.

It is an inspirational letter that the bishop might have sent any young priest heading for a missionary posting. But for Riel it would grow in symbolic importance. The Bishop of Montreal would become a hero, mentor and spiritual fountainhead. As Louis wrote:

I put my trust
In the Lord of Mount-Royal [Monseigneur Bourget].
He allows me to suffer

So he can see the extent of my patience.
He seeks to graft me
To his strong and healthy vine.
He will help me triumph
Through humility and sorrow.

During the summer of 1875, Riel was still trying to sort out his future in the everyday world. He had to make a living and he wrote his mother that he planned to settle in the place of his former exile, St. Joseph in Dakota, near the Canadian border. It wouldn't be such a bad life. Perhaps he could farm or become involved in the Gingras' businesses. Since St. Vital was only forty miles away, he could remain in close contact with family and friends. He could offer advice on the Riel farm and keep an eye on his land holdings—a government commission had finally been established to distribute the promised acreage among the Métis population and Riel wanted to see that his family got their share. And he would not cease his political activism. On July 12, 1875, he wrote to Julie Riel, "During the five years I will spend in exile, I will have only one thing to do and that is to tell the Métis: remain Métis, become more Métis." Certainly his family and friends were anxious to have him close by. "I am happy to learn that you will soon be in St. Joseph," said his mother.* "We will visit you there and, if you like, we are ready to stay with you. Your friends and relatives want to see you also. Nanin will go with his wife, also Octavie and Louison, Paul, Charles, Benjamin and many of your friends."

On October 21, Louis wrote Julie from Albany, New York, that he had thought of leaving for St. Joseph that week but something unforeseen had come up that prevented him from doing so. Within a few days he was in Indianapolis talking to a powerful American senator about invading Manitoba. Father Barnabé had mentioned it in a letter to Riel.

The references to a mysterious plot had continued to ripple through letters to and from Riel since the previous winter. Father Richer had alluded to "an expedition", Father Barnabé had promised he would send the address of a nitroglycerine manufacturer. The plan finally emerged that fall.

What Riel intended was to re-establish the provisional government in Manitoba. He calculated that he could round up enough of a force throughout the Northwest to accomplish this: both the Métis and English Half-breeds were being abused by the administration of Lieutenant-Governor Morris; the Indians were upset at the government's interpretation of their newly signed treaties; several

---

Julie Riel was illiterate. All letters signed by her were written by someone else, usually one of her daughters. Similarly, letters sent to her were read to her.

hundred of those French-Canadian émigrés Riel had been hectoring would follow him, he was sure; and then there were the fiery Irish immigrants, when they heard what Riel had in store for them—a province entirely to themselves, west of Manitoba in what is now Saskatchewan—they would flock to his cause. Quebec would certainly support him. All that was required was the co-operation of influential American politicians. Their involvement was critical on three accounts: a base of operation in the United States from which to organize and then dispatch the invading force was essential; a source of money was urgently required for his campaign; and the U.S. government must be persuaded to again prohibit Canadian and British troops from travelling across its territory. This time a Métis army of sharpshooters would be ready to take on the English soldiers; guerrilla tactics would be used without mercy. Once the provisional government had taken root, Riel believed, the Canadians would be forced to renegotiate the Manitoba Act; this time he envisioned a quasi-independent state only loosely associated with Canada and Britain.

It was not such a hare-brained scheme as it may seem. The Indians and mixed-bloods numbered some 48,000 and were seething with discontent. If they rebelled there would be little defence. The North-West Mounted Police had been formed just two years before, but they numbered only a couple of hundred scattered across the vast Northwest. The militia consisted of a few greenhorns in Winnipeg and environs and they had already displayed their ineptness during the Red River resistance. The weak link in Riel's plan was the United States. There were plenty of American speculators hungry to make a quick buck, so raising money by issuing bonds was not such a far-fetched idea. But Riel's reading of the realpolitik of the day was out of whack. He promised "a plan of action deferential to the United States", which probably meant that Manitoba and the Northwest would sit within the American sphere of influence. The problem was that the dream of Manifest Destiny, the Americas as a vast U.S. state, as least as far as Canada was concerned, was fading fast; Americans were finally learning to live with the idea of a separate northern nation.

Still, Riel remained determined to round up U.S. support. At the end of October, he travelled alone to Indianapolis to meet with Oliver P. Morton, Republican senator for Indiana. Morton had a reputation for vociferously sticking up for underdogs; he more than anyone else was responsible for the amendment to the Constitution which gave blacks the vote. Although a stroke had partially paralysed him in 1865, it hadn't undermined his energy or influence, and he planned to run for the Republican presidential nomination in 1876, which is most likely why Louis chose him as a potential ally.

Senator Morton met with Riel, and was most courteous towards him, but in the end would not commit himself to the scheme. Riel's subsequent letter to him reveals how nervous and ill at ease he had been during the meeting (the following text is a draft; the polished letter, if there was one, probably did not contain the spelling and grammatical errors):

> Perhaps it is not entirely out of place to say, Mister Senator, that during my visit to Indianapolis, I have been so slow in developping you my plan, I felt this time such a difficulty to exprès my thoughts in english, that I caused you to believe my plan impossible. The fact is I have only shown you the skeleton of it. I have exhibited none of the details which would have made it look different. Your objections are sound. They are forseen in my plan. But I am not discouraged As I told you I hope the divine Providence will help me.

Ten years later, while waiting in jail to be hanged for treason, Riel wrote about a strange incident that occurred after this encounter. The stroke had left both of Morton's legs paralysed, and in this Riel thought he saw an opportunity. If he could cure him, the senator would be obliged to help him. But then, he reasoned, if both legs were restored at the same time, Morton might think it was a result of natural causes. Better, thought Riel, that he pray for the healing of only one leg. That would demonstrate the power of divine Providence and convince the senator that a little help to the Métis cause might result in the other leg being restored. Riel discussed the idea with his confessor, Father Primeau of Worcester, Mass. The priest laughed and told him to go ahead and try, at which point Louis was so grateful for his encouragement that he kissed the priest's knees and feet. Riel related this story when he was under great duress and it is probably at least somewhat apocryphal. Still, there is no doubt that by late 1875 Louis was losing his grip on reality.

After leaving Indianapolis, he travelled to Washington and stayed at the home of his friend Edmond Mallet, who would later write a most telling and, in many ways, a pathetic description of him:

> [Riel] was so far as I could judge an exemplary Catholic. His life was in keeping with his religion. His language as his deportment was as chaste and as modest as a virtuous young girl's. He neither drank nor smoked. He ate sparingly, generally milk, bread, cold meat, celery etc. He was exceedingly neat in his person and dress and was easily polite to the few persons he met—my wife, children, sister-in-law and a few choice friends. He would not go into society. He went to mass every morning, and crept into some dark spot in some church at night to recite his evening prayers.

In fact, Riel was turning more and more inward to a strange spiritual realm of his own making, away from the world that had wounded him so badly. The years of being hunted like animal prey, of seeing his hard-fought ambitions for Manitoba and the Métis shattered, of being caught up in the intense and consuming ultramontane cult, took their toll emotionally. Even Washington, the city of politics, which he had once loved, intensified his bleak state of mind. Economic depression had brought poverty and crime, especially among the blacks, and as Riel wandered the streets he seemed to see nothing but vagrants, cripples, the homeless. The American writer and judge W.F. Bryant claimed that each day while walking to and from church, Riel gave money to a blind Italian immigrant who sat begging in front of the Presbyterian church, until all of the $1,000 donated by Bishop Bourget had disappeared. The story may be exaggerated, since the amount seems exceedingly large, and oddly there is no mention of it in Riel's or Bourget's papers. Still, there's likely a kernel of truth to it.

At the beginning of December, yet more bad news arrived; Louis's brother Charles had died a month before, on his twenty-first birthday.

"Meunier", as his family liked to call him, had not had an easy life. Ten years old at the time of his father's death, he had been looked after for several years by an aunt. Forced to go to work early to help support the family, he had not received the education his siblings had. He was the wayward, mischievous child of Julie's brood. Three months before his death, his elder brother had sternly written, "I hope that Charles is a good boy. May he remember the respect and obedience he owes my aunt.... As he grows older, he will see that we do not grow up to do what we please, but to become wiser. I speak to him in this way, because I fear that he will cause my aunt offence."

Meunier had been hired on the work gang building the branch railway which was to connect Winnipeg with the Northern Pacific at Pembina. In October he became ill and was taken to his aunt's house in Ste. Agathe. For twenty-two days his fever raged and abscesses formed on his body. His brother-in-law Louis Lavalleé wrote that finally, "He was well prepared for death and he died quietly like a little child."

Riel had always felt guilty that he had not done enough for this brother and he was distraught at the news. "My dear brother Meunier, how his death has caused me pain," he wrote. "I recall the circumstances because on the same day as his death, without knowing what had happened, I remembered that this was his birthday, and had holy mass said for him, and after I received the bad news, I realized with some emotion that the soul of my beloved brother might have appeared before God at the same moment I was placing his destiny under the protection of the heavenly Host."

Only days after news reached him of Charles's passing, Riel underwent another intense religious experience—not unlike his otherworldly "visitation" after Marie's death, when he received his father's final blessing.

December 8 held special meaning for Louis. On that date, exactly six years before, the Métis provisional government had been proclaimed. As well, it was the Feast of the Immaculate Conception, the favourite holy day of Pope Pius IX, at the time a hero to the ultramontanes. And it was just two days after Louis had watched the opening of Congress by President Ulysses S. Grant, a ceremony that had impressed and excited him.

Riel was sitting in his usual place at the back of St. Patrick's, an unpretentious, rather shabby edifice which had once been a cultural centre for Irish workers. Solemn mass was being offered. Then, as he put it:*

> At the same moment as the priest, having finished his sermon, was saying the Credo and while the people were standing up, I suddenly felt in my heart a joy which so possessed me that to hide the smile on my face from my neighbours I had to unfold my handkerchief and hold it with my hand over my mouth and cheeks. Despite my precautions, a young boy about ten years old, who was a little in front of me, saw my great jubilation.

> After rejoicing thus for about two minutes, I immediately felt an immense sadness of the soul. And if I had not made a great effort to contain my sobs, my cries and my tears would have exploded throughout the church. For discretion's sake, I bore in silence the almost intolerable sadness that I was feeling in my soul. But that great pain, that had been as great as my joy, passed in a while. And my spirit rang with one thought: the joys and the sorrows of man here on earth are but brief.

Within a week, Riel would undergo several other intense religious experiences, all involving encounters with the "Divine Spirit". By now he had begun to believe that God had designated him a prophet of the New World.

It's not surprising that Riel should fling himself into mysticism at a time when his emotions seemed on the verge of short-circuiting. His boyhood had

---

* *The original of this document and many of the poems accredited to Riel during this time have been lost, but copies were found in an essay entitled "The Madness of Riel". The unknown author was intent on proving that Riel was insane and may have either doctored or added materials to prove his point. Historians, however, have repeatedly used this source when writing about the Métis leader. I remain suspicious about how much of it was truly penned by Riel. On the other hand, not to use it would mean remaining silent about some of the most dramatic events of his life.*

been filled with the dramatic and imaginative spirituality that was the Métis religion. As one anonymous poet described it, "A nervous tic, a flight of birds, a strange, new sound, all had importance and prophecies were built from these signs." His mother and his sister Sara both recorded incredibly rich spiritual encounters. And the Catholic church, indeed the entire Judeo-Christian tradition, has a long history of acclaiming such supernatural occurrences. A legion of saints—Augustine, Thomas of Aquinas, Teresa of Avil (Sara Riel's favourite), Marguerite-Marie, to name a few—underwent visions that dramatically transformed their lives. Louis Riel's whole psyche would be geared for such experiences.

And there was his artistic sensibility. In another, perhaps more rational time, the Canadian painter Emily Carr wrote in her diary: "Every artist I meet these days seems to me to leak out the fact that somewhere inside him he is groping religiously for something, some in one way, some in another, tip-toeing, stretching up, longing for something beyond what he sees or can reach." She might have been talking about the poet Riel.

And Louis's belief that the Métis people were about to experience the Millennium, with him as the Messiah, was hardly a foreign one in the nineteenth century. As the historian J.M. Bumsted has pointed out, his mysticism was closer to Protestant millennialism than to Catholic charismatic phenomena. The nineteenth century saw the creation of a myriad of new Protestant sects, and many of the faithful dreamed of establishing themselves in a sacred new land, Joseph Smith and Brigham Young, spiritual leaders of the Mormons, being among the most prominent.

Certainly, during the first weeks of December, Riel's behaviour was growing increasingly erratic, as a letter to Edmond Mallet clearly reveals. It's written in a mixture of English and French which may account, at least in part, for its awkwardness.

> Very Dear Major.
>
> I have come to see you. I find that you are at church, of course.
>
> I would wait for you or go and see where you are, if I were not so busy at my place in our common interest, in the interest of all [polishing the Manitoba invasion plan]. I have to go back immediately; because though the doors of my habitation are well locked, it is nevertheless true that strangers may get in after all by the windows, or break the doors.
>
> There are so many curious, indiscreet and even bad people to be feared, in this world.

In the same letter he describes an encounter with a young woman, probably Mallet's cleaning woman.

A virgin has helped me during the greatest part of the time which I have spent in writing this earnest appeal to your charity for myself and those I have to work for. The virgin, so candid and fair has sometimes knelt down near me, sometimes stood up over my desk. She has watched my works closely. She has uttered of her own spontaneous mouth and heart or[a]lly the hour of our meeting before three o'clock today.

No wonder Edmond began to feel that his friend was losing his mind.

Sometime between December 10 and 15, 1875, using a false name, Riel had a private audience with the President of the United States. It wasn't the first time he had met Grant; Mallet had arranged a similar encounter the previous summer, although no record of what happened then remains. In the December meeting, Riel was to present his Manitoba invasion plan, now full-blown and accompanied by an annotated map. Louis was probably nervous and tense; his English may well have escaped him. The president may simply have thought the scheme unworkable. Whatever happened, according to Mallet, "He [Riel] failed utterly and it was that failure which was the immediate cause of his being placed in the insane asylum of Montreal."

Riel had become so disturbed that he needed around-the-clock attention, and Mallet, who had a delicate wife, several small children and a demanding job in the treasury department, felt he could no longer handle the situation. He asked Father Barnabé for help, but the priest wrote back, regretfully, that his mother was deathly ill, so that his household was completely caught up in nursing her. Finally, Edmond decided to take Louis to Father Primeau in Worcester, Massachusetts. Primeau had been Riel's confessor; perhaps he could calm him.

The two men arrived in Worcester at breakfast time. Sitting in the rectory dining room with Father Primeau was Honoré Mercier, who had greeted Riel when he arrived in Montreal more than two years before. The previous evening the journalist-turned-politician had given a speech at a charity banquet. With him at the breakfast table was the proprietor of the local French-language newspaper, Ferdinand Gagnon. Mallet took the three aside and told them that Riel had suffered a nervous breakdown in Washington. Interestingly, Gagnon later said Riel seemed quite rational at that point.

However, Louis's sojourn at Worcester, which lasted only eight days, was a nightmare for Father Primeau. Riel was a constant source of embarrassment and irritation, especially since he kept insisting that the priest was treating him as if he were crazy only to prepare him for his responsibility as the Messiah. Primeau's letter to Mallet on New Year's Eve, a week after Louis left, reveals that he had been at his wits' end.

Friday he asked me if he could, without disobeying me too much, begin to announce, in the city of Worcester, what he would soon have to proclaim throughout the world.

The poor child! When I told him that some of the things he wanted to do were impossible illusions, he started to weep and said: "But we have to do miracles. Command me then...."

In my view nothing but a miracle will restore him to his normal state— very probably his role is finished— May God lead him to an honourable and Christian end.

Like a hot potato, Louis was passed on to the parish priest at Suncook. It was thought that if anybody could understand Louis, it would be Évariste Richer.

The trip on Christmas Eve from Worcester north to Suncook, through rolling hills heavy with snow, was described in an article written ten years later by Ferdinand Gagnon for his newspaper, *Le Travailleur*. Riel was accompanied by Father Primeau and an unnamed man from Worcester who served as a guard.

By this time Riel had grown adept at creating realities of his own, and, for someone who only a few years before had rebelled against the establishment and proudly set up the first democratic government in Canada's Northwest, these illusions created a strange world indeed. He saw himself as part of an unholy trinity of cast-off monarchs, the other two members being Count de Chambord, the Bourbon claimant to the French throne, and Don Carlos, the pretender to the Spanish throne. Both nineteenth-century would-be royals represented the repressive, loyalist forces in their respective countries and their cause had been taken up by the ultramontanes in Canada. Riel saw the pretenders as he saw himself—divinely chosen by God to lead his people and yet unjustly kept from doing so by his liberal enemies. In his overheated mind, each member of the trio was represented by a different-coloured bull. The Count de Chambord had lost his chance at the throne because he had insisted on replacing the republic's tricolour with the Bourbons' white flag, so naturally he was designated the white bull. Don Carlos's colour was black, perhaps because so much death had occurred during the First Carlist War. Riel was represented by red, for the blood of Christ and all martyrs. The trip to Suncook must have been interesting, because Louis kept insisting he was now a bull. Father Primeau had to give him stern looks to stop the embarrassing snorting.

Guarded by the man from Worcester and cared for by the increasingly perplexed Richer, Riel stayed twenty-five days in the pleasant village of Suncook. During this period he wrote letters to Archbishop Taché and Father Ritchot, the last communication he would make with friends at home for over a year. They were sad, pathetic, angry letters, yet quite rational.

By January 18, 1876, Riel was on his way to Keeseville in New York State. Father Richer felt that Louis was not improving under his care; the Barnabé family that loved him so much might offer the warmth and comfort that would help him. But during the ten days Louis stayed with them, he kept the household in a constant uproar. He slept neither day nor night, he paced incessantly up and down, up and down, and he cried and howled so horribly that the priest's mother was terrified of him and wouldn't go near him. (No mention is made of Evelina being there, or what she thought of Riel's outlandish behaviour.) Finally, in desperation, Father Barnabé telegraphed Louis's uncle in Montreal for help.

As soon as he got the wire, John Lee left for Keeseville. As he stepped off the train, he spotted Fabien Barnabé. "What's wrong?" he demanded.

The priest looked terrible, haggard and distraught. "Poor Louis! He is out of his mind!"

Staying for the night at the rectory, Lee got a taste of what the Barnabé family had been through. Hour after hour, his beloved nephew roared like a bull.

The train trip back to Montreal was a nightmare. John Lee would later tell the story himself: "He [Louis] continued to cry in the train. I told the travellers that he was a poor lunatic and to please excuse him. When they talked or laughed, Louis said, 'Keep still. Do not laugh, I beg you. I am a prophet.'"

Since he was in contravention of the government-imposed exile, Riel was entering Canada illegally. John Lee decided to avoid the crowded Bonaventure Station in downtown Montreal, and wired ahead for a carriage to meet them at the village of St. Lambert. All went well as they crossed the frozen St. Lawrence, until they mounted the bank and passed the old Bonsecours Church. Louis tried to scramble out of the carriage and had to be restrained. Only after Lee promised to take him to mass after lunch did he quiet down a little.

Riel's Aunt Lucie, his uncle and a trusted friend, Henri Flageolle, looked after him during this disturbing time. For the first six days of his stay, Louis refused to sleep or be quiet, and "had contortions like a man in a rage". According to Lee, three times he locked himself in his room, stripped naked and tore all his clothes and bed coverings to shreds. He would never say why he had done such a thing. He had to be re-dressed like a little child.

He was locked in his room, but often he would try to escape, pleading that he wanted to go to church. And to mention that he might be ill was to bring on terrible frenzy. He would rant, "No, I'm not crazy! Never say I'm crazy! I have a mission to perform and I am a prophet.... I am sent by God!"

Yet as the days passed, the calm of the Lee home—Louis was particularly fond of his Aunt Lucie—had its effect. He became less excited and more rational. After a few weeks he was finally allowed to attend mass at St. Jean Baptiste

Church. As the long and rather intense sermon ended, Louis stood up and in a loud and dramatic voice sang out three times: "Hear the voice of the priest!" He made no effort to resist when his uncle and others bundled him out the door.

The Lees finally admitted that they were "all tired out". Another of Riel's old schoolmates, with whom he often stayed when he was in town, Dr. Emmanuel-Persillier Lachapelle, was called on to help. John Lee asked the doctor how he could get Louis committed to an insane asylum and Lachapelle obligingly told him.

Louis was often taken out for rides in the family's carriage, and on March 6, 1876, a fine sunny day, he was promised a trip to the village of Longue-Pointe to visit his old friend the doctor. On their arrival, Louis realized at once that he was being committed to the Hospice of St. Jean de Dieu, an asylum for the insane. He never forgave his uncle, believing, quite rightly, that he had been tricked.

The physician who received him, Henry Howard, later described his first impression of Riel: "He had the appearance of a gentleman, frank and honourable," he wrote, "and judging from his appearance I would never have supposed that he was guilty of the crime of which he was accused [the murder of Thomas Scott]. At that moment I felt great pity for him; and I thought that his friends ought to have done something better for him than to send him to a lunatic asylum."

The Sisters of Providence who ran the institution insisted that Riel's identity be hidden to avoid "an incident", and his uncle had decided on the surname of David. "I am happy to see you, Mr. David," said Dr. Howard. Riel looked surprised. "Why do you call me David?" he asked. "My name is Louis Riel." Louis then took out a small prayerbook from his pocket, and handed it to the doctor. "Look at my name there, Louis Riel, written by the hand of my beloved sister [Sara]." Immediately a nun seized the little book, tore out the page and snapped, "You are known here only under the name of Mr. David." Riel was naturally very upset. "When he calmed down," wrote Howard, "the poor fellow wept, and turning to me, said, 'That was a gift given to me by my dear sister on my birthday, and in all my wanderings I always kept it near my heart.'" It was not an auspicious beginning.

From the outside, L'Hospice St. Jean de Dieu, better known as Longue-Pointe Asylum, seemed a shining example of a new, enlightened attitude towards the insane that was just taking shape in the Western world. Instead of being confined like vicious animals, the inmates were to be "morally resuscitated" by being kept in a healthy, pleasant environment. Situated on six hundred acres of rolling farmland in the suburbs of Montreal, Longue-Pointe had been constructed only the year before Riel arrived. Made of bright red brick, with what seemed like plenty of windows, the complex consisted of a large, six-storey main building attached by long corridors to two annexes, each five storeys high. The gardens were nicely laid out, and there was a working farm with animals. From the outside it seemed quite pleasant—the interior was another story.

Seven years after Riel had been confined there, Dr. Harold Tuke, a prominent British reformer advocating more humane treatment for the insane, made a tour of the asylums of North America. He said of Longue-Pointe, "In the course of seven and thirty years I have visited a large number of asylums in Europe, but I have rarely, if ever, seen anything more depressing...."

It was horribly overcrowded, it stank, there wasn't a picture or coat of paint on the walls, and the food was disgusting. Each inmate was confined to a tiny, narrow room—Tuke said it was more like an animal pen than a cell—where there was hardly enough space for a bed; many patients slept on straw mattresses on the floor. Each cell had a small opening at the top of the door which was closed or opened by the keepers; this was the occupant's only source of light. Privacy was unheard of.

Treatment revolved entirely around the idea of authority; the inmate was to do what he or she was told or face punishment. Although physical assault was not uncommon, discipline primarily involved constraint: most often the kind of iron handcuffs used on criminals were employed, but so were leather cuffs, strait-jackets and crib beds. And it wasn't necessarily violent behaviour that resulted in such harnessing. Since the province paid only $100 a year for each patient, the nuns had to pinch every penny, and one of the worst offences was to tear one's clothes; that would land you in a strait-jacket for days. Longue-Pointe truly was, as Dr. Tuke pointed out, "a chamber of horrors".

Louis Riel naturally loathed the place, and never stopped pleading to be released. In fact, his confinement was probably illegal under Quebec law. The Act Respecting Private Lunatic Asylums specified that an individual could be involuntarily confined under certain conditions: a family or friend could apply to have someone admitted to an asylum—in Riel's case this was John Lee—but the patient had to be carefully examined and then certified by two doctors who were not relatives, friends or connected with the institution. Dr. Lachapelle likely signed the certification form. How carefully he examined Riel is not known, but certainly his being a close friend, and therefore hardly an objective examiner, ran counter to the law's intent. More significantly, there is no record of a signature of a second doctor, and there probably never was one.

Dr. Howard's role in all of this is most suspect. He was not an employee of the hospital, but supposedly an independent agent working for the government to ensure the rights of the patients. Howard's concept of mental illness was, in

some aspects, very simple. If someone had committed a crime, especially murder, that person was automatically insane, no questions asked. Howard would
write, "According to my observation, Louis David Riel had a perfect knowledge
of what he believed to be right and wrong, but being a great criminal, and
guilty of bad conduct, I considered him a fool, in virtue of a teratological defect
in his psycho-physical organization." That Riel had never been convicted in a
court of law didn't seem to faze the doctor, nor did the fact that he had
absolutely no knowledge of the circumstances surrounding Thomas Scott's execution. He believed Riel guilty of murder and therefore crazy.

Louis Riel fought the prison of Longue-Pointe Asylum with all the strength
and passion of his highly developed instinct for survival. He could see that the
treatment offered was bad for his health. In writing Bishop Bourget, he pointed
out, "Dr. Lachapelle prescribed for me a walk of several miles a day, to make
sure that I'm tired and sleep better at night. And this very same doctor puts me
in a place where I am allowed only to walk behind the house under a guard
who has orders to constrict my every step and where I spend the night with
chains around my feet and hands. How can I sleep like this?"

Louis always carried a suitcase full of correspondence with him wherever
he went. The letters, he explained to Dr. Howard, were his link to his friends
and family, their support and their protection. One evening shortly after he had
been incarcerated at Longue-Pointe, he returned after dinner to find that his
valise had been cut open and all the papers were missing. He was beside himself, and, as he put it, "made a row". For that he was stripped naked and
slapped in a strait-jacket. Thereafter, as Dr. Howard rather cutely put it, "he was
sad, and seemed suspicious of everyone surrounding him, and particularly of
his friends."

On several occasions he took off his clothes, considered a great travesty in the
asylum, but he explained to Bishop Bourget, "The spirit of charity told me, 'The
one who is good must show himself naked. Because he is beautiful. The one who
disobeys is the one who must hide himself. Because he is ugly.' Afterwards the
good Lord said: 'In truth, in truth, the day is coming when all men will stand up
naked from the bowels of the earth.'" Bishop Bourget wrote Riel a reply telling
him that God wanted him to be "well dressed", and Louis immediately gave up the
habit of stripping, much to the relief of the nuns running the place.

Louis's one comfort was attending mass, but that led to further provocation.
Like the rest of the institution, the chapel was filthy; the sanctuary was dusty,
the altar linens stained and the candles lopsided and broken. As he would later
write Bishop Bourget, Louis believed that God spoke out: "I do not see as much
dirt on the Jewish altars as the Catholic. Tell those who are in charge. And if

they don't listen, you will roar, you will bellow my fury." Riel did just that, as well as toppling everything within his reach and breaking the glass of the chapel door. His punishment was to be strait-jacketed again and placed in solitary confinement.

He was thereafter banned from the chapel and this led to a four-day hunger strike. There was real concern that he might starve himself to death, which the nuns realized would cause a major scandal. So when Louis finally asked permission to consecrate the food offered himself, and eat it as the flesh and blood of Christ, the chaplain, who thought he was crazy anyway, told him to go ahead.

During his time at Longue-Pointe, Riel wrote non-stop to Bishop Bourget, eight letters in the first half of May alone. (The bishop may have been the only one he corresponded with, as no other letters from this time have been found.) These are a mixture of rational thought, bursts of religious exaltation, visions— "I saw a turtle. I said: Lord what's the meaning of this? And the Lord answered: this is the government of Ottawa which walks like a turtle"—strange biblical references and cries of help, with the "mission" Bourget supposedly had sanctified as the pivot. A single paragraph in a letter dated April 20, 1876, gives a feel for his writings at the time:

Monseigneur,

I have received your letter of March 17. For a long time, I have wanted to respond. But in the state I find myself, I can't write when I want, neither as I like, nor what I like. The Holy Spirit who fills you with his gifts which you so charitably communicated to me, pushes me with one hand and holds me back with the other, so strongly that I feel that I'm being crushed by a mountain at the same time as I leap into action on the wings of my mission. When will you help me? I have been dying for seven years, and five I have spent in the heat of fire....

Whether it was through the intervention of Bishop Bourget—Riel kept pleading, "for the love of God, try to get me out of here!"—or because the Sisters of Providence were fed up with his disruptive behaviour—they claimed that the Orangemen of Montreal had got wind that Riel was confined there and threatened to burn the asylum down—or because, as Dr. Howard admitted, there was real fear that Louis would commit suicide, it was decided in May that he should be moved to another institution near Quebec City. His old friend and one of the defence lawyers for Ambroise Lépine, Joseph-Adolphe Chapleau, who was now provincial secretary, made the arrangements.

Louis was accompanied by Chapleau, another supporter and the member of parliament, Joseph Mousseau, as well as two doctors. Being incarcerated in yet another mental asylum wasn't exactly what Riel had had in mind for himself, and there was a struggle to get him aboard the boat. "I made myself go limp, and they were hard put to hold me up. I looked at old Mousseau, his face covered with sweat, and I laughed up my sleeve," he later recalled.

On the afternoon of May 19, 1876, he was admitted to the St. Michel-Archange Asylum at Beauport under the name of Louis Larochelle.

Beauport Asylum was not much better than Longue-Pointe. In fact, the physical surroundings were even more gothic; a massive structure of grey limestone, it was the oldest asylum in the province. The year before, a fire had swept through the women's section, killing twenty-six inmates; several of those who lived were badly scarred, but luckily for Riel they were well hidden in the women's dormitory. Privately operated for profit, the place was over-crowded, dark and depressing. Riel made no secret of how he felt.

> The impious attacked my work, taking away
> My rights. They have done everything to destroy me.
> I know they wanted to lead me to the tomb of death.
> Many of my friends wanted to do as much.
> In order to topple these satanic plots
> The son of man pretended to persecute me.
> These judases have felt a great thrill
> Of Joy. And idiots came to rig me
> As they constrained those possessed by the devil.
> Ignorant doctors recommended the medicine
> Of heavy leather harnesses you use on animals.

In certifying him as insane, Dr. Lachapelle filled out a medical history in which Riel's problem was summed up succinctly: "In religious matters he thinks himself a prophet."

And yet, as the days went by, Louis became calmer, more rational. It may be that the environment at Beauport was not as authoritarian or, more likely, he may have at last found the perfect release valve for his troubled psyche—his writings. A myriad of poems, letters and revelations poured from Riel's pen during the time he was in Beauport, and perhaps it was this self-administered therapy that gradually made him well again.

All his life, Louis Riel had been courteous, even formal, in addressing people, both in letters and in his private writings. Few harsh words were ever expressed against anybody, even his enemies. Now, like a pressure cooker that has to explode, Louis railed against people and institutions that he felt had betrayed him. The language was sometimes crude, the structure occasionally amateurish, the sentiment juvenile, but at last the anger was being released. (It must be remembered that Riel probably never thought the poems would be published, at least not in their raw, unpolished state. They were his form of private diary.) A song composed at Beauport simply entitled "Ottawa" is a prime example.

> Ottawa, you're totally lost,
>> Smoking your cigars.
> *Chorus:* If anyone has known your bad faith
>> It's surely me!
> Your cohorts all two-faced
>> Ferocious bums
> *Chorus:* If anyone has known your bad faith
>> It's surely me!
> You live a lie
>> And your fury gnaws at me.
> *Chorus:* If anyone has known your bad faith
>> It's surely me.*

But it was at those people, many intimate friends, who had disappointed him, that he aimed his sharpest, most mocking barbs. Joseph-Adolphe Chapleau, the lawyer who had accompanied him to Beauport, was an example. Riel purposely spelled his name wrong in a poem entitled "Chapeleau-the-Conservative", and had him speaking in the first person of his botched attempt to defend Ambroise Lépine. A few verses give the flavour:

> When I get there
> Everything goes wrong.
> I'm so embarrassed
> To truly defend him
> Would be my downfall.
> I can see
> The hangman's noose.
>
> I declare that
> With a flick of the hand
> I could have proven
> His innocence;
> And without even resting
> Driven the scum
> To despair....

---

* *Translation by Wilfrid Dubé.*

I was prodigal with the wine
Of sympathy.
I softened the tone
Of my harangues.
I was amiable.

I have the grace
Of my place.
Ambroise is in jail.
My sweet tongue
Had him plead guilty
And cut the cord.
That's good enough.*

There were others on whom Louis wreaked revenge in this same spiteful but harmless way. Among them were Hector Langevin, the man who had replaced Cartier as the Conservative Party's chief Quebec lieutenant—"You call yourself conservative/But all your heart conserves/Are wicked games"—and Marc-Amable Girard, lawyer, MLA for Manitoba and one-time Riel loyalist—"While the métis, with much toil/Sowed together/Girard and his gang harvested/Right behind them/The mustard seed,/Before it even grew."

But the man who had disillusioned him the most was his former soul-mate, Joseph Dubuc. After Riel was exiled in 1875, Dubuc was elected in Louis's old riding of Provencher. Thereafter, Dubuc's correspondence to Louis dried up. That same summer Julie Riel hinted that all was not well with their relationship—"They [the Dubucs] have not the same courtesy towards us any more," she wrote. Not only was Riel upset at thus being abandoned, but he had heard that Dubuc was not defending the Métis cause as strongly as he should have. His response, naturally, was to write a long poem expressing his outrage.

What gall you have!
Betrayed Métis are dying.
You serve their hated tyrants.
Deep in your shameless soul you say:
"I do for them
What any other coward would."

Throughout this period, Riel was also wrestling with his own sense of self. He now believed that the divine hand had touched him. "I have become priest

---

* Translation by Wilfrid Dubé.

in the middle of suffering/I have acquired my titles by the grace of God." And the image of himself as prophet, messenger of God, was more central than ever. He liked to refer to himself as, of all things, a telephone* with a long-distance connection to heaven:

> When I speak to you, it is the voice of God that sounds
> And everything I say is essential to you.
> I am the happy telephone
> Who transmits to you the songs and messages of heaven,
> I help in a special way....

Riel also envisioned himself as carrying on his shoulders the burden of mankind's wickedness. This is made clear in some of his most controversial verse, "Oh! Que j'ai fait attention...."

> I confess in the name of those who sin.
> I mediate for them; I take on their being.
> I speak for them in gracious tones.
> Man has traded his spirit for the heart of a beast.
> I will resurrect his soul, enlighten it,
> Kindle the original flame of reason in him.

He then gave a long, rather naive recitation of man's sins:

> Every day I commit horrible sins
> That I hide and repress.
> I feel that my whole life is drained.
> I avoid what's right: my heart whores.
> I have given myself to indecency.
> I drink my money: renounce my health....
>
> I don't work: I rob my boss.
> I show off a lot
> But truly am good for nothing: and honest folk
> Treat me as a worthless bum.
>
> I hang out in restaurants.
> Pockets always full of sweets.**

Some historians have taken this literally, as Riel's personal confession of a

---

* *News of Alexander Graham Bell's great invention filled the newspapers that year. Riel was fascinated by it.*
** *Translation by Wilfrid Dubé.*

shocking, debauched past.* Given the previous verse and the austere and dedicated life he had lived to date, the more logical interpretation is that the poem is a symbolic confession of the sins of all humanity—Riel as a kind of Jesus Christ of the nineteenth century (although he never once called himself the son of God).

Very soon after he was admitted to Beauport, Riel began signing his prose, and later his poetry, "Louis David Riel, Prophet, Infallible Pontiff, Priest King". It should be emphasized again that, with a few exceptions—primarily the letters to Bishop Bourget, whom he considered his private mentor—documents signed this way were for his own personal rumination, not for public consumption. A letter sent to Archbishop Taché during this time closed with his usual sign-off, "with the greatest respect and strictest obedience, your servant, Louis Riel"; a letter to his mother concluded, "Your affectionate son, Louis." Some letters to Bishop Bourget included the middle name "David" but none of the other accolades. It was probably one way of bolstering his own ego against the criticism and name-calling he had suffered.

Embracing David, ancient King of the Hebrews, as a kind of alter ego was a fascinating development, and not a totally far-fetched one. There were striking similarities. Both men had been snatched from obscurity to accomplish great things: David was a shepherd, the youngest son in a not very important Bethlehem household, when he was anointed king; Riel was an insignificant Half-breed living in the "wilderness" of Red River when he was sent to be educated in Montreal. Both were mixed-bloods: David was one-eighth Gentile, Louis one-eighth Indian. Both achieved success very young; David killed Goliath with one whirl from his sling; Riel fought off the Canadians and effectively established the province of Manitoba. Both spent time in exile: David was on the run from the vicious King Saul; Riel hid in Vermette's woods after the warrant for his arrest was issued. Both men were called crazy: David saved his life by feigning insanity after he was captured by the Philistines; Riel claimed he was pretending to be out of his mind to hide himself from assassins. Finally, David and Louis both had long conversations with God and both expressed these revelations in poetry; some of Riel's verse of the time had a decidedly psalm-like ring to it. Louis must have found encouragement in David's success story; the latter was finally made king and ruled a huge empire for over thirty years. However, prudish Riel probably didn't draw parallels with the lascivious aspects of King David's life—his reputation as a great womanizer, his fifteen wives and his infamous lust for Bathsheba—or his love for Saul's son, Jonathan,

---

* Most particularly, Thomas Flanagan, Riel: Prophet of the New World, page 74.

which may have been more than platonic, or the fact that family feuding finally drove King David to despair.

Louis had a great admiration for the ancient Hebrews—he called himself the Messiah of the Jews—and it was their moral code that, in the universe of his imagination, he decided to adopt—with certain alterations. He thought that Mosaic Law, with its strict and disciplined observance, would serve as a defence against society's liberalism. In politics, liberal ideology had, for Riel, come to be represented by John Schultz and his friends, and their determination to make a buck no matter what the consequences. In Louis's moral sphere, liberalism meant "to turn one's back on God, to flee the duties of lasting virtue for the life of ease, of self-indulgence and of sensual pleasure." The law of Abraham, Isaac and Jacob would put a stop to such decadence.

Polygamy was to be encouraged; the sovereign would be allowed fifteen wives, the exact number David had, lesser mortals would be permitted fewer. (Did Riel realize how much trouble David had with the domestic politics that emerged from his harem?) This was not to satisfy man's lust, Riel emphasized. A woman was *never* to be forced into a marriage she didn't want. In a time when there was little else for females but domesticity and child-rearing, Riel believed that polygamy would mean more women could marry—few would be left to suffer the ugly existence of spinsterhood—and multiple marriages would permit a sharing of child care and housework.

He believed in incest in special cases; if a daughter was over thirty, for example, and her brother did not have his full complement of, say, five wives, then she could join the group. Riel also decided that if the head of the household died and the eldest son stepped in as the bread-winner, and if he was too poor to find a wife, he should be allowed to ask for the hand of one of his sisters. Was Louis thinking of his beloved Sara? Perhaps, but there's no evidence that the Riel siblings had an incestuous relationship; Louis would likely have died of guilt if he had even thought of such a thing. Later on there would be hints that an entirely different family might have served as his inspiration.

How was Riel's version of the Mosaic Law to be implemented? Certainly not through the Roman Catholic hierarchy. For one thing, Pius IX, whom the Quebec ultramontanes had for so long idolized, had suddenly become an enemy.

Bishops Bourget and Laflèche had insisted that their clergy could dictate politics to their parishioners; Archbishop Taschereau had objected to this, especially to priests withholding sacraments from those who had committed the terrible sin of voting for the Liberals. The dispute had turned fierce and the Vatican had been forced to mediate. The ultramontanes ultimately lost, and never forgave Pius IX. As for Riel, he no longer believed in the doctrine of papal infallibility.

In his recreated society, Riel got rid of "Vatican corruption" by simply naming Bishop Bourget the new pope. This fit into his cosmology because, according to Riel, the spiritual head of the Catholic faith was about to leave the Vatican and come to New France. Then, in the year 2333 AD, the church would move again—this time away from Montreal to Riel's birthplace of St. Vital. He wrote:

> The Queen of the Lakes has become heiress
> She is the Vital church. She is the last in line.
> She will vanquish the proud empire of Satan
> She will behold the end of the whole world.

Why St. Vital? Because the Métis were a people chosen by God primarily because of their Native blood. Riel came to believe that North American Indians were a lost tribe of Israel, and therefore a direct link with Abraham, Isaac, Jacob and David. Writing to Bishop Bourget, he explained:

> Here, My Lord, the Holy Ghost revealed to me that the primitive nations of North America are Jewish, the pure-blooded descendants of Abraham, except the Eskimos, who came from Morocco.
>
> While we exposed Moses on the water of the Nile in order that he be rescued, an Egyptian ship got lost at sea, unable to find its way back. The crew was composed of forty-four persons, twenty-seven from the Egyptian nation and seventeen from the Jewish nation.
>
> The Egyptians consisted of twenty-two men and five women. The Jewish of three mature males, a young boy and thirteen females.
>
> Those seventeen Hebrews were members of three different tribes who had fled tyranny to find a more welcoming country. The three men were married....

Riel then proceeded to create an elaborate and very specific family tree for the lost tribes of Israel, and to explain how they spread across North America. He concluded, "the Holy Ghost told me.... 'You are the David of the Christian era....'"

It was all very rational to Riel, and he couldn't understand why so many people had difficulty following his logic.

Like the parables composed in his student days under the influence of the Sulpicians, Louis's writing of this time was full of dramatic imagery, as God wreaked vengeance on an assortment of wicked cities and nations. In Spain the liberal regime of Alfonso XII would be destroyed. Because it promoted slavery, the southern U.S. would once again be ravaged. Washington would be crushed. "Great capital! With one kick of my heel I will make your hills bend like the back of a bull when he struggles to his feet, aroused from sleep by a kick from the herdsman."

Much has been made of the authoritarianism displayed by Riel in these writings.* With such a philosophy, how could he be the humane and free-dom-loving revolutionary portrayed by the Métis and their sympathizers? What must be remembered is the time and place in which Riel's new religion emerged. While he certainly was not pathologically insane in the way we understand that concept today, he was under great emotional stress.** At Red River only six years before, he had displayed remarkable egalitarianism. The ultramontanes had taken him under their wing when he desperately needed somebody on his side, and their rigid, elitist philosophy did leave its mark on him. But nowhere in his writing did he advocate cruelty to persons; his hunger for revenge was directed not at individuals but at abstract authority which had used its power to humiliate and thwart the likes of Riel and the Métis people. His religion was, in fact, inclusive; anti-semitism, bigotry towards blacks or aboriginal people, were entirely absent. What he seemed to be struggling for was an idealized system where the morally upright pre-vailed, and maybe, in the wicked world he had experienced, coercion—forced adherence to a superior moral system—was necessary.

As Riel worked out on paper a universe more to his liking, he also began to come to terms with the real world around him. He began to acknowledge that he was ill, that his sickness, as he saw it, was not mental illness so much as "a great physical and moral exhaustion"—which was probably closer to the truth than any of the diagnoses of "megalomania" and other quack diseases. "I really want to be cured," he wrote to Bourget in May of 1876; thereafter he began to conform to what the officials at Beauport expected, and he was therefore con-sidered on the mend.

His old mentor, Archbishop Taché, visited Riel in November or December of 1876. Louis tried to make up for the angry letter written the previous January, pleading with him: "Be my liberator. I want to reach the United States." But Taché considered him "mentally dead" and thought that Beauport Asylum was exactly where Louis should be. He made no effort to have him released. He did, however, revive contact by post between Louis and his family, which may have done more good than any other therapy. Julie Riel wrote on January 21, 1877, "It has been a year now since I've received a letter from you. You can believe that I find that a very long time. You could probably say as much about us, but

---

* *For a particularly critical and negative view of Riel see Flanagan,* Riel: Prophet of the New World, *pages 95–96.*
** *For further discussion of Riel's insanity see the "Letter to Father Joe," Addendum Three, page 453.*

we did not know where you were...." Riel quickly wrote back a very long and quite rational letter full of love and concern for his family. Shortly afterwards, Father Barnabé would write from Keeseville: "The sooner you become submissive and obedient, the sooner you will find good health, and the sooner it will be the pleasure of your friends to find you among them again." The letters from his family and the priest struck a chord; from that time on, Riel's health improved. He was allowed to send out for books on history. He was asked to join discussions in the Cercle Catholique, a group of ultramontane adherents which included Clément Vincellette, manager of the Beauport Asylum. Louis became so friendly with Vincellette and his family that he often went on outings in the country with them.

By the end of 1877, Louis's health had improved so much that preparations began for his discharge. In the judgement of Dr. François-Elzéar Roy, Louis Riel had been cured—"more or less".

– 12 –

I would kiss you ten times in a quarter of an hour
If each time my soul felt better
But the sweet kisses are drunken pleasures
That would make the most earnest spirit fall.
The wise one enjoys it; but he must slow it down
The delight can upset the heart.

On January 29, 1878, the day Louis Riel was released from Beauport Asylum, he was whisked to the American border. The last thing the officials of the asylum wanted was the scandal that would surely result if it was ever discovered he had been living in Canada illegally for two years. He immediately headed for Keeseville and the comfort of the Barnabé household. He felt welcome there; Father Fabien had written as a New Year's message: "I send you the embraces of the most affectionate and holy friendship—Mother and Evelina say: Amen." And, he suggested, a year of rest at Keeseville was just what Louis needed to recuperate.

Once Louis was settled, his first thoughts were of how to make a living. He had no money at all, but he did own six valuable parcels of land near Winnipeg, including one near St. Vital referred to as Bodé's land, on which was located a house; a lot near St. Boniface where his father's old mill had been; and farmland at Ste. Agathe. On February 26, 1878, he wrote Julie: "If you haven't sold it [the land] you must be pretty low on funds, because I know that you have hardly any income. And you have bought all the clothing and many other things."

Louis also mentioned that he himself needed money because he had big plans—he wanted to buy farmland in Nebraska. Good homesteads were still available there, the climate was a little warmer than Dakota or Montana, and, far away from political turmoil, he could devote himself to farming. As he wrote his mother, "I assure you that after all these years of struggle, I am very anxious to establish a home for myself." He thought his Red River property might bring in as much as $1,000, which would set him up nicely in Nebraska.

His letters had something of a desperate ring about them—"I am waiting for your letter anxiously. Spring is quickly coming and I would like to get some land soon, in time for sowing." In March 1878, he signed an affidavit assigning power of attorney to his mother, but although the land was valuable, money was still scarce in Manitoba; the incredible boom that would hit Winnipeg and make millionaires out of all the speculators waiting in the wings was still a couple of years away. In July, Julie sent word that she had finally sold the Ste. Agathe property to Joseph Delorme for $550, but because of legal complications, the money would not be handed over until June of the following year.

Louis soon had to admit to himself that his dream of a Nebraska farm was premature. Instead of heading west, he would farm near Keeseville. With the help of Father Barnabé, who lent him $125, he rented three acres of land at $10 an acre and planned to sow corn and potatoes. It was a time of happiness for him, as he himself would write: "In the fields around Keeseville, my! how we laughed/George, Regis and I, while farming the land."

And Fabien Barnabé was determined to help Riel fully regain his health. In a letter to his Aunt Lucie, Louis described how kind Fabien had been to him. Besides lending him the money to rent the small farm, "He is lending me his horse, so that I may do the work I would otherwise be unable to do. He has supplied me with the seed. His hired man helps me continually. Since milk was making me feel better, he bought a cow specifically for that. He has given me much of his clothing. He has given me some money to buy medicine." Since it was recommended that the medication be accompanied by drinking a small amount of strong liquor daily, the priest obtained some, the total coming to at least $120.

But there was another reason Louis wanted to stay in the East for a while. He had fallen in love with Evelina Barnabé, and she with him.

The romance must have started almost immediately upon Louis's arrival in late January, because two months later he wrote her a poem entitled "If my love pleases, and if my joys suffice".

> Oh sweet Evelina! Whom I find so lovable
> And for whom I wish such happy days!
> If you frequently taste the delectable bread
> And love holy communion;
> I beg God that he answer my prayers
> And unite us both as soon as possible....

In Riel's papers were found three versions of this particular poem to Evelina; in the second draft the first couple of stanzas are identical, but a second part hints at something very mysterious and black. Riel began by reminding Evelina that she was already twenty-seven years old and still "a maid" but "Your cheeks have the freshness of Spring./You are sweet and charming." God likely didn't want her to marry sooner, he said, so that she could experience the world and acquire the knowledge it takes to become a "wise mother". But, he went on, many people had tried to seduce Evelina, setting in her path many traps and temptations. Then he continued:

Look back today
And remember how in your life
As a young woman
No day has gone by
Without a mighty struggle.
You who wish to serve God as a Christian woman
Know what wisdom it takes
To escape the world and all its dangers.
You know how she must behave
To avoid the corrupt and shallow.
And, forgive my frankness,
For I do not wish to speak to you in muddled words,
Although family be a revered sanctuary
It is more often than not
Soiled even between brother and sister.
And if ever God should want you to be a mother
Remember, Evelina,
That Ammon, the son of David,
Committed incest with his sister Thamar.
And divine anger
Was around to punish this fatal disorder.*

It's hard to imagine what Riel meant by this. Both Fabien and Evelina seemed so frail, upright and devout, such total innocents, that it's almost impossible to think that anything sexual occurred between them. Some historians** have suggested that Louis was referring to an incestuous relationship between himself and his sister Sara. But given the context of the poem, this interpretation seems far-fetched. What is more probable is that Louis and Evelina had talked

---

* *Translation by Wilfrid Dubé.*
** *E.g., Flanagan,* Riel: Prophet of the New World, *page 86.*

about their deep, but not necessarily sexual, feelings for Sara and Fabien. Riel was simply commenting on their conversation. Having been immersed in the saga of King David and his tribulations for so long, perhaps he simply had the possibility of incest on his mind. Whatever the case, the passage remains one of the most baffling in all of Riel's vast writings.

But Evelina likely never saw this strange reference; Riel sent her the third and most innocent version of the letter. There was no question of her feelings; she was madly in love. From that time on, her letters and poems were full of her passion for him. "I'm going to bed hoping to dream about you. I love you and I kiss you." "Please accept as a souvenir for your birthday, these flowers. You will find among them an oleander...; it is an emblem of my vital and sincere love." "Return, return quickly/My heart throbs at this thought/You are so lovable to me/That I am yours inseparably."

Two years before, Evelina had watched the fits of madness that had so terrified her household. She knew Louis had been confined in an asylum and was considered insane by some. None of this mattered to her. He spoke so beautifully, so uniquely, and, as a picture taken in 1878 reveals, he remained an exceptionally handsome man, even if his face was now etched with a certain indelible sadness. As Louis and Evelina walked the beautifully treed streets of Keeseville that spring and summer, they must have found great joy in each other.

In March 1876, Riel had written his old friend and political mentor, Father Ritchot, a long letter. It was so elegant and reasoned that the priest, who had heard all about Louis's insanity from Taché and others, must have wondered if they were talking about the same person. The letter was a rather sad analysis of his actions since the Red River Rebellion. "I have always been opposed to those small political promises. I hate these compromises with no meaning, that the first to arrive can thwart. And thinking of a person like you, Father, I tried to do what a man would want done to himself, I have tried to do what my conscience says I have to do for my fellow man." Riel also suggested to Ritchot that the priest himself might be interested in buying some of his land. Ritchot didn't take him up on the offer.

Riel was obviously struggling with himself, as his writing at this time poignantly suggests:

> Lord calm in me this political drive.
> Make it rest in me for at least five more years.
> My health is still too fragile.
> Deliver me from my constant worries.
>
> O God I pray you
> To give me, please, peace of mind.

Remove this passion for literature
And give it back to me when your tender care
Has restored my health completely.
The farming, the fields
Will have brought me prosperity.

Remove this wanderlust;
And give me stability.
I will raise cattle
And horses.
O God! may your heavenly grace
Favour all my labours.
Help me discover a sound homestead
With good and rich earth
Where the harvest will be plenty....*

Yet the political fray would soon prove irresistible to him, and he never did establish himself on that homestead in Nebraska.

By the early fall of 1878 it was obvious that Riel was not going to make much of a living working the small farm he had rented near Keeseville. His corn harvest had turned out all right but, as he wrote his Aunt Lucie and Uncle John Lee in Montreal, insects had almost completely destroyed his potatoes. But then there wasn't much for anyone in Keeseville at that time.

The depression that had descended in 1873 had ravaged the industrial towns in the United States. Wages had dropped to $1.50 a day for ten hours of work, unions had been weakened and unemployment was rampant. In Keeseville, a millhand started a blaze as a protest and it swept through the town, destroying factories and flour mills, the new Methodist church and ten homes. Riel was visiting friends at Glens Falls, a town about sixty miles south, at the time, and Barnabé wrote him, "Keeseville was already very poor—this catastrophe reduces it to nothing."

Louis was a well-educated man; surely, Father Barnabé insisted, he would be able to find a good position in a larger city. By the end of September Louis was in New York looking for a job.

His two-month stay there would leave him despondent and physically exhausted. He himself did not write about this period, but Barnabé's letters suggest he tried for several positions—as a journalist, a law clerk, a salesman of newspaper ads—all to no avail. It's unclear what happened, whether Louis was never hired or whether looking for work was simply not his chief interest. He

---

* *Translation by Wilfrid Dubé.*

apparently spent most of his time trying to round up support for yet another armed invasion of Manitoba.

Just before Riel's death in 1885, the *New York Herald* published a story, without a byline, claiming that he had purposely gone to New York at the same time as two famous Irish revolutionaries, just released from a London jail, were arriving to great publicity. It was at that point, said the newspaper article, that he had proposed to the Fenian leadership, like O'Donoghue before him, a plan for a "Manitoban rebellion".

In fact, since Louis had returned to Keeseville in January 1878 there had been hints that he was again promoting a grand scheme to invade Manitoba, similar to the one he had presented to President Grant and Senator Morton three years before. According to the newspaper report, "He promised to found a great northwest republic in the event of a victorious outcome of the proposed war." All he needed was money, and this was what he asked the Irish revolutionaries to provide. But the Fenians had had enough of disastrous invasions of Canada, and they turned him down flat.

His "revolutionary" efforts exhausted him, but there was no question of another mental collapse. On October 12, 1878, Father Barnabé wrote to Edmond Mallet, "His mind shows perfect lucidity, the greatest agility. You could truthfully say that he had never experienced a breakdown, if you knew nothing of his past."

By November Louis was back in Keeseville, but only to pack his belongings and say goodbye to Evelina, who was now his declared, although secret, fiancée. (Madame Barnabé apparently did not approve of the match. Maybe she was remembering the nights of the roaring bulls.) At last he was heading west again, to the vast and open prairies he loved so much.

It had been Fabien Barnabé's idea. He was acquainted with John Ireland, Bishop of St. Paul, whose ambitious Catholic Colonization Bureau was attracting attention throughout the church establishment. Founded two years before, in 1876, its purpose was to pluck factory workers and the unemployed from their wretched living conditions in the cities of Europe and eastern North America and to settle them on prairie farms. Since much of the land was owned by the railways, the bishop was in effect an agent for these companies, and a highly successful one. Under his patronage, over the next five years ten Catholic villages would spring up in western Minnesota.

Here was a healthier and more spiritual future for those pinched and religiously bankrupt French-Canadian émigrés in New England. And given his ambition and experience, Riel was surely the man to organize such a scheme, with the help, of course, of Bishop Ireland's Colonization Bureau. Father

Barnabé, who had been frustrated for some time by his inability to save the French-Canadian souls of Keeseville, wanted to go west too. He saw himself buying land for an orphanage where he could turn Catholic city boys into dedicated farmers. The priest decided to send his friend the bishop a letter introducing Riel; once Louis was established, Barnabé and his family—including, of course, Evelina—would follow.

By early December 1878, Louis was on his way to St. Paul. Perhaps he hadn't realized how deeply homesick he had been, for he wrote: "Minnesota, which I now entered,/Filled my heart with longing/For my home strung along its border." He went at once to visit his Uncle François Riel, a stonecutter by trade, who lived in Minneapolis, and then he settled down to wait for an interview with Bishop Ireland. It came sometime during the Christmas holidays. The bishop received Louis cordially enough but responded by doing nothing—he didn't even send a letter accepting or rejecting the idea. Barnabé would write months later, "He [the bishop] has found me perhaps too belligerent. Perhaps he thinks that I will be working for the movement in his diocese." After stewing for several weeks, Riel finally decided to head for St. Joseph, Dakota Territory.

The year before, Louis's old friend Antoine Gingras, the heart of St. Joseph, had died at age fifty-seven. A clever businessman to the end, he left his two sons general stores in Winnipeg, Pembina and St. Joseph, and a trading post on Mouse River. The younger son, Norman, was a close friend of Riel's and invited him to stay at his farm near the village.

The country had changed remarkably since Louis had taken refuge there nine years before. Scandinavian and Icelandic immigrants had flooded into the area, the post office was already called Walhalla and soon the name of St. Joseph would disappear altogether. Almost all the Métis had left. The buffalo had become all but extinct in the area; the few that were sighted now and then were always west of the White Earth River. The Gingras family business was indicative of this great change; not long before it had consisted of trading posts with pemmican and buffalo hides as the important items of commerce. These posts had now been transformed into general stores where scythes, tea and silk for fancy dresses were sold.

The seven months he spent in the St. Joseph and Pembina area were a happy time for Riel. As soon as the roads were passable, a procession of his relatives, friends and political allies made its way to the Gingras farmhouse. These were joyful reunions. His mother was almost overcome with emotion as she embraced "her beloved son, her Louis". Octavie, Riel's second-oldest sister, now a charming woman of twenty-six, had married during his absence. Her husband was Louis Lavallée, who had corresponded with Riel but had never actually met him; the two men fell into each other's arms and became lifelong friends. Eulalie, the third sister, married not long after Louis arrived. It caused consternation in the family—Julie was beginning to feel the effects of all her children leaving. Alexandre was studying at St. Boniface College. That left only Joseph, who was hoping to marry soon, and Henriette, the youngest daughter in the family, at seventeen a tall, beautiful young woman. Louis hadn't seen her for four years, and he was overwhelmed.

To his delight, Riel was caught up in a rather delicate family conundrum. Twenty-one-year-old Joseph had his eye on the daughter of prominent Métis Edouard Marion, a trader and farmer who lived near St. Joseph. The young woman was called Marie-Rose and was considered a beauty. Louis visited the Marions often on behalf of his brother and grew to like them more and more.

> During the winter holidays
> It is to them
> That I owe
> Much of my enjoyment
> After supper, dancing;
> the fiddle:
> I will visit the little house
> of Marion.

Marie-Rose had a sister, Louise-Anne, who was thought to be even more attractive. Louis certainly thought her so.

> Your name is beautiful, Louise Anne.
> Your parents can glory in it.
> Oh! the Havana sun!
> Is not as brilliant as your eyes.

The problem was that the Marion sisters were already spoken for. Both Riel brothers eventually gave up, but it was a pleasant interlude for Louis.

And Evelina had not been forgotten. Father Barnabé had written that she was very ill, probably with the first stages of tuberculosis, a disease that plagued almost every member of the family. Louis had sent her several love poems (since lost) and letters. She had responded, "I often go and sit under the lilacs, which are about to bloom. I hasten to gather a few blossoms to give you. I am carried back to that time when we were so happy, both of us seated on the same bench." Evelina supposedly enclosed in that letter those few blossoms, nicely pressed, and legend has it that Riel carried the keepsake in his breast pocket until the day he died. It probably is only a romantic myth. By the time Louis came to his sorry end, Evelina was nothing more than a vague, pleasant memory.

Early in the morning of January 20, 1879, Riel borrowed horses and a cutter from Norman Gingras and drove the twenty-five miles to the railway station at St. Vincent, just across the river from Pembina. Shortly after his arrival, the train from Winnipeg stopped and off stepped Joseph Dubuc. Louis's old friend was on his way to Ottawa and the opening of Parliament. Given what Riel now thought of him—a sell-out, a betrayer, a hen-pecked husband—and given that he was the member for Provencher, the very position that should have been Louis's, their first meeting in four years was probably strained. But they shook hands cordially enough and went to the Hotel Desaulets, where Ambroise and Maxime Lépine and several other Métis were waiting for them. It must have been a joyful reunion; the Lépine brothers made it clear that their respect and love for Riel had not diminished one bit.

They talked the whole day, and at one point the difficult topic of Louis's mental illness came up. Joseph Dubuc told him flatly that none of his friends believed for a moment that he was deranged. Either he had been arrested by the government and held in the insane asylum or he had faked the madness. Riel's reply was interesting:

> What is believed about my stay in the asylum is correct, at least in one regard. No, I was not confined through vengeance or as a result of persecution; but I did pretend to be mad. I succeeded so well that everybody believed that I really was mad. And why did I do it? Because I held the two governments of England and Canada in check for twelve months, the governments of those countries wanted to see me dead. But because I was still alive, and in spite of their efforts and those of their police to arrest me, I had been able to get myself elected; therefore they took the revenge they sought against me on my people, by refusing them their rights and by persecuting them. Seeing this, I said to myself, they are still afraid of me; but if I should disappear, or if I should lose my mind, their relentless persecution might be relaxed. A poor fool would be pitied, his past overlooked.

Almost every historian has dismissed Riel's explanation as a self-serving fabrication, an opportunity to tell his followers what they wanted to hear. But his rationale warrants more consideration than that. All the scenes that have been described of Riel's fits of madness, from turning himself into a snorting bull to ravaging the asylum's chapel, could feasibly have been faked by someone determined to prove himself insane. And in his poetry written at the time, he stated emphatically that he was indeed faking his insanity. "I have taken the great cross, the yoke of obedience./Sacrificing myself even so far as passing for insane." ("En me sacrifiant jus'qu'à passer pour fou.") Finally there are the opinions of those who were close to him. André Martineau, a St. Joseph farmer with whom Louis stayed for several months in 1878–79, wrote to his brother in 1887:

> I remember that on one occasion he [Riel] set himself to look at me fixedly, and to demand of me what I thought of him, of his past life, and especially of the insanity attributed to him by certain people in Canada. I answered that I did not believe that he had ever been insane, and upon that he explained to me how often and for what reasons he had pretended on many occasions to be mad, for the purpose of better attaining his ends and foiling his enemies.

It may be that both phenomena were going on at the same time: Riel was mentally and emotionally exhausted, as he claimed, and he thought, at least in his own tired mind, that as part of his never-ending struggle for his people, he had staged a madman's act. He had lived in constant fear of his life for five years, and through his irrational behaviour he may have been providing for himself, even subconsciously, a respite that he desperately needed.

Whether Riel's absence from the Canadian political scene shielded his people from even greater revenge by the Orangemen and the politicians the order influenced, as he hoped, is hard to ascertain; certainly, since the Red River resistance, the Métis had suffered deliberate and blatant betrayal that amounted to persecution.

Almost the entire Métis community at Red River was suffering economic hard times. The thousands of miles of steel that had been laid in the United States, and the branch line connecting Winnipeg with Pembina, had largely destroyed the carting business that had been a mainstay of the Métis bourgeois. Once-thriving families, the Brelins, the Brélands, the Lagimodières, suddenly found that their prime source of income had almost completely dried up. For a few years, they were saved by the business of harvesting buffalo bones for fertilizer. The prairie was littered with these macabre white skeletons; whole families would spend weeks loading them into carts and transporting them to the nearest railway depot. But it was only temporary relief because soon the bones had disappeared, just as the live specimens had.

Many, of course, had turned to farming as their main livelihood, just as the Riel family had, but in this they were thwarted too. In February 1870, Sir John A. Macdonald wrote, "These impulsive half breeds ... must be kept down by a strong hand until they are swamped by the influx of settlers." And that's exactly the modus operandi that was followed: the government of Canada carefully worked out a strategy to deprive the "impulsive half breeds" of the land that had been promised them. The chief weapon was delay.

The Métis of Red River had thought that their community would be greatly strengthened under the Manitoba Act. There were two sections that supported this view: section 31 promised to distribute 1.4 million acres among Métis children—a recognition that they were part Indian and therefore had a right to aboriginal claims on land—which eventually worked out to be about 240 acres for each individual; section 32 stated that the Métis would receive title from the dominion government to those lands they already occupied, mostly their long strip farms fronting on the Red and Assiniboine rivers. In this way, much of the area south and east of Winnipeg—the parishes of St. Vital, Ste. Agathe, Ste. Anne-des-Chênes—would remain French-speaking, Catholic enclaves, "locking out" the Anglo-Saxon settlers who everybody knew would soon arrive in huge numbers. The Riels would have been one of the families that benefited immensely, increasing their small holdings by 2,160 acres. It would have made Louis's dream of becoming a prosperous farmer quite feasible.

The government's first delaying tactic was to say that no lands could be registered until after a thorough land survey and census of the Manitoba population had been completed. That might have seemed logical enough, except that an Order-in-Council dated May 26, 1871, allowed all newcomers to stake vacant land wherever they found it. All the homesteader had to do was register his claim at the land office in Winnipeg. In one of those incredible flights of logic that marked the whole sordid episode of Métis land claims, the government officials ruled that the old settlers were not allowed this privilege because supposedly their lands were already protected under the Manitoba Act. By 1873, as the historian D.N. Sprague puts it, "Three years had passed. Not one promised patent to a river lot had emerged. Not one of the 1.4 million acres was allotted."

In subsequent years, the act was altered through a series of orders-in-council—which may well have been totally illegal*—to suit the situation as the government saw it. In 1874, for example, section 32, which had guaranteed legal ownership of land already occupied, was amended. Originally it was thought that all an individual land owner had to do was to swear in front of witnesses that certain property was rightfully his. The amendment to the Manitoba Act made it necessary for an individual to have made significant improvements to the land—fences erected, crops planted, houses and barns built, livestock kept—for the property to be assigned to him. This was a major blow to the

---

* This is the basis of a complicated lawsuit currently wending its way through the court system. The Manitoba Métis Federation is arguing that the Métis were deprived of prime Manitoba real estate by unconstitutional acts of the federal and Manitoba governments during the 1870s and 1880s.

Métis buffalo hunter, whose business dictated that he remain for only short periods in Red River; such improvements would have been almost impossible for him to carry out. A second amendment the next year stated that the owner had to have resided on the land on July 15, 1870, when many of the Métis were away doing what they usually did in July—hunting bison.

As well as changes to the Manitoba Act, other government action worked insidiously against the Métis. The official land surveyor simply didn't bother including Métis families in the parish lists—either those people he considered would not make "true farmers" became invisible to him or he did his job superficially. Perhaps most important, in disputes between Métis and newly arrived homesteaders over ownership of land, the new settlers almost always won. Many Métis families were thrown off land they had occupied for decades; in Rat River, eighty-four of the ninety-three Métis families were slapped with "writs of ejectment" from river lots they thought they owned. The result was exactly as Sir John A. had envisioned: by 1883 more than seventy percent of the Métis and more than fifty percent of the English-speaking Half-breeds had seen the land they occupied in 1870 patented to others, mostly incoming settlers.

Section 31 of the Manitoba Act, the distribution of the 1.4 million acres to Métis children, fared no better. Under the act, the lieutenant-governor was given authority to resolve the land issue, and Adams Archibald tried to come up with a quick and easy way to distribute the promised acreage. He asked the Métis themselves to stake out the properties they wanted. These claims would then be publicized through signs or newspaper advertisements. If nobody objected, the land claim would be considered legitimate; if there was opposition, a board of inquiry would determine the distribution in a particular area. It would have been an efficient and equitable method of carrying out the land provisions of section 31. But the government was having none of it; large tracts of Métis-owned land did not fit into its plans for a vast prairie grain basket cultivated by "real" farmers, nor did the section satisfy the speculators, people like John Schultz, who could see the value of river lots in the Winnipeg area soaring. Eventually, it was decided that the 1.4 million acres were to be located on the bald prairie. Historically the mixed-bloods had never liked this type of environment, preferring instead wooded areas with plenty of water. Living on the prairies was in fact abhorrent to them. Individual Métis began selling their portions of the promised acreage for as little as $25 a claim. Speculators rubbed their hands in glee.

The distribution of land came to an abrupt halt when another wrinkle developed. The question of who was eligible to receive a portion of the 1.4 million acres was up in the air. Originally the term "Métis children" was interpreted as meaning anyone having a mix of English or French and Indian ancestry. But the government subsequently changed that, so that only those who were children—not the adult heads of households—were eligible. Almost overnight four thousand people were dispossessed of their land entitlements. Naturally there was a great outcry among the Métis, especially since, two weeks later, the same government gave the old English settlers 140 acres a head each, no questions asked. Finally a compromise of sorts was reached: each Métis head of household would be issued a piece of paper worth a specific amount—a kind of money—which would be used to purchase any land that was open to homesteading. In this way the insidious idea of Métis scrip was born. Speculators had a heyday. By 1882 less than six hundred thousand acres of land was still retained by Half-breeds, while two million acres in land scrip had been diverted to quick-buck artists.

Meanwhile, the Red River Valley was being flooded with homesteaders. Between 1871 and 1881, Manitoba's population tripled, and almost all the newcomers were English-speaking Protestants. By the time Louis Riel returned to St. Joseph, many of the Red River Métis had simply given up trying to make it in this strange new society. For one thing, they were quickly losing political power in the Manitoba legislature. They couldn't resist the temptation to sell land claims to speculators for a song and migrate to more remote areas.

Right from the beginning Riel had understood that great vigilance would be needed to ensure that the Métis got what the Manitoba Act was supposed to guarantee them. It was the main reason he had decided, in 1873, to run for both the House of Commons and the provincial legislature, with the intent of becoming premier of Manitoba. That was the year he stepped aside for Cartier; the single condition he set for this sacrifice, and it was more important to him than his own amnesty, was that the Métis land-claims issue be resolved in their favour. Nothing happened; Cartier was too ill and Macdonald was unwilling.

The warrants issued in the fall of 1873, which resulted in Lépine's capture and Riel's flight into exile, had as much to do with greed as they did with Orange revenge for the death of Thomas Scott. The entire cabal who had conspired against the Métis leaders—Francis Cornish, Henry Clarke, John Schultz—were enthusiastic speculators, eager to get their hands on as much Métis land as possible. They were desperate to get rid of the one person who was strong and clever enough to obstruct their endeavours—Louis Riel. His exile imposed by the House of Commons in 1875 was fuelled by the same motives. Riel's five-year absence from the country would be just long enough to make the fortunes of many a man. And that was exactly what had happened.

As Riel listened that January day in 1879, as Dubuc, the Lépine brothers and others described the hoodwinking and intimidation the Red River Métis were being subjected to, he must have realized with bitterness how crucial his leadership had been and how much the Half-breed community had suffered without it. And he agonized over how cruelly he had been deceived by the politician he had once been so loyal to. A few months later he wrote the best-known of his poems. Entitled "To Sir John A. MacDonald" (the incorrect capitalization is Riel's), it is five hundred lines of rhymed satire, revisionist history in which Riel vents his frustration and anger on not only Macdonald but many important figures who have injured him and the Métis—William McDougall, John Schultz, Edward Blake, Alexander Mackenzie. In the preface to his English translation, the poet John Glassco described it as a "curious mixture of wit verging on buffoonery and rhetoric spilling over into the absurd." In his poetry Louis could be as vindictive and disrespectful as he felt like. After all, it was his own private journal, his catharsis. A few verses give the flavour.

> Sir John A. MacDonald doth govern proudly
> The provinces from which his power flows;
> While his bad faith perpetuates my woes —
> And all his countrymen applaud him loudly.
>
> Despite the peace he owes me, and despite
> His pledge to honour in deed and fact
> What was our Pact
> And is my right,
> For ten years now Sir John has warred with me.
> A faithless man is a vulgar man, be he
> Either a wise man or a witling born:
> And so I hold him up to scorn.

A few lines jump off the page—they may be wishful thinking on Riel's part or they may be uncannily prescient. He is referring to Sir John A.:

> You will be the seen prevaricator
> And on you history will lay the blame.
> I pine away in exile but remain
> In spite of you my nation's true leader.

Riel was now totally disillusioned with the political system. If he was to continue in his mission of renaissance for the Métis people, he would have to work outside that system. His grand plan had been years incubating; his earlier schemes of invading Manitoba represented one manifestation, but his thinking had developed from there. No longer would he rely on skeptical presidents or timid Fenians.

What Riel now envisioned was a confederacy of Great Plains Indians: the Blackfoot, the Cree, the Sioux, the Gros Ventres, the Crows, the Bloods and the Peigans would form a vast alliance, the purpose of which would be to set up an independent, self-governing Native state in the Canadian Northwest. This would come about through either an armed invasion, or maybe merely a show of force which would persuade the dominion government to negotiate terms. The catalysts in this political action would be the Métis, whose numbers were estimated at over 7,500 throughout the prairies. It was the peripatetic mixed-bloods who for more than a century had wandered from tribe to tribe trading furs and other valuables. It was they who had relatives in all the Indian tribes scattered across the plains. And it would be they—under Riel's leadership—who would be instrumental in establishing this great Native confederacy.

It wasn't such a far-fetched idea. The Great Plains Indians were in such desperate straits in the year 1879 that it was surprising there hadn't been a bloody uprising already.

The tragedy had begun the year before. The winter of 1877–78 had been unusually mild, with little snowfall. The prairie was very dry and in the spring grass fires erupted along the Canada–U.S. border. The resultant lack of grazing prevented the already depleted herds of buffalo from making their usual trek northward into Canada. But as bad as the situation was that year, it was merely a portent of the calamity that was to follow.

In the spring of 1879, while Riel was in St. Joseph, another series of grass fires broke out along the border, turning the prairie into an ugly black wasteland. Once again the bison wintering in the United States were prevented from travelling northward, and those that had remained in the north of Canada stayed there. Because the fires had started almost simultaneously along the line, it was obvious that arson was involved. The Blackfoot were accused of committing the crime, but it was unclear why they should do such a thing, as they suffered as much as anybody. Historians now believe the fires were set by mercenaries paid by the American government; the idea was that the renegade Sioux who had taken refuge in Canada would be forced back across the border by starvation, to be brought to justice for their many perceived crimes. Whoever set the blazes achieved their purpose: the buffalo were trapped in the United States and the American army prevented Canadian hunting parties from travelling south. What followed was famine. One North-West Mounted Police constable described thirty ravaged Indians he had come across just outside Fort Walsh: "They looked like a delegation from some graveyard. There were men, women and children with their eyes sunk back in their heads, and all with the look of despair about them." Another Mountie wrote of a band of Blackfoot, "I have seen them, after I had an animal killed, rush on the carcass before the life was out of it and cut and tear off the meat, eating it raw." The Canadian government finally organized a relief effort which managed to prevent mass starvation, but not before an indelible scar was left on the Native psyche. Riel felt that if there was ever a ripe time to promote his confederacy scheme, this was it.

In the summer of 1879, he bade his friends at St. Joseph and Pembina good-bye and started off on the rugged journey to Wood Mountain, just north of the American border, about eighty-five miles southwest of what eventually would be called Moose Jaw, Saskatchewan. He later wrote his mother:

> We have taken twenty-eight days to reach Wood Mountain. Not an hour of sickness but we have spent half the time on buttes. Joseph Gariépy wasn't following the road, he was following his mind. That is how he is. I was rocked in my wagon as I haven't been rocked for a long time. I assure you, dear mother, that I was happy to see the prairie. It gives me strength.... Every day, I think affectionately of you....

Riel had one purpose in going to Wood Mountain—to confer with the famous Sioux chief Sitting Bull, whom the American authorities considered the most "blood-thirsty" of the Indian "bandits".

In 1868, the U.S. government had signed an agreement with the Black Hills Sioux that no one was to enter the latter's territory unless permission was granted. With the first scent of gold, of course, prospectors began pouring onto the reserve; by 1874 the American public was clamouring for a geological survey of the Black Hills. To oversee this, the arrogant and reckless Lieutenant-Colonel George Armstrong Custer was sent in with 1,200 soldiers, four Gatling guns, sixty scouts and a great wagon train of supplies. For two years the Sioux remained remarkably patient despite this outright violation of their treaty, until Custer informed the world, "There's gold in the grass roots. Come and get it!"

Inevitably there had to be a showdown. But what surprised and outraged the Americans was that, at the valley of the Little Bighorn, the U.S. Army suffered the most humiliating defeat imaginable. When the shooting finally stopped, the lieutenant-colonel himself had been slaughtered and so had 264 men of the Seventh Cavalry.

Even as he surveyed the scene of his great victory, Chief Sitting Bull knew he had lost the war. He knew the wrath of the entire U.S. Army would soon descend, and to prevent the genocide of his people he ordered a march northward. By the time Riel travelled to Wood Mountain, the Sioux warrior had been in Canada for two years and both he and his people were in a sad state. Since the Canadian government was under no obligation to feed them during the great famine, they were suffering terribly.

No record has been found of Louis Riel's meeting with Sitting Bull, if indeed it actually occurred. But it would have been quite an encounter—the wavy-haired Métis, still a little effete-looking, his expression full of intelligence and dreaming, and the old warrior, his eyes characteristically hooded and his face so pitted with remnants of smallpox that it looked like old, grainy wood. It is not known what kind of impression Riel's plan for an Indian state made on Sitting Bull or whether an agreement was reached. But the meeting certainly didn't discourage Louis. In a few days he left to set up his base of operation in northern Montana.

– 13 –

The States have harboured me.
For what the English have taken
Of my own, they'll pay a fee.
They'll pay. I am a citizen.

The territory in which Louis Riel chose to make his home for the next four and a half years is as vivid and dramatic a landscape as found anywhere. The mighty Rockies monopolize Montana's western frontier, but moving east, the mountains slip into cleft foothills, steep valleys, outlandish flat-topped mesas. Then comes the Great Plain rolling towards the Dakota boundary, in Riel's day a virtual ocean of luxuriant knee-high grasses. Montana's split personality is also revealed in its climate: on summer days the temperature can climb to 110 degrees F.; during some winter nights it plunges to minus 60 degrees F.; and the wind never stops blowing. Drought threatens in two out of every ten years. Dust storms are so thick that a calf can lose its mother in a blink of an eye. The grass fires are controlled now, but they were phenomenal. Sheets of flame swept across the plains with the speed of wind, faster than a horse, bringing with them rolling masses of thick black smoke that would hang like a curtain of doom for weeks. If the gophers hadn't been burned to death, they starved for lack of anything green to eat.

And yet there was something compelling about this country. Early settlers talked about the other-worldly landscape, particularly the sandstone buttes, flat as a cucumber slice on top, like giant altars where sacrifices were made to spectacular gods. And then there was the glorious colour—to this day there remains the fascination with the colour—the yellows and reds and purples that constantly played on the ridges, the gullies, the towers, the eccentric conglomeration of sandstone looking like some awesome gothic cathedral stuck in the middle of sagebrush desolation. It was a landscape extraordinary to even the most mundane mind; to someone with a hyper-charged imagination, it could easily become a realm of the gods.

When Riel arrived, there were only 38,000 people living in this territory, which was larger than Italy or Greece. While white settlers, cattle ranchers mostly, were just moving onto the Great Plain, the Indians still made up the vast majority of the population. The warrior-like Blackfeet were situated in the far north of the territory, the Assiniboine in the far east, the Atsina in the centre, the Crow in the southeast, the Shoshoni in the southwest and the Flathead, Pend d'Oreille and Kutenai in the Rocky Mountain region. The Sioux, who were considered among the most warlike of the tribes, also occasionally appeared. Friction had periodically flared among the various tribes, but it was nothing compared to the all-out warfare waged against the whites.

When Louis Riel arrived in the fall of 1879, he immediately joined a band of about 150 Métis families, buffalo hunters, camping not far from the Big Bend in the Milk River. He probably already knew a lot of these people, or at least their relatives, because many of them had come from the St. Joseph–Pembina area.

Actually the Métis had been living in the rugged country of Montana for over thirty years by the time Louis got there. They came first as trappers settling along the Missouri River. These were the famous mountain men of American lore, utterly fearless, remarkably skilful. Wolves, bobcats, mountain lions swarmed the country, which didn't bother these people as long as their traplines were full. They were guides and traders for the American Fur Company, and when gold was discovered at the beginning of the 1860s, and mining camps sprang up like mushrooms, it was Métis trip men who transported the ore out and the provisions in. But the buffalo hunters were the most numerous. As the shaggy beasts deserted the Turtle Mountains in Dakota, the great trek west began. By the mid-1870s, a substantial community had established itself on Frenchman River, close to its confluence with the Milk River.

The area between the Milk and Missouri rivers, north central Montana, is relatively tame compared to the badlands, a sometimes flat, sometimes rolling country of thick grasses on which the buffalo thrived. The many deep, wooded coulees provided shelter in the winter. In 1879, it was the last place in the midwest where bison herds were still spotted. In only three more seasons of hunting they would disappear from the Missouri River country as surely as they had from everywhere else. Meanwhile, hunters gathered in the neighbourhood for one last taste of the life they had enjoyed for centuries.

The Métis had always presented the Americans with a dilemma. Were they

Frenchmen or were they Indians?—nobody quite knew, but they were certainly people to turn your nose up at. They were, after all, associated with the dreaded redskins. The 1870s and 1880s were a savage period in Montana history, a time of nonstop guerrilla skirmishes and outright warfare. After the Battle of Little Bighorn in nearby Dakota Territory in 1876, the whites were nursing their wounded pride, eager to get even. The Métis living near the U.S.–Canada border were thought to be the main arms-dealers to the Sioux, and therefore were not trusted. The editor of the *Fort Benton Record* would feel free to write: "These Canadian half breeds pay no taxes; they produce nothing but discord, violence and bloodshed wherever they are permitted to locate. They are a worthless, brutal race of the lowest species of humanity, without one redeeming trait to commend them to the sympathy or protection of any Government."

American authorities were sure of one thing about those people with strange French names—they were British subjects, and therefore the wards of the Canadian government. It was untrue—most of them, and often their grandmothers and grandfathers, had been born in Dakota Territory and were therefore American citizens. But there was no hesitation in forcing them north across the border if circumstances warranted it. In 1875, just as the war with the Sioux was starting to heat up, the Half-breeds were accused of supplying Indians with guns (there was probably some truth to this, but not nearly to the extent of the American accusations). That indefatigable Indian fighter General Alfred Terry ordered that the Half-breed encampment on Frenchman River be scattered across the border. But as soon as the U.S. Army left the area, the Métis returned and, with some Lakota Sioux, re-established their ramshackle community. In the summer of 1879 another army commander, Colonel Nelson Miles, chased them once more into Canada, but by the time Riel arrived in the fall of that year, they had wandered back again.

The band that Louis latched onto was located a little south of the Frenchman River, on Beaver Creek, not far from Wolf Point about seventy miles north of the Missouri River. Around them were camped many tribes that traditionally lived north of the Canadian border—Sioux, Blackfoot and Cree—eager to hunt the few remaining buffalo sighted in the country.

This was the first time that Riel had actually lived the traditional life of a Métis buffalo hunter, and if he didn't exactly fit into this culture, he certainly became absorbed by it. He wrote his mother in October 1879, telling her how healthy he felt. "The buffalo meat is a good remedy because I feel stronger."

To reside in a wintering camp of Métis buffalo hunters was to live in constant bedlam. As one writer put it, "horses, dogs, women and children, all intermingled in a confusion worthy of an Irish fair." Crowded together in a clump of woods were some thirty to forty huts built mostly of logs, with pine branches and tanned skins stuck here and there to keep out the winter wind. Buffalo bones, particularly the dramatic skulls, were strewn about the ground. Buffalo robes were stretched out on poles and other smaller skins were dried by being tacked to the hut walls or being stretched on miniature frames hanging from trees. Each hut was home to three to five families, mostly relatives. To avoid utter chaos, the clutter inside was kept to a minimum, the furniture consisting of a few beds made of spruce boughs and covered with buffalo robes, a roughly hewn sideboard, a table, a stove on which sat a few blackened kettles. On the walls was displayed an armoury of guns, powder-horns and bullet-bags. But there was always enough room for a good-sized crucifix and a picture or two of the Virgin or of favourite saints.

The Métis loved parties; most nights the sound of the fiddle and the thud of moccasinned feet rang throughout the camp. During the day, the women, of course, were kept busy feeding and clothing their brood; the children played or, under their mother's supervision, studied their letters. It was the men who had not enough to do. Some spent their time gambling and drinking, mostly rum and in huge quantities.

The camp was still governed in the traditional manner, with the election of guides and captains and a supreme commander. Louis wrote his brother Joseph in December 1879 that the buffalo hunters "have done me the honour of electing me chief of the camp." He quickly assumed the role of leader, adviser, translator, spiritual confidant.

The federal agent administering the Indian reservation at Wolf Point was a little startled by the sudden appearance of this articulate, well-educated, well-known revolutionary in its midst. He informed his superiors that fall, "The Half Breeds are in force on the Milk River. They also have been very importunate in regard to staying in this country, and latterly one Riel (the leader of the trouble in Manitoba in 1869) has acted as their ambassador. He is staying with them, with what object I am unable to say. He can wield the Half Breeds at will, and also probably the crees."

It was necessary for the Métis to obtain permission from the U.S. Army to spend the winter on an Indian reserve, and this was Riel's first task. He travelled back and forth from Fort Belknap to Fort Assiniboine trying to persuade various officials. Finally, General Alfred Terry agreed that the band could winter on the large Belknap Indian Reserve, the home of Gros Ventres, Yankton Sioux and Assiniboines. But, he insisted, the Métis would have to leave as soon as spring arrived.

Among Indian agents there had been growing resentment against the Half-breeds, who were wanderers, free spirits, and therefore a bad example for the

Indians; the permission to camp on the sheltered reserve was considered an accomplishment and Riel a hero. And financially his first year was something of a success: he managed to accumulate eight horses, four carts and some other goods. One serious problem remained; there was little hard cash around, and Louis had borrowed money in St. Joseph to come west. He was desperate to pay it off.

Life with the buffalo hunters was not easy. For one thing, Louis absolutely detested the excessive drinking, and didn't hesitate to moralize on the subject.

> Booze is responsible
> For almost all unhappiness
> It is a thing
> Full of weeping
> It robs the country
> Of its talented men
> And the disciplined armies
> Of their valiant warriors.

Not surprisingly, some of the old-timers grew deeply resentful of his constant sermonizing and Riel found himself in one battle after another.

He wrote three poems which give a unique and vivid portrait of life in the camp, especially its seamy side. All are about individuals with whom Riel came into conflict. Thomas Larance, for example, was a horrible boozer:

> You serve Satan well, in your role as drunkard
> > You do his work
> > With as much success
> > As he himself
> > You are guilty of excessive
> > And supreme wickedness.
>
> ————
>
> > You aim with your firearms
> > At your friends, fearless of God
> > Your abominable drunkenness
> > Is the cause of their distress.

George Hyacinthe was not only a drinker, but beat his wife and neglected his children:

> If you only hunted
> As you should, reasonably
> You would not suffer the disgrace
> Of being a ne'er-do-well.

You would pay all your debts
As honest people do.

————

You would not be rejected
By everyone, like an old skinny buffalo,
You would be loved and respected.

But you were born in a mire
You love only dancing and the clash of cymbals
You are a wastrel
One party leads to another....*

The worst of the bunch was Joseph Parisien, a violent troublemaker. Louis had watched in shock as he had assaulted three men with his fists, and had thereafter felt in danger himself: "One day you accosted me with a fist in my chest/You tried to frighten me. You made a racket/Because in camp, I put people like you/In their place...." He suspected that Parisien was an undercover agent for the North West Mounted Police.

The excessive boozing wasn't only morally repugnant to Riel; he had seen first hand what terrible conflict it brought. He still envisioned the Métis as the chosen people, but how could they carry out the task of building a new nation if they were divided and without hope?

The Indian agent at Wolf Point had good reason to wonder what Louis Riel was doing in the area. Everybody realized that with the beasts vanishing into thin air there was hardly a future in buffalo hunting. In fact, Riel was acting as a grassroots activist, a kind of Che Guevara of the Métis people. By living with the exploited, he felt, he could best give expression to their grievances. And of course he had already formulated his grand scheme—the confederacy of Indian and mixed-blood peoples who would fight for a country of their own.

Over the winter of 1879–80, he and his followers met with several Indian tribes, trying to forge agreements to engage in military action in Canada's Northwest Territories. Two accounts describing these encounters are available, but both are somewhat suspect. They were written some time after the events, by white officials, and both were self-serving documents designed to impress their superiors—they both claimed to take credit for smothering a major Indian uprising.

Superintendent James M. Walsh was in charge of the North-West Mounted Police post at Wood Mountain. Although Walsh had some empathy with Native

———————————————————

* *Translation by Wilfrid Dubé.*

peoples, in particular Sitting Bull, Louis Riel neither liked him nor trusted him, and the feeling was mutual. According to Walsh, he had heard rumours that the Assiniboines had agreed to become involved with Riel's confederacy plan. He claimed he rode into their camp on the Milk River near Wolf Point and confronted Chief Red Stone. Under the Mountie's prodding, a document was produced, supposedly signed in either red ink or blood by Riel and Red Stone. Its basic contention was that the country belonged to the "Indian blood of the prairie", the Indians and their brethren, the Half-breeds. All would unite into a "loyal confederation" of Indian tribes and Half-breeds from the Saskatchewan to the Missouri. Walsh stayed overnight in the Assiniboine camp and, according to him, succeeded in convincing the Indians that Riel was an impostor and his grand scheme foolishness. Red Stone would not hand the signed document over to Walsh, but agreed to burn it and send word to the Métis camp that he was calling it quits.

Walsh also claimed that he extracted a promise from Chief Sitting Bull not to join Riel before his band left Wood Mountain to winter in Montana. Sitting Bull did meet with the Métis chief sometime in January of 1880. No record is available of what went on, except that the Sioux did not participate in the foray into Canada that Riel planned for that summer. The courageous and wily old chief was almost a spent force anyway; the next year he would surrender to the U.S. Army and dejectedly retire to the Standing Rock Reserve in North Dakota.

Riel put an interesting spin on his meeting with Sitting Bull. In March 1880 Riel wrote Colonel H.M. Black at Fort Assiniboine thanking him for allowing the Métis to spend the winter on the Indian reserves: "Having no other way to acknowledge efficiently such a favor, those métis have exerted themselves during the whole winter to pacify the Sioux; Sitting Bull himself and all his band."

Another individual who witnessed meetings between Riel and Indian nations at the time was Jean L'Heureux, a French Canadian who acted as translator for Crowfoot, one of the chiefs in the Blackfoot Confederacy. Like many Canadian Indians in the terrible famine of 1878–79, Crowfoot's people had decided to winter in Montana, hoping to hunt the few buffalo spotted there. They had travelled from the Rocky Mountain foothills in what is now Alberta and set up their camp on the Milk River, about fifteen miles from Riel's group. According to L'Heureux, almost immediately some of the Métis approached the Blackfoot and started talking up the confederacy scheme. A few days later Riel himself, accompanied by four advisers, arrived at the camp, and it was then that he met L'Heureux. Louis asked the translator, who had considerable influence with Chief Crowfoot, to attend an important meeting of Métis that was coming up. L'Heureux did so and during the assembly learned interesting details of

Riel's plans. Using the excuse of preventing horse theft, which at the time was rampant in the West, an army of Indians and Half-breeds would occupy the North-West Mounted Police post of Wood Mountain. With a southern base secured, the confederacy would overwhelm other Mountie forts farther west and north. Once these were occupied, a democratically elected and representative provisional government would be established, and negotiations with Ottawa would then begin. The invasion was to take place the following June; the Indians and Métis would meet in the Tiger Hills on the Milk River and advance from there.

Riel hoped that L'Heureux would persuade Crowfoot and the Blackfoot to join his confederacy, but according to the translator he not only talked the chief out of any involvement, but, fearful that young Blackfoot braves might be enticed by Riel and his plot, persuaded Crowfoot to move camp away from the Métis, south to the Missouri River. Riel's envoys visited the new camp to trade with the Blackfoot and to propagandize, but according to L'Heureux this was without success.

Bands of the plains Cree were also wintering around Milk River and they too were part of Riel's plans. Louis had a high opinion of them, noting, "The crees are the most civilized indians of the Canadian Northwest, because they have been for a good many years in constant communications with the half-breeds." He met with them several times in January, and L'Heureux reports that in an encounter with Chief Little Pine, Riel grabbed the parchment papers authorizing Treaty No. 6, which had been signed in 1876 setting up Little Pine's reserve, and trampled them underfoot. It was utter folly to keep faith with such lies, he declared. But it was Big Bear whom Louis Riel considered a man "of good sense" and who he hoped would agree to his invasion plan. The burly Cree chief had so far refused to sign a treaty pinning his people on a reserve, and his spunk attracted Riel. There is no record of the encounter but the Cree and Métis had a history of distrust, so that it would have been a near impossible feat to unite the two groups. Although Riel's Indian confederacy scheme collapsed, Big Bear and Riel continued to maintain contact until the North-West Rebellion flared.

By March 1880 Riel probably realized that his grand plan for a summer campaign in the Northwest Territories was premature. There were many reasons for this. The Indian tribes Riel was trying to unite had been deadly enemies for years, and didn't trust each other or him. As well, most of the Indians had recently negotiated treaties, and despite years of terrible deprivation, they still considered the "pieces of parchment" binding contracts which precluded any conflict with the Canadian government. And, despite the close relationship between the Half-breeds and various members of tribes, there had been a history of antagonism between the two peoples—to suddenly trust in Louis Riel as the supreme leader was asking too much. Finally, the Indian chiefs may have sensed what Riel truly felt about them. In his vision of the New World, recorded in his diaries, the tribes in Manitoba would interbreed with the French Canadians, and the Indians in the Northwest would amalgamate with the Italians, Irish, Bavarians and Poles who would soon be living there. The result would be a new race, "the Métis race". The Indians, according to Riel, would "quietly and gradually" disappear.

As the harsh winter began to soften, the buffalo hunters had to keep their promise to move off the Indian reserve. Some families headed towards the North Saskatchewan River in Canada, but most decided to trek south, still in pursuit of the elusive buffalo. Riel would go with them, but first he travelled to Fort Assiniboine, Montana, to sell his band's pemmican and furs and to reassure the commanders there that his people were doing what they were supposed to.

Fort Assiniboine, nestled on the northwestern side of the Bear Paw Mountains on the Milk River, was not the cluster of ramshackle shacks that constituted most army posts in those days. It was a compound of impressive red-brick buildings constructed in 1879 with a multi-million-dollar appropriation handed over by a panicky Congress. Riel may have chuckled when he heard why the politicians had been so generous—not only were they unnerved by the presence of Sitting Bull in nearby Cypress Hills and the continuing warfare between the Indians and settlers, but they had been in a constant stew about the success of Louis Riel's rebellion at Red River ten years before.

Riel rejoined the Métis and they continued travelling south until they came to the Missouri. It was spring and the swollen brown river had turned into a torrent. Patrice Bellehumeur, a member of the group, recalled the following: "In the spring we decided to cross the Missouri River to the south bank. For crossing the river, we made rafts out of skins and the horses had to swim across. We lost seven horses that were drowned." Louis himself would later write, "The Saintly Virgin is powerful. It is she who saved my life several times on the Missouri."

Once the Musselshell River, with its startlingly clear, greenish-yellow waters, was reached, the hunting band travelled along its banks south a hundred miles through lonely prairie until they came to the confluence of Flat Willow Creek. From there they turned west and journeyed another seventy-five miles until they found what they considered an appropriate spot to set up camp. They all knew it would be a hard summer with the buffalo hunt so poor; they must all turn their energy to trying to scrape out some kind of livelihood. It would be a collective agreement, for under Riel's leadership the band conducted its business in a most democratic manner. A council was elected which met in regular business sessions, deciding on such issues as the by-laws and punishments that ordered everyday life, the camp's movements, the sales and purchases of supplies, etc.

As soon as camp was struck, Riel undertook a long 190-mile trip to Fort Benton, on the most northern loop of the Missouri River. This was the most money-hungry, bustling place in all of Montana at the time; its unwritten motto was "Walk in the middle of the street and mind your own business. This is a tough town." It had burst to life in 1862, when the great gold rush began. The steamboats that brought in the booze and brought out the gold all stopped at Fort Benton. When the gold bubble burst, it went through a dry period, but by 1875 it was thriving once again. At that point the cheapest and fastest route to the Canadian Northwest was not through Winnipeg—the railroad had not been built yet—but by steamboat along the Missouri River. At Fort Benton, settlers or Mounted Policemen or Indians could stock up on everything from bullets to fine silks to illegal whisky; the traders, or "merchant princes" as they were called—T.C. Power, I.G. Baker, the Conrad brothers—were as aggressive as any on the American frontier.

Fort Benton was also the judicial centre for Choteau County, and it was to the courthouse that Riel went when he arrived in town. He had made the decision to become an American citizen, and on May 17, 1880, he made a legal declaration of his intention.

It hurt him to do so. He would later say, "It sored my heart. It sored my heart to say that kind of adieu to my mother, to my brothers, to my sisters, to my friends, to my countrymen, my native land." He was intent, however, on making a new career for himself in a country where he had never been labelled a villain. And, as he wrote his brother Joseph that July, "I think I would be able to help the Métis just as well in this country as another."

In fact, he was still deeply bitter over the treatment he had received from the Canadian and British governments. He expressed his resentment in disjointed verse he wrote about this time. It was also obvious that he still considered himself the valiant defender of the Métis people.

> Albion,* you were mistaken.
> You'll reap your just reward.
> Your dreams will lie forsaken,
> Slain by my valiant sword.

---

* *Poetic name for Great Britain.*

I will break the bonded cage
That your moneyed reign affords.
From the people's boundless rage
Naught will protect your lords.

You will be forced to swallow
Dirty, briny seawater.
Heavy your heart, and hollow,
You'll cry, you too will suffer.*

By August Riel was back at Flat Willow Creek. For decades, the country along the Musselshell River had been the scene of fierce Indian resistance, particularly by the Sioux. White settlements and trading posts had come and gone, and by 1879 it was an isolated place. The Métis, desperate to find some way to survive, decided to ask the American government to designate the area a Half-breed reservation where agriculture would be their primary livelihood. Riel wrote a petition to Colonel Nelson Miles, the highest-ranking officer in the region. It was a sad comment on the plight the Half-breeds found themselves in:

> We ask the government to set apart a portion of land as a special reservation in this territory for the halfbreeds, as, scattered amongst other settlers, it becomes a very difficult matter for us to make a living and owing to our present limited means and want of experience in economy, we cannot compete with the majority of our fellow countrymen.
>
> Our want of legal knowledge has also been a stumbling block in our way, as often defrauded by tricky men, we have again been as individuals put to expense in the law courts uselessly. This alone has rendered us often unable to remain more than four or five years at a time in our place without being completely impoverished.

The petition went on to promise that liquor would be banned from the reservation. Riel realized that the Métis community would need a substantial sum of money to build schools and buy agricultural implements, seed and livestock. In return for a loan from the government, the Half-breeds promised to use their influence among the Indians to bring peace. The petition was signed by 101 men, primarily heads of households. Although the document is in Riel's handwriting, his signature is not attached, an indication, perhaps, that he didn't feel himself a genuine member of the hunting group, or perhaps he was fearful his reputation would get in the way of success. Interestingly, among those who

---

* *Translation by Wilfrid Dubé.*

did sign were Joseph Parisien, Thomas Larance and George Hyacinthe (although his name was transposed into Hyacinthe George), the three men whose rowdy excesses had caused Riel so much trouble.

With the petition in hand, Louis travelled the hundred miles east to the junction of the Tongue and Yellowstone rivers, where Fort Keogh (today called Miles City) was situated. Colonel Miles was headquartered there and Riel presented him with the petition.

Miles was quite impressed with the idea. He wrote that the Half-breeds "running over the country results in no benefit to themselves, and a very injurious influence upon the different Indian tribes". He recommended "favourable consideration" and sent it on to General Alfred Terry, commander of the army's Department of Dakota in St. Paul. After that the document was passed from one government department to another, often receiving favourable comment, until it finally arrived on the desk of Indian agent A.R. Keller in Montana. In his reply, Keller paints an interesting picture of Métis culture at the time:

> They are very rarely long in any one place as they are natural barterers, trading in anything and everything, in demand in an Indian camp from a cartridge to a gallon of whiskey. They talk fluently nearly all the languages of the northern latitude including our own. They move in bodies of from one hundred to one thousand carts and are deemed very formidable warriors, always on good terms with all tribes no matter what relation they may sustain to our Government. During all the incursions of the hostile Sioux into our country, they were almost constantly into contact with these half-breeds but never in a hostile manner. In fact I have never yet heard of a collision between them even in an individual capacity. They dress like Americans and are experts in hunting fishing and trapping. They have intelligence and some education....

Keller could be describing the quintessential Yankee trader, but as a typical white Indian-hater he sadly saw little value in the Métis contribution. "As usual in such cases they imbibe the evils of civilization without its virtues. They would certainly be an undesirable class of population to settle in this Territory." Besides, he pointed out, ignoring the fact that most of them had been born in either Dakota or Montana territories, they were British subjects. It was excuse enough to deny them their reserve. Soon the American Half-breeds would be forced to make a choice—were they Indians or whites? In a very few years their culture would all but die out in the United States.

Riel spent the winter of 1880–81 in the buffalo hunters' camp at Flat Willow Creek. The old-timers said it was the worst winter in memory. The blizzards began in December and continued with hardly a break until May; temperatures stuck at minus 40—minus 20 was considered balmy. But it was more than the terrible weather that brought hardship to the Métis camp. Many of the Half-breeds made their living buying and selling horses, and the Indians, mostly camping across the border in Canada, never ceased stealing them. The situation was so serious that a deputation was finally sent to Captain Leif Crozier of the North-West Mounted Police at Wood Mountain. Crozier didn't believe the three Métis who confronted him, and did nothing. Riel was most indignant.

The Métis were fearful of the Indians, particularly the Sioux, and tried to keep out of their way. Patrice Bellehumeur described one encounter.

> Early in the fall Riel and I made another trip to Benton. We met a band of Indians who gave us a fright. They were forty in number and well armed, but they didn't attack us; but they asked to search our cart. Riel succeeded in calming them. They sat on the ground around the cart and Riel gave them some tobacco. We hitched up and continued our journey, but they followed us for three or four miles.

Louis seems to have become totally absorbed in the fight for survival. Almost all letters to his family and friends in Manitoba ceased at this point. In May 1881, Joseph Riel complained that Louis had not written in nine months; it would be another year before the elder son finally made contact again with his family at St. Vital. Evelina Barnabé seems to have been completely forgotten as she sat stewing in Keeseville, wondering what had happened to her betrothed. It would be another year before she found out—Louis had found someone far more suitable to take as a wife.

Marguerite Monet *dit* Bellehumeur was a pretty, petite Métisse. She was sixteen years younger than Riel, having just turned twenty when Louis began courting her. She had been born at White Horse Plains near Red River on January 15, 1861, to Marie Malaterre and Jean-Baptiste Monet *dit* Bellehumeur, both from old Métis hunting families. After they left Red River the Bellehumeurs had settled at Fort Ellice, directly west of Fort Garry, on what is now the Manitoba–Saskatchewan border, and there Marguerite spent most of her childhood. When the buffalo became scarce, the family followed the herds into Montana, and they were part of the band which had elected Louis Riel chief.

Jean-Baptiste's nickname Bellehumeur was quite appropriate; he was a good-natured, kind-hearted man and his wife Marie was a charming woman. Riel would grow very fond of them both.

In the one photograph that exists of Marguerite Bellehumeur, she is a compact, neat-looking young woman as nicely dressed as any Victorian lady. A couple of contemporary descriptions of her disparagingly mention her dark skin.

But in the photo there is no evidence of this, and her daughter, Angélique, was very fair with flaxen hair. Riel was drawn to Marguerite because she was devout, sweet and without pretence.

> Her faith so deep and her righteousness
> Are a beauty to behold.
> Ah ... she is a tender creature
> Always attentive to her duty.
> I have the privilege of knowing
> That her love is unfailing.
> When she loves, she loves through and through.
> Her gaze beckons me on.

By February he had decided to ask for her hand in marriage.

When the rest of the Métis found out about his intentions, they responded by ridiculing the match, much to Riel's dismay. The reasons for this are not clear. Were these hard-living men merely teasing Riel and he took it the wrong way? Had Marguerite already been spoken for? Or was there deep resentment at the ethical high horse Riel had ridden? At any rate Louis was deeply hurt and, naturally, turned to verse to express his feelings.

> All the boys in the world
> Can choose their girl.
> I also have a sweetheart
> That I long to see every day.
>
> But people are doubting
> Of my simple and good faith.
> And seeking to hurt me
> By gossiping behind my back.
>
> The nation I love
> Takes pleasure in insulting me
> And goes to great lengths
> To give me trouble.
> They turn this sublime love
> This God-given
> Simple and tender feeling
> Into a crime.
>
> If my own people blame me,
> It is since I have wanted
> To take a woman.
> My own oppose my wishes.

Ten years of my life
I have toiled for them
They want to deprive me
Of all legitimate pleasures,
And want me to live
Without joy and friends....*

Riel married Marguerite on April 27, 1881. Since there were no priests available, the ceremony was probably conducted by the bride's father. Louis would feel guilty about this until a priest finally sanctified the union about a year later.

Riel's bitterness towards those Métis who had taunted him about his marriage did not ease. And he was growing more impatient with the violence and ugliness in the camp. He had grown weary of men like Sévère Hamlin who in a fit of temper had assaulted his own mother, dragging her on the ground by the hair. This same individual had repeatedly tried to seduce Marguerite. Riel despised him:

Sévère Hamlin, you had better
During the remainder of your life
Do enough penance
To soften the blows
That God's wrath may shower on your head.

Louis began to distance himself from daily life in the buffalo hunters' camp. Still, he didn't abandon them. When, in a few months, they voted to move to Rocky Point on the Missouri River, the couple packed up their few belongings and went with them.

---

* *Translation by Wilfrid Dubé*

– 14 –

Every known crime
Almost always happens there
Where the scum thrives and teems.

In January 1881, three months before marrying, Louis Riel had received good news. Winnipeg was booming, land prices were soaring and a lot he owned in St. Boniface had finally been sold for $410. Then in April his property in St. Vital fetched $450. There is no record of any delay, so Louis probably received the money (minus debts he may have owed) by May. In all likelihood he used this windfall to set himself up in business as a trader. He had already made contact with Thomas O'Hanlon, a good-natured Irish Catholic who was an agent for T.C. Power and Bro., wholesale merchants, traders and freighters—they owned the upper Missouri's largest steamboat line. And, most important for Riel, they were kings of the buffalo-robe trade. O'Hanlon wrote a letter of introduction to the company and Louis became a buyer, seller and fixer.

Although T.C. Power was based in Fort Benton, the company operated an outlet at a small settlement called Carroll or Carroll Landing, and it was in this area, near Rocky Point, that Marguerite and Louis settled, along with the rest of the hunting band.

The huddle of shacks that made up Carroll Landing was testimony to the folly of the get-rich fever that was raging in the territory at the time. By 1882, when Riel frequented it, it was nothing more than a collection of mud and log huts, too squalid even to be called cabins. There was only one ranch within twenty-five miles.

Riel travelled from place to place—Carroll, Fort Assiniboine, Fort Benton,

Fort Belknap, Helena—trading the catch of his buffalo-hunters' band for such necessities as nails, corn, wood and calico.

His wanderings took him through the badlands, Missouri breaks country, hundreds of miles of canyons and coulees, of grotesquely shaped buttes, of sand, cacti and sagebrush. Some honest men lived there: the cattle and sheep ranchers, the fur trappers, buffalo hunters and those who made their living chopping wood for the steamboats plying the Missouri (as Riel himself would do on occasion). But this territory was also a last outpost of the freebooters, mostly horse thieves, cattle rustlers, illicit whisky traders, claim jumpers, who thrived in a place where law enforcement was almost non-existent, where citizen vigilante groups were often the only protection against thieving marauders, where murders and hold-ups happened every day. In the small derelict towns, and in the outbacks, the saloons thrived, mixtures of dance halls, houses of prostitution and gambling dens. Here a dude could chugalug illicit whisky, meet the *femme fatale* of his dreams and take on those polished gentlemen, recently off the Mississippi steamboats, who were most obliged to relieve him of his cash in any game of blackjack.

It's hard to imagine an environment less suited to Louis Riel's strait-laced personality; indeed he loathed the debauchery rampant in the territory. As usual, he expressed his aversion in vivid verse. "To me all canteens are filthy./You go there the way you run to the outhouse....

> Saloons are filthier
> Than stables.
> Nothing but poison-selling shops
> And houses of ill repute.
> Every known crime
> Almost always happens there
> Where the scum thrives and teems....

In that same poem, Riel writes: "I have myself sold booze./And of all those I supplied,/I believe the whisky vendor is always the sorest loser." This is a startling admission, because by that time he had kicked off his campaign to curb the selling of liquor to Indians and Half-breeds. As he put it in a letter written for the Helena *Independent* of May 29, 1882: "When he [a Métis] visits a store with the produce of his chase, if the trader meets him with intoxicating liquor and trickery, he throws him into demoralization and poverty and retards his final settlement." Louis grew determined to do something about the "deterioration of Half-breed morals".

Riel had liked the trader Simon Pepin when he first met him, thinking him friendly and rather jolly. He soon discovered that Pepin was anything but an honourable businessman. He exploited Indians and Métis alike, selling them illegal whisky, tobacco and cartridges, all the time charging outrageous prices. Pepin was an early pioneer from Quebec, a freighter, rancher, stockraiser and financier who was in charge of the territory from Salt Lake to Fort Benton for the Diamond R Transportation Company. He often hung out at the company's trading outlet at Wilder's Landing, a short hop east of Carroll, but he also worked the surrounding Indian reserves. Riel was offended by the man's dishonesty; "It has been my intention to remind him that there is a justice to be observed by him as by any other man," he wrote. He then sent three documents outlining his complaints, with eyewitness accounts, to Deputy Marshal J.X. Beidler, and when he heard nothing, Riel approached U.S. Marshal Alexander C. Botkin at Fort Benton. Botkin later wrote a description of that encounter:

> a figure appeared in my room that was quite sufficient in itself to fix my attention and excite my interest. It was that of a man of magnificent stature six feet in height, with broad shoulders slightly rounded, and finely proportioned throughout. He had brown hair reaching to the neck, and a full beard of the same colour. His complexion was that of a Caucasian, and there was nothing in his appearance save prominent cheek bones to suggest Indian blood. There was a notable dignity in his carriage and he had a courtliness of manner that we are in the habit of regarding as characteristic of the French.

In September 1882, Botkin appointed Riel a special deputy marshal and paid him as such. As Botkin later said, "I encouraged him to procure the necessary evidence and promised my cooperation." With this endorsement, Louis decided to prosecute Pepin in the courts. It was a decision that would eventually cost him dearly.

His dealings with Marshal Botkin pitched him into the political stew then boiling in the territory, and, as usual with Riel, he was forced into making an important decision. Would he be taken in by the powerful, moneyed people who found him, as an educated, sophisticated Métis, an interesting exotic, who went out of their way to woo him, offering him a comfortable living in their trading establishments, or would he again embrace the cause of the poverty-stricken Half-breed buffalo hunter? Not unsurprisingly, he came down solidly on the side of the underdog.

Like the dramatic topography and climate, the politics of early Montana were extreme. There were radical Republicans and radical Democrats, with only a few moderates in the middle. And the philosophies of both parties were of a far different colour than they would become in the twentieth century.

Montana had been made a territory in 1864, and the first governor, appointed by President Ulysses S. Grant, was a staunch Republican. James M. Ashley was an outspoken critic of slavery and the South, like most of the radical members of his party in Montana. However, the Democrats, whose trademark was their insistence on the superiority of the white race, were a more powerful force in the territory, and by 1882 one of their number, Martin Maginnis, had been elected five consecutive times to the U.S. Congress. Maginnis's chief contribution was to shrink the reservations that had been negotiated with various Indian tribes and open them up to homesteaders. In October 1882, a riot almost broke out at Fort Benton as hungry speculators lined up to get their hands on acreage that had been seized from the Blackfeet. Because he was a "good ol' boy" and had dedicated himself to opening the country to cattle ranchers, homesteaders, entrepreneurs, anybody who was white and sympathetic to the capitalists, Maginnis was solidly backed by the powerful moneyed interests in the territory. The bankers and merchant princes and copper kings all supported him. One of Maginnis's chief boosters was C.A. Broadwater, the man who managed the Diamond R Transportation Company and was Simon Pepin's boss.

Maginnis had said over and over that he wasn't the least interested in running for Congress for a sixth time, and the Republicans wanted to believe him— any Democrat named as his successor would be easier to beat than he. But by early August 1882 the Democratic mouthpieces that passed as newspapers began trumpeting his cause—no one could serve the territory as well as he could, they insisted; though he didn't even have a vote in the House (representatives from territories with small populations didn't at the time), through magnificent lobbying he had succeeded in getting much beneficial legislation (at least to the whites) passed. By September Maginnis had changed his mind and was nominated by acclamation.

The Republicans were now eager to find someone strong enough to challenge him, and they decided on Alexander Botkin, the man who had made Louis Riel a special deputy marshal.

Botkin had been born in Wisconsin two years before Riel. He had been a high-spirited journalist with the *Chicago Times* and the Milwaukee *Sentinel*, eventually becoming editor-in-chief of the latter. He resigned that position, supposedly because of ill health, and was then appointed United States marshal in Montana. In 1878, while tracking down horse thieves, he was caught for days in a horrible blizzard and suffered a stroke that left him paralysed in his lower limbs. He was often mentioned in the same breath as Senator Oliver Morton of Indiana, and Riel, too, must have thought of the man he had once tried to make his champion. Certainly he discussed with Botkin in detail his plan for a republic of Indians and Half-breeds in the Canadian Northwest.

Although his position on the shrinking of Indian reservations was not much different than Maginnis's, Botkin was more sympathetic towards the Indians and Half-breeds. Riel and the others appreciated his civility, because the Democrats had nothing but contempt for them. One incident vividly illustrates the treatment they received at the hands of Democratic ward heelers.

Sheriff John J. Healy was a larger-than-life character, a former whisky trader who had been chased out of Fort Whoop-Up by the North-West Mounted Police. He was also a devoted Democrat and this made him nearly untouchable. In March 1882, he and a posse raided a buffalo-hunters' camp on the Milk River near Medicine Lodge, supposedly because the Half-breeds had not paid custom duties on certain goods when crossing the Canada–U.S. border. It was later revealed that there was no hard evidence of this. What Healy and his men did was to confiscate (or more accurately, steal) 1,500 buffalo robes, and a number of beaver, elk and antelope pelts, everything that the camp owned. Not unexpectedly the hunters turned on the sheriff and his companions, tied them up, seized their guns and repossessed their valuable merchandise. Once Healy telegraphed for help, the U.S. Army went after the hunters, but they had already disappeared over the Canadian border. It was these too frequent outrages that left the Natives feeling defenceless. But the Half-breeds did have one advantage over the Indians—they could vote. And with only 23,000 electors in the entire territory, even a bloc as small as theirs was important.

The election for both the territorial government and the congressional representative was slated for November 7, 1882. Louis Riel spent most of October stumping the campaign trail for Marshal Botkin, travelling to remote Half-breed communities along the Missouri River. It must have felt good to be back in the thick of politics again, and his magic powers of persuasion were obviously in full force because he had no trouble persuading his listeners of Botkin's virtues. Commentators over the years have criticized Riel, claiming that, because he was not yet an American citizen, he was somehow acting illegally. But the law was clear: any male twenty-one or older who had declared his intention of becoming a citizen, as he had, and had lived in the territory for six months was eligible to vote, and, of course, participate in the election campaign.

It was a dirty one. The Irish were flooding into the territory, employed on railway construction gangs, and their votes were bought outright; the Mormons were promised a homeland; the cattle ranchers were guaranteed that the Indians would be strung up for stealing horses. Riel himself claimed that he was offered a large amount of money if he would persuade the Half-breeds to vote the Democratic ticket. At Rocky Point, where the Democrats were represented by Simon Pepin, ten men were accused of casting 720 votes for Maginnis.

When the dust settled, the Democratic incumbent had been returned for the sixth time. But it was a closer race than anyone had anticipated. Maginnis won by only 1,484 votes out of a total of 23,312. All of the precincts where Riel had campaigned voted solidly for Botkin, who was thankful and would remain an admirer of Louis Riel. In 1900 he wrote an article calling him "The John Brown of the Half Breeds", and concluding that "he offered up his life on behalf of a poor and oppressed people."

During 1882, Marguerite and Louis had settled into a comfortable and happy marriage. Much to Riel's relief, their union had been properly blessed. On March 12, a Jesuit missionary had sanctified it in a solemn and much-appreciated marriage ceremony.

Two months after, on May 9, 1882, Marguerite gave birth to a son. He was called Jean, a name associated in Riel's mind with the sun. Louis had yearned for a child for many years, and it must have been a happy time for both him and Marguerite. Yet even this peace was marred when, in February 1883, a letter arrived that proved an emotional bombshell for Riel. It was from Evelina Barnabé.

She had learned of Riel's marriage from a story in an American newspaper. Shocked and hurt, she had written Louis's sister Henriette asking if the news was true. Henriette quickly answered her letter but could tell her little. "I deeply regret that I am not able to give you reassurances concerning the marriage of my brother. We heard something to that effect last fall but we here don't believe it, although it is possible. He hasn't written to us for over two years...."

Evelina finally found a Montana address for Riel and wrote him a short, emotionally overwrought letter. Although it had been five years since he had left Keeseville, and he had abruptly terminated his correspondence to her, she had never forgotten him and apparently still considered that they were engaged. She begged him to write and tell her if the reports of his marriage were true. "If you do not do so you will bring on yourself the greatest curses God can utter, for having destroyed forever the future of one who, if this is the case, has a single regret, having known and loved you."

Riel must have ached with guilt. The Barnabés had been so kind to him, taking him in at a time when he needed them. To the day he died he carried Evelina's papers with him, so he must have loved her deeply. But she represented the world of lilac bushes, lace-curtained rectories, sunny verandas and pleasant tree-lined streets, whereas he lived in a rugged, dirty, frontier society. How could she, with her frail health, her delicate constitution, have survived?

Only a rough copy of his reply has been found, and it is not known whether the letter was ever sent.

In it he explained that her correspondence to him in the spring of 1879 had led him to believe that she was having doubts about the marriage. She had ordered him not to mention their engagement in his letters "until you have the means" to marry. And, as he explained, he was very poor at the time. On another occasion she wrote, "I've told you that if you come for me, I will be nothing but an embarrassment to you ... it appears to me that I don't possess the qualities that you want in a wife. I am a lowly woman who has little courage and consequently I don't know about the high position you will occupy if you succeed."

That Riel could be so insensitive, indeed cruel, to a woman who loved him—and to his sister Sara whom he had also ignored for years—is an indication of how much he had become absorbed in the culture of the Montana buffalo hunter. The fight for even primitive existence seems to have precluded all niceties, sympathy or even respect.

Both Evelina and her brother were seriously ill with tuberculosis. "The illness has prevented me from helping in the church for the last two months," she wrote. Only two months after Louis received her letter, Fabien Barnabé died of the disease, aged forty-four. Louis wrote a poem-prayer in his memory praising his charity and his piety. "He has finished his days; but his dear soul/Lives. My God! you known that/He loved your commands/Remember, I pray you/His last sigh of faith." The priest's body was returned to L'Assomption, and Evelina and her mother remained in Quebec. It would be another nine years before Riel's "beloved betrothed" finally married.

The winter of 1882–83 was another ferocious attack. The temperature sank lower every day, blizzards raged, white-outs flared. It could have served as a warning that a miserable year was in the offing.

On the first day of March 1883, Riel was standing on the banks of the Missouri River when suddenly before him appeared his "dear papa", pale, and looking as though he feared his son. Then, as Riel wrote:

> I went straight to him and he came straight to me, although we met each other in the middle of a crowd of people. Before reaching him, I fell to my knees to receive his benediction. And I saw him stretch his arms out towards me in order to fulfil what he wished for me. And I saw that he blessed me, as though to make twice as strong and twice as lasting the benediction which Sister Ste. Thérèse had passed on to me [ten years before at the convent at St. Norbert].

Two weeks later Louis finally became an American citizen. This, coupled with the vision of his father, touched off an emotional crisis. "I began to experience very strong moral sadness," he wrote at the time. The rupture with his past, with the native land he had once loved so much, was not so easily accomplished as he had thought it would be.

His depression may also have had something to do with his financial condition. After the terrible winter the Indians and Half-breeds were suffering— horses had died out on the frozen prairie, the buffalo had disappeared altogether. There was little pemmican, and few hides or pelts to sell, and nobody had any cash to buy calico or even ammunition. The Riels too were in desperate straits, especially since Marguerite was pregnant with their second child.

Henry Macdonald was a Scottish immigrant and sheep rancher around the Musselshell area. He later claimed that in March 1883 he hired both the Riels, Louis as a shepherd and Marguerite as a domestic. She was to look after the children in the family and do the housework. "Mrs. Riel assumed her duties stolidly. She worked well, though slowly and in contrast to her voluble mate, talked little. She took a great deal of pleasure in the baby." Macdonald decided Louis was not conscientious enough in his job—"He felt little responsibility for the sheep"—and in a few days let him go.

By this time Riel had found a more suitable position anyway. Father Joseph Damiani had offered him a job as a schoolteacher at St. Peter's Mission.

Most of the early Protestant clergy in Montana came with the white settlers, and stayed in their communities; it was the Catholics, the Jesuits in particular, who took on the formidable task of converting and "civilizing" the Indians. The Blackfeet were among the most difficult; for years they simply refused to swallow the religion the white man was trying to force down their throats. As early as 1846, the Jesuits began following them around during their glorious buffalo-hunting days. In 1873 they established St. Peter's Mission in the foothills west of the Missouri River and south of the Sun River. Very quickly, marauding Indians drove them away. They returned in 1874, full of enthusiasm because the Blackfeet at last seemed ready to convert and settle down. But the church had been reopened for only a couple of weeks when the U.S. Congress passed legislation moving the southern boundary of the Blackfeet reservation about eighty miles north to the Birch Creek–Marias River, far from St. Peter's Mission. After all their effort, the Jesuits weren't ready to give up. They converted the mission into a boarding school for boys, hoping in this way to keep in contact with the Blackfeet. But many parents would not agree to send their sons so far away, and soon boys from a variety of tribes had taken their place. White settlers also sent their sons to St. Peter's, but they were carefully segregated from the Natives.

In 1882 a fine stone residence and school was constructed and a year and a half later Father Joseph Damiani was named mission superior, in charge of about five priests and teachers.

In the 1870s, about twenty-five families of Half-breeds had also settled in the area; Damiani had taken them on as a special project. They were still trying to hunt buffalo and the priest hoped that if their acknowledged leader, Louis Riel, was on site, they would gravitate towards him and settle down.

The job of schoolteacher at St. Peter's offered many advantages to Riel. It would provide a small salary and a permanent home, and now, with a second baby on the way, a place where his children could receive a proper education and religious instruction. He'd have a chance for conversations with the priests there, educated, ethical men whom he liked. And he would still be available to advise and guide the Half-breeds.

The Riels arrived in April 1883, and either because there was no place available or because they were too poor to build a cabin, they moved in with the family of James Swan. Swan was a fifty-four-year-old Métis who had been born at White Horse Plains, near Red River. He considered Riel a great hero and so apparently didn't mind that the family of three would take up residence with him. "We have to ourselves one corner of his little house," Riel wrote his brother Joseph.

Louis was ready now, he said, to enjoy a quiet life with his family, but if a single theme dominated his life it was that peace would forever elude him.

His job as teacher didn't start until the following September, and in the meantime he had to earn some money. In mid-May 1883, he was working as a general hand on a ranch above the Sun River. To his amazement he found standing in front of him, blotting out the sun, Sheriff John Healy, the same Healy who had the year before stolen the buffalo hides from the Métis of Milk River. The sheriff whipped out a warrant for Riel's arrest, and then escorted him to jail at Fort Benton. Riel had been charged with election fraud.

The mud-slinging had never ceased since the election of the previous November. Both sides had accused each other of padding the ballot box. Marshal Botkin had gone so far as initiating legal action against several Democrats, perhaps an unwise thing to do since they, after all, were in power. They in turn promised, according to the *Benton Weekly Record*, "at the proper and not very far distant time ... to show that gentleman [Botkin] that two can play at his little game." The person the Democrats chose as a target of their retaliation was Louis Riel.

A county grand jury at Fort Benton had become convinced that Riel had induced Half-breeds who were not U.S. citizens to vote—the indictment stated that he "willfully, fraudulently and feloniously ... aided, abetted and assisted Louis Jerome and Urbain Delorme [who were] not citizens of the United States...." As later evidence would show, the whole thing was patent nonsense; both the Métis referred to were American citizens and had the papers to show it. Meanwhile Louis was slapped in jail in Fort Benton. He spent his time writing long, awkward poems in English and feeling sorry for himself.

> Last fall, I had a vote to give.
> Then I found friends by the hundreds.
> But now that for their cause I grieve.
> They do not come near me, they dread....
>
> You know that I have no money.
> The poor have always shar'd my funds.
> Good help is as sweet as honey.
> Who will, amongst you, go my bonds?
>
> My wife and my child have no bread.
> They suffer deeply for your cause.
> They weep all day long on my bed.
> Love and friendship also has laws.

In fact the Benton Republicans quickly raised the $900 in surety needed for his bail and he was released in a few days. Still, his forthcoming trial would weigh heavily on his mind.

In June of 1883, Riel decided that after an absence of ten years, it was time for a visit to Manitoba. His period of imposed exile was long over, and he could freely do so. He longed to see his family at St. Vital and it seemed just the time for a family reunion—his beloved youngest sister Henriette was getting married in July.

Another important reason for his return to his birthplace concerned the matter of land and scrip. Many Métis living around St. Peter's Mission who had been born at Red River were entitled to either or both of these—their 240-acre allotment under section 31 of the Manitoba Act or scrip worth $160 received by "half-breed heads of families". They had left Manitoba before the complicated legislation was passed and the land was still owed them. There were also some individuals who had sold their allotments at very low prices, and now wished to pay out the original purchaser and resell the land for more money—this also was permitted under amendments to the Act. Twenty people signed powers of attorney giving Riel the authority to sell their scrip and land at the best possible price. It's not clear whether he was to receive a commission from these sales.

He himself still owned land he had bought previously, and as the child of a "half-breed head of family" he was entitled to his own 240 acres. As well, Marguerite, having been born at White Horse Plains, could claim the same amount. She signed the power of attorney with a large X, for Riel's wife was totally illiterate.

Besides the land owed to him under the Manitoba Act, Louis still owned parcels that he had staked out twelve years before. And that spring, despite their poverty, the Riels had made a most generous gesture. They had donated a piece of prime Red River Valley land to the Sisters of the Precious Blood in St. Hyacinthe, Quebec. For several years, Louis had been corresponding with Mother Catherine-Aurélie, the founder of the order, and he believed that her prayers had cured his sister Eulalie of a serious illness. The land, wrote Louis, "is situated in a good central location, although there are not yet many buildings around it; but it is in the neighbourhood of Monseigneur Taché's seigneurie; it is seven or eight miles from Winnipeg, no more than a mile from the railroad, near the Seine River." William Gladu, Eulalie's husband, agreed to pay the taxes each year. On receiving the generous gift (which they sold in 1888 for a substantial sum) the nuns sent a beautifully scripted document—a "holy Union of Prayers, sacrifices and good deeds between Mr. and Mrs. Louis Riel and the Sisters of Precious Blood in St. Hyacinthe"—and promised to pray "for Monsieur and Madame Louis Riel in perpetuity, during their life and after their death."

In the first week in June, Riel left St. Peter's Mission for Manitoba. Since Marguerite was now seven months pregnant, it was felt the trip would be too hard on her, so she stayed behind with Jean. On the way Louis stopped at Pembina and talked with the postmaster, deputy of customs and judge of the probate. He had been told by the two men involved in the charges against him, Louis Jerome and Urbain Delorme, that documents would be found there proving that they had been born in the United States. And he did manage to collect some important evidence.

Louis's arrival in St. Vital set off a jubilant family reunion. His mother was now sixty-one, suffered from ill health and looked old beyond her years, but she was overjoyed as she hugged her beloved son. All Louis's brothers and sisters were there to greet him except Sara, still labouring as a missionary at Île-à-la-Crosse. With Henriette's wedding pending, it was a busy, happy time. The parade of friends and relatives dropping by Julie's house never ceased; Riel jokingly complained that "I have hardly been able to sleep on account of the large number of visitors."

And it must have been comforting for Louis to see for himself that a modicum of prosperity had finally come to the Riel family. They lived rather well.

His brothers and brothers-in-law had made the farm viable. They were building homes of their own and Julie's house was now a comfortable and nicely furnished abode. The women of the family were impeccably dressed and well groomed. The grandchildren would no doubt receive good educations. They were a family of respectability and, at that point, high expectations.

News of Riel's presence quickly reached the English-speaking community of Winnipeg, and just a few days after his arrival on June 28, a reporter for the *Free Press* drove out to St. Vital seeking an interview. The following day a journalist from the *Daily Sun* did the same. Both wrote interesting descriptions of Riel:

The Daily Sun:

He wore a black slouched hat, beneath which was a full face with broad forehead and keen brown eyes of marked intellectuality. His black curly hair was rather shorter than that worn by the average half-breed. He has a full beard, pointed, of a darkish brown colour. He has a straight, large, prominent, well-shaped nose, and a most expressive mouth. He has extraordinary self-possession, but when relating some stirring fact or exciting reminiscence his eyes danced and glistened in a manner that riveted attention.

The Free Press:

His appearance was something of a surprise to one who had expected to see a rather desperate-looking character. He is a man of medium size and powerful build. His features are prepossessing and almost handsome— aquiline nose, large dark expressive eyes, and a high forehead—while his general expression is mild and thoughtful.... Throughout the whole interview his tone was subdued, and the serious expression of his face was only occasionally relieved by a pensive smile.

Riel had reluctantly agreed to talk to the reporters. He told them he was astounded at the prosperity of Winnipeg, but predicted the phenomenal growth would end in about twelve years. Most of the interviews, however, were given over to his justification of his actions during the Red River Rebellion, and particularly to the execution of Thomas Scott. "I am more and more convinced every day, without a single exception, I did right," he said.

And yet he felt sadly alienated from the French-speaking elite of Manitoba. He had looked forward to seeing Archbishop Taché, but he had an unfortunate misunderstanding with the prelate. The details are not known, except that it involved money which Taché apparently held in trust for Riel. Louis would later write, "We exchanged several unpleasant words. Finally, the archbishop mentioned the name of an Englishman to me. And he said, 'It is he who has your money.'" Ever after, the Riel family believed that the archbishop had cheated them.

Riel also spent a few days at the home of his old friend Joseph Dubuc, now a judge, but it was an uncomfortable visit. Shortly after, he turned down an invitation to attend a concert and banquet put on by the now influential St. Jean Baptiste Society, to which he had been especially invited. In a letter to Joseph a year later he would write, "No one wanted me in the influential political circles of Manitoba." He would go even further and say, "I am forgotten as if I were dead."

They may not have wanted him because they were concerned he might raise embarrassing questions. While the French of the community might have prospered, and some of the Métis bourgeoisie as well, the vast majority of the Half-breeds had suffered terribly under Canadian rule, and the French-speaking politicos had been powerless to do anything about it. They had been unable, and perhaps unwilling, to prevent what became the most profound diaspora in Canadian history.

As early as 1870, when the provisional government was still in power, some thirty or forty families left on the spring hunt and never came back. Riel and his council had already capitulated to the Canadians, and the Métis were frightened that the influx of white immigrants that would surely follow would change forever their way of life. Some headed south to form communities like those Riel had encountered at Milk River in Montana. Many more left for the Canadian Northwest, settling around Qu'Appelle in present-day Saskatchewan, St. Albert near Edmonton, and St. Laurent on the South Saskatchewan. The exodus continued during the 1870s, mostly among the buffalo hunters. By 1878, however, the affluent and educated were deserting the French parishes of Red River, most heading for the Saskatchewan River area. By the time Riel visited his birthplace in 1883, 4,000 Métis had moved from the Red River area. In the process the make-up of Manitoba had changed drastically. In fifteen years the population had increased almost tenfold, to 108,640, and most of the new arrivals were English-speaking Protestants. Whereas in 1870 the Métis had represented forty percent of the population, they now made up only seven percent.

The onslaught of settlers with a different language and culture was one reason for the exodus; another was the unrelenting attempt by the dominion government, in league with money-hungry merchants and speculators, to pry the Métis from their valuable land around Winnipeg. Half-breed land claims had become so bogged down in a quagmire of government legislation and bureaucratic red tape that many Métis abandoned their land or sold their scrip for the pitifully small amounts the speculators offered. They then headed west to unin-habited country where river lots were still available for the asking.

There was another, less obvious but equally insidious, reason for their departure en masse. In the Catholic parishes, the political power had gravitated to the more educated and wealthy French Canadians. The church itself seemed to have turned its back on the ordinary Métis, and had begun buying up their land and scrip. Riel must have frowned on all this, and it may have been one reason he was cool to the French-speaking elite and they to him.

Many of Riel's old friends had gone, including those who had been embroiled in the Red River resistance—Ambroise Lépine, André Nault's two sons, Louis Schmidt, Pierre Parenteau, Charles Nolin. But they kept in close con-tact with their families at Red River, and Riel listened carefully to the stories passed on about life on the South Saskatchewan River.

Henriette's wedding was one of the great social events of the season, for it was a union of two great Métis families, the Riels and the Poitras—Henriette was marrying Jean-Marie, son of François and nephew of Pierre, both renowned hunters of the White Horse Plains. The religious ceremony was held on July 10, and then, as in most Métis weddings, the celebrations went on for two long, boisterous days.

The Riels and Poitras were part of the bourgeoisie, religious and rather sedate people, so that the festivities probably lacked the wild abandon of those in the buffalo-hunting camps. But traditions were followed. In all likelihood, after the religious ceremony was concluded, every single one of the two hun-dred or so guests would line up to kiss the bride. Henriette would be busy guarding the shoes on her feet, because bachelors in the crowd were waiting to snatch one or the other and then demand a hefty sum from the groom (most often used to buy more liquor). There would have been a succession of fiddlers grinding out "The Red River Jig", "Pair O'Fours", "Reel O' Cats". The men would have pounded the floor and, as they had for centuries, shouted, "Ho! Ho!" as if they were taking off on their horses. All the guests—men, women and chil-dren—would have danced the night through. The banquet tables would have groaned under the weight of "Red River salmon" (a fancy name for catfish), buf-falo stew, galettes, fried dough cakes, berry puddings and pies. Only after the entire wedding party was near collapse would the horses be harnessed up and families loaded into their carts to make their way home.

Old friends and family had come from all over to attend Henriette's wed-ding, including Napoléon Nault and Damase Carrière, who had travelled all the way from Batoche on the South Saskatchewan River. Riel spent a great deal of time with them and they could not stop talking about the trouble that was brewing in the district over Métis land claims. The name Gabriel Dumont was mentioned time and again.

Two days after the celebrations finally wound down, Louis wrote his wife, Marguerite. He had not had much luck in carrying out the business end of his trip, he told her. The incredible land boom of 1881–82 had come to an abrupt halt as the Canadian economy spiralled downward, and Riel was finding it near impossible to sell Métis land or scrip at decent prices. He also asked Marguerite to pray for him, because he had been warned that once again the Orangemen of Winnipeg were planning to assassinate him. On June 28, Cyprian Audet had sworn an affidavit before Justice of the Peace Charles Sauvé: "I heard at St. Boniface on the 25th day of June a man say in presence of several other persons that there was a bullet made to kill Louis Riel and that said Louis Riel will die by the bullet, and the same person profered in my presence other threats against the life of Mr. Riel." Louis became anxious to return to the United States.

On his departure his mother extracted a promise from him that he would return soon, possibly that winter, with Marguerite and her grandson, Jean— "*mon petit-petit*", as she fondly called him and the new baby.

By August 20 Riel was back at St. Peter's Mission. His Manitoba visit must have inspired him for he wrote an ode called "The French-Canadian-Métis", a long paean of praise to his people. It was one of the most accomplished works of his later years. In it he expressed his vision of an independent Métis nation in the West, formed on the principle of natural law and guided by God. An amalgamation of the Métis, French Canadians and French (hence the hyphens in the title), it would embody the superior characteristics of all three peoples. The first part of the ode is the most romantically poetic:

> With unstinting love I give praise
> To French-Canadian-Métis:
> A young people whose yesterdays
> Are now alive as history.
>
> Their eyes have seen the glory
> Against Minnesota bands.
> They've only tasted victory
> Against the Dakota clans.
>
> Flowers strewn across prairie beds
> Or on Nor'western mountain shields,
> Remembering, incline their heads
> And tell their stories to the fields.

The cart paths that proliferate
Around the town of Regina
Serve as reminders of roads laid
Reaching deep into Montana.

Their humble, friendly habitat
Has served as refuge for strangers.
Their proven valour in combat
Has warded off many dangers.

Peace loving, never ill-bred.
Warrior blood runs in their veins.
Let them by Laurier be led.
They'll be fearsome on the plains.

Manitoba, still a sapling,
Dibbled by deft hands in firm ground,
With sacerdotal nurturing
Its taproot is secure and sound....*

Riel had been home only a few weeks when Marguerite gave birth to their second child, a girl they named Marie-Angélique. It was as though Riel's ideas of mixing the races had become reality. She was as fair as a Scandinavian—many old-timers said she looked just like her grandmother, the lovely Marie-Anne Gaboury Lagimodière—with huge Métis-like brown eyes, delicately proportioned with a pixie-like face. She would grow into a lovely child with a happy, sunny smile. Louis would write about her, "She is a well-loved crybaby who doesn't mind waking us up often during the night; and seems to want to keep our eyes open from twelve to one." The proud father would come to adore her more each year.

Riel would not begin teaching school until late November, and until that time his lawsuits occupied his time and energy. The election-fraud case against him was scheduled to be heard on September 22. With the documents he had obtained in Pembina, Louis was fairly confident of exoneration. He rushed to Fort Benton only to be told that the case would be held over until the spring session. Meanwhile, the newspapers were having a field day. The Republican *Helena Weekly* called him "a gentleman and scholar, a worthy and desirable friend" and "an American citizen with as full rights and infinitely more character than his persecutors". The Democratic Benton *Record* had a different opinion. "The majority of mankind would recognize Louis Riel for just what he is, a low

---

* *Translation by Paul Savoie.*

scoundrel whose fox-like cunning has alone kept him out of jail for these many years; whose sole and confessed occupation for a long time has been peddling liquid hell-fire to the Indians in defiance alike of United States and Territorial Law." The editors had obviously not read Louis's sermonizing poetry.

Riel had yet another lawsuit wending its way through the court system. Despite every effort to talk him out of it, he remained determined to prosecute Simon Pepin for selling illicit liquor to Indians and Half-breeds. Between October 25 and November 8, 1883, he rented a team of horses from Charles Crawford's livery stable at Fort Benton which he used to travel to remote Métis settlements at St. Peter's Mission, Big Spring Creek and Fort Maginnis. Subpoenas were issued to eight witnesses who had agreed to give testimony against Pepin. This endeavour cost Riel $265, which he certainly couldn't afford; fortunately he eventually was reimbursed for some of it by Marshal Botkin and the Republicans. The Pepin prosecution was also scheduled for the spring assizes.

In early January 1884, the Riel family received another terrible blow. Sara Riel, or Sister Marguerite-Marie as she now called herself, had died of tuberculosis two days after Christmas. For months there had been signs that she was fading. In July she had written her mother that she was very ill, suffering dreadfully, spitting blood all the time. The Riel family had tried to arrange for her to be returned to St. Vital—she had not come home once since she had left twelve years before—but they had soon realized she would never survive such an arduous trip. Fortunately, only months before, on January 9, 1883, she had finally made contact with her beloved brother. For years Louis had not written her, rather cruel neglect given how much she adored him, and yet obviously her feelings hadn't changed.

> For a long time, my loving and dear Louis, I thought of writing to you but the difficulty which kept my pen silenced was that I didn't have your address and I knew the family was in the same position, not being able to correspond with you. Having been told by Reverend Father Rapet that you might spend part of the winter at Benton, I hasten to write. Excuse the scribbling. I become more careless about my handwriting the older I get, but as for my feelings, believe me brother, they are the same as they were in the good days of our childhood when we loved one another without expressing it in words. Despite silence and separation there must not be the slightest suspicion of change in our feeling for each other....

Sara had written to her new sister-in-law: "I want to assure you of my tender and deep love; from now on your troubles are my troubles, your joys will be my joys, your hopes my hopes and your happiness my happiness."

Now the self-sacrificing Sara was gone. As had occurred on the deaths of his other two siblings, Marie in 1873 and Charles in 1875, Riel's reaction to Sara's passing was intense religious upheaval.

It began with the letter written by Bishop Bourget in which he said that God had ordained Riel with a unique spiritual mission. Louis's confessor, Father Frederick Eberschweiler of Fort Benton, insisted that the bishop had been misunderstood and suggested that Louis ask Bourget to clarify the meaning of his famous missive of July 14, 1875. In February 1884, after he had learned of Sara's death, Riel wrote five drafts of a letter to Bourget, although whether any of them was ever sent is unknown. More than asking for an explanation from the bishop, they revealed what Riel's divinely inspired assignment had meant in his life. There was a ring of bitterness, even of martyrdom, in his words:

> With God's help, and always according to your word, I held back nothing that belonged to me, or that touched me. My wife and children and I, we have no home. We live with others. We have neither beds nor pillows. We sleep on straw.

> I wish ardently to procure the glory of God as much as possible. And yet I am considered an eccentric. People scorn me, they laugh at me, they shrug their shoulders when they speak of me. I work unceasingly for the honour of religion; and people point at me; I work without ceasing for the good of society. And the newspapers vilify me. I am put in prison.... I work without ceasing for the salvation of souls, and I am told: let us do what we want, it is none of your business. And for all my deeds I am treated as a public nuisance.

Riel probably realized how pathetic and sorry for himself he sounded, for the next four renditions of the letter mention not a word of his and his family's unhappy circumstances. He did describe private revelations that he had experienced over the years, a direct result, he said, of Bourget's inspirational words. The most astounding of these occurred in 1878, when Riel was at Glens Falls and saw an American eagle soaring in the sky. Suddenly it turned its head to the northwest, all the while smiling at Louis. The eagle, thought Riel, was a symbol of the long-dead Senator Oliver Morton. The Indiana politician had come to represent, in Riel's mind, the first in a succession of popes who, in his vision of the church's future, would reign in North America. This was described in the second version of the letter to Bourget and it is doubtful that it was sent either.

Louis's disillusionment with his role as champion of the underdog was further reinforced in March 1884. Simon Pepin's trial was finally heard at Fort Benton. Although Riel had mustered several witnesses who swore they saw the trader sell liquor to Half-breeds, there were few who had admitted to having seen him do the same thing with Indians. The judge ruled that it was not illegal to sell intoxicating spirits to Half-breeds and dismissed the charges against Pepin. The Democratic newspapers laughed out loud at Riel's humiliation and he was deeply offended. He wrote to his brother Joseph, "I was not successful in my trial to prevent the sale of liquor. Although the law is clear, and my evidence strong, I did not win anything.... Everything seems to have been turned against me by the power of money." He complained that the trial had left him in debt to the tune of $137 and he had only two months to pay it. Joseph borrowed $250 and sent it to his brother immediately.

On April 16, 1884, the case of the Territory of Montana vs. Louis Riel in regard to charges of election fraud was heard at Fort Benton. The fact that Louis had dug up documents proving that the two men who were alleged to be British subjects and therefore ineligible to vote had in fact been born in Dakota territory was by now well known. Also, they were waiting in the wings to testify under oath that they were indeed American citizens. On a motion of the district attorney, the charges were summarily dismissed.

That evening Louis attended the Catholic church at Fort Benton, where he lit "a most beautiful candle" to Saint Joseph, who he believed had delivered him from "the wickedness of my enemies".

Throughout this time, Riel was carrying on his duties as schoolmaster at St. Peter's Mission. He taught some two dozen boys, divided into three grades; the subjects were reading, writing, spelling and arithmetic, all in English, and catechism in both French and English. He seems to have been a dedicated and well-liked teacher. Mrs. M.C. Murphy, the mother of two of his students, wrote: "Many heartfelt thanks from a devoted mother for all the kindnesses you have shown my little children, with many kind wishes to yourself and family."

Yet Louis found the job tiring and unsatisfactory. He wrote his brother-in-law Louis Lavallée, "My health, my occupation as schoolteacher and study master are overwhelming me." And on June 3 he confided to one of the Jesuit missionaries, Father Camillus Imoda:

> I have not been well for two weeks. My health suffers from the fatiguing regularity of having to look after children from 6 in the morning until 8 at night, on Sunday as well as on the days of the week. I am interested in the progress of the children and in the welfare of the school. I have its success at heart. And as a result I try to do my best. I do not know if my work is worth very much; but I do it conscientiously. I do not get enough rest.

But something else may have been responsible for Louis's ennui. During April and May he had undergone the most intense emotional trauma. Night after night he suffered terrifying dreams: ten hours after he had died he found himself in an other world where there was "stifling, appalling heat"; voices told him to detach himself completely from the world; he heard a soft, sad chanting, "Riel, thirty years in purgatory," which he recognized as the voice of God singing his Libera, a prayer for the dead. There were also periods of exaltation. While he was praying, a heaven-sent messenger told him, "You must march out in front." And two days later, he suddenly heard the Latin words *statue cum fiducia*, "believe with confidence". Both of these incidents he took as signs that his mission was about to begin.

As usual, he described these revelations in his writings. Whenever he had a moment he would scribble feverishly; as he himself put it, "The jug of my spirit has come uncorked." The outpouring of words was overwhelming and took many forms: a number of anguished prayers to the Virgin Mary; long and rather lovely litanies addressed to Saint Joseph in which he asked the "glorious carpenter" to intercede on behalf of just about everybody he cared about; a series of adulatory poems, paeans of praise, to the various priests who had played important roles in his life.

Much of Louis's verse throughout this period is laced with images of the landscape surrounding St. Peter's Mission. It was so dramatic, so striking, that it surely had a profound effect on his flights of mysticism.

The grounds of St. Peter's Mission were quite beautiful; a stream meandered through the Sullivan Valley, which was full of cottonwood trees, willows, currant bushes, lovely pastel sweet peas, wild prairie roses. But it was the strange, rocky buttes jutting into the sky that dominated the place and gave it its otherworldly character—Eagle Rock, Nipple Butte, Piagan's Butte, Rattlesnake's Buttes, Little Prickly Pear Butte, Priest's Frock Butte and the mammoth outcrop that dominated everything, Birdtail Rock. These bluffs were more than just startling to look at; they were dangerous places swarming with rattlesnakes and wolves—Firman Harris shot a wolf in the hills surrounding St. Peter's that was seven feet six inches long. All of this must have been fuel for the heated-up imagination of Louis Riel.

As the lovely spring of 1884 turned warmer, Louis's mystical theorizing grew ever more intense. In mid-May he wrote the first entries of what would become an eighteen-month-long diary, "a notebook of meditations and prayers", as he put it. That month's entries were an exercise in self-torment. He was too much interested in comfort; he must divorce himself from the world's pleasures and live an ascetic life.

At my table, I will have only what is strictly necessary—water or milk to drink, no dessert, no syrup.

I do not even want to sit comfortably. I want to punish myself, mortify myself in everything.

He even came to doubt his own mission. Was it merely an act of pride to think that God would mark him as someone special? "Who am I? Who am I to attempt to lead events?" he wrote in obvious distress.

But by June the journal entries sounded a more optimistic, confident note.

Leader of the Manitobans! You know that God is with the Métis; be meek and humble of heart. Be grateful to God in complete repentance. Jesus Christ wants to repay you for your labours. That is why He is leading you gradually along His way of the cross. Mortify yourself. Live as a saint, die as one of the elect.

This was written on June 2. Had Riel any idea that two days later he would again be asked to sacrifice himself to the welfare of the Métis people? On May 1 the Riels had finally moved into a house of their own, a sparsely furnished cabin provided by the Jesuits on the grounds of St. Peter's Mission. Marguerite had quickly made it a comfortable home. Despite that, Louis felt utterly exhausted. The never-ending teaching chores, the nerve-racking legal cases and his intense spiritual quest had all taken their toll. On May 27, 1884, he wrote his brother Joseph, congratulating him on his recent marriage to Eléonore Poitras and adding, "I'm not enjoying very good health, my heart doesn't permit me to write as I would like." He could hardly wait until the children left for their summer vacation and he could, at last, enjoy some peace. Perhaps he'd work on his poetry manuscript.

On Sunday June 4, Louis attended early mass at St. Peter's. He loved the little church, for although it was primitive, made only of wood, it was beautifully whitewashed, the interior trimmed with as bright a blue as the dazzling sky out-side. There were colourful statues of Saint Joseph and the Virgin both holding the baby Jesus, and the sanctuary was resplendent with gold leaf. It was a lovely sunny day and the sun was streaming through the windows. Father Damiani was just concluding the offering, Riel was deep in prayer, when an old Métisse named Madame Arcand whispered to him that visitors had arrived. Louis was a lit-tle annoyed at the interruption, but promptly left the church. As he walked towards James Swan's house, he caught sight of four men standing together. They were crusted with dust, and haggard-looking, as though they had been on the road for days. The stockiest of them came towards him with his hand outstretched. Riel took it and held on to it. "You are a man who has travelled far. I don't know you, but you seem to know me."

"Yes," the other replied, "and I think you may know the name of Gabriel Dumont."

"Of course, quite well," answered Riel. "I know it well. It is good to see you but, if you will excuse me, I am going to hear the rest of the mass. Please go and wait for me at my home, over there, the house near the small bridge. My wife is there and I will join you shortly."

It was only twenty minutes or so before Riel appeared again. The other three members of the delegation, James Isbister, Moïse Ouellette and Michel Dumas, introduced themselves and explained their mission. They had travelled almost seven hundred miles—it had taken seventeen days—from St. Laurent on the Saskatchewan River to St. Peter's. They had been delegated by members in the community to ask Riel to direct their struggle for justice from the Canadian government. Gabriel Dumont would later say that Riel looked surprised and flattered. But he said to them, "God has helped me understand why you have made this long trip, and since there are four of you who have arrived on the fourth, and you wish to leave with a fifth, I cannot answer today. You must wait until the fifth. I will give you my answer in the morning." If the delegation was a little confused by his mystic response, they were not puzzled by his answer the next day. Dumont remembered him saying, "It has been fifteen years since I gave my heart to my country. I am ready to give it again now." Riel then wrote a memo in straightforward if awkward English.

> Gentlemen, your personal visit does me honor and causes great pleasure. But on account of its representative character your coming to me has the proportions of a remarkable fact. I record it as one of the gratifications of my life. It is a good event which my family will remember. And I pray to God that your delegation may become a blessing amongst the blessings of this my fortieth year.

Riel did not try to hide the fact that he was also going on his own business. "The Canadian Government owes me two hundred and forty acres of land according to the thirty-first clause of the Manitoba Treaty." And he would attempt to collect. He added that he wanted to be back at St. Peter's Mission by September.

But there was something else not mentioned in the stilted prose. Surely this was the God-given opportunity he had been waiting for. Could it be that his grand scheme, so long fermenting, of an independent, Roman Catholic, Métis republic, might at last be realized?

St. Peter's Mission, Montana, where Riel taught at a boys' school during 1883–84.

Father Alexis André, the superior
of the Oblate missionaries during
the North-West Rebellion. He
and Riel quickly became
adversaries.

Métis scouts at St. Laurent, 1874.

Louis Riel *ca* 1883 in Montana, while he was acting as a kind of Che Guevara for the Métis. He looks not so much like a buffalo hunter as like a French poet.

Although this picture has not been positively
identified, it is likely Riel's wife, Marguerite.
It was found in Louis's private papers.

Marguerite and Louis's two children, Jean and
Angélique, in 1886, after the death of both
their parents.

Major-General
Frederick D. Middleton,
commander of the
Canadian expeditionary
force for the North-West
Rebellion, 1885.

The first shot fired
at the battle
of Batoche,
May 9, 1885.

Canadian troops
sleeping in the
zareba trenches
during the battle
of Batoche,
May 10, 1885.

Graves of the Métis killed during the North-West Rebellion. They are situated at Batoche, with the St. Antoine de Padoue Church and rectory in the background.

Gabriel Dumont, the "Prince of the Plains".

Councillors of the provisional
government who had
surrendered or been
captured, beside the
Regina courthouse at
the time of their trial, 1885.

The Scarth building in Regina,
rented by the dominion
government as a courthouse
for Riel's trial. Built in 1885,
it burned down in 1886.

Louis Riel's defence attorneys.
Left to right: F.X. Lemieux, Charles Fitzpatrick and James Greenshields.

Members of the jury that convicted Riel. *Standing, left to right*: Walter Merryfield and Henry J. Painter; *seated, left to right*: Francis Cosgrove (foreman), P. Deane, E.J. Brooks and Ed Evett.

Hugh Richardson, the stipendiary magistrate who presided over Riel's trial.

Louis Riel on trial.

Louis Riel's mother, Julie, with his son, Jean, a few years after his death.

Louis Riel photographed outside his tent shortly after he gave himself up to Major-General Middleton, May 1885.

Louis Riel at the time of his trial, August 1885.

PART IV
TRAGEDY

– 15 –

Lovable Spirit
Of Jesus Christ.
Lend me your power and insight
That Through my labour over this petition
Of the Northwest people, I may register the urgency
Of their grievances and the injustice of their plight.

Louis Riel told Gabriel Dumont he needed time to prepare for the trip; he had to wrap up his work as schoolmaster and Marguerite had to ready their children for the 680-mile journey. So it was not until June 10, 1884, that the little caravan set out in the hot morning sun. Dumont and the others had arrived with three carts, and into one of these were loaded the family's possessions. Not Louis's important papers, though. Afraid that Canadian government agents might intercept them, he entrusted his precious documents to another Saskatchewan Métis, Pierre Gariépy, a relative by marriage of Cuthbert Grant's, who was visiting relatives in Montana and would return to Canada later.

About forty-five miles north on the Mullen Road, the party reached the pretty town of Sun River. Riel must have thought it necessary to make a public announcement of his departure, because he and Michel Dumas dropped in to the office of the town's newspaper, the *Rising Sun*. The next day it reported, "He [Riel] is an American citizen, and ... he considers the land over which the stars and stripes wave his home, and now only goes to assist his people as much as lays in his power, and after which be it much or little, he will return to Montana."

By a curious fluke, the editor, David B. Hall, had been a young soldier in Wolseley's army. "It was queer to sit and talk to this man," he wrote of Riel, "and remember how, as a drummer boy of 15, we longed to spill his blood." Nevertheless, Hall wished Louis "success in his mission".

From Sun River, the party of eight followed the Missouri River to Fort Benton. There the horses could be rested for a day or two and supplies bought. Riel took the opportunity to attend mass and talk with his confessor, Father Eberschweiler. The priest was dubious about Riel's plans, and when Louis asked him to bless the expedition, he refused. The next day, however, Riel returned and pleaded with him so fervently that Eberschweiler finally acquiesced. Louis ran to collect the others, but of the four-man delegation only Gabriel Dumont was willing to join them. Although he did it out of politeness, it would become an experience that both men remembered with emotion. Riel described it thus:

> The holy priest put on his surplice, made us kneel at the altar rails, took his vessel of holy water, and sprinkled on us the divine benediction. While he was blessing us, with his approval and permission, I offered the following prayer to God. "Dear God, bless me according to the light of your Providence which is loving and without measure. Bless me with my wife, with our little son, Jean, with our little daughter, Marie-Angélique, and with Gabriel Dumont."

As far as Louis Riel was concerned, his mission was divinely endorsed.

The procession now headed north. The Canadian government had already been warned about Riel's imminent arrival. Lawrence Clarke, chief factor of Fort Carlton, the Hudson's Bay Company's trading centre in the Saskatchewan Valley area, had pointed out in a letter that the Métis were becoming poorer and poorer and that they were at the point of rebellion—shades, he said, of 1869–70. Riel, he insisted, should be taken prisoner as soon as he stepped on Canadian soil, and while he admitted that this would infuriate the Métis, a contingent of North-West Mounted Police could quickly squelch any protest, he advised.

But the government did not act on Clarke's suggestions, probably because it would have been totally illegal to do so. The Riels were not interfered with once during their journey.

The spring festival of pale purple crocus, yellow flowers of the prickly pear and the reddish-violet blooms of purple cactus had already faded, and the hazy gold of what is a prairie summer was settling. It was a little warm but still comfortable as the party travelled northward through the dry, short-grass section of the Great Plains, camping under a star-pricked sky at night. Riel had plenty of time to get to know his companions.

James Isbister, fifty-one, was an English-speaking Half-breed who had started farming in the Prince Albert region in 1862, the first person to do so. He came from an illustrious family. His first cousin was Alexander Kennedy Isbister, who had been an explorer for the Hudson's Bay Company and then at age twenty had emigrated to Britain, where he became a prominent barrister. Alexander Isbister never forgot his roots, and worked hard championing the rights of Métis and Half-breeds against the HBC's monopoly. It was he who presented the 1846 petition demanding free trade to the British Parliament, and for this he would have been well regarded by Louis Riel's father. To Riel himself, James Isbister was an important member of the delegation because he represented the English-speaking Half-breeds of the South Saskatchewan River. During the Red River resistance, the Métis leader had learned how important it was to have the English on side.

Michel Dumas, a handsome man of thirty-five with bright blue eyes and sandy hair, had been born in Red River, had grown up in the Half-breed parish of St. James and had been educated at St. Boniface. Although Riel doesn't seem to have recognized him immediately, he must have known him. For one thing he was a cousin of Louis Schmidt, Riel's old school chum and political ally. He had moved to the Northwest Territories just four years before, with Schmidt, and was trying to scrape out a living as a farmer. He was one of the leaders among the Métis activists.

The third man, Moïse Ouellette, Gabriel Dumont's brother-in-law, was not an official part of the delegation. Originally Louis Schmidt had been asked to go to Montana. He had agreed, but on May 12 was appointed to a rather lucrative position in the Prince Albert land office which he did not want to jeopardize, and so had declined. Ouellette went instead.

The Ouellettes were among the most prosperous of the Métis in the Batoche area. The patriarch of the family, Joseph, had come from Red River to the South Saskatchewan area in early 1874, with his four sons, including Moïse. They were good farmers, with the best herd of cattle and the most modern machinery. At age eighty, the elder Ouellette still trapped muskrat and fox all through the winter.

But the most celebrated member of the delegation was certainly Gabriel Dumont, the generous, hard-living, buffalo hunter known as the "Prince of the Prairies".

Gabriel's grandfather, Jean-Baptiste Dumont, had been a French-Canadian voyageur working for the Hudson's Bay Company. Around 1800 he had married a full-blooded Sarcee. (As with so many Native women of the time, little is known about her; even her name is lost to history.) This marriage produced three sons, all of whom grew to be over six feet tall, and as strong as the buffalo bulls they hunted. Gabriel's father, Isidore, was a sensible, clever man, but the uncle after whom Gabriel was named was flamboyant, violent, hard-drinking and addicted to gambling. In later years Gabriel the second also developed a reputation as a frightening man while in his cups—he adored Hudson's Bay Company rum—and he was, as a friend once put it, "an inveterate gambler, would gamble sometimes for three days on end, stopping only to eat."

Gabriel's father, Isidore, married Louise Laframboise, of a prominent White Horse Plains Métis family. The couple returned to the Saskatchewan River territory where Isidore had spent most of his life, but by the late 1830s they had decided to taste the settled life at Red River. Here Gabriel was born in December 1837, the third child and second son. But Isidore loathed farming, and in 1840 the family loaded their possessions in Red River carts and headed back to the North Saskatchewan country.

Gabriel grew up a nomadic child of the plains. He received no formal schooling; he couldn't read or write although he could speak six languages—French and five Indian tongues (no English). His education was of another sort: by age ten he could not only ride a pony but break one in; he could shoot a bow and arrow with deadly accuracy; and, unusual for a Métis, he could swim miles without fatigue.

In 1851, when Gabriel was thirteen, the Dumont family left for the usual mid-summer trek to the northern United States in search of buffalo. Their relationship with the Sioux Indians had been deteriorating for years, for a number of reasons, and the Métis hunting bands that were not travelling together agreed to warn each other if they spotted war parties. In early June, the Dumonts were alerted to a large group of Teton Sioux camped in the hilly country of the Grand Couteau. Scouts were sent out and soon spotted an encampment of about 500 lodges and 2,500 warriors. The Métis immediately made a barricade of their 200 carts and dug in to defend themselves.

The Sioux were sure of victory and attacked with confidence, but they soon found to their dismay that the Métis fortification was impenetrable. When hours later the Indians finally gave up, eighty of their own had been killed while only one Métis had perished, and he had been taken prisoner earlier. The defence preparations were credited with giving the Métis the greatest victory of their history, and were used ever after. Young Gabriel Dumont had taken his place with the sharpshooters in the rifle pits. The Battle of Grand Couteau would remain etched in his memory, and the details of the strategy used there with such success would be important during the North-West Rebellion.

With the encroachment of white settlers, and the American government's war on Indians and Half-breeds, it did none of the plains people any good to fight each other. In 1862, Gabriel was part of a delegation—his father and uncle were the leaders—who met with the Dakota Sioux at Devil's Lake and negotiated a peace agreement. From that time on, antagonism between Métis and all Indian tribes greatly eased, and Gabriel came to realize that an alliance between Métis and Indians was the only way to survive in a white-dominated culture. He was naturally intrigued, then, by Riel's plan of a Native people's republic.

Dumont was a celebrated buffalo scout. As a white hunter once said, "Gabriel knew the prairies as a sheep knows its heath and could go anywhere blind-folded." He was supposed to be able to call the buffalo, just as some moose hunters can entice their prey from hiding. By the time he was twenty-five he was chosen leader of the hunting bands along the South Saskatchewan River, a position he held until the final hunt of 1881.

Dumont understood the consequences of the dwindling herds as well as anyone. In 1872, he staked out the first land he ever owned, a patch of meadowland and aspen on the slopes of the South Saskatchewan River. Over the next decade he cleared about twenty acres, grew potatoes and barley and mowed hay for his horses. The house he built was the talk of the neighbourhood; it was quite large and in the parlour stood Dumont's prize possession, a much-used billiard table. His wife's most cherished object was a hand-operated washing machine, probably the first in the Northwest.

In the same year he moved onto his land, Gabriel began a more lucrative enterprise. His property was located beside a path that was used as a short-cut to Fort Carlton. For years the Hudson's Bay Company had kept a scow moored at the spot for convenient crossing of the river, but now they had abandoned it. In the autumn of 1872 Dumont took it over and made a business out of what became known as Gabriel's Crossing. A primitive barge was towed upstream by a rope tied to horses' tails and set free into the current. The passengers were then left on their own to row as hard as they could to the opposite shore. The enterprise brought in some money, since it serviced a well-used trail, but Gabriel seems to have been an indifferent ferryman. If there was anything more interesting to do, he'd leave his post. Weary travellers would arrive only to find the scow tied up for the day. In 1882, he finally sold the business.

Dumont had made one truly smart decision in his life; he had married Madeleine Wilkie. She was born in 1830 in Pembina to Jean-Baptiste Wilkie, a Scottish Half-breed who was for years president of a large band of Métis hunters. Madeleine had been educated a little, could speak and read English and sometimes traded the product of Gabriel's hunt at Red River. She was a kind, conscientious woman who became well known for her knowledge of medicinal plants and her nursing ability. According to those who knew the Dumonts well, Madeleine and Gabriel's marriage seemed blessed by heaven.

There was only one dark cloud—they were never able to have children of their own, although they eventually adopted a daughter and a son.

Even after the buffalo hunt ceased, Gabriel remained a leader of his people, and it was natural that he would be sent to fetch Louis Riel. The relationship of these two men remains one of the most fascinating in Canadian history. They made a striking contrast: the strait-laced and hypersensitive Riel, intellectual, pious and serious, fastidious in his clothing (a photograph taken in 1880 shows him dressed elegantly; indeed he looks more like a French poet than a leader of buffalo hunters) and the hard-living, risk-taking Dumont, known for his courage and recklessness. Although at five foot eight he was not the giant his father and uncles had been, he seemed huge with his big head, massive shoulders and barrel chest. With his black curly hair to his shoulders, and a long scraggly beard, he looked much like the buffalo he slaughtered. And like so many clever men who are illiterate, he was in awe of educated people. Almost from the beginning he was enthralled by Louis Riel. What Riel thought of Dumont is harder to discern, although he certainly considered him a close friend. While Riel was still in Montana, an admirer had given him a carved wooden staff from Mexico which he loved. This he gave as a token of friendship to Gabriel Dumont.

By the end of June the Riels and their escorts had reached the edge of the flat prairie and could see the beginnings of the cool, green parklands, with their groves of aspen, poplar and birch. On July 1 they reached Tourond's Coulee (called Fish Creek in English), named after a well-known Red River Métis family that had played an important role in the 1870 resistance and at whose St. Norbert farm the Métis had gathered in the fall of 1873 to elect Riel to the House of Commons. Like everyone else, the family had found living in the new Red River uncomfortable and had joined the exodus to the Saskatchewan Valley.

At Tourond's Coulee were waiting sixty carts filled with Métis, the women and children cheering and clapping as loudly as they could, the men shooting volleys into the air, everyone singing Pierre Falcon's anthem, "Ah, would you have seen these Englishmen...!" It must have been sweet solace for Louis to realize that after years of ridicule and obscurity, here he was considered a true hero, his deeds during the Red River Rebellion still appreciated, his belief that the Métis were a special people still honoured.

Gabriel Dumont's house was located not far away, and Madeleine welcomed Marguerite Riel and the two children—Jean was now two, Angélique 10 months—and made them comfortable for the night. Most of the crowd that had greeted Riel stayed as well, camping outside on Dumont's property.

The next morning the entire entourage left for the little village of Batoche, on the banks of the curving South Saskatchewan River about ten miles north of Gabriel's Landing. Dumont had thought the newly constructed St. Antoine de Padoue Church, about a half-mile from the village, would be a convenient place for Riel to address the people. But news of Louis's arrival spread quickly and by the time he got to Batoche there were so many people congregated, English and Half-breeds as well as Métis, that they could not possibly all crowd into the church. They gathered instead on the grassy terrace at the back, and there Riel made his first speech to the Saskatchewan Métis. Almost nothing was recorded of it, except that Dumont remembered he spoke of "rights, treaties and other matters".

Among the crowd that gathered that sunny day at Batoche was Riel's cousin Charles Nolin, who had been at the centre of a dangerous anti-Riel plot during the Red River resistance that had almost caused the collapse of the provisional government. Ironically, after the rebellion he had been rewarded for his support of the Canadians; he had been elected to the Manitoba legislature from 1874, and had even served as minister of agriculture for a brief time. But after he lost his seat in 1878, he too decided to join the exodus from Red River and head west. He staked several claims at Touchwood Hills, near Qu'Appelle, and in the Batoche area, selling them shortly afterwards for substantial amounts. Indeed, by 1884 land speculation had made him a well-off man.

Riel and Charles Nolin had been reconciled in 1871 when Louis had returned to St. Vital after a brief exile in Dakota Territory. Indeed, Nolin had been most enthusiastic about asking Riel to come to the Saskatchewan Valley. The two cousins probably greeted each other warmly, and since Charles owned the second-grandest establishment in the entire district, a bright, roomy two-storey house, he invited the Riels to stay with his family. As everybody said Marguerite and the two children would be most comfortable there, Louis agreed. But there was one disadvantage of staying at Nolin's home—it was a little out of the way, situated as it was at St. Louis de Langevin, about fifteen miles north of Batoche. The Riels, however, would remain the guests of Charles Nolin for four months, until it became essential that Louis reside closer to the scene of action.

The first organized meeting at which Louis would speak was to be held on July 8. Meanwhile, he had seven days to absorb the history and peel back the layers of grievances that now infected the place.

No less than the Métis of Red River, the hunters of the Northwest had grown deeply concerned about the dwindling buffalo herds. In the summer of 1871 a number of Métis families, including much of the Dumont clan, who were camping near Fort Carlton, asked for a priest to serve among them. The Reverend Alexis André, who had been an Oblate missionary among the Crees and Sioux of Dakota and Manitoba for ten years, and his assistant, joined the group of about fifty families that October. A temporary church and residence for the missionaries were constructed in a spot near the HBC Fort called La Petite Ville. At André's urging, in December of 1871 a general meeting of the winterers was organized and a resolution put forward calling for the formation of a permanent Métis colony. The gathering was presided over by Lawrence Clarke, the chief factor at Fort Carlton. He gave the Métis a long lecture about the disadvantages of continuing the buffalo hunt. If they didn't settle down, he said, "They could never hope to rise in the world but must remain forever the slaves and helots of their more intelligent fellow citizens." It was a bit exaggerated, but many of those attending the meeting agreed with him. Louis Letendre *dit* Batoche said, "The country is opening up to the stranger and the Métis must show his white blood and not be crushed in the struggle for existence."

Lawrence Clarke—who had suggested Riel be taken prisoner as soon as he arrived in Canada—would play a most devious role in subsequent events in the Northwest. His employer, the HBC, wanted the four thousand or so Métis in the West to settle in one area because the Company needed freighters to carry out its business; if a large number of Half-breeds found themselves competing for jobs, wages would come tumbling down. Furthermore, an anchored population would rely on the HBC for its everyday supplies.

Few of the Métis realized Clarke's true motive, however; won over by him and Father André, they passed the resolution to establish a Métis settlement unanimously and to great applause. A committee consisting of Gabriel's father, Isidore Dumont, and several recently arrived Red River patriarchs, Joseph Gariépy, Joseph Hamelin and Joseph Parenteau among others, was set up to find a suitable site. Dumont said he knew the perfect place—south of Fort Carlton in the valley of the Saskatchewan, thick with groves of aspen and poplar. It was suitable for agriculture, with plenty of timber for building and fuel and good grass for horses, and, perhaps most important, it was located not far from buffalo country. In 1873 the settlement was officially named the parish of St. Laurent, in honour of both the martyred saint of that name and Father André's brother, Laurent, who was a priest in France. The next year a church was built of large pine logs, with a thatch roof; even on the grimmest winter Sundays, it was packed.

As the community had now taken root, some form of authority would have to be put in place. At that time, the Canadian government's administration did not stretch as far as the parkland—the Northwest Territorial Council had not yet been established—and it was decided the community should set up its own government, modelled on the regulations of the buffalo hunt. In December

1873, the people of St. Laurent gathered outside the church and chose by acclamation Gabriel Dumont as their first president. Eight councillors were also elected, and a code of law "wide-ranging in scope and application" was devised regulating such things as taxes, breach of promise to marry, horse theft, lighting fires on the prairie and free Sunday passage on the ferry. Significantly, one clause specified that this was not an attempt to form an independent state and that the Métis were "loyal and faithful subjects of Canada".

In February of the next year, 1874, a public assembly approved the landholding regulations, which allotted to each family head, and to sons aged twenty and over, a river lot with a quarter of a mile water frontage, extending back two miles to grazing land, very much on the pattern of the farms of the Red River Valley.

After land distribution was taken care of, the first priority for Dumont and his councillors was the excessive slaughter of the buffalo. The 1874 hunt had been a poor one, and it was beginning to dawn on even the most sanguine that the animals were near extinction. A law was formulated which stipulated that each spring a public assembly would determine the date of departure of the buffalo-hunting brigade; no one could leave before that time.

In late spring of 1875 a party of Métis and Indian families was spotted contravening the code by running the buffalo ahead of the main party. While supposedly "free hunters", they were in fact working for the Hudson's Bay Company. At least three of the leaders were residents of the Métis settlement and had taken part in the formation of the buffalo-hunt regulations. Dumont first warned the group to stop breaking the rules; when this was ignored, he and forty men armed with rifles rode into the camp, seized horses, carts, provisions and personal possessions, and levied fines against some of the group. Lawrence Clarke, the only justice of the peace in the region, wrote a letter full of exaggeration to Lieutenant-Governor Morris at Red River, claiming that the Métis of the Saskatchewan had "assumed to themselves the right to enact laws, rules and regulations ... of the most tyrannical nature...." The Métis "court" had levied "by violence and robbery large sums of money on inoffensive persons". The newspapers in Winnipeg and elsewhere in Canada got wind of Clarke's alarming letter, and reported the event as though it were a major revolution. It certainly terrified the lieutenant-governor and his bosses in Ottawa, who still remembered clearly, and with fear, the Red River resistance. A detachment of fifty Northwest Mounted Police was immediately dispatched to Fort Carlton. Gabriel Dumont was out of the country, but as soon as the Mounties arrived, two of the Métis who had been involved in the incident approached them and apologized for their action—the confiscated goods and horses had long since been returned. "We had no idea we were acting against the law," they said. Nevertheless, Clarke insisted that Dumont be arrested when he returned from the hunt. Fortunately, the investigating officer, Commissioner George Arthur French, refused. "What I have seen of the Half-breeds, I consider them a well-disposed law-abiding people, the few infractions of the law that do occur, being mainly due to ignorance of laws...." Although Gabriel Dumont and his council were entirely vindicated, it was the end of the Métis government. "The humble legislature of the St. Laurent colony, having no longer the right to punish delinquents, naturally lost all its sanction and died while just out of the cradle," the missionary Vital Fourmond later wrote. The incident caused deep resentment against the Hudson's Bay Company and suspicion of Clarke, both of which were still festering when Louis Riel arrived on the scene.

As the influx of Red River and other migrants continued, the new community expanded, stretching untidily along the shores of both sides of the South Saskatchewan River for about twenty-five miles. By 1880 the population had reached a thousand, and three communities had taken root; the village of St. Laurent at the northern boundary, Tourond's Coulee on the south and Batoche in between.

While the entire area was referred to as the St. Laurent settlement, by 1878 the village itself had been losing prominence. The land around it was marshy and unproductive and, more important, the most enterprising, successful businessman had established himself ten miles south.

François-Xavier Letendre's background was not unlike Louis Riel's. In fact, Jean-Baptiste Lagimodière and Marie-Anne Gaboury were supposed to have met Xavier's grandparents in 1808 in the region of Fort des Prairies. In 1825 the Letendres had moved to Red River, and Xavier had been born there. His father was a hunter and trapper, and gradually, as the buffalo moved south and west, he had begun to again spend winters in the Northwest. Finally, in 1872, the family had moved to the South Saskatchewan River.

Xavier was not so much interested in hunting as he was in making money; he had established himself south of St. Laurent just where the Carlton Trail, the main route between Winnipeg and Edmonton, crossed the South Saskatchewan. Letendre's father had been called Batoche by the Indians—this was why he was called Louis Letendre *dit* Batoche—and Xavier too retained the name. The village which he dominated was named after him.

At Batoche Xavier set up a ferry service. (He was in direct competition with Dumont, but with Xavier's father in charge it was a more efficient operation than Gabriel's.) Xavier also began a freighting business—by 1884 it consisted of over a hundred carts—and a chain of trading posts. When his large new store opened in Batoche in 1880, it was considered a major event. An advertisement in the *Saskatchewan Herald* claimed it had "First-class goods, suitable for the family or the camp and embracing groceries, dry goods, provisions."

Letendre lived in what he liked to boast was "the grandest house west of Winnipeg". Built by a master carpenter from Quebec, it was a wood-frame building two and a half storeys high, with a rounded tower on one side and a large veranda with gabled columns in front. One visitor described it thus: "Up stairs were six roomy bedrooms, sumptuously furnished with marble-topped dressers and carpets on all floors." The rest of the house was equally elegant. Letendre entertained lavishly there, sometimes hiring the Grey Nuns from Île-à-la-Crosse to cater fantastic meals.

When Louis Riel arrived, Batoche consisted of Letendre's complex of buildings, a huddle of other stores, houses and outbuildings, most built of white-washed logs, a post office in the rectory, a cemetery and, half a mile to the southeast on a broad terrace overlooking the river, the church of St. Antoine de Padoue, which had been built that year. Batoche seemed a pretty, prosperous place; at least the Kerr brothers, also merchants at Batoche, found it so:

> Each family has a comfortable dwelling and outhouses and also the imple-
> ments for farming. They are also well supplied with cattle and horses—each
> Breed [sic] possesses an abundant supply of wood. There is always a ready
> market at Batoche for their grain and vegetable. Our firm has paid on an
> average $1.75 per bushel of wheat, $1.00 for potatoes and $1.25 for oats. I
> do not know any grievances they may possess...."

The Kerrs must have been trying to put the best spin on things, for, in reality, the Métis were in desperate straits. The demise of the buffalo had shattered their economy. The steamboat—the Hudson's Bay Company had two plying the Saskatchewan, the *Northcote* and the *Marquis*—had displaced many freighting jobs and, since so many were contending for the little work that remained, wages had plunged. The HBC had traditionally paid paltry amounts for the furs they bought from trappers but now the prices were ridiculous: twenty-five cents for a skunk or three muskrats, a dollar for a mink and a dollar or two for a fox. The Métis knew that their very existence now depended on agriculture, and that was the reason ownership of their land had become such an important, anxiety-ridden concern.

Almost from the moment their St. Laurent Settlement had been established, the Métis began worrying about the security of their property. No surveys had yet been done to give legal boundaries to their lots, and there was no land office set up to register their claims. Already many lots had been bought and sold without any legal recording. Over the next ten years, letters and petitions from not only the Métis but also the English Half-breeds and white settlers flooded into Ottawa. Either they were ignored entirely or the answers were inadequate and condescending. Priests, influential businessmen and officials who tried to press the Métis cause received just as cool a reception.

The Métis of the Northwest Territories wanted two things: patents for the lands they had already settled on and access to more property in the form of scrip—an acknowledgement that they shared with the Indians in the original title to land. This was not a far-fetched notion, as it was part of the underlying philosophy of the Manitoba Act.

Canadian politicians—in particular Sir John A. Macdonald, who had been returned to office in 1878—held an arrogant and confused attitude towards the Métis. Having never visited Manitoba and experienced the situation for themselves, they blamed the mess in Red River entirely on the Métis, rather than on the complicated, insidious legislation they had passed to help their friends the land speculators. Now they claimed that the Half-breeds of the Northwest would only "squander" their land grants. The politicians' response to an increasingly chaotic situation was simple: they "procrastinated with a fatuity almost beyond comprehension".

In 1878, petitions from St. Laurent, St. Albert, Cypress Hill and Prince Albert were written which pleaded: "It is of the most urgent necessity that the Government should cause to be surveyed, with the least possible delay, the lands occupied and cultivated by the half-breeds, or old residents of the country, and that patents therefore be granted to them." It was first sent to the Northwest Territorial Council (the appointed committee advising the lieutenant-governor, set up in 1875), which emphatically backed the Métis demands, believing that everyone who had relied on the buffalo for their livelihood should get help to readjust to a new life. But the Ottawa politicians were, as usual, lukewarm. The Minister of the Interior, David Mills, avoided the question of Half-breed land grants, but he did assure the Métis that the surveys of lots already settled would proceed as quickly as the government found the money to do the job.

In summer 1878 surveyors arrived in Prince Albert, with strict instructions to make the survey conform to the existing configuration of land ownership rather than merely slap the traditional system of rectangular townships on the district. They moved south and eventually arrived at the St. Laurent Settlement, but, since the end of the summer was fast approaching, they completed only about one-fifth of the area. The next summer, for reasons which remain obscure, the rest of the St. Laurent Settlement was surveyed on the square-lot principle. The

Métis river-front farms played havoc with the township-section squares the surveyors neatly drew.

Naturally, this outraged the Métis, many of whom had lived on their land for a half-dozen years or more by this time, and they demanded a resurvey. The government steadfastly refused to spend the money and the Métis stubbornly continued to carve out their long, thin river lots.

The Métis demand that scrip be issued to compensate them for the aboriginal title to lands was faring no better with the politicians. In 1879 Parliament passed a vaguely worded amendment to the Dominion Lands Act that gave the government the power to give the Northwest Métis what they wanted, but years went by and nothing was done.

In 1881, an incredible land boom saw homesteaders fanning all over the Northwest. Word spread that Batoche would soon become a commercial hub servicing the new settlers. The Métis remembered the same thing happening in Winnipeg, where they were cheated and crowded out by speculators. They became even more anxious about their status as "squatters" with no title to their land. On top of that, the opening of the Dominion Lands Office at Prince Albert that year was inexplicably delayed. There was still no place to register their land.

In September 1882 yet another petition was sent, written by Charles Nolin and signed by Gabriel Dumont and forty-six others. There was nothing obsequious about it; the pride of nation was still there.

> Having so long held this country as its masters and so often defended it against the Indians at the price of our blood, we consider it not asking too much to request the Government to allow us to occupy our lands in peace, and that exception be made to its regulations, by making the half-breeds of the North-West free grants of land. We also pray that you would direct that the lots be surveyed along the river ten chains in width by two miles in depth, this mode of division being the long established usage of the country.

The Minister of the Interior's reply caused more consternation. "When the proper time arrives the case of each bona fide settler will be dealt with on its own merits; but as regards the surveying of the land in question ... all lands in the North West Territories *will be surveyed according to the system in force* [italics added]."

All along the Métis had been concerned that the land they occupied would be sold from under them to white settlers. In summer 1883, their worst fears were confirmed. An entire section on the west side of the river at Batoche was purchased from the dominion government by W.J. Johnston of Prince Albert on behalf of an Ontario real estate firm. Abraham Montour, who had farmed a quarter section of this land since 1873, was told nothing of this transaction until Johnston showed up at his door. The government eventually claimed that the property had been sold in error, and tried to silence Montour so as not to create panic among other Métis by offering him a special grant in an adjoining section. When Montour finally understood what was going on, he spread the word very quickly. The community was enraged.

The petitions and letters continued to pour into Ottawa until, by the beginning of 1884, the government finally decided something had to be done. Dominion Lands Inspector William Pearce was sent to investigate, arriving at Prince Albert in January. Although the government had given him the power to deal with the river-lot problem, he soon announced that he didn't have time to resurvey the square blocks and there was no other surveyor readily available who had the expertise to do the job. He suggested that the existing rectangular sections could somehow accommodate the long river lots without the trouble and expense of a new survey. The problem was that Pearce did not speak a word of French, and he was an arrogant man who believed that "halfbreeds were a worthless lot". The Métis were by now so suspicious and upset that they dismissed his complicated compromise as another political trick.

But it was not just the Métis who were frustrated and anxious. Both the English-speaking Half-breeds and the white settlers were furious at Sir John A. Macdonald's government. Their anger, however, stemmed more from economic collapse than land-ownership problems. From 1881 onward, a succession of drought and early frosts had devastated harvests. After the 1883 crash, the price of wheat fell from $1.25 a bushel to forty cents. At the same time the cost of transportation and machinery had spiralled upwards. Life on the prairie was not at all what the homesteaders had expected.

All through 1883 and early 1884, meetings were held in the various communities of South Saskatchewan. Over and over again the settlers' grievances and fears welled up, but everyone seemed stymied as to what to do. No leader had emerged to mould the grumblings into an effective protest movement. James Isbister was well liked, but he didn't possess the stature. Michel Dumas was considered too impetuous and he drank too much. Nobody trusted Charles Nolin. And Gabriel Dumont? Everybody held him in high esteem, but not only was he illiterate, he himself admitted he was not politically astute.

At a meeting at Abraham Montour's house in Batoche on March 24, 1884, the name of Louis Riel popped up. It's not clear who first mentioned it, but it probably was Napoléon Nault who had met Riel the previous summer while he was attending Henriette's wedding. It was an inspired idea. Métis still remembered with great pride the accomplishments of the Red River resistance and the

Manitoba Act. It certainly wasn't Riel's fault that the promises had not come to fruition. The notion of enlisting Louis as an adviser quickly gained currency.

But if the Métis had learned anything from the Red River resistance, it was that there must be solidarity if any protest was to succeed. In April another meeting was called, this time with Métis and English-speaking Half-breeds. So many people showed up that the gathering had to be held outdoors, at the back of Gabriel Dumont's house. Huddled against the nippy wind and ankle-deep in slushy snow, the three hundred or so men talked for five hours. This time Louis Riel's name was raised by the Half-breed Andrew Spence. Eventually it was decided that Dumont and others would personally make a trip to Ottawa to present the government with a list of grievances, and on the way would stop in Montana to garner Riel's advice. First, however, they would seek the concurrence of the white settlers of the Saskatchewan Valley.

On May 24, delegates of all three contingents, Métis, Half-breeds and whites, gathered at the Lindsay schoolhouse at Red Deer, situated between the St. Laurent Settlement and Prince Albert. Again grievances were hashed over, the federal government's indifference and procrastinating condemned. Finally, the question of Louis Riel was raised. There was much debate—some whites and Half-breeds did not want to be associated with such an infamous revolutionary—but, although it was not unanimous, a resolution was passed specifying that a delegation be sent to invite Riel to the South Saskatchewan area. His task would be to formulate a petition setting out their grievances and listing means of resolving them. So instead of travelling to Ottawa, Dumont and the other three emissaries found themselves headed for St. Peter's Mission, Montana.

Six days after he had settled at Charles Nolin's house, on July 8, 1884, Louis Riel spoke to his first organized public meeting. It was a lovely sunny day as some stood and some settled on the ground outside Nolin's spacious home on the banks of the South Saskatchewan. First, the delegation to Montana reported:

> We were received by Mr. and Mrs. Riel in a very friendly manner; their courtesy was sincere, simple and true. Generally, when one enters the dwelling of a very poor man, the feeling of the visitor is more or less painful. But entering Mr. Riel's house, our impression was different. The humble condition of his home reminded us of the opportunities he has had for several years to become rich and even to make an exceptional fortune, and how, at all risks, he stood firm by the confidence of this people. We know how he worked for Manitoba and how he struggled on behalf of everyone in the Northwest, and having seen how little he had worked for his own benefit, we have returned after a long journey of almost fourteen hundred miles, with double the confidence we had in him when we left to seek him out in a strange land.

The guest was next up and it was vintage Riel: "Your voice is more than friendly, it is the voice of loving compatriots.... I say to you: it is the voice of my country." In light of future events, the conclusion of his remarks was interesting:

> I thank you for the delicate and flattering invitation to remain with you. It would be assuredly most sweet to me to pass my life in the midst of such grateful compatriots. The love I have for my native country is strong enough to keep me here, but the adopted country to which I belong has taken hold of my heart. I have promised it my devotion. I belong to it as long as I live.

The *Prince Albert Times* commented that "He [Riel] spoke of their grievances which he seemed to thoroughly understand...."

Three days later Riel travelled ten miles north to the Lindsay school. The speech he would give there would be more challenging; his persuasiveness, his personal charm, his ability with English would have to rise to the occasion. In a warm and calm voice he stressed to the several hundred people who had turned out what was to him the essential ingredient in any attempt to influence a government—unity and harmony among disparate groups. It was a theme he would repeat over and over.

> I salute you all with the cheers of my heart, because your different interests are finding the way to the grand union: the grand union of feelings, of views, of endeavours, without which a people can never have any influence, without which a people can never accomplish anything of importance and without which you could not be happy.

It was not exactly a fiery speech, though, and some of the younger men were disappointed. What kind of revolutionary was this who spoke so softly and calmly? The majority, however, thought him a huge success.

A few days later, an invitation arrived requesting him to speak in Prince Albert. Louis was taken aback because he was unprepared for any support coming from that town, at least immediately.

Prince Albert was the commercial hub of the entire Northwest. Founded in 1866 by the Reverend George Nesbit as a Presbyterian Indian mission, it had gradually attracted white settlers, especially after the Cree, Assiniboine and Chipewyan tribes signed Treaty No. 6 in 1876, handing over a tract of land bigger than all of Great Britain—much of it, especially around the North Saskatchewan River, prime farmland. The community thrived during the 1870s and early 1880s. Churches, stores, doctors' and lawyers' offices sprang up. A drygoods store on River Street was the first building constructed of brick west of Winnipeg. After 1875 a flood of settlers descended, many of whom came from the Red River Valley. The most prominent was none other than the poet Charles Mair.

Although Mair had at first prospered in the town of Portage la Prairie, where he settled after the Red River resistance, by the mid-1870s he had grown disillusioned. The great land boom which he had counted on to make his fortune wouldn't occur for a few more years. He felt there was "a sullen discontent" about the place. In 1877, he decided to move to the greener pastures of Prince Albert. On his arrival he immediately opened a large retail store which was considered the ultimate in modernity because it had glass-enclosed display cases.

At first it looked as though Mair had made a brilliant move. Battleford, 125 miles from Prince Albert, had been made the capital of the Northwest Territories, the proposed route of the Canadian Pacific Railway snaked right through Prince Albert, and the surrounding farmland was considered superb for wheat farming—during the 1870s almost every harvest seemed unbelievably bountiful. Speculators, Charlie Mair and Lawrence Clarke among them, had a field day. Every square foot around the town was snatched up; a quarter-section on the outskirts which had been priced at $1,000 in November 1881 sold for $15,000 three months later. The population in the District of Lorne swelled from five hundred to five thousand; Prince Albert itself housed seven hundred people. Then the bubble burst with a horrible pop. The CPR switched routes; the railway would run far south, through the drylands of Saskatchewan and Alberta, and it would be years before enough money could be found to lay spur lines to towns like Prince Albert. The Territories capital went with the railway; in 1883 Regina took Battleford's place as the queen city. On top of all that was the depression and drought of the early 1880s. The white settlers were so hard-up that they would look to anyone who provided real leadership, even Louis Riel.

Still, Louis was nervous about appearing there. Many of the townspeople were much like Charlie Mair—Anglo-Saxons with a pronounced Orange streak. The *Prince Albert Times*, which Mair himself had helped found, was hardly friendly. On July 18, it sniffed, "We must express our surprise and regret that any of our citizens should ... let the utterly false impression go forth to the world that Prince Albert is so destitute of able, educated, experienced and intelligent men as to require the guidance of an alien French half-breed."

And there were forces at work trying to stop Riel. The powerful chief factor at Fort Carlton, Lawrence Clarke, wrote the Roman Catholic priest in Prince Albert, Alexis André, warning that a riot might break out if Riel spoke in the town. André then urged Riel not to accept the invitation. Louis complied with his judgement and wrote a polite refusal, stating that he thought that his presence might cause the English-speaking community to split around the issue of his leadership—exactly what he didn't want to happen.

He was truly surprised when, a few days later, a petition arrived signed by eighty-four people, all but four of them white settlers, pleading with him to come to Prince Albert. Then Father André, who must have been listening to his parishioners, did an abrupt about-turn. He wrote to Louis,

> Opinion is so pronounced in your favour, and you are so ardently desired, that it will be a great disappointment to the people of Prince Albert if you do not come. So you must absolutely come; you are the most popular man in the country and, with the exception of four or five persons, everyone awaits you with impatience. I have only to say to you: come, come quickly.

How could Riel refuse such a appeal?

On July 19, about five hundred people packed into Treston Hall, the largest auditorium in Prince Albert. Again Riel was calm, moderate, thoughtful. It was a careful, rather tame address. Again he played his refrain of unity, but this time he suggested something more concrete: the three Northwest communities, Assiniboia, Saskatchewan and Alberta, should band together into one provincial government. As the *Prince Albert Times* reported, "There were many men in his [Riel's] opinion at present in the country who were able to govern it. Lets all help to get responsible government, as the first thing to be acquired."

Riel's speech was considered a great success. Said the newspaper, "This was a mass meeting, such as Prince Albert has never seen; people came from the country to meet Mr. Riel, from everywhere, and they went back struck with the quiet and gentle way he spoke to them." There was a lone dissenter. Captain Richard Deacon had been a volunteer in Colonel Wolseley's expeditionary force to Red River. He tried to tell the crowd "to be careful who they selected as their leader, for Mr. Riel had been a failure before, and they had no guarantee that he would not be so again." The crowd went into an uproar and the captain was manhandled out the door.

The one person who could have led the anti-Riel forces was conveniently out of the district. As early as the summer of 1882, Charles Mair had sensed that Métis discontent might lead to another rebellion and he had moved his family to Windsor, Ontario. He retained his businesses in Prince Albert still, and so found it necessary to reside in that city for six months of the year. In the summer of 1884 a business colleague wrote him in Ontario telling him about Riel's arrival and, probably wisely, he did not return to Prince Albert that fall.

Even Father Alexis André, a man who did not like his authority challenged one bit, had nothing but praise for Riel. The priest was a friend of Edgar

Dewdney, the Lieutenant-Governor and Indian Commissioner of the Northwest Territories, and provided a regular conduit of news to Ottawa which many people felt amounted to nothing less than constant undercover surveillance. On July 21, 1884, he wrote: "Since my last letter to your honour nothing has happened to disturb my belief that Riel in coming to this country has not any bad design in view.... Everywhere Riel goes he is creating the most favourable impression...."

– 16 –

Never go out without a hat, whether it's hot or cold....
Ripe peas, well prepared, are good for a weakened constitution.

Something other than hot air resulted from all these meetings Riel had been attending. A committee consisting of representatives from the Métis, the Half-breeds and the whites had been organized to draw up the petition of grievances that would be sent to Ottawa. The secretary's job would be an important one in this task, and Riel carefully looked around for the right person.

He first thought of his old school chum and fellow agitator, Louis Schmidt, who in 1880, with his wife, three children and cousin Michel Dumas, had moved to the South Saskatchewan Valley and begun farming.

As soon as Louis arrived at Batoche the two men fell into each other's arms. As Schmidt wrote in his memoirs, "It was not without emotion that I saw him again, knowing full well all the reverses he had suffered. From being the master of his country he was coming back to it now, a stranger without sanctuary." Schmidt offered to become secretary of Riel's committee, but Louis urged him not to give up his clerical job in the Prince Albert land office, pointing out that he could be a great help to the Métis in that position. Riel then had to cast about for another secretary. It wasn't difficult; one of the most politically committed and passionate people in the Northwest simply took it on himself to do the task.

William Henry Jackson was a small, delicate-looking young man of twenty-three, an intellectual trying to make a living as a farmer. He was the power behind the radical Farmers' Union, a devoted enemy of Sir John A. Macdonald and his Conservatives, and a long-time and passionate admirer of Louis Riel.

Although the cultural backgrounds of Riel and Jackson were quite different, there were similar strains. Jackson had been born in 1861 in Toronto, although he had been brought up in the small town of Wingham in the heart of Orange country. His father, Thomas Gethyn Jackson, owned a general store and the family—William, his mother, Elizabeth, his brother, Thomas Eastwood, and his sister, Cecily—lived above it. Both parents were devoted Methodists, and dancing, drinking and playing cards were strictly prohibited. They were also well read and believed strongly in education, saving as much as they could for their children's schooling.

Will was ten years old when his father took him to his first political rally. Jackson senior was a devoted reformer, an admirer of political activists, especially William Lyon Mackenzie, and his children were brought up believing that it was a right to oppose any oppressor and a duty to fight for the underdog, a philosophy Will would live by his entire life.

When Will turned sixteen he entered his first year at the University of Toronto and managed a first in mathematics and logic. His specialty, however, was classics. (Even when he was in the thick of the North-West Rebellion, he carried around his Greek and Latin grammars. He was a natural linguist, spoke French fluently and quickly learned some Cree.) He might well have become a professor, but in his third year the family's business went bankrupt—a fire had almost destroyed Wingham and Jackson senior could not collect his accounts. There was no longer any money to support Will at university. Meanwhile, Eastwood had moved to Prince Albert to set up the town's first pharmacy. His parents followed a few months later and William and Cecily, who took a teaching position, in 1882. Both Will and his father took homesteads near the junction of the North and South Saskatchewan rivers, and Thomas Gethyn started a farm machinery business. But Will's only real interest was political agitation.

He had plenty of opportunity. Farmers in the West were so dissatisfied with the policies of Macdonald's government that the first of those agrarian protests which would so often flash across the prairies was fermenting. In the spring of 1883, branches of what was called the Settlers' Rights Association sprang up in small towns. In December of that year a huge convention was held in Winnipeg at which the Manitoba and Northwest Farmers' Union was officially conceived. Taking their lead from Louis Riel, the union drew up a bill of rights outlining what the farmers wanted—an end of the CPR's monopoly was at the top of the list. Its first action was to send a delegation to Ottawa to present its bill of rights to Sir John A. and his Cabinet. Although the politicians were polite enough, the farmers came back angry and empty-handed. The government's only concrete response to their request was to authorize a new militia battalion of Winnipeg's 90th Militia Regiment.

Another convention of the Farmers' Union was held a few months later, in March 1884. The hostility and frustration were so fierce that cracks quickly appeared in the union's solidarity. The radical idea that the West should secede from Confederation and form a new country of Manitoba, the Northwest Territories and British Columbia had been bubbling for some time, but the moderates had managed to keep a lid on it. At the March meeting the radicals gained control and the talk of secession grew stronger. It was just what the Tories in Ottawa wanted. In newspapers across the land, they were able to play on people's fear of separatism, and they successfully linked the Farmers' Union with the Liberal Party extremists. By the time spring seeding had been completed, the union was all but dead.

It had been an important unifying force in the Saskatchewan Valley. Throughout the winter of 1884, union members gathered in one another's homes to plan their action against the government, and one of the things they talked about most was how to get the French on side. The previous summer the first election for the Northwest Territorial Council had been held and, almost to a man, the Métis had voted against the union's representative. If they were to succeed at all in their protest, the French would have to be won over to the idea of common action.

The well-read, well-educated Will Jackson was a skilful writer of petitions, memoranda and letters and was therefore a natural for the position of secretary of the union. When the executive asked him to do something about the Métis question, he approached Gabriel Dumont, Michel Dumas and Maxime Lépine. From that stemmed the meeting of March 24, 1884, at which Louis Riel's name was first mentioned.

Jackson was excited that such a great man was coming to Saskatchewan. He told a Prince Albert audience in July that in the Ontario Orange country where he grew up, Riel had always been portrayed as "a cutthroat, an outlaw, a bold braggart, and indeed the embodiment of nearly all that is evil." But Will had never thought that way. Louis Riel had always been as much a hero to him as that great champion of the oppressed, Mr. Mackenzie.

The day after Riel's arrival, Will lagged behind. He began talking to Louis and their conversation lasted well into the night. Louis Schmidt recorded what happened next.

"'What is he looking for?' Maxime Lépine asked, intrigued by the nervous little Englishman who was monopolizing the chief. 'The Canadians have decided to resort to arms,' replied Riel. 'They believe that we will also take up arms. They want to join us and he is their delegate.'"

Schmidt says that after that the two men became inseparable, and that Jackson "simply elected to stay with Riel at Nolin's house."

As well as being Riel's secretary, Will also acted as a kind of public relations agent for him. He sent Louis's Prince Albert speech off to the *Winnipeg Free Press* for publication. Writing on July 23, he gave an account of the preparation and arm-twisting he himself was doing on behalf of the movement. What he aimed for was a "clear, concise, logical petition", well researched with plenty of facts and figures. Such an impressive document "will strengthen our hands more than a month of speechifying". One paragraph of the same letter reveals how much in tune the two men had already become: "I am in good health except [for] a slight cold and enjoy good rest & hope that you also are in good shape. We will not get much respite until after the petition, but we can rest calm and peaceful as to the result, while the enemies of our God are tossing on their beds devising evil things against themselves."

While the Métis and English-speaking settlers had grievances against the government, the Indians in the Northwest had been outrageously abused. With the buffalo gone it was a question of either starving to death or living as wards of the state on reserves. By 1884, most of the Indians of the plains had signed various treaties with the government but they quickly discovered that they hated the confinement of reserve life. Often the soil was too poor to make farming a money-making proposition, and the government provided inadequate help in supplying cattle (which were often eaten by hungry Indians anyway), farm equipment and seeds.

When the depression descended on Canada in the early 1880s, the budget of the Indian Department was substantially cut. The government bureaucrats, who almost to a man were not only unsympathetic to the clients but seemed to take a perverse pleasure in their suffering, set in place a rigid system of rations. The result was widespread starvation and scurvy in the winter of 1883–84. A description of the Cree chief Piapot's reserve near Indian Head, written in May 1884 by a *Winnipeg Free Press* reporter, said it all:

> The bodies of the dead were strung up in trees as is the Indian custom. Spring found some fifty or more ghastly corpses dangling from limbs of trees surrounding the teepees of the remaining members of the band. Warm weather increased the number of deaths alarmingly. The deadly malaria arising from the sloughs in the vicinity carrying them off at the rate of seven or eight a day....

Violent confrontations flared between Indian bands and the North-West Mounted Police for the first time since the Mounties had arrived in the West.

In the spring of 1884 Cree Chief Big Bear sent runners to all the plains Indians, even his long-time enemies, the Blackfoot, inviting them to a thirst dance and council on the adjoining reserves of Poundmaker and Little Pine near Battleford.

Over two thousand Indians gathered—perhaps the largest assembly of plains chiefs in history. It was abruptly terminated. A showdown with the Mounted Police occurred which nearly escalated into a full-fledged war. If it had not been for the older chiefs, who managed to cool down younger warriors, Superintendent Leif Crozier and his force of thirty men might well have been massacred.

After his arrival at Batoche in July, Riel made contact with the various Indian bands. It was probably Dumont who organized this effort, sending emissaries to the various chiefs, mostly Cree but also Assiniboine and Blackfoot. In late July, Chief Beardy called a council of plains Indians beginning on July 31, 1884, to be held on his reserve at Duck Lake. Louis Riel was invited. He refused to take part in the actual meeting, but he met with twelve chiefs, including Big Bear and Poundmaker, days before the main gathering. Again he emphasized that a united front of all Northwest tribes was the only way to put real pressure on the government. The strategy of sending a petition to the dominion government, signed by the chiefs, was talked about for a long time. Significantly, Riel insisted that although he would gladly help in the technicalities of writing such a document, he would not advise the chiefs on what the petition should say. Riel understood that the Métis, while sympathetic to the Indians' plight, did not want to become involved in their actual struggle.

Three weeks later Riel met with Big Bear at the Prince Albert home of Eastwood Jackson. The two leaders had, of course, linked up four years before in Montana while the Cree were camping on the Milk River. Since then Big Bear had finally been forced into signing a treaty with the Canadian government, but he had refused so far to choose a reserve. He wanted to settle adjacent to Poundmaker and Little Pine near Prince Albert, but the government was alarmed at the thought of such powerful chiefs residing so close together and had refused Big Bear's request. After that he had steadfastly refused to pick another location. His tenacity and independence were much admired by other plains Indians, many of whom now believed that they had made a dreadful mistake in signing any treaty with Canada. Louis Riel liked and respected the old chief.

Eastwood Jackson was at the meeting between Riel and Big Bear and he later wrote that the two men talked about the Indian treaties and how the Canadian government had acted in such bad faith; it was necessary, both agreed, that Big Bear's people fight for better terms. According to Jackson, Big Bear pleaded with Riel that once the rights of Métis had been secured he would help the Indians. It's not known whether Louis agreed.

By the end of summer, it was obvious that the Riel family was not going to return to Montana in time for the school term. Louis was too embroiled in the movement and his main task, the formulation of the petition, had not been completed. Not only that, but he was obviously enjoying himself. At the end of July he had written his brother Joseph and brother-in-law Louis Lavallée an exuberant letter:

> Not long ago I was a humble schoolmaster on the distant banks of the Missouri and here I am today in the ranks of the most popular public men in Saskatchewan. Last year no one in the influential political circles of Manitoba wanted me, this year in the heart of the Northwest people are stirred by my words. The bankers invite me to their table. And their kindness, their handshaking, their gestures of approval! They applaud me with the rest of the crowd. The poor money-bags who regarded me in past years with an air of pity is worried at present. He opens his eyes in astonishment, he is alarmed, he is getting angry. What has brought all this about? Dear Joseph, dear brother-in-law, you know that it is God. I humble my soul to the ground....

The bankers and powerful people of Prince Albert might be in Louis's corner, but he discovered to his shock that the clergy were not.

Of the four missionary priests who worked in the St. Laurent area, Father Alexis André was by far the strongest character. A tough Breton, he had served with the Métis buffalo hunters at Pembina before coming to the Saskatchewan Valley in 1868. He had been instrumental, as adviser and promoter, in the formation of the St. Laurent community. A man of unrelenting energy and zeal, he was also something of a tyrant. He would brook no opposition—he had been known to slap parishioners who crossed him—and he certainly wasn't going to tolerate someone like Riel trespassing on his turf. André was deeply conservative in his politics, a fervid supporter of John A. Macdonald and his party. He was a close associate of Lawrence Clarke, the HBC boss at Fort Carlton, and a confidant of Edgar Dewdney, the Indian Commissioner and Lieutenant-Governor of the Northwest Territories from 1881 to 1888. It was André who had convinced the Métis, in the 1883 election of the Northwest Territorial Council, to vote for the establishment candidate against the Farmers' Union representative. There was strong suspicion that during the election Clarke had used HBC funds to bribe as many Métis as André could think of. Since André saw himself as part of the establishment, he had no difficulty in supplying the upper echelon with information. Letters are full of references to him—"L. Clarke Esq, a priest [André], and one or two Indians are reporting and have promised to report..." is typical.

Father André was blunt and impetuous in his speech, and he hardly knew what etiquette meant. He was as tough as the Métis buffalo hunters he preached at, but far more austere. A NWMP officer has left this description of him: "He always reminded me of those priests of the Greek Church who one sees hanging around wharfs of Galatia. He wore a lofty cap of beaver and a greasy cassock very much the worse for wear. In addition he sported an uncared for beard of iron grey."

He was not the kind of man Louis Riel would appreciate. Very quickly the two would grow to loathe each other, until eventually all-out warfare was declared. In a few months André would say of Riel: "He is a diabolical spirit."

The antagonism began on August 10, when Riel made a speech suggesting that the clergy were lacking in enthusiasm for the Métis cause. A week later, after mass at Prince Albert, Louis and Maxime Lépine had their first angry showdown with André. Riel accused the clergy of being too much in cahoots with the government. He tried to get across his idea that the Métis were a distinct people with a special mission, but André would have none of it. He retorted that Riel's ideas were utopian and unrealistic, and declared him "a veritable fanatic". Riel, in turn, called André "a coward" and "a man sold to the government".

Louis had probably been looking for an adviser in the spirit of Belcourt, Ritchot, Dugas and Bourget. He would not find that person among the Oblates of Saskatchewan.

Sir John A. Macdonald was receiving alarming bulletins about the possibility of common cause between Métis and Indians. With 26,000 Indians and 7,000 Métis in the Northwest, this was a terrifying idea. Macdonald decided to send his own personal emissaries to sniff out the situation. They were Judge Charles Rouleau, who could speak French, and Deputy Superintendent of Indians Lawrence Vankoughnet. The two men nosed about for a few days in late summer.

Both found that the rumours of a looming Half-breed and Indian revolt had been "greatly exaggerated", although they agreed there was reason for concern. In his letters to Prime Minister Macdonald, Judge Rouleau bluntly pointed out the reason for this:

> My own impression is this: unless the Govt come to the help and assistance of the Indians with food and clothing, there will be great misery and starvation among them during this winter. On almost all the reserve, the crops are a failure and in order to avoid perhaps some depredation on their part during the winter, I would humbly suggest that more supplies than usual should be bought.

Hayter Reed, Assistant Indian Commissioner and another powerful bureaucrat who weighed Rouleau's suggestions, expressed no such sympathy. He was a hardliner who believed the Indians' suffering was entirely their own doing. In Canadian history, there have been few senior bureaucrats as insensitive, dishonest or self-seeking as Hayter Reed. Even his bosses in Ottawa considered his recommendations outrageous and immoral, and yet he continued to have near-absolute control over the lives of the Natives.

Sir John A. Macdonald's response to the pleas for more food for the Indians, and for the resolution of Métis land claims, was to increase the police force in the Northwest by a hundred men.

Late in the summer the Conservative government let slip another opportunity to defuse the troubles in the Saskatchewan Valley. The Minister of Public Works, Sir Hector Langevin, was travelling throughout the Northwest and planned to visit the St. Laurent Settlement in August, as the governor-general, Lord Lansdowne, said, "to set Riel's head the right way." The Métis and others of the Saskatchewan Valley were glad of the opportunity to show the Cabinet minister around. A huge welcoming committee, a gala banquet and ceremony were planned; the minister would be presented with a list of grievances and Riel would give a speech outlining the idea of the Métis as a separate nation. But when he reached Regina, Langevin suddenly changed his plans. Perhaps he couldn't be bothered travelling the three hundred and fifty miles over dusty trails, or more likely some mysterious but important political manoeuvring was behind his change of heart. On August 19, he wired Judge Rouleau excusing himself. But either Rouleau didn't get the message or he didn't pass it on, for the Métis community knew nothing of the cancellation. For days they roamed the roads looking for him. When Langevin returned to Ottawa, after being wined and dined by the Conservative elite across the West, he reported that all was well. He had met only two disgruntled settlers during his entire trip.

Meanwhile, there were those who were growing impatient with Riel because they thought he was moving too slowly and too moderately. Where was the petition, they wanted to know. The farmers were desperate. Snow had arrived in early September, killing off almost the entire wheat crop; many had no idea how they were going to feed even themselves during the winter. They needed redress from the government. James Isbister touched a nerve that was growing ever more sensitive with Riel when he wrote, "we Protestants have learnt from very good authority lately, your Clergy are doing their utmost to break the existing unity between the French and English half-breeds."

In September, the Métis leaders got a chance to express their frustration at clergy reticence when Vital Grandin, the Bishop of St. Albert in Alberta, paid one of his periodic visits to the St. Laurent community. He arrived on September 1. There was a lot to do: the confirmation of some eighty children, visits to the sick and elderly, consultations with the local priest. He was about to bless the new bell at Batoche's St. Antoine de Padoue Church when a schoolteacher passed him a letter written by Riel outlining Métis grievances. The bishop then agreed to a public meeting to be held September 5 at the church.

Despite cold, rainy weather, a large number of people turned out; fortunately for the Métis leaders, André was not among them. Gabriel Dumont, who in preceding weeks seemed to have faded into the background, once more assumed a leader's role. He spoke first, simply but emotionally. He complained about the lack of support by the clergy, how they shunned the community's meetings and refused to discuss the issues. He recalled the formation of the St. Laurent community in 1873 and contrasted Father André's support then to his present lack of commitment. Dumont concluded on a conciliatory note—he and the others would listen with as much submissiveness as usual to what the priests had to say. Following him, Riel, Lépine and Nolin also spoke with "great excitement".

Bishop Grandin, who was much more of a politician than André, listened politely. After the Métis leaders had spoken, he told them that he and his clergy were being asked to endorse a movement about which they had little information. They had been kept in complete ignorance, he complained. Riel took this criticism to heart and immediately planned ways to rectify the situation. The entire Métis community felt better after the encounter with the mild-mannered bishop.

Travelling with Bishop Grandin was Amédée Forget, who was both clerk of the Northwest Territorial Council and Lieutenant-Governor Dewdney's secretary. He was in the St. Laurent area to collect information for his boss. While the bishop was busy performing his duties, Forget had a few days to wander about, talking to as many people as he could. At one point he let drop the bombshell that if the people wanted, Riel could probably be appointed to the Northwest Territorial Council. He'd be able to help the Métis in a concrete way, and there would be a $1,000 per annum salary. Then he added, perhaps he could even be made a senator. When Nolin and Lépine got word of this, they hurried to tell Riel. His reply was what they had expected: "Do you think I would dirty my name by accepting such an appointment?"

The day after the community meeting with Bishop Grandin, Amédée Forget went to visit Gabriel's Crossing, spending the night at Joseph Vandal's house. That evening Gabriel Dumont went to see him. "I'm glad your business has brought you around this way," he said. "It gives me an opportunity to make known our grievances. You are an officer of the government, but you are also our friend, and as such will, I'm sure, help us with the governor." Gabriel was emphatic about one thing: any attempt by the government or the police to arrest Riel would meet with strong resistance. "We need him here as our political leader," Dumont said, and then, in a reassertion of his own authority, added, "In other matters I am the chief here." Since there had been so much concern about the Métis fanning Indian discontent, he explained the relationship between the two people: "They are our relatives and when they are starving they come to us for relief, and we have to feed them. The government is not doing right by them." Dumont continued, "We want the Indians fed, our rights recognized and Mr. Riel as our leader, but," and he emphasized this, "we don't desire to create any disturbance." Gabriel then gave Forget a document explaining the grievances of the Métis and suggesting some solutions—Riel's answer to the bishop's complaint that he had no information about the agitation. It listed the usual grievances about land claims and lack of responsible government, but there was one portion of it that never appeared again in subsequent drafts, although it was one of the most interesting concepts Riel had developed. Basically it was an ingenious method of extinguishing Indian land title claimed by the Métis. Two million acres of land would be set aside for Half-breeds, both Protestant and Catholic. The government would sell these lands, put the money in the bank and use the interest to set up schools, orphanages and hospitals. For the poor, carts, seed and farm equipment would be purchased. It wasn't such an outlandish idea. The Homestead Act stipulated that in every township, two sections were to be earmarked as "school lands" and sold by auction at a time when the value of land had reached its peak. The proceeds would be placed in dominion securities and the interest paid to provincial governments to support public education. Riel's plan was merely a take on this, but everyone knew that the federal government would never be so generous towards Native people, so the proposal was dropped. In fact it would have provided a much brighter future for the Métis.

When he returned to Regina, Forget wrote a long report to Dewdney:

> The agitation is not, at present as noisy as in the beginning but none the less serious, I believe. It comprises nearly all the French and English Half-breeds and a number of unprincipled white settlers at Prince Albert. These latter are opponents politically of the present party in power and would delight in causing trouble that might embarrass the present Government.

Forget then put his finger on what was the thorniest problem:

> Another remarkable feature of this agitation, and perhaps the most alarming, considering the religious nature of the Half-breeds, is their loss of confidence in some of their old missionaries, such as Father André, Fourmond and [Julien] Moulin. These missionaries have long lived with them and always had their full confidence, but have lost it for not greeting Mr. Riel more cordially.

He concluded his report on a positive note: "Were free schools established in their various settlements and some aid in the form of farming implements and seed from grain to the more destitute, I believe it would stop all ill feeling against the Government." His recommendation, like so many others, was never acted on.

Forget also described Riel's comings and goings during the short time he was there. The Métis leader was certainly busy—Indian chiefs, English Half-breeds, farmers from Prince Albert had all trekked to Charles Nolin's house for sessions with Riel.

By October 1, a draft of the long-awaited petition to be sent to the dominion government was finally ready. There was something for everyone but, perhaps because the Indians were the most hard up, they were mentioned first: "the Indians are so reduced that the settlers in many localities are compelled to furnish them with food, partly to prevent them from dying at their door, partly to preserve the peace of the Territory." What was to be done about this was not stated. For the Métis there was the demand for land grants and patents for the land they had already settled on. For the white settlers, reduction of the tariff on machinery, and reform of the homestead regulations. For all residents, responsible government coupled with provincial status, vote by ballot and control of natural resources. And as an acknowledgement to Riel, there was a long section complaining of the treatment he had received during and after the Red River resistance.

This document was circulated to the committee of white settlers, Half-breeds and Métis. In a letter written to Will Jackson at the time, Riel nicely stated his philosophy of grass-roots democracy.

> Be careful. Do not argue too much in favor of it [the draft petition]. It would be good to take notice simply of the different opinions expressed about that petition or any of its clauses.... The committee members must be left free altogether. And if any of their views have to be changed or modified, no other way than friendly persuasion ought to be made use of to that end: and if they do not see as you do; if they do not wish to alter the ideas let it be so.

The petition would be discussed and haggled over throughout the various Saskatchewan Valley communities for a month and a half, yet, in the end, hardly a word was changed.

After Bishop Grandin's visit in September, Louis began keeping a diary-notebook of religious contemplations. Over the winter of 1884–85, he once again used his writing as a kind of catharsis. These were the contemplations of a deeply religious man, a long prayer-conversation with his God. He seemed to be letting loose some pent-up exuberance through a stream of consciousness.

My God! Be kind to Marguerite and me as well as to our children. As they grow and mature, watch over them for me, we beg you. Grant us, in union with our dear father and mother, brothers and sisters, nephews and nieces, uncles and aunts, cousins and close relatives, our benefactors and friends, the grace to think, pray, understand, comprehend, speak, write, act and serve You in everything, always and everywhere, according to Your Holy Spirit of truth, right, justice, accuracy, true propriety and prompt dispatch, so that we may do much good....

These writings are also laced with rather grandiloquent images of himself and others:

Oh my God! I beseech You in the name of Jesus Christ, be in me like the sap which gives the laurel its glory. Deck me with flowers as You embellish the prairie every spring. Please make me fruitful, even as You fructify the most fertile and the best cultivated gardens and fields. For the love of Christ, hear me.

Riel's personality is most vividly revealed in the sections he called "Prophetic Admonitions". This was the ascetic worrier forever lecturing himself, laying down rules and regulations to curb any animal urges he might have. He was evidently having ongoing health problems, though probably not serious ones.

You eat a third too much.

Do not be too sure of yourself.

You have medicines with you that you bought without getting proper advice. Don't use them very much. I warn you: if you continue to take them, you will be sick when you get where you are going.

Adopt a regimen. Regulate your life.

Eat blood cooked into a good broth. Take it clear. Be careful. Your stomach is weak. Do not eat heavily before you go to bed. Control your appetite when you eat. In the middle of the day, have a good meal of foods suited to your state of health. When you have breakfast, only eat about two-thirds as much as you would like.

Never go out without a hat, whether it's hot or cold.

I think bean soup is excellent for a person who is run down.

Ripe peas, well prepared, are good for a weakened constitution.

Corn is a dish that persons whose nervous systems have been disturbed should never forget to have on their table.

What his journals did not reveal during this period was any indication of the hot-blooded rebel. There was one hint of what was looming in the future, and that was a reference to the Métis as a separate people. "Saint John the Baptist, intercede unceasingly with Jesus and Mary for me and my chief friends, so that, being meek and humble of heart, we may inculcate in our Métis nation all the principles of goodness."

While Bishop Grandin was in Batoche, Riel had asked that a new religious society specifically for the Métis people be set up and that Saint Joseph be named the patron saint. This was supposedly an attempt to heal the widening fracture between priests and their parishioners, and so the bishop agreed. He could not have known, of course, that it would be used as an organization for revolution.

September 24 was set as the day to inaugurate the Union Métisse St. Joseph. Hundreds of people packed into the little St. Antoine de Padoue Church in Batoche. Father Julien Moulin insisted on giving the sermon even though he had been absent from the St. Laurent area for a month. A French Oblate missionary who had come to Canada in 1858 and had served in missions across the Northwest ever since, he was loved by his parishioners—they called him "Père Caribou"—because he had, as they said, "given his heart and purse to the Métis." He wasn't exactly a sophisticated man, however. His sermon that day tackled his favourite topic—temperance—but during it he kept talking about Saint Jean Baptiste rather than the newly appointed Saint Joseph. Those squirming in the pews realized that he had simply assumed that the patron saint of the French Canadians would be adopted by the Métis. Another priest finally whispered in his ear, and he corrected himself, but he had already pinched the nationalist pride of his parishioners.

To make matters worse, Father Jean-Vital Fourmond, the parish priest at St. Laurent village, also made a gauche exhibition of himself. Louis Schmidt described it thus: "The good P. Fourmond, who was quite a poet and musician in his day, wished to enhance the solemnity by composing himself a chant. But his enthusiasm was so great that he started singing his canticle so that only he could follow it, an octave too high and he muffled each verse."

These clerical *faux pas* were all the more embarrassing when compared to the eloquence of the speaker who concluded the ceremony. Riel was at his best that day—passionate, cogent, dramatic. He spoke for three-quarters of an hour, much of it on his main theme—as he said over and over, "We Métis have now been established as a nation." But he also stressed the obedience that Catholics owed their priests, especially such self-sacrificing missionaries as Fourmond and Moulin. He concluded with an expression of loyalty to the Pope, the bishops, the clergy and Her Majesty Queen Victoria.

Such sterling performances endeared him all the more to the people of the Saskatchewan Valley. As Father Fourmond himself put it, Riel was now thought of as "a Joshua, a prophet, even as a saint."

The formation of the Union Métisse St. Joseph did not bring the expected reconciliation between the clergy and the people; in fact the tension became greater. In November Father Fourmond, who seemed not to have an ounce of political savvy about him, sent his own petition to the federal government, without conferring with the Métis leaders. In it he asked for an annual subsidy of $1,000 to support a school run by the Faithful Companions of Jesus. Riel knew immediately what kind of embarrassment this would cause, since the debate over religious schools was raging at the time. Sure enough, the *Prince Albert Times* picked it up on November 28, denouncing the establishment of parochial schools in the Northwest, and blaming the whole thing on Riel. At that point, Riel and Jackson were trying to drum up support for their own petition with the English-speakers in the settlement, and Fourmond's action caused great damage. Riel apologized to the English, insisting he knew nothing about the petition, and Will Jackson wrote a letter to the *Times*. "Mr. Riel availed himself of the first opportunity afforded by a public gathering to oppose the petition.... He was supported by all the French half-breeds present with the effect that no further signatures were obtained and the petition is believed to have been abandoned." Fourmond was humiliated and Riel was furious. He was growing more impatient with Oblates by the day. That same month he ran into Father Valentin Végréville, pastor at St. Louis de Langeville Church, at Moïse Ouellette's house, and berated him for his lack of support for an hour. For the first time Louis revealed that he had a divine mission as revealed by God. That set alarm bells ringing. On December 5, Louis attended mass at Prince Albert, and afterwards had another violent argument with Father André.

Riel never wrote about his conflict with the Oblate fathers; only on very rare occasions did he say anything bad about anybody, least of all the clergy. Almost all the descriptions of his run-ins with André and the others come from their own records—Fourmond's *Petite Chronique de St. Laurent*, André's and Végréville's letters and other Oblate papers—and from Louis Schmidt, who eventually sided with the clergy against Riel. Most accounts were written after the North-West Rebellion, when the missionaries had lost the confidence of the Métis and were trying to justify their actions in the months preceding the agitation. For these reasons, their reports remain very suspect. The following is a particularly vivid example.

In December, the Oblate missionaries were holding their monthly retreat when, they claimed, Riel suddenly showed up. Again he began berating them for not showing enough enthusiasm or support for the Métis cause. Father André lost his temper and began ranting at Riel that, from now on, the Oblates would treat him as their enemy. Louis immediately burst into tears, fell to his knees and begged for forgiveness. He was then accompanied to the chapel by the priests, where he pledged never to lead an uprising against a civil government. Even after this pledge, the Oblates debated whether they should declare Riel a heretic and deny him the sacraments. They finally decided against this extreme action because, as Father Fourmond put it, his outbursts were a result of "the spiritual ordeals and misfortunes of his past, which were enough ... to put his unstable mind into a state akin to madness, where he was not really responsible for what he said."

This incident has been cited by many historians as the beginning of Riel's mental collapse, but there are many things wrong with this interpretation. No one else, including the white settlers and Half-breeds, thought Louis was the slightest bit mad. There is nothing to indicate insanity in his letters or journals at this point. As well, his subsequent actions did not signify that he was ever obsequious towards the St. Laurent clergy. And finally, what Father Fourmond did not admit was that if he and his colleagues had excommunicated Riel, their parishioners would have risen up in revolt. What the clerics were really upset about was that they had lost control; Riel was far more highly regarded by the Métis than they were.

The strong-willed André was particularly incensed and mortified by this. He wanted to get Riel out of the country and one way of doing so, he thought, was to bribe him. The priest arranged for the district's representative on the Territorial Council, David H. Macdowall, to meet with Louis. Macdowall owed André a debt because the priest had delivered up the important French vote in the last election, and this would be one way of repayment, as well as getting rid of a nuisance. On December 23, 1884, André and Macdowall travelled to St. Laurent and for four hours conferred with Riel.

When Louis had been first approached by the delegation from Saskatchewan, he made no bones about the fact that he had an outstanding debt he wanted to settle with the federal government. He felt that not only did he have a right to his land claim but he was owed other compensation: for the months he ran the provisional government in Manitoba; for his organization of the Métis against the Fenians; for recognition of his stepping aside for George-Étienne Cartier; for the humiliation and deprivation he had suffered while in exile; for his leadership of the Métis in the last few months in St. Laurent. He had told both Nolin and Lépine that he'd like to ask the government for money owing him—he thought about $10,000 or $15,000—but he wasn't sure how to go about it. When André said he could arrange such a payment, the Métis held a meeting to discuss it. As Napoléon Nault later recalled, "We talked at length about the figure to ask. Charles Nolin thought $100,000, but finally we agreed to settle for $35,000, the sum which was thought necessary to purchase a printing press and all the equipment to start a newspaper."

Macdowall's account of the meeting, sent to Lieutenant-Governor Dewdney, painted a portrait of Riel totally out of character. The politician insisted Louis had come to Canada for no other reason than to enrich himself.

> He [Riel] proceeded to state that if the Gov't. would consider his personal claims against them & pay him a certain amount in settlement of these claims, he would arrange to make his illiterate and unreasoning followers well satisfied with almost any settlement of their claims for land grants that the Gov't. might be willing to make and also that he would leave the N.W. never to return.... Riel made it most distinctly understood that "self" was his main object and that he was willing to make the claims of his followers totally subservient to his own interests.

Macdowall's letter continued in a sarcastic vein: "His claims amount to the modest sum of $100,000, but he will take $35,000 as originally offered.* I believe myself that $3,000 to $5,000 would cast the whole Riel family across the boundary." Riel certainly met with Macdowall and André, but it's highly unlikely that he would have asked for so high a sum as $100,000; it had already been decided that $35,000 would buy the Métis newspaper. More important, it would go against the character of the man, everything he had ever stood for, his fifteen years of working for the oppressed, to suggest that he would have sold the Métis out for "almost any settlement of their claims". It was a vicious, self-seeking and in all likelihood total distortion of Macdowall's meeting with the Métis leader that would have serious repercussions. Unfortunately, there is no account of Riel's version of the encounter.

The *Prince Albert Times* on November 21 had hinted at what André and Macdowall's plot was all about. Instead of voting for the establishment Tory, the

---

* *Riel always claimed that he was offered $35,000 by Sir John A. Macdonald in the fall of 1873 to leave the country. On several other occasions, he claimed, he was offered similar bribes, but always turned them down.*

newspaper worried, the French might elect someone "who would keep warm the place until M. Riel may have by an increased term of residence qualified for the position." Father André spelled out exactly their concerns in a letter to Edgar Dewdney: "I know that if Riel is satisfied, all the half-breeds will be united in the next election, and, as a man, they will vote for Mr. MacDowall, and we will carry everything before us; so I strongly recommend you to use all your influence at Ottawa to obtain for Riel that sum." André added, "Now you will ask if Riel is satisfied will the other half-breeds be satisfied. Really, I believe most of them will be, for their grievances are fanciful." André might well have asked himself why Riel was so much more popular than he was.

The whole question quickly became irrelevant because the prime minister stuck up his nose at the very idea of giving Riel any money. Macdonald, as Dumont's biographer George Woodcock perceives, had "suddenly developed scruples of an uncharacteristic delicacy about settling the problems of the Northwest by means of a cheap bribe; he probably knew Riel well enough to understand that the bribe would be rejected."

The whole unsavoury episode did irreparable damage. Sir John A. had always had a low opinion of the Métis. Now he purported to be so shocked at Riel's attempt "to extract money from the public purse" that he no longer had any sympathy for them whatsoever. This was unfortunate because it was exactly at this time that the Cabinet should have been dealing with the well-thought-out requests of the people living in the Northwest. The petition written by Riel and Will Jackson, which had been making the rounds for the last month and a half, had finally, on December 16, been sent off to the governor-general, with copies going to the government.

Jackson was delighted when just three weeks later there arrived a return note signed by the Under-Secretary of State acknowledging receipt of the petition. Surely this meant that at last Macdonald and his Tories were going to do something, he told Riel. Then the days began slipping by and nothing more was heard from the government. Like all their other entreaties to Macdonald and his Cabinet, the petition which had been written with such care and then circulated and thoroughly debated disappeared into thin air. If the citizens of St. Laurent had received the slightest sign of sympathy, a hint even, that their very legitimate grievances were being considered, the North-West Rebellion undoubtedly would never have happened.

– 17 –

Give me that gift
Not to anger them
Grant that I may show the way
Without upsetting them
Make them all be charmed
By the benevolence of my words.

January 1, 1885, must have been one of the most enjoyable days in Louis Riel's life. Two hundred residents of the St. Laurent community, from St. Louis de Langevin in the north to Tourond's Coulee in the south, gathered at Baptiste Boyer's house for a huge New Year's Day banquet in Riel's honour. Everyone, grandmothers, infants in arms, young girls, elderly men smoking pipes, attended. The fiddlers played all night and the dancing never stopped. The tables groaned under the weight of the feast dishes. Madeleine Dumont had arranged that a new dress be made for Madame Riel. Marguerite had developed a bad cough and had not been feeling well over the winter. The two children, Jean and Angélique, were thriving, though, and they were rambunctious with all the other kids. For Louis, the most wonderful part of the evening was when the letter from "the Inhabitants of St. Louis de Langevin" was read. It made very clear how much the Métis loved and honoured him.

> We do not want to let the opportunity of this New Year pass by without acknowledging the respect, gratitude, and affection we have for the one who we justly regard as the true father of the French populations inhabiting the vast territories of the Northwest.

> To us, you are, as in the Roman days, the valiant leader of this popu-
> lation that is strongly confident that, God willing, you will one day bring to
> victory our just claims.

This was followed by many toasts. It was the year, they all said, that great
honour and wealth would finally come to Louis Riel. He responded by saluting
all the Métis women in the room, and Queen Victoria.

Life was rather pleasant right then. There was still hope that the government
might respond to the petition. The war with the Oblate fathers had eased a little.
And the Riel family finances were not quite as tight; a cash subscription had
been raised for their immediate use. In November, the Riels had left the Nolin
home at St. Louis de Langevin and had moved into a cabin on Moïse Ouellette's
farm. For Riel it was a weaning away from the Manitoba émigrés and their
emphasis on caution, and a move, both physically and intellectually, towards the
Saskatchewan Métis dominated by the activist Dumont clan. William Jackson
took the opportunity to be near his hero and moved in with the Riels right away.

Métis undercover agents had discovered as early as September that Will was
being watched by the police and that his mail was being censored. Louis had
written to Eastwood Jackson, "If your brother finds himself unsafe, tell him that
the french Halfbreeds invite him to come and remain this way amongst us. And
if we are to be arrested, we will be together." Will finally accepted the invitation. He became mesmerized, not only by Louis, whom he worshipped, but by
the entire Métis culture. As the historian Donald B. Smith put it, "Perhaps he
romantically saw personified in the old Métis buffalo hunters, dressed in buckskin jackets, home-made cloth trousers, and moccasins, his heroes of antiquity.
Like the early Greeks and Romans, they were simple and direct, hospitable and
generous, brave in the hunt and in battle, men who felt not the slightest degree
of subserviency to anyone except to their prophet, Riel." But there was a more
concrete reason for Jackson's being enthralled by this culture—he had fallen
head over heels in love with the Ouellettes' sixteen-year-old daughter, Rose.

The long winter evenings were spent in discussions that often ended up in
heated debate. As attached as Will was to Louis Riel, he had a fundamental difference with the Métis leader. Jackson did not believe in private ownership of
land—all greed stemmed from this one evil, he thought. Riel, on the other hand,
based his concept of a Métis nation on the fact of their original proprietorship
of the Canadian soil. Still, Jackson remained close to Louis, becoming more and
more caught up in Riel's spirituality.

On January 28, 1885, the federal government finally got around to doing
something about Métis land claims. A three-man Halfbreed Land Claims
Commission was set up, but its only mandate was to compile a list of all those

living in the Northwest Territories who might be entitled to receive land grants. Those who had received scrip in Manitoba were to be excluded from any such largesse in the Northwest. A telegram announcing the commission was sent to the lieutenant-governor and he was shocked by it. It gave the Métis almost nothing they wanted. Of the 1,300 who believed they had a claim, only 200 fit into the purview of the commission. To make matters worse, there was not a word about the thorny question of river lots. Nor was there a mention of Riel's personal claim.* Dewdney thought it might very well incite the Métis to violence, and so he reworded the official version to vaguely read: "Government has decided to investigate claims of Half Breeds and with that view has already taken preliminary steps." This was passed on to the territorial representative, David Macdowall, who in turn gave it to Charles Nolin. Riel finally saw the Dewdney telegram on February 8. It was not until almost a month later that Dewdney showed Father André the original version from Ottawa.

The Dewdney version of the government's proposal caused much excitement. Another "investigation" was not what the Métis wanted, but at least it was a response to the petition. Riel himself felt that his job was all but done. In the second week of February, he made arrangements with Louis Marion to drive him and his family to Winnipeg in mid-March. He planned a visit to his family before he returned to his teaching job in Montana.

On February 17, a forty-hour prayer marathon took place at St. Laurent de Grandin Church, concluding with the unveiling of a special dedication, written by Riel, of the Métis nation to the Sacred Heart of Jesus. Some thought it was a little like a war cry. "Sacred Heart of Jesus! Give us the light! Instruct us! Protect us! Defend us! Strengthen us! Save us! with all those to whom we are united by blood."

On February 24, 1885, a community meeting was held at St. Antoine de Padoue Church at Batoche. The place, as usual, was packed. Ostensibly the subject was Dewdney's telegram but the talk quickly shifted to the real concern that night. Riel told the crowd that the work he had promised to do—draft the petition—was completed and they had an answer of sorts from the government.

---

* There are some historians, D.N. Sprague in particular, who believe that Macdonald was purposely provoking the Métis, so that they would rebel. Why? Because the Canadian Pacific Railway was precariously close to bankruptcy. If troops and supplies had suddenly to be rushed to the Northwest, he might be able to persuade the Canadian public to cough up yet more money for the railway. As far-fetched as this theory may sound, it is given credibility by documentation revealing Macdonald's thinking at the time.

Now, given his notoriety, he would be nothing but a hindrance to their movement. He had received reports that the NWMP were secretly conspiring to arrest him. He had always said he would return to the United States; now he planned to do just that. The entire church erupted with shouts of "No! No!" People jumped to their feet. One old Métis yelled, "If you leave, nephew, we will go with you!" A white settler from Prince Albert boomed out that Riel must stay in the country. Charles Nolin, according to his friends, "would have continued to clamour NO! forever if someone hadn't interrupted him." Even the priest, Fourmond, got in the mood and blessed Riel for his patriotism. When the racket had subsided, Riel asked quietly, "And the consequences?" Almost to a man, they answered, "We will suffer the consequences!"

On March 1, Riel addressed the congregation on the steps of the little St. Laurent de Grandin Church. According to the memoirs of Louis Schmidt, written after he had turned against his old friend, Riel upped the ante considerably. Peace and compromise had achieved nothing, he suggested; maybe it was time for the Métis "to bare their teeth". Then, according to Schmidt, he spoke quite irrationally, "For I have only to lift my finger and you will see a vast multitude of nations rushing here who are only awaiting the signal on my part."

The next day Riel, Napoléon Nault and Damase Carrière set off for Prince Albert. Twelve years before, Father André had assisted them in setting up a government in the newly formed St. Laurent district. Perhaps he could give them some advice, even his blessing, for some kind of provisional government. They obviously had no idea how much André loathed Riel, or they wouldn't have bothered. He hadn't stopped writing Lieutenant-Governor Dewdney pleading for bribe money to get Riel out of the country. His letter of February 8, 1885, was typical: "I am aware that his [Riel's] name has already caused you considerable annoyance, and that you would be glad to hear no more about this notorious character. I share your feeling in this regard...." Naturally, André was not going to sanction any government that Riel would lead. At first Louis was polite towards the priest. But once André, in his usual condescending and sarcastic manner, began belittling the idea, Louis became enraged. He abruptly turned on his heel and left. From that time on there would be open warfare between the two men.

On March 3, Riel, with Dumont and sixty other intimidating-looking Métis, attended a meeting at Halcro Village with white settlers and English-speaking Half-breeds. Riel said the reason his companions were armed was that he needed protection; the Mounties, he had heard, were about to arrest him. Although he did not talk of open rebellion, he railed against the government. That night many of the settlers decided to distance themselves from the Métis and their movement.

But William Jackson provided the most astonishing news of the evening. He announced he was resigning as secretary of the Farmers' Union to study and meditate, and "to look to the salvation of my soul".

On March 5, a secret meeting was held at Gabriel's Landing. Attending were Louis Riel and ten other Métis, including Gabriel Dumont, who was still very much in command of these people. Four others were members of the Dumont clan. A revolutionary oath written by Riel was taken and it was vintage Riel, a strange mixture of politics and religion:

> We, the undersigned, pledge ourselves deliberately and voluntarily to do everything we can to
>
> 1. save our souls by trying day and night to live a holy life everywhere and in all respects.
>
> 2. save our country from a wicked government by taking up arms *if necessary* (italics added).
>
> We particularly pledge ourselves to raise our families in a holy way and to ceaselessly practise the greatest trust in God, in Jesus, Mary, Joseph and Saint John the Baptist and in all our patron saints. For our banner we take the commandments of God and the Church and the inspiring cross of Jesus Christ our Lord.

There followed the mark X of ten men. Louis Riel's signature was not on the document, probably because he considered himself only an adviser. As George Woodcock points out, the coming together of this secret society indicated "the old Saskatchewan clans of hunters who had dominated the earlier council at St. Laurent were once again moving into the leadership."

There was a reason for the rising militancy in the early days of March. Bad news had been filtering into the St. Laurent settlement for weeks.

On February 20, the prime minister had finally made a decision about Louis Riel's own demands—the large sum André and Macdowall had said they would get him. Sir John A. was blunt: "We have no money to give Riel. He has a right to remain in Canada and if he conspires we must punish him. That's all." There was indignation throughout the entire Métis community.

On March 4, the full details of the government's telegram to Dewdney announcing the Halfbreed Claims Commission were, at last, released. For most in the community the idea of getting a few more acres of land in the vast Northwest vanished. The day after this announcement was made, March 5, the secret oath of Métis militants was taken.

But there was something even more serious to worry about. The summer before, in 1884, two hundred heads of households had submitted applications for patents to their river lots. All but forty-five land owners in the St. Laurent settlement area had finally caved in and made the boundaries of their land conform to the government's survey. Since they had done what was expected of them, they had assumed that, after years of pleading, they would finally get title to their land. However nine months had passed without a word. Finally in February the Prince Albert land office received its instructions. All but six had been allowed only the right to "enter" for their property. This meant they would have to perform further homestead duties—cultivate more land, remain on their properties for months at a time—and pay fees. If their farms were over the 160-acre limit, the maximum allowable under a "free grant", they would be charged $1 or $2 an acre, money most of them didn't have. Worse, they were required to go through the whole application process again, including inspection by a Dominion Lands Office agent. These bureaucrats were notoriously patronizing and often bigoted in their attitude towards Half-breeds and Indians. If they felt for any reason that an applicant was not living up to the Homestead Act—perhaps the fields were not ploughed neatly enough—they would recommend denial of the patent. And the officials in the land office in Prince Albert and in Ottawa's Department of the Interior were even worse tyrants. No wonder many Métis felt the chance of ever owning their land was slim indeed. Not only that, but about thirty families were still living on land the government had sold to the Prince Albert Colonization Company; that problem was simply ignored. The government could claim that it was acting within the rules and regulations set down by the Dominion Lands Act, but that meant nothing to these people. They were desperate. With the buffalo gone for good, and freighting jobs shrinking every year, their only chance for survival was on their land. To lose it would be to face an unspeakable future.

The Métis received the bad news from the land office on March 7. Once again they gathered at the little church in St. Laurent village in their usual large numbers. A correspondent for the Toronto *Mail* was mysteriously on hand to record the events. Riel announced that he believed it was time to form a provisional government, an action that had produced results fifteen years before at Red River. It was a good time to do so, he added, because England and Russia were about to go to war, and imperial troops would surely not be spared for Canada. As the reporter told it, "Nolin and Riel then moved that, as the Government had for fifteen years neglected to settle the half-breed claims, though it had repeatedly ... confessed their justice, the meeting should assume that the Government had abdicated its functions through such neglect; and should proceed to establish a provisional Government." A bill of rights was

introduced, probably written by Will Jackson. It contained many of the sentiments of the earlier petition, but set out in a much clearer, more straightforward
way.* The river-lot question was addressed in point number 2, "That patents be
issued to all half-breed and white settlers who have fairly earned the right of
possession on their farms." But there were several other new clauses—"the lawful customs and usages" of the Métis should be respected, and the region "be
administered for the benefit of the actual settler, and not for the advantage of
the alien speculator." It was far from being a revolutionary document, indeed it
was quite moderate, and Riel made it clear that if the government appointed a
commission with an adequate mandate to deal with the Métis land question, the
provisional government would be dissolved immediately.

Gabriel Dumont insisted that messengers be sent out to the various Indian
chiefs informing them of what had happened and asking for their support. Riel
realized it was going to be extremely risky to rely on their co-operation. There
were even Métis who had been utterly committed only a few days ago and now
were getting cold feet—Riel's cousin, for example.

Charles Nolin faced a terrible dilemma. His wife, Rosalie, the sister of
Maxime and Ambroise Lépine, had for the last ten years suffered a disabling illness which left her limbs weak and withered. Nolin was an extremely devout
man and one day he was reading a book about Our Lady of Lourdes when a
revelation suddenly came to him that the saint would do something for his wife.
He discovered that the nuns of St. Laurent had some waters from the river
which flows into the French town of Lourdes and were willing to give him a
sample. Rosalie was advised to begin a novena with a promise to donate a gift,
perhaps a statue of the Virgin, at the end. On December 18, 1884, relatives and
neighbours gathered at the Nolin house for what turned out to be a most curious ceremony. They sang the Hymn of our Lady of Victories, chanted the litanies of Lorette and recited the rosary. The youngest member of the family then
patted the holy water from Lourdes onto Rosalie's body. Wherever the child's
hands touched, she felt a burning sensation. Then she cried out—the weakness
in her legs and arms had disappeared. She was totally recovered. (In fact, she
would enjoy another forty-two years of robust health.)

For the people of St. Laurent, the recovery of Rosalie Nolin was indeed a miracle. Father André took every advantage of it; he wrested a promise from Charles
Nolin that, in thankfulness to the Virgin, he would not engage in any civil disobe-
dience. Until that time Nolin had been devoted to the Métis cause; in January
he had been asked by Riel and Dumont to withdraw his tender to construct the

---

* *For the full Bill of Rights, see Addendum Two, page 452.*

telegraph line between Edmonton and Duck Lake to vividly indicate his dissatisfaction with the government. It would have been a very lucrative job, but he said he would do it if Riel agreed to stay in the area and run for the House of Commons.

On March 5, after the oath was taken by the Métis militants, the group rode over to Nolin's house at St. Louis de Langevin, and asked him to join them. All Nolin could think of was the promise he had made to André; he must not renege, his wife's health was too important. Scrambling for time, he came up with the idea of a novena—nine days of public prayer and confession—in which, he hoped, the entire St. Laurent community would rethink their irrational scheme of an armed uprising. It was to begin March 10 and conclude on March 19, which was also the feast day for Saint Joseph, the newly acquired patron saint of the Métis.

On the first day of services Father Fourmond, who said mass, and Father Végréville, who had travelled from his own parish at St. Louis de Langevin to assist, were very pleased with the large turnout. Over the next few days, they did not hesitate to use the special services to preach obedience to the civil authorities—and to themselves. Never did they mention or sympathize with those Métis who were worrying about whether in the future they would have a piece of land to call their own.

Riel did not show up until March 15, and on that day the entire militant society were with him. Indeed, St. Laurent de Grandin Church was packed. The usually mild-mannered Father Fourmond rather foolishly took advantage of this to press his views on armed revolt. He ended his sermon on a threatening note; he would refuse the sacraments to anyone who participated in such a thing. The worshippers crowded into the pews were stunned. Riel rose in his place and denounced the priest. "You have turned the pulpit of truth into one of politics, falsehood and discord. How dare you refuse the sacrament to those who would take up arms in defence of their most sacred rights!" Fourmond must have sensed that the congregation sided with Louis, not with him, for he said not another word.

Riel's diaries reveal that he had indeed decided on revolution, albeit not a bloody one:

> Lord our God, through Jesus, Mary, Joseph and Saint John the Baptist, allow us, in this month of March in the year eighteen eighty-five, to take the same position as we did in '69; and to maintain it most gloriously for Your sovereign domain, most honourably for religion, most favourably for the salvation of souls, advantageously for society, and most suitably to procure in this world and the next the greatest sum of happiness for all those who

will help us directly and even indirectly. Change our clergy, as well as Charles Nolin and William Boyer [a Métis merchant living at Batoche and a close friend of Nolin's]. Transform all of us together.

Throughout this period, the North-West Mounted Police had a pretty good idea of what was going on from the information supplied by their undercover agents, who were everywhere. Actually Major Crozier, stationed in Prince Albert, had been rather sympathetic to the plight of the Métis and had warned his superiors there could be violence if nothing was done about their land claims.

On March 11 Crozier reported to NWMP headquarters in Regina that "a great deal of excitement had prevailed amongst the Half-breeds for some days past. The leaders are continuously travelling about amongst their men and these are getting arms ready for use." They refused to carry freight or do other jobs for the Mounties, and he had heard that they were planning to attack Fort Carlton. Without waiting for orders from higher-ups, he had decided to leave for the Hudson's Bay post immediately with a troop of fifty.

Lieutenant-Governor Dewdney received a copy of Crozier's letter and sent it on to Ottawa with a condescending sneer: "If the half-breeds mean business the sooner they are put down the better. They are like Indians, when they gather and get excited, it is difficult to handle them, but if they are taken unawares there is little difficulty in arresting the leaders." Dewdney obviously did not know Riel or Dumont well.

On March 13, Crozier and his men arrived at Fort Carlton. He immediately telegraphed Dewdney, "Halfbreed rebellion likely to break out any moment. Must be prepared for consequences. Troop must be largely reinforced. French Half-breeds alone in this section number seven hundred men. If Half-breeds rise Indians will join them."

The commander of the NWMP, Colonel Acheson Gosford Irvine, was ordered to lead a force of one hundred men from Regina to Prince Albert "as soon as possible". They set out on March 18. There was no thought of proposing negotiations with the disaffected Métis.

On March 17, Michel Dumas, Napoléon Nault and others happened to run into Lawrence Clarke, the chief factor at Fort Carlton, who had been in Winnipeg doing business. They asked him if he had heard anything, was the government doing anything about their land claims? In his usual "domineering and authoritative manner" he jeered, "the only answer you will get will be bullets." He then claimed that on his way northward he had passed a camp of five hundred policemen who were preparing to capture the Half-breed agitators.

They especially wanted Riel.* This was incredible news and it quickly spread throughout the French communities. Father Fourmond was told that the police were coming "to exterminate the Métis, women and children." What nobody knew at the time was that five days before, after first conferring with Father André, Lawrence Clarke had met in Regina with Police Commissioner Irvine, Indian Commissioner Hayter Reed and Stipendiary Magistrate Hugh Richardson (who would later preside over Riel's trial for treason). Clarke's advice was that "Mr. Riel and his band of discontents should not be allowed to keep up sense-less agitation, destroying the faith in the country and ruining its peaceable inhabitants." On March 17, Dewdney sent Clarke a telegram, "Put in PA Times that an additional force is being sent.... Get paper to enlarge and state that gov-ernment intend to have peace in the district." So all Clarke was doing was carry-ing out the government's propaganda plan. What he accomplished was to jump-start the North-West Rebellion.

In the evening of March 17, Riel had been visiting families living around the Tourond's Coulee area, and he spent the night at Joseph Vandal's house. He left early in the morning and before noon arrived at the home of Baptiste Rocheleau. Soon a doctor from Saskatoon, John Willoughby, and a Half-breed trader, Norbert Welsh, knocked at the door. Since all had met before, they exchanged pleasantries. Suddenly about seventy Métis, most armed, rode up. "Can you imagine my feelings?" Willoughby would later testify. "I had no revolver and decided to let them take me quietly." Riel faced him and said, "The time has come, doctor, when it was better for a man to have been good." Willoughby had no idea what he was talking about, but Louis went on to explain. Because of Clarke's warning, the revolution would begin before the novena ended. "He and his people were going to strike a blow to get posses-sion of the country, which had been stolen from them and misruled by the Canadian Government.... He said, 'I and my people have time and time again petitioned the Government to redress our grievances, the only answer we received each time was an increase of the police.'" Over dinner, Riel told the doctor all about his plans. There was to be a new God-fearing nation where parliamentarians wouldn't spend all their time smoking cigars and lounging about reading rooms. It would be free of Orangeism. It was to be divided into regions, one each for Bavarians, Hungarians, Poles, Italians, Germans and Irish

---

* There are several versions of this encounter, supposedly by eyewitnesses. Dumont's rendition has Clarke claiming that only seventy police were on the way. However, he wasn't there and may have been inaccurate. The above is an amalgam of several reports.

plus Métis and Indians. According to Willoughby, Riel then told him what he had been planning ever since he had left Montana; it sounded a lot like the Indian–Métis republic he had been dreaming about for years. "He said the time had now come when those plans were mature, that his proclamation was at Pembina, and that as soon as he struck the first blow here, that proclamation would go forth and he was to be joined by half-breeds and Indians and that the United States was at his back."

Riel and the others left right after dinner and Dr. Willoughby made a dash for Clarke's Crossing, about forty miles away, to send a telegram to the police in Regina. He was too late. The wires had already been cut.

Riel's party headed north towards Batoche. As they approached the village they ran into Gabriel Dumont. He had just taken two prisoners, John Lash, the Indian agent for the Carlton district, returning from Chief One Arrow's reserve, and his interpreter, William Tompkins. Lash later testified that Riel went up to him and told him he was going to detain him. The rebellion had begun and they were going to fight until the entire Saskatchewan Valley was in their hands, he said. The two men were imprisoned in the Church of St. Antoine de Padoue at Batoche.

Riel and the others then moved on to the Kerr brothers' store on the south side of Batoche. They walked in and demanded all guns and ammunition. "I told them," remembered George Kerr, "that they were up on the shelf, that the store was with cross beams and the guns were on the cross beams. I told him to take them." Riel responded, "Give my men what they want and charge it." A keg of powder, a box of Ballard rifle cartridges and six double-barrelled shotguns were quickly hauled out of the store. The Métis then left. Sometime later, the Kerrs went to tend their cattle, a distance of three miles. On the way back they came across a parade of Métis and Indian women with packs on their backs. George yelled to his brother, "Hey, isn't that frying pan ours?" When they got to the store it "was upside down". The only thing left was the Fairbanks scales, and even those had been tipped over.

When Riel arrived at the Batoche church, a huge crowd was waiting for him. According to Father Moulin's memoirs, Riel asked if he could hold the meeting inside, but the priest refused. Louis, by this time, had lost his patience with the vacillating Moulin, and he shouted, "Look at him, he is a Protestant!" Then, turning to his followers, he said, "Rome has fallen." When Moulin, an elderly, small-boned man, still refused to let them in his church, Louis ordered, "Take him away! Take him away!" Once inside, the community made plans to establish their own authority.

Gabriel Dumont recalled:

I told the crowd the latest news: "The police are coming to take Riel." I also asked the people, "what are you going to do? Here is a man who has done so much for us. Are we going to let him slide through our hands? Let us make a plan."

Then Riel spoke. "We send petitions, they send police to take us— Gabriel and me. But I know very well how this works. It is I who have done wrong. The government hates me because I have already made them give in once. This time they will give up nothing. I also think it would be better for me to go now. I must leave you and I feel I should go now. Once I am gone you may be able to get what you want more easily. Yes—I really think that it would be better if I went back to Montana."

The whole crowd interrupted and told him, "No, we won't let you go. You have worked hard for our rights and you can't quit now."

Dumont then asked the crowd: "All in favour of taking up arms raise your hands." Instead of raising only one hand, the whole crowd rose as one. There were cries of joy and they yelled, "If we are to die for our country, we will die together."

Later Dumont didn't hesitate to place the blame for igniting the rebellion on Lawrence Clarke. "It was Clarke who put fire to the powder by reporting the news. The news was false. It was invented to scare off the organizers of the meeting."* But it was done. The rebellion had indeed begun.

By now it was six o'clock and quickly growing dark. A contingent of armed Métis crossed the Saskatchewan to the west side, where the Walters & Baker store was located. Riel said, "Well, Mr. Walters, it has commenced," and asked him for all the arms and ammunition in the store. The shopkeeper retorted, "Well, you can't have them." The Métis merely shoved him aside and gathered up all they found. They then arrested Walters and detained him in the second floor of his store. Later that night the other prisoners joined him there; Riel thought they would be more comfortable in his building than at the church.

---

* *There has been much speculation about Lawrence Clarke's true role in the North-West Rebellion. Not only was he the HBC factor, he was a significant land speculator, who like many of his friends in Prince Albert had lost a lot of money when the railway moved south. So desperate was this business elite in those hard times that some historians speculate that Clarke, knowing what a huge infusion of cash would result from hundreds of soldiers suddenly arriving in the district, purposely goaded the Métis to rebellion. Subsequent acts of his give credence to this theory.*

The Métis army continued to secure the Batoche area. At ten p.m. they arrested a Métis, Louis Marion, the very man who was supposed to have driven Riel and his family to Winnipeg. He had refused to join the movement. Riel said to him, "Unhappy man, think of your soul and not of earthly things." Marion still objected, so he joined the white prisoners huddled in the Walters & Baker's second floor.

At four a.m. in the pale moonlight, a Métis patrol came across Peter Tompkins and John McKean near Duck Lake fixing the telegraph lines. The party crowded upstairs at Walters & Baker grew even larger.

The first day of the revolution had certainly proved a busy one.

Early the next morning, in a slushy snowfall, people began gathering at Batoche. The men arrived with Winchester repeating rifles, pistols and even old trading muskets. This was the end of the novena, the feast of Saint Joseph, and it was the day that William Henry Jackson was to be converted to Catholicism.

It had not been easy for Will. His Methodist family were horrified when they discovered his intention. His brother, Eastwood, had written Louis two weeks before and then showed up at Ouellette's house in St. Laurent, pleading that Will be sent home to his father. "He must be quiet or his mind will give way," he wrote. He reminded Riel that the Jackson family had made very real personal sacrifices for the cause, and said now they believed that the revolutionary route Riel was taking would "kill the movement amongst Canadians and English." This would prove a deadly accurate analysis. Will elected to stay with the Métis, whom he had grown to admire, and to convert to their religion. Later he would write his family, "I am confident that God has at last led me to a place where he wishes me to work."

Having just gone through the intense conversion process, Jackson was horrified when, the day before he was to be baptized, Riel came to him and told him he planned to break with Rome. Louis intended to establish his own corruption-free church, with Bishop Bourget of Montreal as pope and Riel as "Prophet in the New World". This would not have been an astonishing idea to someone who had known of Riel's previous reflections on the church, but to Jackson it was a thunderbolt. He understood the significance of this at once: "There was no middle course. If he spoke the truth then I must accept him in place of the priest—lose my soul even as Jesus of old, on the other hand if he were an impostor or deluded fanatic, then to accept was damnation, for he would be anti-Christ." Will decided to say nothing for the time being, but it caused him great mental anguish.

The baptism went ahead,* the Métis fired their guns into the air in salute and Will frenchified his name, calling himself thereafter Honoré Joseph Jaxon.

Much to Father Moulin's dismay, St. Antoine de Padoue had been turned into a kind of tactical control centre. Peter Tompkins, the man who had been fixing the telegraph wires before he was taken prisoner, was at the church on March 19 and described it as "a council room, barracks, prison and restaurant, all together." It was here that most of the meetings of the militants would be held, including the important one that day to establish a provisional government.

Although he never officially became part of it, Riel called this government the Exovedate, from the Latin "ex", out of, and "ovile", fold. Louis explained it this way: "I prefer to be called one of the flock; I am no more than you are. I am simply one of the flock." The majority of the flock, however, had a hard time getting their tongues around his Latin mixture. Most times they called the government simply *le petit provisoire*, to distinguish it from the Red River provisional government.

It wasn't exactly a democratically elected body, but then these were times of emergency. Riel nominated Gabriel Dumont as the "Adjutant General ... at the head of the army", which was ratified by thunderous applause. Dumont then selected his councillors. In keeping with the buffalo-hunt tradition, a senior statesman, Pierre Parenteau, was named president; the others included Dumont's two brothers-in-law, Moïse Ouellette and Baptiste Parenteau, as well as his close friends Maxime Lépine and Damase Carrière. In all, twenty men—they were called Exovede by Riel—would serve on the council, seventeen Métis, two French Canadians and one Indian, the Sioux chief White Cap. Elections may not have been held for officers, but the decision-making was certainly democratic, perhaps too much so. The Exovedate gnawed over everything, from whether Riel should become the official prophet to what kind of hats, if any, the soldiers should wear.

One person had been named *in absentia* to the Exovedate—Charles Nolin had been selected commissar, a job he definitely did not want. Since the early fall, the Catholic clergy had been looking for a prominent Métis around whom those loyal to the church might gather. Charles Nolin seemed to fit the bill; he had prestige in the community—after all, he had once been a Cabinet minister

---

* *There is confusion as to the date of Jackson's baptism. The plan was always to celebrate it on the feast of Saint Joseph, March 19, and Riel was supposed to have told the Métis men to bring guns for the salute afterwards. Yet some documents, including a letter from Jackson himself, say he was baptized the night before. It was written months after the event so he may simply have made a mistake.*

in Manitoba—and was pious and, most important, pliable. Father André had had little difficulty in persuading Nolin, after his wife's miraculous cure, to pledge that he would not join Riel's rebellion. Nolin had always been more talk than action anyway; in fact he was terrified at the very idea of an armed revolution. On March 15, he met with the Oblate missionaries and agreed to try to split the Métis community, and he persuaded the Half-breed trader William Boyer to help him. (He had tried something very similar at Red River, fifteen years before.) But early on March 19, he was arrested on his doorstep by four of Dumont's men. Whether he sided with the clergy was of no concern to the Métis, but it was suspected that he was feeding information to the police.

Nolin and William Boyer joined the others who had spent the night at the Walters & Baker store under guard. At ten that night Nolin, Boyer and Louis Marion were tried for treason—the first official act of the Exovedate. The trial was brief. Riel gave an impassioned speech pointing out the many ways his cousin Charles was a traitor. There are several versions of what happened after that. When Nolin was giving evidence against Riel and saving his own neck in the process, he testified that he had defended himself by "proving" that the Métis leader had made use of the movement to enrich himself. Nolin said that he was acquitted by the council but that Riel vigorously protested the decision. Nolin then realized that to save his life he would have to agree to join the provisional government. A more likely rendition of this event has Riel talking privately with Nolin until an understanding was reached. The two men then walked arm in arm into the Exovedate headquarters. Riel cried, "Here we have the big wheel in the movement with us again." Replied Nolin, "I am in the movement now, body, heart and soul. Before I was with you only in body."

Whatever version is correct, the whole thing seems to have been a farce, staged to put the fear of God into Nolin and any others who might have similar subversive ideas.

Indeed, the episode can be seen as a metaphor for the entire rebellion to this point. It's obvious from statements made by men like Philippe Garnot and Maxime Lépine that most of the Métis, especially Riel, never thought they would actually take up arms against Canada; they were trying to catch Ottawa's ear in an attempt to intimidate Macdonald's do-nothing government into giving them serious consideration. But such games sometimes take on a life of their own; this one was already ricocheting towards disaster.

The Exovedate also discussed military strategy that day. There were two very distinct points of view. The majority, mostly the old buffalo hunters, wanted to round up a huge force of Indians and strike at once, before the NWMP reinforcements could arrive. Fort Carlton would be captured first, then

Prince Albert and Battleford. From that position of strength, negotiations with the Canadian government would begin.

Riel was strongly opposed. If he could help it, no blood would be shed. Not only that, but from his previous experience in Montana he didn't trust the Indians' dedication to his plan; they had very few guns and were in a weakened position. Riel's strategy was more complicated: he wanted the Métis to arm themselves, but to fight only if they were attacked. He did agree, however, that the weapons and rations stored in the Hudson's Bay Company depot should be confiscated, just as Fort Garry had been taken during the Red River resistance. Riel knew Dumont would need supplies for his armed force, whether they were going to fight or not.

Ever since the Hudson's Bay Company had built it in the 1790s, Fort Carlton had dominated the Saskatchewan Valley. Located on the south side of the North Saskatchewan, about twenty miles northwest of the St. Laurent settlement, it had been a busy commercial centre where the Indians and Métis had traded the products of the buffalo hunt and the fur trap for goods from eastern Canada and Europe. As well as the main fort, there were a few outbuildings, including a large storehouse which the North-West Mounted Police had made into a make-shift barracks. Despite its importance as a trading centre, it was isolated, on the fringes of the parkland forest, thirty miles from the nearest large settlement of Prince Albert. On the south, steep wooded hills shot up three hundred feet; on the east lay low sand hills. The only trail north was a steep, rutted cart track. It was not exactly impregnable from a defence point of view—twenty sharpshooters could pin a force of hundreds inside. The Exovedate members could see that Riel's strategy was manageable and the following compromise was recorded in the minutes of the meeting. It was a call to supporters:

> Moved by Boucher, seconded by Carrière, that we desire to effect the capture of the fort without spilling any blood, and the greater our force the more certain of attaining our object, but in the case we are compelled to fight, justice compels that we should take up arms, and do you join us. We have ammunition.

Superintendent Leif Crozier had arrived at Fort Carlton on March 3 with a force of fifty Mounties. He knew that Colonel Irvine was on his way from Regina with a hundred more police, but he decided to raise a militia force of fifty volunteers in Prince Albert to add to his manpower at the fort, at least until the reinforcements arrived. Among these recruits was a Scottish Half-breed lawyer, Thomas McKay, whom one writer described as a "strong character, with unusual ability and resourcefulness and quite fearless." He was also a police informer and Lawrence Clarke's brother-in-law. McKay talked Crozier into allowing him and the Prince Albert merchant Hillyard Mitchell to travel to Batoche to confer with Riel. On March 21 the two set out, and by afternoon they reached the Walters & Baker store, where they were stopped by sentries. They were then conducted to Norbert Delorme's small house, not far from the church where the Exovedate was in council. Riel shook the hands of the two men and invited them to sit as he and the others were just finishing their noon meal. McKay said,* "There appears to be a great deal of excitement here, Mr. Riel." Louis responded, "There is no excitement at all, it was simply that the people were trying to redress their grievances ... and they had decided to make a demonstration." The two men quickly got into a heated argument, Riel charging McKay with having done nothing for the Half-breeds, and McKay accusing Riel of using the movement for his own ends. McKay was waving his arms about and he knocked over a cup that contained bull's blood, which Louis habitually took as a medication, and it spilled onto the plates. Later McKay would tell reporters that he had seen blood splashed all over Riel's dishes. Stories of savage rites introduced by Riel and practised by his followers appeared in newspapers all through eastern Canada.

Riel became so infuriated with the Half-breed that he decided to indict him for sedition and try him on the spot. The dishes and cups were taken from the corner of the table, Philippe Garnot took notes on a rough piece of paper, and Gabriel Dumont, sitting on a wine keg, was the judge. Riel acted as prosecutor and called witnesses who testified to McKay's earlier obnoxious behaviour, in particular to his declaration that nobody else in the settlement was in favour of the Métis militancy. Riel was called away on business. McKay continued to defend himself until somebody offered him something to eat. That tired him out and he fell asleep in the corner of the room, at which point the trial seems to have been completely forgotten. When Riel returned he was his normal polite self, and said that he meant nothing personal. When McKay suggested that the Métis leader go to Fort Carlton to talk with Crozier, Riel replied, no, he would surely be arrested. He did, however, agree to send two emissaries, Charles Nolin and Maxime Lépine.

---

* *McKay gave the version of events usually used by historians while he was giving evidence against Riel at his trial. Much of it is so far-fetched as to be unbelievable. Riel was supposed to have shouted at him: "You don't know what we are after—it is blood, blood, we want blood; it is a war of extermination, everybody that is against us is to be driven out of the country." This is entirely out of keeping with Riel's usual behaviour.*

McKay returned to Fort Carlton and with Captain Henry Moore prepared to meet with the two Métis that evening. Nothing is known about this conference except what was revealed in a letter sent by Will Jackson to a Métis sympathizer. "Since their visit to us on Saturday Capt Moore and Mr McKay have greatly endangered the situation and the lives of the hostages held by us by threatening to attack us in the midst of our efforts to prevent bloodshed. Please, inform our friends of the increasing danger incurred by such a course of action...."

The same day Riel wrote the police major a letter that demanded nothing less than total surrender:

> ...You will be required to give up completely the situation which the Canadian Government have placed you in, at Carlton and Battleford, together with all government properties.
>
> In case of acceptance, you and your men will be set free, on your parole of honor to keep the peace. And those who will choose to leave the country will be furnished with teams and provisions to reach Qu'Appelle.
>
> In case of non-acceptance, we intend to attack you, when tomorrow, the Lord's Day, is over, and to commence without delay a war of extermination upon all those who have shown themselves hostile to our rights.

It was signed by all the members of the Exovedate, including "Louis 'David' Riel, Exovede".

To surrender was not in Crozier's nature. He didn't respond to Riel's infuriating letter; he decided to simply sit and wait for his superior officer, Colonel Irvine, to show up with his hundred-man force. Riel didn't attack on the following Monday; he had never intended to, no matter what his letter said. Nor did he order his men dispersed. Twenty miles apart, both sides anxiously waited— who would make the next move?

– 18 –

I have seen the giant; he is coming, he is hideous.
It is Goliath.

It was cold for the end of March; a thick crust of brownish snow still covered the ground. The sun hadn't come out in days, which may have contributed to the gloom and impatience both the Métis and the Mounted Police felt as their nervous waiting continued. Finally Gabriel Dumont couldn't stand it any longer. It was obvious to him that the police were using the village of Duck Lake as a base for spying on the Métis population. He said to Riel, "We have taken up arms and we just sit here. If we wanted to move now we could catch them by surprise."

"But," said Riel, "it won't be easy. They won't just let us get away with it."

"Give me ten men and put me in charge," replied Dumont. He planned to establish a military base at Duck Lake and intercept the police as they crossed the frozen expanse.

The village of Duck Lake was situated between Batoche and Fort Carlton, just east of Chief Beardy's reserve. It was a mixed community of white and Métis farmers with the Stobart, Eden and Company general store, run by Hillyard Mitchell, forming the hub. When Dumont arrived there, he immediately went to the store but found it locked. He was about to smash in the door when a local farmer came scurrying over with a key. The Métis were disappointed to discover that all the guns had disappeared; the only thing found was some lead shot in the latrine ditch.

Meanwhile, Riel and another contingent of armed men had arrived, and, together with Dumont, they went to Beardy's reserve to give the horses and themselves a rest. As night fell, Dumont ordered two scouts, Baptiste Arcand

and Baptiste Ouellette, to watch the road. They soon returned. They had seen two men who they were certain were police. Dumont and several others took after them, and in the bright light of the moon were soon able to spot them.

"Stop!" Dumont commanded. "If you try to escape I will kill you."

"Why?" asked the rider. "I am a surveyor."

"What are you trying to tell me?" Dumont asked. "There is nothing to survey out here at this time of night." The two men were taken prisoner and detained in Mitchell's store, which soon became the holding place in Duck Lake for all the Métis hostages. (Dumont persisted in his belief that the prisoners were Mounties. In fact one was the surveyor J.W. Astley, and the other, Harold Ross, was deputy sheriff of Prince Albert. Nevertheless, they were spying on behalf of the police.)

Dumont and his men stayed up all night watching the Carlton Trail. When morning finally arrived, they decided that Crozier was unlikely to send his men out in broad daylight, so they went back to Duck Lake to sleep. They had hardly unbridled their horses when another alarm was sounded, "More police!" The major had sent a contingent of fifteen Mounties and seven militia to secure Mitchell's supplies. Tom McKay was with them.

Dumont and his men quickly saddled up again, and soon spotted three police scouts who quickly took off towards the main body of Mounties and volunteers. When they caught up to them, the Métis quickly slid off their horses and the police contingent did the same. There was a lot of belligerent yelling—"If you don't stop I'll kill you." "I'll kill you first!" "Look out: it will be the end for you!" etc.

The free-for-all continued. Dumont swung his gun at McKay but only hit the buttocks of his horse. A policeman in a sleigh aimed his gun at Gabriel but didn't fire. Somebody pushed Edouard Dumont into the snow. Finally the man in charge, Sergeant Alfred Stewart, wisely ordered all the police sleighs turned around. Quickly the Mounties took off in the direction of Fort Carlton. Dumont shouted at Tom McKay, "You watch out. This is all your fault, all of it. You brought the police and whatever happens will be your responsibility. Don't you realize there are Canadian Métis fighting to the death with us?"

Gabriel later said that he was proud he had listened to Riel and had not attacked without the police firing first.

Meanwhile, Riel was not present at the confrontation between Dumont and the police group, but scribbling away in his diary:

> The Spirit of God informed me that a battle had taken place about two miles this side of Duck Lake. This was not told to me in words, but was communicated to my spirit in a more tangible way than is usually the case with a simple

thought. I am convinced that an event of this kind has occurred, for it was revealed to me that the Crees had rendered us a great service there. The divine communication ended more precisely, saying: you will give Tchekikam [a Duck Lake Indian known as Boss Bull] whatever he asks of you.

By the time the police contingent arrived back at Fort Carlton, Major Crozier already knew about their run-in with the Métis—after watching the brawl, a scout had swiftly reported. The major found himself in a dilemma. He knew that he should wait for his superior officer, Colonel Irvine, and his detachment of a hundred men. They were scheduled to arrive later that day, in fact. On the other hand, he had all those Prince Albert volunteers goading him to do something. If he didn't act quickly, they said, the Indians and Métis in other areas would rise up in mass revolt. Lawrence Clarke was there and he went so far as to say that Crozier was a "bloody coward". "Are we to be turned back by a parcel of half-breeds? Now is the time, Crozier, to show if you have any sand in you." Certainly the major agreed that the "Force had been insulted", and he was not a patient man when either his honour or that of his beloved North-West Mounted Police was being sullied. He gave a command; the "fall-in" was sounded. Not only were all available men mustered, fifty-six policemen and forty-three militia, but so was the seven-pounder cannon.

At ten a.m. on March 26 the force started out, some mounted, some in horse-drawn sleighs. His superiors would later write that it was a shame Crozier's better judgement had been "over-ruled by the impetuosity displayed both by the police and volunteers."

Meanwhile, the Métis returned to Duck Lake to round up their comrades; estimates differ but Dumont claimed there were two hundred Métis as well as dozens of Indians. Gabriel was feeling pretty good; after all, the Mounties had been forced to turn back without any serious violence. His men were laughing about it and eating their lunch when they received yet another warning that police were approaching.

Quickly Dumont and his men—at first there were only twenty-six—saddled their horses and took off. Gabriel said to his brother Isidore, "I don't want to start killing them, I want to take prisoners. But if they try to kill us then we will kill them."

Dumont had no intention of meeting Crozier head on. The police had better weapons than the Métis, and they were trained in battle formation. He chose a shallow depression near the Carlton Trail two miles from Duck Lake that had plenty of low bush and a log cabin on one side that would offer protection. He ordered his men to take cover there.

Crozier had attempted to outmanoeuvre the Métis forces by following a trail through the Indian reserve, which was situated directly between Fort Carlton and Duck Lake. The police stopped at the house of Chief Beardy, who told them that they had no right to intrude on his reserve; he also said he had nothing to do with Riel's agitation. He sent along an old headman, the near-blind Assiyiwin, as a mediator. When Crozier and his party had just reached the edge of Beardy's reserve, scouts came running with news of a possible ambush up ahead. The major immediately ordered his men to halt. They arranged their sleighs across the trail as a protective barricade, but that meant they were stuck in one place. Shortly they noticed that Métis were creeping forward until eventually they would form a semicircle right around them.

Assiyiwin had gone to confer with the Métis and they had decided the best thing was to parley with Crozier. The old Cree and Gabriel's brother, Isidore, walked towards the police, waving a white blanket. Crozier responded by greeting the two: "What is it you want?" Suddenly, according to Dumont, Joseph McKay, a Half-breed translator who had a rifle and carried a revolver in his belt, moved his horse forward. This startled the unarmed Indian. Assiyiwin said to McKay, "If you haven't come to fight what are you doing with so many guns, grandson?" and then made a grab for his rifle. The two scuffled until McKay finally jerked his gun away and fired at the old man. Assiyiwin toppled over dead. Thus an elderly, unarmed Indian mediator became the first victim of the North-West Rebellion.

Crozier immediately responded, "Fire away boys!" Isidore, Gabriel's beloved elder brother, was the next to fall. "He was killed without firing his gun—we found it by his side," Dumont said afterwards.

Bedlam broke out after that. For the next twenty minutes the two sides blasted away at each other. Now there were more Métis than police officers, and they were better protected, hidden behind the cabin on one side of the road and in the shallow wooded coulee on the other. And they were far superior shots. As one young police officer described the scene, "Bullets fell like hail. We were catched in a nice trap and flanked on three sides." Even the Mounties' seven-pounder didn't help. When they finally got it in place, Crozier was positioned in front of it, so the gunners couldn't fire.

Dumont himself was wounded, his head grazed by a bullet. When Delorme saw him fall off his horse, he yelled, "Oh no—they got you!" But Gabriel, always the joker, responded, "As long as you don't lose your head, you're not dead." As Dumont lay wounded in the snow, his cousin Auguste Laframboise toppled beside him. "I crawled and dragged myself over to him, saying to myself: 'I am going to say a little prayer for him,' but wishing to make the sign of the cross with my left hand, since my right side was paralysed, I fell over on my side and, laughing I said, 'Cousin, I shall have to owe it to you.'" Laframboise was already dead.

In the midst of all this Riel was invoking the name of every saint he could think of. Dumont remembered: "He was in the small hollow with us. He was on his horse, a crucifix in his hand, held up in the air. He would not get down from his horse. He was very exposed—the small hollow was not deep enough for a mounted man to be in cover."* The story of the unarmed Riel sitting high on his horse as bullets whizzed around him quickly made the rounds, and the Métis began to believe that he was invincible and truly blessed by God.

Finally Crozier gave the signal and somehow his men managed to hitch the horses to the wagon, pick up some casualties—the Métis always claimed the police looked after their own and left the volunteers on the battlefield—and in full retreat gallop back towards Fort Carlton. Twelve Mounties and militia had been killed, eleven were wounded. The Métis had lost five of their own.

After the police left, Gabriel Dumont's head was bandaged and he was helped onto a horse. "When I passed my brother Isidore, I got down but I couldn't tell if he was dead. [He was.] A little further on I was told, "Behind that bluff there is a young volunteer, wounded in the leg." I went around the fence and came up to him: I was going to finish him off. I told him it would be quick and painless. I reached for my revolver, but it was right in the middle of my back and I couldn't reach it from the left or the right. While I was trying to get my gun, Riel arrived and stopped me from killing him."

Dumont was eager to pursue the police and militia and there's no question that if he had had his way there would have been a massacre. But Riel pleaded with Dumont, "in the name of God do not kill any more. There surely has already been too much bloodshed." Gabriel agreed to call off his soldiers.

The Métis were overjoyed at what seemed like such an easy victory. There was little celebration, however. Louis insisted that they spend the rest of the day

---

* Contemporary historians have tended to rely on the accounts of whites who were at the battle, or who heard reports of it afterwards, in particular Tom McKay, Joseph McKay, John W. Astley, Thomas Sanderson, Harold Ross and Leif Crozier. Their evidence is most suspect for two reasons: they were trying to justify a humiliating defeat and they longed to take revenge on Louis Riel. George F.G. Stanley, for example, quotes three witnesses at Riel's trial as saying that Louis ordered "in the name of the Father, the Son and the Holy Ghost to return the fire of the police." Dumont denied this and it does seem unlikely. Gabriel was always in command of military operations, and as events immediately after the battle indicate, Riel deplored violence.

praying for the souls of the dead. He maintained to the end of his life that there had never been any intention by the Métis of shedding blood.

The day after the battle at Duck Lake, the Métis council met to map out their future strategy. They argued fiercely about whether to present the Mounted Police with another ultimatum of surrender. Finally a letter to Crozier was written, dated March 27, 1885:

> Sir
>
> A Calamity has fallen upon the country yesterday. You are responsible for it before God and men.
>
> Your men cannot claim that their intentions were peaceable since they bringing along cannons. And they fired many shots first.*
>
> God has been pleased to grant us the victory; and as our movement is to save our rights, our victory is good: and we offer it to the Almighty.
>
> Major, we are christians in war as in peace. We write you in the name of God and of humanity come and take away your dead whom we respect.

It was signed by all the members of the Exovedate, including Riel.

One of the prisoners, Tom Sanderson, was chosen to carry the message to Crozier at Fort Carlton. Colonel Irvine was there by that time, and he believed the letter an enticement to ambush. Much to the disgust of the volunteers, he refused to allow the bodies to be picked up. Sanderson too was enraged and said that if he could borrow a sled and horses, he'd do the job himself. Irvine's response was to imprison the luckless teamster, claiming he was a spy.

Colonel Irvine decided that the fort was not worth protecting. With his men, the remnants of Crozier's force and several dozen frightened white farm families taking refuge, over two hundred people were cooped up in the dilapidated old fort. The wounded were not receiving the treatment they needed; two had already died. And the hills that rose to the north made the place almost indefensible; as one of the volunteers quipped, it was "a beautiful spot for sharpshooters to pot us as we walked by." Not only that, the once cocky militia, now that they had tasted real fighting, wanted to get back to Prince Albert. To protect their families, they said.

Colonel Irvine decided to abandon Fort Carlton. The men under his command spent March 27 bundling up as many supplies as they could carry (ignoring the loud protests of the now discredited Lawrence Clarke, who scurried around

---

* *Gabriel Dumont always thought that Isidore might have been killed by McKay even before Assiyiwin.*

taking inventory). The wounded would need to rest comfortably on the seventy-five-mile journey to Prince Albert, so hay was used as stuffing for makeshift mattresses. As this was being done, the hay was scattered about. Suddenly someone yelled that the stove was ablaze. There was barely time to get the wounded outside before the storehouse went up like a torch. The police and civilians were just winding their way up the steep trail to the north when the northern palisade burst into a sheet of flames. The Hudson's Bay Company store, however, was not as much damaged as the Mounties thought it would be. The next day the store, which still held all kinds of provisions, was looted by the Indians and Métis. Also found were important papers that were delivered to Louis Riel.

Dumont wanted to ambush Irvine's force right then but, as he later remembered, "Riel was against that, saying it was too savage to go and attack them at night. I was very upset by Riel's opposition, and told him, 'If you are going to give them the advantage like that, we cannot win.'" It was the beginning of a serious rift that would soon widen between the two men.

The Mounties and militia arrived in the now terrified town of Prince Albert late in the afternoon of March 28. One of the first persons they encountered was Charles Nolin. He had taken advantage of Riel's and Dumont's preoccupation to seize a small pony and, as Dumont put it, "ran just like we knew he would, just like a fox." To Nolin's annoyance, Colonel Irvine suspected he was a spy and promptly slapped him in jail.

On March 31, the Exovedate met for the last time at Duck Lake to discuss strategy. They had discovered in the papers found in the Fort Carlton ruins that a Canadian armed force was on its way to the West. It was time, they decided, to move back to Batoche to prepare for the onslaught.

But the Exovedate also spent much time, as it always did, on spiritual matters. Already Riel had been able to impose his peculiar world vision on the Métis of St. Laurent. Before the Battle of Duck Lake, the community had met at St. Antoine de Padoue Church and had passed a resolution exactly as he dictated it: "that the commandments of God be the laws of the Provisional Government; that we recognize Louis David Riel to direct the priests; that Archbishop Ignace Bourget be recognized from today by the French-Canadian people of Saskatchewan as the Pope of the New World."

Since they had not been privy to the long, tortuous history that had created Riel's strange theology, they probably didn't have the slightest idea what he was talking about. But they worshipped him so much that they would have done almost anything for him.

The March 31 meeting of the Exovedate went even further—in a resolution Louis was made a full-fledged prophet: "That the Canadian half-breed

Exovedate acknowledges Louis David Riel as a prophet in the service of Jesus Christ and Son of God and only Redeemer of the world...."

While Louis was obviously behind the campaign to make himself a divine soothsayer, his diaries reveal that he wasn't entirely confident. "O my God! Help me, guide me so that I do not do anything rash. Do not let me confide in anyone unless it is reasonable and proper. Assist me, direct me, so that I do not jeopardize the cause." He seemed constantly to find it necessary to boost his own morale: "My ideas are right; they are well balanced. They are level and clear; there is no mourning in my thoughts. My ideas are like the sights on my rifle. My rifle is upright. It is the invisible presence of God which holds my rifle straight and ready."

There was some opposition to Louis's mystical elevation. Riel's host, Moïse Ouellette, was growing more skeptical of the Métis leader by the day, so much so that Charles Nolin had tried to talk him into running away with him. Ouellette had said he would stay with his own people, but he didn't hesitate to speak out, not against Riel, but against his campaign to cast off the Catholic church.

But the great problem for Riel was not the skepticism of his fellow Métis, but what to do with his "special friend" and devoted admirer, William Jackson. Riel's advisers had decided that the Exovedate's secretary was as mad as a hatter.

Just before his baptism, Will had been confronted with Riel's decision to break with Rome. He decided that Louis was wrong in this and sent him a note saying so. But, as Jackson would write to his family, "To my surprise he re'd my decision with calmness and said that he left me as free in regard to leaving Rome for him as he had left me in regard to leaving Protestantism for Rome, but told me I would suffer for my lack of faith." Jackson, however, couldn't bear to break with his political mentor, whom he regarded as the "voice" of the "aboriginals throughout the world". "I became aware," he wrote, "that Mr. Riel was endowed with the power of reading my mind and was acquainted with passages of my past life known only to myself." Despite this, nagging doubts remained, and as the Métis moved towards open rebellion, Will became even more anxious. "To one side I was allied by blood, to the other by ties of religion, friendship and concurrence in certain political views." He decided to remain neutral, although he would continue to act as Riel's secretary.

In that capacity one night, he was writing a long letter about land claims. Louis was beside him, and suggested they stop and pray for inspiration. Jackson described what happened next:

> while he was praying a peculiar convulsion or something of the kind seemed to take possession of me under the influence of which I became rigid and helpless sinking back upon the bed on which I was sitting.... Mr.

Riel and some of the attendant councillors then rubbed my limbs until I recovered, but I believe from a remark which I fancied I caught from Mr. Riel's lips that he considered me hopelessly prejudiced against his views....

On the evening of March 25, when Riel left for Duck Lake, Jackson finally became convinced that "God was with him rather than the priests." That night he set out after his now acknowledged spiritual master.

Jackson decided that God had sent him a specific message, ordering him to go among the Indians as a missionary. Will had always idealized Native peoples—they were, he wrote, "incomparably nearer to God than that of any average man taken from ... what we call our civilization." Now he believed that, like Riel, he had a special mission. The Métis, however, thought differently. They were convinced that he was a lunatic, and detained him under guard.

The citizens of Prince Albert were furious when they heard that Colonel Irvine had not picked up the fallen volunteers on the battlefield. They convinced him to release Tom Sanderson from prison, and to allow him, another teamster and Will Jackson's brother, Eastwood, to retrieve the bodies. Relatives of the dead were sure, they said, that their loved ones had already been scalped and horribly mutilated "by the savages". In reality, the Métis were horrified when, the next day, they discovered the corpses still lying in the sun. Sleighs were sent to pick them up and they were stored in two houses near Duck Lake. The delegation from Prince Albert finally arrived and performed their sad job as quickly as possible, although the Métis would not help load the bodies. They were insulted at Irvine's lack of trust.

Eastwood Jackson had an ulterior motive in coming with the teamsters. When Tom Sanderson told him that his brother, Will, was "out of his mind", he became intent on rescuing him. But when he met both Riel and his brother at Duck Lake, Will seemed at least rational, and so he decided to leave him.

A few days later Eastwood was working in his pharmacy when a Métis friend told him that he had seen Will at Fort Carlton and that he was much worse. The druggist asked for a pass from Irvine to travel to Duck Lake to see his brother. The colonel, suspicious that Jackson was passing information to the Métis, refused, until at last Eastwood's mother and minister prevailed on him. On April 7, Jackson arrived at Batoche and immediately went to see Riel. Their conversation was pleasant enough, but when Eastwood asked that his brother be released, Louis said he would have to ask the council. After that, for some reason, Riel became convinced that Eastwood Jackson was a spy. He ordered him detained along with his brother, although the Jacksons were allowed more freedom of movement than the other prisoners.

When Eastwood had come to Duck Lake the first time, to transport the bodies back to Prince Albert, Louis Riel had given him a letter addressed "To the People of Prince Albert". Jackson was supposed to distribute it widely and even hold public meetings, but he had destroyed it on the way back to Prince Albert because he thought he would be arrested if it was found on his person. (His mother somehow made a copy; perhaps Eastwood dictated it to her from memory.) In his letter Riel had emphasized that he held no antagonism towards the white settlers, even though some of them had fought against the Métis; it was the Hudson's Bay Company, in the person of Lawrence Clarke, and the Canadian government that were at fault.

In fact, Riel had begun to lose the sympathy of the settlers months before. The terror of an Indian uprising remained and many whites had not approved of including Native grievances in the petition that went to Ottawa. Then the Farmers' Union had lost most of its clout, especially after Lawrence Clarke was allowed to join. And the March meeting in Halcro, at which Louis showed up in the company of sixty armed Métis and railed against the government, had been the last straw for most white settlers. They were not interested in open rebellion.

He didn't fare much better with the group he felt much closer to, the English-speaking Half-breeds. During the first months, they had idolized Riel as much as the French-speakers. But they had not experienced the surge of pride that Riel's dream of a separate nation, a separate people, had inspired in the Métis. Not being caught up in the powerful spiritual vortex Riel spun, they were not prepared to risk everything by taking that fatal step towards armed rebellion. They sent the Exovedate a note that they "would continue to sympathize, as they have always done, with the French half-breeds in their desire to obtain their legal rights, by all constitutional means," but they would not resort to arms. Riel replied, "Gentlemen, please do not remain neutral. For the love of God, help us to save the Saskatchewan." Emissaries were dispatched to try to persuade them. It was to no avail; neutral they remained.

That left the Indian nations, and they would represent a powerful and frightening force if ever they were to unite. Throughout the fall and winter, Dumont's emissaries had been in constant contact—had even sent tobacco as a token of alliance—with the tribes of the North Saskatchewan.

In a letter the Exovedate members begged the Indians, "do what you can ... take the stores, the provisions and the munitions. And without delay, come this way; as many as is possible." A general uprising of plains Indians did not occur; the pacifism of Chief Crowfoot and the mighty Blackfoot Confederacy ensured that. However, support did come from the south branch of the Saskatchewan; scores of warriors arrived from the One Arrow, Beardy, Okemasis, Chakastapaysin and Petaquakey reserves. In other areas, encouraged by the news of the Métis victory at Duck Lake, the Indians staged revolutions of their own.

Three days after Duck Lake, on March 29, a group of Stoneys from the Eagle Hills demanded flour and ammunition from James Payne, hired by the dominion government to teach the Natives the elements of farming. He was a stern taskmaster and the Indians hated him. When he refused, a Stoney named Itka shot him dead.

The next day, the same Stoneys ran into Barney Tremont, a Belgian-born rancher who had made a fetish out of his loathing for Indians, threatening them whenever they came near his property. They murdered him with two shots to the head and an arrow in the heart.

On March 30, Crees moved on Battleford. They were hungry and frustrated; as their chief, Poundmaker, who had tried hard to adapt to reserve life, said, whites promised everything but delivered only disease and poverty. The townspeople had just time to flee their houses and take refuge in the fort, located on the south bank. From there, five hundred people crowded together "like chickens" watched the sack of Battleford.

Then on April 2, at Frog Lake, young warriors from Big Bear's band, led by Little Big Man and Wandering Spirit, killed nine whites, including the Indian agent and two priests, and burned down Fort Pitt. The federal government's refusal to negotiate properly with Big Bear had led to the old chief losing prestige and the young radicals taking charge.

Louis Riel's reaction to these episodes is not part of the historical record, but he must have been ambivalent. He hated the idea of bloodshed, and yet, as the days passed, a concerted Indian uprising was obviously the Métis militants' only hope.

Shortly after Duck Lake, the Exovedate and the entire Métis fighting force returned to Batoche. They commandeered every building in the village for their own use, and distributed any supplies, from wheat to farm implements, that were still in the stores. Letendre's huge house was Dumont's central control; he and Madeleine lived there while he directed the military operation from the parlour.

The Riel family occupied one of the smaller houses in the village, probably the one owned by the merchant John Fisher.

April 5, Easter, was a glorious morning. Everyone in the village gathered at St. Antoine de Padoue. Father Moulin celebrated mass and then took the opportunity to give one of his sermons on obedience to the Catholic clergy and the government—in that order. Riel, who was in the church, remained quiet throughout the service, but outside in the bright sunlight he reprimanded the priest for not applauding Métis heroism. Moulin called Riel a heretic and an apostate. Not long after, Louis wrote in his diary, "Priests are not religion. The spirit of God has told me that this was, is and always will be true."

That night Louis had another intense spiritual vision—like others in his past, this came at a time of chaos, when death was in the air. The Zouaves, the Canadians who, with the encouragement of Bishop Bourget, had enrolled in a papal army to defend Rome against Italian forces fifteen years before, had ever after been part of Easter celebrations in Quebec. In his dream that Easter night in Batoche, Riel had seen their commander, Captain Taillefer, come to Montreal to celebrate the installation of Bishop Bourget as the first North American pope. His vision of a newly constituted Catholic church always seemed to dominate his thinking when his own world was in turmoil, when he was in need of a new, more moral and structured society. Once again Riel needed to establish a universe, no matter how metaphorically, where the oppressed minorities, the Métis, Indians, Irish, Slovaks, could live with dignity and equality. To suggest, as has been done endlessly for over a hundred years, that this vision was nothing more than the rantings of a madman is to say that a unique spirituality is beyond the pale, that conformity must smother all alternatives.

On April 6, incredible news reached the Métis. General Frederick D. Middleton and a force of men were in the neighbourhood, getting ready to attack Batoche.

Even before the Battle of Duck Lake, the Prime Minister of Canada had decided that the North-West Mounted Police were not enough to deal with the Métis and Indian problem in the Northwest. Interestingly, on March 23, 1885, the very day that Sir John A. called up the militia, his Cabinet refused to grant the Canadian Pacific Railway any more money. Macdonald's great dream was a hair's breadth away from bankruptcy. But in his usual way, the wily politician managed to intertwine these two disasters into a victory wreath.

According to historian D.N. Sprague, mobilizing the militia was at first conceived by the prime minister only as a show of force; he fully expected that the insurgents would give up once they saw Canada's military might. "What Macdonald seems to have envisioned was a sudden dash to the Prairies, a mysterious 'escape' of Riel back to the United States, conciliatory gestures to the surrendering Métis, and aid for the railway after it played such a key role in breaking up the 'outbreak' so 'speedily and gallantly.'" Once Duck Lake had flared, the situation became far more dangerous. The railway, thank God, would become even more important.

The man Macdonald put in charge of the North-West Expedition was Major-General Frederick D. Middleton, the commander of the Canadian militia.

Middleton was fifty-nine years old, and had already served in the British artillery for forty-three years. Born in Belfast of an Anglo-Irish military family, he had been educated at Royal Military College, Sandhurst, and was fighting the Maoris by the time he was twenty-one. A whole series of "colonial" wars had followed—during the Indian Mutiny, Middleton was twice recommended for the Victoria Cross, gaining a reputation for reckless courage. But, unfortunately for Middleton, the overweight British military establishment in the mid-nineteenth century was not an institution of rapid advancement. He was the third son of a not very wealthy family, and he suddenly found himself on half-pay. Duty in Canada was one means of alleviating his financial plight and in 1869 he ended up in Montreal. By then a widower, he shocked his Protestant friends and family by marrying Eugenie Doucet, a young French-Canadian Catholic. In 1870, Middleton returned to Britain, where he had landed a well-paying, cushy job at his alma mater, Sandhurst—in 1874 he became commandant. That appointment ran out in 1883, and Middleton seemed destined to face a retirement of genteel poverty on half-pay pension. However, his in-laws intervened and the Canadian government offered him the command of the militia. He had only been back in Canada eight months when the North-West Rebellion broke out.

"Old Fred", as his men liked to call him, suffered the unhappy coincidence of looking exactly like the cartoon character Colonel Blimp: he was short, stocky, with a beet-red face and a huge walrus moustache. He was a dedicated snob, the very model of Gilbert and Sullivan's model major-general; indeed one of the reasons he came to Canada was that that very title came with the job. He didn't think much of colonials, especially their untrained civilian volunteers who had the presumption to call themselves soldiers.

Once the prime minister had called out the militia, Middleton travelled to Winnipeg by train, arriving on March 27, the day after the Battle of Duck Lake. With the Militia Regiment of Winnipeg, "the 90th Rifles", he left immediately for Qu'Appelle, the nearest railhead to Batoche. There he would establish his headquarters, train his raw recruits from Winnipeg and wait for reinforcements to arrive by rail.

And reinforcements there would be. Back in eastern Canada, young men were dying to fight and thousands flocked to enlist—eight thousand by the end of the rebellion. This would be the first all-Canadian war—a short, nasty skirmish massing huge manpower and artillery, including a machine gun, against Native peoples who wanted nothing more than for the government to live up to the treaties they had signed, or hand over deeds to the land they had lived on for years. It was not a war to be proud of.

From the moment the Canadians arrived at Qu'Appelle, Métis scouts watched their every move; one of Dumont's spies, Jérome Henry, actually worked as a teamster for the major-general. It wasn't hard keeping track of them, for Middleton's army wore bright red tunics and blue serge pants; they stood out on the white-brown prairies like ring-necked pheasants.

Dumont and his captains had an intricate plan of guerrilla warfare ready. It was exactly the kind of fighting that suited them. All the Métis fighters knew the prairie like the back of their hand, the coulees, the sloughs, the groves of aspen, balsam, poplar and willow, the clumps of bush—a perfect terrain for sabotage.

Dumont planned to blow up bridges and railway tracks, so the trains full of soldiers could not get through. He would make quick raids on the prairie outposts where food for Middleton's men and hay for their horses were being stored. And he would never stop menacing them, until their life became a terror. "I prepared to go ahead of the troops," he later wrote, "harass them by night, and above all prevent them from sleeping, believing this was a good way to demoralize them and make them lose heart." Given that the soldiers were green as grass, these tactics probably would have driven them to distraction. But they were never carried out because Louis Riel refused to allow it. Since Dumont's head wound had not completely healed, he was worried about Gabriel's health. He argued that with the police force sitting in Prince Albert, the Métis could not afford to divert soldiers away from Batoche. He said night raids were too much like savage Indian warfare. And he felt that French Canadians who had joined Middleton's forces might be injured. Maybe most important, deep down he still hoped that the Canadian government might sue for peace, might negotiate with him and the Métis people. Dumont was still so much in awe of Riel, he wrote, "I yielded to Riel's judgement although I was convinced, that from a humane standpoint, mine was the better plan: but I had confidence in his faith and his prayers and that God would listen to him." A letter of instruction was sent to various outposts outlining Louis's philosophy.

General Middleton had by this time evolved his own plan. The North-West Expedition would consist of three different campaigns. Major-General T.B. Strange would go after Big Bear, marching from Calgary to Edmonton, eastwards along the North Saskatchewan River; Lieutenant-Colonel William Otter would liberate Battleford, where the citizens were still cooped up in the fort, and then pursue Poundmaker; Middleton himself would attack the Métis at Batoche. On April 6, on a cold, windy morning, he left Qu'Appelle with 402 men and a wagon train of 120 vehicles. By April 13 the troops had reached Humboldt, a hundred miles from Batoche.

As the Canadians lurched forward mile by mile, the tension at the St. Laurent settlement mounted. The Métis soldiers grew more nervous as they realized the might of Middleton's force. Perhaps Dumont was right, perhaps they should have harassed, intimidated, terrorized. Now it was becoming too late for such tactics. The Indian warriors they had daily expected had not shown up. The women and children from the outlying farms were crowding into Batoche for protection, setting up camps on both sides of the river. Riel himself was becoming more and more anxious. On April 21, he would write in his diary:

> I have seen the giant; he is coming, he is hideous. It is Goliath. He will not get to the place that he intends to occupy.
>
> I see him: he is losing his body, he is losing all his men. Nothing but his head remains. Because he will not humble himself, his head is cut off.

The Métis leaders had grown increasingly impatient with the unyielding clergy of the St. Laurent. Father Végréville, Fourmond's assistant at the St. Laurent de Grandin Church, was the most outspoken critic of the Métis rebellion. When he came to visit Father Moulin at Batoche, Dumont had him brought before the Exovedate and chastised for his lack of support. He was told Father Moulin would offer him a place to stay, his horse and buggy were taken away, and he was made to sign a document stating: "I promise to keep perfectly neutral and I will not leave here without consent of the Provisional Government."

Métis scouts had spotted Charles Nolin, flanked by police guards, making nocturnal visits to St. Laurent rectory. They were sure Fourmond was passing information to the police via Nolin. The next day the priest was brought under guard from St. Laurent, and hauled before the Exovedate. Riel asked the reasons for these visits and Fourmond, furious, answered him sharply. Riel shot back, mockingly, "Why he's a little tiger!" The priest was escorted back to the now crowded rectory at Batoche. A few weeks later Father Touze was ordered to come from Duck Lake. The clerics ensconced at Father Moulin's manse were allowed to celebrate mass and administer the sacraments to anybody who wanted them. And they were also free to wander about, as long as they didn't leave Batoche.*

Finally Gabriel Dumont had reached the end of his patience. The very idea of the alien Middleton and his greenhorn soldiers roaming around his country without interference was abhorrent to him. Dumont thought the enemy had already shown signs of fearfulness by not advancing as quickly as they could, and he wanted to take advantage of that. And his army, with so much time to

---

* *The accounts of what happened to the clergy are based primarily on their writings, Father Végréville's diary, for example. And they are very one-sided. The Métis have a quite different rendition, but it is based, to some degree, on oral history, until recently not accepted by academics. I've tried a mixture of both.*

think of the intimidating force approaching, was slipping away. "I told Riel that I could no longer accept his humanitarian advice, that I intended to go out and shoot at the invaders, and that my men supported me." Riel finally gave in. "Very well! Do what you wish!" he said. Then he warned Gabriel to take care of his wounded head, and "to fear his own boiling courage and his habit of recklessly exposing himself!" Dumont replied that he and his men would deal with Middleton's soldiers "as we would the buffalo".

The place where Gabriel Dumont chose to take a stand was Tourond's Coulee, the very spot where the Métis community had gathered to welcome Riel, Marguerite and their children eight short months before. It was the southernmost farm of the St. Laurent settlement, and therefore the boundary of what the Métis considered their territory.

Middleton's force now numbered 800. At Clarke's Crossing, thirty-five miles from Batoche, where the troops had rested, several Indians had been captured who had told the Canadians that the Métis force numbered at most 250. That was exactly what the major-general had anticipated, and he began to worry that after all this effort, the rebels might not even put up a fight. He then made a curious decision. He split his army, sending 370 men under the command of Lord Melgund, his chief of staff, to the west side of the river. The rest would remain with him on the east side. The wide, fast-flowing South Saskatchewan now separated the two forces and they had difficulty communicating, let alone coming to each other's relief. It would prove a grave mistake.

Late in the evening of April 23, Dumont, Riel, about two hundred Métis soldiers and thirty Sioux and Cree set out from Batoche. About four miles south, they came to Robert Goulet's farm and stopped to eat. By this time it was midnight. Just as they were finishing, Emmanuel Champagne and Moïse Carrier arrived to tell them that a troop of Mounted Police had been spotted on the trail from Qu'Appelle and it was assumed they were going to attack Batoche. Many of Dumont's men wanted to go back to protect their families, but Gabriel convinced them that a force of fifty would be sufficient. Riel agreed to lead them back. Dumont wasn't particularly unhappy about this. All along the path Louis had insisted on stopping to pray; now, with Riel gone, as Dumont quipped, "This time we won't be saying rosary so much, so we'll move faster." Not only that, Dumont felt much freer to carry out his own version of warfare. "My plan had been to surprise the enemy camp during the night, to spring a prairie fire on them, take advantage of their confusion, and massacre them. If we had found the English camp that first night, Middleton's soldiers would have been lucky to get out alive." But they didn't find the camp, and so they decided to return to Tourond's Coulee and wait for the enemy to arrive.

The spot for ambush was chosen carefully. All along the steep banks of the meandering Fish Creek sat dense clumps of willows and underbrush. The trail which Middleton's column would use followed the Saskatchewan River, then swung inland and climbed upwards to the prairie for an easier crossing of a creek and ravine. Dumont positioned most of his men in the wooded coulees near the upper trail so that they could get a clear shot at the enemy, walking either upward towards them or downward after they had passed them.

Dumont ordered his men to remain hidden in the bushes and to leave no signs of their presence on the prairie. But, as he later wrote, "They paid little attention to my orders, and when I returned they had made many fires right on the path." It would prove to be a serious mistake; Middleton's scouts would spot the tell-tale signs of their presence.

Dumont was so eager to fight that he and Napoléon Nault went out to search for enemy scouts. "I wanted to get behind them, kill them, and take their guns. That was always my first thought: to get more guns." They found no one and returned to Fish Creek.

Dumont now positioned his men for an ambush. Most of them would be hidden in the ravine just off the main trail, but they would wait to fire until Middleton's advance guard had made its way past them, and then a group of sharpshooters would attack from the rear. It might well have worked if the Métis presence had remained a secret.

The next morning was dull and grey, with a low-lying mist; it would rain or snow for much of the day, adding to everyone's misery. Just as Dumont was finishing breakfast, Métis guides arrived, reporting that the enemy was breaking camp. One of the Canadian scouts spotted the Métis horsemen—there were still no leaves on the trees—and he ran back to warn Middleton. Dumont's opportunity for an ambush evaporated.

The Winnipeg 90th Rifles advanced and the Métis opened fire—the Battle of Fish Creek had begun. It was a long-drawn-out affair, the Métis firing from deep in the ravines, behind a cover of trees and bushes, the Canadians on higher ground near the crest. A nervous Sioux in full war paint suddenly sprang out of his protected spot and ran towards the enemy, screaming his war cry. He was quickly gunned down, the first casualty of the battle.

As the hours of chaos passed, Dumont had difficulty in keeping his men from fleeing—the Canadians were so many, and had such formidable guns, including nine-pounder cannon. Eventually the number of Métis fighters was reduced to fifty-four. Fortunately Edouard Dumont, Gabriel's brother, who had returned to Batoche with Riel, heard the shooting and galloped to the battle with seventy reinforcements. Dumont himself displayed tremendous courage, scurrying on his hands and knees from one group of soldiers to another, encouraging them. Somebody began singing the Métis national anthem, Pierre Falcon's song about the similar battle years before at Seven Oaks. What Dumont didn't tell his soldiers was that he was worried the Redcoats might outflank his men. They didn't. In fact Middleton had decided that his casualties were already too heavy; he would not even try to pry the Métis from that densely wooded ravine. Dumont later recalled how the battle ended:

> When we got down to our last seven bullets, I said, "we are going to start a fireline in front of the police." The wind was blowing toward the enemy. We started the fire.... I told my men "we are going to make a sweep, yelling and screaming. March right behind the flames." I always stayed right behind the biggest flames, and when we were about forty yards from the police the fire went out. It was at the edge of a small wet wood. The police were in flight. As we advanced, we found many dead, and no doubt there were many more dead in the underbrush because the water in the little creek was red. We didn't find any rifles or cartridges. The sun had gone down.

The Métis lost four of their own, and two were wounded. Two of the dead were members of the Tourond family, on whose property the battle was fought. Middleton's forces suffered much greater losses—ten dead and forty-five wounded. For that reason alone the Battle of Fish Creek was considered a victory for the Métis. Middleton sent Ottawa his impressions by coded telegram: "the troops behaved well on the occasion of their first meeting with the enemy, but I confess to you that it was very near being otherwise, and if it had not been for myself and A.D.C.'s it would have been a disaster."

The next day a heavy, wet snowstorm blanketed the prairie. Middleton's army, now huddled in their camp on a flat plain south of the battlefield, was so quiet, so despondent, as to seem almost lifeless.

At Batoche, Dumont's men prepared for the next battle, which they knew would be the crucial one. Guerrilla warfare was out of the question; their mobility had been hampered by the loss of horses during the battle, fifty-five in total. (Riel had an explanation for the death of these animals; he wrote in his journal: "Oh my Métis Nation! For a long time you have offended Me with your horse races, by gambling on these detestable races, by your obstinacy, by your odious wrangling about your wicked horse races. 'That is why,' says the Eternal Christ, 'I killed your horses while sparing you.'")

Dumont's tactics had worked at Fish Creek; Riel's Goliath had at least been kept at bay. The same strategy of entrenchment would be applied at Batoche. Immediately the Métis set to work constructing a honeycomb of trenches and rifle pits. The Church of St. Antoine de Padoue, with the rectory next to it, sat up on a flat terrace south of the village. To the west the banks of the Saskatchewan descended sharply, a tangle of shrubs, underbrush and small trees. To the north the terrain sloped gently downwards for a half-mile to the little cluster of houses and stores at Batoche. And not far away was the landing where the ferries plied the Saskatchewan. It was between the village and the church, in open rolling grassland protected only here and there by clumps of trees, that the Métis constructed their rifle pits. They were about eighteen inches deep, with a foot-high embankment of logs placed on top of each other, each pit holding two or three men, and spaced about fifty feet apart. They skilfully took advantage of the topography so that, as the soldiers advanced, they'd be in full view of the sharpshooters.

The atmosphere in the St. Laurent settlement grew more tense with each passing day. Scouting parties, some even including Riel, were continuously monitoring the countryside for Canadian military activity. Métis and Indian women and children were flooding in from the countryside now, taking up residence in the camps, which were growing larger and more ramshackle by the day. The Métis councillors had rounded up all the cattle they could find, but as the days went by food would be in short supply, with strict rations imposed.

The biggest problem for the Métis was weaponry. The Canadians possessed the modern guns—Sniders, Winchesters, Peabodys—each soldier carrying as much as a hundred rounds of ammunition. A few of the old buffalo hunters had good rifles, but most had only old unreliable equipment, like muzzle-loaders. Then there was the crisis of ammunition; Dumont spent much of his time running around trying to find bullets. The most terrifying weapon used by the Canadian side was a relatively new invention—the Gatling gun. It was the first time a machine gun had been used in Canada—and that against its own Native peoples.

The Métis were now desperate for the Indian tribes to join in the revolution. Letters were dispatched and on May 1 a message of support arrived from Poundmaker, promising reinforcements would be sent. But shortly after, he became involved in his own bloody battle with Middleton's forces, and none could be spared. Outside of Chief White Cap, who with about twenty Sioux had camped at Batoche, the Métis were left to fight their battles alone.

During the Battle of Fish Creek, Riel had spent the day at Batoche praying unceasingly with the women of the village. His arms had remained stretched out to form a cross; when his strength had given out, the Métisses had taken turns holding them up. And a miraculous victory had indeed happened. When the Métis fighters returned, Louis had ordered four days of fasting, prayer and penance to ask for God's help in the upcoming struggle. As he wrote, "Properly performed, four days of fasting is enough to turn a nation of dwarves into a nation of giants."

The struggle with the St. Laurent clergy continued daily. Because the priests refused to give the sacraments to anyone taking up arms, Riel became even more intent on remodelling the Catholic church to his own liking. A little log chapel had been set up by the Métis. Situated in a cluster of willows, it was adorned with the crucifix which Louis had held high during the Battle of Duck Lake, the flag decorated with a picture of Our Lady of Lourdes which the Métis had flown during the Battle of Fish Creek, the letters from Bishop Bourget declaring Riel's mission and the Latin benediction which Bishop Grandin had recited when he had visited in September. It was here the Métis women and children had prayed during the Battle of Fish Creek, not at St. Antoine de Padoue, and it was Louis Riel who had led them in prayer, not Father Fourmond, Moulin or Végréville.

On April 26, on Riel's urging, the Exovedate had passed resolutions giving life to Louis's new church. They reflected his fascination with the Old Testament and the Hebrews. The Sabbath was no longer to be held on Sunday, but on Saturday, "as determined by Your Holy spirit in the person of Moses Your Servant." The Exovedate resolved that May 1 would be a special Easter, and following that May 2 would be the first Saturday Sabbath.

Riel was also determined to create his own ministry. Each member of the Exovedate would be ordained a priest with the power to administer the sacraments and to hear confessions. If he expected the Métis people to confess to old buffalo hunters like Maxime Lépine or Damase Carrière, he would have to set an example. The day before the Battle of Batoche, when the possibility of death made the act of confession even more important to the soldiers, Riel had a group kneel down in front of the altar of their little chapel. All the members of the Exovedate were asked to crowd around. Then Riel himself owned up to the sin of gluttony and asked forgiveness. Old Baptiste Boucher, who liked a good meal himself, mumbled that Louis should say five Paters and five Aves.

Riel's religious doctrine was changing during this time as well. In many ways, it was a far more humane theology than the one he had been immersed in during his formative college days, or the rigid doctrine of the ultramontanes: hell would not last forever because such a philosophy was "contrary to divine mercy"; the church was to be more ecumenical, reaching out to all creeds, and more open to the needs and desires of its people, particularly minorities such as the Indians or Métis.

One of the strangest quirks in Riel's thinking was his insistence on changing the names of the days. Monday was to be named Christ Aurore, Tuesday, Vierge

Aurore, Wednesday, Joseph Aube, Thursday, Dieu Aurore, Friday Deuil Aurore, Saturday Calme Aurore, Sunday Vive Aurore. Riel thought the new names were much nicer sounding, and he considered the old ones had a pagan ring to them.

Naturally, the Catholic clergy at Batoche were horrified at these heresies. On April 30 they excommunicated Riel and his followers (who still seemed to be the majority of the Métis at Batoche). Louis responded with his own, rather wise, theological answer. "Priests have been ordained to support the spirit of religion. They have authority only in as much as they are faithful to their mission. As soon as they stray from that, they have lost their position and their usefulness. Priests are not religion."

Interestingly, about this time Riel seems to have given up on the idea of ever returning to the United States. For one thing, he still believed he could reach an accommodation with the Canadian government. On April 29, he wrote:

> I used to live wretchedly in the United States among serpents, amid poisonous vipers. I was so surrounded that wherever I wished to set foot I saw them teeming. The ground was crawling with them. The United States are hell for an honest man. A respectable family is in disrepute there. It is ridiculed, scoffed at. Oh, what a great misfortune it is to be obliged to seek refuge in the United States.
>
> O my God, for the love of Jesus, Mary, Joseph and Saint John the Baptist grant me the favour of speedily reaching a good arrangement with the Dominion of Canada.... Guide me, help me to secure for the Métis and Indians all the advantages which can now be obtained through negotiations.

But it was much too late for that.

For two weeks, not a rifle was fired in the Batoche area. Middleton and his men busied themselves in their camp, burying their dead and slowly recovering their spirits from what the eastern Canadian newspapers had screamed was a major defeat. They were also waiting for the *Northcote*, a HBC steamer, to come down the South Saskatchewan bearing reinforcements and supplies. The Métis were also occupied, digging what they hoped would be impenetrable fortifications.

Still, a hush of terror hung over Batoche. Riel wrote in his diary:

> I see the redcoats very close to us. I walked ten feet from their guns, but they didn't do me any harm. They were stunned, and so was I, almost as much ... there I realized that our men were only little boys and their wives were little girls, fit only to play games together. They were faced with real soldiers. God alone has saved us.

On May 7, Middleton felt confident enough to break camp and move towards Batoche. He now had eight hundred soldiers, four cannon, a machine gun and 150 wagons full of supplies and equipment. As his troops moved northward, they broke into every Métis farmhouse (and some white settlers' homes) along the way, looting and smashing everything in sight. They killed cattle and stole horses wherever they encountered them. As it was later revealed in a House of Commons debate, "they demolished Madame Tourand's house at Fish Bay, broke her furniture and broke up the clock and bedsteads and strewed the floor with the rest of the furniture, and then set fire to the house." The Canadians could hardly wait to get to Dumont's Landing, where they camped on Gabriel's land. They burned his house to the ground—what upset him the most was the thought of his beloved pool table going up in flames. They also tore down his stable. Middleton had decided to turn the *Northcote* into a makeshift gunboat, and they wanted the wood from Dumont's stable to build up the main deck.

Middleton planned a two-pronged attack. The *Northcote*, with a troop of artillery aboard, would steam along the Saskatchewan River in the hope of diverting the Métis from the fortifications near Batoche. At exactly the same moment, the Canadians would mount a surprise attack on the village from the south. But the plan was flawed right from the beginning.

Gabriel Dumont had quickly realized exactly what Middleton's strategy was. When the Canadians started to advance early on May 9, he placed 30 soldiers along the banks of the river; the rest, about 155, remained in their fortifications near the village. Gabriel was intent on capturing the boat, for he knew that a cache of prisoners would make for advantageous bargaining with the Canadian government. And he longed to get his hands on the supplies and ammunition stored on two barges that were being pulled by the steamer.

Middleton was slow and cautious, fearful of ambush at every turn as he moved towards Batoche, so much so that the steamer proceeded well ahead of him. The *Northcote* whistled around the bend in the river at Batoche a full hour before Middleton's troops arrived. Dumont's sharpshooters on both sides of the river suddenly shook the little boat with a wild, noisy barrage of gunfire. The helmsmen dived for cover, and the *Northcote* struck a sandbar and then lurched uncontrollably into the main current. Meanwhile, Dumont was galloping along the riverbank, ordering his troops to man the ferry cable at Batoche Landing. But there was time to lower it only to the point where it injured but did not disable the vessel. It sliced off the *Northcote*'s smokestacks and scraped the top of the pilot house. A fire burst out on deck but it was quickly smothered. The steamer staggered downstream for two miles before it lurched to a stop. And there it sat out the battle, no good to either Middleton or Dumont.

In all the excitement, the Métis soldiers were lured away from their rifle pits at Batoche. Dumont ordered them back in place and then remembered that he hadn't carried out an important part of his strategy. He had wanted to start grass fires in front of Middleton's advance; these were designed to produce a great deal of smoke which the Métis hoped would irritate the eyes and impede the vision of the Canadian soldiers. Dumont's men would then attack from the surrounding bushes. However, Isidore Dumas, scouting out the enemy, reported that Middleton's forces had already passed La Belle Prairie, where they had planned to set the blaze. The only avenue left to Dumont was for his soldiers to hunker down in their rifle pits between the village and the church. The Métis at Batoche, men, women and children, could hear the bugle sounding as Middleton officially announced the beginning of the battle.

Dumont was surprised that the Canadians were attacking from the south rather than the east as he had expected, but his men were quickly readied. The Redcoats advanced, the cannon were placed on the knoll of a hill near the church, the Gatling machine gun was aimed at the cabins below the cemetery. There was a furious outburst as several Métis rushed forward and tried to steal one of the guns. When the Redcoats regained their composure and attacked, Dumont's men melted into the bushes. So completely hidden was the honeycomb of rifle pits that some of the Canadians in the very front lines did not set eyes on an actual Métis shooter until the last hours of the battle.

Suddenly a white flag was seen flying from the church. Father Moulin for one was ready to give up. For a short time he conferred with Middleton's men, planting the suspicion in Métis minds that nagged all through the Battle of Batoche. They were sure the clergy were feeding information to the enemy. By the end of the fighting the priests would be regarded as traitors.

The fierce fighting continued. The cannon pounded away, knocking down several houses at Batoche. The Gatling gun rapidly spewed out a deadly stream of bullets. Neither one of these did much damage to the men dug into well-protected rifle pits, but later analysis concluded that the guns might have prevented the rout of the Canadian army.

It was late afternoon when Middleton ordered his troops to stop firing. They would retreat to the zareba, a kind of makeshift stockade, which had been built at a nearby farm. The first day of fighting had ended in what historians have traditionally called an inconclusive battle, a stalemate, overlooking the fact that 800 well-armed soldiers with deadly guns had not budged 175 entrenched Métis one inch.

Dumont's men harassed the Redcoats all night, shooting into their camp from the bushes and howling bloodcurdling war cries. The Canadians had to take shelter under their wagons, taking turns walking among the horses to prevent a stampede.

Louis Riel's note in his diary that evening summed up the situation: "The Spirit of God made me see two Métis, two dark men. They were about to be shot dead in the battle, but God allowed Himself to be moved by fasting and prayer. They were only wounded."

When reveille sounded at five a.m. the next morning, the Canadians found a layer of ice covering their water buckets and, hidden in the bushes, mocking Métis taking pot-shots at them. The Redcoats pushed their guns forward near the cemetery until they could see the village down below. The fighting began in much the same manner as the day before. Although he had more than five times as many soldiers as Dumont, Middleton didn't feel strong enough to take the village of Batoche by storm. By six o'clock, the Canadians had not managed to get within two hundred yards of their furthermost advance of the previous day. Middleton ordered them to fall back once again to their zareba, where they would spend another night being harassed by Métis sharpshooters.

For Dumont's men, the ammunition problem was now acute; pieces of metal, nails and even stones were being used. Dumont later recounted how precious each bullet was. "Each night the police returned to their camp, and often there were bullets left on the ground, usually at the foot of a tree, where they had stopped to reload. Often we found machine gun belts which held forty bullets each. These were the same calibre as many of the Métis twelve-shot hunting rifles. We also took the guns of the dead. At the end we had sixty or seventy."

Dumont realized that the general knew they were short of ammunition. "One report said that Middleton planned to make us use up our bullets, no doubt on the advice of Father Végréville." He, for one, never forgave the priests for the devious role they played during the battles of Batoche.

Dumont was particularly incensed when he was shown some exploding bullets used by the Canadian soldiers.

> We thought it was understood between nations that only mortars could be explosive, as their debris was very destructive. But for a man in combat to be exposed to exploding bullets was to cause a terrible wound and certain death, which was against the basic principles of war.... The government troops committed a huge crime against humanity and against the rights of the men of the Métis nation.

Ottawa denied that such bullets were used, but Métis maintain to this day that they were seen by many people. Fortunately few of Dumont's men were hit by the Canadians.

During these battles Riel tried to bolster his soldiers' morale. He wandered from one rifle pit to another, crucifix in hand, praying, reading from the Bible, speaking words of encouragement. He pointed out to the men that, although the village stores and houses had been subjected to two days of intense bombardment, the Métis flag, painted with the image of Our Lady of Lourdes, was still flying unscathed above the Walters & Baker store.

The third day, Monday May 11, was a dreary repetition of the previous drama—shelling by the Canadians, to be returned, now very carefully because of the shortage of bullets, by Dumont's sharpshooters. Both sides were worn down. Many of the Métis and Indian soldiers had remained for as long as seventy hours straight in their rifle pits, which were chock full of used ammunition, blankets, shirts, damaged rifles, Indian ceremonial items. The enemy's zareba had turned into a filthy stockade, full of dust and horse manure. However, the Canadians, after three days of shooting practice, were growing more confident, while the Métis, with almost no bullets left, were becoming desperate. Middleton came to a decision: "Our men were beginning to show more dash, and that night [May 11] I came to the conclusion that it was time to make our decisive attack." He might have added that 150 Mounted Police under the command of Colonel Irvine had joined his army, so he now had 950 men to fight 160 Métis and Indians.

The general's strategy was not a complicated one. Middleton, with about 150 men, the Gatling gun, and a cannon, would approach Batoche in a wide sweep from the northeast. His men would start firing from that position, and with the Métis soldiers thus diverted, the main body of Middleton's infantry force coming from the south would attack the village head on.

In mid-morning, Lieutenant-Colonel Bowen Van Straubenzie, commanding the main force, heard Middleton's cannon ring out three or four times, but there was no racket from small arms. Van Straubenzie concluded that something had gone wrong and did not advance.

The major-general returned to camp at noon in a terrible rage because his orders had not been obeyed. But, perhaps unbeknownst to him, his strategy had worked. Dumont had been perplexed by Middleton's sudden appearance on his northeast flank—if the Canadians attacked on two fronts, Gabriel knew the game was over. He moved reinforcements to that position, leaving the southern area around the church vulnerable.

Then an important sign came that the rebels were worried. One of the Métis hostages, J.W. Astley, carrying a white flag, had galloped into Middleton's camp with a letter from Riel:

If you massacre our families, we are going to massacre the Indian agent [John B. Lash] and other prisoners.

Louis "David" Riel
Exovede.

Middleton immediately wrote a note on the reverse side of Riel's letter:

Monsieur Riel

I am most anxious to avoid killing women and children and have done my best to avoid doing so. Put your women and children in one place and let me know where it is and no shot shall be fired on them. I trust to your honour not to put men with them.

Fred Middleton
Com' N.W. Field Force

Louis quickly sent back a message agreeing to what Middleton had suggested. The Métis thought that Riel had begun negotiations for peace and relaxed their guard.

After a miserable lunch in the stockade, the major-general ordered his forces back to the same position near the cemetery they had occupied for days. Once again his soldiers could see themselves being picked off by Métis sharpshooters, not moving forward an inch. One of the officers, Lieutenant-Colonel Arthur Williams, finally, as was later reported, "had a belly-full up to his eyeballs." Instead of creeping up slowly to feel out Métis strength, Williams and his men rushed forward. Soon they had occupied the church, walking into the welcoming arms of the priests and nuns. Middleton then established his base there. The major-general was still fearful and ordered a reconnaissance action. The troops ignored him and with a piercing, defiant scream charged forward towards the rifle pits. The Métis, unable to reload quickly, were soon overcome and the Redcoats barrelled on. The rifle pits were held to the last possible moment; then the rebels fled to stations lower down the hill. Many were barefoot, having gotten into the habit of kicking off their boots or moccasins while in the pits.

One young Canadian plunged his bayonet into the stomach of an enemy, then stopped a moment to look at his victim—the body was skinny and shrunken, the hair pure white. Later the dead man would be identified as Joseph Ouellette, ninety-three years old, father of Riel's host. The old man had refused to stay at home. Dumont would later confess: "What kept me there [on the battlefield], I should say, was the courage of old Ouellette. Several times I said to him: 'Come on, Father, we must pull back!' and the good old man always replied: 'Just a minute! I want to kill another Englishman!' Then I said to him, 'Very well, let us die here.'"

The Canadian onslaught continued. Soon all the rifle pits were abandoned and the Métis had retreated into the village, the Canadian soldiers following after them. Letendre's house came under siege. Dumont and several of the Métis old guard remained underneath it firing at the enemy. Then Fisher's store was taken. Then Gariépy's house. Within an hour, most of the resistance was crushed, although rifle fire continued from across the river for another four hours, until seven p.m.

The Métis started counting their casualties, which they reported as twelve dead and three wounded, but two of these were not soldiers; a young girl had been killed by a burst of shrapnel—ten-year-old Marcile Gratton had been shot dead on the doorstep of Fisher's store, where she had gone looking for her mother—and a nine-month-old baby had died from machine-gun fire. All the Métis fatalities were suffered on the last day of fighting. The official count for the Canadians was ten dead, thirty-six wounded. Lieutenant-Colonel Williams succumbed a short while later to typhoid fever, although some people claimed he died of a broken heart caused by the tongue-lashing he received from Major-General Middleton.

In the late afternoon of May 12, Louis Riel and Gabriel Dumont met in the woods on the outskirts of the village.

"What are we going to do?" Riel said as soon as he saw his friend.

"We are defeated," Gabriel responded. "We shall perish. But you must have known, when we took up arms, that we would be beaten. So, they will destroy us!"

After the battle, the women gathered the children along the riverbank. Many were sobbing, they were so frightened, hungry and tired. They were also thirsty, so much so that they licked the dew off the leaves. Food had been short for days, but now it was nonexistent; many families killed their pet dogs and ate them. At night the defeated hid in the wooded areas, or in caves along the riverbank. Gabriel Dumont ran from one group to another trying to comfort them. "It was sad to see those poor souls lying in the hay like animals," he later wrote. "When I saw the children's bare feet I made them little shoes out of raw-hide." And he added, "The women were very courageous and even joked about the state they were in."

The Canadian soldiers, of course, ached for revenge and went after the entire Métis population. A reporter for the Toronto *Mail* left an account of the plundering in the days immediately following the Battle of Batoche:

What a distressing picture is offered by these Half-breed families; cruelly plundered and stripped by the volunteers. The soldiers only came out of the houses of the Half-breeds after having broken whatever they could not carry away; stoves, clocks, bedsteads, tables etc. were all mercilessly destroyed by these raving maniacs [soldiers]. Poor mothers of families who had only one bed and one blanket were brutally deprived of these articles. The soldiers being unable to carry off the bed, took hold of the blanket, and splitting with their knives the ticking, which contained the feathers, enjoyed the sport of throwing them to the wind ... the soldiers have robbed and destroyed everything they could lay their hands on in that region, leaving the residents in the most destitute conditions.

The day after the final battle, little groups of men and women carrying white flags showed up at Middleton's tent to give themselves up. The fifteen men who were thought to be on Riel's council were imprisoned; the others were disarmed and allowed to return to their farms. But among the list of dead, wounded and taken prisoner, the name of neither Louis Riel nor Gabriel Dumont appeared.

Dumont was roaming about trying to round up blankets and food for the impoverished Métis. Twice he went back to Batoche and stole supplies from under the soldiers' noses. He would remember one occasion: "I saw a policeman standing in the doorway, and I weeded him out. Another of them came out to look at the body, and I killed him too. I took two blankets and two counterpanes which I carried to my wife...."

Madeleine and Gabriel had come across Marguerite Riel and her two children in one of the caves. They were shivering with the cold and they hadn't eaten for a day. Dumont arranged for blankets and food to be brought to them. Marguerite said she had no idea where her husband was, except that he had gone off with one of the Exovedate. For the next two days, Dumont combed the hills around Batoche, all the time eluding the soldiers, searching for Louis Riel. He and Louis might not always have agreed on military tactics—if Gabriel had been of a different personality he might have blamed him for the defeat—but he remained utterly devoted to his "spiritual leader."

The day after the battle, Middleton had written a letter to Riel saying he would receive him and his council and offer them protection until the government decided what to do with the rebels. The letter was given to Moïse Ouellette, who showed it first to Dumont and then to Riel. Dumont's response was typical: "You tell Middleton that I am in the woods and that I have 90 cartridges to use on his men." But so was Riel's. He would not continue fighting, he would not exile himself again in the United States, not even with his friend

Gabriel Dumont, not even for the sake of his wife and children. He would give himself up to Canadian justice. Métis accounts quote Riel as saying to Napoléon Nault, "I'm the one they want and when my enemies have me, they'll be overjoyed: but my people will be at peace and they will get justice. I still have writing to do for a day or two, then I shall go. Let's say adieu, cousin." He wrote Middleton on May 15: "I have received only today yours of the 13th inst. My council are dispersed. I wish you would let them quiet and free [*sic*]. I hear that presently you are absent. Would I go to Batoche, who is going to receive me? I will go to fulfill God's will."

Later that afternoon, two Canadian scouts and an army translator of Cree found a weary, dishevelled Métis dressed in a Hudson's Bay coat, with a white handkerchief tied around one sleeve, an out-of-shape Stetson, and his pants rolled up over sockless feet, walking on the trail near Guardepuis crossing. They asked him who he was and he answered, "Louis Riel." Armed only with Middleton's letter, he had come to surrender.

– 19 –

And when His evidence
Decides my acquittal,
Let the Multitude dance
In a move immortal.

When Louis Riel was brought into the sprawling, bustling camp of the North-West Field Force, he was immediately taken to Strategic Command. "How do you do, Mr. Riel," General Middleton asked. "Please take a seat."

Middleton questioned his prisoner for the rest of the day, interrupted now and then by curious soldiers trying to catch a peek at the "fabulously famous" Métis leader, or by newspaper reporters hammering after interviews. The two men talked on a whole variety of subjects, including religion. "He told me Rome was all wrong and corrupt, and that the priests were narrow-minded and had interfered too much with the people ... he thought religion should be based on morality and humanity and charity," Middleton later said.

The major-general was rather surprised to find he had a cultured gentleman on his hands, rather than the ranting savage he had expected. "He [Riel] was a man of rather acute intellect. He seemed quite able to hold his own upon any argument or topic we happened to touch upon."

A small, bell-shaped tent was set up for Riel right beside Middleton's, guarded by two sentries with "loaded arms" and bayonets. A young staff sergeant working for the camp's doctor dropped in to see if Louis needed any medical attention. He wrote, "the prisoner was lying down as I entered. He scrambled to his feet as I came in. His small piercing eyes were so bright and so searching that I almost forgot to survey the powerful physique that confronted me. He greeted me in a low musical voice and placed rather a delicate soft hand in mine. His hat was off showing a great mass of brown hair, all well kept ... he wore a gray Northwest Mounted Police shirt ... a pair of bull-hide moccasins, gray tweed pants and vest completed his apparel." Later that afternoon Louis was handed over to the officer who would be responsible for getting him to Regina.

It was a strange twist of fate that Captain George Holmes Young should have been chosen for the job. He was the son of the Reverend George Young, the Methodist minister who, fifteen years before, had comforted Thomas Scott as he was being led to his execution in the courtyard of Red River's Fort Garry. When Young introduced himself to the Métis leader and told him who he was, Louis responded, "And how is your father, the fine old gentleman?"

Captain Young would spend nine full days with Riel; much of the time the two would be shackled together—they slept in the same room. They talked and debated during the entire journey. Young would later say, "I found that I had a mind against my own, and fully equal to it; better educated and much more clever than I was myself."

The captain and his prisoner did not travel alone; they were accompanied by sixteen well-armed soldiers and a Presbyterian minister, Charles Bruce Pitblado.

The first leg of the journey, from Batoche to Saskatoon, was undertaken on the hapless *Northcote*, now recovered from its war wounds. As well as Riel and company, there were several wounded soldiers aboard. They had such fierce hatred for Riel, or so they boasted, that Young feared for the Métis leader's life—one of the reasons he kept him shackled. From Saskatoon they travelled south by cart—thirteen horses in all were used. Young was worried that Wood Mountain Métis and Indians would attempt a daring rescue, and so whenever the road went through a hilly or wooded area, the soldiers accompanying them would fan out to scout out the neighbourhood. Finally, at Moose Jaw, they boarded the CPR for the short ride to Regina.

During all this time, Riel had long conversations with both Young and Pitblado during which he explained in detail the strategy of the Métis during their rebellion. One thing that emerged was the great importance placed on taking prisoners; Dumont and Riel had hoped to capture the Mounties during the Battle of Duck Lake and the Canadian soldiers aboard the *Northcote*, hold them as hostages and then deal with the Canadian government. These negotiations would have been especially effective if an Indian uprising had flared at the same time.

The three also talked a great deal about religion, and Reverend Pitblado set down in point form the bare bones of Riel's new theology; it now had a decidedly Protestant flavour about it.

1. We believe that all true believers constitute the true church. Believers in the Lord Jesus Christ are christians, and all christians make the church holy, catholic and vital.

2. We do not believe in the infallibility of the Pope.

3. We believe in the inspiration of the Holy Scriptures and the right of every man to read and learn the truths they contain.

4. We believe in a regularly ordained ministry. We would accept the ministers of all the denominations, Episcopalian, Presbyterians and Congregationalists in our ministry without re-ordaining. We would be somewhat doubtful about the Baptists....

5. We believe in a form of church government. We prefer the Episcopate. We would like [to] see a head bishop for the Dominion or for the new world, who would be independent of Rome.

6. We believe there is one God. We believe in the Trinity, though not in the ordinary sense.

7. We pray to God, to Christ, to Mary, to the saints. The three persons of [the] Trinity are in these three first. God the Father is perfect and highest. God the Son is perfect and Savior. Mary is pure but not perfect, and in her dwells the Holy Ghost. The saints are our friends, who have access to the persons who are powerful.

8. We believe in the final salvation of all men.

It became clear during this trip why Louis Riel had so readily given himself up—he was determined that the Canadian people hear his justification of the events, with his religious beliefs at the centre of his rationale. And, naively, he sincerely believed that he would be exonerated. But as he chatted with his companions on the train from Moose Jaw to Regina, Riel learned something that must have given him an awful premonition of coming darkness.

Since Regina, although the capital of the Northwest Territories, was still not much more than a cluster of ragtag huts and squat wooden structures, there was no appropriate jail available except the guardhouse of the North-West Mounted Police headquarters, west of the city. Traditionally the Métis had never trusted the force, judging, quite correctly, that many of the enlisted men had a decided Orange tinge to their thinking. Since Duck Lake, when they had become convinced that the Mounties had deliberately provoked them into taking up arms, they hated them even more. When, on May 23, Riel was placed in the dingy little cell, a shackle connected to a chain in the wall slapped on his leg, he realized he had been delivered to the enemy.

And the rebel leader was indeed to be made an example of. He was not to have a comfortable time in jail. The food was terrible—mostly potatoes with a little greasy beef. His daily exercise consisted of walking up and down in the courtyard carrying a ball that was connected by a heavy chain to his ankle. All his mail was heavily censored, he could write to no one except his family and his lawyers and these letters were carefully scrutinized, he was allowed no newspapers and only those books which the authorities thought suitable. And worst of all, the government was determined to smother his propaganda—he was allowed no visitors except by the prime minister's written consent. Only one or two reporters who had shown sympathy for the Conservative Party would be allowed to interview him.

The man in charge of the prison was a thin-faced, heavily moustached Mountie, R. Burton Deane. He had been a British career officer and after serving in India had come to Canada. In 1883 he had been appointed inspector of the North-West Mounted Police. He was a stern, no-nonsense jailer who didn't want to talk to Riel and certainly had no interest in listening to him.

As he always did in times of emotional trauma, Riel turned to his writing for comfort. He wrote a poem in English called "To the Commanding Officer of the Mounted Police in Regina". It was sent to the inspector, but whether Deane realized the satirical, mocking nature of it is not known:

> Your heart, Captain Dean,
> Must be worthy, great.
> By what I have seen,
> You are upright, straight.
> Without flattery,
> Your face, your stature
> Speak of your merry
> And Noble nature.

Riel quickly made clear why he was appealing to the solemn Deane; he planned to write his own account of the North-West Rebellion, and he wanted it published:

> Would the governor
> And the government
> Grant me a favor
> In my detainment?
> My wife, my children
> Are poor, have no bread.
> Could I use my pen
> In Jail, for their aid?

Deane was not the kind of man to be moved by such poetical implorings.

Neither the Mounties nor the government had any intention of allowing Riel a forum to spread his message.

Louis was very worried about his wife and children. He had left them at Batoche in the care of a cousin, Cuthbert Fayant, but Marguerite was suffering badly. All during the Battle of Batoche she had had terrible coughing fits, and had been spitting up blood. The previous winter she had had a miscarriage and now she was pregnant again, with her third child. She was, his sister Henriette wrote, very worn out and very dismayed. Full of anguish, Louis wrote a reminder to himself, in English: "Margaret! I told/You and your father/Before we enroll'd/Our lives together,/That my future was/Still clouded with storms."

Riel was relieved when he heard that Joseph had gone to fetch his family. Louis knew that they would be well taken care of at the family home in St. Vital.

It was not all gloomy news for Louis Riel. The Quebec Liberal establishment, including many of his old friends at the Collège de Montréal, was rallying to his support. The National Association for the Defense of the Imprisoned Métis had been set up, with a star-studded executive, including the lawyer Louis had worked for so many years before, Rodolphe Laflamme. The prime mover was one of Louis's classmates, J.B.R. Fiset. A physician and devoted Liberal—although he was temporarily not in office, he had been a member of Parliament and would be again—he was the man who eleven years before had accompanied Riel to Parliament, when he had daringly signed his name in the members' register.

Riel wrote a long letter to Fiset thanking him for his help and sketching some of the reasons for the North-West Rebellion. He emphasized that he had voluntarily walked into Middleton's camp. He could have chosen exile in the United States—Gabriel Dumont and Michel Dumas had easily escaped south of the border and, after being detained by the U.S. Army for a couple of days, were wandering about freely. Louis said he gave himself up because he thought the wrath of the government would then descend on his head and the Métis would be left in peace. To a large extent, he was right.

On behalf of the defence committee, who would pay their fees, Fiset had already sought out Riel's team of lawyers. They included two young hot-shots from Quebec, François-Xavier Lemieux and Charles Fitzpatrick.

Lemieux had been born in 1851 on a farm in the parish of Lévis, across the St. Lawrence River from Quebec City. Educated at Lévis College and Laval University, he was called to the bar in 1872, and almost immediately made a name for himself as a brilliant criminal lawyer. After he won a spectacular murder case, a reporter said of him, "If anyone can cheat the gallows it is François-Xavier Lemieux," and that became his signature.

Fitzpatrick was even younger than Lemieux—only thirty-two years old. Born in Quebec City, he was the son of an Irish lumber merchant. Educated at St. Anne's University and Laval, he was the top student in his class; unlike Lemieux, he was not a particularly forceful speaker, but he was known for his brilliant legal arguments. He had acted as both defence lawyer and prosecutor in the Trois Riviéres area. He was a devoted Liberal—Wilfrid Laurier liked to call him "my dear Fritz".

Both men had come from rather humble origins but they had married into the cream of Quebec society. Lemieux's wife was Diane Plamondon, daughter of a superior court judge, and Fitzpatrick's was Corinne Caron, whose father was Quebec's second lieutenant-governor and whose brother was Sir Adolphe Caron, federal Minister of the Militia.

Two other associates made up Riel's defence team—James N. Greenshields of Montreal, and T.C. Johnstone, who had moved from Toronto to Regina in 1882.

On July 6, 1885, Louis Riel was to be formally charged. Since the police were sure that an attack by Métis and Indians to free their leader was imminent, there was great debate as to how to get him to the courthouse. Finally it was decided to disguise him as a police officer. Thus, dressed in a white helmet and blue cape, he was driven in an open carriage the three miles to downtown Regina, three genuine Mounties sitting beside him.

Riel was accused of committing high treason—waging war on the representatives of the queen's government. In 1885 his crime was as serious as it had been five centuries earlier, when in 1352 the Statute of Treasons was passed by the British Parliament during the reign of Edward III. At that time, the law called for the guilty person to be "hanged, drawn and quartered and to have all his possessions confiscated by the Crown." The physical mutilation and seizure of goods had gone by the wayside, but still there remained only one option open to a judge when sentencing a person convicted of high treason—death by hanging. There was another, lesser offence with which the government could have charged Riel. By the nineteenth century it was felt that execution was sometimes too harsh a punishment for insignificant rebellions against the state, and so the crime of treason-felony had been introduced. In this case the court was allowed complete discretion—sentences ranged anywhere from a couple of days in prison to life. But treason above all was a political act. With so many headlines, at least in English Canada, screaming for revenge, there was no way the government could consider anything for Riel but the most serious crime on the books.

The man who swore out the information against him was the chief investigator in the case. Alexander David Stewart, Hamilton's chief of police, had been chosen partly because he was a noted Liberal and his signature on the indictment would give the case a supposed non-partisan flavour. On his way west through Winnipeg, Stewart gave a brief interview to the *Sun*. The reporter wrote: "He [Stewart] intended to get all the evidence he could against Riel and by any means, for said the chief, with a sly laugh, 'I guess the idea is to hang him.'" Riel's sympathizers were upset at Stewart's appointment because he was an avid member of an Orange lodge in Hamilton.

Riel had sent the same letter to his lawyers as he had to Fiset, outlining the reasons for the rebellion. Lemieux had responded with a telegraph full of optimism: "Your admirable letter received and creates great enthusiasm, great prospects—going up next week." At that point the lawyers said that Riel was guilty only of "the folly of loving his country too much".

Fitzpatrick and Lemieux arrived in Regina at three in the morning on July 15, 1885. A terrible thunderstorm, followed by a deluge, had made the roads almost impassable with mud. There was no space available at the local hotel—reporters had taken all the rooms—and they ended up sleeping on the floor the first night.

The next morning a press conference was held with Riel in attendance. The *Daily News* reported that the prisoner was "almost overcome when they [his lawyers] entered his presence ... [his] voice choked with emotion." He was so pleased that "each gentleman was of a representative nationality." Subsequently, the prisoner and his lawyers met in private. Exactly what went on in that meeting is of vital importance in the Riel saga. Fitzpatrick and Lemieux came away saying they had talked with a "madman or a damned hypocrite, maybe both". They would write shortly afterwards to Archbishop Taché, "We visited Riel today—his words, his deportment, and his conduct in general confirm ... that he was not of sound mind."

It has often been assumed that it was at that point that insanity jelled as the only defence open to the lawyers. But there is another, more logical scenario. Riel was insistent that the trial provide him with a forum to explain and rationalize his actions during the Red River resistance and North-West Rebellion. He was sure he could prove that he had not committed treason at all, that his Métis had set up their own government only when the established one had ceased to function in their interests, that the rebellions therefore were necessary and legal. It would have been a more difficult defence than insanity, but not unreasonable. "The logic was sophisticated, political and maybe, dangerous," political scientist Gerald B. Sperling has written. "It was not complicated; it had been worked out in Manitoba." But it was a defence the lawyers were definitely not prepared to pursue. Knowing that Louis had been hospitalized in Quebec mental asylums in the 1870s, Fitzpatrick and Lemieux may well have had the defence of insanity already worked out; certainly they had contacted doctors at Beauport Asylum before they left. They would not deny that Riel had rebelled against the queen; instead they would prove that he had been crazy as a loon while doing so. No matter how appropriate it may have seemed to legal minds, it was a strategy doomed to failure. First, Riel was not insane.* Secondly, if the lawyers had known anything about him, his history, his sense of mission, his pride, they would have realized he would never agree to act like a lunatic—not even to save his own life.

The trial was to take place in a rented building in dusty downtown Regina. "On a spot," waxed the *Regina Leader*, "where three years ago the only sign of life was the trail of the savage or the footprints of the buffalo, or the sweet short song of the prairie lark—what do we have? The highest expression of civilization—an organized court of law." Whether this trial was "civilized" is another question. In fact, it made a mockery of justice—a shabby trial in a shabby little courtroom that would have incredible historic significance.

The courtroom was located on the ground floor of a two-storey brick building constructed only the year before. There was nothing dignified about it; the walls weren't even painted. It was only fifty feet long and twenty feet wide, so that the participants and spectators were packed in like sardines. A special area was set aside for "ladies" so that the wives of all the important personages—Judge Richardson, Major-General Middleton, the crown attorney—could "enjoy the spectacle". They were all dressed very "prettily" in light summer dresses, adding colour, along with the scarlet-coated Mounties, to an otherwise drab crowd.

The first order of business was again to read the charge of high treason against Riel. As the clerk droned on and on, Louis leaned forward in his seat listening intently. The language was as medieval as the law itself. "Louis Riel, then living within the Dominion of Canada and under the protection of our Sovereign Lady the Queen, not regarding the duty of his allegiance nor having the fear of God in his heart, but being moved and seduced by the instigation of the devil as a false traitor against our said Lady the Queen...." There were six counts in all; for each of the three battles, Duck Lake, Fish Creek and Batoche, there were two identical charges, one distinguishing Louis as being "a subject of our Lady the Queen", the other identifying him as "living within the Dominion of Canada and under the protection of our Sovereign Lady the Queen". This was an attempt by the crown to ward off Riel's defence that he was an American citizen and therefore could not commit treason against Queen Victoria. And they would prove successful. Riel's citizenship never became a real issue.

---

* For a discussion of the controversy over Riel's insanity, which has raged for over a hundred years now, see "Letter to Father Joe", Addendum Three, page 453.

Once the indictment had been read, the clerk asked the accused how he pleaded—guilty or not guilty. Before he could answer, the defence counsel challenged the jurisdiction of the court. This was something Riel desperately wanted; he felt that he could only get a fair trial in Quebec before a French-speaking jury of twelve. It was not an outrageous request.

For many years trials for capital crimes committed in the Northwest Territories could only be heard in Upper or Lower Canada, before a judge and full panel of jurors. But in 1877, to relieve the overly burdened judiciary, the stipendiary magistrate system was introduced. A stipendiary magistrate was a lawyer with at least five years' experience who served as a part-time judge. He received a stipend for the hours he put in; he was appointed by the government, and continued only at its pleasure. He was, in other words, a servant of the party in power.

Fifty-nine-year-old Hugh Richardson, a handsome man with a well-tended beard and moustache, was the stipendiary magistrate who would try Riel. He was typical of the breed. Born in London, England, he had come to Canada with his family in 1831, settling near Toronto, where his father worked as a bank manager. Richardson was called to the bar of Osgoode Hall in 1847, practised law in Woodstock, Ontario, and was the chief clerk in the department of justice from 1872 until he left in 1876 for Battleford, to take on the job of stipendiary magistrate the next year. He was very much part of the ruling elite of the Northwest. He had been a lieutenant-colonel in the militia, and was often called upon by the establishment to give his opinion on military matters. He was also deeply involved with political issues, almost always siding with the Conservatives. In 1880, for example, he wrote a letter to the Deputy Minister of the Interior urging the government to deal with Métis grievances because the "halfbreed colonies had been latterly subjected to the evil influences of the leading spirits of Manitoba troubles." In March 1885, the judge had attended the meeting with Lawrence Clarke, NWMP Commissioner A.G. Irvine and Indian Commissioner Hayter Reed, at which it was determined that a hundred mounted police should be sent from Regina to Fort Carlton to squash the Métis rebellion. How Richardson could consider himself at arm's length from either the accused or the alleged crimes is hard to fathom. Riel's lawyers were disgusted by the judge's close links to those who were prosecuting their client. Lemieux wrote his wife, "How can you expect justice, any justice, to be done?"

Richardson overruled the defence's challenge that his court could not legally hear the case. In this he was backed by legal precedent; only three days before Riel's trial, a man had been hanged for the murder of his room-mate in Moose Jaw. The basis of his appeal had been the legality of the stipendiary magistrate hearing capital cases, and the Manitoba appeal court had ruled in favour of the prosecution.

Once that legal tangle had been dealt with, the clerk of the court asked Riel once again how he pleaded. He responded with dignity: "I have the honour of answering the court I am not guilty."

The next day was entirely spent debating whether the trial should be post-poned. The crown was eager to get on with it: a panel of thirty-six potential jurors and the seventeen witnesses for the prosecution were all waiting—the NWMP had set up a special boarding tent for them across the street from the courthouse, but it was not very comfortable. Any delay would therefore be most inconvenient, said the chief prosecutor. There was, however, one difficulty: Riel's attorneys, who had arrived in Regina only eight days before, had had neither time nor money to call any witnesses. As Riel's third lawyer, James Greenshields, told the judge, "Counsel for the defence feel that it is utterly impossible to do justice to the prisoner if we are forced on at the present time." That was putting it mildly. In fact, they had no case at all. They needed at least a month to get ready, they said.

Affidavits were filed that day that indicated that there were already sharp differences between the accused and his lawyers: the lawyers were eager to prove that Riel was insane, Louis was determined to prove his innocence by showing that his rebellion was justified. To that end, he asked that Gabriel Dumont, Michel Dumas and Napoléon Nault, who were all safely in Montana, be guaranteed immunity from prosecution to give evidence. Dumont was eager to tell the court that he alone was responsible for the military operation; that Riel had been asked by the Métis to come to St. Laurent and had done so with nothing but peaceful intentions—he had never so much as held a gun; and that it was the entire fourteen-member Exovedate who had voted for armed rebellion—Riel was not even an official member.

Lawyer Greenshields, temporarily bowing to Riel's request, said, "We intend to ask this court to order all documents, petitions, writings and representations—prayer after prayer, petition after petition was presented to the Government by people asking for redress—be brought before the court." The means of doing this would be to subpoena the keepers of these documents, A.M. Burgess, Deputy Minister of the Interior, and Lawrence Vankoughnet, Deputy Superintendent of Indian Affairs.

Judge Richardson found both these requests rather ridiculous. He was not going to guarantee the Métis rebels immunity from prosecution—if they wanted to help Riel they could give themselves up and face trial. And he was certainly not going to trouble such senior civil servants as Burgess and Vankoughnet. As the crown asked, what possible bearing could such documents have on Riel's defence? This was a showcase trial that was designed to focus the Canadian public's attention on one scapegoat, to divert it away from the real economic and political reasons for the North-West Rebellion. There was no way the

420 / RIEL: A LIFE OF REVOLUTION

scapegoat was going to be allowed to dredge up the government's incompetency and cruelty in its treatment of the Métis and Indians of the Northwest.

Once these witnesses had been contemptuously disallowed, there was no possibility for Louis Riel to get a fair hearing.

Judge Richardson did permit an adjournment, but only of one week, enough time to bring to Regina the witnesses that Riel's defence lawyers wanted. These were two doctors from Ontario and Quebec insane asylums and the priests André and Fourmond. During the entire trial, not one witness for the defence gave evidence that was sympathetic to or supportive of Riel. Those who were called by his legal team were only too anxious to show how crazy he really was.

Three days after proceedings adjourned, another trial took place which fortified the defence lawyers' intention to rely on Riel's perceived insanity. It took a judge and jury less than thirty minutes to find Will Jackson not guilty by reason of insanity.

Jackson had been arrested at Batoche by Middleton and eventually charged with treason-felony. Through documents found at the Métis headquarters implicating Jackson in Exovedate decisions, the crown felt they had a good case against him. His family, however, waged a campaign to convince the politicians that, as his father put it, "Willie had received such cruel treatment at the hands of Riel, that his mind is quite unhinged and he is sinking into idiocy." By the time his case got to trial, a deal had been worked out between the crown and defence. The logic was simple: Jackson was the only white man among the Métis and Indians who participated directly in their rebellion, and therefore he must be insane. The judge ordered that he be sent to the Selkirk Lunatic Asylum, but since that institution was not ready for him, he was temporarily detained at Lower Fort Garry. On November 2, with the help of his sister, he escaped and fled to the United States. Canadian authorities never attempted to pursue him. Despite what his father had written, he remained utterly devoted to Louis Riel, referring to him as one of "the greatest patriots and statesmen" Canada had ever produced. He never stopped calling himself Honoré (or Henri, as he sometimes used) Joseph Jaxon, in memory of the time he had lived with the Métis.*

---

*Jackson had a remarkable career until his death in 1951 at age ninety in New York City. Among other things, he was a union organizer in Chicago, the administrator of the Anarchist Defense Fund, a Métis spokesman in the United States, a successful construction contractor, a member of the Baha'i. In the mid-1940s, he became a janitor and furnace man for a New York City apartment building. For five years he toiled at this, until he became ill, couldn't pay his rent and was evicted. It took three men six hours to remove his boxes of papers. Almost all were destroyed. They contained invaluable records of the North-West Rebellion and other events involving the Métis.

Louis Riel spent the nerve-racking wait for his trial to resume in a tiny jail cell hastily built beneath the courtroom building. One of the longest letters he ever penned in his long letter-writing career was to Archbishop Taché at St. Boniface. Taché had sent Riel's old friend Father Georges Dugas to comfort him and the other Métis prisoners being held in makeshift Regina jails, and Riel thanked him for that. There was a long explanation of his religious thought and a justification for his break with the established church. Riel's great hero, Bishop Bourget, had died just a month and a half before, and Louis now informed the archbishop that he, Taché, had been "divinely elected" Bourget's successor.

> Now that I am imprisoned, accused of High Treason, without any means of defence, unable to call my witnesses and with my best witnesses displeased with me, I entrust myself to the paternal Providence of God who has every-thing and everybody in His care. Today, July 24, 1885, I proclaim humbly from the padlocked compound of Regina prison that you are the pontiff chosen by God to instruct, console, succour, guide, bless, and save the New World through the grace of Jesus Christ.

The problem was that the archbishop didn't want the job. He had long ago concluded that Riel "was a miserable madman and lunatic".

On the hot, dry morning of July 28, Louis Riel's trial began again. The little courtroom was, in effect, a national stage where many of the antipathies and hatreds which had bedevilled Canadian society since the British conquest were played out. As the historian George F.G. Stanley put it, it was a drama of "east vs west, Ontario vs Quebec, Orangeism vs Catholicism, Anglo-Saxon vs French." And in the middle of it was one man fighting to save his life.

There had been rumours circulating for weeks of a plot to free Riel and smuggle him across the border. In fact Pascal Bonneau, a French-Canadian busi-nessman living in Regina and a close friend of Louis's, later insisted that he was approached by Lieutenant-Governor Dewdney to organize a getaway for Riel. Certainly the Canadian government had much to gain—Quebec votes, for one— if Riel's trial was aborted. Bonneau was arranging the horses he needed for the plan when Charles Nolin found out about it. He supposedly reported it to the authorities and that was the end of the plot to free Riel. Still, precautions were taken; an enormous number of armed guards encircled the Regina courthouse.

Once the court was called to order, its first business was to select a jury. It would consist of only six men; because of the sparse population in the Territories, the stipendiary magistrate was allowed to work with this number. Riel's counsel had tried to argue that the right to a twelve-man jury trial for capi-tal crimes had been won by the Magna Carta and defined in imperial statutes for hundreds of years. Judge Richardson dismissed the argument out of hand, simply saying the law permitted the smaller jury so that was that.

Among the panel of thirty-five possible jurors, two had French names; neither was chosen to sit. All six jurors selected—Francis Cosgrove, the chairman, Walter Merryfield, Henry J. Painter, Edwin J. Brooks, Bell Deane and Ed Everet—were Anglo-Saxon Protestants. Only Brooks, who had been born in Quebec, could speak French. Riel's lawyers didn't care so much about the jurors' language as their religion. Lemieux and Fitzpatrick did not believe that Protestants could understand the significance of Riel's rejection of the Catholic church—an important plank in their defence of insanity.

Juror Edwin Brooks, a merchant from Indian Head, scribbled down notes during the trial, including a description of Riel:

> A good-looking man, fair complexion, high forehead, wavy black hair, of medium height, full beard, like John the Baptist, sharp flashy eyes, small sensitive hands that twitch all the time and which he uses a great deal in talking, waving them around like the arms of a windmill. Like the half-breeds we know, he wore a dark, poor-fitting suit, open red flannel shirt and moccasins on his feet.

Louis Riel and his counsel faced a formidable team of prosecutors. The chief crown counsel was Christopher Robinson, son of John Beverley Robinson, Ontario's chief justice, a man who had done more to shape the law in Upper Canada than any other individual. Christopher Robinson was considered one of the most elegant and polished courtroom performers in Canada. Britton Bath Osler of Toronto was judged by the press as simply "the finest, most quick-witted" criminal lawyer of his day. George Burbridge was the Deputy Minister of Justice and would become the architect of Canada's criminal code. David Lynch Scott was a barrister and mayor of Regina. The only French Canadian on the crown's side, Thomas Casgrain of Montreal, was a professor of law at Laval University. With all these heavy guns present, it was obvious the government felt there was a lot at stake. B.B. Osler would put it bluntly: he told the jury it was "the most serious trial that has ever probably taken place in Canada."

In his opening remarks, Osler gave much importance to the note sent to Major Crozier before Duck Lake: "In case of non-acceptance [of Métis demands that the Mounties leave Fort Carlton], we intend to attack you, when tomorrow, the Lord's Day, is over, and to commence without delay a war of extermination upon all those who have shown themselves hostile to our rights." The prosecutor emphasized that Riel had asked the Canadian government for money and promised in return to go back to Montana. Finally, the crown prosecutor made much of Riel's break with the priests. All of this was used to paint as black a portrait of the accused as possible. Osler pulled no punches:

> The prophet of the Saskatchewan was the cry under which his poor dupes, and many of them should have known better, were supposed to rally ... it is not a matter brought by any wrongs and grievances that have existed, so much as a matter brought about by the personal ambition and vanity of the man on trial ... the evidence shows that he was utterly careless of his methods, and had but one object, his own power, or money, and he did not care whose lives he sacrificed.

Since Riel had not been an official member of the Exovedate and had never taken up arms, let alone killed anybody, it was important to establish that he had absolute power over the Métis, and commanded them in their armed uprising. To this end, many of the white men who had been taken prisoner during the rebellion were called to give evidence. Some of it was very damaging indeed. John Astley, the surveyor who, after the Battle of Batoche, had been sent with a message to Middleton, testified that Riel had admitted that he had ordered the Métis to open fire at Duck Lake, and said that he himself had actually seen Louis command the Métis to fall in line.

The crown's prime strategy—to show that Riel had been the brains and spirit behind the rebellion—was very successful. The tightly controlled testimony of the witnesses, those who had been prisoners of the Métis, and others such as General Middleton and Captain George Young, came together like an elaborate, well-managed jigsaw. That it was a completely distorted picture of the truth, of course, mattered not at all. Neither did the fact that much of the testimony was hearsay.

Eastwood Jackson, Will's brother, participated in the character assassination. Riel had spoken to him about the money he felt the dominion government owed him. "He disclosed his personal motives to me on this occasion. He became very much excited and angry, and attacked the English and the English constitution, and exhibited the greatest hatred for the English, and he showed his motive was one of revenge more than anything else."

The defence's tactics were obvious from the onset of the trial. There would be no aggressive, energetic cross-examination to reveal contradictions, mistakes or even lies in the testimony of crown witnesses. Counsel for the defence would try to coax out of even the most reluctant crown witness evidence that portrayed Riel as a lunatic. Dr. John Willoughby, the Saskatoon physician who had encountered Riel a week before the Battle of Duck Lake, was the first witness called. He described for the prosecutor the conversation he had had with the accused, in which Louis had explained his plan to divide the Northwest Territories into individual states for Bavarians, Poles, Italians, etc. Riel's lawyer, Charles Fitzpatrick, jumped on this:

> *Q.* Of course the plan he unfolded to you about the conquest of the North-West then did not strike you as anything extraordinary for a man in his position to assert?

> *A.* It did, certainly.

> *Q.* It appeared to you a very rational proposition?

> *A.* No, it did not.

Riel sat quietly as witness after witness gave testimony by which the prosecution attempted to portray him as the devil incarnate, and the defence to paint him as an utter fool. He finally lost his composure when his cousin Charles Nolin appeared as the crown's star witness.

Nolin was obviously seeking revenge against Riel for the humiliation he had suffered during the North-West Rebellion. His interpretation of events was as sinister as his rather limited imagination could manage. In one instance, he described a book in which he claimed Riel had written that he would destroy England, Canada, Rome and the Pope, in that order. Nolin testified that "He [Riel] said before the grass is that high in this country you will see foreign armies in this country. He said I will commence by destroying Manitoba, and then I will come and destroy the Northwest and take possession of the Northwest." This was meaty material for a defence intent on proving insanity. Lemieux managed to elicit from Nolin not only that Riel had shown him such a book, but that the prophecies had been written in buffalo blood. It was all too much for Louis. He jumped up and pleaded with the judge, "If there was any way, by legal procedure that I should be allowed to say a word, I wish you would allow me before this witness leaves the box." What had obviously been a festering sore between the accused and his attorneys finally burst into the open.

Right there in the open courtroom, Fitzpatrick and Riel struggled over how the case was to be conducted, over the very competence of the defence counsel. Red in the face, the lawyer angrily spat out, "this man is actually obstructing the proper management of this case ... and he must be given to understand immediately that he won't be allowed to interfere in it, or else it will be absolutely useless for us to endeavour to continue any further in it."

But Riel was not easily subdued, even if his lawyers were threatening to quit. His perception of what was happening in the court was reasonable and logical and has been shared by those standing trial throughout time:

> My counsel come from Quebec, from a far province. They have to put questions to men with whom they are not acquainted, on circumstances which they don't know, and although I am willing to give them all the information that I can, they cannot follow the thread of all the questions that could be put to the witnesses. They lose more than three-quarters of the good opportunities of making good answers, not because they are not able...; they are learned, they are talented, but the circumstances are such that they cannot put all the questions.

After the judge promised him that he would get a chance to address the jury before they retired to consider their verdict, Riel finally gave in and agreed to keep quiet for the rest of the trial. But not before a final outburst. "I cannot abandon my dignity," he cried. "Here I have to defend myself against the accusation of high treason, or I have to consent to the animal life of an asylum. I don't care much about animal life if I am not allowed to carry with it the moral existence of an intellectual being."

As the trial proceeded, the weather got hotter, but still spectators packed the courtroom. The antics of Judge Richardson's wife, a large, flamboyant woman who sat close to her husband, were getting on the defence's nerves. Lemieux wrote, "It was enough to make you sick, she had the indecency to laugh heartily when most had tears in their eyes."

The defence's case began at ten a.m., July 30. It would last only one day. Riel's lawyers called a mere five witnesses, none of whom had any sympathy whatsoever for the accused. What the defence lawyers had to prove under law, if they were to obtain a verdict of not guilty by reason of insanity, was that Riel was so irrational as to be unable to comprehend the illegality of his acts.

Riel's sworn enemy Alexis André was the first witness to take the stand. Lemieux made a half-hearted attempt to establish the reasons for the North-West Rebellion, by asking him about the petitions and letters that had been sent by the Métis to the dominion government. When André testified that many had not yet received the patents for their lands on the South Saskatchewan, crown prosecutor Osler quickly cut him off at the pass. "My learned friends have opened a case of treason, justified only by the insanity of the prisoner; they are now seeking to justify armed rebellion for the redress of these grievances. These two defences are inconsistent." There was no way the government was going to be put on trial if the crown attorneys had their way. And they did get their way. Lemieux acquiesced and the questioning turned abruptly to the defence he was the most comfortable with—Riel's state of mind. André, who despised the Métis leader, was only too happy to oblige. "On the question of religion and politics," he said, "we considered that he was completely a fool. In discussing these questions, it was like showing a red flag to a bull."

In cross-examination, the crown brought up the $35,000 Riel had supposedly demanded from the government for self-imposed exile to the United States. André testified that Riel was quite prepared to sell out the interests of the Métis if he received the money. The priest, in fact, did great damage to the defence's case, because the so-called bribery attempt made Riel appear not a lunatic but a manipulative and shrewd bargainer.

Finally crown attorney Casgrain asked the Oblate: "A man may be a great reformer of great religious questions without being a fool?" André answered: "I do not deny history, but the reformer must have some principle which the prisoner never had." He would have made a great witness for the prosecution.

The scholarly-looking Father Vital Fourmond was also eager to express his opinion of Riel's character.

> Before the rebellion, it appeared as if there were two men in the prisoner. In private conversation he was affable, polite, pleasant and a charitable man to me. I noticed that even when he was quietly talked to about the affairs of politics and government, and he was not contradicted on these subjects, then he was quite rational; but as soon as he was contradicted on these subjects, then he was a different man and would be carried away with his feelings. He would go so far as to use violent expressions to those who were even his friends. As soon as the rebellion commenced, then he became excited and was carried away and he lost all control of himself and of his temper. He went so far that when a father contradicted him, he became quite excited and had no respect for him, and he often threatened to destroy all the churches.

Interestingly, during the trial neither priest expressed his opinions about Riel as vehemently as he had in the past. They may have realized that the Métis were already seething with resentment against them, that they considered them traitors, and that it would take years for the church to overcome Métis antipathy. Even that great apologist for the Catholic clergy in the Canadian West, the historian Marcel Giraud, would write, "the memory of the schism that had taken place could not be effaced immediately. For a long time it prevented the re-establishment of the reciprocal confidence that hitherto had united the Métis and their missionaries. Even today the mere evocation of these events reawakens the animosity of the two parties."

Philippe Garnot, who had served as Riel's secretary when Jackson was incapacitated, was the third witness. He was questioned about Riel's religious beliefs, but his responses were so abrupt and uninformative as to be useless. The crown didn't even bother to cross-examine him.

The last two witnesses were psychiatrists and both would turn out to be disasters for the defence's position.

Dr. François-Elzéar Roy had been the superintendent and part owner of the Beauport Asylum in Quebec City when Riel had been hospitalized there ten years before. Roy testified that while the accused was in his institution, he suffered from "megalomania". When asked what the symptoms of the disease were, he replied: "They [the ill] sometimes give you reasons which would be reasonable if they were not starting from a false idea. They are very clever on those discussions, and they have a tendency to irritability when you question or doubt their mental conditions, because they are under a strong impression that they are right and that they consider it to be an insult when you try to bring them to reason again." (One juror would later tell his family that he thought Dr. Roy was describing a normal human condition, and that he often acted that way himself.) Roy then went on to say that from what he had heard in the courtroom that day, Riel's mind was "unsound".

Crown attorney B.B. Osler made mincemeat of this, and Louis Riel publicly congratulated him for doing so. Obviously the doctor had not prepared well for his testimony, even though he had come all the way from Quebec City to Regina. He had not brought any documents pertaining to Riel's case, neither the certificate of involuntary confinement nor the written medical history. Throughout his cross-examination Osler kept hounding the witness, until Roy's answers became ever more vague and muddled. Finally the doctor admitted: "I am not an expert in insanity."

Dr. Daniel Clark, superintendent of the Toronto Lunatic Asylum, was called as an expert witness for the defence. On the basis of what he called "cursory" interviews he had had with Riel, three over two days, he was prepared to say he was insane. But his testimony wasn't much good to Riel's case because he also insisted: "they [the insane] often know what they do and can talk about it afterwards; it is simply all nonsense to talk about a man not knowing what he is doing, simply because he is insane." Riel, he said, definitely knew right from wrong.

Fitzpatrick was flabbergasted, indeed furious, at Clark's testimony, but the psychiatrist reminded him, "I might say, if the court will allow me, that when I come to cases of this kind, I am not subpoenaed for one side more than another. I am here only ... to give a sort of medical judicial opinion."*

---

* After Riel's death, Clark made a career of his brief encounter with the revolutionary. He gave many papers and lectures at various scholarly functions on the subject of Riel's insanity. These were full of vicious lies—he claimed, for example, that Riel's mother was a "semi-imbecile", his father "deranged"—and gross interpretations that were patently unfair.

With that the defence rested its case. Even the prosecutors were surprised at how weak it had been.

The crown called two other medical doctors in rebuttal, who claimed that Riel was perfectly sane.

The next day, July 31, Fitzpatrick gave his two-hour summation to the jury. It would be his only chance to extricate his case from a swamp of incompetence and weakness. He tried, in a long-winded, tortured, emotional kind of way.

> It is right for me to say, gentlemen, that the government of Canada had wholly failed in its duty towards these Northwest Territories ... and, I say, gentlemen, that it is a maxim of political economy that the faults of those whom we have placed in authority necessarily injuriously affect ourselves, and it is thus that we are made the guardians of each other's rights. The fact that the government and the people placed in authority have committed faults towards the Northwest to a large extent do not justify the rebellion; but, gentlemen, if there had been no rebellion, if there had been no resistance, is there any one of you that can say to-day, is there any one of you that can place his hand on his conscience and honestly say that the evils under which the country has complained would have been remedied?

Most of the summation, of course, attempted to prove Louis Riel's insanity. After the poor performance of his witnesses, all Fitzpatrick was left with was the logic that the very act of leading a few hundred Métis against the mighty Canadian force was proof of insanity, as was questioning the Catholic hierarchy in Rome, or trying to express a reformed religion.

At last Riel had his chance to speak. He had been preparing for days, scribbling notes, reciting out loud to himself. He would address the jury. Fitzpatrick tried to stop him, but Judge Richardson insisted it was the accused's right to do so.

Riel was dressed more formally on this occasion, in a frock coat and a stark white shirt. The trial had been a terrible ordeal for him, and he admitted he had trouble keeping his emotions under control. "I hope with the help of God I will maintain calmness and decorum as suits this honourable court, this honourable jury." Since almost nobody in the courtroom spoke French, and he did not want to rely on a translator, he was forced to speak English. As a result some of his language was a little awkward, even simplistic—the eloquence and forcefulness that would have been his in French were missing, and yet it was a superb speech, one of the classics of Canadian history.

He asked the jurors not to take as a mark of insanity the little prayer with which he would begin his testimony. It was typical Riel: "O, my God, bless me, bless this honourable court, bless this honourable jury, bless my good lawyers who have come seven hundred leagues to try to save my life, bless also the lawyers for the crown, because they have done, I am sure, what they thought their duty."

He realized it was imperative right at the beginning to give the motivation for his actions as clearly and forcibly as he could:

> When I came into the Northwest in July, the first of July 1884, I found the Indians suffering. I found the Half-breeds eating the rotten pork of the Hudson's Bay Company and getting sick and weak every day. Although a Half-breed, and having no pretension to help the whites, I also paid attention to them. I saw they were deprived of responsible government, I saw that they were deprived of their public liberties. I remembered that Half-breed meant white and Indian, and while I paid attention to the suffering of Indians and the Half-breeds I remembered that the greatest part of my heart and blood was white and I have directed my attention to help the Indians, to help the Half-breeds and to help the whites to the best of my ability. We have made petitions, I have made petitions with others to the Canadian government asking to relieve the condition of this country. We have taken time; we have tried to unite all classes, even if I may speak, all parties. Those who have been in close communication with me know I have suffered, that I have waited for months to bring some of the people of the Saskatchewan to an understanding of certain important points in our petition to the Canadian government and I have done my duty. I believe I have done my duty.

While he thanked his lawyers several times during his address, he also made it clear what he thought of their defence:

> when I saw the glorious General Middleton bearing testimony that he thought I was not insane, and when Captain Young proved that I am not insane, I felt that God was blessing me, blotting away from my name the blot resting upon my reputation on account of having been in the lunatic asylum of my good friend Dr. Roy. I have been in an asylum, but I thank the lawyers for the crown who destroyed the testimony of my good friend Dr. Roy, because I have always believed that I was put in the asylum without reason.

Riel tried to explain the religious beliefs that had been so mercilessly ridiculed in the courtroom over four days:

My insanity, Your Honours, gentlemen of the jury, is that I wish to leave Rome aside, inasmuch as it is the cause of division between Catholics and Protestants.... If I have any influence in the New World it is to help in that way and even if it takes two hundred years to become practical [a reality], then after my death that will bring out practical results, and then my children's children will shake hands with the Protestants of the New World in a friendly manner. I do not wish these evils which exist in Europe to be continued, as much as I can influence it, among the Half-breeds. I do not wish that to be repeated in America. That work is not the work of some days or some years, it is the work of hundreds of years.

When he finally concluded his speech, there was hardly a dry eye in the house. Even Mrs. Richardson kept quiet.

For fifteen years I have been neglecting myself. Even one of the most hard witnesses on me said that with all my vanity, I never was particular to my clothing; yes, because I never had much to buy any clothing. The Reverend Father André has often had the kindness to feed my family with a sack of flour, and Father Fourmond. My wife and children are without means, while I am working more than any representative in the Northwest. Although I am simply a guest of this country—a guest of the Half-breeds of the Saskatchewan—although as a simple guest, I worked to better the condition of the people of the Saskatchewan at the risk of my life, to better the condition of the people of the North-West, I have never had any pay. It has always been my hope to have a fair living one day. It will be for you to pronounce—if you say I was right, you can conscientiously acquit me, as I hope through the help of God you will. You will console those who have been fifteen years around me only partaking in sufferings. What you will do in justice to me, in justice to my family, in justice to my friends, in justice to the Northwest, will be rendered a hundred times to you in this world, and to use a sacred expression, life everlasting in the other.

Christopher Robinson gave the summation for the crown immediately after Riel had finished. It was cold, logical and without emotion, incisively massing all the evidence against the accused. He probably realized that he no longer had to worry too much about the question of insanity—through his performance Riel had already proved he was rational. "Well, gentlemen," Robinson said,

we have the evidence to show that this rebellion was designed, contrived, premeditated and prepared, that it was carried out with deliberation and intention, that it was the result of no sudden impulse, that it was no outburst of passion, but it was clearly, calmly and deliberately opened and carried out.... Those who are guilty of this rebellion, and those who have not a proper excuse have taken the step upon their own heads, and they must suffer the punishment which the law from all time, and which the law for the last five centuries has declared to be the punishment of the crime of treason.

Once Robinson had concluded, Judge Richardson began his address to the jury; time soon ran out, however, and he continued it the next day, August 1.

Richardson had presided over the trial with some impartiality until the moment he gave his summation. Then his bias against Riel became crystal clear. He did recite the law and portions of evidence, but he did not hesitate to express his opinion on such things as Riel's insanity. Finally he told the jurors, "Not only must you think of the man in the dock, but you must think of society at large. You are not called upon to think of the government at Ottawa simply as a Government, you have to think of the homes and of the people who live in this country, you have to ask yourselves: Can such things be permitted?"

With that loaded question in their minds, the jury retired to consider their verdict. It was two p.m.

The courtroom relaxed. The ladies burst into loud chatter; the lawyers gathered in a cluster, already beginning the post-mortem; the reporters scribbled furiously—the story must be ready to telegraph the moment the verdict was announced. Suddenly the din of conversation wavered; everyone turned to stare at the defendant's box. Riel was on his knees, praying softly but audibly to his God in both French and Latin. Sometimes he would scramble up to ask his lawyer about something that had popped into his head. But always he would return to his prayers. Mrs. Richardson told her dinner guests that night that it was all very embarrassing.

At 3:15 the door to the courtroom slowly opened and the six men of the jury filed in, flanked by two red-coated Mounties.

Riel jumped to his feet and gripped the railing of the prisoner's dock. With all the effort he could muster, he would remain calm.

The clerk asked the foreman to read the verdict. Even though it was very short, the man struggled with it—he had tears in his eyes. "Guilty," he whispered and then added in a louder voice, "Your Honour, I have been asked by my brother jurors to recommend the prisoner to the mercy of the crown."

The foreman of the jury, Francis Cosgrove, had wanted to acquit Riel altogether. According to his daughter, he said, "Riel should have been set free and allowed to go somewhere in the Northwest Territories and have a place of his own with other Métis." Another juror, Edwin J. Brooks, left a description of the debate that went on. The jurors had been sequestered and closely guarded all during the trial. "Even if we went to the washroom, a Mountie went with us," wrote Brooks. "All we did was discuss, discuss, discuss":

> On the subject of whether Riel was insane or not. We argued that back and forth for hours at a time. A couple of the fellows believed he was; but I couldn't agree, although there was a good deal of evidence against him on that score. He had twice been committed to an asylum in Montreal and some of his actions seemed to show him crazy, but his behavior in the court-room, the close way in which he followed the case and the sharp questions he put, proved to me that he was quite sane and of right mind.
>
> We had hot discussions also as to whether Riel was entirely to blame or whether the Government wasn't just as much so.
>
> Another difficult point was whether to recommend mercy. Some of the fellows wanted him hanged outright. I was strongly against that and in the end we were unanimous.

What became clear was that once the jurors had decided that Riel was not mad, there was no way to acquit him. No other defence but insanity had been presented. It is possible—a question mark that has hung in history—that if the reasons for the North-West Rebellion had emerged clearly, a hung jury or even an acquittal might have resulted. The defence called not one witness who was non-white, not one person who had been privy to the Exovedate or its decisions. Yet around the corner from the courthouse sat the jail where twenty-one Métis activists were awaiting their own trials. If they had testified, another more genuine version of the truth might have emerged.

Before he was sentenced, Riel was given an opportunity to address the court. Somehow he managed to keep his composure during a speech that went on for three hours. He had not prepared at all, so it was a much more rambling, less logical address than the precise discourse he had given just before the jury retired.

He actually seemed relieved that he had been found guilty, that he didn't have to live with a judgement of madness: "Should I be executed—at least if I were going to be executed—I would not be executed as an insane man. It would be a great consolation for my mother, for my wife, for my children, for my brothers, for my relatives, even for my protectors, for my countrymen." And there was the hope, of course, of clemency.

Much of the long speech, however, was a justification for his life of revolution, or as he put it, his "fifteen years' war". He was supremely proud of the Manitoba Act and the part he had played in its creation. His ideas about immigration and land ownership, which had been offered up time and again as the rantings of a madman, flowed directly from his experience at Red River. He wanted all sorts of people, Irish, Bavarians, Swiss, to divvy up the vast amount of empty land in the Northwest. What was so insane about that? he asked.

His opinion of the rights of land ownership for Métis and Indians was particularly poignant. Referring to the Anglo-Saxon settlers flooding into the area, he said:

> When they have crowded their country because they had no room to stay any more at home, it does not give them the right to come and take the share of all the tribes besides them. When they come they ought to say, well, my little sister, the Cree tribe, you have a great territory, but that territory has been given to you as our land, it has been given to our fathers in England and France and of course you cannot exist without having that spot of land. This is the principle. God cannot create a tribe without locating it. We are not birds. We have to walk on the ground....

Finally Riel told the court he wanted two things. He wanted a commission of doctors to examine him, not to judge whether he was insane, but to decide whether he was an impostor. Was he someone who had struggled for the Métis people, or had he cared only for his own gain? And he wanted another trial, a trial that would cover fifteen years of his life. "I wish my career should be tried."

At last the long, rambling, emotional plea was finished. Judge Richardson sat up straight, took a deep breath; he had obviously had enough of this tiresome man. He said to Riel, standing directly in front of him:

> It is now my painful duty to pass the sentence of the court upon you, and that is, that you be taken now from here to the police guardroom at Regina and that you be kept there till the eighteenth of September next, that on the 18th of September next you be taken to the place appointed for your execution, and there be hanged by the neck till you are dead. And may God have mercy on your soul.

– 20 –

Death will come as a thief
In that very moment when my heart
Worried by sickness
Still hopes to come back to life
Death will come. But when I recognize her,
Trembling all over between her icy hands,
I will then glimpse the web of my thoughts.
Will I then be freed from her?

Louis Riel's lawyers immediately appealed his sentence.
    For about a month Riel succumbed to a black despondency. The first thing he did was to recant his heresies. Just two days after he was sentenced to hang he wrote Father Fourmond: "Please write and compose yourself the formula which I should sign to place myself in perfect harmony with the good Lord and with the Church of Jesus Christ, of which you are an authorized priest. I will make that formula mine. Obedience is the bread with which I should nourish myself."

The repudiation was drawn up the next day by fathers Fourmond and Louis Cochin, an Oblate missionary stationed near Battleford. It was an uninspired document; as the political scientist Thomas Flanagan put it, "Fourmond was more concerned with dogma and ecclesiastical discipline than with the essentials of Riel's thinking." Basically, Louis was to renounce his "false mission of prophet" and affirm the orthodox teachings of the Catholic church. He didn't like the document one bit, but on August 4 he signed it. Shortly after, a mass was held for all the Métis prisoners, at which Louis publicly answered questions about his change of face. He was very frank about the reasons he had signed the document; he was Catholic to his very bone, and now, in the shadow of death, he wanted to partake of the sacraments. Writers in the past have made much of this capitulation to the establishment he had so long fought against; the recantation, said one, "was the most tragic record to be found in all the original papers of the Métis movement." Yet Riel was not capable of suppressing his flights of fancy, his nonconformist beliefs. Just days after he had recanted, Father Cochin would write, "I saw Riel this morning. At first he appeared to be very subdued. But when he started to talk about his alleged mission he began to [sound] like a prophet and to say he had connections with the Holy Ghost. He told me he had seen his Bishop Bourget. He was an extremely brilliant sun...."

Riel's diaries at the beginning of August were full of compliance: "Everything I will write in this notebook is subject to the approval of his Excellency Monseigneur Alexandre-Antonin Taché, Archbishop of St. Boniface. At the outset, I renounce anything in my writings which, in Monseigneur's opinion, deserves condemnation." But by October his old, exuberant, heretical imagination was back at work. Once again he was busy redesigning the universe. "The Lord wants the pagan name of the Atlantic to be discarded and replaced by that of Saint Paul. If nations and navigators adopt this glorious name, the ocean will be less stormy, says the Lord...."

The Riel family, waiting anxiously for news in St. Vital, were, of course, shocked at the verdict; they hadn't fully realized the significance of the treason charge against Louis. Once again, there was no doubt, no question, that they would stick by him. On August 3, his sister Henriette had written on behalf of them all:

> My dearest brother,
>
> Ah! Yes, if I could only do as the dove which left the ark to look for firm land and to bring back the olive-branch, in the hope that there might be a spot of land that was not drowned or submerged by injustice and abomination. Lord, the time has come for your Merciful Hand to stop this torrent; the glory and honour of Your Name beseech Your Infinite Kindness to prevent this last crime....We have heard the fatal verdict; but NO there is Someone there, between the Hangman and the victim. This cannot happen!...
> Courage! cherished brother; we all kiss you.

In mid-August, Louis Lavallée, the husband of Louis's oldest sister, Octavie, was finally given permission to see Louis in jail. Nothing is recorded of their conversations but Riel did write his mother that his brother-in-law's visits were a great consolation. What probably cheered Louis up was that Lavallée was able to tell him that the support and sympathy for him in Quebec and the French parishes of Red River were overwhelming.

By the time Riel's trial had ended, the French-speaking population of Canada and the eastern United States was convinced that it had all been a sham, rigged to ensure that Louis was hanged even before the first witness was called. When the verdict was reached there was an outpouring of exasperation, rage and grief. There was no doubt in the minds of Francophone journalists that Riel was condemned to hang because he was French-speaking, Catholic and a Half-breed. When Will Jackson was quickly found not guilty by reason of insanity, they were reinforced in their conviction. *Le Courrier de St-Hyacinthe* bellowed: "If the sentence is carried out, ... Riel will have been hanged because he's not English; and because the French-haters of Ontario wanted to see him ... dance at the end of a rope."

Just a few days after Riel's trial was completed, Arthur Dansereau, a newspaper editor well known for his Conservative views, wrote to Joseph-Adolphe Chapleau, who years before had helped transfer Riel from Longue Pointe to Beauport Asylum. "Don't even ask me about Riel—the people have gone completely wild from one end of the province to the other. You can be sure that the Liberals will have their revenge ... if Riel is hanged. You can't imagine the violence with which even our best friends express themselves."

If there was a sour note in all this for Louis, it was that his lawyers and the priests had convinced the population of Quebec that he should be saved, but because he was a "pathetic, helpless maniac".

Sir John A. Macdonald had told his worried ministers to ignore the storm, insisting it would soon blow over and Riel could be executed as expeditiously as possible. "The conviction of Riel is satisfactory," he telegraphed Lieutenant-Governor Dewdney. "There is an attempt in Quebec to pump up a patriotic feeling about him—but I don't think it will amount to much."

Meanwhile, Riel's lawyers were busy attending to his appeal. In September they appeared before a panel of three judges of the Manitoba Queen's Bench. Their argument centred on the validity of the six-man jury, but the question of insanity was also raised. Surely if the jurors urged clemency, there must have been real doubt in their mind about Riel's state of mind. There was no attempt to argue other errors which might have been made during the trial—the judge's prejudicial charge to the jury, for example. The justices quickly ruled that there were no grounds for appeal. "Heresy is not insanity," wrote one, and that succinctly summed up the opinion of them all.

There was still one other avenue of appeal that Riel's lawyers would try— the judicial committee of the Privy Council in London, England.

Riel would have liked to engage in his own debate, but his jailers allowed no political writing at all to leave the prison; only letters to his family were permitted, and they were heavily censored. He did manage to smuggle one document out via his lawyer Lemieux. It was a petition "To His Excellency [Grover] Cleveland President of the United States and to His excellency's Cabinet", explaining the history of the Red River Resistance, the saga of his promised amnesty and the justification for his actions during the North-West Rebellion. He proposed that Métis and Indian territory be made one vast region under the protection of the U.S. government.

Louis must have known that an American invasion at this point was wishful thinking. A short time later, he sent the authorities a note requesting that, upon his execution, his body be given into the care of Father André and that it be sent back to St. Boniface.

Indeed, as his diaries reveal, he had become obsessed with death, in an eccentric love–hate relationship that seemed to horrify but comfort him at the same time.

> Death has gained a day on me since yesterday.
> Death is now busily taking today away from me.
> Death is stealing my time as fast as the pendulum of
> the clock can count the seconds. My God, help me to get ready.
>
> Death hovers over me like a great bird of prey hovering
> over a chicken that it wants to carry off.
> Death keeps guard at the door of my cell.
> Death peers at me behind my prison bars.
> Death watches at my door like a Labrador retriever
> keeping watch in front of the house.

September 17 was the second birthday of the Riels' little girl and also the day Riel's execution was postponed from the original date, September 18, to October 16. Louis wrote to his wife:

> My little girl, Marie-Angélique, at two years old, can pronounce my name
> with a joyful smile of hope and contentment. Thank God for September 17,
> the birthday of your little Marie-Angélique. Thank God for the day when
> His Holiness deigns to bestow his grace so charitably; the day that was the
> eve of my death has been changed to a day of thankfulness. And you, my
> dear Marguerite; pray to the good Lord that he receives my thanks.

Louis must have been worried about his wife. She was having a difficult pregnancy and as a result had not been able to visit him. He did write her occasionally, but his letters were never passionate or very loving, although he may simply have been protecting her from embarrassment since she was illiterate and all his correspondence had to be read to her and read by censors, too. A poem written about this time, oddly in English, says a great deal about the relationship; he remained a combination father, teacher, messiah. How much he was the lover was only hinted at:

> Margaret: be fair and good.
> Consider the sacred wood
> On which the perfect Jesus
> Died willingly to save us.
>
> Truly Christ will save us all
> Beleive it: and hear his call.
> His spirit always teaches you
> What your dear soul has to do....
>
> The body dies: but not the soul.
> Perhaps tonight death on its roll
> Will in a sudden call our names
> To stand before God with our shames.
>
> Begin the work which is thine own.
> Amongst your friends you are alone
> If you miss god, by doing wrong.
> Life is short: the next is long
>
> Margaret! we be the prey
> Of bad spirits? no let us pray....
> Be sweet to my words: and listen
> When I write you with a golden
> > Pen

The Riel family had not told Louis how ill his wife really was. Her ordeal at Batoche had taken a terrible toll, and Louis's trial had also done its damage. On October 21, Marguerite would give birth to the couple's third child, a little boy, but the infant lived for only two hours. Marguerite herself was near death. It was another shattering blow for Louis, and his letter to Henriette was full of anguish:

> The pain that I feel at seeing my little, little one taken away from me, without my even being able to cover him with tenderness penetrates to the depth of my soul. At the same time, I thank God for having, in his charity, let the baby live a few hours just long enough to be baptized. The holy

water on his forehead and the holy words on his very little soul made him a child of God.

At the instant of the baby's death, Riel had a vision of him. "He appeared to me on earth for only a fleeting moment and only long enough for me to make the sign of the cross." The tragedy was almost too much for Riel. He scribbled in his diary: "Now, O my God, we need the benefit of Your paternal mercy; for my wife lies on a sickbed.... And as for me—O my God, I am condemned to death!"

As he waited out the long, lonely hours in his jail cell, Riel's writings were his one comfort. Yet he included no entries in his diary during the month of September. Father André was visiting him frequently, and under his close scrutiny Louis may not have felt free to express himself. In the last entry for August, he wrote, "Circumstances make it preferable to do what I would prefer not to do," and for weeks after he wrote nothing.

By October, though, he was back in full swing as the irrepressible prophet, all restraint forgotten.

October 2, 1885

God made me see that I was climbing the holy mountain step by step. Mankind was to help me ascend it. The things men were doing on my behalf put me in a joyful and encouraging state of mind. Although I was walking carefully, I was serene, not anxious. Gigantic forces were going ahead of me. Without appearing to do so, I was guiding them.

The rest of the diary is a melange of prophecies, revelations, parables. His dreams were full of people he had known. "My brother Charles is a famous jurist. His books are recognized everywhere. He dies of old age. His hair is white, but of a whiteness kind and pure." "I saw Eastwood Jackson. The bed that I had made for his politics was rather hard." The journal also contained a meditation on temperance, a lengthy game of renaming everything he could think of—"God wants the Big Dipper to be called the 'Fabien Barnabé', God wants the North Star to be called 'Henriette', God wants the planet Saturn to be called 'Sophia'"—and a restructuring of the international order—"God revealed to me that He would be pleased to see the two Englands [Great Britain and the United States] enter into a legislative union to further their interests in commerce and world affairs." What is lacking in these last entries is any terror of death, any pleading for his soul to be saved. Either he had reconciled himself to his end, or right up to the last moment he believed the people of Canada would save him.

Riel received word of a postponement of his execution to October 22; by then his lawyer Fitzpatrick was on his way to London to argue his application to appeal before the judicial committee of the Privy Council. It was a long, involved constitutional argument which didn't seem to make much impression on the court. On October 22, leave to appeal was denied. The crown hadn't even bothered to submit a brief.

The ball had now been bounced back into Sir John A. Macdonald's court and he was forced to grant yet another postponement.

The jury in the Riel trial had done a great disservice, the prime minister felt, when they recommended clemency. It would have been so much more expedient if they had just decided to hang the man. The protest in Quebec had not died down as he had predicted. Petitions, telegrams, letters demanding Riel's life be saved were flooding into his office daily. And they weren't just from French Canadians; the bid to save Riel was now an international cause célèbre. Eight hundred people in Chicago appealed for the remission of the death sentence. From Holyoke, Massachusetts; Nashua, New Hampshire; St. Paul, Minnesota; St. Louis, Missouri came outraged telegrams pleading for the Métis. French intellectuals and German counts sent cables. Even Chinese revolutionaries sent protests.

But, of course, there was the other side, opponents of Riel who were vicious and threatening. The Orangemen of English Canada, remembering Thomas Scott, were adamant that Riel be hanged, and on schedule. Even before the trial, some had suggested that he be executed no matter what the verdict. If the government didn't do the job, they'd lynch him. A letter from the Orangeman J.C. Gilroy to the prime minister was typical. If Riel was not hanged, he wrote, "in a few months there will be the greatest rebellion, one of the mightiest struggles for freedom and liberty from French domination by the loyal, intelligent, Protestant people of Ontario that our beloved Dominion had ever witnessed."

Riel had an opinion, of course, as to what Macdonald should do (in English).

> This
> is
> Sunday, eighteenth of october
> Eighty five
> If Sir John does not remember
> that it is right to keep me alive.
> If he does not let me go free;
> If he does not open to me
> The Hustings, to work and to speak,
> He will become so sick and weak
> that he will cease to be member

of the House, and he will have to eat
the bitter fruit of his defeat
      Before any cucomber
Next summer can florish
      For his dish.

Macdonald had never had any intention of saving Louis Riel's life. He had been terribly embarrassed by the tiresome rebel during and after the Red River resistance. Now, seventy years old, exhausted from the prolonged battle to save the CPR, longing for retirement, he had run out of patience. Still, he had to somehow appease the outraged people of Quebec and the French-Canadian members of his party. The answer he finally came up with was the appointment of a medical commission to judge once and for all whether Riel was insane, whether he knew right from wrong—now, not at the time of the rebellion. It was a political farce. Macdonald, the great master of manipulation, fully intended to pull the strings of the two puppets he appointed. He wrote that the job shouldn't take more than three or four days. He added that the doctors should interview Riel and others (as few as possible), until "you are convinced that Riel knows right from wrong and is an accountable being." This would not exactly make for an objective finding. Meanwhile, Riel's execution was postponed once again.

Before the commissioners arrived, NWMP surgeon Augustus Jukes was invited to give his opinion, since he had seen Riel held as a prisoner in a Mountie jail many times. He dutifully telegraphed on November 6 that the prisoner was eccentric but not insane. Jukes had grown to like Riel. "For my own part I confess I should be well pleased if justice and popular clamour could be satisfied without depriving this man of life...." But a few days later, Jukes suddenly changed his mind, and telegraphed that he now felt it essential that Riel's writings should be studied by another commission before his sanity was decided on. Sir John A. ignored the second recommendation.

By this time the two physicians appointed to the commission were rushing to Regina.

Dr. Michael Lavell had been a professor of obstetrics but was now the warden of the Kingston Penitentiary. "You have under your charge criminal lunatics and are, therefore, an expert," the prime minister said, justifying his appointment. What he didn't write was that Lavell was a staunch Tory from Macdonald's own constituency who could be counted on to do the right thing. Posing as a newspaper reporter, Lavell chatted with Louis. There was no doubt in his mind that the condemned man was quite sane. Riel, wrote the doctor, had "a manly expression of countenance, sharp eyes, intelligent and pleasing address. His conversational prowess was remarkable...."

It had been obligatory for Macdonald to include a French Canadian on the commission. Dr. François-Xavier Valade of Ottawa certainly appeared to be someone who was pliable: he had no special training or expertise in mental illness; he was relatively young and therefore would defer to the senior Lavell; he was a protégé of Joseph Caron, a Cabinet minister in Macdonald's government; and, as the historians Bob Beal and Rod Macleod pointed out, best of all, he was on the government payroll, making over $1,000 a year testing food samples for the Inland Revenue Department. But unexpectedly, he refused to play the role Macdonald had assigned him.

Valade also interviewed Riel without telling him he was a doctor, and he had long talks with Father André. His findings were quite different from those of his older colleague.

> After having examined carefully Riel in private conversation with him and by testimony of persons who take care of him, I have come to the conclusion that he is not an accountable being, that he is unable to distinguish between wrong and right on political and religious subjects, which I consider well-marked typical forms of insanity under which he undoubtedly suffers, on other points I believe him to be sensible and can distinguish right from wrong.

Valade's report could have created embarrassing problems for Macdonald's government, if Lieutenant-Governor Dewdney hadn't simply deleted all the facts about not being able to distinguish right and wrong in political and religious matters. In his telegram Dewdney simply said that Valade's and Lavell's reports were essentially the same—both considered that Riel understood right from wrong—except for minor semantic differences. The House of Commons would see only the falsified report.

On Wednesday November 11, Macdonald's Cabinet met. There was some debate; the French-Canadian members were hesitant, especially J.A. Chapleau, Riel's old schoolmate. Now secretary of state in Macdonald's Cabinet, he had stayed up all night composing his resignation letter, but at the last moment decided against presenting it because, he said, it might promote "a racial war".

Rodrigue Masson, the son of Louis Riel's old patron, was trying everything he could to save the Métis leader. Masson was now Lieutenant-Governor of Quebec, and so could not make his feelings public, but he discreetly approached Sir John and pleaded with him to change his mind. "In this day and age the death penalty is not applicable to this kind of crime." Masson warned Macdonald of the dire political consequences; he predicted that both Liberal and Conservative forces in Quebec would combine to form a nationalist movement. In fact what he foresaw was the creation of the Parti National and the obliteration of the Conservative Party in Quebec for the next hundred years. The Prime Minister of Canada would listen to none of this advice. He growled an answer that would echo down through history: "He shall hang though every dog in Quebec bark in his favour."

The next day, November 12, a special messenger bearing the governor-general's warrant for execution left Ottawa for Regina. Even Riel's lawyers didn't know the decision had been made. Lemieux sent Louis a telegram on Friday November 13: "If no respite is granted by Saturday then write ... parting words.... Courage. FXL."

Riel had already written his will—two versions of it. The first draft contained a list of political grievances against the state and argued that the government as his executioner had a financial responsibility to his family. If such money was forthcoming, he would ask that a chapel in honour of the Sacred Heart of Jesus and another for the Sacred Heart of Mary be erected and he entrusted this task to his wife, his family and André. He also listed his debts to various people in Benton, Montana, and Montreal, including the $250 he still owed the long-deceased Father Fabien Barnabé; it was to go to his estate, meaning Evelina. All of this was missing in the second draft, which was simply the testament of a good Christian. He made peace with the Catholic church; he bade farewell to his "good and tender mother who loved me so much and who had such Christian love for me"; and he insisted he bore no grudges or hatred against those "who persecuted me ... who made a mockery of the process and who condemned me to die." He thanked Marguerite for being so loving and loyal and he blessed his son and daughter.

At seven p.m. on November 15, the messenger sent by Ottawa arrived at Regina. Riel was told immediately that he would be executed the next day.

His mother and his brothers, Alexandre and Joseph, had visited him in October, and Riel had convinced them that there was such a demand for clemency in the country that he would surely escape the hangman's noose. Julie had returned to St. Vital cheerful and reassured. Now he must tell her that he had been wrong. He had truly adored his mother his entire life; it must have been excruciatingly difficult for him to write the final words.

> May you be blessed from generation to generation for having been so good a mother to me.
>
> May your faith, your firm hope, and your exemplary charity be like trees laden with good fruits in the future. And when your last day shall come, may God be so pleased with you that your pious spirit will leave the earth on the wings of the love of the angels.

It is two hours past midnight. Good Father André told me this morning to hold myself ready for tomorrow. I listen to him, I obey. I am prepared for everything according to his counsel and his recommendations.

But the Lord is helping me to maintain a peaceful and a calm spirit, like oil in a vase which cannot become agitated.

I am doing everything I can think of to be ready for any eventuality, keeping myself in an even calm, according to the pious exhortations of the venerable Bishop Bourget....

I embrace you all with the greatest affection....

Dear Mother,

I am your affectionate, submissive and obedient son

Louis David Riel

But of course it was his wife to whom he owed the most courageous words. Marguerite was so broken-hearted, so ill now, that she would not live to see summer. There was not much to the letter; Louis seemed already to have left her.

Dearly Beloved Marguerite,

I am writing to you early in the morning. It's scarcely 1 a.m. Today is the 16th. It is a remarkable day.

I send you my best wishes. I counsel you today according to the charity which you showed me on the subject. Take good care of your little children. Your children belong more to God than to you. Try to give them care that is the most consistent with religion, make them pray for me.

Write often to your good father. Tell him that I don't forget him for a single day. He must take heart. Sometimes life appears sad, but the times which seem the saddest are sometimes those which are the most agreeable to God.

Louis "David" Riel
Your husband who loves you in our Saviour

I write a word of kindness according to God, to my little, little Jean; a word of kindness and tenderness also to my little, little Marie-Angélique.

Take courage. I bless you.

Your father,
Louis "David" Riel

The last meal that Louis asked for consisted of three eggs and a glass of milk. All night he could hear hammering outside his cell window, as the scaffold was slowly being erected. He tried to keep calm. Father André was with him and hour after hour they prayed together. Finally at five a.m. the priest said mass and Louis received his last communion. At seven a.m. André administered extreme unction. Riel then asked permission to bathe. He was a little upset because the clothes given him to wear—a short black coat, grey tweed trousers, a wool shirt, moccasins—were rather shabby.

It was a cold, clear morning, and Regina's citizens had already gathered in the field before the square. A strong cordon of Mounties was on hand to keep anyone from drawing near. Louis could hear the noise of the curious through the walls of his cell.

At 8:15 the sheriff arrived. "You want me, Mr. Gibson?" Riel asked. "I am ready."

A crowd of officials and several priests followed Louis as he walked slowly along the corridor to the guardhouse.

There Louis knelt in prayer with the priests around him, often stopping to kiss a small ivory crucifix. He was hatless and his thick brown hair, the one vanity of his life, shone in the sunshine. He asked God to bless his mother, his wife and children. "My Father bless me according to the views of Thy Providence which are beautiful and without measure."

Louis mounted a ladder that led to a window, and climbed outside onto the scaffold without help, even though Father André himself was close to collapsing. He stood on the platform for a moment. He had hoped to make one last statement, one last justification for his life of revolution, but Father André had said no. Riel had argued, but he believed now that submission was his only salvation.

The hangman stepped forward to place the hood on his head, fumbling with the noose around his neck. "Louis Riel," he whispered, "you had me once and I got away from you. I have you now and you'll not get away from me." Jack Henderson had been a prisoner in Fort Garry in 1870 and had sworn then to take revenge not only for his humiliation, but for the death of his friend Thomas Scott. Now he was doing just that, and getting paid $50 for it.

Father André began to cry openly. "Courage, Father," whispered Riel, who was standing very erect, very calm. Then the clergy together led the prayer. "Our Father, who art in heaven, hallowed be thy name. Thy kingdom come. Thy will be done...."

The trap-door suddenly snapped open. The rope jerked, swayed back and forth violently, and then came to a dead stop.

EPILOGUE

It took three weeks of unconscionable delay before the government finally gave permission for Louis Riel's body to be shipped back to St. Boniface. When it arrived by train on December 10, 1885, there waiting was a crowd of loyal supporters, most of them openly weeping. The coarse wooden casket was hoisted onto strong Métis shoulders and carried six miles to the Riel family home at St. Vital. There, that day and the next, it lay in state.

Julie's parlour was draped in mourning black. A beautiful metallic coffin, which had replaced the shabby wooden one, stood on a bier in the corner of the room. At its head a small altar had been erected, brilliantly illuminated and adorned with emblems. On a couch near the casket lay the widow, Marguerite Riel. She was so ill she could hardly greet the mourners as they gave their condolences.

On December 12, a mile-long funeral cortège made its way to St. Boniface Cathedral. Rumours had spread that a posse of Orangemen planned to attack the procession, and most of the Métis men carried guns. Among the pallbearers were Louis's cousin André Nault and his uncles Joseph and Romain Lagimodière. Archbishop Taché had tried to discourage a requiem mass for Riel, thinking it would cause trouble in the community, but the Riel family and his parishioners ignored him. Louis's old schoolfriend Abbé Dugas celebrated the funeral mass in front of hundreds of sobbing, solemn mourners. There were as many people waiting outside as in the cathedral.

As he had wanted, Louis Riel was buried beside his beloved father. A small, simple marker identified the gravesite until 1891, when the Union Nationale Métisse de St. Joseph erected a monument.

On May 24, 1886, Marguerite finally succumbed to the tuberculosis and intense emotional trauma that had afflicted her at Batoche. She was buried beside her husband.

Marie-Angélique and Jean continued to live with their grandmother, although their Aunt Henriette had a lot to do with their upbringing. The children attended school at St. Vital. Marie-Angélique was adored by everybody, a pretty, blonde, blue-eyed "angel", as her father had once called her. From a letter written to an uncle and aunt at age twelve, it seems she was a bright, sensitive girl. But the misfortunes that had so often plagued the Riel family continued. Just before her fourteenth birthday, in 1897, she died of diphtheria.

Like his father before him, Jean Riel was a bright student; in 1899–1900 he attended St. Boniface College and in 1902 he went to Montreal to study at the École Normale Jacques Cartier. His support was provided by a handful of Louis Riel's old friends and sympathizers, including Honoré Joseph Jaxon. In 1904, having decided that he didn't much like teaching, Jean got a job in the Ministry of Mines and Fisheries in Quebec City. and soon became an apprentice civil engineer. Jean Riel was a handsome young man, over six feet tall with the black eyes of his mother. He was also very reserved and serious. In 1908 he married Laura Casault, the daughter of a prominent Quebec family.

That year he returned to St. Vital, working as an engineer for the Grand Trunk Pacific Railway. Since Jean was based at a construction camp twelve miles away, his wife lived with his Uncle Joseph. That June Jean was returning home to his bride when his buggy overturned and he suffered a rib fracture. It seemed like a minor injury at first, but then it became inflamed. He was finally taken to a hospital at St. Boniface, and on July 31 he died there. He was twenty-six years old. He left no children, and thus there are no direct descendants of Louis Riel.

Yet the name has not faded in Canadian history. With each generation Louis Riel's persona has taken on different colours, different nuances. As long as the notion of Anglo-Saxon imperialism prevailed, and with it the neglect or, more accurately, contempt of cultures other than the European, Louis Riel was denigrated. His achievement of bringing Manitoba into Confederation as a province, and his assumption that aboriginal people could have a distinct and equitable place in North America, were ridiculed. For years his image was that presented by the imperialists, the Schultzs, Boultons, Middletons, Macdonalds, who saw him as an unrepentant traitor to Canada and the British empire. In the mid-twentieth century that perception shifted, but hardly for the better; he began to be called a "messianic prophet", his charisma even likened to Hitler's—someone who, with his egocentric, heretical notions of religion and nationhood, had led a primitive and unsuspecting people astray. Even Quebec, which has long used

Louis Riel for its own nationalistic ambitions, never wholly embraced him. He remained for the French-speakers a pathetic victim of Anglo-Canadian tyranny, executed unfairly because he was insane. It is only recently that our society has slowly taken off its blinkers of prejudice and come to understand, often with shocked amazement, that Native cultures have their own uniqueness and value—great value in a world polluting itself to death. With this understanding came the first progress towards Louis Riel's exoneration. When his story is read for its own sake and not swathed in the constraint of political ideology, we find a man who was truly a humanitarian, who gave up prestige and wealth to fight for the underdog, who led a life of dedicated revolution even though his instincts, conservative and devout as he was, might not naturally have led him in that direction. He was a complex man full of contradiction and angst, certainly, but what makes Louis Riel so intriguing is that he managed to straddle two cultures, Native and white, and came as close as anyone to envisioning a sympathetic and equitable relationship between the two. That Canadians may someday achieve this vision remains Louis Riel's legacy.

ADDENDUM ONE

The List of Rights as Drawn by the Executive of the Provisional Government.

I. That the Territories heretofore known as Rupert's Land and North-West, shall not enter into the Confederation of the Dominion of Canada, except as a Province; to be styled and known as the Province of Assiniboia, and with all the rights and privileges common to the different Provinces of the Dominion.

II. That we have two Representatives in the Senate, and four in the House of Commons of Canada, until such time as an increase of population entitle the Province to a greater Representation.

III. That the Province of Assiniboia shall not be held liable at any time for any portion of the Public debt of the Dominion contracted before the date the said Province shall have entered the Confederation, unless the said Province shall have first received from the Dominion the full amount for which the said Province is to be held liable.

IV. That the sum of Eighty Thousand ($80,000) dollars be paid annually by the Dominion Government to the local Legislature of this Province.

V. That all properties, rights and privileges engaged [*sic*: enjoyed] by the people of this Province, up to the date of our entering into the Confederation, be respected; and that the arrangement and confirmation of all customs, usages and privileges be left exclusively to the local Legislature.

VI. That during the term of five years, the Province of Assiniboia shall not be subjected to any direct taxation, except such as may be imposed by local Legislature, for municipal or local purposes.

VII. That a sum of money equal to eighty cents per head of the population of this Province, be paid annually by the Canadian Government to the local Legislature of the said Province; until such time as the said population shall have reached six hundred thousand.

VIII. That the local Legislature shall have the right to determine the qualification of members to represent this Province in the Parliament of Canada and in the local Legislature.

IX. That in this Province, with the exception of uncivilised and unsettled Indians, every male native citizen who has attained the age of twenty-one years, and every foreigner, other than a British subject, who has resided here during the same period, being a householder and having taken the oath of allegiance, shall be entitled to vote at the election of members for the local Legislature and for the Canadian Parliament. It being understood that this article be subject to amendment exclusively by the local Legislature.

X. That the bargain of the Hudson's Bay Company with respect to the transfer of the Government of this country to the Dominion of Canada, be annulled; so far as it interferes with the rights of the people of Assiniboia, and so far as it would affect our future relations with Canada.

XI. That the local Legislature of the Province of Assiniboia shall have full control over all the public lands of the Province and the right to annul all acts or arrangements made, or entered into, with reference to the public lands of Rupert's Land, and the North West now called the Province of Assiniboia.

XII. That the Government of Canada appoint a Commission of Engineers to explore the various districts of the Province of Assiniboia, and to lay before the local Legislature a report of the mineral wealth of the Province, within five years from the date of our entering into Confederation.

XIII. That treaties be concluded between Canada and the different Indian tribes of the Province of Assiniboia, by and with the advice and cooperation of the local Legislature of this Province.

XIV. That an uninterrupted steam communication from Lake Superior to Fort Garry be guaranteed, to be completed within the space of five years.

XV. That all public buildings, bridges, roads and other public works, be at the cost of the Dominion Treasury.

XVI. That the English and French languages be common in the Legislature and in the Courts, and that all public documents, as well as acts of the Legislature be published in both languages.

XVII. That whereas the French and English speaking people of Assiniboia are so equally divided as to number, yet so united in their interests and so connected by commerce, family connections and other political and social relations, that it has, happily, been found impossible to bring them into hostile collision— although repeated attempts have been made by designing strangers, for reasons known to themselves, to bring about so ruinous and disastrous an event—and whereas after all the troubles and apparent dissensions of the past—the result of misunderstanding among themselves; they have—as soon as the evil agencies referred to above were removed—become as united and friendly as ever—there- fore, as a means to strengthen this union and friendly feeling among all classes, we deem it expedient and advisable—that the Lieutenant-Governor, who may be appointed for the Province of Assiniboia, should be familiar with both the French and English languages.

XVIII. That the Judge of the Supreme Court speak the English and French languages.

XIX. That all debts contracted by the Provisional Government of the Territory of the Northwest, now called Assiniboia, in consequence of the illegal and inconsiderate measure adopted by Canadian officials to bring about a civil war in our midst, be paid out of the Dominion Treasury; and that none of the members of the Provisional Government, or any of those acting under them, be in any way held liable or responsible with regard to the movement, or any of the actions which led to the present negotiations.

XX. That in view of the present exceptional position of Assiniboia, duties upon goods imported into the province, shall, except in the case of spirituous liquors, continue as at present for at least three years from the date of our entering the Confederation and for such further time as may elapse until there be uninterrupted railroad communication between Winnipeg and St. Paul and also steam communication between Winnipeg and Lake Superior.

ADDENDUM TWO

The Revolutionary Bill of Rights passed on March 8, 1885, St. Laurent.

1. That the half-breeds of the Northwest Territories be given grants similar to those accorded to the half-breeds of Manitoba by the Act of 1870.

2. That patents be issued to all half-breed and white settlers who have fairly earned the right of possession on their farms.

3. That the provinces of Alberta and Saskatchewan be forthwith organized with legislatures of their own, so that the people may be no longer subjected to the despotism of Mr. Dewdney.

4. That in these new provincial legislatures, while representation according to population shall be the supreme principle, the Métis shall have a fair and reasonable share of representation.

5. That the offices of trust throughout these provinces be given to the residents of the country, as far as practicable, and that we denounce the appointment of disreputable outsiders and repudiate their authority.

6. That this region be administered for the benefit of the actual settler, and not for the advantage of the alien speculator.

7. That better provision be made for the Indians, the parliamentary grant to be increased and lands set apart as an endowment for the establishment of hospitals and schools for the use of whites, half-breeds, and Indians, at such places as the provincial legislatures may determine.

8. That all lawful customs and usages which obtain among the Métis be respected.

9. That the Land Department of the Dominion Government be administered as far as practicable from Winnipeg, so that the settlers may not be compelled as heretofore to go to Ottawa for the settlement of questions in dispute between them and the land commissioner.

10. That the timber regulations be made more liberal, and that the settler be treated as having rights in this country.

ADDENDUM THREE

The controversy over Riel's insanity has raged since his execution in 1885. The following letter is a telling contemporary examination of the issue. It is written by Douglas Daniels, Associate Professor of Sociology and Social Studies at the University of Regina, to Father Joseph Curcio, a long-time activist priest who has administered to the poor and oppressed in Canada and Latin America. Father Curcio is currently working in North Battleford, Saskatchewan.

Dear Father Joe:

Thanks for the tapes on the Church in Nicaragua, and for the Riel book.* I am not as saddened by the book's message as you have been. Flanagan, it must be remembered, is an intellectual who has moved so far to the right that even the Reform Party is too soft for his ideology. Thus he repeatedly turns nearly every interpretation of Riel's theology in a negative direction, whether to megalomania, lunacy, petty hearsay, or plain old religious irrationalism that he—as "liberal" rationalist—cannot abide. Flanagan even scratches through the diaries for supposed obsession with incest and masturbation, which he can find only by microscope and even then only by innuendo. His is the work of a modern Inquisitor, armed not with the Malleus Malleficarum but with neo-Freudian psychology and what is ultimately illiberal liberal rationalism.

So much of the denigration of Riel comes from a condescending view of his times. Riel is struggling with the same things rural Quebec Catholics are struggling with—the saints, papal infallibility, the eternality of hellfire, the corrupt Vatican bureaucracy, justice and injustice in the church, miraculous cures for physical diseases, intercessions by various saints, angels and biblical figures in

---

Flanagan, Thomas, Riel: Prophet of the New World, 1979.

aid of human suffering, and of course human political causes. Catholics and many other religious people of the time are also obsessed with sexual issues and a good part of the 19th century is spent in debates—religious and secular—on the good/evil nature of masturbation! Everyone who is confined by the religious structure of the time is open to the voice of God, voices of angels, visitations from the prophets, invitations to sainthood, revelations, "calls" to prophecy, to mission. They are also open to great fear since the calls may be false—not from angels but from demons, not from God but from the Devil. Or the devil of egotism. Or from the weakness of an ego that refuses a Holy Mission from fear of the physical suffering involved—spirit willing but weak of flesh. Riel proved his physical courage in face of exile and death, but perhaps was never entirely certain that his spirit was a strong and pure enough vehicle for God's work on earth. Certainly his highly "political" advisors in the church played on these fears.

How could Riel know for certain which are the true and false voices, what is courage or cowardice, God's call or ego's call, prideful insubordination or the explosive prophetic breakthrough, the "heresy" of Jesus against the Pharisees and the old lawgivers. If one thinks small and acts small, such problems will never arise and your doubts and anguishes will be small ones easily resolved by a weekly confession. But to think of changing the historic oppression of one's people and indeed all of humanity—how can one poor brain handle all the politics, economics, the religious bureaucracy of Christendom, family life, clash of cultures, personal material survival on the frontier, political persecution, etc. etc? It's hardly surprising that this poor mind—really a magnificent instrument of consciousness and access to the dynamics of life—but a finite instrument—can be overloaded from time to time and appear to break down.

Remember too how Riel is a clever young half-breed boy who is "elevated" from log shacks on the prairie to Montreal seminaries and contact with the highest levels of the church and state—all by the skills of his mind and the devotedness and intensity of his spirituality. But he's still a frontier boy who doesn't really understand the depth of crass Machiavellian power in the Quebec/Roman Church and the British Imperial state. The amazing thing is just how much this prairie boy was able to learn, and how skillfully he used his mind and spirit against the overwhelming forces aligned against his people.

That his mind became sometimes exhausted and over-energized is hardly surprising. That his mind tried to resolve its internal dilemma and external historical problems in religious terms was virtually inevitable, given the times, his people, his background. The British psychiatrist R.D. Laing has a most helpful view of the period of mental-spiritual retreat commonly called "schizophrenia" (Greek "broken soul"). According to Laing, many people whose lives are overloaded with apparently impossible contradictions seem to escape into a world and a language that is incomprehensible to most observers. But Laing's long experience as a humanistic doctor led him to believe that there is much more going on in the schizophrenic experience than mere babble and hallucinatory nonsense. People having severe problems in living who cannot face these problems directly—due to social oppression, family oppression, fear of retaliation etc.—are forced to speak in similes, metaphors, visions, "hallucinations". With religious people, needless to say, much of the imagery that is readily available to this hyperactive mind will be of a religious sort—a whole bible of characters to draw on for the play going on inside one's head. More importantly, Laing points out that many people who are allowed to seek out a place of sanctuary during these periods of highly energized mental activity ("schizophrenic episodes") end up essentially curing themselves. This is especially so if they are treated with compassion, unmolested by electroshock, lobotomies or other varieties of negation of humanity.

Riel's stay in a mental hospital in Quebec is both horrifying and amusing. Many of his supposedly "insane" acts—stripping naked in front of the nurse sisters, for example—can also be seen as typical acts of defiance against an oppressive institution. Indeed, this is how much of the behaviour in closed, "total institutions" is seen by the sociologist Erving Goffman, author of *Asylums*. Riel at this time seems to be on an emotional binge. Had he been a big drinker perhaps he could have gone on a passionate two week bender, and history would not have had to wrestle with the sanity question. Certainly Riel had much to be broken-hearted about—his American backers had ceased their support for the Fenians and Metis. The Metis, like so many "small peoples" today, abandoned to their fate after the end of U.S.–U.S.S.R. Cold War, became as expendable as Kurds and Timorese. So Riel had much real, historic anguish in his heart. What is so remarkable was how his feverishly energized mind at this time not only cured itself, but also helped him lay the foundations for a theology which was to become clearer, more universalistic and more humane over the rest of his life.

The amazing thing is that his diaries track very well the movement from metaphysical spiritual struggles with spirit figures to ever more practical matters—the same direction that liberation theology moves (and incidentally the direction that most millenarian and cargo-cult movements also take). At the time of his 1876 internment in a lunatic asylum he was literally under enough pressures to drive a man "insane". How could this fellow from the prairies dare to go against the pillars of the Church, the representatives of God and Jesus on earth, the people who had plucked him from the sod and educated him, especially in the duties of obedience? How could he oppose the depredations of British colonial capitalism—which he first saw as Orangeman "liberalism", when the elite

Catholic Ultramontanes who opposed "liberalism" really did very little in fact to protect his people, the Metis and Indians and others on the prairie? The amazing growth which shows the true greatness of the man is how seriously he takes his theology, how each break with the past and each step forward puts tremendous strain on his sanity and a deep toll on his health. His theology tries to transform the elitist, conspiratorial Ultramontanes, whose anti-democratic, anti-liberal stance is the direct progenitor of Opus Dei and the Catholic right of today. He transcends Catholic–Protestant sectarianism nearly a century before ecumenism. He learns that it is Orange bigotry at the service of Central Canadian land speculators that was the enemy of his people, not ordinary Protestants.

In 1876, all these challenges to his strict Catholic upbringing are enough to incapacitate him from daily life for a while, but he does indeed "work things through" and emerge as a sane and intelligent man using his talents for his people. Like many great men who open their thoughts to poems, diaries and journals he remains plagued to the end of his life with the great questions—is he really a prophet doing God's work, or merely carried away by pride? Is it necessary for him to rupture with the corrupted church of Rome and to set up a new church in the New World, a more genuinely small "c" catholic Church that would serve all good people regardless of nationality or nominal faith, or is he simply a disobedient child of the Church? How surprising that we can recognize the anguish of priests in Latin America facing the same problem today or Martin Luther centuries ago, but somehow deny the dignity of genuine spiritual suffering to Riel. Need we point out that many observers of the Third World have warned of a potential schism between the Church of the oppressed people of the South and the complacent Church of the North?

Riel was dealing with the same problem a century earlier. Given the limited intellectual material and political resources of his time, his achievements are all the more remarkable. That he proved his sanity before psychiatrists who wanted to nullify his message and a court that wanted to hang him (albeit needing to prove him sane to do so) was merely another obstacle which he overcame after a lifetime of obstacles.

His life was as troubled as those of so many officially canonized saints, yet perhaps he is scrutinized so intently because he kept more exhaustive diaries of his spiritual struggles than most other saints left us. Indeed, the medieval saints were proud of their spiritual suffering and struggles. One wonders what the modern psychiatric profession would do to the whole panoply of saints if psychiatrists were in charge of canonization. Louis Riel had the misfortune to protect his people with bible and vision while the colonizers had gatling guns and psychiatrists. Thus Riel and his role in history really do represent the intersection of two worlds, two epochs, the rural religious age and the calculating capitalist era.

Even after death he has suffered because of the coincidence of times. This coincidence has made it difficult to recognize him in direct line with centuries of martyrs who sacrificed themselves for righteousness but seem locked outside the kingdom of heaven by continued misunderstanding on earth. Perhaps the cruellest part of Flanagan's examination of Riel's theology is the period after Louis is sentenced to hang, and is writing to various political and religious figures for intercession to stay the execution. It is a time of frenetic activity, of all night vigils and writing in his cell, of all night conversations with Father André and other visitors. It is hardly surprising that a man about to die should try to complete his life's work for posterity and to tie up the many loose ends of his theology.

Less serious is Riel's plan to rename the days of the week to get rid of pre-Christian influences (the Roman gods Mars, in Mardi, Saturn in Saturday, etc.) and to rename continents and planets to more Christian names. This may be a somewhat foolish project, similar to the fanciful euphemisms of the "politically correct" in our time, but it is hardly evidence of insanity. Such massive renaming has been done in reality in both religious and secular revolutions—the Puritans in England and the metric converters of the rationalist French revolution. Similarly, many Catholics since Riel have repudiated the notion of eternal hellfire, believing that no God as compassionate as Jesus could be so unforgiving.

Finally, much is made of Riel's attitude to the church and immortality in his last days. Flanagan notes that Riel's various letters to Catholic and Protestant Church figures, seeking their support for clemency, emphasize only those aspects of his theology least likely to upset the recipient of the letter. This would only seem prudent or politic for one whose neck is almost literally in the noose, but Flanagan presents this prudence as though Riel is welching, backing down from his role as true prophet. Imagine the opposite, that Riel should beg support from church leaders in time of sectarian strife between Catholic and Protestant, French and Irish and English, and tell such leaders that if he lived Riel would spend his life working to end all churches and have only a highly democratic Christian community on the prairies, without hierarchical structures, where spiritual leaders would both have secular power but also be simply "Exovedate" (Latin for from the flock). This vision of the Christian commonwealth, very close to that of the first Christians, would have guaranteed Riel's repudiation by churchmen to whom even ecumenism was a threat. Indeed one must look to the social gospel advocates of the 1920's and 1930's and even later before one finds tangible achievements of ecumenism on the prairies. In any case, Riel is demeaned by Flanagan no matter what he does. If Riel specifies all the details of his theology (including renaming the days of the week) he is portrayed as a crank. If Riel withholds some of his theology from those whose ears are not ready to hear, he's portrayed as an opportunist trying to preserve his neck. Flanagan presents the same cynical portrayal of Riel's final relations with the Church and Father André, his confessor and companion on the death watch. Riel and André jointly draw up an "abjuration" of Riel's formal heresies against the church, which Riel signs. But Riel makes a copy, given to the prison warden, which he signs Louis "David" Riel, as though to reassert his prophetic role. Is Riel not playing both sides of the fence, trying to save his neck and possibly his eternal soul by appearing to submit to the church hierarchy? Or is he, to the end, in genuine turmoil, torn between a life of obedience to the will of God and not really sure which is the true path of obedience—to his inner prophetic voice or the external voice of the structures of the Church? "Thy will not mine!" Interestingly, Riel the orator refrains from giving a speech from the gallows, on the advice of Father André who suggests silence as a final act of humility (Christ having spoken only seven words on the cross).

In the most demeaning paragraphs of the entire book is Flanagan's portrayal of Riel's attitude to death and immortality in his final hours before execution. In the days immediately after his trial Riel is busy writing letters to politicians. At one point in this flurry of activity he jokes in his journal, "I almost forgot that I've been sentenced to death." But as the final hour draws near it is hardly surprising that he wonders what will happen after his death. Will he suffer, will he be recognized as a saint for his work and sacrifice and even—will *he* be resurrected after three days, like Christ? The last speculation Flanagan "documents" literally from scraps of paper from Riel's past in Montana, and the testimony of a Dr. Jukes who visited Riel before his execution. Yet nowhere in his writing does Riel talk about his own resurrection and certainly he never claims to be a new Christ. In his absolutely final letter Riel repudiates anything "too presumptuous" in his writings. But in the way Flanagan presents Riel's final ruminations on mortality one can see the persistent attempt to dismiss him as an unstable megalomaniac, rather than an intelligent, devoted man loyal unto death to his God and his people. One can only speculate how Thomas Flanagan would write about the vigil in the Garden of Gethsemane and the passion of Calvary. Was Christ driven by ego? Why did he drag in God to back up his radical politics? Why was he such a publicity seeker to allow himself to be captured by the centurions? Why was he so neurotic as to curse a tree that didn't bear fruit? What were his true intentions with Mary Magdalene? Why couldn't he figure out what was God's will and his own will? And, worst of all, if he really believed it all, why did he utter those last words on the cross about betrayal? Indeed, if Flanagan was writing 2000 years ago he would have done a good nullification of Jesus for the Romans and the Pharisees, both of whom were far more "rational" by Flanagan's criteria than Jesus.

Of course Riel was human, and humans have flaws. Certainly his theology had elements of irrationality, but so do the theologies that classify eating meat on Friday as a mortal sin, or proscribe forever the eating of beef or pork, or worry about incubi, succubi and how many angels dance on the head of a pin, or whether the trinity is three separate entities. Nor is irrationality a prerogative of religion. Nineteenth century utopian socialism is full of all sorts of wild and wonderful ways of re-organizing sexuality and family life—tendencies which continue to this day in the name of secular rationality. And secular "rational" capitalism continues to destroy the planet's very life.

So let us judge Riel a little less harshly. And since Riel was human, he had a life, a body and a selfhood, and wanted to lose none of these. Those who judge him as flawed for wanting to live and be heard have standards that only incorporeal angels can meet. Riel, with his "flaw" of human vulnerability, will forever confound his critics, both with his life—and with his death. The highly politicized, partisan psychological attacks by establishment historians will diminish him no more than similar attacks can wipe away the beauty of Vincent Van Gogh's sunflowers and starry nights, or, embarrass every other soul that loved humanity too much for his/her own good.

Well, I hope all this cheers you up a bit for the struggle that seems to have no end.

All the best to you,

Doug

NOTES

AAStB	*Archives de l'archevêché, St. Boniface*
AOM	*Archives Oblates Montréal*
AUStJB	*Archives de l'Union St. Jean-Baptiste, Woonsocket*
CMSA	*Canadian Missionary Society Archives*
CSP	*Canadian Sessional Papers*
Glenbow	*Glenbow-Alberta Institute Archives*
HBCA	*Hudson's Bay Company Archives*
NAC	*National Archives of Canada*
PAA	*Provincial Archives of Alberta*
PAM	*Provincial Archives of Manitoba*
PAQ	*Provincial Archives of Quebec*
QUL	*Queen's University Library*
SAB	*Saskatchewan Archives Board*
StBHS	*Saint Boniface Historical Society*
USL	*University of Saskatchewan Library*

All references to Louis Riel's writing are found in The Collected Writings of Louis Riel. They are listed by volume and number. Thus, CW2-020 refers to volume 2, number 20.

PROLOGUE

p. xv   *"Oh my God!..."*: Thomas Flanagan, ed., *The Diaries of Louis Riel* (Edmonton: Hurtig Publishers, 1976), p. 108. All writings of Riel's in the Prologue are from the diaries.

p. xv   *As W.W. Harkins...*: CW A3-104; also Harkins's letter to R.D. Redford, Aug. 12, 1896, private collection.

CHAPTER 1

p. 3   *"Indian Blood throbs..."*: CW 4-074.

p. 4   *The first Lagimodière ancestor...*: Robert Gosman, *The Riel and Lagimodière Families in Métis Society, 1840–1860*, Parks Canada, Manuscript Report no. 171, 1977, p. 97.

p. 4   *Louis Riel's grandfather...*: Gosman, page 123.

p. 6   *There is no record of Jean-Baptiste Lagimodière...*: Marcel Giraud, *The Métis in the Canadian West*, trans. George Woodcock (Edmonton: University of Alberta Press, 1986), vol. 1, p. 269.

p. 6   *Marie-Anne was gorgeous...*: Z.M. Hamilton, "The Story of Beautiful Marie Gaboury", p. 1, SAB, SHS 31.

p. 7   *he already had a wife and three children...*: Abbé George(s) Dugas(t), "The First Canadian Woman in the North-West", Historical and Scientific Society of Manitoba, p. 13.

p. 7   *These marriages, à la façon du pays...*: Sylvia Van Kirk, *Many Tender Ties: Women in the Fur Trade* Society 1670–1870 (Winnipeg: Watson and Dwyer, 1980), p. 28, 34.

p. 8   *The journey from Lachine...*: Dugast, p. 3, Hamilton, p. 2.

p. 9   *How Lagimodière thought he could avoid disaster...*: Dugast, p. 5.

p. 10   *She delivered the baby...*: Joseph Kinsey Howard, *Strange Empire: The Story of Louis Riel* (New York: Houghton Mifflin Co., 1952), p.61.

p. 10   *At the end of May, Lagimodière...*: Agnes Goulet, *Marie-Anne Gaboury: Une femme dépareillée* (Saint Boniface: Editions de Plaines, n.d.), p. 9.

p. 10   *James Bird, the HBC factor...*: Giraud, vol. 1, p. 382.

p. 11   *Lagimodière and his partners...*: Dugast, p. 7.

p. 11   *In August of 1808...*: Hamilton, p. 3.

p. 12   *When spring arrived...*: Dugast, p. 12.

p. 13   *Fort Gibraltar had become...*: William Douglas, "'The Forks' Becomes a City", *Historical and Scientific Society of Manitoba*, 1944–45, p. 51; Jill Wade, "Red River Architecture, 1812–1870", (Unpublished MA thesis, University of British Columbia, 1967), p. 103; W.L. Morton, "The 1870 Outfit at Red River", *The Beaver*, spring 1970.

p. 13   *Thomas Douglas, fifth Earl of Selkirk...*: material on Selkirk and his colonies from: Howard, p. 35; Donald Purich, *The Metis* (Toronto: James Lorimer, 1988), p. 32; John Morgan Gray, *Lord Selkirk of Red River* (Toronto: Macmillan, 1963), p. 34, 62, 75.

p. 15   *On August 29, 1812...*: Gray, p. 63, 67, 73.

p. 15   *The Indians who for centuries...*: Giraud, vol. 1, p. 391.

p. 15   *Actually the settlers' predicament...*: Giraud, vol. 1, p. 385.

p. 16   *if it had not been for the shortsightedness...*: Giraud, p. 396.

p. 19   *Brushing aside warnings...*: Howard, p. 38; Gray, p. 146; Margaret Arnett MacLeod and W.L. Morton, *Cuthbert Grant of Grantown: Warden of the Plains of Red River* (Toronto: McClelland and Stewart, 1963), p. 43.

p. 20   *Marie-Anne Lagimodière was one of those...*: Dugast, p. 23; Hamilton, p. 7.

p. 20   *Jean-Baptiste had been making his way...*: Hamilton, p. 5; Goulet, p. 45; Dugast, p. 22.

p. 22   *It was triangular in shape...*: Gosman, p. 98.

p. 22   *On July 16, she experienced...*: Goulet, p. 63; Dugast, p. 29.

p. 23   *Out on the prairie...*: Giraud, vol. 1, p. 490.

p. 24   *Jean-Baptiste continued to hunt bison....*: Gosman, pp. 88, 99.

p. 25   *The first Riel to immigrate....*: Antoine Champagne, "La Famille de Louis Riel: Notes généalogiques et historiques", *Mémoires de la Société Généalogique canadienne-française,* vol. XX, no. 3, 1969. Also Gosman, p. 80.

p. 26   *Riel spent the long winter nights...*: Gosman, p. 80.

p. 27   *There's no record of how...*: Giraud, vol. II, p. 207.

p. 28   *There is some indication...*: *Dictionary of Canadian Biography*, vol. IX, p. 663.

p. 28   *HBC records first mention....*: HBCA, Lac la Pluie District Accounts Outfit 1838, B105/d/50 Fo. 13d, B105/d/52, Fo. 2, 3, 13, and B. 105/d/53, Fo. 3, 30, 31.

p. 29   *Jean-Louis's young wife died...*: Gosman, p. 84.

p. 29   *By the spring of 1843....*: AOM, Registre des prises d'habits—1841–1884.

p. 29   *Through Oblate connections....*: Correspondance de Mgr Bourget, Rapport de l'Arch. de Québec, p. 423; Bourget to Provencher, April 25, 1843. StBHS, Collection Louis Riel Famille.

CHAPTER 2

p. 30   *"In my rapture...":* CW 4-054.

p. 30   *Even as a child....:* notes by Henriette Riel-Poitras, StBHS, Collection Louis Riel Famille.

p. 30   *"Family prayers, the rosary...":* CW 3-077.

p. 31   *"She [Julie] was suddenly enveloped...":* Riel-Poitras.

p. 31   *Louis's early childhood...*: PAM, Riel collection, no. 78, Sara Riel to Louis Riel, Feb. 5, 1871.

p. 31   *Colouring all of Riel's early years...*: CW 3-077; Gilles Martel, "Louis Riel, prophete du nouveau monde: les sources psycho-sociales de sa conscience prophetique", Les Cloches de Saint-Boniface, vol. 78, 1979, p. 281.

p. 32   *His sister Henriette described...*: Riel-Poitras.

p. 32   Much of the descriptive material on the Red River Settlement is taken from Wade, "Red River Architecture, 1812–1870" (Unpublished MA thesis, University of British Columbia, 1967).

p. 33n   *There is irony here...*: Frits Pannekoek, *A Snug Little Flock: The Social Origins of the Riel Resistance 1869–70* (Winnipeg: Watson & Dwyer, 1991), p. 93.

p. 34   *For years, the Métis...*: material on the buffalo hunt comes primarily from Joseph Kinsey Howard, *Strange Empire: The Story of Louis Riel* (New York: Houghton Mifflin Co., 1952), p. 254; Frits Pannekoek, "The Fur Trade And Western Canadian Society, 1670–1870", Canadian Historical Association, Historical Booklet no. 43;

John E. Foster, "The Plains Metis" in R.B. Morrison and C.R. Wilson, eds., *Native Peoples: The Canadian Experience* (Toronto: McClelland and Stewart, 1986), p. 392; Marcel Giraud, *The Métis in the Canadian West* (Edmonton: University of Alberta Press, 1986), vol. II, p. 140; G. Herman Sprenger, "The Métis Nation: Buffalo Hunting vs. Agriculture in the Red River Settlement", *Western Canadian Journal of Anthropology*, vol. 3, no. 1, 1972.

p. 34n   *For example George F. Stanley...*: George F.G. Stanley, *The Birth of Western Canada: A History of the Riel Rebellions* (London: Longmans, Green, 1936), p. 8.

p. 38   *After his marriage...*: Robert Gosman, *The Riel and Lagimodière Families in Métis Society, 1840–1860*, Parks Canada, National Historical Sites Branch, manuscript report no. 171, 1977. p. 84.

p. 38   *he saw himself...*: Diane Payment, *Riel Family: Home and Lifestyle at St-Vital, 1860–1910*, Parks Canada, Historical Research Division, 1980, p. 2.

p. 39   *He was ordained...*: Pannekoek, *A Snug Little Flock*, p. 80; Gosman, p. 9.

p. 39   *Early on, Belcourt...*: Pannekoek, *A Snug Little Flock*, p. 94.

p. 40   *Pierre-Guillaume Sayer...*: material on the Sayer trial from Giraud, vol. 2, p. 236; Margaret Arnett MacLeod and W.L. Morton, *Cuthbert Grant of Grantown: Warden of the Plains of Red River* (Toronto: McClelland and Stewart, 1963) p. 135; Alexander Ross, *The Red River Settlement: Its Rise, Progress and Present State* (Minneapolis: Ross & Haines, 1957), p. 372; Auguste Henri de Tremaudan, *Hold High Your Heads: The History of the Metis Nation in Western Canada* (Winnipeg: Pemmican, 1982), p. 46.

p. 41   *The place was seething...*: Pannekoek, p. 209.

p. 42   *In 1830...*: Jennifer S.H. Brown, "Changing Views of Fur Trade Marriage and Domesticity; James Hargrave, "His Colleagues and 'The Sex'", *The Western Canadian Journal of Anthropology*, vol. VI, no. 3, 1976.

p. 42   *The most furious battle...*: Pannekoek, p. 119.

p. 43   *The man they despised...*: Pannekoek, p. 114; Giraud, vol. 2, p. 237.

p. 44   *Jean-Louis Riel was the main instigator....*: W.L. Morton, introduction in Alexander Begg, *Alexander Begg's Red River Journal & Other Papers Relative to the Red River Resistance of 1869–70* (Toronto: The Champlain Society, 1956), p. 34; Giraud, vol. 2, p. 243; Tremaudan, p. 45.

p. 44   *Jean-Louis, weary of farming...*: Gosman, p. 88; Payment, p. 2.

p. 45   *His sister Henriette...*: Riel-Poitras.

CHAPTER 3

p. 46   *"The other day...":* CW 4-009.

p. 46   *On June 1, 1858...*: Donatien Frémont, *The Secretaries of Riel* (Prince Albert: Les Editions Louis Riel for La Société canadienne-française, 1985), p. 7; Sister Marie Bonin, "The Grey Nuns and the Red River Settlement", *Manitoba History*, vol. 11, 1986, pp. 12–14.

p. 49   *Among the institutions...*: Alastair Sweeny, *George-Étienne Cartier: A Biography* (Toronto: McClelland and Stewart, 1976), p. 27; George F.G. Stanley, *Louis Riel* (Toronto: Ryerson Press, 1963), p. 23.

p. 49   *"Alone and far..."*: CW 1-002.

p. 50   *The curriculum which...*: Stanley, p. 35; Gilles Martel, *Le messianisme de Louis Riel* (Waterloo: Wilfrid Laurier University Press, 1984), p. 391.

p. 51   *"A young man from..."*: Eustache Prudhomme, *L'Opinion Publique*, Feb. 19, 1870.

p. 51   *"All the students..."*: J.O. Mousseau, *Une Page d'Histoire*, 1887, pp. 7, 8, 10.

p. 52   *"My inattention..."*: CW 4-001.

p. 52   *"One day a student..."*: Mousseau, p. 10.

p. 53   *" La Souris"*: CW 4-022.

p. 55   *They were invited to stay...*: Fremont, p. 9.

p. 56   *While in Montreal...*: Robert Gosman, *The Riel and Lagimodière Families in Métis Society, 1840–1860*, Parks Canada, National Historic Parks and Sites Branch, manuscript report no. 171, 1977, p. 92.

p. 56   *"some time ago..."*: CW 1-002.

p. 57   *The tour de force...*: CW 4-029; Glen Campbell, "Poetry: Riel's Emotional Catharsis", *Humanities Association of Canada Newsletter*, vol. XIII, no. 2, spring 1985; Thomas Flanagan and John Yardley, "Louis Riel as a Latin Poet", *Humanities Association Review*, vol. 26, 1975.

p. 58   *He had been a dedicated...*: Soeur Élisabeth de Moissac, "Les Soeurs Grises et les événements de 1869–1870", *Société Canadienne d'Histoire de l'Eglise Catholique*, vol. XXXVII, 1970, pp. 215–28.

p. 58   *"Dearest Mother"*: CW 1-003.

p. 59   *"That death caused him..."*: affidavit of John Lee in *L'Etendard*, April 26, 1886.

p. 60   *"The other day..."*: CW 4-009.

p. 61   *"My daughter is .."*.: CW 4-010.

p. 62   *"We have no regret..."*: AAStB, Lenoir to Taché, Aug. 26, 1865.

p. 62   *"The dark fall..."*: CW 4-008.

p. 64   *"Amid the teeming crowd..."*: CW 4-036.

p. 65   *Rodolphe Laflamme's politics...*: Sweeny, p. 228.

p. 66   *On June 12, 1866...*: CW A1-003.

p. 66   *"I must go..."*: CW 4-038.

CHAPTER 4

p. 69   *"One day ontario..."*: CW 4-058.

p. 69   *According to his friend...*: Louis Schmidt, "Mémoires" in *Le Patriot de l'Ouest*, Feb. 8, 1912.

p. 71   *Bishop Taché...*: cited in W.F. Bryant, *The Blood Of Abel*, p. 43.

p. 71   *"You are always..."*: CW 1-007.

p. 72   *"They penetrated..."*: Charles Mair, Toronto *Globe*, Feb. 16, 1869.

p. 72   *"I have heard.."*.: George Young, Toronto *Globe*, Nov. 27, 1868.

p. 72   *Julie had given up the mill...*: Diane Payment, *Riel Family: Home and Lifestyle at St-Vital, 1860–1910*, Parks Canada, Historical Research Division, 1980, pp. 7, 8, 9.

p. 73   *In January 1869*: Payment, p. 11; Thomas Flanagan, "Louis Riel's Land Claims", *Manitoba History*, spring 1991, p. 4.

p. 74   *Since his return to Red River...*: Donatien Frémont, *The Secretaries of Riel* (Prince Albert: Les Editions Louis Riel for La Société canadienne-française), p. 11.

p. 75   *A bizarre scandal...*: Frits Pannekoek, *A Snug Little Flock: The Social Origins of the Riel Resistance, 1869–70* (Winnipeg: Watson & Dwyer, 1991), p. 146.

p. 76   *"What a spectacle..."*: CMSA, John Chapman to the secretaries, Feb. 19, 1863.

p. 80   *The year that Riel arrived back...*: Auguste Henri de Tremaudan, *Hold High Your Heads: The History of the Metis in Western Canada* (Winnipeg: Pemmican, 1982), p. 55; Lionel Dorge, "The Métis and Canadien Councillors of Assiniboia", *The Beaver*, winter 1974.

p. 81   *By the summer of 1868*: Jill Wade, "Red River Architecture 1812–1870" (Unpublished MA thesis, University of British Columbia, 196), p. 100.

p. 81   *"He could speak..."*: William Healy, *Women of Red River* (Winnipeg: The Women's Canadian Club, 1923), p. 128.

p. 84   *Clearing the bush...*: Joseph Kinsey Howard, *Strange Empire: The Story of Louis Riel* (New York: Houghton Mifflin Co., 1952), p. 80; Alexander Begg, *Alexander Begg's Red River Journal & Other Papers Relative to The Red River Resistance of 1869–70* (Toronto: The Champlain Society, 1956) p. 155.

p. 86   *"I received hospitalities..."*: letter from Charles Mair to Holmes Mair printed in the Toronto *Globe*, Jan. 4, 1869.

p. 87   *Mrs. Bannatyne...*: Norman Shrive, *Charles Mair: Literary Nationalist* (Toronto: University of Toronto Press, 1965), pp. 72, 73.

p. 87   *"At the pointe de chênes..."*: CW 4-040.

p. 88   *"The half-breeds are..."*: Mair, Toronto *Globe*, Jan. 4, 1869.

p. 88   *"Please be so good.."*.: CW 1-010.

p. 90   *In the following months...*: Shrive, p. 87.

p. 92   *"After you left"*: Sara Riel to Louis Riel, Sept .7, 1868, PAM, Riel letters.

p. 96   *Colonel Dennis....*: Colin Read, "The Red River Rebellion and J.S. Dennis, 'Lieutenant and Conservator of the Peace'", *Manitoba History*, vol. 3, 1982, pp. 11–19.

CHAPTER 5

p. 98   *"I am a Métis girl"*: CW 4-041.

p. 99   *Being named lieutenant-governor...*: George Woodcock, "Louis Riel: Defender of the Past", *The Beaver*, no. 290, 1960, pp. 24–29.

p. 100   *Alexander Begg laughed...*: Alexander Begg, *Alexander Begg's Red River Journal & Other Papers Relative to the Red River Resistance of 1869–70* (Toronto: The Champlain Society, 1956), p. 174.

p. 101   *"That learning through..."*: CW 1-076.

p. 105   *John Harrison O'Donnell...*: Joseph Kinsey Howard, *Strange Empire: The Story of Louis Riel* (New York: Houghton Mifflin Co., 1952), p. 99.

p. 106   *On the evening of...*: J.J. Hargrave, Montreal *Herald*, Nov. 27, 1869; Auguste Henri de Tremaudan, "Louis Riel's Account of the Capture of Fort Garry, 1870", *Canadian Historical Review*, vol. 5, 1924, p. 153.

p. 107   *Alexander Begg described him...*: Begg, p. 176.

p. 107   *Provencher was just leaving...*: Hargrave, Montreal *Herald*, Nov. 27, 1869; Donatien Frémont, *The Secretaries of Riel* (Prince Albert: Les Editions Louis Riel for La Société canadienne-française, 1985), p. 20.

p. 108   *Meanwhile at exactly the same time...*: Hargrave, Montreal *Herald*, Nov. 27, 1869.

p. 108   *McDougall had rented...*: W.L. Morton, introduction in Begg, pp. 54, 55, 59; Howard, p. 107; *The Canadian Illustrated News*, Dec. 25, 1869; Nancy L. Woolworth, "Gingras, St. Joseph and the Metis in the Northern Red River Valley: 1843–1873", *North Dakota History*, vol. 42, 1975, pp. 16–27.

p. 109   *"A King without a Kingdom..."*: St. Paul *Daily Press*, Nov. 21, 1869.

p. 109   *On the morning of November 2...*: Auguste Henri de Tremaudan, "Letter of Louis Riel and Ambroise Lépine to Lieutenant-Governor Morris, January 3, 1873, *The Canadian Historical Review*, vol. 7, 1926, p. 137.

p. 110   *Governor Mactavish was confined...*: Dr. Cowan's deposition, Canada, Parliament, *Journals* (House of Commons), "Report of the Select Committee", 1874.

p. 111   *On the morning of November 16...*: Hargrave, Montreal *Herald*, Dec. 13, 1869; Howard, p. 115; George F. Stanley, *Louis Riel* (Toronto: Ryerson Press, 1963), p. 68.

p. 112   *Ross was one of a huge...*: Sylvia Van Kirk, "'What if Mama is an Indian?'", *The New People: Being and Becoming Métis in North America*, p. 207.

p. 113   *Riel realized that...*: Stanley, p. 70; Begg, pp. 205, 210.

p. 114   *Much to Riel's amazement...*: Riel himself made extensive notes on the convention from November 16 to December 1, in CW 1-017, translated in Begg, p. 420.

CHAPTER 6

p. 117   *"We stormed Schultz's house..."*: CW 4-041.

p. 117   *Back in mid-November...*: Alexander Begg, *Alexander Begg's Red River Journal & Other Papers Relative to the Red River Resisitance of 1869–70* (Toronto: The Champlain

Society, 1956), pp. 183, 188; Schmidt, "Mémoires", Feb. 15, 1912; Peter MacArthur, "The Red River Rebellion", *Manitoba Pageant*, spring 1973, vol. 18, no. 3.

p. 118   *The Fire-Engine House...*: Begg, p. 185

p. 120   *"McDougall fumbled with..."*: Joseph Kinsey Howard, *Strange Empire: The Story of Louis Riel* (New York: Houghton Mifflin Co., 1952), p. 127.

p. 120   *Colonel Dennis started out...*: Colin Read, "The Red River Rebellion and J.S. Dennis, 'Lieutenant and Conservator of the Peace'", *Manitoba History*, vol. 3, 1982, p. 11; "Memorial of the people of Rupert's Land and North-West" to President Ulysses S. Grant, Oct. 3, 1870, CW 1-076.

p. 121   *He had hired...*: George-É. Cartier to the imperial government, June 8, 1870, NAC, Blue Book, 1874, p. 176; Begg, p. 71.

p. 122   *Dennis meanwhile set about...*: Read, p. 15.

p. 122   *Schultz's Winnipeg establishment...*: material on storming of Fort Schultz from Howard, pp. 135, 136; notebook of James Ross, Dec. 1–14, 1869, PAM, Ross papers; Begg, pp. 205, 209, 211, 215; Schmidt, Feb. 15, 1912, p. 4.

p. 125   *All through the previous night...*: Louis Riel, "Mémoire sur les causes des troubles du Nord-Ouest et sur les négotiations qui ont amené leur règlement amiable. CW 1-188; Thomas Flanagan, Political Theory of the Red River Resistance: The Declaration of December 8, 1869", *Canadian Journal of Political Science*, vol. 11, 1978, pp. 153–164.

p. 125   *"The obligation of subjects..."*: as quoted from Thomas Hobbes's *Leviathan*, in Lawrence Berns, "Thomas Hobbes", in Leo Strauss and Joseph Cropsey, eds., *History of Political Philosophy* (Chicago: Rand McNally, 1963), pp. 366–67.

p. 126   *On Friday, December 10*: Begg, p. 225; James Ross, Notebook of James Ross, PAM; Schmidt, Feb. 15, 1912, p. 4.

p. 128   *"He was one of the finest..."*: Rev. R.G. MacBeth, "On the Fighting Line in Riel's Day", *Maclean's*, July–Nov. 1914, Feb. 1915; Schmidt, Feb. 15, 1912.

p. 128   *The third person...*: Robert Cunningham, Toronto *Globe*, Jan. 28, 1870; Schmidt, Feb. 15, 1912.

p. 130   *Immediately after Christmas...*: Sir Charles Tupper, *Recollections of Sixty Years in Canada* (Toronto: Cassell, 1915), p. 143.

p. 132   *De Salaberry would...*: Begg, p. 261.

p. 132   *Although Smith...*: Peter C. Newman, *Merchant Princes* (Toronto: Penguin, 1991), p. 21.

p. 134   *Louis Schmidt has his number...*: Schmidt, Feb. 22, 1912.

p. 134   *Donald Smith was the ultimate...*: Association of Métis and Non-status Indians of Saskatchewan, *Louis Riel: Justice Must Be Done* (Winnipeg: Manitoba Métis Federation Press, 1979), p. 40; E.B. Osler, *The Man Who Had to Hang: Louis Riel* (Toronto: Longmans, Green & Co., 1961), p. 81.

p. 134   *"It is hoped here that..."*: Macdonald to Rose, Dec. 5, 1869, NAC, Macdonald papers, Letter Books, vol. 13, p. 648.

p. 134   *And the prime minister...*: George F.G. Stanley, *Louis Riel* (Toronto: Ryerson Press, 1963), p. 86.

p. 135   *Almost immediately, support...*: Schmidt, Feb. 22, 1912.

p. 135   *One night, Louis...*: Begg, p. 300.

p. 135   *The Canadians who had been smoked...*: Stanley, p. 101; Henry Woodington, "Diary of a Prisoner in the Red River Rebellion", *Niagara Historical Society*, vol. 25, 1913, p. 32; MacArthur, p. 23.

p. 137   *Then there occurred...*: Stanley, p. 87; Begg, p. 262; Schmidt, p. 468; Smith to Howe, April 12, 1870, NAC, Secretary of State of the Provinces, 1869, 1043.

CHAPTER 7

p. 139   *"Grant me righteousness..."*: CW 3-195.

p. 139   *It was a sharp...*: materials used in the account of the public meetings of Jan. 19 and 20, 1870, include Joseph Kinsey Howard, *Strange Empire: The Story of Louis Riel* (New York: Houghton Mifflin Co., 1952), p. 146; George F.G. Stanley, *Louis Riel* (Toronto: Ryerson Press, 1963), p. 88; Alexander Begg, *Alexander Begg's Red River Journal & Other Papers Relative to The Red River Resistance of 1869–70* (Toronto: The Champlain Society, 1956), pp. 261, 270.

p. 142   *"I came here with..."*: Begg, p. 276; Stanley, p. 91.

p. 143   *That evening the Mactavish...*: Begg, p. 263.

p. 144   *"The devil take it..."*: New Nation, Feb. 11, 1870.

p. 145   *That evening Bannatyne...*: Begg, p. 297.

p. 146   *The Nolin brothers...*: Stanley, p. 95.

p. 147   *"On my life..."*: New Nation, Feb. 18, 1870.

p. 147   *It was ten p.m.*: Begg, p. 303; Louis Schmidt, "Mémoires", *Le Patriot del'Ouest*, April 4, 1912, p. 3.

p. 148   *The community's leading light...*: Charles Boulton, *Reminiscences of the North-West Rebellions* (Toronto: Grip Printing and Publishing, 1886), p. 24.

p. 150   *After a "good, hefty dinner"*: Materials used in the account of the Boulton uprising include Stanley, pp. 103–7; Frits Pannekoek, *A Snug Little Flock: The Social Origins of the Riel Resistance 1869–70* (Winnipeg: Watson & Dwyer, 1991), p. 184; Begg, pp. 307, 312; Schmidt, April 12, 1912; Irene M. Spry, "The 'Memories' of George William Sanderson, 1846–1936", *Canadian Ethnic Studies*, vol. 17, no. 2, 1985, p. 115.

p. 150   *Schultz had not been...*: William Healy, *Women of Red River*, pp. 232–33; Howard, pp. 152–53.

p. 153   *Norbert Parisien...*: Howard, p. 159; Begg, p. 314; Auguste Hendri de Tremaudan, "The Execution of Thomas Scott", *Canadian Historical Review*, vol. 6, 1925, p. 222.

p. 154   *"Fellow Countrymen..."*: CW 1-033.

p. 155   *At eleven o'clock...*: Begg, p. 313.

p. 156   *"Riel had sent word..."*: Spry, p. 128.

p. 157   *In a farmhouse near Kildonan...*: W.L. Morton introduction in Begg, p. 108; Begg, p. 317; W.J. Healy, *Women of Red River* (Winnipeg: The Women's Canadian Club, 1923), p. 226; August Henri de Tremaudan, *Hold High Your Heads: The History of the Metis Nation in Western Canada* (Winnipeg: Pemmican, 1982), p. 85; Donald Smith, report to Howe in W.L. Morton, *Manitoba: The Birth of a Province* (Winnipeg: Manitoba Record Society Publications, 1965), p. 36.

p. 158   *On February 24...*: Begg, p. 321.

CHAPTER 8

p. 159   *"My dealings with Canada..."*: CW 4-058.

p. 159   *His background naturally...*: *Dictionary of Canadian Biography*, vol. IX (1861–1870), p. 707.

p. 160   *He certainly had a deep...*: Joseph Kinsey Howard, *Strange Empire: The Story of Louis Riel* (New York,: Houghton Mifflin Co. 1952), p. 162.

p. 160   *George William Sanderson...*: Irene M. Spry, "The 'Memories' of George William Sanderson 1846–1936", *Canadian Ethnic Studies*, vol. 17, no. 2, 1985, pp. 129–30.

p. 160   *Henry Woodington...*: Henry Woodington, "Diary of a Prisoner in the Red River Rebellion", *Niagara Historical Society*, vol. 25, 1913, p. 51.

p. 161   *"When Riel came in..."*: Spry, p. 130.

p. 161   *"The Métis said..."*: Auguste Henri de Tremaudan, "The Execution of Thomas Scott", *The Canadian Historical Review*, vol. 6, no. 3, 1925, p. 231n.

p. 161   *The trial took place...*: George F.G. Stanley, Louis Riel: (Toronto: Ryerson Press, 1963,) p. 113; Schmidt, "Mémoires", *Le Patriot de l'Ouest*, April 4, 1912, p. 3

p. 163   *Almost every historian...*: J.M. Bumsted, "The 'Mahdi' of Western Canada? Louis Riel and His Papers", *The Beaver*, Aug./Sept. 1987, p. 49.

p. 163n *For years incredible rumours...*: Alexander Begg, *Alexander Begg's Red River Journal & Other Papers Relative to the Red River Resistance of 1869–70* (Toronto: The Champlain Society, 1956), pp. 331, 342.

p. 163   *The American consul...*: quoted in Harold C. Knox, "Consul Taylor of Red River", *The Beaver*, March 1949, p. 18.

p. 164   *"Let anyone put himself..."*: quoted in W.F. Bryant, *The Blood of Abel* (Hasting, New York, published by author, 1887), p. 80.

p. 164   *In April the Toronto* Globe...: *Globe*, April 3, 1870.

p. 164   *"The people generally now have..."* New Nation, March 11, 1870.

p. 165   *Although he had been born into...*: Maurice Prud'Homme, "The Life and Times of Archbishop Taché", *Historical and Scientific Society of Manitoba*, series 3, no. 2, 1904, p. 4; Lionel Dorge, "Bishop Taché and the Confederation of Manitoba", *Historical and Scientific Society of Manitoba*, series 3, no. 26, 1969–70, p. 93; Donatien Frémont,

"Archbishop Taché and the Beginnings of Manitoba", *North Dakota Historical Quarterly*, vol. 6, 1931–32.

p. 165   *As a member of the governing body...*: Robert Gosman, *The Riel and Lagimodière Families in Métis Society, 1840–1860,* Parks Canada, National Historic Sites Branch, manuscript report no. 171, 1977, pp. 26–27.

p. 166   *I have always feared...*: Taché to Cartier, Oct. 7, 1869, Taché papers, AAStB.

p. 167   *The bishop would say...*: Taché to the governor-general, Lord Dufferin, Nov. 14, 1877, AAStB.

p. 167   *"I have seen him..."*: CW A3-012, p. 530 .

p. 170   *But it was the Saint...*: Begg, p. 338.

p. 171   *"It is almost refreshing..."*: quoted in Howard, p. 133.

p. 172   *On March 25, 1870...*: Begg, pp. 343, 365.

p. 174   *During those lovely April days...*: Begg, pp. 326, 355.

p. 175   *"Riel...has a fine physique..."*: Letter from N.P. Langford to J.W. Taylor, July 10, 1870, J.W. Taylor papers, Minnesota Historical Society Collections.

p. 175   *That night a rally...*: Toronto *Globe*, April 7, 1870.

p. 177   *Ritchot had been optimistic...*: Rev. N.-J. Ritchot kept an extensive diary of his negotiations, originally in the parish archives of St. Norbert. A translation is available in W.L. Morton, ed. *Manitoba: The Birth of a Province* (Winnipeg: Manitoba Record Society Publications, 1965)

p. 178   *"Everything looks well..."*: Macdonald to Rose, Feb. 23, 1870, NAC, Macdonald Papers, vol. 517.

p. 179   *As historian D.N. Sprague has concluded...*: D.N. Sprague, *Canada and the Métis 1869–1885* (Waterloo: Sir Wilfrid Laurier Press, 1988), p. 58.

p. 181   *"His Excellency told us..."*: Ritchot's Journal, May 19, 1877, Morton, *Manitoba: The Birth of a Province*, p. 154.

p. 181   *"Without setting too much store..."*: CW 1-057.

p. 182   *"I would give up my place..."*: *New Nation*, March 18, 1870.

p. 182   *"We are waiting..."*: Canada, *Report of the Select Committee 1874*, Taché deposition.

p. 183   *"if anyone in Toronto..."*: quoted in Norman Shrive, *Charles Mair: Literary Nationalist* (Toronto: University of Toronto Press, 1965), p. 114.

p. 183   *The Americans, realizing...*: Begg, p. 347.

p. 184   *"These impulsive half-breeds..."*: Macdonald to Rose, Feb. 23, 1870, NAC, Macdonald papers, vol. 517.

p. 184   *"Instead of [becoming a priest]..."*: Garnet Joseph Wolseley, "Narrative of the Red River Expedition", *Blackwoods Magazine*, vol. CVIII, Dec. 1870, p. 710.

p. 188   *I remained in view...*: CW A3-013, p. 551.

CHAPTER 9

p. 191   *"You glide above..."*: CW 4-044.

p. 191   *After Wolseley's "victory"...*: George F.G. Stanley, *Louis Riel* (Toronto: Ryerson Press, 1963), p. 157; Auguste Henri de Tremaudan, "Louis Riel's Account of the Capture of Fort Garry, 1870", *The Canadian Historical Review*, vol. 5, 1924, pp. 146–59.

p. 192   *"Pray for me..."*: CW 1-066.

p. 192   *She had every reason...*: materials on the behaviour of Wolseley and his expeditionary force include: Joseph Kinsey Howard, *Strange Empire: The Story of Louis Riel* (New York: Houghton Mifflin Co., 1952) pp. 184, 185; Donatien Frémont, "Archbishop Taché and the Beginnings of Manitoba", *North Dakota Historical Quarterly*, vol. 6, 1931–32, p. 131; Marcel Giraud, *The Metis in the Canadian West* (Edmonton: University of Alberta Press, 1986), vol. II, p. 377; Auguste Henri de Tremaudan, *Hold High Your Heads: The History of the Metis Nation in Western Canada* (Winnipeg, Pemmican, 1982), p. 103.

p. 194   *"I cannot help but..."*: Garnet Joseph Wolseley, *The Story of a Soldier's Life* (New York: Kraus, 1903, 1971), vol. II, p. 219.

p. 195   *After some discussion...*: Stanley, p. 161; John P. Pritchett, "The Origin of the So-Called Fenian Raid on Manitoba in 1871", *The Canadian Historical Review*, vol. 10, 1929, p. 26.

p. 196   *"That not a single pledge..."*: CW 1-076.

p. 197   *"I was sorry to hear..."*: Sara Riel to Louis Riel, Oct. 25, 1870, PAM, Riel papers.

p. 197   *"I hear the joyful..."*: CW 4-046.

p. 198   *"Oh! An angel..."*: CW 4-043.

p. 198   *"Québec, our motherland..."*: CW 4-045.

p. 199   *"God has not turned..."*: CW 1-085.

p. 199   *"Poor friend", he wrote...*: Louis Schmidt, "Mémoires", in *Le Patriot de l'Ouest*, April 18, 1912, p. 5.

p. 200   *"I regret that..."*: Joseph Dubuc to Louis Riel, Dec. 8, 1870, PAM, Riel papers.

p. 200   *"Mr. Dubuc ... suffers..."*: Sara Riel to Louis Riel, Jan. 29, 1871, PAM, Riel papers.

p. 201   *"Ah, dear Louis..."*: Sara Riel to Louis Riel, Feb. 20, 1871, PAM, Riel papers.

p. 201   *The Ontario party...*: D.N. Sprague, *Canada and the Métis, 1869–1885* (Waterloo: Sir Wilfrid Laurier Press, 1988), p. 76.

p. 202   *"The more I endure..."*: Sara Riel to Mrs. Louis Riel Sr., Louis Riel and family, Aug. 8, 1871. PAM Riel papers.

p. 203   *O'Donoghue had been...*: materials on the attempted Fenian raids include: Howard, pp. 191–97; Stanley, p. 170, 171; Pritchett, Canada, *Report of the Select Committee, 1874*.

p. 204   *Father Ritchot, who seemed...*: *Report of the Select Committee, 1874*, Ritchot to Archibald, October 4, 1871.

p. 204   *"You know perfectly..."*: *Report of the Select Committee, 1874*, Taché depostion.

p. 205   *"the Rielites hoped..."*: P.R. Mailhot, "Ritchot's Resistance: Abbé Noel Joseph Ritchot and the Creation and Transformation of Manitoba", Unpublished PhD thesis, University of Manitoba, 1986, p. 182.

p. 206   *On a mild winter evening,*: Le Métis, Dec. 21, 1871; Tremaudan, *Hold High Your Heads*, p. 105.

p. 207   *"I have spared neither..."*: *Report of the Select Committee, 1874*, Taché to Cartier, May 6, 1871.

p. 208   *"You must remember..."*: *Report of the Select Committee, 1874*, Taché depostion.

p. 209   *William Devlin, a young carter...*: affidavit of W. Devlin and J. Mager, St. Paul, March 20, 1872, PAM, Riel papers; Riel to Taché, March 21, 1872, CW 1-121.

p. 210   *"Don't worry about us..."*: CW 1-130.

p. 210   *"It is a crying shame..."*: Archibald to Cartier, Jan. 19, 1872, NAC, Macdonald papers.

p. 210   *On April 28...:* "Letter of Louis Riel and Ambroise Lépine to Lieutenant-Governor Morris, January 3, 1873", CW 1-158.

p. 211   *"It seems to me..."*: Riel to Taché, April 27, 1872, CW 1-131.

p. 212   *"Alexandre, I thank you..."*: Louis Riel to Julie Riel, May 17, 1872, CW 1-138.

p. 212   *He wrote to Dubuc...:* CW 1-137.

p. 212   *"I received your kind letter..."*: CW 1-143.

p. 215   *"The oxen gasped..."*: Sara Riel to Mrs. Louis Riel Sr., and Louis Riel, July 2, 1871, PAM, Riel papers.

p. 215   *"Dear Mamma..."*: Sara Riel to Mrs. Louis Riel Sr., and Louis Riel, August 11, 1873, PAM, Riel papers.

p. 216   *"Goodbye, God..."*: Sara Riel to Mrs. Louis Riel Sr., and Louis Riel, n.d., PAM, Riel papers.

p. 217   *"Oh! I wish..."*: CW 1-161.

p. 218   *"I love the world..."*: Riel to Taché, Jan. 8, 1876, CW 2-007.

p. 218   *"I went to bed at nine..."*: CW 1-173.

CHAPTER 10

p. 220   *"Those of homeland dispossessed..."*: CW 4-054.

p. 220   *"Death will come as a thief..."*: CW 4-050.

p. 222   *"For sustenance..."*: CW 4-052.

p. 224   *"was very lonely..."*: Henriette Pierrette to Veuve Riel, Jan. 25, 1874, PAM, Riel papers.

p. 225   *"They have been very..."*: CW 1-182.

p. 225   *"I have decided to write..."*: Barnabé to Riel, Jan. 19, 1874, PAM, Riel papers.

p. 226   *"Let each say..."*: Mason Wade, *The French Canadians, 1760–1967* (Toronto: Macmillan, 1968) vol. 1, p. 360.

p. 227   *"I made two visits..."*: CW 1-190.

p. 228   *"This man [Riel]..."*: *Report of the Select Committee 1874*, Taché to Dorion, Jan. 3, 1874.

p. 229   *As the new members arrived...*: George F.G. Stanley, *Louis Riel* (Toronto: Ryerson Press, 1963), p. 202; J.M. Bumsted, "The 'Mahdi' of Western Canada? Louis Riel and His Papers", *The Beaver*, Aug.–Sept. 1987, p. 50; Vernon LaChance, "The Métis Rebellions", *Maclean's* , Oct. 15, 1930; Edgar Collard, *Canadian Yesterdays* (Toronto: Longmans, Green, 1955), p. 41.

p. 232   *In the spring of 1873...*: For materials on Father Ritchot and amnesty see P.R. Mailhot, "Ritchot's Resistance: Abbé Noel Joseph Ritchot and the Creation and Transformation of Manitoba" (Unpublished Ph.D. thesis, University of Manitoba, 1986).

p. 234   *"The times are exceedingly..."*: Joseph Lemay to Louis Riel, March 20, 1874, PAM, Riel papers.

p. 235   *"By giving me this little book..."*: CW 4-053.

p. 236   *"One could not speak..."*: Robert Rumilly, *Histoire des Franco-Américains* (Woonsocket, R.I.: l'Union Saint-Jean-Baptiste d,'Amérique, 1958), p.34.

p. 237   *"Everyone is for us..."*: CW 1-204.

p. 238   *"Lépine, why is..."*: CW 4-049.

p. 239   *Lépine's trial...*: Stanley, p. 210; Z.M. Hamiltonto F.J. Collyer, Aug. 9, 1944, SAB, SHS 179.

p. 242   *"The sound of Lépine's..."*: *Le Travailleur* (Worcester, Mass.), Dec. 24, 1874.

p. 243   *"Those of homeland dispossessed..."*: CW 4-054.

CHAPTER 11

p. 244   *"I am mad in the eyes..."*: CW 4-055.

p. 245   *"In the great republic..."*: CW 4-080.

p. 248   *"I have received your letter..."*: CW A1-014.

p. 248   *"I put my trust..."*: CW 4-062.

p. 249   *"During the five years..."*: CW 1-245.

p. 249   *"I am happy to learn..."*: Mrs. Louis Riel Sr. to Riel, Aug. 14, 1875, PAM, Riel papers.

p. 251   *"Perhaps it is not entirely..."*: CW 1-250.

p. 251   *"[Riel] was so far..."*: Edmund Mallet, "Notes on Riel", AUStJB.

p. 252   *"I hope that Charles..."*: CW 1-247.

p. 252   *"My dear brother Meunier..."*: Riel to Paul Proulx, May 10, 1877, CW 2-039.

p. 253   *"At the same moment..."*: *Le Courrier du Canada*, June 11, 1885.

p. 254   *"Every artist I meet..."*: NAC, Emily Carr papers, diary, Sept. 9, 1933.

p. 254   *And Louis's belief...*: Peter Beyer, "La vision religieuse de Louis Riel: L'ultramontanisme canadien-français au service de la nation métisse", *Studies in Religion*, vol. 13, 1984, p. 93; J.M. Bumsted, "The 'Mahdi' of Western Canada? Louis

Riel and His Papers", *The Beaver*, Aug.–Sept. 1987, p. 51; Gilles Martel, "Louis Riel, prophete du nouveau monde: les sources psycho-sociales de sa conscience prophetique", *Les Cloches de Saint-Boniface*, vol. 78, 1979, pp. 281–295.

p. 256   *"Friday he asked me…"*: Primeau to Mallet, Dec. 31, 1875, AUStJB.

p. 256   *He saw himself…*: *Le Travailleur* (Worcester, Mass.), December 11, 1885.

p. 257   *"He [Louis] continued to cry…"*: affidavit of John Lee in *L'Étendard*, April 26, 1866.

p. 258   *"He had the appearance…"*: Dr. Henry Howard, "Medical History of Louis David Riel during His Detention in Longue Pointe Asylum", *Canada Medical and Surgical Journal*, June 1886, pp. 641–49.

p. 258   *From the outside…*: material for the account of L'Hospice St. Jean includes Daniel Francis, "Minds in Chains", *Horizon Canada*, vol. 7, pp. 1790–95; Henry M. Hurd, ed., *The Institutional Care of the Insane in the United States and Canada*, vol. IV (New York: Arno Press), p. 189.

p. 259   *"In the course of…"*: Tuke in Hurd, p. 193

p. 259   *"Dr. Howard's role…"*: Thomas Flanagan, *Riel: Prophet of the New World* (Toronto: University of Toronto Press, 1979), p. 58.

p. 260   *"Dr. Lachapelle prescribed…"*: CW 2-017.

p. 260   *Dr. Howard rather cutely…*: Howard, p. 646.

p. 261   *"I have received your letter…"*: CW 2-010.

p. 262   *"The impious attacked my work…"*: CW 4-066.

p. 262   *Dr. Lachapelle filled out…*: Hôpital St-Michel-Archange, dossier no. 3697.

p. 263   *"Ottawa, you're totally lost…"*: CW 4-056.

p. 263   *"When I get there…"*: CW 4-057.

p. 264   *"You call yourself conservative…"*: CW 4-072.

p. 264   *"I have become priest…"*: CW 4-063.

p. 265   *"When I speak to you…"*: CW 4-065.

p. 265   *"I confess in the name…"*: CW 4-077.

p. 268   *"The Queen of the Lakes…"*: CW 4-068.

p. 268   *"Here, My Lord, the Holy ghost…"*: CW 2-010.

p. 268   *"Great capital! With one kick…"*: CW 2-041.

p. 269   *"It has been a year…"*: Mrs. Louis Riel Sr. to Riel, Jan. 21, 1877, PAM, Riel papers.

p. 270   *"The sooner you become…"*: Rev. F. Barnabé to Riel, April 21, 1877, PAM, Riel papers.

CHAPTER 12

p. 271   *"I would kiss you ten times…"*: CW 4-086.

p. 272   *"I assure you that…"*: CW 2-049.

p. 272   *"He is lending me his horse…"*: CW 2-058.

p. 272   *"Oh sweet Evelina!..."*: CW 4-082, 4-083, 4-084.

p. 274   *"I'm going to bed..."*: Evelina Barnabé to Riel Oct. 4, 1878, Jan. 9, 1879, April 13, 1879. NAC, Department of Justice misc., Riel papers, II.

p. 274   *"I have always been opposed..."*: CW 2-053.

p. 274   *"Lord calm in me this political..."*: CW 4-078.

p. 275   *"Keeseville was already..."*: Rev. F. Barnabé to Riel, March 29, 1878, PAM, Riel papers.

p. 276   *Just before Riel's...*: *New York Herald*, May 17, 1885.

p. 276   *"His mind shows..."*: Barnabé to Mallet, Oct. 12, 1878, Mallet papers, AUStJB.

p. 277   *"Minnesota, which I now entered..."*: CW 4-088.

p. 277   *"He [the bishop] has found me..."*: Barnabé to Riel, Feb. 1, 1879, PAM, Riel papers.

p. 278   *"During the winter holidays..."*: CW 4-091.

p. 278   *"Your name is beautiful..."*: CW 4-089.

p. 278   *"I often go and sit..."*: Evelina Barnabé to Riel, May 13, 1879, PAM, Riel papers.

p. 279   *"What is believed about my stay..."*: Joseph Dubuc, "Mémoires d'un Manitobain", ms, PAM.

p. 279   *"I have taken the great cross..."*: CW 4-066.

p. 280   *"I remember that on one..."*: n.a. "Testimony from Dakota" *The Riel rebellion...: How it began, how it was carried on, and its consequences*, n.p. p. 28.

p. 281   *The Métis of Red River had thought...*: sources for the account of the Métis land claims issue include: D.N. Sprague, *Canada and the Métis, 1869–1885* (Waterloo: Sir Wilfrid Laurier Press, 1988), pp. 109–39; Thomas Flanagan, *Metis Lands in Manitoba* (Calgary: University of Calgary Press, 1991), pp. 29–37; Donald Purich, *The Metis* (Toronto: James Lorimer, 1988), pp. 60–79; Nicole J.M. St-Onge, "The Dissolution of a Métis Community: Pointe à Grouette, 1860–1885", *Studies in Political Economy*, no. 18, autumn 1985, p. 149; David Boisvert and Keith Turnbull, "Who are the Métis?", *Studies in Political Economy*, no. 18, autumn 1985, p. 107; P.R. Mailhot and D.N. Sprague, "Persistent Settlers: The Dispersal and Resettlement of the Red River Métis, 1870–1885", *Canadian Ethnic Studies*, vol. XVII, no. 2, p. 1; Gerhard Ens, "Métis Lands in Manitoba", *Manitoba History*, spring 1983, p. 2.

p. 284   *"Sir John A. MacDonald..."*: CW 4-094; translation by John Glassco in *Canadian Literature*, vol. 37, 1968, p. 40

p. 285   *What Riel now envisioned...*: "Dans l'Etat du Minnesota", CW 4-088; Evelina Barnabé to Riel, March 12, 1879, PAM, Riel papers.

p. 285   *The tragedy had begun the year...*: Maggie Siggins, *Revenge of the Land: A Century of Greed, Tragedy and Murder on a Saskatchewan Farm* (Toronto: McClelland & Stewart, 1992), pp. 73–76.

p. 286   *"We have taken twenty-eight..."*: CW 2-065.

p. 286   *In 1868, the U.S. government...*: Siggins, p. 70.

CHAPTER 13

p. 288   *"The States have harbored me...":* CW 4-101.

p. 290   *To reside in a wintering camp...:* N. Anick, *The Metis of the South Saskatchewan*, vol. 1, Parks Canada, manuscript report no. 364, 1976, pp. 154, 186.

p. 292   *"Booze is responsible...":* CW 4-108.

p. 292   *"You serve Satan well...":* CW 4-098.

p. 292   *"If you only hunted...":* CW 4-097.

p. 293   *"One day you accosted me...":* CW 4-099.

p. 293   *Superintendent James M. Walsh...:* Walsh papers, PAM, quoted in J.P. Turner, *The North-West Mounted Police 1873–1893* (Ottawa: King's Printer, 1950), vol. 1, pp. 410–14.

p. 294   *"Having no other way...":* CW 2-070.

p. 294   *Another individual who witnessed...:* Jean L'Heureux to J. A. Macdonald, Nov. 1, 1886, NAC, Macdonald papers, vol. 110, p. 44891; Jean L'Heureux to Indian Affairs Commissioner Edgar Dewdney, Sept. 1880, NAC, Indian affairs records file 34527; letters from Superintendent Crozier of Fort Walsh, March 24, March 29, May 7, 1880, NAC, Mounted Police Records, vol. 2233.

p. 295   *"The crees are...":* CW 2-154.

p. 295   *He met with them several times...:* L'Heureux to Macdonald, Nov. 1, 1886, NAC, Macdonald papers; John Maclean, *Canadian Savage Folk*, p. 380.

p. 296   *"In the spring...":* William McCartney Davidson, *Louis Riel, 1844–1885*, p. 127.

p. 297   *"It sored my heart...":* CW A3-013, pp. 550, 551.

p. 297   *"Albion, you were mistaken...":* CW 4-101.

p. 298   *"We ask the government...":* CW 2-073.

p. 299   *"They are very rarely...":* Thomas Flanagan, "Louis Riel and the Dispersion of the American Métis", *Minnesota History*, vol. 49, 1984–85.

p. 300   *Early in the fall...:* Davidson, p. 127.

p. 301   *"Her faith so deep...":* CW 4-100.

p. 301   *"All the boys in the world...":* CW 4-103.

p. 302   *"Sévère Hamlin, you had better...":* CW 4-105.

CHAPTER 14

p. 303   *"Every known crime...":* CW 4-110.

p. 303   *Winnipeg was booming...:* Thomas Flanagan, "Louis Riel's Land Claims", *Manitoba History*, Vol. 21, Spring 1991, p. 7.

p. 304   *"To me all canteens...":* CW 4-110.

p. 304   *Riel had liked the trader...:* CW 2-087, 2-094.

p. 305 *"a figure appeared in my room..."*: Alex C. Botkin, "The John Brown of the Half Breeds", *Rocky Mountain Magazine*, vol. 1, no. 1, Sept. 1900.

p. 307 *Sheriff John J. Healy...*: Fort Benton *River Press*, April 5, 1882, p. 6.

p. 308 *Yet even this peaceful...*: Evelina Barnabé to Louis Riel, Oct. 16, 1882, NAC, Department of Justice, misc., Riel papers.

p. 308 *"I deeply regret..."*: Henriette Riel to Evelina Barnabé, May or June 1882, PAM, Riel papers.

p. 309 *In it he explained...*: CW 2-101.

p. 309 *"He has finished his days..."*: CW 4-117.

p. 309 *"I went straight to him..."*: CW 3-173.

p. 310 *Henry Macdonald was a ...*: Eleanor Banks, *Wandersong* (Caldwell, Idaho: Catson Printers, 1950), pp. 253–54.

p. 311 *"We have to ourselves..."*: CW 2-132.

p. 312 *"Last fall, I had..."*: CW 4-12.

p. 313 *The land, wrote Louis...*: CW 2-103.

p. 314 *"He wore a black slouched hat...*: *Winnipeg Daily Sun*, June 28, 1883.

p. 314 *"His appearance was something..."*: *Winnipeg Daily Times*, June 29, 1883.

p. 314 *"We exchanged several..."*: CW 2-151, p. 356.

p. 317 *"With unstinting love..."*: CW 4-114.

p. 319 *Between October 25...*: CW 2-121.

p. 319 *"For a long time..."*: Sara Riel to Riel, Jan. 9, 1883, PAM, Riel papers.

p. 320 *"With God's help..."*: CW 2-126.

p. 321 *"I was not successful..."*: CW 2-133.

p. 321 *"Many heartfelt thanks..."*: Mrs. M.C. Murphy to Riel, PAM, Riel papers, March 3, 1884.

p. 321 *"I have not been well..."*: CW 2-150.

p. 323 *"At my table..."*: CW 2-151, p. 354.

p. 323 *"Leader of the Manitobans!..."*: CW 2-151, p. 355.

p. 323 *"I am not enjoying..."*: CW 2-137.

p. 324 *"You are a man..."*: Gabriel Dumont, *Gabriel Dumont Speaks*, trans. by Michael Barnholder (Vancouver: Talonbooks, 1993), p. 43.

p. 324 *"Gentlemen, your personal..."*: CW 3-002.

p. 324 *"The Canadian Government..."*: CW 3-004.

CHAPTER 15

p. 327 *"Lovable Spirit..."*: CW 4-128

p. 327 *"He [Riel] is an American..."*: *Sun River Sun*, June 12, 1884.

p. 328   *"The holy priest..."*: CW 3-140, p. 143.

p. 328   *Lawrence Clarke, chief factor of Fort Carlton...*: Clarke to Grahame, May 20, 1884, NAC, Macdonald papers, incoming correspondence, pp. 42244–42250.

p. 329   *But the most celebrated member...*: materials on Gabriel Dumont include: George Woodcock, *Gabriel Dumont* (Edmonton: Hurtig Publishers, 1975); John Andrew Kerr, "Gabriel Dumont: A Personal Memory, *The Dalhousie Review*, vol. 15, 1935–36, pp. 53–59; Sandra Lynn Mckee, ed., *Canadian Plainsmen: Gabriel Dumont, Jerry Potts*, (Surrey, B.C.: Frontier Books) 1982; Victor Carl Friesen, "Gabriel's Ferry", *The Western Producer*, May 9, 1985, p. 8.

p. 331   *She was born in 1830...*: "A Pictorial History of the Métis and Non-Status Indians in Saskatchewan." SAB R-E 1710, p. 18.

p. 333   *In the summer of 1871...*: Materials used in the account of the St. Laurent Settlement and its government include: Woodcock, pp. 95–100; Diane Payment, *Structural and Settlement History of Batoche Village*, Parks Canada, manuscript report no. 248; Anick, *The Metis of the South Saskatchewan*. Parks Canada, National Historic Parks and Sites Branch, manuscript report no. 364, 1976.

p. 335   *Lawrence Clarke, the only justice...*: Woodcock, pp. 106, 109.

p. 336   *François-Xavier Letendre's background...*: A. Anick, pp. 296–98; "A Pictorial History of the Métis and Non-Status Indians in Saskatchewan", p. 24; Diane Payment, "Monsieur Batoche", *Saskatchewan History*, vol. 32, no. 3, pp. 81–100.

p. 337   *"Each family has a comfortable..."*: quoted in Diane Payment, *Structural and Settlement History of Batoche Village*, Parks Canada, National Historic Parks and Sites Branch, manuscript report no. 248, 1977, p. 676.

p. 338   *they "procrastinated with a fatuity..."*: Z.M. Hamilton to F.J. Collyer, August 9, 1944, p. 48, SAB, SHS 179.

p. 338   *In 1878, petitions from St. Laurent...*: Materials used in the account of the Métis land issue include: Joseph Kinsey Howard, *Strange Empire: The Story of Louis Riel* (New York: Houghton Mifflin Co., 1952), pp. 315–18; Bob Beal and Rod Macleod, *Prairie Fire: The 1885 North-West Rebellion* (Edmonton: Hurtig Publishers, 1984), pp. 44–48; A. Anick, pp. 311–42; D.N. Sprague, *Canada and the Métis, 1869–1885* (Waterloo: Wilfrid Laurier Press, 1988), pp. 141–55.

p. 341   *"We were received by Mr...."*: NAC, Dewdney papers, vol. 6, pp. 2230–32.

p. 342   *"I thank you for the delicate..."*: ibid.

p. 342   *"I salute you all with the cheers..."*: CW 3-006.

p. 343   *Speculators, Charlie Mair and...*: Maggie Siggins, *Revenge of the Land: A Century of Greed, Tragedy and Murder on a Saskatchewan Farm* (Toronto: McClelland & Stewart, 1992), p. 264.

p. 344   *"Opinion is so pronounced..."*: André to Riel, n.d., NAC, Dewdney papers, vol. 6, p. 2226.

p. 344   *"There were many men..."*: Prince Albert *Times*, July 25, 1884.

p. 345   *"Since my last letter..."*: CSP, 1886, #52c, printed in *Epitome of Parliamentary Documents in Connection with the North-West Rebellion, 1885.*

CHAPTER 16

p. 346   *"Never go without a hat..."*: CW 3-194, p. 371.

p. 346   *William Henry Jackson was a small...:* Cyril Greenland and John D. Griffin, "William Henry Jackson (1861–1952): Riel's Secretary", *Canadian Psychiatric Association Journal*, vol. 23, 1978, pp. 469–78; Donald B. Smith, "Honoré Joseph Jaxon: A Man Who Lived for Others", *Saskatchewan History*, vol. 34, no. 3, 1981, pp. 181–91, and also "William Henry Jackson: Riel's Secretary", *The Beaver*, spring 1981, pp. 10–19.

p. 347   *Farmers in the West...:* Bob Beal and Rod Macleod, *Prairie Fire: The 1885 North-West Rebellion* (Edmonton: Hurtig Publishers, 1984), pp. 33–36; Howard Adams, *Prison of Grass: Canada from a Native Point of View* (Saskatoon: Fifth House Publishers, 1989), pp. 75–76.

p. 348   *"a cutthroat, an outlaw..."*: quoted in Smith, "William Henry Jackson".

p. 348   *The day after Riel's arrival...:* Louis Schmidt, "Notes: Mouvement des Métis à St-Laurent, Sask., 1884", AAStB.

p. 349   *"I am in good health..."*: Jackson to Riel, July 23, 1884, NAC, Macdonald papers, vol. 105.

p. 349   *While the Métis...:* materials used in the account of the plight of Indians include: George F.G. Stanley, *Louis Riel* (Toronto: Ryerson Press, 1963), p. 282; Beal and Macleod, pp. 78–80, 85–91; Desmond Morton, *The Last War Drum, The North West Campaign of 1885* (Toronto: Hakkert, 1972), pp. 16–17; R.S. Allen, "Big Bear", *Saskatchewan History*, vol. 25, no. 1, Winter 1972, pp. 1–17; Walter Hildebrandt, "Battleford 1885...: The Siege Mentality", *NeWest Review*, May 1985, p. 21.

p. 349   *The bodies of the dead...: Manitoba Free Press*, May 17, 1884.

p. 351   *"Not long ago I was..."*: CW 3-009.

p. 351   *There was strong suspicion....:* Don McLean, "The Metis Struggle for Independence in the West", *New Breed*, July–August 1985, pp. 31–32.

p. 352   *"He always reminded me..."*: quoted in George Woodcock, *Gabriel Dumont* (Edmonton: Hurtig Publishers, 1975), p.78

p. 352   *"My own impression is this..."*: Rouleau to Dewdney, Sept. 5, 1884, Glenbow, Dewdney papers, pp. 1402–5.

p. 353   *James Isbister touched a...:* Isbister to Riel, Sept. 4, 1884, PAM, Riel papers.

p. 354   *"I'm glad your business..."*: Quoted in Woodcock, p.151.

p. 355   *Basically it was an ingenious method...:* Beal and Macleod, p. 123.

p. 355   *"The agitation is not, at present..."*: Forget to Dewdney, Sept. 18, 1884, NAC, Macdonald papers, vol. 107.

p. 356   *"Be careful. Do not argue..."*: CW 3-018.

p. 357   *"My God! Be kind to Marguerite..."*: CW 3-109, p. 355.

p. 357   *"Oh my God! I beseech You..."*: CW 3-109, p. 368.

p. 357   *"You eat a third..."*: CW 3-109, pp. 371–72.

p. 358   *September 24 was set as the day...*: Stanley, p. 290.

p. 359   *As Father Fourmond himself put it...*: Fourmond to the Superior-General, Dec. 27, 1884, Missions des Oblats de Marie Immaculée, XXIII.

p. 360   *In December, the Oblate missionaries...*: Fr. Fourmond, *La Petite Chronique de St. Laurent*, 1885, Missions des Oblats de Marie Immaculée, North West Rebellion file, 71.220.

p. 360   *When Louis had been first...*: sources for the land bribery issue in include: Stanley, pp. 294–96, Beal and Macleod, pp. 125–26; Auguste Henri de Tremaudan, *Hold High Your Heads: The History of the Metis Nation in Western Canada* (Winnipeg: Pemmican, 1982), p. 147n; Donald Creighton, *John A. Macdonald: The Old Chieftain* (Toronto: Macmillan, 1955), pp. 413–14.

p. 361   *"He [Riel] proceeded to state..."*: Macdowall to Dewdney, Dec. 24, 1884, NAC, Dewdney papers, vol. 4, pp. 1329–34.

p. 362   *"I know that if Riel..."*: André to Dewdney, Jan. 21, 1885, NAC, Dewdney papers, vol. 1, pp. 28–30.

CHAPTER 17

p. 363   *"Give me that gift..."*: CW 4-128.

p. 363   *"We do not want to let..."*: presentation to Riel, Jan. 1, 1885, PAM, Riel papers.

p. 364   *"If your brother finds..."*: CW 3-020.

p. 364   *"Perhaps he romantically saw..."*: Donald B. Smith, "William Henry Jackson: Riel's Secretary", *The Beaver*, Spring 1981, p. 16.

p. 365   *"Sacred Heart of Jesus..."*: CW 3-028.

p. 366   *Then, according to Schmidt...*: AAStB, Schmidt Notes.

p. 366   *"I am aware that his [Riel's]..."*: André to Dewdney, Feb. 8, 1885, NAC, Macdonald papers, vol. 107.

p. 367   *We, the undersigned, pledge...*: CW 3-194, pp. 381–82.

p. 368   *Finally in February the Prince Albert...*: D.N. Sprague, *Canada and the Métis, 1869–1885*, (Waterloo: Sir Wilfrid Laurier Press, 1988) pp. 171–72.

p. 368   *"Nolin and Riel then moved..."*: Toronto *Mail*, April 13, 1885.

p. 370   *"You have turned the pulpit..."*: Fr. Vital Fourmond, *La Petite Chronique de St. Laurent*, 1885, PAA, Oblate papers: files re Rebellion (71.220).

p. 370   *"Lord our God, through Jesus..."*: CW 3-194, p. 382.

p. 371   *"a great deal of excitement..."*: Crozier to Irvine, March 11, 1885, NAC, Macdonald papers, vol. 105.

p. 371   *"If the half-breeds mean business..."*: Dewdney to Macdonald, March 11, 1885, NAC, Macdonald papers, vol. 107.

p. 371   *"Halfbreed rebellion likely..."*: Crozier to Dewdney, March 15, 1885, NAC, Macdonald papers, vol. 105.

p. 371 *On March 17, Michel Dumas...*: George F.G. Stanley, *Louis Riel* (Toronto: Ryerson Press, 1963), p. 305; George Woodcock, *Gabriel Dumont* (Edmonton: Hurtig Publishers, 1975), p. 164.

p. 372 *What nobody knew at the time...*: Sprague, p. 172.

p. 372 *"Can you imagine my feelings..."*: Willoughby's testimony in Desmond Morton, *The Queen v Louis Riel* (Toronto: University of Toronto Press, 1974), pp. 75–83.

p. 373 *"I told them," remembered George Kerr...*: Kerr's testimony in Morton, *The Queen v Louis Riel*, p. 153.

p. 374 *"I told the crowd..."*: Gabriel Dumont, *Gabriel Dumont Speaks*, trans. by Michael Barnholder (Vancouver: Talonbooks, 1993), pp. 46–47.

p. 374 *"Well, Mr. Walters, it has commenced..."*: Walters's testimony in Morton, *The Queen v Louis Riel*, p. 159.

p. 375 *"I am confident..."*: Will Jackson to his family, Sept. 19, 1885, USL.

p. 377 *Nolin and William Boyer joined...*: Stanley, p. 308; Philippe Garnot, PAA, Mémoire, Oblate papers (71.220).

p. 380 *"You will be required..."*: CW 3-032.

CHAPTER 18

p. 381 *"I have seen the giant..."*: CW 3-195, p. 396.

p. 381 *"We have taken up arms..."*: Gabriel Dumont, *Gabriel Dumont Speaks*, trans. by Michael Barnholder (Vancouver: Talonbooks, 1993), p. 51.

p. 382 *"Stop!" Dumont commanded...*: ibid; p. 52.

p. 382 *There was a lot of...*: ibid; p. 53.

p. 382 *"The Spirit of God informed..."*: Thomas Flanagan, ed., *The Diaries of Louis Riel* (Edmonton: Hurtig Publishers, 1976), p. 57.

p. 383 *By the time the police...*: sources for the account of the Battle of Duck Lake include: George F.G. Stanley, *Louis Riel* (Toronto: Ryerson Press, 1963), pp. 315–17; Joseph Kinsey Howard, *Strange Empire: The Story of Louis Riel* (New York: Houghton Mifflin Co., 1952), pp. 329–39; Bob Beal and Rod Macleod, *Prairie Fire: The 1885 North-West Rebellion* (Edmonton: Hurtig Publishers, 1984), pp. 151–59; Dumont, pp. 56–58; Charles W. Jefferys, "Fifty Years Ago", *Canadian Geographical Journal*, vol. 10–11, 1935, pp. 258–69.

p. 384 *He sent along an old...*: Blair Stonechild, *Saskatchewan Indians and the Resistance of 1885: Two Case Studies* (Regina: Saskatchewan Education, 1986), pp. 23–27.

p. 385 *"He was in the small..."*: Dumont, p. 56.

p. 385 *"When I passed my..."*: ibid., p. 58.

p. 386 *"A Calamity had fallen upon..."*: CW 3-046.

p. 388 *"O my God! Help me..."*: Flanagan, *The Diaries of Louis Riel*, p. 58.

p. 388 *"My ideas are right..."*: ibid., p. 60.

p. 388   *"I became aware," he wrote...*: W.H. Jackson to "My Dear Family", Sept. 19, 1885, USL.

p. 392   *"Priests are not religion..."*: CW 3-195, p. 406.

p. 392   *According to historian D.N. Sprague...*: D.N. Sprague, *Canada and the Métis, 1869–1885* (Waterloo: Sir Wilfrid Laurier Press, 1988), p. 175.

p. 394   *"I yielded to Riel's judgement although..."*: George F.G. Stanley, "Gabriel Dumont's Account of the North West Rebellion 1885", *Canadian Historical Review*, Sept. 1949, p. 256.

p. 395   *"I have seen the giant..."*: CW 3-195, p. 396.

p. 396   *"I told Riel that I..."*: Stanley, "Gabriel Dumont's Account of the North West Rebellion 1885", p. 258.

p. 396   *The place where Gabriel Dumont...*: Sources used for the account of the Battle of Fish Creek include: George Woodcock, *Gabriel Dumont* (Edmonton: Hurtig Publishers, 1975), pp. 196–205; Beal and Macleod, pp. 229–34; C.P. Stacey, "The North-West Campaign 1885", *Canadian Army Journal*, vol. 7, no. 3, July 1954, pp. 10–20; Carman Miller, "Lord Melgund and the North-West Campaign of 1885", *Saskatchewan History*, no. 3, autumn 1969, pp. 80–108; Jefferys, pp. 258–69; Daniel M. Gordon, "Reminiscences of the N.W. Rebellion Campaign of 1885", *Queen's Quarterly*, vol. XI, July 1903, pp. 3–20; R. H. Roy, "With the Midland Battalion to Batoche", *Saskatchewan History*, vol. XXXII, spring 1979, pp. 41–60.

p. 396   *"My plan had been to surprise..."*: Dumont, p. 61.

p. 398   *"When we got down to our last seven..."*: ibid., pp. 63–64.

p. 398   *"the troops behaved well..."*: *Report of the Rebellion in the North-West Territories, 1885*, CSP, no. 6a, p.1.

p. 398   *"Oh my Métis nation..."*: Flanagan, *The Diaries of Louis Riel*, p. 73.

p. 401   *"Priests have been ordained..."*: CW 3-195, p. 195.

p. 401   *"I used to live wretchedly...*: Flanagan, *The Diaries of Louis Riel*, p. 78.

p. 401   *"I see the redcoats very close..."*: ibid., p. 84.

p. 402   *Middleton planned a two-pronged...*: Sources used in the account of the Battle of Batoche include: Desmond Morton, *The Last War Drum: The North West Campaign of 1885* (Toronto: Hakkert, 1972), pp. 69–94; Beal and Macleod, pp. 256–75; Dumont, pp. 8–79; Stanley, *Louis Riel*, pp. 335–38; Walter Hildebrandt, "The Battle of Batoche", *Prairie Forum*, vol. 10, no. 1, 1985, pp. 17–63; Stacey, pp. 10–20; Iris Allan, ed., "A Riel Rebellion Dairy", *Alberta Historical Review*, summer 1964, pp. 15–25; Jefferys, pp. 258–69; Roy, pp. 41–59.

p. 404   *"The Spirit of God..."*: Flanagan, *The Diaries of Louis Riel*, p. 87.

p. 404   *Each night the police...*: Dumont, p. 70.

p. 404   *"We thought it was understood..."*: ibid.

p. 406   *"If you massacre..."*: CW 3-053.

p. 406   *"What kept me there...*: Stanley, "Gabriel Dumont's Account of the North West Rebellion 1885".

p. 407   *"What are we going..."*: ibid.

p. 408   *"What a distressing picture..."*: Toronto *Mail*, June 19, 1885.

p. 408   *"I saw a policeman..."*: Stanley, "Gabriel Dumont's Account of the North West Rebellion 1885".

p. 409   *"I'm the one..."*: quoted in Auguste Henri de Tremaudan, *Hold High Your Heads: The History of the Metis Nation in Western Canada* (Winnipeg: Pemmican, 1982), p. 141.

CHAPTER 19

p. 410   *"And when His evidence..."*: CW 4-135.

p. 410   *"He told me Rome..."*: Middleton's testimony in Desmond Morton, *The Queen v Louis Riel* (Toronto: University of Toronto Press, 1974), p. 186.

p. 410   *"He [Riel] was a man..."*: ibid., p. 277.

p. 410   *"the prisoner was lying down..."*: *Brantford Courier*, Jan. 28, 1904.

p. 411   *"I found that I had..."*: Young's testimony in Morton, *The Queen v Louis Riel*, p. 275.

p. 412   *"1. We believe that..."*: CW A3-011.

p. 413   *"Your heart, Captain Dean..."*: CW 4-133.

p. 414   *"Margaret! I told..."*: ibid.

p. 414   *Riel wrote a long...*: CW 3-065.

p. 416   *"He [Stewart] intended..."*: Winnipeg *Sun*, June 29, 1885.

p. 416   *"almost overcome when they..."*: Ronald L. Olesky, "Riel: Patriot or Traitor?" *Canadian Lawyer*, April 1991, pp. 20–25.

p. 416   *"We visited Riel today..."*: Lemieux, Fitzpatrick, Greenshields to Taché, July 15, 1885, AAStB, also Dugast to Taché, July 17, 1885, AAStB.

p. 418   *In 1880, for example...*: CSP, no. 116, p. 80.

p. 418   *In March 1885, the judge...*: D.N. Sprague, *Canada and the Métis, 1869–85* (Waterloo: Sir Wilfrid Laurier Press, 1988), p. 172.

p. 420   *"Willie has received such..."*: quoted in Cyril Greenland and John D. Griffin, "William Henry Jackson (1861–1952): Riel's Secretary", *Canadian Psychiatric Association Journal*, vol. 23, 1978, pp. 469–78.

p. 421   *"Now that I am imprisoned..."*: CW 3-077.

p. 422   *"A good-looking man, fair..."*: Murray G. Brooks to Michael Kennedy, Feb. 1, 1954, Historical Society of Montana.

p. 423   *"The prophet of the Saskatchewan..."*: Morton, *The Queen v Louis Riel*, p. 74.

p. 423   *"He disclosed his personal motives..."*: ibid., p. 174.

p. 424   *"Q. Of course the plan..."*: ibid., p. 83.

p. 424   *"He [Riel] said before the grass is high..."*: ibid., p.195.

p. 424   *"If there was any way..."*: ibid., p. 205.

p. 425   *"My counsel come from Quebec..."*: ibid., p. 207

p. 425   *"It was enough..."*: quoted in Olesky, p. 24.

p. 426   *"On the question of religion..."*: Morton, *The Queen v Louis Riel*, p. 233.

p. 426   *"Before the rebellion..."*: ibid., p. 240.

p. 427   *"They [the ill] sometimes..."*: ibid., p. 245.

p. 428   *"It is right for me..."*: ibid., p. 287.

p. 429   *"O, my God..."*: CW A3-012, p. 523.

p. 429   *"When I came into the North-West..."*: ibid., p. 524.

p. 429   *"when I saw the..."*: ibid., p. 529.

p. 430   *"My insanity, your Honours..."*: ibid., p. 531.

p. 430   *"For fifteen years I have been..."*: ibid., p. 536.

p. 430   *"Well, gentlemen," Robinson said...*: Morton, *The Queen v Louis Riel*, p. 339.

p. 431   *"Not only must..."*: ibid., p. 349.

p. 431   *"Riel should have been..."*: quoted in *The Globe and Mail*, July 22, 1955.

p. 432   *"On the subject of whether..."*: Murray G. Brooks to Michael Kennedy, Feb. 1, 1954, Historical Society of Montana.

p. 432   *"Should I be executed..."*: CW A3-013, p. 540.

p. 433   *"When they have crowded..."*: ibid., p. 547.

CHAPTER 20

p. 434   *"Death will come as a thief..."*: CW 4-050.

p. 434   *"Please write and compose..."*: CW 3-084.

p. 434   *"Fourmond was more concerned..."*: Thomas Flanagan, *Riel: Prophet of the New World* (Toronto: University of Toronto Press, 1979), p.163.

p. 435   *"was the most tragic..."*: Joseph Kinsey Howard, *Strange Empire: The Story of Louis Riel* (New York: Houghton Mifflin Co., 1952), p. 458.

p. 435   *"I saw Riel this morning..."*: Cochin to Taché, August 14, 1885, AAStB.

p. 435   *"Everything I will write in this..."*: Thomas Flanagan, *The Diaries of Louis Riel* (Edmonton: Hurtig Publishers, 1976), p. 94.

p. 435   *"The Lord wants the pagan..."*: ibid., p. 164.

p. 436   *"If the sentence is..."*: *Le Courrier de St-Hyacinthe*, Aug. 15, 1885, as quoted in A.I. Silver, "The French-Canadian Press and 1885", *Native Studies Review*, 1984, vol. 1, pp. 2–15.

p. 436   *"Don't even ask me..."*: Arthur Dansereau to J.A. Chapleau, Aug. 5, 1885, NAC, Chapleau papers, correspondence, as quoted in Silver.

p. 436   *"There is an attempt in..."*: Macdonald to Dewdney, Aug. 17, 1885, NAC, Macdonald Letter Book 23.

p. 437   *"To His Excellency..."*: CW 3-095.

p. 437   *"Death has gained a day..."*: Flanagan, *The Diaries of Louis Riel*, p. 130.

p. 437   *"My little girl..."*: CW 3-101.

p. 438   *"Margaret: be fair and good..."*: CW 4-145.

p. 439   *"He appeared to me on earth..."*: Flanagan, *The Diaries of Louis Riel*, p. 159.

p. 439   *"God made me see..."*: ibid., p. 144.

p. 439   *"My brother Charles..."*: ibid., p. 150.

p. 440   *If Riel was not hanged...*: J.C. Gilroy to Macdonald, Oct. 29, 1885, NAC, Macdonald papers, vol. 108.

p. 440   *"This is Sunday..."*: CW 4-146.

p. 441   *"you are convinced..."*: Macdonald to Lavell, Oct. 31, 1885, QUL, Lavell correspondence.

p. 441   *"For my own part..."*: Glenbow, Riel papers, Jukes report, Nov. 15, 1885.

p. 442   *as the historians...*: Bob Beal and Rod Macleod, *Prairie Fire: The 1885 North-West Rebellion* (Edmonton: Hurtig Publishers, 1984), p. 335.

p. 442   *"After having examined carefully..."*: ibid., p. 337.

p. 443   *"May you be blessed..."*: CW 3-140.

p. 444   *"Dearly Beloved Marguerite..."*: CW 3-142.

BIBLIOGRAPHY

BOOKS, MANUSCRIPTS

Adams, Howard. *Prison of Grass: Canada from a Native Point of View.* Saskatoon: Fifth House Publishers, 1989.

American Frontier Life: Early Western Painting and Prints. New York: Portland House, 1987.

Anick, N. *The Metis of the South Saskatchewan,* two vols. Parks Canada, National Historic Parks and Sites Branch, manuscript report no. 364, 1976.

Association of Métis and Non-status Indians of Saskatchewan. *Louis Riel: Justice Must Be Done.* Winnipeg: Manitoba Métis Federation Press, 1979.

Banks, Eleanor. *Wandersong.* Caldwell, Idaho: Catson Printers, 1950.

Beal, Bob, and Rod Macleod. *Prairie Fire: The 1885 North-West Rebellion.* Edmonton: Hurtig Publishers, 1984.

Begg, Alexander. *Alexander Begg's Red River Journal & Other Papers Relative to the Red River Resistance of 1869–70.* Toronto: The Champlain Society, 1956.

Boulton, Charles. *Reminiscences of the North-West Rebellions.* Toronto: Grip Printing and Publishing, 1886.

Brown, Jennifer. *Strangers in Blood.* Vancouver: University of British Columbia Press, 1980.

Bryant, W.F., *The Blood of Abel.* Hastings, Nebraska: published by the *Gazette Journal,* 1887.

Campbell, Marjorie Wilkins. *The North West Company.* Toronto: Macmillan, 1957.

Charette, Guillaume. *Vanishing Spaces: Memoirs of Louis Goulet,* trans. by Ray Ellenwood. Winnipeg: Editions Bois Brûlés, 1980.

Chartier, Armand. *Histoire des Franco-Américains de la Nouvelle-Angleterre, 1775–1990.* Sillery, Quebec: Septentrion, 1991.

Collard, Edgar. *Canadian Yesterdays.* Toronto: Longmans, Green, 1955.

Creighton, Donald. *John A. Macdonald: The Young Politician.* Toronto: Macmillan, 1965.

————. *John A. Macdonald: The Old Chieftain*. Toronto: Macmillan, 1955.

Davidson, William McCartney. *Louis Riel, 1884-1885: A Biography*. Calgary: Alberta Publishing Co., 1955.

Davis, Ann. *The Logic of Ecstasy: Canadian Mystical Painting, 1920–1940*. Toronto: University of Toronto Press, 1992.

Dugas, Georges. *The First Canadian Woman in the Northwest*. Winnipeg: Manitoba Free Press, 1902.

Dumont, Gabriel. *Gabriel Dumont Speaks*, trans. by Michael Barnholden. Vancouver: Talonbooks, 1993.

Flanagan, Thomas, ed. *The Diaries of Louis Riel*. Edmonton: Hurtig Publishers, 1976.

————. *Metis Lands in Manitoba*. Calgary: University of Calgary Press, 1991.

————. *Riel and the Rebellion: 1885 Reconsidered*. Saskatoon: Western Producer Prairie Books, 1983.

————. *Riel: Prophet of the New World*. Toronto: University of Toronto Press, 1979.

Foster, John E. "The Plains Metis", in *Native Peoples: The Canadian Experience*, R.B. Morrison and C.R. Wilson, eds. Toronto: McClelland & Stewart, 1986.

Fourmond, Fr. Vital. *La Petite Chronique de St. Laurent*. 1885, PAA, Oblate papers: file re rebellion (71.220).

Frazier, Ian. *Great Plains*. New York: Farrar, Straus Giroux, 1989.

Frémont, Donatien. *The Secretaries of Riel*. Prince Albert: Les Editions Louis Riel for La Société canadienne-française, 1985.

Friesen, Gerald. *The Canadian Prairie: A History*. Toronto: University of Toronto Press, 1987.

Giraud, Marcel. *Le Métis canadien: son role dans l'histoire des provinces de l'Ouest*. Paris: Institut d' Ethnologie, 1945. Trans. by George Woodcock as *The Metis in the Canadian West*, 2 vols. Edmonton: University of Alberta Press, 1986.

Gosman, Robert. *Riel House, St. Vital, Manitoba*. Parks Canada, National Historic Parks and Sites Branch, manuscript report no. 171, 1975.

————. *The Riel and Lagimodière Families in Metis Society 1840–1860*. Parks Canada, National Historic Parks and Sites Branch, manuscript report no. 171, 1977.

Goulet, Agnes. *Marie-Anne Gaboury: Une femme dépareillée*. Saint Boniface: Editions des Plaines, n.d.

Gray, John Morgan. *Lord Selkirk of Red River*. Toronto: Macmillan, 1963.

Healy, W.J. *Women of Red River*. Winnipeg: The Women's Canadian Club, 1923.

Heller, Joseph. *God Knows*. New York: Alfred A. Knopf, 1984.

Howard, Joseph Kinsey. *Strange Empire: The Story of Louis Riel*. New York: Houghton Mifflin Co., 1952.

Hurd, Henry M., ed. *The Institutional Care of the Insane in the United States and Canada*, vol. 4. New York: Arno Press, 1973.

Jordan, Mary V. *To Louis from your sister who loves you Sara Riel.* Toronto: Griffin House, 1974.

Maclean, John. *Canadian Savage Folk: The Native Tribes of Canada.* Toronto: Briggs, 1986.

MacLeod, Margaret Arnett, and W.L. Morton. *Cuthbert Grant of Grantown: Warden of the Plains of Red River.* Toronto: McClelland & Stewart, 1963.

Malone, Michael P., Richard B. Roeder and William L. Lang. *Montana: A History of Two Centuries.* Seattle: University of Washington Press, 1976.

Martel, Gilles. *Le messianisme de Louis Riel.* Waterloo: Wilfrid Laurier University Press, 1984.

McKee, Sandra Lynn, ed. *Canadian Plainsmen: Gabriel Dumont, Jerry Potts.* Surrey, B.C.: Frontier Books, 1982.

Morton, Desmond. *The Last War Drum: The North West Campaign of 1885.* Toronto: Hakkert, 1972.

————. *The Queen v Louis Riel.* Toronto: University of Toronto Press, 1974.

Morton, W.L. *Manitoba: A History.* Toronto: University of Toronto Press, 1957.

————. *Manitoba: The Birth of a Province.* Winnipeg: Manitoba Record Society Publications, 1965

————. *The Critical Years: The Union of British North America 1857–1873.* Toronto: McClelland & Stewart, 1964.

Newman, Peter C. *Merchant Princes.* Toronto: Penguin, 1991.

O'Donnell, John H. *Manitoba As I Saw It.* Winnipeg: Clark Bros., 1909.

Osler, E.B. *The Man Who Had to Hang: Louis Riel.* Toronto: Longmans Green & Co., 1961.

Pannekoek, Frits. *A Snug Little Flock: The Social Origins of the Riel Resistance 1869–70* Winnipeg: Watson & Dwyer Publishing, 1991.

Payment, Diane Paulette. *Structural and Settlement History of Batoche Village.* Parks Canada, National Historic Parks and Sites Branch, manuscript report no. 248, 1977.

————. *Riel Family: Home and Lifestyle at St-Vital, 1860–1910.* Parks Canada, Historical Research Division, Prairie Region, May 1980.

————. *The Free people—Otispemisiwak", Batoche, Saskatchewan, 1870-1930.* Environment Canada, Parks Service, 1990.

Pelletier, Emile. *A Social History of the Manitoba Métis.* Winnipeg: Manitoba Métis Federation Press, 1977.

Peterson, Jacqueline, and Jennifer S.H. Brown. *The New Peoples: Being and Becoming Métis in North America.* Winnipeg: University of Manitoba Press, 1985.

Purich, Donald. *The Metis.* Toronto: James Lorimer, 1988.

Riel, Louis. *The Collected Writings of Louis Riel/Les Ecrits Complets de Louis Riel,* George F.G. Stanley. Edmonton: University of Alberta Press, 1985.

————. *Selected Poetry of Louis Riel,* trans. by Paul Savoie, ed. by Glen Campbell. Toronto: Exile Editions, 1993.

Ross, Alexander. *The Red River Settlement: Its Rise, Progress and Present State.* Minneapolis: Ross & Haines, 1957.

Ruest, Agnes M. *A Pictorial History of the Métis and Non-Status Indians*. Prince Albert: Saskatchewan Human Rights Commission; Association of Métis and Non-Status Indians of Saskatchewan, 1976.

Rumilly, Robert. *Histoire des Franco-Américains*. Woonsocket, R.I.: l'Union Saint-Jean-Baptiste d'Amérique, 1958.

St. Louis Local History Committee. *I Remember—A History of St. Louis and Surrounding Areas*. Altona: Friesen Printers, 1980.

Shrive, Norman. *Charles Mair: Literary Nationalist*. Toronto: University of Toronto Press, 1965.

Siggins, Maggie. *Revenge of the Land: A Century of Greed, Tragedy and Murder on a Saskatchewan Farm*. Toronto: McClelland & Stewart, 1992.

Sissons, Constance Kerr. *John Kerr*. Toronto: Oxford University Press, 1946.

Sprague, D.N. *Canada and the Métis, 1869–1885*. Waterloo: Sir Wilfrid Laurier Press, 1988.

Stanley, George F.G. *The Birth of Western Canada: A History of the Riel Rebellions*. London: Longmans, Green, 1936.

——————. *Louis Riel*. Toronto: Ryerson Press, 1963.

Stonechild, Blair. *Saskatchewan Indians and the Resistance of 1885: Two Case Studies*. Regina: Saskatchewan Education, 1986.

Strauss, Leo, and Joseph Cropsey, eds. *History of Political Philosophy*. Chicago: Rand McNally, 1963.

Sweeny, Alastair. *George-Étienne Cartier: A Biography*. Toronto: McClelland & Stewart, 1976.

Tremaudan, Auguste Henri de. *Hold High Your Heads: The History of the Metis Nation in Western Canada*. Winnipeg: Pemmican, 1982.

Trofimenkoff, Susan Mann. *The Dream of Nation: A Social and Intellectual History of Quebec*. Toronto: Macmillan, 1982.

Tupper, Sir Charles. *Recollections of Sixty Years in Canada*. Toronto: Cassell, 1914.

Turner, J.P. *The North-West Mounted Police 1873–1893*, vol. 1. Ottawa: King's Printer, 1950.

Van Kirk, Sylvia. *Many Tender Ties: Women in the Fur Trade Society 1860-1870*. Winnipeg: Watson & Dwyer, 1980.

Wade, Mason. *The French Canadians, 1760–1967*. Toronto: Macmillan, 1968.

Wolseley, Garnet Joseph, Viscount. *The Story of a Soldier's Life*, vol. 2. New York: Kraus, 1903, reprinted 1971.

Woodcock, George. *Gabriel Dumont*. Edmonton: Hurtig Publishers, 1975.

JOURNALS, MAGAZINES

Allan, Iris. "A Riel Rebellion Diary". *Alberta Historical Review*, summer 1964.

Allen, R.S. "Big Bear". *Saskatchewan History*, vol. 25, no. 1, winter 1972.

An officer of the Force. "Red River Expedition of 1870". *The Manitoban*, Dec. 1891–Oct. 1892.

Anderson, Frank W. "Louis Riel's Insanity Reconsidered". *Saskatchewan History*, vol. 3, no. 3, autumn 1950.

Arnold, Abraham. "If Louis Riel Had Spoken in Parliament, or, Louis Riel's Social Vision". *Prairie Fire*, vol. 6, no. 4, autumn/winter 1985.

Artibise, Alan. "The Crucial Decade: Red River at the Outbreak of the American Civil War". *Historical and Scientific Society of Manitoba*, Transaction Series III.

Austin, James M. "Some Experiences of the Expedition of the North West Field Force as Copied from a Diary Kept in My Possession". *Saskatchewan History*, vol. 38, no. 1, winter 1985.

Baptie, Sue. "Edgar Dewdney". *Alberta Historical Review*, autumn 1968.

Barbeau, Marius. "The House that Mac Built". *The Beaver*, Dec. 1945.

Barclay, Robert George. "Grey Nuns Voyage to Red River". *The Beaver*, winter 1966.

Barrhead, Allen Ronaghen. "Charles Mair and the North-West Emigration Aid Society". *Manitoba History*, nos. 13–16, 1987–88.

Bartlett, Fred E. "The ordeal of William Mactavish". *The Beaver*, autumn 1964.

Bell, Charles N. "A Day with the Buffalo Hunters". *Alberta History*, winter 1982.

Bell, J. Jones. "The Red River Expedition." *Canadian Magazine*, vol. 12, 1898–99.

Beyer, Peter. "La vision religieuse de Louis Riel: L'ultramontanisme canadien-français au service de la nation métisse". *Studies in Religion*, vol. 13, 1984.

Boisvert, David, and Keith Turnbull. "Who are the Métis?" *Studies in Political Economy*, vol. 18, 1985.

Bonin, Sister Marie. "The Grey Nuns and the Red River Settlement". *Manitoba History*, vol. 11, 1986.

Botkin, Alex C. "The John Brown of the Half Breeds." *Rocky Mountain Magazine*, vol. 1, no. 1, Sept. 1900.

Bourgeault, Ron. "Metis History". *New Breed*, Jan. 1985.

—————. "The Struggle Against British Colonialism and Imperialism". *New Breed*, Feb.–June 1985.

Brasser, T.J. "Métis Artisans". *The Beaver*, autumn 1975.

Brebner, J.B. "John Brown of the Half-breeds". *Nation*, vol. 175, 1952.

Brown, D.H. "The Meaning of Treason in 1885". *Saskatchewan History*, vol. 28, no 1, winter 1975.

Brown, Jennifer. "Changing Views of Fur Trade Marriage and Domesticity: James Hargrave, His Colleagues, and 'The Sex'". *Western Canadian Journal of Anthropology*, vol. 6, 1976.

—————. "'A Colony of Very Useful Hands'". *The Beaver*, spring 1977.

—————. "Ultimate Respectability: Fur-trade Children in the 'Civilized World' ". *The Beaver*, two-part series, winter 1977, spring 1978.

Bryce, George. "Worthies of Old Red River". *The Historical and Scientific Society of Manitoba*, no. 48, Feb. 1896.

Bumsted, J.M. "Flood Warnings". *The Beaver*, April–May 1986.

—————. "The 'Mahdi' of Western Canada? Louis Riel and His Papers". *The Beaver*, Aug.–Sept., 1987.

Burt, Larry W. "In a Crooked Piece of Time: The Dilemma of the Montana Cree and the Metis". *Journal of American Culture*, vol. 9, no. 1, 1986.

Campbell, Glen. "The Political Poetry of Louis Riel: A Semiotic Study". *Canadian Poetry*, vol. 3, 1978.

—————. "Teaching the Fables of Louis Riel". *Alberta Modern Language Journal*, vol. 20, 1982.

—————. "Les Chansons de Louis Riel". *La Revue Littéraire de l'Albert*, vol. 1, no. 2, 1983.

—————. "Poetry: Riel's Emotional Catharsis". *Humanities Association of Canada Newsletter*, vol. XIII, no. 2, spring 1985.

Carter, Sarah. "The Woman's Sphere: Domestic Life at Riel House and Dalnavert". *Manitoba History*, vol. 11, 1986.

Champagne, Antoine. "La Famille de Louis Riel: Notes généalogiques et historiques". *Mémoires de la Société Généalogique canadienne-française*, vol. XX, no. 3, 1969.

Cherwinski, W.J.C. "'Honoré Joseph Jaxon, Agitator, Disturber, producer of plans to make men think, and Chronic Objector...'". *Canadian Historical Review*, vol. 46, 1965.

Clark, Daniel. "A Psycho-Medical History of Louis Riel". *The American Journal of Insanity*, vol. XLIV, 1887–1888.

Claude, Jean-Paul. "The American Metis". *The New Breed*, vol. 15, no. 7, July 1984.

Clubb, Sally. "Red River Exodus". *Arbos*, Jan.–Feb. 1965.

Cooke, Britton B. "Riel before the Jury". *Canadian Magazine*, vol. 44, 1914–15.

Cooper, Barry. "Alexander Kennedy Isbister, A Respectable Victorian". *Canadian Ethnic Studies*, vol. 17, no. 2, 1985.

Deane, R.B. "Augustus L. Jukes: A Pioneer Surgeon". *Calgary Associate Clinic Historical Bulletin*, vol. 2, no. 4, Feb. 1938.

Desjardins, Edouard, et Charles Dumas. "Le complexe médical de Louis Riel". *L'Union Médicale du Canada*, Sept. 1970.

Dorge, Lionel. "Bishop Tache and the Confederation of Manitoba". *Historical and Scientific Society of Manitoba Transactions*, series 3, no. 26, 1969–70.

—————. "The Métis and Canadien Councillors of Assiniboia". *The Beaver*, three parts, summer, autumn, winter 1974.

Douglas, William. "'The Forks' Becomes a City". *Historical and Scientific Society of Manitoba*, 1944–45.

—————. "New Light on the Old Forts of Winnipeg". *Historical Society of Manitoba*, series 3, no. 2, 1955.

Dusenberry, Verne. "Waiting for a Day That Never Comes". *Montana, the Magazine of Western History*, April 1958.

Ens, Gerhard. "Métis Lands in Manitoba". *Manitoba History*, spring 1983.

Flanagan, Thomas. "Louis Riel's Religious Beliefs: A Letter to Bishop Taché". *Saskatchewan History*, winter 1974.

—————. "The Religion of Louis Riel". *Quarterly of Canadian Studies for Secondary Schools*, vol. 4, 1975–77.

——————. "The Riel 'Lunacy Commission': The Report of Dr. Valade". *Revue de l'Université d'Ottawa,* vol. 46, 1976.

——————. "Louis Riel: A Case Study in Involuntary Psychiatric Confinement". *Canadian Psychiatric Association Journal,* vol. 23, 1978.

——————. "Political Theory of the Red River Resistance: The Declaration of December 8, 1869". *Canadian Journal of Political Science,* vol. 11, 1978.

——————. "Louis Riel and the Dispersion of the American Métis". *Minnesota History,* vol. 49, 1984–85.

——————. "Louis Riel's Land Claims". *Manitoba History,* vol. 21, spring 1991.

Flanagan, Thomas, and John Yardley. "Notes and/et Documents: Louis Riel as a Latin Poet". *Humanities Association Review,* vol. 26, 1975.

Flanagan, Thomas, and Neil Watson. "The Riel Trial Revisited: Criminal Procedure and the Law in 1885". *Saskatchewan History,* vol. 34, spring 1981.

Foster, J.E. "The Métis: The People and the Term". *Prairie Forum,* vol. 3, 1978.

Frégault, Guy. "Louis Riel, patriote persécuté". *L'Action Nationale,* vol. 25, 1945.

Frémont, Donatien. "Archbishop Taché and the Beginnings of Manitoba". *North Dakota Historical Quarterly,* vol. 6, 1931–32.

Friesen, Victor Carl. "Gabriel's Ferry". *The Western Producer,* May 9, 1985.

Garay, Kathleen. "John Coulter's *Riel:* The Shaping of 'A Myth for Canada' ". *Canadian Drama,* vol. 11, no. 2, 1985.

Gibson, Dale. "The Judge and the Serving Girl: A Scandal at Red River". *The Beaver,* Oct., Nov. 1990.

Glassco, John. "To Sir John A. MacDonald [sic]". *Canadian Literature,* vol 37, 1968.

Gluek, Alvin C., Jr. "The Riel Rebellion and Canadian–American Relations". *The Canadian Historical Review,* vol. 36, 1955.

Goldring, P. "Lower Fort Garry". *Canadian Antiques Collector,* vol. 6, no. 8, Nov./Dec. 1971.

Gordon, Daniel M. "Reminiscences of the N.W. Rebellion Campaign of 1885", *Queen's Quarterly,* vol. XI, no. 1, July 1903.

Greenland, Cyril, and John D. Griffin, "William Henry Jackson (1861–1952): Riel's Secretary". *Canadian Psychiatric Association Journal,* vol. 23, 1978.

Gutteridge, Don. "Riel: Historical Man or Literary Symbol?" *Humanities Association of Canada Bulletin,* vol. 21, 1970.

Hafter, Ruth. "The Riel Rebellion and Manifest Destiny". *Dalhousie Review,* vol. 45, 1965.

Harrington, Lyn. "Prairie Battlefield". *Canadian Geographical Journal,* vol. 66–67, 1963.

Hildebrandt, Walter. "The Battle of Batoche". *Prairie Forum,* vol. 10, no. 1, 1985.

——————. "Battleford 1885: The Siege Mentality". *NeWest Review,* May 11, 1985.

Hind, H.Y. "Red River Settlement and the Half-Breed Buffalo Hunters". *The Canadian Merchants' Magazine,* vol. 3, 1858.

Howard, Henry. "Medical History of Louis David Riel during His Detention in Longue Pointe Asylum". *Canada Medical & Surgical Journal*, vol. 14, 1886.

Huel, Raymond J.A. "Louis Schmidt: Patriarich of St. Louis". *Saskatchewan History*, vol. 40, no. 1, 1987.

Ireland, Mabel Sauke. "A Pictorial History of the Sun River Valley". *Sun River Historical Society*, Feb. 1989.

Jefferys, Charles W. "Fifty Years Ago". *Canadian Geographical Journal*, vol. 10–11, 1935.

Jonasson, Jonas A. "The Background of the Riel Rebellions". *Pacific Historical Review*, vol. 3, 1934.

——————. "The Red River Amnesty Question". *Pacific Historical Review*, vol. 6, 1937.

Kennedy, Howard Angus. "Memories of '85". *Canadian Geographical Journal*, vol. 70–71, 1965.

Kerr, John Andrew. "Gabriel Dumont: A Personal Memory". *The Dalhousie Review*, vol. 15, 1935–36.

Knox, Harold C. "Consul Taylor of Red River". *The Beaver*, March 1949.

——————. "The Question of Louis Riel's Insanity". *Historical and Scientific Society of Manitoba*, series 3, no. 6, 1951.

LaChance, Vernon. "The Metis Rebellions". *Maclean's*, Oct. 15, Nov. 1, 1930.

Laliberte, Larry. "St. Laurent's Metis Council". *New Breed*, July 1984.

Larmour, Jean. "Edgar Dewdney and the Aftermath of the Rebellion". *Saskatchewan History*, vol. 23, autumn 1970.

Lee, David. "The Métis Militant Rebels of 1885". *Canadian Ethnic Studies*, vol. 21, 1989.

Lehmann, P.O. "Louis Riel, Patriot or Zealot". *Scarlet and Gold*, no. 67, 1985.

Littmann, S.K. "A Pathography of Louis Riel". *Canadian Psychiatric Association Journal*, vol. 23, 1978.

——————. "Louis Riel's Petition of Rights, 1884". *Saskatchewan History*, vol. 23, no. 1, 1970.

Lussier, A.S. "Msgr. Provencher and the Native People of Red River, 1818–1853". *Prairie Forum*, vol. 10, no. 1, 1985.

MacArthur, Peter. "The Red River Rebellion". *Manitoba Pageant*, vol. 18, no. 3, spring 1973.

MacLeod, Margaret Arnett. "Winnipeg and the HBC". *The Beaver*, June 1949.

——————. "Songs of the Insurrection". *The Beaver*, spring 1957.

Mailhot, P.R., and D.N. Sprague. "Persistent Settlers: The Dispersal and Resettlement of the Red River Métis, 1870–1885". *Canadian Ethnic Studies*, vol. 17, no. 2, 1985.

Mallory, Enid Swerdfeger. "The Life of Lower Fort Garry". *Canadian Geographical Journal*, vol. 66–67, 1963.

Manroe, Jack. "Mr. Dawson's Road." *The Beaver*, Feb./March, 1991.

Markson, E.R. "The Life and Death of Louis Riel: A Study in Forensic Psychiatry". *Canadian Psychiatric Association Journal*, vol. 10, 1965.

Martel, Gilles. "Louis Riel: ferveur nationaliste et foi religieuse". *Relations*, vol. 39, 1979.

_____. "Louis Riel, Prophète du nouveau monde: les sources psycho-sociales de sa conscience prophetique". *Les Cloches de Saint-Boniface*, vol. 78, 1979.

_____. "Les multiples expressions littéraires d'une experience mystique: Louis Riel, 8 décembre 1875". *Humanities Association of Canada Newsletter*, spring 1985.

Martin, Chester. "The First 'New Province' of the Dominion". *The Canadian Historical Review*, vol. 1, 1920.

McConnell, John G. "The Geography of the District of Saskatchewan in 1885". *NeWest Review*, May 1885.

McLean, Don. "The Metis Struggle for Independence in the West". *New Breed*, July–Aug. 1985.

Miller, Carman. "Lord Melgund and the North-West Campaign of 1885". *Saskatchewan History*, no. 3, autumn 1969.

Miller, J.R. "From Riel to the Métis". *Canadian Historical Review*, vol. LXIX, no. 1, 1988.

Mitchell, Elaine Allan. "A Red River Gossip". *The Beaver*, spring 1961.

Moissac, Soeur Elisabeth de. "Les Soeurs Grises et les événements de 1869–1870". *La Société canadienne d'histoire de l'Eglise Catholique*, vol. XXXVII, 1970.

Morton, Desmond. "Reflections on Old Fred: Major General Middleton and the North-West Campaign of 1885". *NeWest Review*, May 1985.

Morton, W.L. "Agriculture in the Red River Colony". *The Canadian Historical Review*, vol. 30, 1949.

_____. "The Canadian Metis". *The Beaver*, September 1950.

_____. "Red River on the Eve of Change 1857–1859". *The Beaver*, autumn 1962.

_____. "The 1870 Outfit at Red River". *The Beaver*, spring 1970.

_____. "Two Young Men, 1869: Charles Mair and Louis Riel". *Historical and Scientific Society of Manitoba*, series 3, vol. 30, 1973–74.

Mossman, Manfred. "The Charismatic Pattern: Canada's Riel Rebellion of 1885 as a Millenarian Protest Movement". *Prairie Forum*, vol. 10, no. 2, 1985.

Neatby, H. Blair, and John T. Saywell. "Chapleau and the Conservative Party in Quebec". *The Canadian Historical Review*, vol. 37, 1957.

Olesky, Ronald L. "Riel: Patriot or Traitor?" *Canadian Lawyer*, April 1991.

Owram, Douglas. "The Myth of Louis Riel". *Canadian Historical Review*, vol. 63, 1982.

Painchaud, Robert. "Les origines des peuplements de langue française dans l'Ouest canadien, 1870–1920: mythes et réalités". *Mémoires de la Société Royale du Canada*, série IV, tome XIII, 1975.

Pannekoek, Frits. "The Fur Trade and Western Canadian Society, 1670–1870". *Canadian Historical Association*, Historical Booklet No. 43.

_____. "Protestant Agricultural Zions for the Western Indian". *Canadian Church Historical Society Journal*, vol.14, 1972.

_____. "Riel House: A Critical Review". *Archivaria*, vol.18, 1984.

Payment, Diane. "Monsieur Batoche". *Saskatchewan History*, vol. 32, no. 3, 1979.

_____. "The Métis Homeland: Batoche in 1885". *NeWest Review*, vol. 10, no. 9, May 1985.

Pearce, William. "A Personal View". *Alberta Historical Review*, vol. 16, 1968.

Peel, Bruce. "Red River Broadsides, 1869–70". *Amphora*, vol. 19, 1975.

Pritchett, John P. "The Origin of the So-Called Fenian Raid on Manitoba in 1871". *The Canadian Historical Review*, vol. 10, 1929.

Prud'homme, Maurice. "The Life and Times of Archbishop Taché". *Historical and Scientific Society of Manitoba*, series 3, no. 2, 1904.

Read, Colin. "The Red River Rebellion and J.S. Dennis, 'Lieutenant and Conservator of the Peace'". *Manitoba History*, vol. 3, 1982.

Rife, Clarence W. "Norman W. Kittson: A Fur-Trader at Pembina". *Minnesota History*, vol. 6, 1925.

Roberts, A.C. "The Surveys in the Red River Settlement in 1869". *The Canadian Surveyor*, vol. 24, no. 2, June 1970.

Rocan, Claude. "Louis Riel: Turmoil in the Nineteenth Century." *Rotunda*, winter 1985–86.

Ross, Howard E. "A Glimpse of 1885". *Saskatchewan History*, winter 1968.

Roy, David. "Monseigneur Provencher et son clergé séculier". *La Société canadienne d'histoire de l'Eglise Catholique*, vol. XXXVII, 1970.

Roy, R.H. "With the Midland Battalion to Batoche". *Saskatchewan History*, vol. 32, no. 2, spring 1979.

St-Onge, Nicole J.M. "The Dissolution of a Métis Community: Pointe à Grouette, 1860–1885". *Studies in Political Economy*, no. 18, autumn 1985.

Scarlett, E.P. "Physicians in Canadian History—VI: Sir John Christian Schultz (1840–1896)". *Calgary Associate Clinic Historical Bulletin*, vol. 8, no. 2, 1994.

Schoenberg, Fr. Wilfred P. "Historic St. Peter's Mission: Landmark of the Jesuits and the Ursulines among the Blackfeet". *Montana, the Magazine of Western History*, winter 1961.

Silliman, Lee. "The Carroll Trail: Utopian Enterprise". *Montana, the Magazine of Western History*, April 1974.

Silver, A.I. "French Canada and the Prairie Frontier, 1870–1890". *The Canadian Historical Review*, vol. 50, March 1969.

——————. "The French-Canadian Press and 1885". *Native Studies Review*, vol. 1, pp. 2–15, 1984.

——————. "Ontario's Alleged Fanaticism in the Riel Affair". *Canadian Historical Review*, vol. LXIX, no. 1, 1988.

Smith, Donald B. "Honoré Joseph Jaxon: A Man Who Lived for Others". *Saskatchewan History*, vol. 34, no. 3, 1981.

——————. "William Henry Jackson: Riel's Secretary". *The Beaver*, spring 1981.

Snell, James G. "American Neutrality and the Red River Resistance, 1869-1870." *Prairie Forum*, vol. 4, no. 2, 1979.

Sprague, D.N. "The Manitoba Land Question, 1870–1882". *Journal of Canadian Studies*, vol. 15, no. 3, autumn 1980.

Sprenger, G. Herman. "The Metis Nation: Buffalo Hunting vs. Agriculture in the Red River Settlement". *Western Canadian Journal of Anthropology*, vol. 3, no. 1, 1972.

Spry, Irene M. "The Transition from a Nomadic to a Settled Economy in Western Canada, 1856–96". *Royal Society of Canada*, vol. 16, no. 4, 1968.

—————. "The 'Memories' of George William Sanderson, 1846–1936". *Canadian Ethnic Studies*, Vol. 17, no. 2, 1985.

Stacey, C. P. "The North-West Campaign 1885". *Canadian Army Journal*, vol. 7, no. 3, July 1954.

Stanley, George F.G. "Riel's Petition to the President of the United States 1870". *The Canadian Historical Review*, vol. 20, 1939.

—————. "Western Canada and the Frontier Thesis". *Canadian Historical Association Report*, 1940.

—————. "Gabriel Dumont's Account of the North West Rebellion 1885". *Canadian Historical Review*, Sept. 1949.

—————. "Louis Riel: Patriot or Rebel?" *The Canadian Historical Association*, Historical Booklet no. 2, 1954.

Street, W.P.R. "The Commission of 1885 to the North-West Territories". *The Canadian Historical Review*, vol. 25, 1944.

Stubbs, Roy St. George. "Law and Authority in Red River". *The Beaver*, summer 1968.

Swainson, Donald. "Rieliana and the Structure of Canadian History". *Journal of Popular Culture*, vol. 14, 1980.

Tremaudan, Auguste Henri de. "Louis Riel and the Fenian Raid of 1871". *The Canadian Historical Review*, vol. 4, 1923.

—————. "Louis Riel's Account of the Capture of Fort Garry, 1870". *The Canadian Historical Review*, vol. 5, 1924.

—————. "The Execution of Thomas Scott". *The Canadian Historical Review*, vol. 6, no. 3, 1925.

—————. "Letter of Louis Riel and Ambroise Lépine to Lieutenant-Governor Morris, January 3, 1873". *The Canadian Historical Review*, vol. 7, 1926.

Trounce, William Henry. "From Saskatoon to Moose Jaw with the Prisoner Riel". *Saskatchewan History*, vol. 34, spring 1981.

Van Dyke, Henry. "The Red River of the North". *Harper's*, vol. 60, no. 160, May 1880.

Walker, Peter. "The Origins, Organization and Role of the Bison Hunt in the Red River Valley". *Manitoba Archaeological Quarterly*, vol. 6, 1982.

Walter, Dave. "The Hundred Year Controversy of Louis Riel". *Montana Magazine*, no. 68, Nov.–Dec. 1984.

Wetton, Mrs. A.N. "When the Metis Rebelled". *The Beaver*, June 1941.

Williamson, Dave T. "Riel, his people, treated unjustly". *The Native People*, Oct. 30, 1981.

Willock, Roger. "Green Jackets on the Red River". *Canadian Army Journal*, vol. 13, 1959.

Wolseley, Garnet Joseph. "Narrative of the Red River Expedition". *Blackwood's Magazine*, vol. CVIII, 1870, vol. CIX, 1871.

Woodcock, George. "Louis Riel: Defender of the Past". *The Beaver*, spring 1960.

Woodington, Henry. "Diary of a Prisoner in the Red River Rebellion". *Niagara Historical Society*, vol. 25, 1913.

Woolworth, Nancy L. "Gingras, St. Joseph and the Metis in the Northern Red River Valley: 1843–1873". *North Dakota History*, vol. 42, 1975.

THESES

Banks, B.J. "The Red River Rebellion: A Peculiar People in Exceptional Circumstances". Unpublished MA thesis, Carleton University, 1980.

Graham, Jane Elizabeth. "The Riel Amnesty and the Liberal Party in Central Canada, 1869–1873". Unpublished MA thesis, Queen's University, 1967.

Mailhot, P.R. "Ritchot's Resistance: Abbé Noel Joseph Ritchot and the Creation and Transformation of Manitoba". Unpublished PhD thesis, University of Manitoba, 1986.

Wade, Jill. "Red River Architecture 1812–1870". Unpublished MA thesis, University of British Columbia, 1967.

INDEX

A

Allan, Sir Hugh, 227, 228
Americans in Red River, 82
Amnesty for leaders of Resistance, 168, 169, 178, 180, 182, 183, 186, 199, 200, 202, 204, 206, 207, 214, 215, 224, 231, 242-43; select committee, 231, 232-33
André, Father Alexis, 74, 333-34, 343, 344-45, 351-52, 354, 361, 362, 365, 369, 372, 377, 439, 442, 445, 457-58; opposition to Riel, 352, 359, 360, 366; witness in Riel's trial, 420, 425, 426
Annexation of the Northwest to Canada, Canadian Party advocates, 77, 78, 79
Annexation of the Northwest to U.S., proposals for, 70–71, 94, 95, 129, 136–37, 171, 172, 196
Archibald, Adams G. (first Lieutenant-Governor of Manitoba), 193, 204, 205, 206, 207, 210, 214, 282
Ashley, James M., 306
Assiyiwin, 384
Astley, J.W., 382, 405, 423
Audet, Cyprian, 317

B

Ballenden, John, 40, 42
Ballenden, Sarah, 42–43
Ballenden scandal, 42–43, 44
Bannatyne, A.G.B., 81, 82, 86, 104, 118, 124, 129, 141, 142, 145, 148, 155, 220, 222, 223, 234
Bannatyne, Mrs. A.G.B. (Annie), 81, 87
Barnabé, Evelina, 225, 234–35, 235–36, 300; learns of Riel's marriage, 308–309; love for Louis Riel, 235, 272–74, 276, 278
Barnabé, Father Fabien, 225, 240–41, 249, 255, 257, 270, 271, 272, 275, 276–77, 309
Batoche, 332–33, 336, 337, 365, 391, 394, 395, 398–99, 401; battle of, 402–407; meetings in church, 365–66, 373–74, 376, 387; plundering following battle, 407–408
Battleford, 394, sacking of, 391
Beal, Bob, 442

Beardy, Chief, 384
Beauport Asylum, 262, 270, 271, 417
Begg, Alexander (customs collector designate), 100
Begg, Alexander (historian of Red River), 78, 81, 100, 107, 118, 136–37, 156, 164, 170, 172
Begg, Katherine, 173
Belcourt, Georges-Antoine, 39, 40, 71, 91, 167–68, 197
Bellehumeur, Jean-Baptiste, 300
Bellehumeur, Marguerite (wife to Louis Riel), see Riel, Marguerite
Bellehumeur, Patrice, 296, 300
Bétournay, Judge Louis, 222
Big Bear (Cree chief), 295, 349, 350; in North-West Rebellion, 391, 394
Bill of Rights for Rupert's Land (1870), 143–44, Addendum One. See also List of Rights
Bill of Rights (1885), 368–69, Addendum Two
Bird, James, 10
Black, Col. H.M., 294
Black, Judge John, 103, 104, 140, 141, 142–43, 144, 145, 169, 178, 181
Blackfeet, 294–95, 310, 390
Blake, Edward, 208–209, 210, 228, 233
Blondeau, Louis, 85
Bonneau, Pascal, 421
Botkin, Marshal Alexander C., 305, 306–308, 311
Boucher, François Firmin, 19
Boucher, Louis, 26
Boucher, Marguerite, 26
Boulton, Major Charles, 148–50, 152, 153, 154, 155, 156, 157, 169
Bourget, Bishop Ignace, 29, 57, 225–27, 241, 246, 247–48, 260, 261, 267, 421; inspirational letter to Riel, 248, 320; Riel chooses as pope, 268, 387
Bowell, Mackenzie, 231, 233
Bown, Walter, 110, 209
Boyer, William, 377
Breland, Pascal, 93
Brooks, Edwin J. (juror at Riel's trial), 422, 432
Bruce, John, 94, 101, 111, 127, 239–40
Bryant, W.F., 252
Buckingham, William, 78, 79
Buffalo, 15; dwindling herds, 36, 72, 82–83, 234, 333, 335; hunting, 34–36; organization of buffalo hunt used as a model government, 101; Riel joins Métis buffalo hunters in Montana, 289–302

Buller, Capt. Redvers, 187, 188, 192, 193

Bumsted, J.M., 254

Bunn, Thomas, 140

Burbridge, George (crown counsel at Riel's trial), 422

Burgess, A.M., 419

Burke, John, 140, 141

Butler, Capt. W.F., 171

C

Cameron, Capt. D.R., 100, 105, 107, 108

Cameron, Duncan, 17, 19

Canada First Party, 85, 175–76, 182, 183, 184

Canadian Pacific Railway, 227, 228, 365n.

Canadian Party, 77–78, 103

Carr, Emily, 254

Carrie, Rev. J., 150

Carrière, Damase, 316–17, 366, 376

Carroll Landing, 303

Cartier, Sir George-Étienne, 50, 64, 65, 133, 166, 194–95, 207, 208, 214, 215, 283; meets with Ritchot, 177, 178, 180, 181, 182; death, 219; hero to most Métis, 199; illness, 215

Casgrain, Thomas (crown counsel at Riel's trial), 422, 426

Catholic Colonization Bureau, 276

"Catholic Programme", 247

Chapleau, Joseph-Adolphe, 239, 247, 261, 263, 436, 442

Chapman, Rev. John, 76

Charette, François, 239

Chicago, Illinois, 69–70

Chipewyans, 26–27

Christian Brothers, 45

Christie, Alexander, 40

Clark, Dr. Daniel, witness at Riel's trial, 427, 428n.

Clarke, Henry J., 213, 214, 221, 231, 283

Clarke, Lawrence, 328, 334, 335, 336, 343, 351, 371, 372, 374, 374n., 386–87, 390, 418

Cochin, Father Louis, 434, 435

Cochran, Rev. William, 41–42, 43, 148

Coldwell, William, 78, 143

Collège de Montréal, 49, 50

Colvile, Eden, 44

Cooke, Jay, 174

Corbett, Rev. Griffiths Owen, 75–77

Cornish, Francis Evans, 221, 234, 239, 283

Cosgrove, Francis (juror at Riel's trial), 422, 431–32

Council of Assiniboia, 37, 38, 39, 44, 75, 76, 77, 78, 80; summons Riel, 103–104; Métis confiscate papers, 114

"Country marriages", 7

Coureurs de bois, 4

Coutu, Henri, 110, 152

Cowan, Dr. William, 109n., 110, 145, 148

Cree Indians, 295, 391

Creighton, Donald, 119

Crowfoot (Blackfoot chief), 294, 295, 390

Crozier, Supt. Leif, 300, 350, 371, 378, 379, 380, 382, 386; battle of Duck Lake, 383–84, 385, 422

Cumberland House, 10

Cunningham, Robert, 220

Custer, Col. George Armstrong, 28

D

Dallas, Alexander, 76

Damiani, Father Joseph, 310, 311

Dansereau, Arthur, 436

Dauphinais, François, 127

Dawson Road, 84

Dawson, Simon J., 77, 84

De la Broquerie, Joseph, 55

Deacon, Capt. Richard, 344

Deane, Bell (juror at Riel's trial), 422

Deane, Insp. R. Burton, 413

Dease, William, 93–94, 104, 121, 150, 152, 221

Declaration of the People of Rupert's Land (1869), 125–26, Addendum One

Delorme, Joseph, 161, 162

Delorme, Pierre, 223, 238, 384

Demeules, Louis, 211

Denison, George T., 175, 182–83

Dennis, Col. John Stoughton, 95, 96–97, 104, 120–22, 123, 125

Desjardins, Senator Alphonse, 224, 227, 229, 230, 247

Devlin, William, 209–210

Dewdney, Lt.-Gov. Edgar, 344–45, 351, 365, 366, 371, 372, 421, 442

Dominion Lands Act (1872), 227, 339

Dorion, Antoine, 228, 229

Dubeau, Alexandre, 233

Dubuc, Joseph, 199–200, 201, 211, 212–13, 222, 223, 237, 264, 279, 315

Duck Lake, battle of, 383–86, 392, 422, 423

Dufferin, Lady, 230

Dufferin, Gov. Gen. Lord, 242

Dugas, Father Georges, 97, 125, 168, 224, 237, 421, 446
Dumas, Isidore, 403
Dumas, Michel, 324, 329, 340, 371, 414, 419
Dumont, Edouard, 397
Dumont, Gabriel, 335, 336, 339, 340, 341, 354–55, 366, 367, 373–74, 376, 379, 387, 414, 419; ancestors, 329–30; battle of Batoche, 402–405, 406–407, 408; battle of Duck Lake, 381, 382, 383–86; battle of Fish Creek, 397–98; childhood, 330; military strategy, 391, 394, 395–96, 398, 403, 411; relationship to Louis Riel, 332, 387, 394, 408; visits Riel in U.S. (1884), 324, 328
Dumont, Isidore, 330, 334, 384
Dumont, Madeleine, 331, 332
Dumoulin, Father Sévère, 22
Dupont, Léon, 221–22

E

Eberschweiler, Father Frederick, 320, 328
English-speaking halfbreeds, see Half-breeds, English-speaking
Everet, Ed (juror at Riel's trial), 422
Exovedate, see Provisional government (1885)

F

Falcon, Pierre, 101, 332
Famine among Indians (1878–79), 285–86, 287; (1883–84), 349, 352, 356
Farmer, William, 221
Fenian Brotherhood, 203–204, 205, 206, 276
Fiset, Jean-Baptiste-Romauld, 230, 414
Fish Creek, battle of, 397–98, 399
Fitzpatrick, Charles, defence attorney for Riel, 415, 416–17, 422, 424, 427, 428, 439–40
Flageolle, Henri, 257
Flanagan, Thomas, 434, 453, 457–58
Flat Willow Creek, 296, 298, 299–300
Forget, Amédée, 354, 355, 356
Fort Assiniboine, 296
Fort Benton, 297
Fort Carlton, 378, 386–87
Fort Daer, 8, 9, 34
Fort Douglas, 18, 22
Fort Edmonton, 11, 12
Fort Garry, 32, 38, 40; occupied by Métis (1869), 109–110
Fort Gibraltar, 12–13, 18–19
Fort Pitt, 391

Foss, Vaughan, 42
Fourmond, Father Vital, 336, 358, 359, 360, 366, 370, 372, 395, 434; witness at Riel's trial, 420, 426
Fréchette, Louis, 69–70
Freemen, 5–6, 17
Free traders in Red River, 81–82
French Canadians in New York, 236, 245, 276–77
French, Commissioner George Arthur, 336
Frog Lake massacre, 391
Fur trade, 4–5, 7, 83

G

Gaboury, Marie-Anne, see Lagimodière, Marie-Anne
Gabriel's Crossing, 331
Gaddy, William, 150, 152
Gagnon, Ferdinand, 255, 256
Gariépy, Pierre, 327
Garnot, Philippe, 377, 379, 427
Gatling gun, 399, 403
Gilroy, J.C., 440
Gingras, Antoine Blanc, 71, 197, 277
Gingras, Norman, 277
Girard, Marc-Amable, 237, 264
Giraud, Marcel, 426
Gladu, Antoine, 192
Globe, The, 77, 78, 98
Goulet, Elzéar, 161, 162, 193–94, 195
Goulet, Robert, 104
Grand Couteau, battle of, 330
Grandin, Bishop Vital, 128, 353–54, 358
Grant, Charles, 197
Grant, Cuthbert, 19, 32, 34, 135
Grant, President Ulysses S., 101, 196, 255
Granville, Lord, 184
Grasshopper plagues, 23, 72, 234
Greenshields, James N. (defence attorney for Riel), 415, 419
Grey Nuns, 29, 44–45, 55, 58, 62, 73, 158
Guernon, Marie-Julie, 60–62, 63, 66, 227
Guillemette, François, 163, 194

H

Halfbreed Land Claims Commission, 364–65, 367
Half-breeds, English-speaking, 9, 75–76, 102, 112, 329; in North-West Rebellion (1885), 390
Hall, David B., 327–28

Hallett, William, 93, 94, 108, 120, 121, 145
Hamelin, Joseph, 229, 334
Hamlin, Sévère, 302
Hardisty, Isabella, 133
Hardisty, Richard, 133, 134, 137
Hargrave, J.J., 112
Harkins, W.W., xi–xiv
Harrison, Damase, 85
Healy, John J., 307, 311
Henderson, Jack, 445
Henry, Jérôme, 393–94
High treason, vs. treason-felony, 415; Riel's trial
  for, 414–33
Hind, H.Y., 77
Hobbes, Thomas, 125, 126
Homestead Act (1862), 355
Homesteaders, 179, 233, 280, 282, 283, 315, 339,
  340, 341, 343, 347, 356, 390, 433
Hospital of St. Jean de Dieu, *see* Longue-Pointe
  Asylum
Houde, Frédéric, 236–37
Howard, Dr. Henry, 258, 259–60
Howard, Joseph Kinsey, 99, 120
Howe, Joseph, Secretary of State for the
  Provinces, 105, 106, 131, 140, 166, 168
Hudson's Bay Company, 5, 10, 27, 76, 77–78,
  84; administers Red River settlement, 78, 81;
  Red River resistance (1869–70), 129, 132, 145,
  173; relationship to Métis, 36–37, 38, 39–41,
  334, 336, 337; Rupert's Land sale, 90
Hyacinthe, George, 292–93

I

Indians: Blackfeet, 294–95, 310, 390;
  Chipewyans, 26–27; clashes with NWMP
  (1884), 349, 350; Cree, 295, 391; famine
  (1878–79), 285–86, 287, (1883–84), 349, 352,
  356; liquor sale to, 5, 89; relations with Métis,
  9, 36, 170, 350, 355; Riel's native confederacy
  scheme, 285, 286, 293, 295; role in North-
  West Rebellion (1885), 390–91, 399;
  Saulteaux, 15, 22, 121, 170; Sioux, 9, 36, 74,
  121, 151, 286–87, 300, 330, 331; women, 7
Ingraham, John, 221–22
Institut Canadien, 65
Ireland, Bishop John, 276, 277
Irvine, Commissioner Acheson Gosford, 371,
  372, 378, 380, 383, 386, 387, 389, 405, 418
Isbister, Alexander, 38
Isbister, James, 324, 328–29, 340, 353

J

Jackson, Eastwood, 347, 350, 375, 389–90, 423
Jackson, William Henry (later Honoré Jaxon),
  346–47, 348–49, 359, 362, 364, 367, 380,
  420n., 436, 447; converts to Catholicism,
  375–76; detained by Métis, 389; found not
  guilty of treason-felony, 420; religious strug-
  gles, 375, 388–89
Jacques, Dr. A.G., 100
Johnston, W.J., 339, 340
Johnstone, T.C. (defence attorney for Riel), 415
Jukes, Dr. Augustus, 441, 458
Jurisdiction of court at Riel's trial, 418
Jury in Riel trial, 421–22, 431–32, 440

K

Kavanagh, Father François-Xavier, 194
Keeseville, New York, 235; Riel farms near
  (1878), 272, 275
Keller, A.R., 299
Kerr, George, 373
Kerr, John, 221–22
Kildonan, 33, 77
Kittson, Norman, 37, 39, 47, 71

L

Lachapelle, Dr. E.P., 234, 237, 258, 259, 260, 262
Laflamme, Rodolphe, 65, 247, 414
LaFlèche, Bishop Loius-François Richer, 238, 267
LaFontaine, Louis-Hippolyte, 50
Laframboise, Auguste, 384–85
Lagimodière, Benjamin, 72, 73
Lagimodière, Elzéar, 104, 161, 162, 242n.
Lagimodière, Jean-Baptiste, 4, 71; character, 4;
  journeys to Montreal, 18, 20–21; lives near
  young Louis Riel, 31; loyalty to the HBC and
  Lord Selkirk, 17–18; marriage, 6
Lagimodière, Joseph, 446
Lagimodière, Marie-Anne (born Gaboury; first
  white woman in the Northwest), 6, 7, 9,
  10–12, 13, 20, 71; trip west, 8; influence on
  Louis Riel, 8
Lagimodière, Reine, 10, 24
Lagimodière, Romain, 446
Laing, R.D., 454–55
Lamarche, Father Godfroy, 245
Land claims of Métis, 73–74, 83, 95–96, 179,
  202, 213, 214, 280–83, 312–13, 315–16, 317,
  337–38, 339–40, 356, 364–65, 367, 368, 369
Land scrip, 283, 312, 315–16, 317, 338, 339

Land speculators, 282, 283, 316, 343

Langevin, Sir Hector, 264, 353

Langford, N.P., 175

Larance, Thomas, 292

Larocque, Bishop Charles, 238

Lash, John, 373

Laurier, Wilfrid, 238

Lavallée, Louis, 252, 277–78, 435–36

Lavell, Dr. Michael, 441

Lee, John (uncle of Louis Riel), 55, 59, 60, 227, 257

Lee, Lucie (aunt of Louis Riel), 55, 60, 227, 257

LeFloch, Father Jean-Marie-Joseph, 45, 46, 192

Lemay, Joseph, 74, 234

Lemieux, François-Xavier, defence attorney for Riel, 414, 416–17, 418, 422, 424, 425, 426, 443

Lépine, Ambroise, 102, 108, 124n., 127–28, 151, 152, 155–56, 161, 162, 168, 191–92, 208, 209, 211, 216, 243n., 279; death sentence commuted, 242; found guilty, 240; tried for murder, 222, 238, 239–40

Lépine, Jean-Baptiste, 93, 161, 162, 194

Lépine, Maxime, 102, 210, 224, 279, 348, 352, 376, 377, 379

Lestanc, Father Joseph-Jean-Marie, 74, 96–97, 141, 162, 168

Letendre, Xavier, 336–37

Léveillé, Pierre, 137, 210

L'Heureux, Jean, 294–95

Liberal Party of Ontario, 208–209

List of Rights (Dec. 1869), 115–16, (Feb. 1870), 143–44, Addendum One. See also Bill of Rights (1885)

Little Bighorn, battle of (1876), 286

Little Pine, Chief, 295

Longue-Pointe Asylum, 258–61

M

McArthur, Alexander, 123

MacBeth, Rev. Robert, 128, 151

McDermot, Andrew, 81, 96

Macdonald, Henry, 310

Macdonald, Sir John A., 77, 98, 99, 166, 206, 207–208, 214, 227, 228, 232, 233, 280, 283, 338, 361n., 362, 365n., 367, 436, 440; and North-West Rebellion (1885), 392, 393; responses to Red River Resistance, 119, 121, 126, 131–34, 176–77, 178–80, 184; appoints medical commission to judge Riel's sanity, 441; response to news of impending revolt (1884), 352, 353; refuses clemency for Riel, 442–43

Macdonald, Stewart, 239

Macdonnell, Miles, 15, 16, 17, 18, 22

McDougall, Daniel, 46, 49, 55

McDougall, William, Lieutenant Governor of Rupert's Land, 84, 86, 91, 93, 98–100, 105, 107, 108–109, 112, 116, 130, 184; Métis resistance to, 99–100, 102, 104, 106, 119; orders survey, 95; proclaims annexation, 119–20

Macdowall, David, 360, 361, 365

McKay, Joseph, 384

McKay, Thomas, 378–79, 380, 382

McKenney, Henry, 78, 79, 80

Mackenzie, Alexander, 228, 229, 242

McLeod, Murdoch, 157, 161

Macleod, Rod, 442

Mactavish, William, 75, 96, 103, 110, 112–13, 129, 145, 147, 148, 165, 166, 173

Mager, John, 210

Maginnis, Martin, 306, 308

Mailhot, Phillipe, 205, 217

Mair, Charles, 85–90, 91, 92–93, 99, 100, 103, 105, 117, 124, 136, 148, 149, 150, 154, 158, 159, 175; moves to Prince Albert, 343, 344; stirs up Canada First, 176, 182

Mair, Eliza, 100, 117, 124, 136

Mallet, Major Edmond, 241–42, 251, 254–55

Malmros, Oscar, 94–95, 113, 129, 136, 171

Manitoba Act, 179, 180, 432; accepted by Legislative Assembly of Assiniboia, 181–82; land distribution to Métis, 179, 202, 213, 281–82, 283, 312, 338

Manitoba and Northwest Farmers' Union, 347–48

Manitoba, Province of, 179, 180, 213; new settlers (1870s), 232

Marion, Edouard, 97, 278

Marion, François, 109

Marion, Louis, 365, 375, 377

Marion, Louise-Anne, 278

Marion, Marie-Rose, 278

Marshall, William Rainey, 174–75

Martineau, André, 280

Masons, 79

Masson, Joseph, 56

Masson, Louis-François-Rodrigue, 56, 209, 230–31, 232, 233, 237, 247, 442–43

Masson, Sophie, 46, 49, 55, 56

"Memorial of the people of Rupert's Land and North-West" (Sept. 1870), 196

Mercier, Honoré, 224, 247, 255

Merryfield, Walter (juror at Riel's trial), 422

Métis, 34; buffalo hunting, 34–36; exodus from Red River (1870s), 315–16; freighting business, 36; harassment following Resistance, 193–95; land claims, 73–74, 83, 95–96, 179, 202, 213, 214, 280–83, 312–13, 315–16, 317, 337–38, 339–40, 356, 364–65, 367, 368, 369; in Montana, 289–302; North-West Rebellion (1885), *see* North-West Rebellion; opposition to Red River Settlement, 17, 18; origins, 8–9; petition to Ottawa, 346, 349, 356, 362; reaction to Rupert's Land Sale (1869), 90, 91, 93–95, 101; Red River Resistance (1869–70), *see* Red River Resistance; relations with half-breeds, 75–77; relations with Hudson's Bay Company, 36–37, 38, 39–41; relations with Indians, 9, 36, 170, 355; upset by bigotry against, 42, 43–44

Métis, Le, 206, 222, 229

Middleton, General Frederick D., 392–93, 394, 401, 423; battle of Batoche, 402–404, 405, 406, 407, 408; battle of Fish Creek, 398; military strategy, 394, 396, 402, 405; opinion of Riel, 410

Miles, Col. Nelson, 290, 298, 299

Mills, David, 338, 339

Mitchell, Hillyard, 379

Monet, Marguerite (dite Bellehumeur), *see* Riel, Marguerite

Monkman, Joseph, 121, 158

Montana: Riel lives as buffalo hunter in (1879–81), 289–302; Riel's involvement in politics (1882), 305–308, 311–12, 318, 321

Montour, Abraham, 339–40

Montreal, in 1858, 48–49

Moore, Capt. Henry, 380

Morris, Lt.-Gov. Alexander, 216–17, 222, 228, 233–34, 335

Morton, Senator Oliver P., 250–51, 320

Morton, W.L., 166

Moulin, Father Julien, 358, 373, 391–92, 403

Mountain men, 289

Mousseau, Dr. J.O., descriptions of Louis Riel, 51, 52–53, 65

Mousseau, Joseph-Alfred, 231, 261, 262

Mulligan, James, 109n., 126

N

National Association for the Defense of the Imprisoned Métis, 414

National Committee of the Métis, 101–102, 106

Native confederacy scheme, Riel's, 285–87, 293, 295

Nault, André, 97, 106, 109, 161, 162, 163, 194, 210, 242n., 446

Nault, Napoléon, 316–17, 340, 361, 366, 371, 397, 409, 419

New Nation, The, 136–37, 155, 171–72

Newman, Peter C., 133

Nolin, Charles, 135, 142, 144, 145, 146, 201, 223, 333, 339, 340, 365, 366, 368, 369–70, 376–77, 379, 387, 388, 395, 421; witness in Riel's trial for treason, 424

Nolin, Joseph, 46, 161–62, 239

Nolin, Rosalie, 369

North West Company, 5, 10, 12–13, 27; opposition to Red River Settlement, 16–17, 18, 21

North West Mounted Police, 250; confrontations with Indian bands (1884), 349, 350; in North-West Rebellion, 371

North-West Rebellion (1885), 367–409; battle of Batoche, 402–407; battle of Duck Lake, 383–86, 392, 422–423; battle of Fish Creek, 397–98, 399; causes, 362, 419–20, 429, *see also* Land claims of Métis; English-speaking half-breeds remain neutral, 390; Fort Pitt burned down, 391; Frog Lake massacre, 391; rebellion begins (March 1885), 367, 368–69; Riel surrenders to Middleton, 409; role of Indians, 390–91, 399; white settlers opposed, 366

Northwest Territorial Council, 338

Northcote (ship), 401, 402, 411

Nor'wester, The (newspaper), 78, 79, 80, 83, 90, 93, 96, 110, 121, 122

Nouveau Monde, Le, 224, 232

O

Oak Point, 89, 97

Oblate Fathers, 224

O'Donnell, Dr. John H., 105, 124, 221

O'Donoghue, William, 128–29, 155–56, 162, 168, 186, 191–92, 203–204, 205, 206, 243n.; has audience with President Grant, 203; promotes annexation with U.S., 129, 136, 172, 196; seeks support from Fenians, 203–204, 205

O'Hanlon, Thomas, 303

O'Lone, Robert, 194

O'Lone's Saloon, 82, 94, 123, 183, 193

O'Neill, General John, 203

Ontario Party, 201

Orangemen, 77, 206; demand Riel be hung, 440; power in Red River following Resistance, 193

Osler, Britton Bath (crown counsel at Riel's trial), 422–23, 425, 427

Otter, Lt.-Col. William, 394

Ouellette, Joseph, 406–407

Ouellette, Moïse, 324, 329, 376, 388, 408

P

Pacific Scandal, 227, 228, 232

Pagé, Quintal, 224

Painter, Henry J. (juror at Riel's trial), 422

Palliser, John, 77

Pannekoek, Frits, 41, 42, 76

Papineau, Louis-Joseph, 50

Parenteau, Baptiste, 376

Parenteau, Pierre, 376

Parisien, Joseph, 293

Parisien, Norbert, 153–54, 160

Parliament Buildings in Ottawa, 230

Patrick, Alfred, 230

Payne, James, 391

Pearce, William, 340

Pembina, 8, 34, 37, 40, 47, 106

Pemmican, 7, 13, 16, 35, 36, 83

Pepin, Simon, 304–305, 319, 320–21

Petition from white settlers, half-breeds and Métis (1884), 346, 349, 356, 362

Pierrotte, Henriette, 224–25

Pitblado, Charles Bruce, 411

Pointe-à-Michel, 197

Poitras, Jean-Marie, 316

Portage la Prairie, 77, 148, 179

Poundmaker (Cree chief), 391; North-West Rebellion, 394, 399

Primeau, Father Jean Baptiste, 251, 255–56

Prince Albert, 342–43

Prince Albert Times, 342, 343, 344, 359, 361–62

Prince, Chief Henry, 111, 121, 170

Prince of Wales, 55

Privy Council, 439–40

Proulx, Paul, 161

Provencher, Bishop Joseph, 22, 29, 33, 38, 39, 107, 165

Provencher, J.A.N., 100, 107, 108, 137

Provincial status, 143–44, 178, 179, 180

Provisional government (1869–70), Bill of Rights redrafted, 169; constitution drafted, 147; established, 125–29; flag, 145, 172, 173; prepares Bill of Rights, 143–44; problems of governing,

129; reorganized, 127; Scott tried and executed, 161–64; success, 171

Provisional government (1885), establishment, 376; mentioned, 390, 391; military strategy, 377–78; proclaims Riel's new church, 387–88, 400

Prud'homme, Eustache, descriptions of young Louis Riel, 50, 51

R

Racette, Georges, 104, 121

Red River carts, 36, 40, 83

Red River Pioneer, 112, 122

Red River Resistance (1869–70), 97, 100–188; "Canadians" attempt attack on Fort Garry, 148–57; chaos following Resistance, 192–95; Hudson's Bay Company, 114; List of Rights, 115–16; National Committee formed, 101–102; Métis occupy Fort Garry, 109–110; provisional government established, 113–14, 125–29; Red River Expedition under Wolseley, 183–88, 192–93; Schultz's party captured, 121–25; Scott's execution, 161–64; Smith debates Riel, 139–42, 146

Red River settlement, 13, 14, 15–17, 18, 19, 22–24; grasshopper plagues, 23, 72, 234; HBC sells Rupert's land to Canada, 90; major groups in (1868), 77–82; protests against Hudson's Bay Company, 38, 39, 40–41; relations between Métis and halfbreeds, 75–77; social disputes, 41–44; surveyors arrive (Aug. 1869), 95, 96–97; undemocratic government, 32

Red Stone, Chief, 294

Reed, Hayter, 352–53, 372, 418

Regina, 412, 417, 418

Richards, Albert, 100, 108

Richardson, Hugh, 372; stipendiary magistrate in Riel's trial for treason, 418, 419–20, 422, 425, 428, 431, 433

Richardson, Mrs. Hugh, 425, 430, 431

Richer, Father Evariste, 241, 242, 249, 256, 257

Riel, Alexandre (brother to Louis Riel), 72, 278

Riel, Charles (brother to Louis Riel), 44, 71, 73, 197, 200, 252

Riel, Eulalie (sister to Louis Riel), 44, 72, 278

Riel, François (uncle to Louis Riel), 60, 233, 277

Riel, Henriette (sister to Louis Riel), 31, 32, 72, 278, 435, 447; wedding, 312, 316–17

Riel, Jean (son of Louis Riel), 308, 317, 332, 363, 447

Riel, Jean-Baptiste (Louis Riel's grandfather), 25, 27, 60

Riel, Jean-Louis (father of Louis Riel), 25, 27–29, 47; business enterprises, 38, 44, 56, 58; defiance of establishment, 38, 39, 40–41, 44, 58; illness and death, 58; marriage, 29–30, 58

Riel, Joseph (brother to Louis Riel), 72, 163–64, 278, 300, 321, 323, 414

Riel, Julie (mother of Louis Riel), 23, 25, 29–30, 45, 47, 71, 158, 191, 192, 201, 206, 249, 264, 269–70, 272, 277, 313; moves family, 72–73; religious life, 30–31; strength of character, 31; visions, 30, 31; Louis writes final letter to, 443–44

Riel, Louis, abandons the priesthood, 59–60, 62–63; accomplishment, 171, 447, 448; American citizenship, 297, 307, 310, 401, 417; amnesty, *see* Amnesty for leaders of Resistance; ancestry, 3–41; appeals for remission of death sentence, 434, 436, 439–40; appearance, xii, xiii, xiv, 61, 93, 127, 170, 175, 235, 305, 314, 410–11, 422, 441; at Collège de Montréal, 49–62; banished for five years, 243, 244; becomes spokesperson for Métis (1869), 83–84, 88–89, 94–95; birth, 3, 25; buffalo hunter in Montana (1879–81), 289–302; courts Marie Guernon, 60–62, 63, 66; descriptions by childhood friends, 50, 51, 52–53; diaries (1884–85), 322–23, 356–58, 370–71, 382–83, 388, 395, 401, 404, 435, 439, 455, 456; early childhood, 30–32, 41, 44–45; elected to House of Commons, 223, 229, 231, 238; execution, 445; family relationships, 49–50, 56, 58–59, 71–72, 92, 200–201, 211–12, 217, 218–19, 225, 252, 269–70, 300, 309, 313, 319–20, 323, 414, 435, 437–39, 443–44; farms near Keeseville (1878), 272, 275; flees to U.S. (Aug. 1870), 191–92, 195, 196–98; friendships, 51, 212–13, 225; honoured by Métis, 363–64; insanity (1875–77), 251, 252, 253–70, 279–80, Addendum Three; jailed in Regina (May 1885), 412–14; law clerk in Montreal (1866), 65–66; love for Evelina Barnabé, 235–36, 272–74, 276, 278, 308–309; Manitoba invasion plan (1875, 1878), 249–51, 255, 276; marriage (April 1881), 301–302, 308, 318; Montana politics (1882), 305–308, 311–12, 318, 321; moves to Chicago (1867), 69–70; native confederacy scheme (1879), 285–87, 293, 295; new church (1876), 267–69, 456, (1885), 375, 387, 392, 400–401,

411–12, 455–56, 457; in North-West Rebellion (1885), 367–409 *passim;* poems, 51–52, 53–55, 57–58, 60, 61, 62–63, 64, 66, 70, 87–88, 197–98, 220–21, 222–23, 235–36, 238, 243, 245–46, 248–49, 262–65, 272, 273, 274–75, 278, 284, 292–93, 297–98, 301–302, 304, 312, 317–18, 437, 438, 440–41; public meeting with Donald Smith, 139–42; in Red River resistance, 97, 100–188 *passim;* relationship with Gabriel Dumont, 332, 387, 394, 408; relationship with his father, 31, 32, 41, 44, 58–59, 218–19, 309; releases emotions in writings, 53, 262–65, 322, 356, 413, 439; religion, 198, 252, 253–54, 267–69, 434–35, 456, *see also* new church (above); religious upbringing, 30–32; relinquishes Commons seat to Cartier, 214–15, 228, 283; returns to Red River (1868), 71–72; in St. Paul (1872), 209–210, 211, (1874), 233, 234; scheme for an independent Métis nation, 317, 324; schoolteacher (1883–84), 310, 311, 321; sees himself as a prophet, xiii–xiv, 253, 254, 257, 262, 264–66, 359, 387–88; speaks at meetings (1884–85), 341–45, 358–59, 365–66; support following trial, 436, 440, 442–43; supports Archibald's government, 205, 206; surrenders to General Middleton, 409; takes additional name of "David", xiii, 223, 266; Thomas Scott's execution, 161–64; trading business (1881), 303–304; travels to Montreal for schooling, 46–49; trial for high treason, 414–33; visions, xiii–xiv, 31, 253–54, 309, 310, 320, 322, 392, 404, 439

Riel, Marguerite (wife of Louis Riel), 300–301, 302, 313, 317, 318, 332, 408, 437–38, 444; death, 447; illness, 363, 414, 438, 446

Riel, Marie (sister to Louis Riel), 44, 71, 73, 197, 200, 206–207, 211, 217

Riel, Marie-Angélique (daughter of Louis Riel), 318, 332, 363, 447

Riel, Octavie (sister to Louis Riel), 44, 72, 201, 277

Riel, Sara (sister to Louis Riel), 31, 44, 130–31, 192, 196; becomes missionary, 202, 215–16; becomes nun, 71; death, 319–20; letters to Louis, 92, 197, 200–201, 319

Ritchot, Father Noel-Joseph, 74, 91–92, 94, 102, 103, 107, 109, 125, 137, 140, 141, 167, 168, 204, 212, 232, 237, 274; negotiations in Ottawa, 169, 175, 177, 178–82

Ritchot, Janvier, 97, 106, 161, 162

Robertson, Colin, 18–19

Robinson, Christopher (crown counsel at Riel's trial), 422, 430–31

Robinson, Major Henri M., 136, 171, 172

Ross, Alexander, 37

Ross, Harold, 382

Ross, James, 111–12, 113, 114, 143, 144

Rouleau, Judge Charles, 352, 353

Roy, Dr. François-Elzéar, 270; witness at Riel's trial, 427

Royal, Joseph, 206, 207, 237, 239, 247

Rupert's Land Sale, 90

S

St. Andrew, 33

St. Antoine de Padoue Church, Batoche, 391, 399; meetings at, 365–66, 373–74, 376, 387

St. Boniface cathedral, 33

St. Joseph, 71, 192, 197, 277

St. Laurent Settlement, 334–35, 336; surveyed, 338–39, 340

St. Norbert, 33, 92

St. Paul, Minnesota, 37, 47–48, 70–71, 209

St. Peter's Mission, 310, 311, 321, 322, 323

Salaberry, Col. Charles de, 131, 132, 145, 169

Sanderson, George William, 156, 160, 161, 163

Sanderson, Tom, 386, 389

Saulteaux, 15, 22, 121, 170

Sayer, Pierre-Guillaume, 40, 41

Schmidt, Louis, 46, 47, 49, 55, 69, 70, 74–75, 102, 107, 124n., 127, 134, 135, 137, 138, 143, 147, 170n., 173, 181–82, 187, 199, 329, 346, 348, 358, 359, 366

Schultz, Anne, 79, 80, 124, 150

Schultz, Dr. John Christian, 78–80, 84, 86, 87, 89, 90–91, 94, 95, 100, 103, 111, 117–19, 121–25, 160, 193, 199, 231; awarded compensation, 201–202, 229; escapes from jail, 150–51; land speculator, 282, 283; opposition to Riel, 80–81, 152–53, 158, 159, 175, 209–210, 234; stirs up Canada First Movement, 176, 177, 182, 184

Scott, Alfred H., 142, 169, 175, 177–78, 181, 186

Scott, David Lynch (crown counsel at Riel's trial), 422

Scott, Hugh, 177

Scott, Thomas, 84–85, 123, 136, 148, 149, 150, 152, 153, 154, 157, 159–61; becomes hero in Ontario, 164, 175; controversy over his execution, 208–209; execution, 163–64; trial, 161–62

Selkirk, Earl of, 13–14, 21–22, 23, 32

Semple, Robert, 19

Settlers, Anglo-Saxon, 179, 233, 280, 282, 283, 315, 339, 340, 341, 343, 347, 356, 433; in North-West Rebellion (1885), 390; relations with Métis, 341, 344, 346, 366

Settlers' Rights Association, 347

Seven Oaks Battle, 19–20, 101

Simpson, Frances, 42

Simpson, George, 27, 39, 40, 42, 43

Sioux, 9, 36, 74, 121, 151, 286–87, 300, 330, 331

Sisters of the Precious Blood, 313

Sitting Bull (Sioux chief), 286–87, 294

Smith, Donald A., 132–35, 137–38, 143, 162, 195, 208, 220, 233; public debate with Riel, 139–42, 157–58

Smith, Donald B., 364

Smuggling between Red River and U.S.A., 37–38, 40

Snow, John A., 84, 85, 86, 89, 92–93

Spence, Andrew, 341

Spence, Thomas, 148, 172

Sperling, Gerald B., 416

Sprague, D.N., 179–80, 217, 281, 365n., 392

Stanley, George F., 34n., 65, 103, 385n., 421

Statute of Treasons, 415

Ste. Thérèse, Sister, 218–19

Stewart, Alexander David, 415–16

Stewart, James, 76, 188

Stewart, Sgt. Alfred, 382

Stipendiary magistrate system, 418

Strange, Maj.-General T.B., 394

Strathcona, Lord, see Smith, Donald A.

Stutsman, Enos, 108, 113, 136, 203

Sulpician order, 49, 57, 58

Sutherland, Hugh, 153–54

Sutherland, John, 153

Swan, James, 311

T

Taché, Archbishop Alexandre-Antonin, 45, 46–47, 55, 56, 71, 73, 90, 96, 164–69, 170, 172, 191, 194, 202, 204, 207, 214, 223, 228–29, 232, 233, 416, 446; meets with Cartier and Macdonald (1870), 166–67, 182, 183, (1871), 207–208; relationship with Louis Riel, 167, 168, 186, 211, 237, 269, 314–15, 421

Tanner, James, 194

Taschereau, Archbishop, 238, 247, 267

Tassé, Joseph, 224

Taylor, James, 163
T.C. Power Company, 303
Terry, General Alfred, 290, 291, 299
Thibault, Very Rev. Jean-Baptiste, 131, 132, 141
Thom, Adam, 42, 43–44
Tompkins, Peter, 375, 376
Tompkins, William, 373
Tourond, Jean-Baptiste, 93, 223
Tourond's Coulee, 332, 336, 396
Treason, High, 415
Treason-felony, 415
Tremont, Barney, 391
Trois-Rivières, 4
Tuke, Dr. Harold, 259
Tupper, Charles, 130–31

U

Ultramontanism, 226, 246–47, 267
Union Métisse St. Joseph, 358, 359

V

Valade, Dr. François-Xavier, 442
Valade, Sister, 47, 48
Van Straubenzie, Col. Bowen, 405
Vankoughnet, Lawrence, 352, 419
Végréville, Father Valentin, 359, 370, 395
Vincellette, Clément, 270
Voyageurs, 4–5, 83

W

Walsh, Supt. James M., 293–94
Walters & Baker store, 374, 375
Welsh, Norbert, 82–83, 372
Wheaton, Capt. Lloyd, 205, 206
White Cap (Sioux chief), 399
White Horse Plains, 34
Williams, Col. Arthur, 406, 407
Willoughby, Dr. John, 372, 373, 423–24
Winnipeg *Daily Sun,* 314, 416
Winnipeg *Free Press,* 314, 349
Winnipeg, Manitoba, 33, 77, 81, 234, 314
Wolseley, Col. Garnet, 181, 184–86, 192, 195
Wood, Chief Justice E.B., 239, 240
Woodcock, George, 362, 367
Woodington, Henri, 160–61

Y

Young, Capt. George H., 411, 423; opinion of Riel, 411
Young, Rev. George, 72, 160n., 162, 163, 193, 411

Young, Governor-General Sir John, 140, 177, 180, 181, 182, 183, 186

Z

Zouaves, 226, 392